PRAISE FOR

BREAKING THE CODE

'A wonderful book. A serious contribution to history, as well as funny and touching, *Breaking the Code* is how politics genuinely is.'
DANIEL FINKELSTEIN, *THE TIMES*

'Searingly honest, wildly indiscreet, and incredibly funny ... *Breaking the Code* is the best book I've read this year.'
LYNDA LEE-POTTER, *DAILY MAIL*

'Brandreth is the true Samuel Pepys of our day.'
ANDREW NEIL, *BBC RADIO FIVE LIVE*

'Brandreth, for my money, offers about the most honest, and the most amusing, account of the demented, beery futility of the Tory-ruled Commons in the 1990s.'
BORIS JOHNSON, *DAILY TELEGRAPH*

'Hilariously acute ... Portraits withering in their accuracy ... Irresistible.'
MATTHEW D'ANCONA, *SUNDAY TELEGRAPH*

'One of the most attractive things about these diaries is that the diarist is (like Alan Clark) one of those who can admit, even to himself, to having human weaknesses ... Extremely touching ... Brandreth emerges as a decent, amusing, talented and charming man.'
SIMON HEFFER, *DAILY MAIL*

BREAKING THE CODE

WESTMINSTER DIARIES

GYLES BRANDRETH

1990–2007, UPDATED, UNEXPURGATED

Biteback Publishing

This edition published in Great Britain in 2015 by
Biteback Publishing Ltd
Westminster Tower
3 Albert Embankment
London SE1 7SP
Copyright © Gyles Brandreth 1999, 2014, 2015

ISBN 978-1-849 4-915-8

10 9 8 7 6 5 4 3 2 1

A CIP catalogue record for this book is available from the British Library.

Set in Minion Pro

Printed and bound in Great Britain by
CPI Group (UK) Ltd, Croydon CR0 4YY

MIX
Paper from
responsible sources
FSC
www.fsc.org   FSC® C020471

For Michèle

who had the worst of it

and made the best of it

CONTENTS

INTRODUCTION

C an history repeat itself?

Not exactly – of course not. But I must say, as I sit here in the summer of 2015, re-reading my diary from the 1990s, there are aspects of the past that seem to be very present.

In 1992, I became an MP at the general election where almost every opinion poll leading up to polling day predicted either a hung parliament or a small Labour majority. In the event, the Conservative Party, led by John Major, won the election and secured an overall majority of twenty-one seats in the House of Commons. The expectations of the pollsters and the pundits were confounded: the voters, it turned out, did not see the Labour leader, Neil Kinnock, as a potential Prime Minister. In retrospect, Mr Kinnock's triumphalist cry of 'We're all right', delivered at a rally in Sheffield eight days before polling, was seen as premature.

At the 2015 general election, where again almost every opinion poll predicted a hung parliament or a narrow Labour victory, the Labour leader, Ed Miliband, a week before polling day, unveiled an eight-foot, six-inch slab of limestone inscribed with six pledges and promised to erect the mighty stone in the garden of 10 Downing Street when he became Prime Minister. It was not to be. The Conservative Party, led by David Cameron, won the election and secured an overall majority of twelve seats in the House of Commons.

Mr Major's re-election in 1992 was unexpected, but he did not have long to savour his success. As you will discover (or be reminded) in the pages that follow, within weeks of his electoral triumph, his party was engulfed in what amounted to a European civil war. And in 2015, within weeks of Mr Cameron's unexpected outright election victory, this is the front-page headline in the *Daily Telegraph* on the day that I happen to be writing this: 'Tory mutiny on EU referendum: Downing Street chaos'.

As a good European, Alphonse Karr, sometime editor of *Le Figaro*, famously put it, way back in 1849: *plus ça change, plus c'est la même chose.*

Of course, things do change. The drama of Mr Cameron's premiership will be different from Mr Major's in many ways, although, incredibly, some of the cast – almost a quarter of a century on – remain the same. (The political cartoon in today's paper features

Ken Clarke and John Redwood, as recognisable as ever and both still MPs.) One thing that the Cameron and Major administrations will have in common, however, is their dependence on the Government Whips' Office.

John Major began his second term as Prime Minister with a majority of twenty-one. As his years in office rolled by, death, disloyalty and defection reduced that majority to nil. David Cameron has begun his second term as Prime Minister with a majority of just twelve. Managing a government with a wafer-thin majority is not easy and the Government Whips' Office is central to the endeavour. And how it does that job is at the heart of this book, which is why, when the book first appeared, a number of good people – friends and former colleagues – viewed its publication as an act of betrayal.

On the first anniversary of the 1997 general election, when extracts from my diary appeared in a Sunday newspaper, the Conservative Chief Whip telephoned me at home. He was a model of quietly spoken courtesy. I would have expected nothing less: James Arbuthnot, MP for North East Hampshire until 2015, is a gentleman. (Eton, Captain of School; Trinity College, Cambridge; in the expenses furore of 2009, he immediately apologised and repaid the public funds he had claimed for the cleaning of his swimming pool.) He said to me, 'Gyles, you do know that you are breaking the whips' code, don't you?'

I did. And it troubled me. Government whips do not talk about their work, do not discuss their role, do not describe the way they go about their business. They never have – or, at least, they never had until I published *Breaking the Code*.

The day after getting the Chief Whip's call I happened to find myself at a BBC studio talking to Anthony Howard, veteran political commentator and then (perhaps appropriately, under the circumstances) obituaries editor of *The Times*.

'I've got a moral dilemma with these diaries,' I said.

'No, you haven't,' said Tony. 'You've got a personal dilemma. It's not a moral issue. Government whips are government ministers, paid for by the taxpayer. What they do and how they do it are matters of legitimate public interest. If by publishing your diaries you'll be burning your bridges, that's a personal matter. That's for you to decide.'

I decided to take the risk, not only for reasons of cash and vanity, not simply because I enjoy reading other people's diaries and I hope that others may enjoy reading mine, but because I was not convinced that the secrecy surrounding the Whips' Office – and much else that happens in Westminster and Whitehall – is either right or necessary.

In my telephone conversation with the Chief Whip, he reminded me that part of the potency of the Whips' Office derives from the mystery surrounding it. He echoed Walter Bagehot's famous line on the monarchy: 'We must not let in daylight upon magic.' But Bagehot died in 1877. We are now well into the twenty-first century and whips are neither magicians nor Freemasons: they are Members of Parliament with a specific job to do. Their task is to manage and secure the parliamentary business of the government of the day and, in so doing, manage and understand their fellow MPs. If they are more open about the way they operate I can see no harm in it, and, even, some good.

On the day *Breaking the Code* was published, a large brown envelope was delivered to my front door. Inside it was a second envelope. Inside that was a sheet of white paper that contained nothing but a large black spot: a mark of shame. I had betrayed the Office and the Office wanted to make that fact clear to me. I was not in any doubt and so not surprised, in the months that followed, to find former fellow whips, when I chanced to meet them or to pass them in the street in Westminster, avoiding my eye or, in some cases, deliberately turning away and cutting me.

It is more than twenty years since I joined the Whips' Office and I believe by most (if not all) of my former colleagues I have now been forgiven – or forgotten. Happily, *Breaking the Code* was well received when it appeared – and not only by the reviewers. Several of the leading characters in the narrative wrote to tell me that I had got it 'about right'. The book played a part in the development of two successful plays about the work-ings of the Whips' Office: *Whipping It Up* by Steve Thompson (2006) and *This House* by James Graham (2012). And in 2005, a former head of the Whips' Office, Tim Renton, Baron Renton of Mount Harry, Chief Whip during Margaret Thatcher's final year in power, published his own account of the history and practice of parliamentary whipping.

These diaries, of course, cover more than my sojourn in the Whips' Office. The extracts begin in May 1990, when I was deciding it was about time I got into Parliament, and end in May 1997, when the electors of Chester decided it was time I got out. Those seven years take us from the fall of Margaret Thatcher to the election of Tony Blair, and in choosing the material for publication – reducing the potential of more than a million words to one manageable volume – my aim has been to provide both an informal record of some eventful years in British politics and one individual's account of the everyday reality of what is involved in becoming a parliamentary candidate, securing a seat, fighting an election, arriving at Westminster, and, once there, attempting to climb the greasy pole. In its way, I hope that aspect of the book is as revelatory as my account of life as a gov-ernment whip.

In 1990, I was working mainly in television and publishing. I was also non-executive director of a successful company (Spear's Games, manufacturers of Scrabble) and dep-uty chairman of a failing one (the Royal Britain exhibition at London's Barbican). In my spare time I was actively involved in the work of the National Playing Fields Association, the national trust of recreational space. Once I became an MP, I was wholly engrossed in my political life. For five years my routine hardly varied: Mondays to Thursdays I was at Westminster, morning, noon and night. I would leave my home in Barnes, south-west London, at 7.00 a.m. and get back at midnight. On Fridays and at weekends I was mostly in my constituency. I hope I was a conscientious MP. I certainly tried to be. The diary was written in various places: in my study at home in Barnes; in bed at our flat in the centre of Chester; on trains and planes going to and from the north-west; at the House of Commons, occasionally in the Chamber itself, mostly in the Silent Room in the House of Commons Library, my favourite place in my favourite part of the Palace of Westminster. I have a wonderful wife and remarkable children. That they barely feature here reflects not only the editing process, but also the fact that the committed MP all too easily loses sight of his family.

When I was at Oxford in the late 1960s, I was interviewed by the *Sun* newspaper and, if the cutting is to be believed, boldly declared that my life's ambition was 'to be a sort of Danny Kaye and then Home Secretary'. My plan didn't quite work out. I became a minor-league TV presenter and a Lord Commissioner of Her Majesty's Treasury. I have no regrets, but no illusions either. These are not a distinguished Cabinet minister's memoirs. These are the daily jottings of a novice backbencher turned government whip. They reveal assorted weaknesses: impatience, intolerance, intemperance, vanity, egoism, faulty judgement, lack of discretion, absurd ambition (quite embarrassing at times), a naive eagerness to please. Alarmingly, I am not sure they reveal any strengths at all – other than a keen sense of the absurd. But they are what they are, edited yes, but undoctored, presented as they were written on the day, without stylistic improvement, without benefit of hindsight.

Meeting Gordon Brown at 11 Downing Street in 1998 (he was not recruiting me to the Third Way: we were having coffee after appearing on *Frost on Sunday*), the then Chancellor of the Exchequer told me that he had enjoyed reading my account of life at the Treasury under Kenneth Clarke and Norman Lamont. 'I was particularly fascinated by the meeting you called "Prayers",' he said. 'We don't have "Prayers".' Times change. Long-serving MPs of all parties tell me that the camaraderie and clubbability of the House of Commons that I knew in the 1990s has gone. The more civilised working hours introduced by New Labour have seen to that. And several MPs from intakes after mine have told me that, having read my diaries, they marvelled at the ready and regular access backbenchers had to the most senior members of the government in John Major's day.

John Major is the principal player in this story. He makes an unlikely hero: he is not 'box office' in the way that Margaret Thatcher was. But to me he is a hero nonetheless and, re-reading these diaries and reflecting on his record and on the way he kept the show on the road in the most inauspicious circumstances, my admiration for him continues to grow. He is more interesting than most people realise, and more achieving. It is not easy being Prime Minister, as Gordon Brown demonstrated.

'A decent man dealt an unlucky hand,' was Douglas Hurd's assessment of Mr Major. What history's judgement will be is still too soon to tell. What is certain is that John Major led the Conservative Party to a remarkable victory against the odds in 1992 and led them to an historic defeat in 1997. What happened in between is what this book is about.

As a postscript, I have added some extracts from my diaries covering the decade following 1997. I have included them to tie up a few loose ends and to give a flavour of 'what happened next', but I have kept them brief because in politics, in my experience, you are either in the game or you are out of it. For a few years I was in it and – for all the horrors I describe in the pages that follow – there is nowhere else that I would rather have been.

Gyles Brandreth
2015

ABBREVIATIONS

A – also known as Drinks – the meeting of a team of supportive backbench MPs specially recruited by the Whips' Office

BNFL – British Nuclear Fuels Ltd

CGT – Capital Gains Tax

CSA – Child Support Agency

DfE – Department for Education

DNH – Department of National Heritage

DoE – Department of the Environment

DoH – Department of Health

DPM – Deputy Prime Minister

DSS – Department of Social Security

DTI – Department of Trade and Industry

ECOFIN – Meeting of the EU Economic and Finance Ministers

EDCP – Ministerial Committee on the Coordination and Presentation of Government Policy

EDM – Early Day Motion

EMU – Economic and Monetary Union

ERM – Exchange Rate Mechanism

ETB – English Tourist Board

FCO – Foreign and Commonwealth Office

GATT – General Agreement on Tariffs and Trade

HRH – His Royal Highness: in the context of the diaries, usually the Duke of Edinburgh

IGC – Inter-Governmental Conference

MBNA – Maryland Bank of North America

MEP – Member of the European Parliament

MoD – Ministry of Defence

NFU – National Farmers' Union

NPFA – National Playing Fields Association

PC – Privy Counsellor

PMQs – Prime Minister's Questions

PPC – Prospective Parliamentary Candidate

PPS – Parliamentary Private Secretary

PR – Proportional Representation

PUSS – Parliamentary Under-Secretary of State

Q – a weekly meeting of backbench MPs supportive of the government

QMV – Qualified Majority Voting

RHF – Right Honourable Friend

SDP – Social Democratic Party

SFO – Serious Fraud Office

SoS – Secretary of State

UU – Ulster Unionist

FOOTNOTING

I have tried to keep footnotes to a minimum, but felt it right to include brief details of the constituencies of Members of Parliament when they make their first appearance in the diary. When their party allegiance is not given they are Conservatives. If they have died since the diary was written I have added their dates as well. I have also provided footnotes introducing members of my family and friends on their first appearance, but not people to whom only passing reference is made or whose names will be familiar already to the general reader.

'Nothing matters very much and very few things matter at all.'

ARTHUR BALFOUR, PRIME MINISTER 1902–6

CHAPTER 1

1990

TUESDAY 1 MAY 1990

I spoke, not very well, at the London Playing Fields Society centenary dinner at the Savoy.[1] The meal was something of a struggle. I was seated next to Field Marshal The Lord Bramall KG, GCB, OBE, MC, JP,[2] whose terrible dandruff was wafted straight from his left shoulder onto my *petit tournedos de boeuf aux echalotes* every time a waiter breezed past. The Duke of Gloucester gave his I'm-rather-shy-but-really-very-willing-decent-and-determined speech (which went down well) and our diminutive Minister for Sport[3] scored with a nice mixture of laughs and exhortation. As he left he said to me, 'When are you joining us at Westminster?' I said 'I don't think I am', but, of course, I want to.

SUNDAY 6 MAY 1990

Breakfast at TV-am[4] with Brian Johnston[5] (who is lovely and up there with the Queen Mother as one of the four or five people in the land who can do no wrong) and Carol Thatcher[6] (who is lovely too in her funny lumpen way and who's played a fairly tricky

---

1   GB has had a long involvement with the National Playing Fields Association: Appeals Chairman 1983–8; Chairman 1988–93; Vice-President since 1993.

2   Chief of the Defence Staff 1982–5; Lord Lieutenant of Greater London 1986–98; President of the London Playing Fields Society from 1990. (The Duke of Gloucester is patron.)

3   Hon Colin Moynihan, MP for Lewisham East 1983–92, former Oxford rowing and boxing blue, Minister for Sport 1987–90; 4th Baron Moynihan from 1997 and chairman of the British Olympic Association from 2005.

4   GB was a presenter with TV-am, the ITV breakfast station, 1983–90.

5   Broadcaster and cricket commentator, 1912–94.

6   Journalist, daughter of the Prime Minister.

hand pretty faultlessly). We talked about Michael Whitehall[7] and Carol said Michael's story about the taxi is quite true. When they were going out, Michael picked her up at No. 10 one evening and asked to use the phone to ring for a cab.

'Where are we picking up from, guv?'

'Downing Street,' said Michael.

'Oh, yeah?' said the voice, 'No. 10 is it?'

'Yes,' said Michael.

'Oh, yeah?' repeated the voice, 'And what name is it?'

'Whitehall.'

'Oh yeah. A likely story.' At which point Carol grabbed the phone from Michael and said, 'We'd like a taxi for Whitehall at 10 Downing Street please.'

'Oh yeah. And I suppose you're called Thatcher are you?'

'As a matter of fact, I am.'

The taxi never came.

BANK HOLIDAY MONDAY, 7 MAY 1990

Simon[8] came for lunch. He's been out of *Noel & Gertie* for two weeks having an ingrown hair removed from under his left arm. We laughed a lot, but he seemed a bit bleak. He went off to see Frankie Howerd's one-man show and we stayed in and watched Ken Dodd's *This Is Your Life*.

TUESDAY 8 MAY 1990

TV-am and breakfast with John Denver.[9] On to Royal Britain[10] and more crisis talks. Walk to the Savoy for the NPFA fund-raising lunch. Prince Philip[11] (in his electric taxi) arrived ten minutes early, but *this* time (unlike last time when I was in the loo) I was on the doorstep ready and waiting. He's very good: easy, relaxed, apparently interested, informed, concerned etc. even though, poor bugger, he's been at it relentlessly for forty years plus. At the lunch – a smallish group, selected high-rollers (at least, that was the idea…) – HRH

---

7   Theatrical agent and producer, father of comedian Jack Whitehall, friend of GB.

8   Simon Cadell, 1950–96, actor, GB's oldest friend.

9   American singer.

10 An exhibition on the history of British royalty, conceived by GB, which opened at the Barbican in London in 1988 but failed to attract sufficient visitors to succeed.

11 President of the National Playing Fields Association from 1948 to 2012.

spoke well: no notes (certainly not the ones I'd provided!) and his usual trick of being sufficiently indiscreet to make his audience feel they were being 'let in' on something. Colin Sanders,[12] bless him, offered £50,000 there and then. So did Roger Levitt.[13]

Supper with Anne Maxwell[14] in her basement flat in Ladbroke Grove. There's a touch of the Carol Thatcher good-hearted jolly-hockey-sticks about her, and, like Carol vis-à-vis Mrs T., Anne manages to be loyal to her awesome parent without apparently becoming his creature. I'm not sure the same can be said about brother Kevin who left the table at ten to return to the office: 'There's a lot still to do tonight. I've got to sign an Australian affidavit. It certainly can't wait till morning.'

WEDNESDAY 9 MAY 1990

At Royal Britain our overdraft has topped the million mark and is being extended little by little (guaranteed by Richard)[15] while we search for extra funds and/or a buyer. John Broome, founder of Alton Towers, came today and declared that he would take it on – for a controlling interest. He'd pick up the overdraft and spend £2.5 million to give the show the 'wow' factor and jack up the marketing. Was it all bluff and bombast? We left it that he'll come again and take a closer look – when he gets back from his day-trip to New York tomorrow…

Lunch at the House of Lords with Lord Raglan,[16] Prince Philip's suggestion as NPFA's man in Wales. Amiable, clear-thinking, amusing – *and* the name has a ring to it. Lord Longford pottered up and asked if I was still standing on my head. Then he tried to persuade me to show him there and then. I told Raglan that Longford was the only man I knew who could embrace a totally naked woman and apparently not notice it.[17]

THURSDAY 10 MAY 1990

TV-am. On air at 6.10 a.m. At 7.30 a.m. breakfast at the RAC with decent, generous

---

12   Colin Sanders CBE, 1947–98, inventor and entrepreneur, friend of GB.

13   Financier and insurance salesman, soon to fall from grace.

14   Contemporary of GB's at Oxford. Daughter of Robert Maxwell, Labour MP for Buckingham 1964–70, publisher, soon to fall from boat.

15   Richard, 7th Earl of Bradford, chairman of the Royal Britain Company, Unicorn Heritage plc, friend of GB.

16   FitzRoy, 5th Baron Raglan, of Usk, Gwent; independent peer particularly associated with the housing association movement in Wales.

17   Frank, 7th Earl of Longford, minister in Labour governments 1946–51 and 1964–6. In 1971 Lord Longford set up an independent inquiry into pornography and invited Malcolm Muggeridge, Cliff Richard and GB, among others, to be part of the team. During the group's fact-finding trip to Copenhagen Lord Longford met assorted strippers and GB stood on his head.

Christopher Laing,[18] who confides that he's going to give £100,000 to the appeal. Brilliant.

At Royal Britain nothing so obviously brilliant, but a glimmer of hope. J. Paul Getty Jr's 'man of business' calls. 'My client is capricious. He might like it very much. He might not like it at all.' What a perfect partner he would make! He is seeing JPG on Monday and will report back. If JPG comes to see the exhibition he will want to be totally alone. 'There must be no one else in the building.'

SUNDAY 13 MAY 1990

Took Benet[19] to see Charles Dance as a wonderful Coriolanus at the RSC yesterday: power politics and a fickle public. Glorious.

Today at TV-am: Brian Sewell[20] (very queeny), Anthony Burgess[21] (getting frail) and Tony Holden[22] (in happy form). Tony told me a story told to him by Basil Boothroyd who was given an office at Buckingham Palace at the time he was writing his authorised biography of Prince Philip. Arriving for work one morning, crossing the courtyard, gravel scrunching under foot, the eyes of a hundred tourists boring into him, Boothroyd encountered the Queen's Private Secretary coming the other way. Boothroyd paused to greet him. Pleasantries were exchanged. Courtesies were extended. The weather was discussed, the Queen's blooming health was touched on, the vigour and charm of the Queen Mother marvelled at, progress on Basil's book reported – then the Private Secretary threw in gently, 'If you'll forgive me, I must be on my way. I've had an urgent call to say my house is on fire.'

TUESDAY 15 MAY 1990

At TV-am 'Dr Ruth', a tiny American agony aunt, soft, round and ridiculous, a little bundle of fizzing energy, squeezed me tight, held my hand, and pressed her card on me with the words, 'Call me, young man, call me anytime. I mean it. That's the number. Be sure to call now. If you've got a problem, I'm here to help.'

---

18   Member of the construction family, vice-chairman of NPFA, friend of GB.

19   GB's son, then aged fifteen.

20   Art critic of the London *Evening Standard*.

21   Novelist and critic, 1917–93.

22   Journalist and biographer, friend of GB.

THURSDAY 17 MAY 1990

I'm writing this on the train to Truro with Michèle.[23] We're off for three days' civilised filming: Trewithian, Glendurgan, Mount Edgcumbe.[24] There's an hilarious picture of John Selwyn Gummer[25] on the front page of *The Times:* 'Where's the beef? Mr John Gummer pressing a burger on his reluctant daughter Cordelia, aged four, at Ipswich yesterday to underline his message that beef is safe.' Jim Henson and Sammy Davis Jr have died. The joy of a train journey like this is it gives you the time and space to read the obituaries with a clear conscience. Jim Henson is one of my heroes: a true innovator. He gave us the original Fozzie Bear to put on show at the Teddy Bear Museum.[26]

TUESDAY 22 MAY 1990

Breakfast with Richard Harris,[27] lunch with Wayne Sleep,[28] late supper with Jo and Stevie.[29] And in between all the laughter and campery, real anguish. Royal Britain is going to fail. Four years' endeavour going up in smoke. It'll cost us £100,000 plus. It'll cost poor Richard [Earl of Bradford] millions.

WEDNESDAY 23 MAY 1990

The word from Bucharest: 'Mrs Edwina Currie,[30] attired in bright red shoes and red polka-dot dress, walked into a Balkan-style controversy yesterday as she praised the conduct of an election won by a crypto-communist landslide that opposition politicians have likened to the vote-rigging practised under Nicolae Ceausescu.'

The word from the Barbican is similarly tragic-comic: J. Paul Getty Jr is not intrigued; John Broome calls to have another look round, but bows out by phone from Heathrow

---

23 GB's wife, writer and publisher Michèle Brown. They met at university and married in 1973.

24 GB and his wife were making a television series about West Country gardens.

25 MP for Lewisham West 1970–74, Eye Suffolk 1979–83, Suffolk Coastal since 1983; Minister of Agriculture 1989–93; Secretary of State for the Environment 1993–7; Baron Deben from 2010.

26 In 1988 GB and his wife opened the Teddy Bear Museum in a Tudor house in the centre of Stratford-upon-Avon.

27 Irish actor, 1930–2002.

28 British dancer.

29 Joanna Lumley, actress, and her husband Stephen Barlow, conductor, friends of GB.

30 MP for Derbyshire South 1983–97, Parliamentary Under-Secretary of State for Health 1986–8, friend of GB since university, was one of a team of parliamentary observers at Romania's elections.

at 4.30 p.m. Richard battles valiantly with Frank (the bank manager) for an extra £50,000 to get us through the next fortnight. Richard: 'We've a man flying in from Canada on Sunday and tomorrow we're seeing Prince Rupert Lowenstein who manages the finances of the Rolling Stones.' (This last provokes a coughing spasm from Michèle and hysterical giggles from me.) Richard keeps going: 'A man is flying in from Canada, Frank. He's coming from Toronto. It's a long way to come to say "no"!'

BANK HOLIDAY MONDAY, 28 MAY 1990

Twenty years to the week since I started my Finals at Oxford (Scholar, President of the Union, editor of *Isis*, *jeunesse d'oré*, so much promise!)

I find myself in a television studio at break of day (5.00 a.m.!), the early morning toast of the ITV Telethon: standing on my head, unravelling the world's biggest jumper, leading the dawn sing-along with Rustie the Caribbean Cook. Something's gone wrong somewhere.

TUESDAY 29 MAY 1990

Went to lunch with Roger Levitt at Devonshire House, 1 Devonshire Street, round the back of the BBC. It was all very smooth and indulgent. I was there to follow through his promise of £50,000 for the appeal. By the time we got to the coffee it was clear it wasn't going to be forthcoming. Instead: 'Now, Gyles, what you should be doing is letting us look after all your insurance and pension and investment business – and introduce us to your show business friends. Give us the names and addresses, bring 'em in, bring 'em to lunch, that sort of thing. You'll be doing them a favour – and you'll get commission – good commission – you can give it to the charity, keep it for yourself, that's up to you.'

He combines the look of a Mexican bandit with the manners of a North Finchley wide-boy. After lunch he took my arm and escorted me down the stairs and into the street. His Roller was waiting, purring, at the door, chauffeur at the wheel.

'Hop in, Gyles, hop in, it's yours – wherever you want to go.'

'I'm only going to the Underground.'

'It's yours, Gyles – get in, get in.'

He positively pushed me into the back seat and slammed the door and stood waving cheerily on the pavement as the car drove off. We turned the corner and I asked the driver to drop me at Great Portland Street tube.

WEDNESDAY 30 MAY 1990

The Canadian saviour flew in and flew out. No go. It's all over. I'm now on the train to Cambridge for a meeting at Bidwells in Trumpington where we are gathering to discuss the timetable and detail of the liquidation. If the bank had allowed us up to £1.5 million, with Richard's guarantee, we would have had the rest of the year to find a purchaser. The banks are bastards. Always have been. Always will be.

SATURDAY 2 JUNE 1990

A bleak week. Late on Wednesday afternoon I saw the staff at Royal Britain one by one and told them the news. I did it as well as I could and stayed pretty steady until I got to the last of them who was so decent about it that I couldn't quite stop the tears welling and the lump in the throat. It was a good idea: we just got it wrong. The liquidators arrived on Friday morning, full of the jolly banter of the professional mortician. And last night we had a late consolation supper with Simon [Cadell] and Stevie and Jo. Jo was wonderful: 'Tchah! bah! baff! piff-paff! Away with despair, to hell with woe!'

SUNDAY 3 JUNE 1990

I am on the sleeper to Liverpool at the end of a funny, thought-provoking day. It began at TV-am where I'm doing Sundays as Ann Diamond's side-kick. Norman St John-Stevas[31] arrived as a complete self-parody: hooded eyes, luminous nose, teasing mouth.

'Gyles is very charming, isn't he?' he murmured to Anne.

'Yes,' said Anne.

'Exactly.' Norman closed his eyes. 'That's why you mustn't trust him. Charming people are never to be trusted.'

Edward Fox[32] and David Owen[33] were the main guests. We invited them to taste-test the new range of British Rail sandwiches designed by Clement Freud[34] and then turned

---

31 1929–2012; MP for Chelmsford 1964–87; Lord St John of Fawsley from 1987.

32 Actor.

33 MP for Plymouth Sutton 1966–74, Plymouth Devonport 1974–92; Labour Foreign Secretary, 1977–9; one of the founders of the Social Democrat Party, 1981, and its leader, 1983–7, 1988–90.

34 Writer, broadcaster, cook, 1924–2009; Liberal MP for Isle of Ely 1973–83.

to the overnight news: the sad death of Rex Harrison.[35] Because Edward had recently been appearing with Sir Rex in *The Admirable Crichton*, Anne looked to him for some appropriate actor-laddie reminiscences. The poor girl didn't get far.

Anne: Did you know Rex Harrison?

Edward: Yes.

Anne: Did you like him?

Edward: Yes. Ver' much.

Anne: What was he like?

Edward: Erm … er … a genius.

Anne: What kind of genius?

Edward: (pause) A genius.

Anne: But how did the genius manifest itself?

Edward: (pause) Either the sun shines. Or it doesn't.

Anne: He was very much a stage actor?

Edward: Yes.

Anne: And films?

Edward: Yes.

Afterwards, I joined David Owen for breakfast in the canteen. He was going on to meet up with his SDP colleagues to decide whether or not to disband their party in the wake of their dismal showing in the Bootle by-election. He said that while his party might now be dismissed as a joke, he believes that he personally still has credibility.[36] He quoted a couple of opinion polls showing that the public would rather have him as Prime Minister than either Margaret Thatcher[37] or Neil Kinnock.[38] He prophesied that the general election will be very close, with Thatcher the victor by a narrow margin ('They vote for her hating her because they know where she stands') and his hope is that in the run-up to the election the polls will show it to be so close that Kinnock will turn to him to deliver key votes in key marginals. He says he will stand out for a few concessions – the Scottish Assembly, proportional representation in the Euro-elections – and in the event of a narrow Labour victory he can see himself as a possible Foreign Secretary. 'It can't be Kaufman.[39] Kinnock would do better to bring Healey[40]

35 Actor, 1908–90.

36 In 1987 the bulk of the SDP membership merged with the Liberals to form the Liberal Democrats. At the 1992 general election the rump of SDP MPs disappeared: David Owen did not stand, and Rosie Barnes and John Cartwright, standing as independent Social Democrats, lost their seats.

37 1925–2013; MP for Finchley 1959–92; Prime Minister 1979–90; later Baroness Thatcher LG, OM, FRS.

38 MP for Bedwellty 1970–83, Islwyn 1983–95; Leader of the Labour Party, 1983–92; later Baron Kinnock.

39 Gerald Kaufman, MP for Manchester Ardwick 1970–83, Manchester Gorton since 1983; shadow Foreign Secretary, 1987–92.

40 Denis Healey, MP for Leeds South East 1952–5, Leeds East 1955–92; Chancellor of the Exchequer 1974–9; shadow Foreign Secretary 1981–7; later Baron Healey CH.

out of retirement for a couple of years.' He isn't bothered that Kinnock's no intellectual titan. 'He'll manage the party and the civil servants can run the country.' I hoovered up the bacon and baked beans. He ate a single orange and then went out into the forecourt where half of Fleet Street seemed to be waiting to photograph him. It was an exciting conversation and it's left me thinking: if I don't stand in this election, I'm going to have to wait another five years. Go for it, boy.

MONDAY 4 JUNE 1990

David Owen hogs the headlines: 'Decade of hope ends in humiliation ... Owen's odyssey from giddy heights to political failure ... Owen – the great might-have-been.' SDP RIP. What does David Sainsbury[41] do with his money now?

Up on the Wirral we have a good day. It's the opening of the Inner City Village Hall. HRH is very mellow. The only problem is the weather. As we await the royal arrival, the wind blows and the hapless ladies in the line-up battle to keep their hats on and their skirts down. Inevitably, as it lands, Prince Philip's helicopter makes matters worse and most of the bobbing up and down, the curtseying and the handshaking, is done with left hands on head and skirts bunched and held steady between knocked-knees.

SUNDAY 10 JUNE 1990

The failure of Royal Britain is the lead story in the *Mail on Sunday* financial section:

> Unicorn Heritage, the brainchild of TV presenter Gyles Brandreth, has folded.
> The company, which raised over £7 million to stage a permanent exhibition of
> the monarchy at London's Barbican Centre, is to go into voluntary liquidation ...
> Unicorn was sponsored by BES specialists Johnson Fry. 'I told investors from Day
> One that the company would either make you a fortune or lose all your money,'
> said chairman Charles Fry.

The truth is the idea was okay, but the product wasn't quite right, the initial management wasn't quite right, the marketing was off-target and the location was a disaster. Bugger. Bugger. Bugger.

---

41   A generous funder of the SDP whose wife, Susie, was at school with GB.

MONDAY 25 JUNE 1990

On Friday I was at the Connaught Rooms for the Unicorn Heritage Creditors Meeting – a humiliation and a nightmare. On Saturday I was back at the Connaught Rooms presiding over the National Scrabble Championship Finals! I am described on the front page of today's *Times* as 'the high priest of trivia'. Michèle says, 'If your claim to fame is that you founded the Scrabble Championships and you go on wearing those silly jumpers, what do you expect? People will take you not for what you are, but for what they see. That's life.' Bah.

Long letter from Windsor Castle. HRH has been brooding about the Inner City Village Hall:

> I think it should be possible to refine the design with a view to reducing costs still further. For instance, there is a lot of wasted space above the changing room and office area. It might be worth looking at the idea of putting the changing rooms etc. area outside the main hall as a 'lean-to'. The 'lean-to' could then be fitted on to the hall in the most convenient place. This would also add some flexibility to the design by adding it either at one end or along one side or the other...

We go to Wimbledon, the royal box. It's a treat and lovely to be asked etc., but we mustn't accept again. The lunch is jolly (ish), but the tennis is wasted on me. I have not the least idea what is going on.

FRIDAY 13 JULY 1990

The hottest day of the year finds us filming in the glorious garden of Hadspen House. Tomorrow, Stourton. Sunday, Stourhead. Also feeling the heat is Nicholas Ridley[42] who looks set to be booted out of the Cabinet having given an interview to *The Spectator* in which he declares that Germany is trying to take over Europe...

MONDAY 20 AUGUST 1990

As the world prepares for war, the Brandreths prepare for Italy. President Bush is planning a lightning strike against Iraq as Saddam Hussein rounds up Americans, Britons,

---

42 1929–1993; Secretary of State for the Environment; MP for Cirencester & Tewksbury 1959–92.

French and Germans in Kuwait. In Barnes we pack our bags because tomorrow we're off on a lightning trip of our own – to Verona in Colin and Rosie Sanders' private jet. It's all right for some … It's all right for *us*. This is typical of Colin: after the Royal Britain collapse he called and said, 'You need cheering up. Let's go to the opera.' And so we are.

WEDNESDAY 22 AUGUST 1990

The Arena di Verona is amazing: a vast, outdoor amphitheatre, the third largest in the Roman world, seating 20,000 and more. Since AD 30 it's seen Christians thrown to the lions, gladiatorial combat, bullfights, public executions, but tonight, for us, it was *Tosca*. We sat in the best seats in the house (of course), slim flutes of champagne in hand (naturally), surrounded by exhausted victims of corporate hospitality. Next to us, bewildered Japanese; immediately in front, a group who had started the day in Ohio and were fast asleep (all eight of them) way before the end of Act One. Even better than the show (a Philistine speaks!) was the post-Puccini supper – a late-night cold collation back at the hotel: *antipasto di frutti di mare*, wafer-thin *carpaccio* with rocket salad and parmesan, washed down with buckets of chilled Prosecco. As a rule I subscribe to the Noel Coward line that 'work is more fun than fun', but once in a while the soft life can be very sweet.

FRIDAY 24 AUGUST 1990

Wednesday night was sensational: the show rivalled the midnight feast! It was *Zorba the Greek*. At first, Colin was disconcerted to find it was a ballet, not an opera, but it was *so* fantastic, and such a surprise, such an unexpected treat, we were all bowled over. Essentially it was the ballet of the movie, with the Mikis Theodorakis score and Mikis in person on the podium! It was a life-enhancing triumph, my best ever night at the opera.

Yesterday was pretty good too. We flew to Venice for lunch. Colin hadn't realised it was only down the road, so we'd hardly taken off before we landed. And in the evening we were back at the Arena for the Verona standard, *Aida*, through most of which Colin kept muttering 'Where are the elephants? Where are the elephants? It isn't a proper *Aida* without elephants.'

At the airport this morning it's back to reality. We buy newspapers ('Angry Bush takes a step closer to war', '40,000 reserve forces called up by US') and, now we've been part of it for seventy-two hours, notice that the private-jet-set get a tangibly mixed reception. We're whisked past the bucket-shop *hoi polloi*, to be sure, but our passage through customs and passport control isn't so smooth: there's a fair bit of that just-because-you're-filthy-rich-don't-think-you're-getting-any-special-treatment-from-me atmosphere in the air.

....

THURSDAY 30 AUGUST 1990

....

This may be the day that changes my life. I hope so.

As far back as I can remember I have wanted to be a Member of Parliament. At Betteshanger, in 1959, I was the Liberal candidate (age eleven). At Bedales, in 1964, I came out for Sir Alec.[43] In 1970, the election that brought Ted Heath to power was held on the last day of my Finals.[44] I took the train to London to vote, went back to Oxford to party, and returned to London again to be on call overnight at Television Centre as the 'Conservative Voice of Youth' (!), alongside Jack Straw[45] for Labour. In the mid '70s I toyed with getting myself onto the candidates list (but didn't follow it through) and I've kept in touch (sort of) with Oxford contemporaries who are in there now, but until this year, this summer really, these past few weeks, I haven't sensed that I was going to go for it, to make it happen. Well, now I am.

It's really rather funny to be forty-two, to be aspiring to be a Member of Parliament, and to have not the least idea how to set about it. I probably appear as cocky and confident as they come: in truth, I'm as diffident and as uncertain as all get-out. Anyway, the point is: this morning I took my courage in my hands and called Jeffrey Archer.[46] I began dialling (only Jeffrey's number could contain the digits 007) and then – suddenly – lost my nerve and hung up. I sat looking at the telephone, staring at it stupidly, and then, saying to myself, out loud, 'Don't be such an idiot, pull yourself together man', I picked up the receiver and dialled again. Jeffrey was there, and easy and helpful and *kind*.

'Yes,' he barked, 'It's about time. As I said to your mother, "If only he'd got on with it when I first told him to, he'd be in the Cabinet by now."'

I don't know quite how or where or when Jeffrey can have met my mother, but never

---

43   Sir Alec Douglas-Home, Prime Minister 1963–4, later Lord Home of Hirsel.

44   GB went to Betteshanger, a prep school in Kent, 1958–61; Bedales, a coeducational boarding school in Hampshire, 1961–6; and was a Scholar at New College, Oxford, 1967–70. Edward Heath, 1916–2005, MP for Bexley 1950–74, Bexley Sidcup 1974–83, Old Bexley & Sidcup since 1983, Leader of the Conservative Party 1965–75, Prime Minister 1970–74, was President of the Oxford Union in 1939. Thirty years later GB was President of the Union and, on one of the Leader of the Opposition's visits to Oxford, GB was presented to him. Unfortunately GB was unwell and, on shaking Heath's hand for the first time, threw up.

45   President of the National Union of Students in 1970; Labour MP for Blackburn since 1979.

46   Novelist; MP for Louth 1969–74; deputy chairman of the Conservative Party 1985–6; Lord Archer of Weston-super-Mare from 1992; a friend of GB since the early '70s.

mind. He explained that I'll only get a seat if I'm on the official candidates' list (which I knew) and that the man I need to see (which I didn't know) is one Tom Arnold, son of the impresario, MP for Hazel Grove[47] and vice-chairman of the party in charge of candidates.

I call Central Office right away. Tom Arnold isn't there. I speak to a terrifying young woman with a triple-barrelled surname and marshmallows in her mouth. I don't say who I am or why I'm calling – I mutter, 'It's not urgent, I'll call back' and hang up. But this afternoon (having discovered from *Who's Who* that Tom Arnold also went to Bedales!) I write to him, saying here I am, this is who I am, and can I come and see you? So the deed is done.

FRIDAY 7 SEPTEMBER 1990

A letter arrives from Mrs Camilla Barnett Legh, Candidates Department, Conservative Central Office: 'Sir Thomas Arnold has asked me to thank you for your letter of 30 August. Perhaps you would be good enough to telephone this office in order to make an appointment to see Sir Thomas at your convenience.' We're on our way! ... Or so I think until I telephone Mrs Barnett Legh who tells me (from a great height) that the earliest, 'absolutely the earliest', Sir Thomas can fit me in is Monday 5 November at 3.20 p.m. An appointment two months down the road at twenty past the hour does not suggest an *urgent* desire to see me nor the prospect of an extended interview, but what can I do? Be grateful I suppose – and hope the election isn't called meanwhile.

I still haven't told Michèle what I'm up to.

SUNDAY 9 SEPTEMBER 1990

Mrs T. is on *Frost* saying she expects to be around for a good few years yet, certainly till she's seventy. 'Some people *started* their administrations at seventy.' She's ridiculous, but wonderful.

SUNDAY 26 SEPTEMBER 1990

The news is not good. The World Health Organization is predicting that thirty million

---

people will have Aids by the year 2000. The Chancellor of the Exchequer[48] is forecasting 'the most difficult few months of the cycle'. And Michèle is saying, 'The recession is coming. We've got to batten down the hatches.'

Hot news: Britain is to join the European exchange rate mechanism on Monday when interest rates will be cut by 1 per cent to 14 per cent. Everyone agrees it's a brilliant move: Major, Hurd,[49] Kinnock, the Bank of England and the TUC. Nigel Lawson[50] is euphoric: 'I warmly welcome this historic decision which I have long advocated.' Mrs T. is giving a press conference outside No. 10. 'Rejoice! Rejoice!' Naturally there's heated speculation about 'a dash to the polls' – and I haven't even had my frigging first interview yet!

Jill Bennett[51] has died. I last saw her not long ago, very drunk at the Caprice. We embraced like long-lost lovers, but she hadn't a clue who I was. I doubt any of the obituaries will feature one of my favourite filthy Coral Browne[52] stories. As a girl Jill had had a passionate affair with a much older actor, Godfrey Tearle I think. Said Coral, 'I never could understand what Godfrey Tearle got out of his relationship with Jill Bennett – until one night I saw her eating corn-on-the-cob at the Caprice.'

These charity lunches are quite a burden. Making it happen, making it work, making it all seem effortless. Anyway, I put Joanna [Lumley] next to HRH at lunch today and it solved everything. She's perfect and he's charming and they looked as if they were actually having quite a jolly time. Small talk with royalty isn't easy. Being normal with royalty is impossible.

There's that great line of Joyce Grenfell's mother: 'When royalty leaves the room, it's like getting a seed out of your tooth.'

---

48 John Major, MP for Huntingdonshire 1979–83, Huntingdon from 1983; Chancellor of the Exchequer 1989–90; Prime Minister 1990–97; later Sir John Major KG, CH.

49 Douglas Hurd, MP for Mid-Oxon 1974–83, Witney 1983–97; Foreign Secretary 1989–95; later Baron Hurd of Westwell CH.

50 MP for Blaby 1974–92; Chancellor of the Exchequer 1983–9; later Baron Lawson of Blaby.

51 Actress, 1931–90.

52 Australian actress, 1913–91.

FRIDAY 19 OCTOBER 1990

The Lib Dems have won Eastbourne with a 20 per cent swing from the Tories, Howe[53] and Major are at loggerheads, the rift on monetary union is rocking the party, and this is the moment I choose to enter the fray! Maybe it won't happen. Maybe I'm right not to have told Michèle. Maybe my destiny is to be the high priest of trivia. Today I had sessions on *Puzzle World*, the Butlin's project, and the *TV Joke Book*. Tomorrow I'm in Stratford leading the Pudsey Bear Parade. And on Monday I'm at Merchant Taylor's Hall hosting 'The Barbie Summit'. Apparently, I'll get to meet the original Ken and Barbie – 'in person'.

So this is it…

'Gyles Brandreth – who was he?'

'Oh, you know – the poor man's Jeremy Beadle.'

FRIDAY 2 NOVEMBER 1990

Geoffrey Howe has resigned in protest over Mrs T.'s attitude to Europe. 'I can no longer serve your government with honour.' There's a wonderful picture in *The Times* of the Thatcher Cabinet in 1979. Eleven years later and there's not one of them left. She's eaten every single one … By way of tribute at the Caprice at lunch I chose *steak tartare* and was delighted Colin Moynihan hadn't cried off. He's fun, puck-like, and friendly. He seemed very sanguine about Mrs T.'s own prospects – rather less so about his own. He's got a majority of 5,000 but on current form reckons that won't be enough. I didn't ask him about Tom Arnold. I'm not sure why. I think it's partly awkwardness, shyness even, partly self-protection. If I don't tell anyone I've put up for something, if I don't get it nobody knows and I can pretend (even to myself) it never happened.

MONDAY 5 NOVEMBER 1990

'Thatcher moves to fight off Heseltine[54] threat' was today's headline. This I did not discuss this afternoon when I had my brief encounter with Sir Thomas Arnold MP. I reached

53   Geoffrey Howe, Deputy Prime Minister, Leader of the Commons and Lord President of the Council, 1989–90; MP for Bebington 1964–6, Reigate 1970–74, Surrey East 1974–92; Chancellor of the Exchequer 1979–83; Foreign Secretary 1983–9; later Baron Howe of Aberavon CH. John Major replaced him as Foreign Secretary in July 1989. Major became Chancellor in October 1989 when Lawson resigned.

54   Michael Heseltine, MP for Tavistock 1966–74, Henley since 1974; Secretary of State for the Environment 1990–92; President of the Board of Trade 1992–5; Deputy Prime Minister 1995–7. He resigned as Defence Secretary in 1986 over the Westland affair.

St James' station at three o'clock and contrived a roundabout route (via Victoria Station!) so that I walked into 32 Smith Square on the dot of 3.15. I was expected. A girl emerged, easy, friendly, and ushered me past a mighty free-standing portrait of Mrs T. in all her glory towards a little side door that led to what felt very much like the back stairs. Up we went, round bends, along narrow corridors, on and on, until we reached the great man's door. She knocked. A grunt, 'Come!' She opened the door and in I went. The office was tiny, more a vestibule than a room, and Sir Tom, my sort of age but looking older, sat behind his small, sparsely covered desk peering over half-moon specs and effortlessly exuding the discreet charm of the seasoned Tory MP. We exchanged pleasantries (it turned out he was only at Bedales for about ten minutes) and then I came to the point. Could I join the candidates list? Sir Tom was cordial but non-committal. Then he turned to gaze out of the window, narrowed his eyes a moment, touched his mouth with a finger and said, as if thinking out loud, hardly above a whisper, 'Officially, the list *is* closed. It's all done and dusted. But … you never know.' He turned back to the desk and flashed a crinkly smile. He opened a buff folder.

'Here are the forms. If you care to fill them in and let me have them back, we'll take it from there.' He opened his diary. 'Let's meet again on, say, 19 December at 6.30 p.m. Will that suit?'

It won't suit at all, but I said, 'Yes, yes, of course, thank you, thank you so much.'

I was out by three-thirty, the conversation was brief and straightforward, but the combination of Sir Tom's manner – the hushed tone, a certain urgency of delivery, a face with a touch of sadness in repose transformed by sudden brilliant smiles – and the smallness of the room itself gave the meeting an oddly conspiratorial quality. At Oxford I always felt a little hurt that no one had approached me about the possibility of joining MI6. I imagine the initial interview would have felt something like this afternoon's encounter.

TUESDAY 6 NOVEMBER 1990

At noon I was at Buckingham Palace, standing outside the Chinese Drawing Room (or is it the Yellow Drawing Room and I think it's Chinese because of the vases and the *chinoiserie* on the walls?), awaiting the arrival of HRH. As the clock struck he emerged from a door at the far, far end of the long corridor and I watched him walk towards me. He was alone and came quite slowly. It's an odd thing to say, but he seemed almost vulnerable and for the first time made me think of my father. Anyway, we went through the ceremony – handing over certificates to worthies in the playing fields movement – and he laughed because I had arranged the group differently from the last couple of times – 'Can't leave anything alone, can you?' – and he did his stuff with the usual aplomb and then wandered off to the next engagement (horologists I think he said).

I went on to meet up with Peter Marsh.[55] From Greek prince to Greek god. Peter is decking himself out as a portly Adonis these days: gold at the wrist, gold around the neck, I swear there's a gold rinse in the hair – and why not? He's being fantastic with the appeal and he said something that struck home: 'If you can't convey the essence of your message in fewer than eight words, you're not clear about your message. Slogans and catchphrases shouldn't be glib; they should go to the heart of the matter.' He's certainly delivered for us. HRH and I burble on about playing fields and playgrounds, and the value of sport and recreation, and the threats and the dangers and the needs and what-not, and Peter has summed it up in seven words: 'Every child deserves a place to play.'

WEDNESDAY 7 NOVEMBER 1990

'Hurd says Heseltine is "glamour without substance".'

'Heseltine says he won't stand against Thatcher this month.'

Just as I need the Conservative Party to start thinking about *me* the buggers seem to have other things on their minds … Undaunted (quite daunted actually) I have now written to my three potential sponsors. The form requires 'Names and addresses of three responsible persons who will support your candidature. These should include, if possible, one MP and a constituency chairman. At least one of your referees should have known you for ten years or more.' I don't know any constituency chairmen, so I've gone for my local MP (Jeremy Hanley)[56] and two Cabinet ministers: one a former party chairman, John Gummer (whom I first met twenty years ago at one of Johnnie and Fanny Cradock's parties when he was squiring Arianna Stassinopoulos) and William Waldegrave,[57] since Saturday the Secretary of State for Health.

SATURDAY 10 NOVEMBER 1990

'By-election disasters in Bradford and Bootle.' 'Heseltine steps up the challenge.' 'The recession will last until Spring.' Very cheery. Yet there is better news in Barnes: I've signed

---

55 Founder of the advertising agency Allen, Brady and Marsh, he was helping market the NPFA's fund-raising appeal. GB and Michèle bought their house in Barnes from him in 1986.

56 MP for Richmond & Barnes 1983–97.

57 MP for Bristol West 1979–97, a contemporary of GB at university. He was promoted to the Cabinet in the reshuffle that followed Geoffrey Howe's resignation. Later Baron Waldegrave of North Hill and Provost of Eton since 2009.

to do my first commercial (should total £20,000) and I've told Michèle what I'm up to on the political front. Sweetened by the former, she seems *fairly* relaxed about the latter. I think she thinks it won't happen. I think she's right.

MONDAY 12 NOVEMBER 1990

My back has gone again. I cannot move at all. At all. I can't get to the osteopath and until the spasm subsides apparently there's nothing she can do here. I hate this when it happens, not just because I hate being trapped like this, but also because I know it happens when I'm tired and tense and anxious – and I don't like to admit I'm ever tired or tense or anxious! Michèle says, 'Oh God, not another mid-life crisis – spare us', but in fact she's being wonderful (as ever) and she's cancelled everything for the next three days. I need to be up by Thursday for the Coopers Lybrand speech in Sutton Coldfield.

WEDNESDAY 14 NOVEMBER 1990

'Howe attack leaves MPs gasping.' I watched it on the box and it didn't seem that devastating. Damaging certainly, but fatal? I wonder.

THURSDAY 15 NOVEMBER 1990

'Heseltine flings down gauntlet for leadership' – and proposes an early Poll Tax review, which has to make sense.

I'm on my feet again and off to see the osteopath at ten. I've used the three days in bed to draft and redraft my application form. 'Why do you wish to become a Member of Parliament?' 'What makes you think you would be a good candidate?' 'What aspects of campaigning do you most favour?' 'What do you feel are your major strengths and attributes?' The easiest page was the last one: 'Is there any serious incident in your life or aspect of your character, either personal or business, which might cause you and the party embarrassment if they were disclosed subsequent to your selection?' No. 'Have you ever been convicted of a criminal offence?' No. 'In a typical year, how many days do you have off work because of illness?' None. 1990 just isn't typical…

William Waldegrave's reply is in: 'Thank you so much for your kind words about my new appointment. It was very thoughtful of you to write. I need all the encouragement and support I can get in what is obviously an enormous job – though a very interesting and challenging one. I would be delighted to be one of your sponsors. Please use my name freely.' Hooray.

FRIDAY 16 NOVEMBER 1990

Gummer says yes. Two down, one to go. Meanwhile, on the main stage the Thatcher camp say they expect her to win on the first ballot, but one of the opinion polls says Heseltine as leader would give us a 10 point lead.

On the train to Sutton Coldfield I read the Muggeridge[58] obituaries. He was a desiccated old tortoise, self-opinionated, self-righteous and when I fell out with the rest of the Longford Committee and published that diary of our antics in Copenhagen he tore me off a strip ('and to think you have enjoyed nut rissoles at my table'). As a performer he had a certain style, but for all his professional piety and late avowal of the ascetic life, he was a dirty old man. I'm trying to remember who told us about having to break his thumb when he tried to jump her when she was making a phone call in the bedroom at somebody's party. It wasn't that long ago.

TUESDAY 20 NOVEMBER 1990

Letter from Jeremy Hanley:

> I would willingly sponsor you for the candidates list although I think you have far more to offer the world than to waste your time traipsing through the lobbies of the House of Commons late into the night when you could be giving brilliant after dinner speeches. Personally I think you would be a superb Member of Parliament, but the life involves very little free time to pursue other careers, quite contrary to the popular view of MPs with their 'noses in the trough' or being very 'part time' members. Frankly I would send you straight to the House of Lords!

WEDNESDAY 21 NOVEMBER 1990

Last night's vote: Thatcher 204; Heseltine 132. She was four short of the 56-vote lead she needed to secure an outright win. I watched it live and the way she swept towards the

---

58   Malcolm Muggeridge, writer and broadcaster, 1903–90.

camera – 'I fight on, I fight to win' – was wonderful to behold. But the feeling seems to be it's all over.

FRIDAY 23 NOVEMBER 1990

There's a magnificent lead letter in *The Times* today. It runs to five words. Peter Marsh would approve. 'Donkeys led by a lion.'

Apparently she began yesterday's Cabinet meeting with tears in her eyes and a written statement in her hand: 'I have concluded that the unity of the party and the prospects of victory would be better served if I stood down to enable Cabinet colleagues to enter the ballot.' I watched her bravura performance later in the Commons. She was quite magnificent. 'I'm enjoying this! I'm enjoying this!' It was so impressive – whatever you thought of her – and rather moving, ditto.

SATURDAY 24 NOVEMBER 1990

A pleasantly late and liquid night with Jo and Stevie and Simon followed by an unpleasantly early start to get to King's Cross by 8.50. I'm touring the New for Knitting shops.[59] Yesterday, Ilkeston. Today, York. Another train journey, another good obituary. Roald Dahl[60] has died. He was a genius, but odd to look at and really quite creepy to be with.

TUESDAY 27 NOVEMBER 1990

I spent a long day at Shepperton making the Birdseye Waffle commercial: eight hours to shoot thirty seconds. In the real world Mrs Thatcher is now backing John Major. I'm backing Douglas Hurd. In the world of Birdseye Waffles no one seems the least bit interested in who our next Prime Minister is going to be.

LATER

The result is in. Major, 185; Heseltine, 131; Hurd, 56. John Major becomes the youngest

---

59   GB was a director of a chain of specialist knitting wool retail shops.

60   Children's writer, 1916–90.

Prime Minister since Lord Rosebery in 1894 and Michèle tells me that my man coming in last is a useful indication of the reliability of my political instincts.

SATURDAY 1 DECEMBER 1990

There are now no women in the Cabinet (a mistake I would not have made) but Ann Widdecombe[61] joins the government for the first time. The paper describes her as 'a doughty fighter'. At Oxford she was a funny little thing. But mock not, Brandreth. She's in the government. You aren't.

SUNDAY 9 DECEMBER 1990

This weekend we went to see Benet's *Twelfth Night* (I love that play), put up the Christmas tree (our best ever – I know I always say that, but I think this time it's true) and, with champagne from Ros and Mart,[62] toasted the house of Thatcher. The Queen has given Mrs T. the Order of Merit and Denis gets a baronetcy. (In due course it'll be 'Arise Sir Mark…' That's the irony.) Tomorrow at 10 a.m. I'll be at the Dance Attic in Putney Bridge Road with a lordly title of mine own. It's Day One of the *Cinderella* rehearsals and I'm reviving my Baron Hardup. Bonnie Langford is Cinders, Brian Conley (whom I don't know at all) is Buttons, and Barbara Windsor (whom I know and like a lot) is the Fairy Queen. I've got third billing, above Barbara, which is all wrong, of course, shaming really, but there we are.[63]

WEDNESDAY 12 DECEMBER 1990

Tonight we are not going to Jeffrey [Archer]'s party. I wanted to go, but Michèle can't face it. 'All that nonsense of "Krug and shepherd's pie", and there are always too many people, and nobody wants to talk to the wives – ever. It's just self-regarding men preening themselves, looking over your shoulder all the time for someone more interesting, more famous, more like them. Ghastly. Never again.'

We didn't cry off from drinks with the Queen last night however. Perhaps it would

---

61   MP for Maidstone, 1987–2010; a contemporary of GB at university.

62   Rosalind Ayres and Martin Jarvis, actors, friends of GB.

63   This was before her television renaissance in the BBC's *EastEnders*.

have been better if we had. Neither of us was in tiptop form. When Her Majesty arrived, Michèle forgot to curtsey – and then remembered forty seconds into the small talk and suddenly, unexpectedly, without warning, bobbed right down and semi-toppled into the royal bosom. My performance was hardly more impressive. As the canapés came round I found myself in an isolated corner, stranded with Her Majesty, frantic for food (I hadn't eaten since breakfast) but obliged to pass up on every tasty morsel that came past because the Queen wasn't partaking and I somehow felt it would be *lèse-majesté* for me to be eating when she wasn't. All I could think about was how hungry I was. My desultory attempt at conversation can best be described as jejune.

GB: Had a busy day, Ma'am?

HM: Yes. Very.

GB: At the Palace?

HM: Yes.

GB: A lot of visitors?

HM: Yes.

(Pause)

GB: The Prime Minister?

HM: Yes.

(Pause)

GB: He's very nice.

HM: Yes. Very.

GB: The recession's bad.

HM (looking grave): Yes.

GB: Set to get worse, apparently.

HM (slight sigh): Yes.

GB (trying to jolly it along): I think this must be my third. Recession, that is.

HM: Yes. We do seem to get them every few years – (tinkly laugh) and none of my governments seems to know what to do about them!

GB (uproarious laughter): Yes. Absolutely. Very good.

(Long pause. Trays of canapés come and go.)

GB: I've been to Wimbledon today.

HM (brightening): Oh, yes?

GB (brightening too): Yes.

HM (We're both trying hard now): I've been to Wimbledon too.

GB (Exhilarated): Today?

HM: No.

GB (Well, we tried): No, of course not. (Pause) I wasn't at the tennis.

HM: No?

GB: No. I was at the theatre. (Long pause) Have you been to the theatre in Wimbledon? (Pause)

HM: I imagine so.

(Interminable pause)

GB: You know, Ma'am, my wife's a vegetarian.

HM: That must be very dull.

GB: And my daughter's a vegetarian too.

HM: Oh dear.

Well, I had had a long day, and she has had a long reign.

THURSDAY 20 DECEMBER 1990

I had my second encounter with Tom Arnold last night. I had been worrying about the logistics of it since he first proposed the date. I think it may well have been what brought on the bad back. Seriously. I knew I had to be – *had to be* – in two places at the same time: on the stage of the Wimbledon Theatre for the technical run-through of *Cinderella* and in Sir Tom's office at 32 Smith Square, SW1. Happily the gods smiled on me and a moment or two before six, as my stomach churned and my back twinged, Michael Hurll (our director), bless him, announced the supper-break: 'Back at seven, sharp.' I had warned him that I had to 'slip out for half an hour' and I'd booked a black cab and had it waiting at the stage-door. I tore off my Baron Hardup costume, threw on my charcoal-grey suit, leapt into the cab and reached Smith Square at just gone 6.20.

I was ushered past a splendid portrait of John Major in the foyer (a month is a long time in politics) and led up the back stairs to the Arnold closet. I stepped into his room on the dot of six-thirty. A moment of banter, no more – 'There seem to have been some changes since I was last here,' I burbled: he laughed softly and gave nothing away – then I handed over my completed forms. He turned the pages. 'Mmm … mmm … very good … Gummer, Waldegrave, Hanley … mmm … Hanley.'

'I went for the local MP rather than the association chairman because I know the MP so much better,' I said, as casually as I could. (I don't know the local chairman at all, of course, but I have tried, consciously, not to lie outright at any stage in the process to date. This is Michèle's influence.) He patted his lips with his fingers and half-closed his eyes. 'Mmm … mmm.' I had decided what I wanted to say before the meeting and I said it: 'I appreciate I'm not on the list, but, while you're processing this, if a possibility crops up, would it be okay for me to throw my hat in the ring?' His face crinkled into a sudden smile. His eyes narrowed. He glanced furtively to left and right and then leant forward and in a voice barely above a whisper said, 'I don't see why not.' He tapped the side of his nose and smiled again, and then opened up his diary.

'Let's see. We'll next meet on Wednesday 23 January. Yes?'

'In the morning?' I said, as lightly as I could (I didn't mention the matinee at two).

'11.00 a.m.?'

'Fine.'

At 7.03 p.m., on the stage of the Wimbledon Theatre the Lord Chamberlain (Ed 'Stewpot' Stewart) announced 'His Excellency the Baron Hardup of Hardup Hall' and I made my entrance – on cue, but in a charcoal-grey suit. The Ugly Sisters had a lot of fun with that.

CHAPTER II

1991

New Year headlines: 'Prospect of early election recedes.' 'Gulf war could mean tax rise, Lamont[64] hints.' 'Visit by Major to Ulster will revive hope on initiative.' 'Marlene Dietrich has briefly emerged from years of seclusion to help save the studios outside Berlin where she made *The Blue Angel*.'

One of my proudest memories is of holding Marlene's left thigh. Outside the stage door of the Golders Green Hippodrome, one night in 1964, Simon [Cadell] and I helped her off the roof of her limousine. Precariously, on spindly heels she teetered about on the roof of the car, blowing little kisses and distributing signed photos to the fans. She was wearing a black mini-skirt slashed to the waist (or so it seemed) and, as we helped ease her to the ground, Simon got the right leg and I got the left.

....
WEDNESDAY 16 JANUARY 1991
....

Iraq rejects last-ditch peace moves as UN Gulf deadline expires. Major wins cross-party support in Commons – though fifty-five Labour people abstained or voted against (quite useful in the longer term). Saddam is promising that 'the mother of all wars will be waged'. Heath wants time for sanctions to work. Naturally. 'No choice but war' says *The Times* leader. No choice but *Cinderella* at 2.30 and 7.30 says GB. Actually, I'm rather enjoying it. It's a good show, glossy, doesn't hang around, and three grand a week.

---

64 Norman Lamont, MP for Kingston-upon-Thames 1972–97, had been John Major's campaign manager in his bid for the leadership in November 1990 and became Chancellor of the Exchequer when Major became Prime Minister. Later Baron Lamont of Lerwick.

Bonnie, Barbara, Brian, Ray Alan (even Lord Charles, *especially* Lord Charles),[65] they're all *troupers*, doing it now just as their forebears would have done it a century ago. It's a cosy company, a nice old theatre – we're cocooned backstage, out there there's the distant rumble of war – it could all have been scripted by J. B. Priestley. He'd have enjoyed a moment with me last night. There's a small corner in the wings where I do several of my quick changes. There's a makeshift screen and behind it propped on a wooden chair a long mirror lit by a single bare bulb. Just before the ghost scene I was standing ready in my knitted nightshirt when one of the dancers popped her head around the screen.

'May I?'

'Of course.'

She came round and pulled off her top and stood naked for a moment shaking her hair loose in front of the mirror. She looked at me and smiled. 'Sorry.'

'Not at all.' I tried to look at her face.

'They're small, aren't they?' she said, pulling on her top again.

'No. Yes. I mean they're charming.'

And she'd gone. I can't help feeling a proper leading man would have handled the situation with rather more *panache*.

THURSDAY 17 JANUARY 1991

'4.00 a.m.: Bombs rain down on Iraqi capital as war erupts in Operation Desert Storm.'

I had a disconcerting experience during the show tonight. I have three spots when I'm alone on stage, burbling to the audience, and during one of them I suddenly felt as if I was up in the gallery looking down on myself – I could see myself from a long way away, as if I was looking through the wrong end of the telescope, and I was this tiny figure in a ridiculous costume and I just wanted to laugh out loud at the complete absurdity of it. Instead, I dried – not noticeably, I don't think – but, just for a second, my mind went blank and I had no idea where I was, what I was doing or what came next.

SATURDAY 19 JANUARY 1991

'After just fifty days in office, Britain's youngest Prime Minister this century has been forced to become a war leader. His hardest passage so far came during the pre-dawn

65 Ventriloquist Ray Alan's dummy.

hours yesterday morning. John Major had slept no more than two hours during Wednesday night as he received intelligence briefings on the first sorties against Iraq. He retired on Thursday night about midnight but aides woke him in the Downing Street flat at 12.45 a.m. The development they feared most had happened: Iraq's launching of missiles against Israel, threatening a belligerent response that could detach the Arabs from the allied coalition.'[66]

How soon will I get to meet him? Will I get to meet him? Benny Hill is coming to the show today. That's who the cast here all want to meet. He's their kind of hero.

WEDNESDAY 23 JANUARY 1991

My third encounter with Tom Arnold. It's the routine as before: I'm trundled up the back stairs, bundled along the corridor, ushered through his door into his cubby-hole as the clock strikes. (I imagine the secretary doesn't come in because the room couldn't fit three at a time.) Tom is as ever – charming, elusive, conspiratorial – but this time I've come prepared. No more pussy-footing, no more amiable small talk leading nowhere in particular. From my briefcase I produce a piece of paper and lay it on the table in front of him:

To: Sir Thomas Arnold MP

Coming from a large family, and as the chairman of a national body with affiliated associations in every English county, and as a director of a retail chain with thirty branches, I can claim links with many parts of the country.

Specifically I have direct business or family ties with each of the following constituencies:

Hertsmere

City of Chester

Croydon Central

Brighton Pavilion

Castle Point

Chingford

I live not far from Croydon, and my associations with Chester and Hertsmere are particularly close, as my father and his family come from the former and my sister and her family live in the latter.

(Okay, so my father came from Hoylake, but Chester's close. And if St Albans isn't in the Hertsmere constituency it ought to be. And desperate times call for desperate measures.)

Tom considered my list and offered a crooked smiled. 'You've been doing your homework.'

---

66 Throughout the diary GB quotes from newspapers, usually either the *Daily Telegraph* or, as here, *The Times*.

'I'm keen.'

'I see.' He lifted the telephone with one hand and put his finger to his lips with the other. He gave me a knowing look and narrowed his eyes. He murmured into the receiver, 'Hertsmere? The list's closed, isn't it? Yes, thanks.'

The upshot is this: I can send my CV to the constituency chairmen at Chester, Croydon, Brighton, Castle Point and Chingford and Tom has said he will send my details to the Central Office agents in the relevant areas with the recommendation that I be considered for an interview. I am to see Tom again on Wednesday 6 March at 11.00 a.m.

At last, progress.

MONDAY 28 JANUARY 1991

The Duke of Edinburgh Birthday Committee meets. HRH will be seventy on 10 June and, with the Duke of Edinburgh's Award Scheme, we're planning a gala bash at Windsor Castle. Prince Edward is *obergruppenführer.* I propose Michael Caine as master of ceremonies and suggest we try Barbra Streisand for the cabaret, but it's a large committee (there's going to be a lot of talk) and it seems on the cabaret-front we're already committed to Harry Connick Jr. (Who he?)[67]

FRIDAY 1 FEBRUARY 1991

Hundreds of Iraqis have been killed in the first real land battle of the war. It's getting dawn-to-dusk coverage on radio and TV, and most nights I tune in briefly after the show. I didn't tonight, because I went with Bonnie and Barbara and Brian to an end-of-run celebration at Joe Allen's. We laughed a lot, gossiped, they talked about their plans. I got Barbara talking a bit about the Krays ('they only ever killed their own') but it was really showbiz-showbiz all the way. The war didn't get a look-in. War in a distant land (even when our boys are involved) is not a topic much touched upon by the Wimbledon Theatre panto players – though I did make Barbara laugh telling her the story Beverley Nichols told me years ago.[68] It was during the darkest days of the Second World War. John Gielgud[69] went to stay with Beverley in the country and,

---

67   American singer and film actor.

68   Writer who had been President of the Oxford Union in 1919. Fifty years later GB had invited him to return to the Union.

69   Actor. GB wrote a biography to celebrate his eightieth birthday in 1984.

on Sunday morning, Beverley got up early to fetch the papers from the village shop. Gielgud had got there first and was sitting in the kitchen surrounded by all the newspapers, with headline after headline blaring doom and gloom, news of setback and disaster on almost every front. Gielgud was ashen-faced, shaking his head in despair. 'John, what on earth has happened?' 'The worst,' wailed Gielgud, 'Gladys has got the most terrible notices!'

SATURDAY 9 FEBRUARY 1991

'Iraqis morale wilts under allied onslaught.' Mine has rather wilted too. And the country has disappeared beneath a blanket of snow.

WEDNESDAY 13 FEBRUARY 1991

Ash Wednesday. Mrs T.'s monetarist gurus have written to *The Times* warning of 'a 1930s style depression' and calling for interest rate cuts. Saddam pledges to talk to Moscow and fight on. And I go to Stratford-upon-Avon to meet Sooty – in person – at the Teddy Bear Museum. Once he's got the glove on, Matthew Corbett suddenly becomes quite charismatic and Sooty (complete with water pistol aimed straight at the local press) is a true star. I present him with the 'Teddy', the Museum's answer to the Oscar, a lifetime achievement award given to those bears who have 'shaken paws with immortality'.

FRIDAY 15 FEBRUARY 1991

Kinnock sacks Short[70] because she won't keep quiet about the war. The jobless figures head for two million. And I head for Croydon where I'm addressing the Croydon Playing Fields Association and, incidentally, hoping to impress any Croydon Conservatives who happen to be in the audience. I sit with Bernard Weatherill,[71] who is easy, urbane, chatty (reminds me of John Profumo) but clearly doesn't see me as a political figure at all. Why should he?

---

70 Clare Short, MP for Birmingham Ladywood since 1983; member of the opposition front bench social security team 1989–91.

71 1920–2007; Speaker of the House of Commons 1983–92; MP for Croydon North East 1964–92.

THURSDAY 21 FEBRUARY 1991

Hallelujah! A letter from the City of Chester Conservative Association: 'The shortlisting has now taken place and I am pleased to say that we would like you to attend an interview on the weekend of 1–3 March. The format of the interview will be questions from the chairman, a ten-minute speech by you without notes on a subject of your choice, followed by further questions from the Interview Panel.' It is simply signed, 'Vanessa. Agent.'

I call her first thing. She sounds friendly, jolly and quite young. I ask to be booked in for the last slot of the weekend: 3.00 p.m. on Sunday the 3rd.

By odd coincidence, tonight we're going for dinner with the Nimmos[72] – one of the last establishments in London (and certainly the only flat in Earl's Court) where they still have liveried footmen waiting at table and the ladies retire to leave the gentlemen to their port and filthy stories. If it hadn't been for Derek I wouldn't have been to Chester even once. He goes there for the racing and, a few years back, suggested Michèle and I take a look at it as a possible location for another attraction like the Teddy Bear Museum. We went for a weekend and liked it a lot, but it was too far from London and the rents were ridiculous.

I told Michèle about the interview and her *first* response was, 'It's fucking miles away!' There wasn't a second response.

WEDNESDAY 27 FEBRUARY 1991

I am writing this in the Reference Room on the first floor of the Chester Public Library. I am speaking in Harrogate tonight and I've come via here for a quick recess. I got the 7.25 from Euston, reached Chester at 9.57 and walked into and around the centre of the town. On the basis that the other candidates will be drawn from the Central Office list, veterans of the circuit with standard set-piece speeches, my aim is to wow them with my local knowledge – and I've got it all here now: the population, the workforce, the balance of services to manufacturing, the unemployment, the poll tax, the county structure plan, the Chester district plan, the proposed park & ride, the works. I've been through six months worth of the local paper – it's as dreary and parochial as they come (and clearly hates us [Conservatives]) but it's full of useful local guff. There's nary a mention of the incumbent,[73] lots on the Labour Euro MP[74] and picture after picture of the Labour prospective candidate, a bearded teacher called David Robinson. I began by

---

72   Derek Nimmo, 1930–99, actor, and his wife Pat, friends of GB.

73   Peter Morrison, 1944–95, MP for the City of Chester 1974–92.

74   Lyndon Harrison, Labour MEP for Cheshire West & Wirral 1989–99.

trawling the *Rolls of the Freemen of the City of Chester (1392–1700)* without much joy, but I'm feeling pretty good all the same. Leafing through *Wills at Chester*, look who I've found: 'Elizabeth Brandreth, deceased, 1591.' A forebear! Who could ask for anything more?

THURSDAY 28 FEBRUARY 1991

I'm going from Harrogate to York, from York to Birmingham, from Birmingham to London. 'Bush calls Gulf ceasefire but warns Iraq not to fight back.' 'Major keen on June poll.' Wouldn't it be wonderful to be selected in March and elected in June? Who *could* ask for anything more?

SUNDAY 3 MARCH 1991

I'm on the train coming home from the initial interview. It went well. I was appallingly nervous, but I don't think it showed. I came up last night and booked myself into the Grosvenor Hotel (owned by the Duke of Westminster who, I imagine, is about the only person who can actually afford to stay there: it's very lush and *very* pricey). I ordered room service for supper and breakfast and lunch and just paced the room running and rerunning my speech. It was personal and passionate (and ridiculous – I know), but it felt as if it was doing the trick: 'It's been my ambition to represent a Cheshire seat in Parliament since I was a small boy. My father, my grandfather, my great-grandfathers going back to Dr Joseph Brandreth who first came to Chester in the 1770s were all born and bred in this part of the world…' I played the local card for all it was worth, gave them my Iain Macleod story,[75] did the family stuff, the visionary stuff, why I am a Conservative ('Why *we* are Conservatives – we believe in building a better world, a world built on principles, the principles of freedom, independence, initiative…') I went for a *ralentando* at the finish to tug at the heartstrings. 'I believe passionately in the values of our party. I know and love the City of Chester. We have such a great cause. This is such a special constituency. How I would love to be your candidate.' Well, I convinced myself anyway. And I liked them. And I think they liked me.

---

75 In 1969 GB, while still at Oxford, had presented a television programme for ITV called *Child of the Sixties* in which he looked back on the '60s and interviewed a range of guests, including the then shadow Chancellor Iain Macleod (1913–70). After the programme, GB asked his hero for advice about a political career and Macleod replied: 'Go away. Get yourself a wife, she'll knock some sense into you. Get some children, they'll knock the stuffing out of you. And do something – build something, make something, achieve something. Then come back and talk to me.'

MONDAY 4 MARCH 1991

Vanessa has called. I'm through to the next round. They're down from around two dozen to about six. There's a candidates' reception on Friday evening ('for yourself and spouse, lounge suit') hosted by the Association's President – i.e. the Duke of Westminster – and a much fuller interview on Saturday. 'This will take the form of a brief summary of your position on the Community Charge, followed by a fifteen-minute presentation on what would be in your manifesto for the election.' I asked if I could again be the last one to be seen. She laughed and said yes. She's rather plain and horsey, but there's a gawky Carol Thatcher energy to her that I like. Tom Arnold's office has also called. My meeting with him is postponed to Thursday, but I'm going to Central Office anyway today to pick up briefing material. As I write I can't pretend to have much grasp of the detail of our policies, but it's still only Monday…

WEDNESDAY 6 MARCH 1991

A rather drunken encounter with Wayne Sleep last night was followed by an extraordinarily indulgent lunch with John and Patti Bratby today. They took us to the Savoy to celebrate John's retrospective at the National Portrait Gallery. Patti was in one of her favourite rubber rigouts and John was looking more like Raymond Briggs's Father Christmas than ever. We had a wonderful window table overlooking the river and so much champagne that halfway through the main course John began to slide beneath the table – literally. *Kaleidoscope* was coming to interview him at 4.00 p.m. so Patti decided to take him up to bed for a recuperative snooze. He pottered off on her arm beaming benignly and waving to his public as he went.

THURSDAY 7 MARCH 1991

Castle Point, Brighton and Croydon Central don't want to see me. Is this because they don't like the look of my CV or because Sir Tom has warned them off me? I don't know and I don't ask. When I'm closeted with him today his manner is more conspiratorial than ever. 'Mmm, mmm, it's going well,' he murmurs, *sotto voce*, 'Going well. They seem to like you. So far. But it's early days. Can't be too careful. Mustn't take anything for granted.' He picks up the telephone and turns away from me and whispers urgently into it. A girl knocks on the door and hands him a document. It's a speech by John Major. He glances around the room. Evidently this is very hush-hush.

'This hasn't been delivered yet, but there's a phrase here I think you might find useful.'
He points to the headline and raises a triumphant eyebrow. '"A society of opportunity".
Mmm. That's the line, isn't it? A society of opportunity. What do you think?'

'Good,' I say. 'Very good.'

'Call me on Monday. Let me know how you get on.'

FRIDAY 8 MARCH 1991

This is my forty-third birthday and John Major's hundredth day as Prime Minister.
We are travelling to Chester on the 11.35 from Euston in the wake of the Ribble Valley by-election. The Lib Dems have overturned our majority of 20,000. 'Setback to
prospect of early election as Conservatives lose their tenth safest constituency.' The
recession and the poll tax are twin killers – but if I've got to explain away the one and
justify the other, I will!

SUNDAY 10 MARCH 1991

It's Mothering Sunday and if Chester went well I've got to put it down to the mother of
my children. At the Friday night drinks with the Duke of Westminster – in the Venetian
Suite of the Grosvenor Hotel – my darling girl was utterly fantastic. She looked exactly
right; she played the part to perfection. She was better than the Princess of Wales would
have been. She worked the room and they lapped her up. The chairman of the women's
committee was Russian-born and Michèle even managed to charm her *in Russian*. What
a woman, what a wife! I tried not to overdo it – not altogether successfully. I said to the
Duke (whom I met years ago, around the time of his twenty-first birthday, when I was
sent to interview him for *Woman* magazine) 'May I call you Gerald?' which was certainly
a mistake. He was easy-going and perfectly charming (great black bags under his eyes,
cigarette constantly on the go), but I sensed he was wary of me, so after my first sortie
with him I steered clear. I don't think he'll be voting for me, but I felt the others might.

On Saturday the format was as before: fourteen inquisitors in a horseshoe around
the candidate seated at a small card table. The Community Charge stuff was fine – I
remembered all the figures and trotted out the Central Office brief.

For my manifesto:

> I begin with first principles. I am a Conservative because I believe in freedom
> – individuality – choice – initiative. I know they can deliver what we want for

ourselves and our children: a society that's happier, healthier, more prosperous, more open – what John Major calls 'a society of opportunity'. A society of opportunity, a compassionate society, a society that prospers and uses its prosperity to create a better quality of life for all.

It felt as if it was working. Thank you, Sir Tom!

I was okay-ish on the questions – except on farming. I'd done no homework on farming. I know nothing about farming. But that didn't seem to matter. The room was with me. When it was over I made for the loo and when I emerged they were all coming out of the interview room. A couple of the women whispered 'Well done!' as they passed, and the chairman – on crutches, he's ex-RAF, avuncular, Mr Pickwick meets Mr Punch – came struggling up, rather embarrassed, and said, 'Good show – but I forgot to ask – anything I ought to know – skeletons in the cupboard – that sort of thing – need your word.'

'I don't think so.' I tried to say it meekly. 'I think you'll be all right with me.'

MONDAY 11 MARCH 1991

We were still in bed with the early morning tea when Sir Tom called.

'It's going well. Going well. But I think you ought to go and see Sir Peter Morrison. I sense he's got one or two reservations.'

'But he's never even met me!'

'Exactly – needs a bit of reassurance. He's not certain about your contribution to the party. Give his office a call and see if he can fit you in.'

Then John Gummer called: 'Peter Morrison will move hell and high water to stop you. He's got his own man and doesn't want you at any price.'

At five o'clock, on the dot, I rang the doorbell at 81 Cambridge Street, SW1. Sir Peter opened the door and beamed. He could not have been more courteous. He is tall, fat, with crinkly hair, piggy eyes, a pink-gin drinker's face, effortlessly patrician, a non-stop smoker and a proper Tory grandee. (I checked him out in *Who's Who* and the credentials are impeccable: Eton, Oxford, White's, Pratt's, son of Lord Margadale, his brother's an MP, his sister is Woman of the Bedchamber to the Queen!) He introduced me to his secretary – 'This is the real Member of Parliament for the City of Chester' – and then we climbed the stairs to a little first-floor drawing room where he sat back on a sofa, glass in one hand, cigarette in the other, and I sat forward facing him, perched on the edge of my seat, willing him to see me as a surprisingly straight bat. Unfortunately he wouldn't lead the conversation. I had to do the talking. I struggled. I asked him about the constituency and he answered in vague generalities. But he said there are going to be boundary changes that'll make it safer. I asked him about the local press. 'I never talk to them,' he said with satisfaction. I asked him why he was giving up (he looks sixty, but he's only forty-six): 'When you've been a Minister of State, deputy chairman of the party, worked with the Prime Minister at No. 10[76] and you know you're not going to get into the Cabinet – and I'm not – it's time to do something else. If I get out now I've got time for a second career. I'm going into business, going to make some money.' After about half an hour we'd both run dry and he was getting restless, so up I got and off I toddled. He wished me luck and said if it went my way in the final round, he'd do whatever he could to help. I don't know what was gained by the encounter, except he will have discovered I don't have green skin and I own at least one sober suit as well as all those ghastly jumpers.

Tonight we had supper down the road with Peter and Sue.[77] They were funny and generous as ever, but I couldn't concentrate at all on the conversation around me. All I could think about was Chester. I've not told any of our friends (or family, other than Michèle, not even the children) what I'm up to. If it happens they'll know soon enough.

TUESDAY 12 MARCH 1991

Dear Gyles,

I am writing to confirm you are now down to the final three in our selection of a prospective candidate. The procedure for the final selection meetings will be as follows:

a) Thursday 14 March, Executive Council Meeting, 7.00 p.m. at Rowton Hall Hotel.

Each candidate after a brief social meeting with executive council members will be asked a few brief questions by the chairman, then asked to make a fifteen-minute presentation on how they are going to retain Chester at the next general election, followed by questions from members of the executive council. Once all three candidates have been presented a ballot will take place. If one candidate gets more than 50 per cent of the vote they may choose to forward only one candidate to the general meeting. If not, at least two candidates will be forwarded to the general meeting.

---

76 He was Margaret Thatcher's PPS 1990–92.

77 Peter Bowles, actor, and his wife Sue, friends of GB and neighbours in Barnes.

b) Friday 15 March, General Association Meeting at Christleton Country Club, 7.00 p.m.

If more than one candidate is presented then the procedure will follow that of the executive council. If only one is presented then they will be asked to make a speech, answer questions and there will be a vote on a motion proposing them as the next prospective candidate.

At both meetings we would be delighted if your spouse could attend.

Yours sincerely,
Vanessa, Agent

SATURDAY 16 MARCH 1991

Well, if that wasn't forty-eight hours that shook the world, it was certainly forty-eight hours that changed our lives.

On Wednesday night we went to St Paul's to see *Nicholas Nickleby* with Saethryd[78] as The Infant Phenomenon. She was gorgeous. When she was on, I concentrated. The rest of the time, my head whirred with my speech, round and round it went, round and round. On Thursday (Michèle's birthday, poor thing) we set off for Chester early and ensconced ourselves in 'our' room at the Grosvenor. (This is proving an expensive business.) At 6.45 p.m. we were at Rowton Hall Hotel, stomachs churning, smiles fixed. The other candidates appeared equally daunted: Sir Peter's young man looked reassuringly unpromising, uncertain, ill-at-ease, but the woman looked – and was – formidable. She is called Jacqui Lait,[79] she's been on the circuit for years, she clearly knows her stuff. Her husband was even larger than her, bear-like, genial, supportive. Sir Peter's candidate didn't appear to have a spouse – another nail in his coffin. Vanessa said to me right away, 'Sorry, you can't go last this time. They're on to you. We're drawing lots.'

For the first half-hour we sipped our orange juice and mingled. This we did (let's face it) so much better than the others. Michèle was a star – smiling, laughing, gladhanding, moving down the aisles, not missing a single row. She looked the business. She did the business. At 7.30 the chairman called the room to order, the executive council took their seats (there must have been about eighty of them in all), and we, candidates and spouses, were escorted to a separate sitting-room on the other side of the hall. The

---

78 GB's elder daughter was fourteen and a pupil at St Paul's Girls' School.

79 Subsequently MP for Hastings & Rye 1992–7, and Beckenham 1997–2010, and, in 1996, the first woman to join the Conservative Whips' Office.

local papers were waiting to take our pictures. We each had to do a sad shot in case we lost and a happy shot in case we won.

The lots were drawn. I was second on. The speech went well. It was a bit of a toe-curler ('If you choose me you will do me great honour. I promise I will do all in my power to do you proud') but it had shape and purpose *and* the society of opportunity and as much local stuff as I could manage. The speech was fine, but the questions were a nightmare. Several I didn't understand *at all*. There were councillors with points about local government that were utterly and completely beyond my ken. One of the first questions was about farm subsidies. I hadn't a clue. I said, 'I've written on my notes, "If you don't know the answer tell them the truth" – I don't know the answer, sir, but I'll find out.' It got a nice round of applause. But when I didn't know the answer to the next question either, I realised I couldn't play the same card twice so I just blathered and blustered and flannelled – and got away with it, *just*.

When I was asked if the children would move to schools in the constituency, I said 'No,' but when when they said 'Will you live in the constituency?' I said 'Yes, of course. Accessibility is everything. If you choose me tonight, I move in on Monday.'

My turn done, we moved back to the sitting-room and Jacqui Lait went in. Michèle went to the loo and on the way back paused by the door to the hall. She came back and took me into a corner and said, 'Don't be very disappointed if you lose. She's very, very good. She's talking about Europe and she knows her stuff.'

I must say when she emerged from the hall, Jacqui looked like a winner. She glowed. While they counted the votes, we stood around, laughing nervously, drinking coffee, making small talk, making banter, saying what a shame it was the three of us couldn't share the constituency – and, in the moment, even meaning it. Then, quite suddenly, the chairman was struggling in on his sticks. He paused, breathless, looked around the group then shot his hand in my direction: 'Congratulations. The vote was decisive. You are to be our prospective parliamentary candidate. Well done.' The others shrunk back, faded instantly, began at once to make their excuses and go. We mumbled hollow commiserations as the chairman and Vanessa pulled us away and led us triumphantly back into the hall. With Michèle I stood on the little platform at the end of the room and surveyed the standing ovation. It felt very good.

What felt best of all was getting back to our room at the Grosvenor and collapsing over a bottle of ludicrously expensive house champagne. I raised my glass to my birthday girl and she raised her glass to me. By George, we'd done it! Five years on the back benches, five years a junior minister, five years in Cabinet, with perhaps a brief spell in opposition along the way. That'll see me through to sixty.

We slept well and woke early. It was the lead story in the *Daily Post*: 'TV STAR IS CHESTER CHOICE'. All day we scurried about, to the constituency office, to the local paper, to the Conservative club, back to the hotel, back to the office. I took calls, made calls, shook hands, slapped backs, even blew my first kiss at a passing baby. What I didn't do, couldn't do, should have done was make time to rewrite my speech, so when we reached the Country Club for the 'coronation' I was painfully aware that certainly a third of those in attendance (there were 200 plus) had heard *everything* I had to say only twenty-four hours before. I struggled on regardless, giving it word for word as I'd done on Thursday night, but with much less brio – the oomph had gone out of me somehow – and, apparently, in floods of tears. On the platform I was seated immediately between the Duke and Sir Peter, who both smoked throughout, and, from start to finish, thick plumes of smoke rose vertically (and viciously) straight up from the ends of their cigarettes bang into my eyes. It was a nightmare. My mouth was dry, my palms were wet, my eyes were streaming. But the crowd was kind. They seemed to think it was a triumph all the same.

And now, it's Saturday afternoon, we're back in London, and – this is the odd bit, the bit I almost dare not admit – I feel flat already. What I've dreamt about for years, what I've striven for *ruthlessly* these past six months, I've got it. The prize is mine. And already I'm thinking, so what? (Aren't human beings strange?)

THURSDAY 21 MARCH 1991

I slipped out of a fairly desultory DoE [Duke of Edinburgh] birthday meeting early to be on parade at the House of Commons for a five o'clock 'briefing' from Peter Morrison. Given that I wasn't his choice, and he's not really my type (and I'm certainly not his), he was as friendly as I could have wished. He marched me down to his subterranean office which was sparse but surprisingly spacious ('I share it with a certain person,' he smirked – I presume he meant Mrs T. – 'that helps') and we sat and looked at one another. The conversation didn't exactly flow, but the gist of it was clear – and helpful: 'You'll need to spend about £2,000 a year of your own money on raffle tickets etc. and write an awful lot of notes. The troops like to get handwritten notes. Sometimes I do twenty a night. When the election's called I'll come down on day one to give you a send-off, then I'll keep out of the way. It's your show. Between now and then if there's anything I can do, let me know. If you want my advice, never talk politics in the constituency. There's nothing to be gained by it. On the great national issues, if you like, take the moral highground. You can't go wrong. But on local issues, keep your head down. There are two sides to every argument. You can't win, so don't try. And anything to do with planning, don't touch.'

He spread his hands out on his desk and pushed himself to his feet. 'Now I am on my way to Committee Room 14.' Another smirk. 'I am proposing to give my colleagues on the 1922 Committee a piece of my mind.'

'What about?'
'Loyalty.'

SUNDAY 14 APRIL 1991

It's a month to the day since I was selected and of the past thirty days I have spent twenty in Chester and ten on the run – rushing up and down West Coast Mainline like a yoyo, attempting to earn a bit of a living while proving to my would-be constituents that I'm all theirs all hours of the day and night. I'm going everywhere, doing the lot – from the King's School Lenten Service to the amateurs in *The Gypsy Baron*. Mostly it's fun – and I am determined to do it well, make it work. The only oppressive part to date is the locals' obsession with my being local too. Whether you're good, bad or indifferent seems to be neither here nor there: your local roots are what really count. I've had the same conversation a hundred times. 'Where do you come from?'

'My father was born in Hoylake.' Slight reassurance.

'Where are your children at school?'

'London.' Faces fall. 'But, of course, when I'm elected I'll have to be in London much of the time and it's important to keep the family together.' Lips purse like a bitter walnut.

'And where are you living now?'

'In Whitefriars, Number 5 – next door to where Basil Nield and his sister used to live.'

Sir Basil was MP here in the late forties.[80] That reassures most of them – but the sharp ones with the angry little faces leave it a beat and then narrow their eyes and go in for the kill: 'Yes, that's where you're renting, but where's your *real* home?'

In fact, Whitefriars is a great success, but it isn't cheap. And the fares aren't cheap. And Sir Peter's £2,000 pa on raffle tickets turns out to be no exaggeration. And what am I earning at the moment? Not enough. This week: the Radio 2 programme on Monday and the speech in Workington on Thursday night.[81] Help!

MONDAY 22 APRIL 1991

I'm sitting in the train travelling from Wolverhampton to Euston when I should be in Stratfford-upon-Avon having lunch with the Prince of Wales. What a ridiculous three days. On Saturday I drove from London to Stratford for the Shakespeare Birthday

---

80   In fact, 1940–56

81   Until the general election, GB continued to work as a radio and TV presenter and to make after-dinner speeches.

Celebrations – I did my stuff: it was fine. I drove on to Chester where I spent Sunday morning tramping the fields on a sponsored walk, went on the Dale Barracks to meet the lads in khaki, on to the police station to salute the boys in blue and on to evensong at All Saints Hoole to reassure one of our ageing activists that I am 'spiritually sound'! This old bird had phoned the office to say that she was concerned that I might not have the right religious values – she's heard rumours – so Gwyn,[82] there and then, volunteered me to go to church with her! In fact she's quite a sweet old thing in a Miss Marplish way and she's loyal to the cause (she's kept every one of the multifarious handwritten notes Sir Peter has sent to her over the past twenty years) and the service itself was a revelation: the church was *packed*, young, old, (many more young than old), families with children, all fresh-faced and bright-eyed with happiness, singing, swinging, praying, swaying, getting the key messages from the deaconess's sermon flashed up onto a screen above the altar. It may not be what John Betjeman and I think of as evensong but it was impressive all the same. I then went on to the Newton Committee Meeting and finally dinner at Hoole Hall.

Today I was up at the crack of dawn and racing down the motorway to get to Stratford in time for Prince Charles's lecture when suddenly, alarmingly, thick black smoke began billowing from the engine. I moved straight onto the hard shoulder, jammed on the brakes, switched off the engine and waited for the belching smoke to subside. It did. I then laughed out loud. It's all so silly – tearing hither and yon, and to what purpose? Anyway, for the first time ever the car phone came into its own. I called Jenny[83] and she called the AA and within an hour I was being towed into Wolverhampton – not before the police had stopped to enquire what I was up to. The policeman recognised me and, when I told him where I had been going, he volunteered to get the police to look after the car while he would drive me personally to my royal luncheon engagement. He was quite pressing, and when I said no I think he was quite put out.

TUESDAY 23 APRIL 1991

I'm back on the train again. This morning the Youth and Sport Conference in WC1. This evening the Younger Women's Supper Club in Chester. (I'm advised that the Younger Women are all supposed to be under fifty – and indeed they were when the group was formed. Now they are of riper years and several bring their mothers, who are comfortably into their seventies.) In the broadsheets Prince Charles gets plenty of coverage: 'It's

---

82   Gwyn Gough, much-valued, much-loved Chester Conservative Association secretary.

83   Jenny Noll, much-valued, much-loved personal assistant to GB.

almost incredible that in Shakespeare's land one child in seven leaves primary school functionally illiterate.' I think the Earl of Chester's observations can be the springboard for my remarks to the Younger Women ... David Owen is getting coverage too. Apparently ministers are 'pressing for Owen to be given a government role'. Somehow, I don't think that's going to swing it on the doorstep.

SATURDAY 27 APRIL 1991

I had my 'briefing' with His Grace [the Duke of Westminster] yesterday. He looks permanently exhausted, but he has a nice manner, an engaging laugh, and he's courteous, friendly and helpful – though it's clear our relationship's not going anywhere. I sit and ask him to tell me what's what and I take notes while he explains that the government doesn't understand the importance of hill-farming, the nonsense of set-aside, the dangers of leasehold reform, the plight of the TA. I realise that I'm a natural for the government as I don't understand these things either! He must wonder why he's having to bother with me. I know why I'm having to bother with him. He's our President and he's local royalty. They love him and all he represents. The activists get a physical thrill from simply saying the words 'His Grace'. Working the room before last night's dinner I said to several of them that I'd had a meeting with him during the day and I sensed as they held my hand they were conscious that they were holding the hand that had shaken the hand of the Duke of Westminster only hours before. The dinner – 'Chester Meets the Brandreths' – was fine, but my speech was too lightweight. They enjoyed the jokes, but they wanted (and didn't get) some political punch and a Churchillian flourish.

Today it's been local election canvassing, plus the Litter Week Photocall, plus the Callin Court coffee morning, plus a couple of mortifying hours standing outside two desolate shopping parades accosting shoppers who don't want to stop: they want to shop. It's becoming clear to me that much of what I'm doing I'm doing *not* to woo the electorate and win over wavering votes but to keep our activists sweet, to boost their morale, to reassure them they've chosen the right man for the job.

FRIDAY 3 MAY 1991

'Any remaining likelihood of a June general election disappeared in the early hours of this morning.' In fact, in Chester we didn't do too badly. We gained one seat from the Lib Dems and the Lib Dems gained one from us and one from Labour. I started the day with a photocall for National Squint Week (no jokes, *please*) and then made my way to

Mold for the Marcher Sound Jobline Launch – a complete waste of time. I went because the Welsh Secretary, David Hunt,[84] was going to be on parade and I thought it would be an opportunity to introduce myself and get a pic for the local paper. In the event when I had forced my way through the crowd to shake the great man's hand he had no idea who I was or why I was there, and the photographers in attendance certainly didn't want me cluttering up the shots.

TUESDAY 14 MAY 1991

Last night we were invited for supper with the Deputy Chief Whip![85] He has a charming house in Lord North Street, a charming wife called Cecilia (birdlike and delightful, with one of those deceptively daffy Kensington manners – don't be fooled by the tinkly laughter…), and a charming, disarming way with him. Lots of quiet chuckling. They couldn't have been more friendly or hospitable. He'd invited us because his is the constituency adjacent to 'mine' and he wanted to 'mark my card'. Also at supper was another Cheshire MP, Neil Hamilton.[86] Dry and droll. I was on best behaviour: didn't drink, didn't talk too much, and didn't find it as alarming as I'd feared.

I was grateful to the Goodlads too because my current acquaintanceship among MPs is pretty limited – though it does include Edwina [Currie], of course, who is in court this week suing *The Observer* over a film review which apparently likened her to a character who undermines her own marriage, sacrifices her children and resorts to murder to further her career. In the movie the part (a glamorous Euro-MP) is played by Charlotte Rampling and you might have thought that Edwina would be thrilled to be mistaken for Charlotte Rampling in any role – but no.

WEDNESDAY 15 MAY 1991

I'm on the 11.25, reaching Chester 2.07, then it's BNFL at Capenhurst, the 'Nursery Education for All' meeting at Queen's Park High School, and the Poster Committee Meeting at the office. Vanessa wants the posters in blue and day-glo pink. The traditionalists want blue and white. I want smiles all round. I predict an hour of wrangling – and Vanessa gets her way.

---

84 MP for Wirral 1976–83, Wirral West 1983–97; later Baron Hunt of Wirral.

85 Alastair Goodlad, MP for Northwich 1974–83, Eddisbury 1983–99; later Baron Goodlad of Lincoln KCMG.

86 MP for Tatton 1983–97.

Edwina wins the day. £5,000 plus costs. Quote of the case: 'I am not interested in personal publicity. Being well-known is an absolute pain.'

SATURDAY 18 MAY 1991

I found a Brandreth in the local phone book – and she lives in Blacon.[87] In fact, she isn't a Brandreth any longer, but her ex-husband is and her son is and this afternoon she's hosting a little tea party in my honour ... and, yes, I have invited the press along. I know it's shaming, but there we are.

Other weekend excitements: the Mill View Primary School May Fayre, the Chester Rugby Club Beer Festival (I've had to sponsor a barrel – £80! – and I hate the taste of beer), the Chester Festival of Transport and the Sponsored Walk for the Hospice ... and it seems I could face another year of this before polling day. The Prime Minister has 'let it be known' that he is prepared to wait until next year before calling the election to reduce the pressure on Norman Lamont for immediate interest rate cuts. Something needs to give. The recession is worsening, not easing, and judging from the doors I'm knocking on the punters are blaming us.

And even our friends don't like us. Yesterday, doing a walkabout in Boughton, one of our elderly activists sidled up to me and said, 'May I have a word?'

'Of course.' He must be in his seventies, small, stocky, cloth-cap, bent, red nose with a drip at the tip, the crooked man on the crooked gate.

'I don't think you're going to hold the seat, I'm sorry to say.' He looked *delighted* to be saying it.

'Oh,' I murmured, as cheerily as I could, 'Why not?' He drew in a long breath. 'Any particular reason?'

'Yes,' he said, shaking his head.

'Well?'

'It's your handshake. It just isn't firm enough.' He put out his hand and I stupidly put out mine and he gripped my hand so hard I wanted to scream.

'That's what you need,' he said. 'You don't mind my telling you, do you?'

SATURDAY 1 JUNE 1991

'Britain remains sceptical about single currency, says Lamont.' Seems quite a good idea

---

87   A Labour stronghold, a district of Chester dominated by a large council estate.

to me – and inevitable. But what do I know? I know that Saethryd has come to Chester and I'm feeling guilty because I'm taking her to the Chester Regatta and Flower Show and there's a photo call and I'm making sure she's in it because the word is that my Labour opponent's marriage is in a rocky state and we can't expect too many happy family snaps during *his* campaign.

THURSDAY 6 JUNE 1991

The birthday lunch for Prince Philip was a complete success. It was Ladies Only (apart from HRH) so I sat in a cupboard in a corner and watched the proceedings through a crack in the door. Michèle was perfect and Joanna [Lumley] was a dream – completely over the top and absolutely right. I allowed myself to attend the drinks beforehand and HRH was genuinely amused by the women-only idea. I told him Jane Asher had done a special birthday cake.

'Didn't she used to go out with Paul McCartney?'

'Yes, but I don't think she likes to be reminded of that.'

'Pity. He's good news.'

'She's good news.'

'Yes, but Paul McCartney's quite special.'

I was convinced the first thing he'd say to Jane was 'Didn't you use to go out with Paul McCartney' but he didn't. When irritated (or sometimes, I suspect, just for the hell of it), he can be perverse. His office get you to provide reams of speech notes which are *never* used. I was convinced he wouldn't use the script provided for the moment when he had to 'Challenge Anneka' to build the playground at Birmingham Children's Hospital within the week – but, apart from calling her 'A-knee-cur' he was spot-on.[88]

SATURDAY 8 JUNE 1991

It's our eighteenth wedding anniversary and for a special treat I take my wife to the City of Chester Conservative Association Annual Salmon Supper at Eaton Hall – courtesy of Their Graces the Duke and Duchess of Westminster, both of whom are on parade, which is jolly decent of them. If I were the richest in the land, is this what I would be doing with my Saturday night? In truth, the event isn't so much at Eaton Hall itself as

---

88 The *Challenge Anneka* television programme, starring Anneka Rice, had agreed to build a playground on behalf of NPFA if Prince Philip issued the challenge.

in the garage at Eaton Hall. We huddle together for warmth as we dine alfresco in a cobbled yard bordered by garages and stables and we are very grateful to be adjacent to such grand surroundings despite the wind and the rain! I sit next to Her Grace and my banter comes across as over-familiarity and as she glazes over I can't think what more to say so I decide to go for votes and work the tables. I then feel ashamed when we get to the auction and she bids a thousand pounds for one of my jumpers! Vanessa forces me to bid 300 plus for an art deco lamp we neither want, need nor can afford.

WEDNESDAY 12 JUNE 1991

Poll puts Labour ten points ahead. Major defends 'unchanged' Euro policy. Brandreth beetles off to Birmingham to be in attendance upon HRH as he arrives at Birmingham Children's Hospital to open Anneka's playground – genuinely built from scratch in forty-eight hours flat.

SATURDAY 15 JUNE 1991

Last night I was at the Northcott Theatre, Exeter, giving the Hans Andersen show as part of the Exeter Festival. The house was full of people expecting Tommy Steele at least, Danny Kaye at best. Instead they got me and I felt – and shared – their disappointment. Tonight we were at supper in Sheen with Tim and Alison Heald[89] and Tim's old chum from his Oxford days, Chris Patten.[90] Clearly Tim assumed that as a prospective candidate I would know Chris and Lavender, know them well, but, of course, I'd never met the chairman of the party and I rather sensed he'd never heard of me. Anyway, we each affected to know one another and the evening was reasonably jolly – except I felt I had to be on my best behaviour in the presence of the 'boss' and I think CP felt he had to be circumspect in the presence of an 'unknown'.

TUESDAY 18 JUNE 1991

The Hilary Howarth Nursery School, the Cherry Grove Primary School, the Blacon Project Adventure Playground, the Farmer's Party at Hatton Hall and, finally, the

---

89   Tim Heald, journalist and writer, and his then wife, friends of GB.

90   MP for Bath 1979–92, chairman of the Conservative Party and Chancellor of the Duchy of Lancaster 1990–92. Later Baron Patten of Barnes, Chancellor of Oxford University and chairman of the BBC Trust.

Euro-constituency AGM – a quiet affair. Up at Westminster Ted Heath is raging at Thatcher's speech on the Union and challenging her to a TV debate (which would be fun) but here in Chester the Euro debate is rather less lively. I toe the line, strike the balance, go for the middle way, but I don't think they're terribly interested.

FRIDAY 19 JULY 1991

We're flying to Venice today. I have mixed feelings about this both because of all the 'vital events' Jill Everett[91] tells me I'm missing in Chester between now and the end of the month and because of my ding-dong with Prince Edward. He sent a pompous letter essentially berating the [Duke of Edinburgh seventieth] Birthday Committee for not pulling our weight – so I called the Palace and spoke to his office and said I thought he had a cheek. Edward called back and I didn't let him get a word in: I just banged on about his pompous letter, reminded him we were all volunteers and said that I didn't like being patronised or cajoled by someone several years my junior when I working my socks off for the good of the cause! He bleated an apology and I felt a whole lot better – but, of course, my response was quite as pompous and uncalled for as his letter. And now I'm leaving the country and I won't even be at the wretched birthday celebrations. Michèle says no one will notice and, of course, she's right.

WEDNESDAY 31 JULY 1991

We bought an English paper and there's the picture of Prince Philip and Prince Edward at the birthday bash meeting Harry Connick Jr, 'the new Frank Sinatra', who pronounced the Duke 'a real cool dude'.

As arranged, at 12 noon, as the clock struck, we met up with Jo and Stevie at the Caffè Florian. The Brandreths and the Barlows took Bellinis in the drawing room of Europe and we raised our glasses to absent royalty and agreed that Michèle had been right – as usual. Tomorrow we are lunching on Torcello, at my favourite restaurant in all the world. Ain't life grand?

TUESDAY 6 AUGUST 1991

Returned to find 'Dear Gyles' letter from Prince Edward: 'In spite of all the crossed

---

91   Deputy chairman of the City of Chester Conservative Association.

wires (for which I apologise) and the bleak economic background, I felt that last weekend's celebrations were a tremendous success. I know there were problems and that egos were bruised along the way ... I trust there are not too many hard feelings about my earlier letter. It may have been a bit heavy handed, but there were a few worried people just prior to the event. Thank you for rallying round; I'm sure it made all the difference.'

Now I feel guilty.

SUNDAY 8 SEPTEMBER 1991

At 12 noon we gathered at Puddington for 'Peter Morrison's Annual Pimm's Party'. This is a gala event in the Association's calendar. Sir Peter provides the Pimm's and the Conservative ladies provide 'the bites'. Until I came to Chester I'd never heard of 'bites' – now I eat almost nothing else. You are what you eat and there are weekends at the end of which I think I've turned into a damp bit of bread and butter rolled round a limp inch of asparagus. The first – fleeting – moment of 'tension' between us and the activists came about because of the bites. Michèle got a message from Jill [Everett] saying she was expected to bring sixty 'bites' to an event and what would Michèle be bringing – sausages on sticks, celery filled with cream cheese, curried stuffed eggs? 'Stuff yours' was my darling wife's reaction. That's not what she said to Jill, of course. That's what she said to me. She also made me phone the hotel and order three trays of canapés as our contribution. We've not been asked for 'bites' since.

The party was fine. We worked the marquee and listened to (but didn't join in) the gossip about our host. Peter's workers fall into two distinct camps: a minority think he's past his sell-by date, that he's let himself go, that he's out of touch, that he gives out all the wrong signals, that he's 'let the seat slide'. The majority simply love the grandeur of the man. 'Have you seen inside the lavatory? The pictures of Peter at Eton. Aren't they *wonderful*?'

WEDNESDAY 11 SEPTEMBER 1991

Lunch at the Old Bailey as a guest of the Sherriff. After we'd eaten we processed along the corridor back towards the courts. I walked at the front with the judge who'd been sitting next to me. We came to a door which was opened by a court flunkey. Thinking that, as a guest, it was appropriate that I should lead the way, I did – and suddenly found myself on the judge's bench in Court No. 1 with the clerk instructing all to be upstanding for Mr Justice Whatever-he-was-called – who followed me in, apparently amused, and invited me to sit next to him on the bench. It was a gripping case – fellow dead in a police cell and the brilliant barrister (Mr Nasty and Mr Smooth all rolled into one) making us believe it wasn't his ugly-looking client, it was the police wot done it. As I left I told one of the clerks how impressed I'd been by the barrister (I believed him completely) and he said: 'He's famous. He's Mr Mansfield.[92] Looks after the IRA and all that sort.'

THURSDAY 12 SEPTEMBER 1991

Last night's Granada drama on the downfall of Mrs T. – *Thatcher: The Final Days* – was gripping stuff. Sylvia Syms was a bit unlikely as Mrs T. and they should certainly have had Martin [Jarvis] as Heseltine – but for us, of course, the fascination was in the characterisation/demonisation of poor Peter M. If it hadn't been for his complacency, his ineffective campaign on her behalf, his somnolence on the watch etc., she might have survived. That was the gist of it – and in the papers the knives are out for him.

This helps explain why he's getting out. It may explain the drinking too. Of course, the programme didn't portray him as either a lush or an old queen, though we can see he's the one and we assume he's the other. I think Jeremy Hanley takes credit for coming up with the line – at the time of Peter's appointment as Mrs T's PPS – 'Ah, at last Margaret's got herself an aide who knows how to carry a handbag.' At Sunday's do at Peter's place one or two were whispering behind their hands about his alleged sexual preferences – but I don't think any of them is aware that Michèle and I have been told *several times* on the doorstep – in no uncertain terms – that the MP is 'a disgusting pervert' who is 'into little boys'.

SUNDAY 6 OCTOBER 1991

Peter invited me to sit in on his regular NFU meeting. On a Sunday morning about four times a year he has six to ten farmers from our part of Cheshire come to his house to tell him of their travails. Peter says whether it's eggs, wheat, beef, poultry, horticulture, they're never happy, but they always arrive in Jaguars. The meeting lasted an hour. The farmers, all looking the part, sat awkwardly, in armchairs and on low sofas. Peter,

---

92   Michael Mansfield QC.

the patrician Tory grandee, sat centre-stage, bolt upright on a dining room chair. He took careful notes throughout, nodded a lot, grunted once or twice, but said nothing and gave nothing away – until the end when he gave us all massive gins and tonics in huge cut glass tumblers. It was a masterly performance: he committed himself to nothing at all and had them eating out of the palm of his hand.

This afternoon, as I was working on my debut speech for the party conference, Francis Maude[93] telephoned. I've not met him – I've met hardly any of them – but he was cordial, businesslike. He explained that he's Financial Secretary to the Treasury (which I know), that he's replying to Thursday's debate on the Citizen's Charter (which I also know), that the Prime Minister regards it as one of the key debates of the conference (which I doubt), and is there any pre-briefing that I need from him or anything that I am planning to say that he should know about so he can respond to it from the platform? I couldn't think what to say or ask, and I didn't like to admit that I've never been to a party conference before so I don't really know the form. I just mumbled thanks and felt wrong-footed.

The moment I put the phone down I went back to the speech. It's four minutes maximum. After three minutes they flash an amber light. After four the light turns red and they haul you off the podium. There really isn't much time to develop an argument. I am trying to give what little I've got to say a bit of shape and substance, but it's still a terrible mishmash of cliches and tub-thumping.

I'm impressed by Maude taking the trouble to call and I'm impressed by the way the whole conference is rigged. There are 1,411 motions submitted by Conservative associations across the land, 98 per cent of them pure grovel ('This conference congratulates Her Majesty's government…', 'This conference agrees with Her Majesty's government…', 'This conference warmly welcomes…', 'This conference wholeheartedly commends…' etc.), 2 per cent mad maverick (Bring back Matron! Bring back hanging! Let's hear it for the birch!), and the ones selected for debate are (quite properly) the ones that will provide the best opportunity for setting out and saluting the government's achievements. All the speakers from the floor are carefully screened and, if you have plans for a future within the party, you'll make sure your contribution does the two essentials: cheers the leader and toes the line.

Apparently in the run-up to a general election they always do their best to give opportunities to prospective candidates. I simply got a call from Central Office saying that my spot would be Thursday at 9.30 a.m.; my theme, the Citizen's Charter; and my position, considered adulation. I didn't argue.

I'm grateful.

---

93   MP for Warwickshire North 1983–92, Financial Secretary to the Treasury 1990–92. MP for Horsham from 1997.

MONDAY 7 OCTOBER 1991

I spent two more hours fine-tuning the speech (two more hours on a four-minute speech – and on the Citizen's Charter to boot!) and then set off to be on parade for the Association's Autumn Lunch, scheduled for 12 noon. (Vanessa is impressing on me that I must start turning up for things on time: if it says 12 noon all the old ladies will be there, ready and waiting, by 11.45 at the latest). Our guest of honour was William Hague,[94] PPS to Norman Lamont, and excellent value: good jokes and a clear message. He also had energy and I'm coming to think that may be the secret of success in this game: controlling, maintaining, sustaining energy. We think we know one another because I was President of the Union about ten years before he was and he seems to recall several of my older jokes. The activists know him because he wowed the party conference as a boy orator aged fifteen. He doesn't look much older now.

From three to seven I was out door-knocking in Christleton and Littleton. The Prime Minister has publicly ruled out a November poll and there doesn't have to be an election before 17 July next, but Jill and Vanessa are insisting we keep hard at it. I suppose they're right.

FRIDAY 11 OCTOBER 1991

What an extraordinary week. The party conference is an extraordinary phenomenon. Last time I was in Blackpool I came to interview John Inman, who was appearing in a summer season spin-off of *Are You Being Served?* Even if there aren't too many of John's kind overtly in evidence among the conference delegates at the Winter Gardens, there's a healthy sprinkling of Captain Peacocks and Mollie Sugdens on parade.

It's only the activists who sit through the debates. Everyone else is junketing, non-stop. MPs, ministers, candidates, party professionals, hacks, broadcasters, lobbyists, hangers-on by the hundreds – moving ceaselessly from one indifferent reception to another. There's a nice freemasonry among the prospective candidates. I was queuing up to have my photograph taken by the BBC for their election night coverage and fell into conversation with the fellow standing in line behind me – gingerish hair, glasses, red braces, prospective candidate standing in some godforsaken northern backwater.

'Do you live in the constituency?' I asked.

'Good God no,' he spluttered, 'Happiness is the constituency in the rear-view mirror.'

Speech of the week: on Tuesday, chairman Patten's opening address, unscripted,

---

94   MP for Richmond, Yorkshire, since 1989.

informal, unexpected, modern. Moment of the week: on Wednesday, when Mrs T. arrived on the platform and pandemonium broke out. She didn't say anything: she just *was* and for five minutes we stood and clapped and stamped our feet and roared. Even Michèle was cheering. There were tears in the eyes. You couldn't not be moved. It was wonderful.

Equally wondrous to behold (in a wholly different way) was the astonishing curly-topped MP for Harlow called Jerry Hayes[95] who bounded up to the podium on Thursday morning to give an apparently unscripted address on the wonders of the NHS and completely and utterly and absolutely lost his way! 'Mr madam chairman' he burbled as he fumbled as he stumbled, concluding (with the rest of us), 'this must be the after-effect of a very bad night.' It made me feel my speech had been quite statesmanlike. I was appallingly nervous, but it was fine – I got a bit of an ovation in the hall, but wasn't much noticed beyond: as I began we hit ten o'clock and the BBC TV conference coverage was interrupted for *Watch with Mother*.

Last night I had my first close encounter with the Prime Minister. It was not an unqualified success. I had been asked to conduct the auction at the Conference Ball (and asked too to donate one of my 'famous jumpers' as an extra auction offering) and consequently Michèle and I were invited to come to the VIP reception and join the line-up for presentation to the Majors. We arrived on time and stood for about an hour, in our gladrags, in the dim and narrow gallery overlooking the Empress Ballroom, sipping our orange juice, shifting from foot to foot, making desultory small talk with the party bigwigs who understandably weren't listening to us because they were anxiously listening out for word that the PM was on his way. It was exactly like waiting for royalty – and when eventually they arrived we treated them like royalty, bicycling Scandinavian royalty perhaps, but royalty all the same. Cameras whirred, bulbs flashed, we all beamed and the PM and Norma worked the line, winning hearts, shaking hands, squeezing arms, grinning resolutely all the way. As they got to us I was thrust forward clutching my 'famous jumper' – powder blue with 'MAJOR TALENT' boldly emblazoned on the chest – and as the Prime Minister caught sight of it I saw a danger signal flash behind his eyes. Whatever happened, he was not going to be photographed with that silly jumper. He started back, he grimaced, he gave a little cough, he muttered 'Good to see you' and moved firmly on.

LATER

We have just watched the Prime Minister give his end-of-conference address. It was exactly right: clear, uncomplicated, compelling. Some good self-deprecating jokes (on

---

95 MP for Harlow 1983–97.

his educational qualifications: 'Never has so much been written about so little') and lots that was quite personal ('the long road from Coalharbour Lane to Downing Street'). I know I'm easily moved, but I found it rather touching. It worked. And best of all, at the end, when John and Norma went walkabout among the cheering delegates, what did we see? Picked out by the TV camera – again and again and *again* – the comely girl who last night bought and is today wearing a powder blue jumper bearing the legend 'MAJOR TALENT'.

So there.

WEDNESDAY 30 OCTOBER 1991

Judy Hurd, wife of the Foreign Secretary, came to Chester to be guest of honour at a charity lunch at the racecourse. She talked about life as the wife of a Foreign Secretary and did it rather well. I introduced myself and we travelled back together on the train. She is the second Mrs Hurd, was his secretary I think, is now quietly grand (not in a nasty way), tall, slim, fair, more presentable than pretty, but friendly, ready to be chatty. Around Rugby (and the second cup of tea) we'd exhausted Castlereagh and Lord Curzon and Anthony Eden and the rest and moved on to star signs (as one does) and we discovered, first, that Douglas Hurd and I share a birthday (8 March – different years, natch) and then, amazingly, that Judy and Michèle share a birthday too – 14 March, same day as Albert Einstein and Michael Caine. (Not many people know that...) I told her the poem that Tom Stoppard sent to me years ago, called simply *14 March*:

Einstein born
Quite unprepared
For E to equal
MC squared

THURSDAY 31 OCTOBER 1991

We were invited to the State Opening of Parliament as guests of the Duke of Edinburgh. This was a real kindness as I have never seen the State Opening, even on television, but somehow, when we woke up this morning, we both felt shattered and decided we wouldn't go. I felt a bit guilty about it, but Michèle was adamant: 'It'll be like a garden party, nobody'll notice.' I wasn't sure, I went on brooding, and, at the last minute, we went. Fortunately. Not only were we expected (our names in elegant italic on dainty cards placed on our gilt and red-velvet seats), we were *awaited*. As we beetled along the red carpet, moments before Her Majesty, white-tied tail-coated flunkeys were anxiously checking their watches. We were seated in a sort of royal stage-box in a narrow gallery to the right of the throne, a ringside seat at a wonderful piece of pageantry and hokum that came over as magnificent and ridiculous all at the same time.

TUESDAY 5 NOVEMBER 1991

Christopher phoned Kirsty[96] and Kirsty phoned Michèle to say: had we heard? Robert Maxwell had committed suicide – thrown himself off his yacht somewhere in the Canaries. Was it suicide or was he pushed? He was an alarming man. I vividly remember my first encounter with him, more than twenty years ago, when I was about nineteen and at Oxford. I was invited by Philip and Anne[97] to an amazingly grand party at Headington Hill Hall where – I am ashamed to say – in the middle of the library, just after supper, I was attempting to amuse a group of fellow guests with an impertinent impersonation of our host when, quite suddenly, a heavy hand landed on my left shoulder. I spun round to find myself face to face with the great tycoon. I blanched. He looked stern, then he let out a loud, alarming, barking laugh, shook me by the shoulder and walked away. His children are devoted to him and I suppose he must have had real friends, although whenever we were at his house I found that fellow guests invariably spent much of their time talking about him in hushed undertones. At the last party we went to – for what seemed like 2,000 of his closer chums – I noticed he'd equipped himself with personal amplification. He was wearing a radio mike and there were speakers scattered about the house and the marquees, so, without having to raise his voice, the great man could address each and every one of us wherever we were. And now he's gone.

Bizarre.

WEDNESDAY 6 NOVEMBER 1991

It may not be suicide. It could be an accident. Or murder. Was he an agent for Mossad? He was a monster. And a crook. I know: I sat in reception at Maxwell House for hours on end, saying 'I'm not leaving without a cheque in my hand' and meaning it – and

---

96 Christopher Hudson, journalist and writer, and his wife, Kirsty McLeod, writer, friends of GB.

97 Maxwell's two oldest children, contemporaries of GB at university.

getting it – after months and months and months of waiting.[98] Maverick, money-maker, MP, rogue, he really *was* Augustus Melmotte in *The Way We Live Now*. I see the Prime Minister has picked the words of his tribute carefully: 'A great character ... I am sure he would not want us to grieve at his loss, but marvel at a quite extraordinary life lived to the full.' Neil Kinnock is completely over the top: 'This is truly tragic news.' That he was ever taken seriously by the Labour Party is amazing. It was pitiful when Peter Jay allowed himself to become his poodle-cum-*chef-de-cabinet*.[99] I remember a lunch at Jeffrey [Archer]'s when Jay was summoned to the phone once, twice, three times, then hauled away altogether. It would be nothing, Jay acknowledged, but when the master flicked his fingers the little dog had to jump. I think it was Jeffrey who had just been at some sporting gathering in Scotland and witnessed Captain Bob put his bearlike arm around the Queen and keep it there. Not even Her Majesty was able to freeze him off. Well, he had *hutzpah*. And for the children it is a tragedy. I must write to Anne, but I'm not sure what to say.

WEDNESDAY 27 NOVEMBER 1991

Creditors force Asil Nadir into bankruptcy. The Maxwell empire is unravelling before our eyes. The recession is deepening and lengthening. And last night, at Buckingham Palace, we set about trying to raise a million pounds for NPFA! HRH and I addressed our potential donors from a little dais in the middle of the magnificent stateroom. I thought as I spoke, 'Isn't this extraordinary, me being here in Buckingham Palace, making a speech like this?' I tried to be amusing. HRH did the business. He went for the jugular. 'Ladies and gentlemen, good evening. The doors at either end of the gallery have been closed. Welcome to the shearing shed.' Of course, we will only fleece them successfully if we follow through ... We went on to the Caprice for supper with Colin and Rosie [Sanders] and he has delivered, bless him: £50,000 *and* he paid for the birthday fireworks at the Windsor bash. A good man.

FRIDAY 13 DECEMBER 1991

Friday the thirteenth. I'm on the train to Chester, on my way to the St Theresa's PTA

98 GB and his wife's editorial services business, Complete Editions, had created a range of books and magazines for two Maxwell companies.

99 Maxwell's chief of staff, 1986–9; later BBC economics editor and non-executive director of the Bank of England.

Karaoke Night, preceded by a 'two-hour in-depth' interview with Chester Talking Newspaper. This morning I was on *Treasure Islands* on Radio 4 talking about children's books and I started the day at TV-am talking about teddy bears. Last night, at the last minute, I found myself standing in for Jeffrey Archer and joining Tony Banks[100] on a programme called *Behind the Headlines* for BBC2. I have just this second opened the *Evening Standard* and read Mark Steyn's review: 'On the last two occasions I saw Brandreth on TV, he was, first, dressed as Rhett Butler to host a *Gone with the Wind* lookalike competition and, second, wearing a fried egg on his head and inviting an adjoining snooker player to join him in a tribute to John Gielgud. Since then, unfortunately, he's been selected as a Tory parliamentary candidate and so is now seen as a ridiculous figure of fun. To correct this impression for *Behind the Headlines*, he has gone to the trouble of wearing a grey suit, sober shirt, discreet tie and asking lots of questions about drugs and inheritance tax. But, behind *Behind the Headlines*, nobody seemed to care. Where most programmes tuck the wires down the back of the presenters' jackets, here they extended from Brandreth's and Banks's ears before disappearing behind the chairs; Brandreth's microphone was off initially, and, later, on when it shouldn't have been; a floor manager crawled into view at one point.' Quite funny really.

TUESDAY 17 DECEMBER 1991

At 10.30 this morning I joined a long queue that snaked its way from the front door of 32 Smith Square all the way through the building to a room right at the back where, for several hours, the poor Prime Minister stood in front of a blue screen waiting to have his photograph taken with each and every prospective candidate in turn. We shuffled forward at a snail's pace, combing our hair and adjusting our ties in the mirror that awaited us at the final bend, and eventually reaching the small, stuffy room where the snaps were being taken. When we entered the room the PM looked weary, but he was equally effusive and engaging with each of us. We all stood in the same position; he held our hand rather limply in his; he offered the same goofy grin; the photographer gave it two shots and we all trusted that our leader's eyes couldn't be closed in both of them. Before we entered into the presence someone must have whispered our names to him because he got every first name spot on and when he realised the woman ahead of me had a child with her (who hadn't come in to the room but hovered near the door) he chased out after the child and led it back into the room himself so it could be photographed too. It's a funny way to lead a country.

---

100   1942–2006; Labour MP for Newham North West 1983–2005.

TUESDAY 31 DECEMBER 1991

199 firms a day are collapsing. We're behind in the polls. Our personal finances are pretty dire because I've spent a year walking the streets and treading water. But this is what I wanted to do and Michèle is supporting me without reproach. (Well, not quite without reproach: every time we're on the motorway for more than four hours trekking between here and Chester she hisses, 'You wouldn't wait, would you? You had to have it; you wouldn't see if something nearer London came up; you *had* to have it; you'd have walked over your dying granny to get it. I know you.' She does.)

Anyway, the year's done now. And there were good things too. Today Dirk Bogarde has a knighthood. And I have a brilliant wife and three good children and one fine cat and plenty of energy and ambition and *hope*. 1992, here we come!

CHAPTER III

1992

Mr Major (who has rather a Pooterish turn of phrase at times) is in the paper rebuking the 'dismal johnnies' for being gloomy about the economy. Apparently he is standing by his man, Norman 'Green shoots/Black eye' Lamont, who is 'doing a difficult job jolly well.' Well, he would say that, wouldn't he? But out here in the boondocks they're still feeling the pain, the recession is bloody, and if you're in debt, out of work and up the creek, homely reassurance from that nice Mr Major at No. 10 doesn't cut much mustard. It's no use telling people they're getting better when they're still hurting. They simply won't believe you. And they don't believe us. It's pretty dismal on the doorstep.

When I last went to Dublin to appear on Gay Byrne's famous *Late Late Show* show, I seem to remember being invited to join Danny La Rue in a couple of choruses of 'On Mother Kelly's Doorstep'. Our hapless Secretary of State for Northern Ireland[101] appeared on the show on Friday and was persuaded to sing solo, giving us a couple of verses of that old saloon-bar stand-by 'Oh My Darling Clementine' – doing so within a few hours of seven men being killed in an IRA bomb attack in Co. Tyrone. I may be new to this game, but I think even I would not have landed myself in that one.

'Brooke hanging on' is the lead story today, along with 'Tories dampen April 9 speculation'. I read in *The Times* that Norman Lamont has rejected 3 March as a possible Budget date and ministers are 'trying to prevent an unstoppable momentum building for a 9 April election.' It seems 7 May is the preferred date. I say two things: 1) Let's stop

---

101 Peter Brooke, MP for City of London & Westminster South, 1977–97; later Baron Brooke of Sutton Mandeville CH.

buggering about and get on with it. 2) It's fascinating to me that, as the adopted candidate in a make-or-break constituency, I know no more of what's going on than what I read in the paper. My only communication with the party I serve is a weekly policy brief sent to me by Central Office (lots of facts and figures on everything from social security to the cost of Trident) which is vaguely interesting but basically useless. I can't use the material when I'm out canvassing because on the doorstep statistics mean nothing, and I can't use it for my press releases because the local press will *only* cover stories with a local angle.

This may be a 'key marginal' but as far as I can tell we're completely on our own. It's just me and Vanessa and our ageing activists against the world! That's not entirely fair. Central Office do send us visiting ministers – usually giving us all of seventy-two hours notice to set up an 'event' that'll do justice to the visiting VIP. Today, for example, I took our dogged-does-it Environment Minister[102] to Chester Zoo where a) I discovered we are working 'with our partners' on a European Zoos Directive (God save the mark!) and b) I had to struggle to ensure that I ended up in the pictures with him when what the photographers really wanted was the Minister and the baby hippo. The trick is to make sure you are in *every shot* and in actual physical contact with the central figure in the picture. If you're on the end of the line they can crop you. If you're in nine of the shots but not the tenth, the tenth is the one they'll use. Pictures are everything. Appear in a couple of photographs, pop up on the local TV news, and the supporters purr, 'Oh, you've been busy!' Kill yourself from dawn till dusk tearing round the constituency doing good works but fail to have your picture in the paper and they look at you reproachfully, lips curling, 'We haven't seen much of you lately, have we?'

SATURDAY 25 JANUARY 1992

I spent the morning 'saving' a nursery school and the afternoon learning about the severe financial challenges facing the Chester Branch of the RNLI. Michèle is currently donning the appropriate gladrags as we ready ourselves for the Newton Branch Twenties Evening. We came up via Wilmslow last night and stayed with Neil and Christine Hamilton at their handsome Old Rectory at Nether Alderley. We were given the Barbara Cartland suite (pink and perfect) and, with due reverence, shown the very loo on which the Blessed Margaret had once sat. Mrs T. is their goddess (you sense they really do *adore* her), but there's a happy photo on display of Christine and John Major in a fond embrace on the night Mr Major made it to No. 10. Christine is loud and splendid and winks a lot. She's Neil's House of Commons secretary and before Neil got in

---

102   David Trippier, MP for Rossendale 1979–83, Rossendale & Darwen 1983–92.

she looked after Gerald Nabarro – whose portrait by John Bratby adorns the drawing-room wall. Because my father was his solicitor I quizzed her about the truth about Nab and the car that went the wrong way around the roundabout, but didn't get very far. Neil is very funny, and wicked, and clearly likes to go as far as he can and then a little bit further. He's a government whip and explained some of the process to me: each whip (there are fourteen in all) is attached to one or two different departments of state and also has a number of MPs in his region in which he takes a special interest. I asked if I'll be in his flock if I get in.

'Oh no,' he said, 'After the election I'll be a departmental minister of some sort.'

'Is that certain?'

'Oh yes. A couple of years in the Whips' Office and then you move on.'

'Aren't you ever moved out?'

'Oh no, the Whips' Office look after their own. That's the whole point.'

SATURDAY 1 FEBRUARY 1992

I am on the 8.45 from Preston, coming from the North West Area Ball at Haydock Park and going towards Saethryd's fifteenth birthday celebrations in London. There are gigantic headlines this morning: 'Leaders hail new world order.' It seems 'world leaders yesterday laid plans to transform the UN into a global peacemaker.' Depressingly, this won't mean a dickiebird on the doorstep – where I'm berated about the recession, asked 'what are you going to do about the schools then?' and invited to get a new bus shelter along the parade, but have never, ever – not once – been cross-questioned on world affairs. I also read that we've had the driest January since 1837, which reminds me that I'm contemplating giving up alcohol for Lent.

FRIDAY 7 FEBRUARY 1992

There's an amusing piece by Matthew d'Ancona in *The Times* today on Churchill the toper. Never averse to a glass of hock at breakfast, apparently Winston as Prime Minister, in his late sixties, could consume a bottle of champagne at lunch, followed by a few brandies. Then, after his siesta, he'd move on to Scotch and soda before returning to champagne and cognac in the evening, coming back to whisky and water once more as he worked into the small hours. Pitt the Younger 'liked a glass of wine very well and a bottle still better.' Asquith's penchant for brandy had him unsteady at the despatch box and Ernest Bevin's secretaries complained that he used alcohol like a car uses petrol. When I first met George Brown[103] – on a television programme with Molly Parkin,[104] in Cardiff in the early '70s – by mid-evening he couldn't stand up. By ten o'clock he and Molly were crawling round the hotel bedroom on all fours. Sober I liked him a lot (the long-suffering Sophie too) and, when we went round to their flat in Notting Hill Gate and he was on the wagon, he was very engaging, but not a great one for detailed reminiscence: he conceded that he'd drunk so much when he was Foreign Secretary that a lot of what had happened had become a blur. He had a fine signed photograph of JFK, but no anecdote to go with it. I never drink before six and I never drink before speaking and I only drink wine, but I'd still like to drink a little less of it. Ash Wednesday here I come.

FRIDAY 14 FEBRUARY 1992

Yesterday, four-and-a-half hours non-stop pounding the beat, followed by the Ball Committee Meeting, the Upton Heath AGM (thirteen of the old faithful in a small hut in a large field), and the Upton Grange Valentine's Evening (as Michèle said, 'You really do know how to show a girl a good time!'). Today, from London word has reached us along the crackling airwaves that the beleaguered Tories have been battered and bruised by the fall-out from 'Black Thursday', a bleak day of grim statistics, the worst of which is the sharp rise in unemployment, while here in Chester our schedule (on what my darling wife is describing as 'a high day of romance') has included breakfast at the Gateway Threatre, the Boughton Branch coffee morning, lunch with the head-mistress at the Queen's School, tea with the Blacon Handbell ringers, drinks with Lord Waddington[105] in the Association Hall (it was good of him to come, I know, and kind of him to speak, I'm sure, but, oh, the *tedium* of it!) and eventually the razzle-dazzle of the Chester Nomads Hot Pot Supper at the Christleton Country Club. This then is the reality of grassroots politics in the '90s.

SATURDAY 22 FEBRUARY 1992

Yesterday I met the Foreign Secretary [Douglas Hurd] for the first time. I was impressed.

103 1914–85; Labour MP for Belper, 1945–70; Deputy Leader of the Labour Party, 1960–70.

104 Writer and artist; in the '70s and '80s, she and GB shared a literary agent.

105 Lord Privy Seal and Leader of the House of Lords 1990–92; MP for Nelson & Colne 1968–74, Clitheroe 1979–83, Rib-ble Valley 1983–90. Later Governor of Bermuda, 1992–7.

I liked him too: he seemed civilised, cool, amused. Central Office told us we could have him in Chester for just forty-five minutes from 3.00 to 3.45, so, at Vanessa's suggestion, we did a walkabout in front of the Handbridge shops and a photocall down by the river. In all we must have encountered thirty to forty shoppers, passers-by, tourists: they all recognised him and were happy to shake his hand. No one raised a political issue of any kind. I kept saying, 'Mr Hurd and I share a birthday, you know' and he kept saying 'Gyles is a good chap' and that was about it. The photographers had us crouching on the banks of the Dee feeding the swans. That was the shot they wanted and that was the shot they were determined to get. The swans were rather reluctant to play ball, however, which meant that the Foreign Secretary and I had to spend a good fifteen minutes waddling on our haunches at the water's edge. Said Mr Hurd with a wan smile, 'I don't think Mr Gladstone did a lot of this, do you?'

Before the Hurd visit I had an interesting lunch with the leading house-builder in these parts. He wants chunks of the green belt released for development. Sir Peter and the senior Conservatives on the city council seem to agree. I sense the Conservative in the street feels differently. Over lunch I sat on the fence, but I may need to come off.

This morning I had coffee with an elderly Tory very much of the old school. Sir Jack Temple[106] was Peter's predecessor. He's old and frail and blind, but he couldn't have been more courteous and sweet. I don't know that his several years at Westminster made much impact on the course of our island history, but he is clearly a good Cheshire man with good Cheshire instincts. He told me that his trademark was spotted ties – 'never wore anything else – people knew who I was' – and that the way to do canvassing was 'to get your driver to take you very slowly through all the villages – you sit on a rug on the bonnet and just wave at the people as you drive past – never stop – never get off – just keep driving through – that way they get to see you, but there are no damnfool questions'.

TUESDAY 25 FEBRUARY 1992

Another of my-kind-of-Tory Cabinet ministers came to Chester today. David Hunt [Secretary of State for Wales] seems utterly straightforward, very friendly, less forbidding than Douglas Hurd, less the statesman more the family solicitor and, consequently, probably a touch more user-friendly on the doorstep and on the box. I took him for lunch to the Sealand Sewage Works where Welsh Water, bless them, organised a brilliant

---

106 1910–94; MP for the City of Chester 1956–74.

photo call amid 20-foot high fountains of raw sewage and served us an alfresco feast of prawn sandwiches. This may sound improbable, but it is true.

....

SATURDAY 29 FEBRUARY 1992

....

A week of memorable evenings. On Tuesday night I was guest of honour at the Sealand Branch Evening at the Deaf Centre in South View Road, where they did not want to hear what I had to say: they wanted to play bingo. I let them have their way. On Wednesday night I was in Paris for the Spear's board meeting[107] and was quite mesmerised by the explicit pornography on the television in my hotel bedroom. (Interestingly, gripping as it was, I switched off after a couple of minutes, thinking that somehow – even though I was quite alone in a locked room a thousand miles from the constituency – I might get caught and it really wouldn't do for a prospective candidate to be found watching porno in Paris in the run-up to a general election.)

On Thursday night I found myself entering the front door of 11 Downing Street for the very first time. The Chancellor and Mrs Lamont were 'at home' and, somehow, I received an invitation. I know Norman slightly: he was President of the Union at Cambridge a few years before I was at Oxford and our paths crossed then, and I've met him since at Jeffrey [Archer]'s lunches, and I like him; he's droll, raffish, a little frayed at the edges – but my problem is I can't quite take him seriously as Chancellor. He may well be excellent at the job – on the stump I say he's outstanding, of course – but the truth is I find it hard to take people altogether seriously when I *know* them. (That's one of the reasons I find it hard to take myself seriously – though I know I must. In this game, taking yourself seriously is part of the job.) Because I was coming in from Paris I was a little late. I bounded in, across a small hallway and up the stairs (past framed cartoons of previous occupants) into a large reception room packed with happy chatterers all taking themselves very seriously indeed. Norman was friendly and welcoming and optimistic. 'We're going to win the election. Of course we are, dear boy. I'm not moving out of *here*.'

Yesterday I was back in Chester – more door-knocking, five hours of it, including a woman in Vicar's Cross who said 'I'm not talking to you – you never come to my door' – 'But I'm at your door, madam!' – 'Go away, I'm not talking to you – you never come to my door' – followed by an evening with the farming folk in Aldford. This evening it's the Guilden Sutton Quiz Night. This is politics in the fast lane.

There's been an IRA bomb at London Bridge, twenty-nine hurt.

---

107   GB was a non-executive director of the games manufacturer J. W. Spear & Sons which had a French subsidiary.

TUESDAY 3 MARCH 1992

Last night we were dined by Shirley Porter[108] at Westminster City Hall which turns out to be a modern office block in Victoria and consequently quite soulless. Shirley, London's own Mrs T., a beady-eyed bundle of energy and obsessive commitment, moved from table to table making sure we were all keeping the faith. She knows what she wants and she gets it, and if, for a nano-second, you look diffident or uncertain she makes you feel utterly ashamed. I'm just watching a lady with a softer centre on the box: it's a giggly Norma Major tossing a Shrove Tuesday pancake. Tomorrow is Ash Wednesday and I go on the wagon.

TUESDAY 10 MARCH 1992

The high points of my Budget Day have been the Blacon coffee morning (in a house that smelled of urine and disinfectant – a smell I'd never encountered before getting this job, but one to which I find I'm now quite accustomed); sherry with the Dean[109] (he drank the sherry; I stuck to orange juice); a talk to some very elderly ladies at the Square One Youth Club on Thackeray Drive; and much the same talk to the Chester Glee Club at the Stafford Hotel. From what I can tell the Budget looks ingenious: the new 20p in the pound income tax rate is attractive and 'a Budget for recovery' is a neat phrase. The line we've been given is that the tax changes will leave the average punter £2.64 better off. Will he believe it? Is it enough? The income support for poorer pensioners going up by £2 (£3 for couples) is certainly good news – though what most of the crumblies really seem to want is a free TV licence. That comes up on the Chester doorsteps several times a day without fail. Standing on the No. 11 doorstep, with the fair Rosemary towering beside him and the boy Hague [Lamont's PPS] grinning in the rear, the Chancellor certainly looks happy enough. Perhaps it will do the trick. Who knows?

WEDNESDAY 11 MARCH 1992

While I was lunching with the Retired Masonic Fellowship at the Upton British Legion Club, the Prime Minister was closeted with Her Majesty at Buckingham Palace.

---

108 Leader of Westminster City Council 1983–91, Lord Mayor of Westminster 1991–2. Dame Shirley's husband, Sir Leslie Porter, was the first chairman of the company that mounted GB's unsuccessful Royal Britain exhibition.

109 Dr Stephen Smalley, Dean of Chester Cathedral, 1987–2001.

Mr Major had a twenty-minute audience with the Queen and the election has been called for 9 April. The game's afoot. The race is on. The BBC's poll of fifty key marginals gives Labour a five-point lead, but that's bridgeable. We can win and, in Chester, we will.

MONDAY 16 MARCH 1992

John Smith's[110] shadow Budget has to be good news. The pundits are saying it'll cost mid-dle managers £1,500 a year. That's exactly what we need. The Conservative voters who have been crucified by the recession (and I've met quite a few and they're angry) will vote elsewhere this time, but the Tories who are simply wavering (they've been bruised, they're fearful of negative equity, they're worried about redundancy, but they've still got a house and a job), they could come back to us at the last minute, clinging on to nurse for fear of something worse.

The buzz from London is that Jeffrey Archer and Norman Fowler[111] are already jos-tling to be the post-election party chairman and Fergie and Prince Andrew are going to split.[112] (I remember a conversation with King Constantine at the time they became engaged: 'Sarah is delightful, so carefree, such fun. She will be a breath of fresh air at Buck-ingham Palace. She will be the making of the modern royal family. You mark my words.')

WEDNESDAY 18 MARCH 1992

A week down, three weeks to go. It's tiring, but it isn't difficult. There are moments I'm hat-ing – assaulting the commuters at the railway station at 8.00 a.m., badgering the mums at the school gates at 3.15 – but the major part of the process – knocking on doors, hour after hour, a minimum of eight hours a day – is relatively stress-free. You shake a hand, proffer a leaflet, mouth a cliché and move quickly on.

Today our star attraction has been Jeffrey Archer who was both brilliant and ridiculous. We started off with him at the Quaker House where we imposed ourselves on a lip-reading lesson for the hard-of-hearing. The old ladies were charmed by Jeffrey, who gave every-one an autograph and then stood in the middle of the room and boomed at them about

110 John Smith, 1938–94; shadow Chancellor of the Exchequer 1987–92; Labour MP for North Lanarkshire 1970–83, Monklands East 1983–94.

111 MP for Nottingham South 1970–74, Sutton Coldfield 1974–2001; later Baron Fowler. In 1990 he left the Cabinet 'to spend more time with his family'. During the 1992 election campaign he was a special adviser to John Major and, after the election, became Conservative Party chairman.

112 Prince Andrew married Sarah Ferguson in 1986. The marriage was formally dissolved ten years later.

Labour's threat to the constitution. He was so loud that they heard every word and loved every moment. Unfortunately, when we went down into the street for the walkabout Jeffrey maintained the volume, which certainly won us glances as we strode purposefully through the shopping precinct, but I'm not sure it won us votes. He became a caricature of himself really, beaming dementedly at visibly shrinking passers-by, thrusting his hand out towards bemused tourists and barking at them in turn, 'Jeffrey Archer. Jeffrey Archer. Jeffrey Archer. This is your candidate, Gyles Brandreth. Jeffrey Archer. Jeffrey Archer. Jeffrey Archer.' Michèle became so embarrassed she separated herself from our group and slipped home. I like Jeffrey. He's like Mr Toad, absurd but still a star. (And I don't forget: he put £30,000 into Royal Britain, lost every penny, and never said a word.)

MONDAY 23 MARCH 1992

Fun and games on the doorstep today. One woman in Vicar's Cross dragged me into her sitting room and said, 'Sit down.'

'No, I can't stay,' I simpered. 'I just popped by to say hello.'

'You want my vote, don't you?'

'Yes, but—'

'Then you'll sit there while I make a cup of tea.'

'No, really, I've got a lot of ground to cover.'

'Look, young man. If you want my vote, you'll sit there and listen to what I've got to say.'

At this point Jill [Everett] appeared to rescue me. 'I'm afraid we've got to get Mr Brandreth back on the road.'

'No you haven't. He's come to see me. He's going to hear what I've got to say.'

'Perhaps Mrs Everett could take notes,' I suggested, edging towards the door, 'and I'll write to you.'

'She'll do no such thing.'

Jill now attempted to lead me through the door. The woman grabbed me and pulled me back towards the sofa. I gave in. I had no choice. I was there for three-quarters of an hour agreeing on the importance of home births, the shameful undervaluing of midwives and the priority of preschool play provision. As I left she said, 'I shall certainly be voting Labour.'

Later, in Boughton, one of our activists reprimanded me for shying away from a particularly ferocious dog. 'You shouldn't flinch like that. They can smell fear. You should go towards them and show them the back of your hand.' She did exactly that and the snarling hound promptly mauled her. We had to rush the poor dear to the hospital and I think she'll need stitches.

The election here seems a million miles from the one on the box. Out there Mrs T. has apparently 'lifted the spirits of the shaken Tories' with a rousing endorsement of her successor and the Prime Minister has impressed the troops with his 'most positive and forceful speech' of the campaign. Says Norman Tebbit:[113] 'At last they've stopped feeding him bromides in his tea.'

WEDNESDAY 25 MARCH 1992

Michael Heseltine flashed in and flashed out today. We had him for half an hour. We took him to the Meadows for the photocall. He had no idea who I was. We shook hands, we posed for the pictures, I made small talk, but I don't think he glanced at me once, and while in a lordly way he gladhanded the forty or fifty faithful we'd corralled to greet him he didn't *engage* with them for a moment. He was grand but not impressive. But I was very glad to have him all the same. I think I have scored on the local issues – nursery education, saving the Cheshire Regiment, more police on the Chester beat – and, notwithstanding Sir Peter [Morrison]'s contempt ('This'll cost you a thousand votes. This could cost you the election'), I think I have been right to be seen to be supporting the Heseltine decision on the Green Belt.[114]

All the old hands say it's the national swing that counts. Local issues, what the candidate does, all the door-knocking, they make a difference of a thousand votes at most. Of course, here a thousand votes one way or another could well be what decides it. That's why we've got to keep at it. And we do.

FRIDAY 27 MARCH 1992

Last night we had the Churches Together *Any Questions* at the Blacon Arts Centre. I survived. I don't think I gave my own supporters the gungho performance they'd have liked: I was too moderate, but my people will vote for me anyway (won't they?); I was wanting to appeal to any middle-of-the-road waverers. I did my best to disconcert the other candidates by being effusively chummy towards them. The Liberal and the Green I like. The Labour fellow is fairly loathsome and he thinks he's going to win.

---

113 MP for Epping 1970–74, Chingford 1974–92. Later Baron Tebbit CH.

114 Heseltine, as Environment Secretary, had rejected a local plan that would have allowed development on Green Belt land in and around Chester.

I'm not wearying yet. I'm not drinking either – and not missing it. The days are very strange though, hour after hour of door-knocking, sudden flurries of excitement when a visiting superstar descends, and then getting home and collapsing in front of *Newsnight* to discover the election coverage on the box bears no relationship at all to the issues that are coming up on the doorstep. On TV and in the papers they are talking about nothing except 'the war of Jennifer's ear'. It hasn't cropped up once on the street.

TUESDAY 31 MARCH 1992

Mr Major brought his soapbox to Chester this morning and it was a triumph. We only had twenty-four hours advance notice and strict instructions not to tell a soul about it. 'If we can't say he's coming, how's anyone going to know he's here?' was my question to Vanessa. 'We can alert the troops to the fact that we're expecting a very important visitor whose name we can't mention and let them draw their own conclusions.'

In the event, our coded signal and the beat of the tom-tom brought out our supporters in their hundreds and we gathered, as instructed, in the pedestrianised part of Eastgate Street at eleven. Equipped with a loud-hailer I stood on a bench in the drizzle and addressed the multitude. This is as close as I get to Agincourt. I don't think anyone was really listening, but it was fun. Old-fashioned street politics. The rain got worse, but the crowd was good-humoured throughout. There was excitement, a sense of occasion in the air. As the minutes passed and word went round the city centre, more and more people thronged the square. The police reckoned there were 2,000 at least by the time the battle bus arrived. The door opened, we all roared, and the Prime Minister with a grin and a wave plunged into the throng. It was amazing. The crush was incredible. I managed to get right by him and stuck to him like a limpet as we moved through the heaving, cheering mass. We were surrounded by police, TV crews, cameramen, and at the Prime Minister's right-hand throughout was Norman Fowler.

As we pushed forward, with supporters and shoppers and gawpers pressing towards us, leaning out to touch the Major anorak, reaching out to shake the great man's hand, Norman Fowler kept up a running commentary, 'The soapbox is just to the right, John. Look towards the balcony now, see the camera, now wave. And now to the left, there's some girls at the window, another wave. That's it, good, good. It's going well. Nearly there.' Major then clambered on to the soapbox and made a proper speech – ten minutes and more – all straightforward stuff, no great rhetoric, but somehow phenomenal. Here was the Prime Minister of the United Kingdom on a soapbox in the rain telling 2,000 of the people of Chester what he wanted to do for his country. It worked a treat. There was some jokey heckling which he handled nicely. We could have done with more.

Stump speech over, he climbed off the box and struggled back through the crush to the bus. We climbed aboard and off we went, round the bend and down to Nicholas Street where our admirable ladies had prepared a sandwich lunch for the prime ministerial party. Making small talk with him wasn't easy. Once we were inside the Association Hall his jauntiness dissipated. He seemed preoccupied – which is hardly surprising.

'How do you think it's going?'

'I'm not sure,' he said, 'It's difficult to tell.'

'The soapbox is working,' said Norman Fowler, still bouncy. 'We've spent a fortune – a fortune – on the set for the talking-to-John-Major rallies, but it's the soapbox that's stealing the show.'

'It's a game,' said Mr Major. 'I did a press briefing last week under a banner that said "The best team in a troubled world" and the photographers managed to catch a picture of me during the one moment when I wasn't smiling under the one word "troubled". You can't win.'

Norma was lovely: normal, friendly, chatty with the troops. She thrilled me: 'I first met you, Gyles,' she said, 'at Heffer's in Cambridge. You were doing a signing session and I queued up to buy one of your books for the children.' I kissed her, which I fear some of the activists thought rather forward. I'm afraid she might have thought so too.

....

LATER

....

Fuck. I cannot believe what has happened. This morning when I was having a high old time in the city centre with the John and Norma cavalcade I should have been at Queen's Park High School addressing the sixth form. I don't know how the cock-up happened. The school had booked me weeks ago, before the election was called, and somehow we didn't transfer the engagement from my regular diary to the election schedule. I cannot believe it. I was due at the school at 10.30 a.m. I was to talk and take questions till 12 and then stay for lunch. Apparently the entire sixth form was sitting in the school hall waiting, waiting, waiting – and now the fact that I failed to show and didn't even let them know I wasn't coming will have gone round the entire school and back to every one of something like a thousand plus families. It is so bloody annoying. I went round to the school in the afternoon and I've got a list of all the sixth-formers and I am writing to each of them personally – but the damage is done. And if it gets to the local press, they will have such fun with it, the bastards.

WEDNESDAY 1 APRIL 1992

Today's poll gives Labour a seven point lead. They're on 42, we're on 35, the Lib Dems 19. I'm scuppered. I have just been watching Mr Kinnock amid flashing lights and fireworks giving a triumphalist oration at a rally in Sheffield. He is so awful, and in ten days he'll be Prime Minister.

FRIDAY 3 APRIL 1992

The front page of the *Chester Standard* is given over to just the right kind of coverage of the Major visit. Couldn't be better. Inside, however, there's a letter that could hardly be worse. It's from 'the committee' of Radio Lion, the in-house radio at the Countess of Chester Hospital, and accuses me of exploiting the hospital and the radio station for political ends. I was invited to be interviewed by them (true), and without forewarning them turned up for the interview with a photographer in tow (also true). I've since used the photo in both the local papers and in my election literature – and they want 'a public apology' from me for having exploited this non-political voluntary organisation in this way! I hate the letter, because it's so prominent, because the tone of it is so nasty, but, mostly, of course, because it contains more than a grain of truth. I did exploit them. To get these wretched pictures into the papers I'm exploiting people all the time. It's inevitable – and I suppose it's inevitable too that sometimes it backfires. (I'm a bit more cautious about taking advantage of the elderly since I was pictured presenting a birthday cake to a virtually gaga centenarian on what turned out to be the morning of the day she died!) There is a decent letter as well. It is from Terry Bennett. 'Full marks to Gyles Brandreth. He talks a lot of sense.' It's a good letter. I know because I wrote it! Our opponents fill the correspondence columns of the local rags with their tiresome tirades and we need to answer back. Our troops aren't good at getting round to letter-writing ('The best lack all conviction while the worst are full of passionate intensity') so I have taken to drafting one or two letters a week for them to copy, sign and send.

The Social Security Secretary Tony Newton[115] was our VIP yesterday and since nobody seemed to have heard of him Vanessa decided that we'd take him to a nursing home. It was the kind of visit Michèle hates. The poor inmates are all siting in armchairs ranged round the walls gazing blankly into the middle distance while the television in the corner blares away from the moment you arrive to the moment you leave. We troop round, shaking the palsied hands, booming our names, grinning inanely at uncomprehending

---

115 1937–2012; MP for Braintree 1974–97; later Baron Newton of Braintree.

faces. Mr Newton, who smokes as much as Sir Peter and the Duke of Westminster, didn't look as if he was enjoying himself. Other than making little jokes about how nobody knows who he is, he had no small talk. He was obviously exhausted. He said he was weary of the campaign and feels it hasn't gone particularly well. The press turned up to photograph us, so I suppose the visit was worthwhile. Let us hope the old dears we were pictured with survive till polling day. (Vanessa has been brilliant with the nursing home vote. The trick she says is to get the matron on your side. She's the one who fills out the postal and the proxy votes … Vanessa's also got me going to see the nuns in Curzon Park: 'You only need to nobble the Mother Superior. If she votes for us, they all will. It's called the rule of obedience.')

The Business Club *Any Questions* was fine. I hit my stride and Robinson was rattled and all at sea. If last night's audience were my electorate, I'd win. They aren't, of course, and I have no idea what the outcome will be. We've been canvassing on the doorstep and by phone and I'm told we've covered about 80 per cent of the constituency, but when I ask Vanessa for the figures she says getting them out of the computer is a nightmare but 'it's looking good' – which suggests to me that it's looking very bad indeed. What the hell. *Que sera sera.* Paddy Ashdown[116] seems to know what to expect. He's demanding four posts in a coalition Cabinet.

TUESDAY 7 APRIL 1992

Peter Lilley[117] came and went. Old Uncle Charisma he ain't, but he was decent and intelligent and businesslike and the (fairly small) crowd we'd gathered for him at the Association Hall liked what he had to offer. The moment he'd gone we went back to Blacon and the worst of the high-rise blocks. They are squalid and soulless, the public parts filthy, the walls covered with mindless graffiti. The Right to Buy has made no impact here. When doors were opened almost every flat looked equally unloved, unkempt – and then you'd find one belonging to an elderly person who opened the door a crack and then opened it wide and you could see how house-proud they were and sense how they must hate having to live where they do with the neighbours they have to endure. Grim places, grim lives. And if and when I become a Member of Parliament, will I be able to make any impact at all on that?

Mr Major has just been on the box setting out ten Tory truths for a golden future. He

---

116   Leader of the Liberal Democrats since 1988–99; MP for Yeovil 1983–2001; later Baron Ashdown of Norton-sub-Hamdon GCMG, KBE.

117   Secretary of State for Trade and Industry 1990–92; MP for St Albans 1983–97; Hitchin & Harpenden from 1997.

believes he 'understands what makes the heart of Britain beat' and the way he says it you believe him. He's no Churchill, but when it comes to simply tugging at the heart strings he's hard to beat. We've also been parading our celebrity circus: Labour have come up with Simply Red, Nigel Kennedy and Steve Cram; we're fielding Ruth Madoc, Lynsey de Paul, Elaine Paige. Not bad. (We seem to be keeping Russell Grant and Bob Monkouse under wraps. Perhaps Chris Patten has locked them in the Central Office cellar, along with Norman Lamont, John Gummer, Peter Brooke, William Waldegrave and all our other missing ministers. I imagine the thinking is 'out of sight, out of mind'.)

THURSDAY 9 APRIL 1992

A depressing start to polling day. The headline in the *Standard*, delivered free of charge through every door in Chester this general election morning, reads 'Brandreth fires back at missed meetings charge'. They've got the wretched missed meeting at Queen's Park High School and they've topped that up with the line that I've 'shirked' public meetings and 'even forced the abandonment of one live radio debate'. In fact I did five meetings with the other candidates (every one a nightmare and of no value – people's prejudices are simply confirmed – which is no doubt why Peter M. very sensibly only ever agreed to do one) and I deliberately turned down the local radio debate because, thanks to the Representation of the People Act,[118] if I didn't show I knew it couldn't happen and I thought 'why give air time to my opponents? What's in it for me?' Still, it doesn't look good and it'll dishearten the troops.

LATER

Michèle and I voted first thing, up on St Mary's Hill, in the nursery school I saved (my one achievement to date!) and then spent the day in John Shanklin's[119] little car criss-crossing the constituency without pause, visiting every one of our twenty-four committee rooms and as many polling stations as we could manage. John is lovely, intelligent, undemanding, easy to be with and 'all I ask is strawberry tea on the terrace when you're elected'.

Everywhere we went we did our best to be jolly, but it's clear it's going to be a close-run thing. The Labour people are certainly more ruthless when it comes to getting out

---

118 During a general election campaign broadcasters are required, when covering a specific constituency, to give equal coverage to all candidates for that constituency.

119 Cheshire county councillor and Conservative activist.

the vote: they turn up at the old folks homes and shovel the old dears into charabancs. They are bolder and, I suspect, more systematic. Our teams were mostly optimistic, the kindly branch chairmen nodding sagely and saying 'It's holding up quite nicely.' (How do they know? I don't think our canvassing has been that scientific!) John Cliffe may have been nearer the mark. Hangdog face, fag cupped in the palm of his hand (he was in the merchant marine and rolls as if he's still on deck), he shook his head mournfully, 'They're not coming out for you. It's a damned disgrace. They don't deserve you. You're too good for them. It's a crying shame.'

David Parry-Jones (from the *Chronicle*) has sent a nice note saying I've fought a brilliant campaign and that the combination of that and the fact that I'm not Sir Peter will give me a majority of 8,000. We shall see.

It's just gone ten. We're watching the box and it don't look good. Ask not for whom the exit poll tolls, it tolls for thee...

FRIDAY 10 APRIL 1992

I am now the Member of Parliament for the City of Chester.

Soon after ten last night we put on clean clothes and brave faces and trudged up the hill to the Town Hall. The entrance and the press room were full of happy Labour activists – buzzy, busy, running from computer to calculator filling in the latest data, the scent of victory already in their nostrils. At the best of times, a Labour activist is not a pretty sight. Good-looking people seem to eschew mainstream politics. (Tom Barker, our young Green candidate is the exception to the rule. He is fresh-faced, fair, pretty – all of which I'd have said to him, except now I don't say that sort of thing. Michèle has even coached me out of the habit of calling everyone 'darling'. It was when I called the Bishop 'darling' that she put her foot down. 'Enough is enough.' 'Yes, darling.') Labour activists on heat, ready for the kill, beards bristling, red faces glistening, the women either appallingly overweight or peculiarly scraggy (not *one* with a normal figure), hunting as a pack – it wasn't nice to see. They *knew* they had won and they couldn't contain themselves. We knew we'd lost and all I really felt was tired.

Inside the main hall, the atmosphere was much more subdued. I had never been to a count before. I couldn't believe how primitive it all is. The ballot boxes are emptied, the papers are sorted and bundled into bunches of fifty and held together with clothes-pegs – yes, plastic and wooden clothes-pegs. They are then carefully placed in lines on long trestle tables and as the night wears on you can see who's line is the longest. For most of the night, Labour's line was longer than mine by far, but gradually I could see I was catching up, and by two in the morning, when word was coming in from around the country that perhaps we hadn't lost after all, I could see that in Chester too we were neck and neck.

The Labour people couldn't believe it. The leader of the Labour Group, whose gross red face had glowed with complacency all evening, now turned purple with anger and dismay. I am ashamed to say it was pleasing to see him looking quite so ugly and unhappy. He wanted recount after recount, and the pegged bundles were checked and rechecked; we argued over the spoilt ballot papers, but there were only a handful of them (where voters had put question marks or squiggles instead of crosses, or placed their mark adjacent to the box not in it), so I conceded the point. And then the moment came: the Returning Officer whispered the final figures to each of us in turn, we accepted them (the Lib Dem and the Green with good grace; Robinson, now ashen-faced, through gritted teeth), and processed onto the stage for the result formally to be announced to the waiting world.

> Brandreth (Conservative) 23,411
> Robinson (Labour) 22,310
> Smith (Lib Dem) 6,867
> Barker (Green) 448
> Cross [Natural Law Party – we never saw him, but apparently he was always 'there'] 98

I have a majority of 1,101 and 44.1 per cent of the vote. In 1987 Peter Morrison secured 44.9 per cent of the vote, so the Conservative vote held and the reduced majority is entirely down to the Liberal collapse: their vote fell by 7 per cent, all of which went to Labour.

Anyway, I've won. And it does feel good. And Michèle has been wonderful. She seems quite pleased. We've had no sleep – well, three hours, but I think I lay awake for most of that. After the count I did radio and television and gabbled away to the local press and we went to the [Conservative] Club and caroused with the victorious troops. They have been fantastic. I didn't have a celebratory drink. Oddly, I wasn't even tempted. On Easter Sunday we are lunching at the Caprice and, then, boy, will the champagne flow...

SATURDAY 11 APRIL 1992

We're going home. I'm about to see London for the first time in four weeks. Thanks to pounding the beat (and laying off the bottle) I've lost a stone – so the election *was* worthwhile. In truth, I'm not sure what impact I had on the result. At constituency level you're not driving the election: it's simply happening to you. Clearly I didn't frighten off our supporters, but I don't think I made much of a difference to the outcome, did I? The activists believe what we do does make a difference, but they have to believe that, don't they?

Chris Patten, Lynda Chalker,[120] David Trippier, John Maples,[121] Colin Moynihan all lost their seats. Two of my friends got in for the first time: Stephen Milligan[122] and Sebastian Coe.[123] Mr Major is starting his reshuffle today. Mr Kinnock is pondering his future. We have an overall majority of twenty-one seats and a majority of sixty-four over Labour. According to the nation's most popular newspaper, 'It was *The Sun* wot won it' and certainly Thursday's front page can have done us no harm among *The Sun*'s more thoughtful readers. Alongside a distorted mug shot of poor Mr Kinnock trapped inside a light bulb ran the headline: 'If Kinnock wins today will the last person to leave Britain please turn out the lights … You know our views on the subject, but we don't want to influence you in your final judgement on who will be Prime Minister. But if it's a bald bloke with wispy red hair and two Ks in his surname, we'll see you at the airport. Good night and thank you for everything.'

....

WEDNESDAY 15 APRIL 1992

....

I got back to Chester on the 11.23. There's a sackload of mail, including a handwritten note from Chevening House, Chevening, Sevenoaks, Kent: 'Dear Gyles, Many congratulations – that's excellent news. I'm sure our stroll among the swans a month ago was decisive. See you soon. Judy joins me in welcome. Yours, Douglas.' The Foreign Secretary finds time to write to the new backbencher. I'm impressed – and pleased. There are lots of gratifying messages. Oddi wrth Ysgrifennydd Gwladol Cymru: 'What a magnificent victory. Many congratulations and welcome to the Commons. I am sure you are just beginning what will be a long and distinguished career and I look forward to working with you for many years to come. Yours ever, David.' Hurd and Hunt are back in post; Kenneth Clarke[124] is Home Secretary, Malcolm Rifkind[125] goes to Defence,

---

120 MP for Wallasey 1974–92; later Baroness Chalker of Wallasey.

121 MP for Lewisham West 1983–92; Stratford-upon-Avon 1997–2010; later Baron Maples.

122 1948–94; MP for Eastleigh 1992–4; journalist and broadcaster, contemporary of GB at university.

123 MP for Falmouth & Camborne 1992–97; Olympic gold medallist in 1980 and 1984; later Baron Coe of Ranmore CH KBE.

124 MP for Rushcliffe since 1970; he had been Secretary of State for Education 1990–92, Secretary of State for Health 1988–90.

125 MP for Edinburgh Pentlands 1974–97; he had been Secretary of State for Transport 1990–92, Secretary of State for Scotland 1986–90. Later MP for Kensington from 2005.

Michael Howard[126] is at Environment and Heseltine goes to Trade and Industry. Two women join the Cabinet (Virginia Bottomley[127] at Health, Gillian Shephard[128] at Employment) but one other (Edwina!) is offered a job at the Home Office and – very publicly – declines. 'Currie snubs Major' is this morning's headline. This morning's rumour is that Chris Patten is going to be Governor of Hong Kong.

THURSDAY 16 APRIL 1992

God save the Queen! And God bless the Duke of Edinburgh! Her Majesty came to Chester today to distribute the Royal Maundy at the Cathedral and to bestow upon us the gift of a Lord Mayorlty in a little ceremony at the Town Hall. When I arrived at the council chamber to take my place it was made pleasantly but firmly clear to me that I am merely the Member of Parliament and consequently somebody of pretty little significance on these all-important civic occasions. At Chester Town Hall, councillors rule, okay? And kindly don't forget it. Suitably humbled I took my allotted place tucked at the end of the third row back. Mayors past and present, sheriffs, councillors, clerks, freemen, county councillors, city and county dignitaries by the score, processed with wonderful dignity to their places. And when everyone bar Larry the Lamb himself was in position, we the riffraff were ordered to our feet and in came the Lord Mayor in all her glory with Her Majesty, small and smiling, and Prince Philip, tanned and gently amused. The ceremony didn't last long and, when it was over, we all stood for the reverse procession. The Queen and the Lord Mayor followed by Prince Philip made to leave, but as they were turning to depart the Chamber Prince Philip suddenly caught my eye. His brow furrowed, he left the procession and moved down the line towards the cheap seats.

'What are you doing here?'

'I'm the Member of Parliament.'

'Good God, are you really? How's it going?'

'Fine, thanks.'

The small talk lasted moments no more, but as HRH chuckled, shook his head and returned to the procession the effect on my 'friends' the councillors was noticeable – and gratifying.

---

126 MP for Folkestone & Hythe 1983–2010; he had been Secretary of State for Employment 1990–92. Later Leader of the Conservative Party, 2003–5, and Baron Howard of Lympne CH.

127 MP for Surrey South West 1984–2005; she had been Minister for Health 1989–92. Later Baroness Bottomley of Nettlestone.

128 MP for Norfolk South West 1987–2005; she had been a Minister of State at the Treasury 1990–92. Later Baroness Shephard of Northwold.

MONDAY 20 APRIL 1992

Frankie Howerd has died and I have started drinking. He was seventy-five, which surprises me (he seemed younger), and I've raised several glasses to him because he was very funny and I was genuinely fond of him – despite the fact that the last time we met he exposed himself to me. He pretended to have a groin strain, thrust a jar of ointment into my hand, pulled down his trousers and threw himself back onto the sofa.

'Rub it in!'

'Where?'

'*There!* Haven't you seen one before? It's perfectly harmless. Treat it like a muscle.'

My first letter from the Prime Minister: 'I am delighted to welcome you to Westminster when there is so much to be done. It will be hard work – but immensely worthwhile. I much look forward to seeing you when the new parliament meets. In the meantime, do take the chance to catch your breath!' A letter too from Michael Portillo[129] whom I've never met. Has he written to all the new boys? Lord St John of Fawsley writes in purple ink, 'My dear Gyles, You will be a wonderful MP but practise a little economy of personality in the Commons. They don't deserve to have too much too soon.'

THURSDAY 23 APRIL 1992

I'm on the 9.03 to Chester, a day of canvassing for the local elections lies ahead. Benny Hill has died and the Prime Minister is allowing Norman Lamont to have Dorneywood, the government's second grand grace-and-favour mansion as his official country residence. We think Rosemary will quite like that.

FRIDAY 24 APRIL 1992

Jeremy Hanley is a good kind man. I caught the 7.39 from Chester and, as arranged, presented myself at the St Stephen's entrance to the Palace of Westminster as Big Ben struck eleven. Tall, broad, beaming, Jeremy was waiting for me on the doorstep and gave me the most wonderful hour-long tour, introducing me to all and sundry in the most extravagant terms. He wouldn't shake my hand. 'Members of Parliament do not shake hands.' The origin of the handshake was physical proof that your hand did not conceal a weapon, that you came in friendship: as at the House of Commons we are all

---

129   MP for Enfield Southgate 1984–92.

'Honourable Members' we don't need to prove our good intentions towards one another so between one another we don't shake hands.

Jeremy's tour started at the Members' Entrance where he introduced me to the policeman and explained that when waiting for a taxi we take precedence over anyone else in the line. There are 651 members and in the members' cloakroom there are 651 coat-hangers arranged in alphabetical order. We found mine! Attached to it, attached to each and every one of the 651 coat-hangers, is a small loop of pink ribbon.

'What's it for?'

'You don't know?'

'I don't know.'

'The pink ribbon – that's where you hang your sword!'

The authorities are clearly keen to discourage sword-fighting within the palace precincts. When we went into the Commons Chamber for the first time (I had never seen inside it before: it was so much smaller than I had expected) Jeremy showed me the two thin red lines woven into the green carpet in front of each of the front benches and said:

> When speaking in a debate, you are not allowed to step over the thin red line. You must 'toe the line'. And the distance between those two lines is the exact distance between two outstretched arms and two full-length swords ... so, you see, they take the business of 'no sword-fighting' very seriously indeed. At the House of Commons, sword-fighting is out. Sword-fighting is taboo. Sword-fighting is definitely not on. (Pause) *Back-stabbing* on the other hand is quite a different matter!

He tells wonderful stories wonderfully well:

> We sit on this side and the opposition sit on this side. You know the Churchill line? 'Never confuse the opposition with the enemy. The opposition are the Members of Parliament sitting on the benches facing you. The enemy are the Members of Parliament sitting on the benches behind you.

Jeremy is now a minister (Under-Secretary of State at the Northern Ireland Office and pleased as Punch) and gets to sit on the front bench. He advised me to sit third seat in, third row up. 'You can see and you're seen.' To bag a place you have to turn up in the morning, any time from 8.00 a.m., collect a small green 'prayer card', fill in your name and put the card on the seat you want. That reserves your place. To confirm your reservation you have to be in position at 2.30 p.m. sharp for prayers. Then the seat's yours for the rest of the day.

MONDAY 27 APRIL 1992

It is difficult to describe quite how miserable I feel. I don't think I should have done this. I fear I may have made a huge mistake and the horror of it is there's no turning back. Joanna and Stevie came to supper. They've only just gone. They were so bright and sweet and full of congratulations, full of the excitement of it all. Joanna kept stroking my hair and saying, 'You are my Prince!' I didn't have the heart – or the courage – or the wit – to tell them how bleak I feel. I haven't told Michèle. She's in the bath as I'm scribbling this.

The plain truth is today has been my first full day at the House of Commons and I have hated it. If you had seen me I don't think you'd have known. I did my best to play the part, but when I got home I felt so low, hollow and quite desperate. It wasn't just the particular humiliation that I'll describe in a moment; it isn't simply that I am forty-four and I have had a day feeling like an awkward fourteen-year-old; it is a sudden horrifying, overwhelming, all-enveloping sense that the Commons and all it stands for just isn't going to be the place for me.

Here's how it went. At 12.30 p.m., as arranged, I met Neil and Christine Hamilton in Central Lobby. Neil and I set off to bag our places in the Chamber. There were prayer cards everywhere, so Neil (who is now a junior minister at the DTI) said we should sit in the second row, just behind the Prime Minister. I said, 'Are you sure?' He said, 'Absolutely.' We filled in our cards and reserved our seats. We then had a jolly lunch in a not-very-jolly canteen somewhere in the bowels of the building.

At 2.30 we were back in the Chamber for the election of the Speaker. The place was packed. I sat immediately behind the Prime Minister, squeezed between Neil and the PM's PPS.[130] I knew at once that I was in the wrong place. I sensed immediately that where I was sitting, literally at the Prime Minister's right ear, was wrong, preposterous, risible. I felt all eyes must be upon me and that every single person in the Chamber must have felt contempt for me and my presumption. In fact, of course, I know that's hardly rational, no one was thinking about me at all, but that's what I felt – and because I felt it I could feel nothing else. The whole amazing process of the election of the Speaker as good as passed me by. Ted Heath, as Father of the House, took the Chair. Some bent old stick[131] proposed Peter Brooke.[132] Tom Arnold seconded him, Tony Benn[133] blathered on against. Peter Brooke then spoke for himself, all very self-effacing and over-fruity at

---

130 Graham Bright, MP for Luton East 1979–83, Luton South 1983–97; PPS to John Major as Chancellor of the Exchequer and Prime Minister 1990–94.

131 Sir Michael Neubert, 1933–2014; MP for Havering & Romford 1974–83, Romford 1983–97.

132 MP for Cities of London & Westminster 1997–2001; later Baron Brooke of Sutton Mandeville.

133 1925–2014; Labour MP for Bristol South East 1950–60 and 1963–83, Chesterfield 1984 – 2010.

the same time. Then John Biffen[134] and assorted others put forward the case for Betty Boothroyd.[135] She spoke so much better than Peter Brooke, but when it came to the vote I voted for Brooke on the basis that I don't know either of them and at least he's a Conservative. (He was obviously also desperate: there were messages from him on both answering machines at the weekend.) When the vote was announced – Boothroyd 372, Brooke 238 – the place erupted. Miss Boothroyd was 'dragged' from her place (in the body of the Chamber, several rows back, needless to say) and we all stood and cheered. The opposition began to clap, so we clapped too. This is not what we do here: we cheer, we wave our order papers and we do not applaud. But we did. History was being made. The Commons has its 155th Speaker and she is the first woman. It was quite an occasion, but because I was so certain I was where I ought not to be I loathed every minute of it. And it went on for two hours.

At 5.00 p.m. I made my way up to Committee Room 10 for the New Members Meeting. All the government whips sat on the platform in a line and we new boys (plus the four new girls) sat, cowed, below at school desks – yes, school desks with ridges for your pencil and square holes for inkwells. It was exactly like a Dickensian school assembly photographed by David Lean in black and white. Even the jokes creaked: 'And when there is a three-line whip you will be here to vote – unless you can produce a doctor's certificate (pause) showing you are dead.' As we shuffled out, my whip[136] hauled me from the crowd. 'I don't know what you think you were doing sitting right behind the Prime Minister. Not a very good start. Don't let it happen again.'

Trembling with the shame of it (and thinking 'Fuck you' at the same time – it is all so stupid) I went down to Central Lobby for my assignation with Angela Eagle.[137] Smallish, youngish, short-lank hair, pointy nose, bloke-ish manner, not my idea of a fun time (as Simon [Cadell] would say, 'She's happier in Holland')[138] she's the victor at Wallasey and the person I'm hoping will provide my 'pair'. On advice, I called her the weekend after the election to ask her if we could pair. She said she'd think about it. She's still thinking. We went down to the bar in the basement to talk it over. I bought her a drink (was that a mistake? I imagine she *lives* for political correctness) and pleaded my cause – rather too desperately I fancy. She's 'seeing one or two others' then she'll let me know. If I don't have a 'pair' I shall be stuck at the House of Commons every night for five years. I cannot believe what I've let myself in for.

---

134   1930–2007; MP for Oswestry 1961–83, Shropshire North 1983–97; later Baron Biffen.

135   Labour MP for West Bromwich 1973–4, West Bromwich West 1974–2000. Later Baroness Boothroyd OM.

136   David Davis, MP for Boothferry since 1987; in the Whips' Office 1990–93; soon to be nicknamed 'DD of the SS' by GB.

137   Labour MP for Wallasey since 1992.

138   'Where the dykes come from'. Ms Eagle 'came out' shortly after joining the government in 1997.

TUESDAY 28 APRIL 1992

My humiliation has not gone unremarked. At the centre of Matthew Parris's political sketch in *The Times* today we read: 'Though Mrs Currie returns to her post as Madam Limelight, Gyles Brandreth (C. Chester) who, *on his first day*, walked straight into the prime TV "doughnuting" space behind the PM and sat down, is already mounting a challenge.' This is exactly what I don't want. If I'm going to play this game, I'm going to play it by the rules. I am going to start at the bottom and work my way up. I'm going to be one of the boys and do it their way.

I'm feeling brighter a) because it's another day, b) because I've always known life was ridiculous anyway, and c) because Jeremy Hanley gave me and Michèle lunch in the Churchill Room. It's the 'grand' restaurant where members can bring guests and we had a sort of window table – it's below ground but on your toes you can see a bit of the river – and the food was rather good and we raised our glasses to one another and, suddenly, the place didn't seem so bad after all. Jeremy is so proud and happy to be a Member of Parliament: 'They can never take it away from you, Gyles. In 1992 you were elected by your fellow countrymen to serve as a Member of Parliament in the mother of parliaments. Ours is the oldest democracy in the world and you're part of it. Whatever happens, in years to come, your family, your descendants will know that you're the one who could put the letters MP after his name.'

THURSDAY 30 APRIL 1992

Last night I did *Wogan* and used several of Jeremy Hanley's stories (without acknowledgment). This morning I'm on the 9.03 pretending to work because with me is a reporter from *The Independent* who is going to spend the day with me on the local election campaign trail. He seems likeable and trustworthy. They're the ones you've got to watch. My besetting sin is saying too much, wanting to please, hoping to ingratiate myself by giving them what they want. Michèle is always telling me I don't need to fill every moment of silence that ever falls, that the responsibility for keeping the conversation going is not uniquely mine – so here I am, head down among my papers, apparently making notes on constituency cases while actually recording the news that Lymeswold (the English answer to Brie – which I loved) has bitten the dust and Fergie and Andrew are exploring the possibilities of a reconciliation.

Until I am allocated an office (which will be in a week or two apparently) I have to collect my Commons post from the post office off Members' Lobby. It comes bundled together with string and I can sort it in the Library or back at home or on the train. I've just been through yesterday's bundle – upwards of sixty bits and pieces, a third of which can go straight in the bin. My vulpine whip, David Davis (DD of the SS), has sent me all his numbers. 'I would be grateful if you could confirm your London number, your principal country number, and any other numbers you have. Please do not divulge my ex-directory number to *anyone*.' I also have a copy of Tuesday's Hansard featuring my name for the very first time. All afternoon we lined up to take the Oath of Allegiance at the Table of the House and then shake the Speaker's hand. At the front of the queue at 2.30 were the government front bench (Hansard reveals their names in full: Michael Ray Dibdin Heseltine, Kenneth Harry Clarke, Michael Denzil Xavier Portillo, Virginia Hilda Brunette Maxwell Bottomley, Sir Patrick Barnabas Burke Mayhew[139] – every name tells a story!), and there I was ('Gyles Daubeney Brandreth, esquire, City of Chester') bringing up the rear three hours later. The poor Speaker must have been punch-drunk shaking so many hundred hands all afternoon and, of course, I cocked up my moment of small talk. She said, 'Welcome to the Commons. It's nice to meet you,' and instead of simply saying 'And it's nice to meet you too, Madam Speaker' I grinned at the one-time Tiller Girl and said 'Do you know, I think we have something in common. We've both appeared in pantomime.' She looked neither amused nor interested. My hope is she wasn't even listening.

WEDNESDAY 6 MAY 1992

The whip is a document as well as a person. The written whip is sent out to each of us each Friday with details of the forthcoming week's business. I received my first whip yesterday. It is a plain piece of A4 marked 'SECRET' and lists what's happening on each day of the week. The funny bit is that it looks as if it's typed on an old-fashioned sit-up-and-beg 1905 Remington and you know whether it's a one, two or three-line whip because the business in question is actually underlined once, twice or three times. One-line business is optional; three-line business compulsory; when it's two lines you have to be on parade unless you have secured a 'pair' and cleared it with the 'pairing whip'. I have just telephoned Angela Eagle to learn that she does not wish to pair with me. She's planning to be in the Commons for many years to come so she's looking for a 'pair' who is a little younger than I am and is likely to be in the House after the next election because he's got a safer seat than mine. The bitch.

This morning I was in my place (third row back, third seat in) at 11.25 a.m. for the State Opening. The House was packed. Black Rod came and did his stuff: 'The Queen

---

139 MP for Tunbridge Wells 1974–97; Secretary of State for Northern Ireland 1992–7. Later Baron Mayhew of Twysden.

commands the honourable House to attend Her Majesty immediately in the House of Peers.' Major and Kinnock led the way and we all trooped from our end of the building to the House of Lords – which I'm told, for some reason, we must never refer to by name. We have to call it 'another place' or 'the other place' or some such tomfoolery. Anyway, by the time tail-end charlies like me got to 'the other place' there was no room to get in so I watched the Queen reading her speech on one of the TV monitors in the Lords' lobby. At 2.30 we were back in our places for the 'proposing and seconding of the motion on the Loyal Address'. This is the traditional start to a five-day general debate on all aspects of the government's proposed programme and it's deemed a great honour to be one of the opening bats. Kenneth Baker[140] kicked off, followed by a bespectacled beanpole who I'd never heard of but who is now 'destined for great things'[141] and was certainly very funny – and cleverly self-deprecatory: 'I'm told the motion is usually proposed by some genial old codger on the way out and seconded by an oily young man on the make.' Kinnock was very good at Kenneth Baker's expense – 'he has seen the future – and it smirks' – 'he is adept at keeping one step ahead of his own debris' – 'he moved from being Education Secretary to becoming chairman of his party, proving that the Tory Party is one of the few organisations where a move from education to propaganda is regarded as promotion.' Dennis Skinner,[142] heckling from below the gangway, was somewhat less subtle: 'He's the big fat slug on *Spitting Image!*'

It was about four when Paddy Ashdown got to his feet – and, as he rose to address the multitude, the whole House emptied. Literally. Labour, Conservative, Unionists, the Welsh, up they got and off they went.

'Is this normal?' I asked my neighbour.

'Oh yes, he's an utter bore. Even the Liberals despise him.'

Apparently the rule is: when Mr Ashdown gets up to speak it's time for tea.

Coming away from the Tea Room (where I treated myself to a toasted teacake) and crossing the Members' Lobby to go back into the Chamber I was stopped by a fellow whose face I recognised but whose name I don't think I've ever known. He said, 'Sign this.'

'What is it?'

'It's a written question.'

'Who is it for?'

---

140 MP for Acton 1968–70, St Marylebone 1970–83, Mole Valley 1982–97; Secretary of State for Education 1986–9; Chancellor of the Duchy of Lancaster and party chairman 1989–90; Home Secretary 1990–92. Later Baron Baker of Dorking.

141 Andrew Mitchell, MP for Gedling 1987–97; he was soon to join the Whips' Office, 1992–5, and then became Parliamentary Under-Secretary of State for Social Security at the Department of Social Security 1995–7. Later MP for Sutton Coldfield from 2001, Secretary of State for International Development, 2010–12, and briefly Chief Whip.

142 Labour MP for Bolsover since 1970.

'The Secretary of State for Employment.'

'What's it about?'

'Oh, I don't know. Just sign it, would you?'

I read the question typed on the piece of paper. It was something about the Concili-ation and Arbitration Service. 'But I don't know anything about this?'

'That's why you're the man we need. Just sign – and you'll get the answer in tomor-row's Hansard.'

'But I don't even understand the question.'

'Then the answer doesn't matter very much, does it? Come on, I need to get it in before six. It's all right. I'm a PPS at Employment. If we want to get something on the record, we plant the question. That's the way it works.'

I signed.

So I have asked my first question in the mother of parliaments and I have no idea what it means.

THURSDAY 7 MAY 1992

Marlene Dietrich has died, aged ninety.

Michèle came with me to meet Mr Fletcher in the Fees' Office. He was friendly and helpful and advised that we should register London as our main residence (which it is anyway) because that'll work to our advantage with the mileage allowance. For trav-elling between London and the constituency it's 68.2p per mile if your vehicle is 2301 cc and above, and 43.4p if you are between 1301 and 2300 cc. Our old Mercedes falls into the lower bracket. Mr Fletcher explained that a number of MPs upgrade their cars to take advantage of the higher mileage rate. I don't think we'll be doing that. Indeed I don't think there's going to be *any* capital expenditure in the Brandreth household for several years to come. My salary is going to be just £30,854 which is a nightmare. Michèle is not amused. 'You didn't think about the money did you? You were so des-perate to find yourself a seat you rushed in regardless.' The only flicker of silver lining is the news that all my train and plane fares to Chester will now be covered (they've cost a small fortune this past year) and Michèle gets fifteen paid 'spouse journeys' *per annum*.

DD of the SS is proposing that I jump in at the deep end and give my maiden speech next week. He's leant me a little paperback guide to Parliament he did for the BBC when they started televising the proceedings and it's rather good. He quotes Harold Macmillan on his 'Maiden': 'Except for "going over the top" in war, there is hardly any experience so alarming as this…'

MONDAY II MAY 1992

Buffet lunch at No. 10. It is infinitely bigger than it appears from the street. There's a long corridor that leads from the front door straight to the Cabinet room, then you turn right and go up a flight of stairs (photographs of previous incumbents in reverse order as you climb) to a series of intercommunicating reception rooms where we mingled and joshed and rubbed shoulders with our genial Prime Minister and felt how good it was to be Members of Parliament and in government again. 'You can fool all of the people some of the time, but you cannot fool all of the people all of the time.' – Abraham Lincoln. 'You can't fool all of the people all of the time, but do it once and it lasts five years!' Eric Forth, MP, Under Secretary of State, Department of Education.[143]

TUESDAY 12 MAY 1992

Having sat in the Chamber from 2.30, through Health questions, through Prime Minister's questions, through the opening stages of the education and local government debate (Bryan Gould[144] v Michael Howard, nothing special), in a nearly deserted House, at exactly 5.35, I was called to give my Maiden speech. It was fine. I stuck to the formula recommended by DD of the SS: a couple of minutes in praise of your predecessor ('whatever they were like'), three or four in praise of your constituency, four or five on the issues under discussion – nothing too controversial, keep it under ten minutes. (When Robert Rhodes James[145] spoke for twenty-three minutes, Ted Heath said, 'Congratulations on both your Maiden speeches.') I opened with a couple of jokes ('humorous sorties' is probably more accurate…) and then led into the challenges of doing the right thing as a 'new boy' at Westminster: 'Sitting in the right place is obviously vital. On the day of Madam Speaker's memorable election, I found myself innocently drawn to the spot immediately behind the Prime Minister – instinctively drawn there, I now realise, by the assumption that it was the correct place for the Member for the City of Chester because that is exactly where my predecessor, Sir Peter Morrison, was wont to sit when he served the Prime Minister's illustrious predecessor so ably and so loyally.' (Interestingly, doing my homework for my paragraph about Sir Peter, I came across this in *The Times* of 24 July 1990: 'The appointment of Peter Morrison as the Prime Minister's Parliamentary Private

---

143 1944–2006; MEP for Birmingham North 1979–84; MP for Mid-Worcestershire 1983–97.

144 Labour MP for Southampton Test 1974–9, Dagenham 1983–94; opposition Environment spokesman, soon to contest for the Labour leadership and deputy leadership unsuccessfully, abandon politics and return to his native New Zealand.

145 1933–99; MP for Cambridge 1976–92.

Secretary may well prove to be as important as any of the ministerial jobs announced yesterday.' Mmm, yes, but perhaps not quite in the way intended.)

The point is: it's over, I've done it, it wasn't too bad. My only real mistake was to speak from notes. It's permissible (especially with a 'Maiden') but a speech without notes earns brownie points. Later on I heard a couple of other new boys on our side (Liam Fox[146] and Jonathan Evans).[147] Their speeches were no better than mine, less elegant, less carefully crafted in fact, but both spoke without notes and I noted the whip on the front bench nodding with approval. Well done them.

At six, I set off to find the Prime Minister's room 'behind the Speaker's chair'. You go left, then right, then down a little corridor, through a pokey ante-room and there you are in a very handsome panelled spacious room, dominated by a large polished oak table, with a little sitting area with sofas and armchairs to the side. There we had a little gathering, not to meet the PM, but to meet his PPS – and a greater contrast between the amiable roly-poly man-of-the-people Graham Bright and the patrician Sir Peter Morrison would be hard to imagine. The one common feature is a certain *embonpoint*, but Graham is altogether smaller and easier and more comfortable. He's Tigger and Bunter and Just William rolled into one: eager, bouncy, friendly, loyal, *fiercely* loyal, and he told us that if ever we needed to relay a message to the PM he's our man. I liked him at once, but he did strike me as very *ordinary*. If these are the eyes and ears of the Prime Minister – if this is the man who must whisper the truth to our great leader in the dark watches of the night – is he really up to it? (This is what I *think*, but, of course, don't *say* to anyone – except Michèle, who points out that Graham is the man who brought 'Sweet 'n' Low' sweetener to the UK and has made a *fortune* – 'which is more than can be said of some of us.')

WEDNESDAY 13 MAY 1992

My Maiden speech looks fine in print. My pigeon-hole contains a one-word note from Cranley Onslow:[148] 'Excellent!' I am rather gratified, until some cynic in the Tea Room points out that Cranley (funny old stick) is standing for the chairmanship of the 1922 Committee and needs my vote. The Chief Whip[149] has got my vote, but he's sent a note too:

---

146 MP for Woodspring 1992–2010; North Somerset from 2010.

147 MP for Brecon & Radnor 1992–7. Both Fox and Evans were promoted ahead of GB.

148 1926–2001; MP for Woking 1964–97; chairman of the 1922 Committee of Conservative Backbenchers 1984–92. Later Baron Onslow of Woking KCMG.

149 Richard Ryder, MP for Norfolk Mid 1983–97; Chief Whip 1990–95. Later Baron Ryder of Wensum.

'*Many* congratulations on your Maiden Speech which I have just read in Hansard.' Of course, he's sent precisely the same letter to everybody, but it's nicer to get it than not to get it, however cynical one is.

LATER

I've just returned from drinks with Virginia Bottomley in the Secretary of State's office in Whitehall. Florence Nightingale on the wall, Virginia, shoeless, curled up by the fireplace. She really is very beautiful, which may be why she seems to irritate so many people.

I'm sitting in the Library. It's a wonderful series of rooms looking out onto the Thames. I'm all alone in the last room, the 'silent' room. You can't 'bag' a space here, but this has become my regular perch. I still don't have an office, but I do have a cubby-hole where I can keep papers and really I'm quite happy camping here. The office I'm likely to get is across the road, above the Underground station, and pretty dingy. I'm waiting now for the ten o'clock vote. It's a bizarre ritual. The bells ring and we then have six minutes in which to get into the appropriate lobby before they lock the doors. We then amble through the lobby at a leisurely pace (it's more a long corridor than a lobby really) and come out at the other end, passing two clerks sitting on high stools recording our names, and bowing our heads as we make our way through the doors. The whole process takes about twenty minutes. Then we head for home. I take a taxi. It's costing me about £15 a time.

THURSDAY 14 MAY 1992

Late this morning DD of the SS found me and handed me a slip of paper, a little strip, no more than two inches deep and four inches wide.

'What's this?' I asked.

'It's a question for the PM,' he smirked. 'You're asking it. This afternoon.'

'But I haven't got a question down for the PM,' I protested.

'Stand up and you'll be called.'

'How do you know?'

'I know. Trust me. Just learn the question. You've got to have it off by heart, no reading, no glancing at notes. Just wait for the Speaker to say your name then spit out the question. We've put a joke in it for you.'

'I ... I...'

'Good man.' And he was gone. And my happy lunch with Michèle in the Strangers' Dining Room (our first lunch in the Strangers' Dining Room) was ruined as over the sliced avocado and prawns I repeated and repeated and repeated DD's wretched question. And it was wretched. The joke – a deliberate slip of the tongue – was as weak as they come.

Lunch ruined, I sat through forty-five minutes of Home Office questions, my stomach churning, and then, at 3.15, we got to Prime Minister's questions. I stood up – along with a hundred others. I thought 'I'm not going to be called after all. Please God, I'm not going to be called. Please God.' Mr Kinnock asked his questions, Mr Ashdown asked his, then suddenly I heard the Speaker say 'Mr Gyles Brandreth', she was pointing at me and I was on. 'Did my Right Honourable Friend happen to see the punch-up in the Italian Parliament yesterday, when it was attempting to elect a new President? Does he see that as an example of the benefits of proportional representation or merely a dress rehearsal for the election of a new loser – er, so sorry – I mean a new *Leader* of the Labour Party.' God, it was so cheap, so contrived, so graceless, but the whip gave it to me and I spoke it as scripted, word for word.

FRIDAY 15 MAY 1992

Matthew Parris is spot-on – and not alone. His verdict on my performance yesterday: 'Chester: *nul points.*'

I have come in to the Commons to take part in the Road Safety debate. I wanted to wipe away the memory of yesterday's humiliation. I was pleased with my speech just now. It wasn't overprepared; I knew what I was talking about (more or less) and I made a couple of points that I believe in and that even have some relevance to my constituency! What's more I have discovered that whatever you say on the floor of the House, you can 'tidy it up' before it's printed in Hansard. After you've spoken you make your way up a narrow flight of stairs behind the Speaker's chair to the Hansard editors' room. There, twenty minutes or so after your speech has been delivered, they'll show you a typed copy of what you've said. They've already touched up the English here and there and corrected any obvious errors and, so long as you don't alter the sense and substance of your contribution, you are permitted judicious fine-tuning.

In the election for the chairmanship of the 1922 Committee I voted for Marcus Fox,[150] pronounced Fux by some colleagues – but with affection. He's dapper, rather delightful, a touch too much of the professional Yorkshire man maybe, and not, I imagine, weighed down by too many 'views', but he's got a twinkle and he's approachable and he won. Cranley Onslow has done it for nine years and looks old and frail and disappointed.

---

150 1927–2002; MP for Shipley 1970–97.

MONDAY 18 MAY 1992

The Tea Room talk is of Thatcher's speech in The Hague. We need to watch out: the Germans are coming and the EC is 'scurrying to build a megastate'. It seems somewhat over-alarmist to me, but Bill Cash[151] and co. evidently agree with every word. 'The lady across the water,' sighed Nick Budgen.[152] 'We miss her so!'

At 6.00 p.m. I had an assignment with DD of the SS. I was to meet him in Member's Lobby. We were both on time (people are pretty meticulous about time-keeping here). He didn't say anything, just gave me a conspiratorial nod implying 'Follow me' and led me into one of the division lobbies where we sat in the far corner, at one of the writing tables, and he whispered to me, 'You're doing well. Keep it up. I'm trying to get you onto a little group we have – good men who can be trusted. We meet in secret, usually on a Monday evening, and look at ways we can undermine the opposition. It's called the Q Committee – named after submarines used in the First World War. Don't mention it to anyone. I'll keep you posted.' It's a very odd place this. Sebastian [Coe] and I thought it was about time we braved the Members' Dining Room, so in we went, à deux, at about eight and, of course, it was full. You can't book. Our lot eat at one end of the room, the Labour people at the other – and the Liberals wait at table. (My little joke: the Lib Dems have a table to themselves, as do the Ulster Unionists.) Anyway, the only table at our end that was free was a table for four right in the corner. We made for it, sat down and waited. As we sat, we sensed a roomful of eyes flick towards us, but thought 'Let's not get paranoid here'. We sat, we waited. We looked expectantly towards the waiters wandering past. None caught our eye. We waited and we sat. Eventually, a colleague from an adjacent table leant over and hissed, 'I take it you *are* waiting for the Chief Whip?' Oh God! We had sat at the table reserved exclusively for the Chief Whip. No one ever – *ever* – sits at this table except by his express invitation. Now they tell us … Pale-faced we got up and searched the room for another perch: all eyes were on us: it was a Bateman cartoon: The New Boys who took the Chief Whip's table.

THURSDAY 21 MAY 1992

A nice letter from Windsor Castle [from Prince Philip]: 'Things have been a bit hectic recently, culminating with the Windsor Horse Show over this last weekend.

---

151 MP for Stafford 1984–97; Stone from 1997.

152 1937–98; MP for Wolverhampton North West 1974–97.

Congratulations on your election. I should think Chester must be a delightful constituency. I cannot see any objection to your remaining as chairman of NPFA as long as there is no clash between its interests and the policies of the government. However, I am sure you will be able to steer a middle course!!' He is a good man.

I wasn't in a state to steer anything this morning thanks to my sustained attendance in the Chamber yesterday. The Maastricht debate (aka Second Reading of the European Communities (Amendment) Bill) began at 3.30 p.m. and concluded at 7.40 a.m.! When Edwina spoke at 5.55 a.m. she noted she was the fifty-fifth speaker called and thanked the Speaker 'for calling me in daylight'. She spoke rather well – notwithstanding repeated interruptions from Sir Nicholas Fairbairn[153] who is mad and brilliant and perpetually drunk. As he weaves his way into and out of the Chamber, the tail-coated flunkies are hovering, at the ready to catch him if he falls.

The debate began with the PM setting out his stall: it was all very measured, moderate and reasonable, strengthening Community law, securing the single market, but resisting the Social Chapter and keeping our options open on the single currency. Who could possibly object? Peter Shore,[154] Teddy Taylor,[155] Austin Mitchell,[156] Nick Budgen, Tony Benn, Bill Cash – all the usual suspects plus Kenneth Baker who was more sceptical than ever and rather impressive. There were several alarmingly good maiden speeches: Roger Evans[157] at 4.45 a.m. was terrific: trenchant and appallingly well-informed; Iain Duncan Smith,[158] another anti, broke the rules, did twenty minutes and certainly didn't avoid controversy, but it was undeniably powerful stuff. I do envy these people who feel so passionately about it and seem to have such a good grasp of the detail. Stephen Milligan did his maiden: good-humoured, easy-going, wonderfully knowledgeable, and not a note in sight. He is ambitious. The government's policy is pro-European, but if you discount the mad women (Edwina and Emma Nicholson[159] – who is *strange*), there aren't that many articulate backbenchers ready to take the pro-European line. Stephen's decided to fill the gap and make his mark.

He will succeed.

---

153   1933–95; for Kinross and West Perthshire 1974–83, Perth and Kinross 1983–1995.

154   1924–2001; Labour MP Stepney 1964–70, Stepney and Poplar 1974–83, Bethnal Green and Stepney 1983–97. Later Baron Shore of Stepney.

155   MP for Glasgow Cathcart 1964–79, Southend East 1980–2005.

156   Labour MP for Grimsby 1977–83, Great Grimsby since 1983.

157   MP for Monmouth 1992–7.

158   MP for Chingford since 1992.

159   MP for Devon West & Torridge 1987–97. Later Baroness Nicholson of Winterbourne.

FRIDAY 22 MAY 1992

High drama last night. In the second division, twenty-two of our side defied the whip and voted against the government, ignoring Douglas Hurd's plea not to inflict 'a savage blow' to John Major's authority. Hurd was good. He's stylish. And Heath was a joy to watch: he is so arrogant, so convinced of his own rightness about everything. He didn't deign to mention Mrs T. by name, but he called her remarks about Germany 'rabid, big-oted and xenophobic'. He rumbled and he thundered, but, oddly, he didn't cut much ice.

I am writing this on the train from Slough. I have been addressing members of the Beaconsfield Conservative Association in the absence of their member who doesn't seem enormously popular.[160] He is, however, very thin, which is more than can be said of some. Now I'm drinking again, and eating toasted teacakes in the Tea Room, the pounds are piling on. Geoffrey Dickens,[161] who is gross but very jolly, is encouraging me to join 'the Currie Club' – 'we eat all the things Edwina's told us not to eat.'

SATURDAY 23 MAY 1992

I see in the paper that Chris Patten has lost a stone and a half and been to a health farm. Also, Elizabeth David[162] has died. I think this calls for a typical Brandreth compromise: steering the culinary middle course, it's going to be a light lunch then something rather good tonight…

TUESDAY 2 JUNE 1992

I am in the Library hiding from rampant Eurosceptics. Word has just come through that the Danes have voted No in their referendum on Maastricht and the Eurodoubters are in a tizzy of excitement. I've just been accosted by Bernard Jenkin.[163] He was bouncing up and down with glee.

'Have you heard? Have you heard?'

'Yes.'

'Isn't it wonderful?'

---

160 Tim Smith, MP for Ashfield 1977–79, Beaconsfield 1982–97; a contemporary of GB at university.

161 1931–95; MP for Huddersfield West 1979–83, Littleborough & Saddleworth 1983–1995.

162 1913–92, cookery writer.

163 MP for Colchester North 1992–7; North Essex 1997–2010; Harwich & North Essex since 2010.

'Well, er—'

'You must sign this.'

'What is it?'

'It's an EDM[164] calling for a fresh start. This is the one chance the government's got to think again. Come on, everyone's signing it.'

He had a lot of signatures already, but I managed to resist, and now I'm lurking in here in the half-light hoping I won't be discovered.

WEDNESDAY 3 JUNE 1992

A bad day. About seventy of our people have signed the wretched EDM to date and the buzz is that at least a dozen junior ministers would have liked to – and probably three or four Cabinet ministers as well. The PM made a statement saying the government is as committed as ever to Maastricht and reminding us that the policy has been endorsed on three occasions: when he came back from Maastricht last December, in the general election, and when we voted for the second reading of the bill a couple of weeks ago. He set the government firmly against a referendum of our own: 'I am not in favour of a referendum in a parliamentary democracy and I do not propose to put one before the British people.' It was a workmanlike effort, but our side certainly weren't cheering him to the rafters. Only eight weeks ago he won us the election against all the odds and could do no wrong. Now there's muttering on all sides.

I came in expecting an all-night sitting, but further consideration of the Maastricht Bill is now postponed and instead we had a rather briefer debate on the Rio Earth Summit. I sat through all five and half hours of it (in a largely deserted Chamber) in order to make a seven-minute contribution. My reward was to witness an extraordinary performance from Sir Nicholas Fairbairn – bizarre yet bravura – in which he seemed to be telling us that famine was necessary in the interests of population control. 'The Queen was in China for ten days during which time the population of China increased by twice the population of Scotland. The people who died in the Ethiopian famine were replaced by new births in six months. The people who died in the earthquake at Mexico City were replaced in sixteen minutes. It is all about death.

---

164 Early Day Motion: a means of setting out backbench opinion on a specific issue. An MP tables a motion expressing a view and invites colleagues to become cosignatories. The motion is printed in the following day's Order Paper in the theoretical expectation it may be debated 'at an early day'. It never is. In the 1939–40 session twenty-one EDMs were tabled. In the '50s around a hundred were tabled annually. Now EDMs are tabled by the thousand and because of the number of them and the range of issues raised – the future of the European Union, the performance of an MP's local football team – the currency has been wholly devalued.

Death is natural and should not be unexpected, postponed or wrong, but births can be prevented. There is no purpose in cutting down a rain forest so that a million bureaucrats can descend on Rio and eat themselves stupid on the world's resources.' He is quite mad, but rather wonderful. I have no idea how the Hansard people will manage to make sense of it.

I am sitting in the Chamber writing this. There are 651 MPs, but right now – registering concern for the future of the planet – there are just a dozen of us. The 'form' is that when you've spoken you always listen at least to the next speaker and then come back to hear the winding-up speeches at the end of the debate. We're nearly through: Mark Lennox-Boyd[165] (Our Man for the Third World) is droning peacefully to a close and at 10.00 p.m. on the dot he'll stop – and then home!

THURSDAY 4 JUNE 1992

An 'Ed Blair' from the Hamilton Oil Company came to bend my ear. I am not sure why I had agreed to see him and I am not at all clear what he wanted. General Peter Martin followed him and we had a good session on the Cheshires.[166] The case for the Cheshires I do understand, do believe in and do want to do something effective about. His briefing was clear and to the point.

At 5.30, with a group of 'arts-minded' colleagues, I went over to the Department of National Heritage for a 'working session' with the new Secretary of State.[167] He's an unlikely-looking specimen, but he's an enthusiast and he made us all feel enthusiastic about both his commitment and the part we might have to play. He wants us to go out as ambassadors for the department and spread the word. This clearly excited Patrick Cormack.[168] 'We'll be like unofficial ministers, will we?' he asked, puffing himself up at the prospect. In the Tea Room they call him the Bishop.

Later it was drinks in the Northern Ireland Office with Sir Patrick Mayhew, a gentleman politician of the old school, Brian Johnston with a bit more up top. Virginia Bottomley saw me setting off up Whitehall on foot and gave me a lift in her ministerial car. 'I take it you're not one of the rebellious new boys? John's doing absolutely the right thing, no question. I'm sure you agree.'

I do – I think.

---

165 MP for Morecambe & Lonsdale 1979–83, Morecambe & Lunesdale 1983–97; Parliamentary Under-Secretary of State at the Foreign Office 1990–94.

166 Major-General Martin had been Colonel of the 22 (Cheshire) Regiment in the '70s and was now one of the leaders of the campaign to prevent the Regiment's proposed amalgamation.

167 David Mellor, MP for Putney 1979–97.

168 MP for Cannock 1970–74, Staffordshire South 1974–2010; later Baron Cormack.

MONDAY 8 JUNE 1992

Our nineteenth wedding anniversary. It began with me declining to comment on the state of the marriage of the Prince and Princess of Wales. All the papers (here and, apparently, right round the world) are full of backwash from the serialisation of Andrew Morton's revelations about Diana – how she's suffered from bulimia, has attempted suicide, is locked in a loveless marriage. I had nothing to offer, but others were less reticent. Lord St John of Fawsley (who now looks like a Tenniel drawing of himself – the Fish Footman meets the Red Queen) was Olympian: 'A warning needs to be uttered that our institutions are fragile.' Peter Mandelson,[169] Labour MP for Hartlepool, declared that the scurrilous book proves there are no longer any boundaries between fact and fiction when it comes to royal reporting. I said, 'I'm taking my wife to lunch at the Royal Oak at Yattenden' – which I did, and it was good, but I wasn't relaxed because all the time I was half-thinking that I ought to get back to Westminster.

I had to be on parade at six for my first meeting of the Q Committee: a mixture of whips and backbenchers (senior and junior) plus some people I'd never seen before (from Central Office, I think) plus the PM's PPS. The object of the exercise is to go through the week's business and work out if there are ways of ambushing the opposition. 'And when the PM gets back from Rio,' concluded our chairman,[170] not one to be frightened of the obvious, 'he's going to need all the support we can give him. Right men?' (There were no ladies present.) We all banged the table in agreement. (It's another odd custom: no clapping in the Chamber, just cheering and waving order papers, and in committee rooms we beat our fingers against the desk in a rapid tattoo while growling a half-swallowed 'Hear! Hear!' at the back of the throat.)

WEDNESDAY 10 JUNE 1992

The round of ministerial briefings for new recruits goes on. Last night it was Gillian Shephard in Room 605 at Caxton House (a pretty dreary gathering) and this afternoon it was tea at the Treasury with Badger Lamont who assured us that all's well, the ERM is working, inflation is conquered, and the recession has blown itself out. So that's all right then. And, as I write, I've just come down from Committee Room 5 where President Heseltine has been giving us a *tour d'horizon* of the DTI. I asked some damnfool question

---

169 MP for Hartlepool 1992–2004; formerly the Labour Party's director of campaigns and communications 1985–90. Later Baron Mandelson.

170 Sir Anthony Durant, MP for Reading North 1974–83, Reading West 1983–97.

(just to fill the air) and the poor man couldn't decipher my name from his crib-sheet. He was clearly anxious to respond to me by name, but simply couldn't.

Rumour is rife that Portillo and Lilley have been caballing with Eurosceptics and don't want the Treaty ratified in its present form. Heseltine was adamant: 'We are committed to it; it's in the national interest; of course we ratify.'

MONDAY 15 JUNE 1992

The PM is back from Rio and has apparently ordered a 'marketing exercise' by whips and ministers to convince us all of the merits of Maastricht. I'm ready to be convinced, but those that aren't never will be.

David Mellor had his first outing as Secretary of State for National Heritage and used it (inter alia) to put yours truly in his place. With a view to triggering some kind words about the Voluntary Arts Network (chaired by Sir Richard Luce,[171] former arts minister of this parish) I asked an agreed question about the need to recognise the contribution of the amateur as well as the professional in the arts. 'Yes,' responded Mellor smugly, 'and I am sure that's true in politics as well.' It was a little sally that produced a good laugh (and I imagine Mellor can't resist a good laugh) and I didn't really mind except that people have been coming up to me ever since saying 'Mellor shouldn't have put you down like that – it's disgraceful'. I'd have preferred them not to notice. Nobody paid much notice to the PM's statement on Rio. The Earth Summit has produced an accord to save the planet, but in London SW1 all we care about is the future of Maastricht.

TUESDAY 16 JUNE 1992

English football fans are rioting in Stockholm, there's been an IRA bomb off Trafalgar Square, the Prince and Princess of Wales are evidently no longer on speaking terms, but the PM didn't do too badly at Question Time. Blubber-lips Hattersley[172] was up for the opposition and all over the place. The people we have to worry about aren't the opposition, of course. It's our own lot – and the trouble is, some of what they say is quite convincing. The interest rates are crippling and because of the ERM we're shackled to them, regardless of what they're doing to the small businesses of Chester (to say nothing

---

171 MP for Arundel & Shoreham 1971–4, Shoreham 1974–92; Minister for the Arts 1985–90. Later Lord Chamberlain to the Queen and Baron Luce KG, GCVO.

172 Roy Hattersley, Labour MP for Birmingham Sparkbrook 1964–97; Deputy Leader of the Labour Party 1983–92. Later Baron Hattersley.

of the assorted Brandreth overdrafts). A good meeting with Kenneth Clarke in the Home Secretary's room at the House. He's very easy, very jovial. I warm to him immediately in a way, I imagine, I couldn't warm to Heseltine in a hundred years.

THURSDAY 25 JUNE 1992

I addressed the massed ranks of the Townswomen's Guild at the Albert Hall yesterday. There were thousands of them – row upon row of good-hearted middle-aged bastions of Middle England. It was fun. I've just come from a long session with Emily Blatch at the DfE.[173] The Townswomen would have loved her. I was seeing her because when I passed her in a corridor last week she said 'Come and see me' so I there I was. We sat on the edge of her sofa for an hour, almost holding hands. We talked about nursery education so intently. She's wonderful and, apparently, very close to the PM, but what the meeting was *about* I'm not quite sure. Bonding, I suppose. That's what the next meeting is going to be for sure: a sandwich lunch with Michael Howard at the DoE. I have to say that I'm impressed by how accessible all these Cabinet ministers are. You can see them whenever you want to – you can catch them in the voting lobby, you can make an appointment to go to their offices, you can hobnob with them in the Tea Room or the Dining Room. No one could accuse any of them of being in any sense remote. I said this to Bill Cash who said, 'Not being remote is not the same as not being out of touch...'

MONDAY 29 JUNE 1992

Lunch with the Foreign Secretary, tea with the Prime Minister. And in between, Mr Major made his statement on the Lisbon Summit. Enlargement, subsidiarity, the GATT round, Yugoslavia – for an hour he batted away with skill and discretion, reiterating the government line but bending over backwards to offend the sceptics as little as possible. When he'd finished I set off for the Tea Room and found myself in the queue with Graham Bright.

'The boss did well, didn't he?' he squeaked, piling the teacakes onto his plate.

'Yes,' I said, 'brilliantly.'

'Come and tell him, he's through here.'

The Tea Room is divided into two. In the first room there's the food counter, the till and assorted armchairs and tables used exclusively by Labour members. The second room is 'our' room, with a couple of tables occasionally occupied by Liberals or Unionists. The

---

173 Baroness Blatch, Minister of State at the Department for Education 1992–4.

PM was sitting at the first table looking remarkably bright-eyed. There was an empty chair beside him. He patted it, 'Now come on, Gyles, how's it going in Chester?' (He knows everybody's name and makes a point of getting it in right away.)

I sat down and he patted my hand. He touches you every time you meet him. It's wonderfully disarming. Graham gave the PM his tea and teacakes and perched on a chair behind him. Nobody could think what to say. Tim Devlin[174] muttered something about how good he'd been just now. The PM nodded. Silence fell. Somehow we knew that talking about Europe, Maastricht, Jacques Delors wasn't what our leader wanted, so to fill the void I suddenly heard myself saying, 'What's happening in Yugoslavia?'

'Ah,' he said, 'Yugoslavia,' and immediately he launched into a fifteen-minute impromptu masterclass on the tragedy of the Balkans. He took us through from the fourteenth century to the briefing he'd had from the UN's General Mackenzie this lunchtime, and his grasp of the detail was astonishing. At one point he fished out his pen and on the back of a paper napkin drew a map of the territory around Sarajevo. He pinpointed the Serb and the Muslim encampments, he knew the names of villages, he seemed to know the names of the head men in those villages. He was very impressive. And when he'd done, he tapped the table twice with the palms of his hands and got up to go. He had only taken a couple of sips of his tea and hadn't touched the teacake. I was eyeing the paper napkin. I thought it might make an interesting souvenir. Graham was ahead of me. He picked it up, folded it neatly and popped it in his pocket. He then popped a bite of the PM's teacake into his mouth and, Bunter-like, toddled off after his master.

Later I was telling Peter Tapsell[175] about the PM's time in the Tea Room and he said, 'Yes, he's an attractive man, intelligent and well-intentioned, but he doesn't frighten anybody, does he? When Margaret came into the Tea Room the teacups rattled.'

WEDNESDAY 1 JULY 1992

I was required to be in Committee Room 12 this morning at 10.30 for a Standing Committee on Statutory Instruments. I arrived at 10.32 and was given a bollocking by the whip. 'You have to be here on time in case the opposition force a snap vote.' There were only two or three opposition in attendance. I have no idea what it was about. The minister spoke, the opposition spokesman spoke, we all voted Aye and that was that. Funny way to run a country.

---

174 MP for Stockton South 1987–97.

175 MP for Nottingham West 1959–64, Horncastle 1966–83, Lindsey East 1983–97, Louth & Horncastle since 1997; Father of the House from 2010.

At six I went for a briefing with Malcolm Rifkind at the MoD. The whole feel of the place dates from a '50s Ealing comedy (you expect the tea to be served by an orderly played by Norman Wisdom), but the beady-eyed Secretary of State comes over as both charming and sharp. This was a general canter round the course for the new boys and an update on Yugoslavia. We are going to be sending up to four RAF Hercules mercy missions a day to Sarajevo and the US are sending the marines into the Adriatic. I have a separate session with Malcolm tomorrow on the future of the Cheshires.

Later I came across Neil Hamilton and Michael Forsyth[176] swooning over pictures of Margaret Thatcher in her Baroness's togs. She was 'introduced' into the Lords yesterday. 'Her Iron Ladyship,' gurgled Forsyth. 'Isn't she beautiful?' cooed Neil. 'It's almost too wonderful to bear.'

THURSDAY 2 JULY 1992

The good news is that, for the first time since partition, leaders of all the Unionist groups have agreed to have talks with the Irish government on the constitution of Northern Ireland. Paddy Mayhew is hailing it as a breakthrough.

The meeting with Malcolm Rifkind was here in his room at the House. He sat on a sofa and listened intently, a couple of officials took notes. Malcolm did a lot of nodding, asked a couple of questions, but gave nothing away. Was he just going through the motions? Do representations like this make any difference or do they do what they want to do regardless? I have no idea – but at least I can do a press release for the local papers declaring that I've 'taken the case to the top'.

The 1922 Committee meets in Room 14 every Thursday at six o'clock. Sir Marcus and the other Committee bigwigs sit on the dais and we backbenchers fill the body of the room. Sitting right at the back, in a single row, are the whips, a line of vultures at the feast. Sir Marcus begins by inviting 'the whip of duty to give us the business for the coming week'. This is read to us and we note what the whipping is and when we have to be on parade to vote. (Having no 'pair' I know I have to be on parade regardless!) Then assorted old boys catch the chairman's eye and get up to make their point – though not tonight, because tonight we had the PM come in to address us. He spoke from very few notes (if any) and spoke well. It's a funny sing-song voice he has, and an odd way of pronouncing certain words (wunt for want etc.); he's not a natural orator, but there's something about his dogged decency that is rather moving. Anyway, when he'd said his piece, we banged our desks and banged and banged them. I was next to Stephen Milligan. He said, 'Keep banging. The whips are watching.'

---

176 MP for Stirling 1983–97. Later Baron Forsyth of Drumlean.

WEDNESDAY 8 JULY 1992

Frankie Howerd's memorial service at St Martin-in-the-Fields. Lots of oohs, aahs and titter ye nots ... no ... yes ... it's wicked to mock the afflicted. The best moment was Russ Conway accompanying the Graveney School Choir from Tooting singing 'Three Little Fishes'; the worst Cilla Black – only because she kept bursting into tears and when the performer cries the audience doesn't. Frank became a regular at Cilla's house every Sunday – 'always by invitation, usually his own'. The house was packed. I sat with Ernie Wise and came back with Fergus Montgomery,[177] a Pickwickian colleague from Cheshire with a distinct theatrical bent.

A six o'clock briefing with Peter Lilley who has a wonderful portrait of General de Gaulle on his wall. Peter plans to make errant fathers contribute towards the upkeep of their children. 'It won't be universally popular; it'll bring a lot of unhappy people to our surgeries; but it needs to be done.' He comes over well. He has a courteous manner and rather a boyish look (given he's forty-nine), but there's nothing camp about him – rumours notwithstanding.

WEDNESDAY 15 JULY 1992

The first gathering of the National Heritage Select Committee. I'm on it because I got a call a couple of weeks back from the Chief Whip, indicating that, as I was a good boy, a place on a Select Committee could probably be mine – they're 'highly coveted'. If you want to be on a Committee you write to the Committee of Selection making your case for consideration. Nominally the Committee then ponders who should go where and then votes you in or not as the case may be. Clearly, though, it's all sorted out by the whips beforehand – who'll get in, who won't and who gets to chair what. At the first meeting, Gerald Kaufman and Paul Channon[178] (as the two senior members) danced a little minuet, both suggesting the other was best qualified to be chairman – but, in fact, it had already been agreed that Kaufman would take the chair. He looks like a tortoise without its shell, but he's elaborately courteous and quite friendly in a spiky sort of way. I think it could be fun. There's already talk of a trip to Australia.

At the end-of-term reception at No. 10, the PM looked preoccupied – as well he might: the pound is sagging, the Euronuts are rampant, Bosnia's in crisis, though what

---

177 1927–2013; MP for Newcastle East 1959–64, Brierley Hill 1967–74, Altrincham & Sale 1974–97.

178 1935–2007; MP for Southend West 1959–97. He was elected in a by-election and succeeded his father, the diarist Henry 'Chips' Channon, who had been MP for Southend-on-Sea 1935–58. Later Baron Kelvedon.

seemed to be exercising him most was the rebellion on the Office Costs Allowance. In the wee small hours (1.00 a.m.) around forty of our side voted with the opposition to increase our secretarial allowance by about £7,000 more than the government wanted. The PM had called for 'restraint' and kept shaking his head saying the vote was 'sending out all the wrong signals'. Of course, we toadies all followed our leader into the lobby, knowing that the rebels and the opposition between them would give us the cash we need anyway. The new amount is £39,960 which – given the size of the mailbag and the level of constituency casework – is hardly excessive. I shall claim the full amount, or near it, and at the same time enjoy the plaudits that come from having voted for restraint.

SUNDAY 19 JULY 1992

Forty-eight hours of relentless good works behind me, I'm on the train back to London and supper with Stephen Milligan in Black Lion Lane. I have the papers laid out before me and the story of the day is sensational: David Mellor, our Minister of Fun, caught with his trousers down and his pecker up. The object of his affections, according to *The People*, not the long-suffering Judith Mellor, but one Antonia de Sancha, thirty-one, 'an unemployed actress'. What next?

MONDAY 20 JULY 1992

Mr Major has rejected David Mellor's offer to resign. The tabloids are in full cry. *The Sun* says: 'The clamour to draw a veil over David Mellor's extra-marital activities reeks of hypocrisy. As the minister responsible for media issues, he has warned the press "it is drinking in the last chance saloon". How can he be left in charge of a privacy bill?' How indeed? It seems *The People* got its story by means of bugging La Sancha's Finborough Road love-nest. That has to be an invasion of privacy, doesn't it? No, according to Bill Hagerty, editor of *The People*: 'Mellor has complained he's been unable to write speeches because he's too tired. Now we know why ... Mr Mellor's love-life has interfered with his effectiveness as a Cabinet minister – and that's a matter of legitimate public interest.'

Stephen [Milligan]'s view is that it's the recess, the silly season is upon us, it's only sex, nothing serious (money is what matters), it'll soon blow over.

By happy coincidence, there's a piece in the paper by Cardinal Hume (fifty years a monk) on the joys of celibacy.

WEDNESDAY 22 JULY 1992

The PM has given Mellor his 'full public support'. Mellor is rounding on the *Mirror* for dragging his wife's health into the picture. It seems Judith has been in danger of going blind with retinitis pigmentosa and the *Mirror* takes the view that the stress of life with David could worsen the effects of the disease. Judith's mum, 75-year-old Mrs Joan Hall, has also thrown in her helpful two-penny-worth: 'He is spending the week trying to save his job. He should be trying to save his marriage.'

John Bratby has died. I'm not surprised, but it'll be grim for poor Patti. They met (I think) through an ad in *Private Eye*, but it was a real love-match as well as a working partnership. Patti, whenever we saw her, dressed in tight-fitting leather (at John's behest), his model and muse as well as homemaker and moral support. We have had some good times at the Cupola and Tower of the Winds. (Isn't it a fantastic name for a house? John *was* fantastic – a true original – and I love the Venice pictures of his we have. He was a crafty bugger too: he lured the great and the good – and the odd minor celeb – to come and sit for him by writing them a beguiling letter saying he wanted to capture 'the individual while we still have a few' and tempting them with the promise of one of Patti's 'bacon sandwiches on the side'. Very few declined the invitation to sit for him and most, of course, then bought the picture.)

SATURDAY 25 JULY 1992

David Mellor seems to have got his in-laws back under control. He is pictured with them, and Judith, and the children, down at Thistle Cottage, somewhere in Enid Blyton country, a happy family, united and strong, grinning inanely at the cameras over the garden gate. Mr Major is determined the tabloids won't drive him out and *The Times* is riding to the rescue: 'Mellor should stay'.

MONDAY 27 JULY 1992

I went to the Department of National Heritage this afternoon. No sign of the beleaguered Secretary of State, but cameramen at the door just in case. My destination was Room 67a on the second floor where I was meeting with Robert Key,[179] amiable cove, MP for Salisbury, Mellor's deputy, and Minister for Sport. I had gone, at his behest,

---

179 MP for Salisbury 1983–2010.

to brief him on playing fields issues and to learn about the government's plans to save school sport. The meeting began quite well; we exchanged pleasantries, Mellor was not discussed (officials were present), tea was served, the minister settled back into his armchair, said 'Fire away' and then fell fast asleep! The note-taking official didn't know what to do. Nor did I. So we both pretended the Minister had just closed his eyes the better to concentrate on my argument. I burbled away and several times the hapless, slumbering Minister rallied, threw in an observation, struggled to keep his eyes open and then gave up the unequal fight and slumped back. After half an hour or so of this charade, I got up to go. The Minister got to his feet, rubbing his eyes, and thanked me profusely. 'That was very helpful. We must keep in touch.' I trust I left him refreshed.

MONDAY 10 AUGUST 1992

The Olympic Games have ended, having totally passed me by. Douglas Hurd has called for UN action to end the horror – 'the intolerable abuses' – of the camps in Bosnia-Herzegovina. The holidays are upon us. Mr Major is off to Spain, staying with Tristan Garel-Jones[180] (who I can't make out at all), and we're off to France, staying with Colin and Rosie [Sanders] at La Dulcinea, St Paul de Vence.

FRIDAY 21 AUGUST 1992

We're driving back from Verona to Nice.

La Boheme was a wow, the Due Torri *comme il faut* (or Italian equivalent), but judging from the English papers we've just bought the world is in turmoil. The UN is halting aid to Sarajevo after one of our cargo planes was threatened. We're sending 1,800 troops to Bosnia and imposing an air exclusion zone over southern Iraq to protect the Shia Muslims. The Cabinet's defence and overseas policy committee has been summoned to Downing Street for emergency talks. Mr Major has returned from Spain, Mr Hurd has broken off his walking holiday in France, Malcolm Rifkind is down from Scotland. Norman Lamont has been left in peace in Italy (the Chancellor jetting back for crisis talks might unsettle the markets) and Michael Heseltine has been allowed to continue his South Pacific idyll: he is studying the flora and fauna of Fiji.

---

180 MP for Watford 1979–97; Minister for Europe 1990–93. Later Baron Garel-Jones.

LATER

We're back at La Dulcinea. Colin is down below in his temperature-controlled cellar looking out a suitable pink champagne. We are going to be raising our glasses to the hapless Duchess of York. She has been staying on the other side of our valley, enjoying a summer break with her friend and financial adviser John Bryan. Unfortunately, unbeknownst to them, lurking up in the hills, was an eagle-eyed jumbo-lensed freelance photographer who has taken a series of gobsmackingly lurid snaps of Fergie, topless, cavorting with her buck at the poolside, tickling his fancy and – wait for it – sucking his toes. (This is not something Michèle has ever thought of doing – at least, so far as I know...) Anyway, these candid holiday snaps have now been relayed right round the globe and (courtesy of the *Daily Mirror*) have even landed on the breakfast table at Balmoral. Poor Fergie. Poor Queen. (And to think it was only ten years ago that Princess Alexandra's lady-in-waiting, Mona Mitchell CVO, told Michèle, so pompously, 'I am afraid divorcees cannot be presented to Her Royal Highness.')

WEDNESDAY 26 AUGUST 1992

Fergie has left Balmoral – probably for the last time. Terry Major, the Prime Minister's brother, has been hit by the recession and can't afford his annual holiday to Bognor. Bugger Bognor: the real news is that Europe's banks are joining forces to defend sterling and the government is signalling its readiness to raise interest rates to maintain the pound's value within the ERM. Ignoring the storm clouds, we set off on Colin and Rosie's boat, the *Snow Queen*, for a very self-indulgent lobster lunch. In the harbour we passed Robert Maxwell's yacht; it is smaller than I imagined, but I don't think he could have toppled over the ship's rail by accident. Either he jumped or he was pushed.

THURSDAY 27 AUGUST 1992

We flew into Heathrow to learn that Saddam Hussein has moved jet fighters to airfields just above the 32nd parallel and George Bush has declared a no-fly zone just below it. We learn too that Norman Lamont is standing firm: 'There are going to be no devaluations, no leaving the ERM. We are absolutely committed to the ERM. It is at the centre of our policy.' But what's really got the nation's juices going in our absence has been the revelation of an intimate telephone conversation between the Princess of Wales and a man called James. It was picked up by a radio ham (a retired bank manager from

Abingdon) on New Year's Eve 1989 and is now available for all to hear, courtesy of *The Sun*'s 'royal hotline'. More than 40,000 have tuned in already – and I met one of them tonight, at Chester Cathedral, at the Cheshire County Youth Theatre's performance of *The Lark*. He said he hadn't listened to it all, but he was convinced it was genuine.

FRIDAY 4 SEPTEMBER 1992

I saw the Prime Minister last night. He came to Eaton[181] to lend his support for Manchester's Olympic bid. He looked pretty unkempt and wild-eyed. I'm not surprised. Lamont has announced that he's planning to borrow about £7.25 billion (*billion*) to defend the pound and my maverick neighbour Nick Winterton[182] is calling for 'an urgent reappraisal of government policy'. 'The economy's on the brink of collapse, Britain's industries are being sacrificed on the altar of Euro-dogma. Let's forget Maastricht and leave the ERM.' Could he be right? The PM was on automatic pilot: genial but a million miles away. He says he's going to be giving a big speech next week, underlining our total commitment to Maastricht and the ERM.

FRIDAY 11 SEPTEMBER 1992

The *Sun*'s serialisation of the de Sancha story has been a joy – if you like that sort of thing. We've had all the gory details: the mattress on the floor, the dressing-up, the toe-sucking … (What is this with the toe-sucking? Clearly, I've led a very sheltered life.) Mr Major is still standing by his man – by his men, indeed. At yesterday Cabinet meeting (the first since July) the PM paid tribute to the Chancellor's 'great skill' and around the table they chorused 'Hear! Hear!'

Last night the PM addressed the Scottish CBI and told industry to 'bite the bullet': 'We will stay in the exchange-rate mechanism of the European monetary system, whatever happens.'

It's strange, we're living in these momentous times, I am a Member of Parliament and yet I have no impact on these events, no input, nothing to offer. If I don't support the government's line to the letter, I'm rocking the boat. If I relay the dismay felt by so many of the smaller businesses up here, I wouldn't necessarily be reflecting the consensus of local opinion (opinion is divided) and I don't believe it would make any difference anyway. The

---

181   Eaton Hall, the Chester home of the Duke of Westminster.
182   MP for Macclesfield 1971–2010.

policy is settled. The government is pursuing it. That's that. To have shared my misgivings with poor exhausted Mr Major when he was up here last week would simply have served to depress the poor man further. So each to his own: Major and Lamont struggle to save the pound, while Brandreth looks forward to a typical backbencher's constituency weekend: Saturday – the jumble sale at St Mary's, lunch at Abbeyfield House, tea with the Civic Trust, supper with the agent; Sunday – the League of Friends charity walk (9.30 start), lunch with the Bangladeshi Community, the war widows' service at Blacon cemetery. All worthwhile, some of it enjoyable, but I'm not sure it's what I expected.

WEDNESDAY 16 SEPTEMBER 1992

Last night we went to see Simon [Cadell] in *Travels with my Aunt* in Richmond. He's wonderful, but it's one of those pieces that's an 'entertainment' rather than a play and it left us (Michèle and me) a little unsatisfied. We didn't say any of this to Simon, who looks shattered but is happy with the way it's going. He has high hopes for it. I doubt it will be commercial.[183]

Today we drove to Stratford, gripped all the way by the radio reports of chaos in the markets. Interest rates went from 10 to 12 to 15 per cent as poor old Badger [Lamont] struggled to save the pound. We've just been watching the humiliation on the box. Blanched, puffy-eyed, the poor bugger made as dignified a fist of it as he could. At least, he didn't fluff his lines. The adventure has cost billions and the end result is that the pound in New York has fallen to DM 2.66, a post-war low. The PM has not surfaced, but filmed going in to see him were Geoffrey Johnson-Smith[184] and Stephen Milligan. Why them?

THURSDAY 17 SEPTEMBER 1992

On the front page of *The Times* Anatole Kaletsky[185] lets rip: 'With one bound we are free. After two years of pointless self-destruction, common sense has finally prevailed. A million people have lost their jobs. Hundreds of thousands have been made homeless or bankrupt. The spirit of British enterprise, so agonisingly reborn in the '80s after two generations of catatonic slumber, has been all but crushed by high interest rates

---

183 GB was completely wrong. The play was a critical and commercial success and Cadell won an Olivier Award for his performance.

184 1924–2010; MP for Holborn & St Pancras South 1959–64, East Grinstead 1965–83, Wealden 1983–2001.

185 *The Times*' economics editor 1990–2010.

designed to punish initiative and risk and to reward idleness and caution. But finally the pound is out of the European exchange-rate mechanism and Britain is free to fashion its economic destiny.'

Stephen tells me he was summoned to see the PM simply because he was a backbencher who happened to be around and the boss wanted 'to settle the troops', show his steady hand at the tiller, prove to us other ranks that – though under fire – as ever he was cool, calm and collected. Stephen was excited, delighted to be in at the kill, but depressed by the outcome. He still believes in the principle of the ERM and says commentators like Kaletsky are way over the top.

'Inflation *is* down and the recession was upon us in any event.'

'But hasn't our policy made it worse?'

'Mmm.'

We're off to a matinee of *The Merry Wives* which means I've not got time for a proper report on the latest twist in the Mellor saga. Mona Bauwens, thirty-one, daughter of some PLO hotshot, is suing *The People* for libel and the hearing of the case has revealed that Mellor and family holidayed with Bauwens in Marbella during the Gulf war – and Bauwens paid the Mellors' air fares. What's more, Mellor has been in the habit of calling on the fair Mona 'on a social basis in the daytime without his wife – for a cup of tea or coffee.' For the tabloids this is a lot more fun than poor old Badger and the ERM. 'I had Mellor – for tea'; 'Tea and sympathy with Mr Mellor'; and my favourite: 'Mellor's Mona Tea-ser'. Watch this space.

SATURDAY 19 SEPTEMBER 1992

The lines are hot. Parliament has been recalled for next Thursday. And we're getting a clearer picture of the week's events. It seems the Treasury knew the game was up for sterling by Tuesday lunchtime. Because of the ERM rules there was no question of throwing in the towel before 4.00 p.m., the Bank of England's official closing time. But we could have pulled out on Tuesday night. Instead Lamont and Major decided to go for broke – to travel the last mile – and pour £15/20 billion of our foreign currency reserves into their doomed defence of our position in the ERM. £15/20 billion down the drain!

What happens to Norman now? I like him. He's amusing – but the truth is he's expendable. There was always something a bit bruised about him: now he's seriously damaged goods. The main plank of the government's economic policy has turned to matchwood. If Norman goes now, he shoulders the blame, we draw a line and move on. But from all I hear he has no intention of going quietly – 'Defiant Lamont intent on riding out the storm' – and gallant Mr Major has saluted his Chancellor's 'courage and common sense'.

If Norman goes, Major can regroup and soldier on. If Norman stays, the stench of failure will stick to the government as a whole and the PM and the Chancellor in particular. We loyal footsoldiers won't smell too sweet either.

MONDAY 21 SEPTEMBER 1992

Major is struggling. Lamont is struggling. Mellor looks doomed. The French have said Yes to Maastricht – by a whisker. And we are just in from an eccentric evening at Poulton Hall, Poulton Lancelyn, with Caroline Lancelyn Green, whom I haven't seen since she played my Cinderella at Oxford twenty-four years ago. Her husband Scirard's family have lived on this same plot of land on the Wirral since 1064. The house is a monument to sixteen generations of delightfully dotty Lancelyns. Scirard's father's desk is as he left it on the day he died – the post still unopened, the copy of *Punch* in just the same position on the floor. Scirard's brother has converted his quarters into a precise replica of Holmes' rooms at 221B Baker Street. Michèle said, 'Given the present, maybe living in the past is the answer.'

THURSDAY 24 SEPTEMBER 1992

There was a tangible sense of excitement in the Tea Room. There's nothing like a crisis for getting the adrenalin going. 'Isn't this fun?' squeaked [Michael] Fabricant.[186] Others, like Winterton, who take themselves seriously (and, bless them, think others take them seriously too), were being rather more pompous about it. But no question: it's been a day of high stakes, high drama. And anti-climax. The PM survived, but he didn't do well. John Smith was magnificent: dry, droll, devastating. We sat glumly and looked on as the poor PM went through the motions, coping as best he could with the sniping from the sceptics (the usual gang: John Wilkinson,[187] Michael Spicer,[188] Nick Budgen), attempting to rally his troops, but, frankly, failing. A few brave souls intervened on Smith (Phil Gallie[189] – good on him; Geoffrey Dickens; Stephen [Milligan]; Judith Chaplin[190] – but he wasn't to be thrown. He was on a roll and it was masterful. Ted Heath was on

---

186 MP for Staffordshire Mid 1992–7; Lichfield since 1997.

187 1940–2014; MP for Bradford West 1970–74, Ruislip Northwood 1979–2005.

188 MP for Worcestershire South 1974–2010; later Baron Spicer.

189 MP for Ayr 1992–7.

190 1939–93; MP for Newbury 1992–3; political secretary to the Prime Minister 1990–92.

something of a roll too: 'I should like to congratulate the Leader of the Opposition on his appointment. He has carried out his duties this afternoon – rather well, in fact – but now we must turn to serious business.' There was plenty of banter with Skinner chirruping away across the aisle. Heath was telling us consideration of the future of the ERM will call for more than a single day's summit: 'We've suffered too much from short summits, most of which are taken up with lunch and dinner.' Skinner: 'You've had a few!' Heath: 'Yes. And I've been trying to lose weight ever since.' The truth is he's gross.

At 4.20 Paddy Ashdown got to his feet, the whole House groaned, got to *its* feet and set off for tea. And while I made for a rendezvous with a teacake, the beleaguered PM went to his room behind the Speaker's chair for a less happy encounter with the unfortunate Mr Mellor. You can only feel sorry for the PM: on a day when he should have been concentrating 100 per cent on making the speech of his life he's been having to waste time on Mellor. Does he stay? Does he go? Can we save him? The Tea Room has decided: he goes, no question. Sir Marcus [Fox] made the point, of course, that had Mellor gone weeks ago, we'd have been spared a summer of silly headlines and the PM could indeed have concentrated 100 per cent on his speech today. Anyway, Sir Marcus telephoned Mellor this morning and gave him the black spot. It's all over – bar the 'personal statement'. That's scheduled for 11.00 a.m. tomorrow.

FRIDAY 25 SEPTEMBER 1992

The wind-ups last night were pretty rowdy. Gordon Brown[191] did well. Norman didn't do too badly. Anyway, we cheered him lustily and did our duty in the division lobbies. The motion to 'support the economic policy of Her Majesty's government' (this week's version) was endorsed by 322 to 296. There were some predictable abstentions.

Today's proceedings began at 9.30 with the debate on foreign policy – 'recent and proposed deployments in the Gulf and Yugoslavia'. It was Jack Cunningham's[192] first outing as shadow Foreign Secretary. The view seems to be that he's got the job because he's got the height, the suit, the demeanour, the glasses, if not the acumen. I like him. He's affable, one of their lot who gets on well with our lot. Of course, he's up against a Rolls-Royce. Douglas was as smooth and impressive as ever. I sat next to Geoffrey Johnson-Smith who muttered, 'Thank God for the grown-ups.'

Naturally, what the children had come to see wasn't Hurd at the despatch box: it was

---

191 Shadow Chancellor; Labour MP for Dunfermline East 1983–2005; Kirkcaldy & Cowdenbeath since 2005. Chancellor of the Exchequer, 1997–2007; Prime Minister, 2007–10.

192 MP for Whitehaven 1970–83, Copeland 1983–2005; later Baron Cunningham of Felling.

Mellor at the gallows. By custom, a personal statement interrupts proceedings, is heard in silence and takes ten minutes. As eleven approached, the *tricoteuses* dribbled in. We looked sorrowful, we put on our funeral faces, we wanted to show we cared. But in our hearts ... (Stephen [Milligan] said to me afterwards: 'Remember the Chinese saying? "There is no pleasure so great as watching a good friend fall off the roof."')

At 11.01 Mellor was on his feet. It was an odd performance, jerky, uneven, conversational (not an oratorical flourish in sight), by turn combative and apologetic, honest, funny, devoid of self-pity but at the same time curiously unsympathetic. 'Having grown heartily sick of my private life myself, I could hardly expect others to take a more charitable view.' He's been a minister for eleven years and he was certainly perfect casting for the job at Heritage. The job was made for him – literally. He hadn't felt, the Prime Minister hadn't felt, that 'in this day and age' his affair was a resigning matter – 'sorry and distressed though I was at the revelations and despite how sordid and cheap it must have looked'. He said he was going because he couldn't expect his colleagues to put up any longer with the ceaseless flow of stories about him in the tabloid press. 'Finally, as I leave the warmth of government office for the icy wastes of the back benches, I want the House to know there is a precedent for this: Captain Oates was born and raised in my constituency.'

At 11.11 it was all over.

LATER

Who goes to National Heritage now? The buzz is either John Redwood[193] or Tristan Garel-Jones. My prediction: a safe motherly type, the Prime Minister's friend, Emily Blatch. I've just been talking to Tom King[194] and we agreed the one good thing to be said about the Mellor debacle is that it's covered the PM's poor showing last night and wiped the ERM fiasco clean off the front pages.

MONDAY 28 SEPTEMBER 1992

Lunch with the Prime Minister. Because No. 10 is being rewired and double-glazed (not to keep the heat in: to keep the bombs out), the PM has decamped and is now ensconced halfway up Whitehall in Admiralty House. There are ten of us for lunch, eight assorted

---

193 Minister of State for Environment; MP for Wokingham since 1987.
194 MP for Bridgwater 1970–2001; later Baron King of Bridgwater.

backbenchers, the Chief Whip and the PM. He's down, feels it, shows it. There's no bounce. He may be letting us see this deliberately, to remind us that he's human, to take us into his confidence, to make us realise he's just like us. But we don't want to be led by someone who's just like us. We don't want a leader who is ordinary. We want a leader who is *extraordinary* – and decent, determined, disciplined, convincing as he is, JM isn't that. The party is profoundly divided, our economic policy is discredited, we're on the brink of being dragged into a Balkan war, and the PM talked about the Citizen's Charter!

Of course, he believes in it, passionately, believes it will change the quality of life of ordinary people. Inevitably, though we all must have thought it, not one of us dared say 'No one gives a toss about the Citizen's Charter, Prime Minister!' All along we skirted the real issues. He did talk about Europe. Maastricht is an international obligation. We are committed to it: we must and we will deliver. Our problem is that we have a majority of twenty-nine and rebellion in the ranks. What's to be done?

During lunch I said nothing. I am aspiring to emulate Iain Macleod's behaviour at Cabinet meetings: 'When he had a point to make he made it with brevity, relevance and force. If he had nothing new to contribute, he did not speak unless invited to do so.'[195]

During lunch I said nothing, but unfortunately as we got up to go and made our way across the room I found myself walking in step with the PM and felt obliged to say *something*.

'Peter Brooke is a brilliant appointment,'[196] I burbled.

The PM paused and looked at me.

'The arts people, the heritage lobby, they'll be relieved, I mean pleased, you know, under the circumstances.' On I went, like an idiot.

His eyes were hard.

My mouth was dry. 'Of course, it shouldn't have happened. Terrible tragedy. Poor David. But Peter Brooke's going to be excellent. Excellent. Congratulations. Well done you.'

He looked at me with complete contempt and said nothing. I put out my hand to shake his, and then remembered we don't shake hands, and laughed nervously, and left.

TUESDAY 29 SEPTEMBER 1992

Bryan Gould has left the shadow Cabinet. He is set to lead Labour's sixty or so Eurosceptics in opposition to his party's support for Maastricht. This has to be good for us, emphasising that there are divisions on all sides. Unfortunately it's evident our divisions go to

---

195 Unnamed Cabinet colleague, quoted in *Iain Macleod* by Nigel Fisher (1973).

196 Brooke had been brought back into government as Mellor's replacement as Seretary of State for National Heritage.

the heart of government. Michael Howard is now saying openly that the treaty needs to be made 'more acceptable' to the British people while Tristan Garel-Jones, our Minister for Europe, is adamant that renegotiation of any kind is simply not on the cards. (Garel-Jones is very odd: supremely self-confident, one of those who denies he knows anything to imply he knows everything, amusing but not comfortable to be with. Whenever I find myself in the Tea Room with him all we talk about is bullfighting, about which I know nothing and he knows a great deal. He's going to write a book on the subject. I am grateful to him for introducing me to a charming phrase to describe the southern Europeans: 'the folk who live below the olive line'.) I am on my way to meet some of them now.

LATER

If they want them, MPs get two expenses paid trips per year to Brussels or Strasbourg. I understand one or two of our colleagues use this facility to take a flying trip over for a good lunch. Stephen [Milligan] and I, of course, have come to Brussels on serious business. We did get lunch, an excellent one, in our elegant downtown embassy, courtesy of our charming ambassador, beady-eyed Sir John Kerr,[197] but we've had good sessions too with the Danish ambassador, with Delors' *chef de cabinet*, with Sir Leon Brittan.[198] The bottom line is that there's a European momentum out here that's totally at odds with the mood back home. Never mind the sceptics, my middle-class middle-of-the-road constituents believe in the single market and are comfortable with the general idea of being part of Europe, at the heart of Europe even. But that's about it. These guys believe in the European dream, they believe in a united Europe, they believe in what they're doing! The Danes, apparently, will come round to the idea of Maastricht. We shouldn't worry about that. So long as Mr Major isn't blown off course by the fringe minority, all will be well. Leon, who has a quaint way with him (a cross between camp and damp), has evidently gone native.

TUESDAY 6 OCTOBER 1992

This year I've got the measure of the party conference. You could come on Monday, stay till Friday, take in four days of debates, a dozen fringe meetings, a hundred receptions

---

197 The UK permanent representative to the European Community 1990–95.

198 European Commissioner, Vice-President of the European Commission 1989–92 and since 1995; MP for Cleveland & Whitby 1974–83, Richmond North Yorkshire 1983–8. Later Baron Brittan of Spennithorne.

offering sandwiches and warm white wine. What the cognoscenti do is come for a couple of nights (max), show a face, take in only those parties where champagne is guaranteed, and make sure that you have accepted a worthwhile dinner or two so that at least in the evening you can sit down for an hour and be properly fed.

The week did not begin well ('Shares plunge in Major's new black Monday – free-fall pound hits all-time low') and it seems to be getting worse. The talk of the town is Norman Tebbit's vulgar grand-standing barn-storming performance on Europe. He savaged Maastricht, poured scorn of monetary union, patronised the PM ('I trust, Prime Minister, you will stand by your Chancellor. After all, it wasn't his decision to join the ERM!'), and brought the conference (or a good part of it) to its feet roaring for more. He stood there, arms aloft, acknowledging the ovation, Norman the conqueror.

I saw Norman Fowler afterwards, 'Not too helpful, was it? I don't think he'd have appreciated it when he was party chairman. Hey-diddle-de-dee.' Douglas Hurd was very gloomy in his civilised world-weary way: 'We are going to break ourselves apart if we carry on like this. We won't last the parliament.' I know he's suffered for the cause of the party (his wife the more so), so we can't say it out loud, but I think there's something quite *nasty* about Tebbit, something mean and twisted.

THURSDAY 8 OCTOBER 1992

Last night, at the Old Ship Hotel, we gave our little drinks party for the activists. We shared it with the Goodlads and Jonathan Aitken[199] – who is tall and handsome and charming and distant. (Talking of the tall and the distant, Heseltine stalked past me in a corridor at the Grand. I flattened myself against the wall like a good Fillipino chambermaid. He glanced towards me, didn't flicker, stalked on. But, but – on the conference platform he's unbeatable: 'If John Smith is the answer, then what is the question?' They lapped it up. They don't like what he is, but they love what he does.)

I'm just in from Norman Lamont's speech. It didn't work. Damp squib, didn't remotely fizzle. He's promising a tight squeeze on public spending and an inflation target of 2 per cent. This may be laudable, but in Chester they think we're obsessed with inflation. They'd be quite happy to see a little more inflation if only we could get the economy moving again. I'm chairing the Family Heart Association lunch and then I'm sneaking back to town. Nobody will ever know. ('Or care,' says Michèle.)

---

199   Minister of State at Defence; MP for Thanet East 1974–83, Thanet South 1983–97.

FRIDAY 9 OCTOBER 1992

The great Denholm Elliott[200] has died (Aids, alcohol and ulcers). Willy Brandt[201] has died. (I remember when we had him as a guest at TV-am. I don't think anyone knew who he was. He sat bewildered on the sofa as Anne and Nick chorused 'Here's Willy!' as though he was going to be our replacement for Roland Rat.) Leslie Crowther,[202] bless him, is struggling for his life. But the news from Brighton (as viewed on the box in our bedroom in Barnes) is that, on the fifth day of the Conservative Party conference, the PM rose again. I have just been watching the PM and he's been magnificent – so reasonable, so reassuring, so right! There wasn't anything new, but the way he did it worked. He played the patriotic card for all he could – we mustn't be left 'scowling in the wings': history requires us to take our place at the heart of Europe where we will best be able to look after Britain's interests and at the same time resist the impetus for a federal Europe. There weren't any fine phrases, but that didn't matter. Today it's his ordinariness that makes him extraordinary.

FRIDAY 16 OCTOBER 1992

A week is indeed a long time in politics. In Brighton just seven days ago my excellent activists stood and cheered our leader to the echo. Today they seem to want his guts for garters. The news that British Coal is going to close 31 pits with the loss of 30,000 jobs has galvanised them in a way I've not known before. They are *passionately* opposed to the policy. There are no mining interests in Chester (and needless to say I know absolutely nothing, zero, zilch, nix, about the subject) but my people are united: Something Must Be Done. To defuse the bomb (at least from a personal point of view) I'm calling a special Association meeting for Sunday morning. Branch officers can consult their branch members and bring me their views. 'Tell me what you think on Sunday and I will tell Mr Heseltine on Monday,' is the line I'm taking.

LATER

A long day, good in parts. Dinner with the county councillors ('We can't betray the

---

200 Actor, 1922–92.

201 1913–1992; Chancellor of the Federal Republic of Germany 1969–74.

202 Entertainer, 1933–96; he had been injured in a car accident.

miners like this'), surgery (nearly three hours of it), a visit to the Oxfam area office at Boughton, a photo call with the war widows, and, best of all, Neil Hamilton with the Chamber of Commerce. Neil was quite brilliant. His theme: the decimation of red tape; his challenge: if there's a bit of unnecessary red tape that's got a stranglehold on your business get me the details and I will deal with it personally. He was effortlessly on top of his brief. He even managed to say all the right things to the market traders. Good turnout, good press, good egg.

He was also very funny. Had I seen the pictures of *Il Presidente*, in full flying fig, flak jacket, helmet, goggles and all, touring the Westland helicopter headquarters? 'Isn't he marvellous? 30,000 miners on the dole today, 120,000 building workers out of work tomorrow, you *know* it makes sense. Fly me, I'm Hezza!'

It also turns out that most of the Cabinet were completely unaware of the decision to close the pits and were taken totally by surprise. Neil says there's no question of a U-turn. There's no going back. 'Drift and dither? That's not our style.' He's wicked.

SUNDAY 18 OCTOBER 1992

It was worth doing the meeting this morning. The troops want the policy reversed – however illogical, whatever it costs. They want the message relayed to the Prime Minister and Mr Heseltine personally. They want me to report back.

We went for a jolly lunch with the Barbours[203] at Bolesworth Castle. Since the *on dit* is that the family fortune was founded on the slave trade, we didn't spend too much time on the plight of the mining community. They are generous hosts. We quaffed and sluiced, admired their pictures, admired their furniture, enjoyed their guests – two of whom I pretended to know but couldn't place and one of whom stole the show by telling us she used to go out with Bill Clinton. This was at Oxford, twenty-five years ago. Was he interested in politics then?

'Not that I remember.'

What was he like?

'What was he like? He was absolutely *gorgeous*.'

MONDAY 19 OCTOBER 1992

Volte-face. U-turn. Climb-down. *Il Presidente* came to the House and ate humble pie.

---

203 Anthony Barbour, High Sherriff of Cheshire 1987–8, and his wife Diana.

Yesterday there was 'no alternative' to the closure of the pits, 'none'. Today he found one. He told us that British Coal will now be allowed to proceed with the closure of only ten of the pits. The future of the rest will be reviewed in due course, 'after consultation'. He's come up with a £165 million aid package to soften the blow in the affected communities and Peter Walker[204] is going to coordinate it. (Apparently Major and Hezza cobbled this together late last night and they had an emergency Cabinet meeting this morning to get it endorsed.)

I arrived too late to bag my seat, so I viewed the proceedings from the members gallery. It wasn't a pretty sight. The jeering was fairly sustained and not confined to the opposition benches. At first Heseltine kept his head down and just ploughed through his script, but eventually the barracking got to him. 'Stop being so plain bloody stupid' he snapped. Almost all the interventions were hostile. Only Edwina rode to the rescue – when the pits closed in her constituency George Brown was the MP and in the government, but no help was forthcoming then, and the South Derbyshire experience shows that, given time, there is life after coal. I'm sure she's right, but I'm not sure anyone wanted to hear the truth. The opposition were baying for blood and – never mind the rights or wrongs of the issue – our side are angry that we've been landed in this mess on top of everything else.

In the Tea Room we loyalists sat silently while the rebels let rip. 'This is typical Heseltine, arrogant, impetuous, thinks he can steamroller anyone and anything. Well, he can't.' Winston [Churchill][205] rode his high horse. Trying to sound Churchillian, he just sounds pompous – but out there, in viewer-land, they're full of admiration for his stand. And Elizabeth Peacock,[206] not I imagine the bear of brightest brain, has become the miners' Joan of Arc. Flushed with the success of her latest interview on the green, she said to me, 'What the Prime Minister asked us to accept was a human disaster and a public relations catastrophe. You have to agree.' I suppose I do. If the closures are inevitable, they should have been phased in, and the announcement has been an undeniable turbo-charged cock-up. The likes of Bill Cash are simply shaking their heads and saying, 'He's simply not up to it.'

Sir Marcus gave an interesting account of his lunch with the PM at the Carlton Club. It was to mark the seventieth anniversary of the creation of the 1922 committee but the festivities didn't go quite as planned. For a start, the poor PM turned up late because of the emergency Cabinet; then the 1922 executive turned on their leader – 'over the lamb chops – in a genial sort of way, you know' – telling him how badly this whole wretched business has been handled; *then* the PM turned on them, admonishing them for not giving him the public backing he needs.

---

204 Baron Walker of Worcester since 1992; MP for Worcester 1961–92.

205 1940–2010, MP for Stretford 1970–83, Davyhulme 1983–97; grandson of Sir Winston.

206 MP for Batley & Spen 1983–97.

As arranged, I met up with Archie Hamilton.[207] I think we're making progress on the Cheshires.

WEDNESDAY 21 OCTOBER 1992

There is an extraordinary story on the front page of *The Times*. 'Mr Major leads a surprisingly solitary life ... Mrs Major spends much of her time in Huntingdon with the children and when her husband first arrived at Downing Street he could find no one to iron his shirts. He would go for days eating little or nothing. Eventually a maid was hired and Wrens brought in to prepare him a breakfast every morning ... He is frequently lonely and unsure of his real friends. He trusts Mr Mellor, Richard Ryder and Lord Archer of Weston-super-Mare.' Oh dear, oh dear.

Well, he could be lonelier still after tonight.

LATER

The great debate came and went and we survived. A full House: 320 to 307, a majority of thirteen. Elizabeth Peacock and the Wintertons were our rebels. Churchill, Cash, Cormack and co. stayed on side. As we filed out after hearing the results, Geoffrey Dickens chuntered, 'That was fun.'

'An utter shambles,' said someone, 'a complete and utter shambles.'

'That's what I mean,' chortled Geoffrey, 'That was fun.'

MONDAY 26 OCTOBER 1992

DD of the SS told me to present myself at the Lower Whips' Office at 5.30 p.m. 'We meet every Monday, just before Q. It's just half a dozen or so good men, ready to go over the top. We call the meeting Drinks. There aren't any, of course. It's a code word. When you get a message saying "Come for Drinks" you'll know what it means.'

In fact, wine was on offer, and nuts, and we sat in the corner, six of us huddled together on low sofas, and Bob Hughes[208] explained to us that we were 'sort of snipers' who had to be ready to lob in the odd grenade, torpedo the enemy, throw the

---

207 Armed Forces Minister; MP for Epsom & Ewell 1978–2001; later Baron Hamilton of Epsom.

208 In the Whips' Office 1992–4; MP for Harrow West 1987–97.

opposition off the scent. The metaphors were mixed, but the message was clear. Risk life and limb and, who knows, promotion could come your way…

Of course, it could be a general election that comes our way. From Egypt (where he is laying wreaths on the field of El Alamein) the PM has let it be known that the consequence of a defeat on Maastricht on Wednesday week could lead him to call an election. 'Idle threats – it's hardly the way to win friends and influence people, is it?' harrumphed some splendid old cove in the Smoking Room. (I think it was Sir Anthony Grant.[209] I've still not mastered all the names. No doubt one of the reasons I'm not Prime Minister.)

TUESDAY 27 OCTOBER 1992

I hosted our President's Club reception down in a marquee on the terrace. Forty or fifty activists donate £100 per year and their reward is a lunch in Chester and this gathering today. The challenge for the member is to come up with a guest speaker to give the event the oompahpah it needs. They have to have a Cabinet minister, but any old Cabinet minister won't do. William Waldegrave? 'No one's really heard of him.' Norman Lamont? 'He's not very popular right now.' Peter Brooke? 'Oh, that's a bit disappointing.' For today's fest I secured David Hunt (who is excellent), but registering the degree of excitement his name engendered when I broke the news, I managed to save the day by adding Jeffrey Archer to the mix. It went well. Jeffrey and David did their bit like old troupers and, despite all the whispering behind the canapés ('is there really going to be an election?'), manfully we toed the line. Inflation's down, the recession's receding, the future's bright.

In fact, we're not being threatened with a general election after all. The latest line from Admiralty House is that if we lose next Wednesday's vote, it's the PM who goes. It's his job on the line. Back me or sack me. And the fix the rebels are in is this: lose Major and who do they get? Clarke? Heseltine? It seems ingenious. Jeffrey thinks it's brilliant. (Perhaps he thought of it?) 'We've got to back John all the way.' I agree and said so later to the lugubrious Sir George Gardiner,[210] who looks like a dying llama, a veritable deaths-head at any feast. 'That's all very well,' he said, moistening his lips and blinking at me through his gig-lamps, 'but he's not helping himself the way he's carrying on. This bullying the party with stupid, meaningless threats, it's infantile.' Ours is not a happy ship.

---

209 MP for Harrow Central 1964–83, Cambridgeshire South West 1983–97.
210 1935–2002; MP for Reigate 1974–97.

TUESDAY 3 NOVEMBER 1992

I am not sure we are going with the grain of the British people. According to the latest MORI poll, 60 per cent think Lamont should go and, if there was a referendum tomorrow, 59 per cent would vote against the ratification of the Maastricht Treaty. Of course, there isn't a referendum tomorrow, but there will be a vote here at ten o'clock. If we win, we soldier on. If we lose, Major goes. And then what?

Willie Whitelaw[211] was at dinner tonight and spent the whole evening sighing, shaking his head, wobbling his jowls in despair. 'I don't know what's become of us.' What is the answer, Lord Whitelaw? 'Unity,' he banged the table with his glass. 'Unity. Unity. It's the Tory Party's secret weapon.' When I said goodnight to him his oyster eyes were brimming with tears.

WEDNESDAY 4 NOVEMBER 1992

We survived. Thanks to the Lib Dems. On the key vote, twenty-six of our side rebelled and six abstained. If Paddy and his merry men hadn't ridden to the rescue, we would certainly have lost and both Major and Hurd would have resigned. As it is, the PM's had a triumph, John Smith looks like an unprincipled opportunist, and it should be fairly plain sailing from now on in.

The debate was rowdy and predictable. The PM was good, John Smith was positively poor. I intervened on him – not because I had anything useful to say but because I wanted to earn brownie points with the whips. (That's the way it seems to work. The only people intervening on the front-bench speakers are either loonies with an axe to grind or those frantic to climb the greasy pole. It's really very silly.) I stayed for the first couple of hours (Heath good, Ashdown excellent) and returned around nine for the wind-ups.

Poor Hartley Booth[212] was the last backbencher to speak on our side. No one was listening. No one at all. As he chuntered on, halting, struggling, the Chamber was filling up, the hubbub growing. Several hundred highly excitable middle-aged men and women, many the worse for wear and all talking volubly, laughing and grunting, meandered back to their places with a complete and utter disregard for poor old Hartley. Several times the Speaker tried to restore order, but no one, no one at all, was the least bit interested in what the hapless bugger had to say. When Cunningham and Hurd got to their feet, we concentrated, the sense of 'occasion' returned, but each side was so busy barracking

---

211 1918–1999; MP for Penrith & the Border 1955–83; from 1983 Viscount Whitelaw KT, CH.
212 MP for Finchley 1992–7.

the other we still couldn't hear a thing. Indeed, the only way to hear was to sit back and put your ear to the amplifier that's built-in to the back of the benches. When it came to the votes, tensions were running feverishly high. Later DD of the SS tried to imply he'd had a pretty good idea of what the numbers would be all along, but I don't believe it. I don't think anyone knew what the outcome would be. When we won the first vote, the one on the Labour amendment, by just six there was uproar. The next vote was inevitably going to be even tighter. The whips were working overtime. You could see Heseltine and Lamont earnestly pleading with the renegades. And when it all came right the whole place went berserk. We stood and cheered and waved our order papers. Those of us who were near enough patted the PM on the back.

There's a rumour going round that it was rather closer than it needed to be. David Lightbown,[213] all twenty stone of him, pursued one of the rebels into the lavatory and was so engrossed in the task of 'persuading' his prey to do the decent thing, he missed the vote himself!

TUESDAY 17 NOVEMBER 1992

This morning I took part in a truly bizarre ritual. It involved my rising at six and spending two and a half hours alone up a turret in a small, deserted, windowless room. As a result of my endeavours I have secured the opportunity to present my first Ten Minute Rule Bill.

What this means is that three weeks from today I will have ten minutes at prime time (after PMQs and before the business of the day) to outline my proposed piece of legislation and present it to the House. To secure this benefit you have to be first in the queue when the Bill Office opens. To be first in the queue you have to be first in the waiting room. To be first in the waiting room you have to be there at eight o'clock. I arrived at 7.30 a.m. and found the Bill Office up eight flights of stairs in a tower off Members' Lobby. The Office itself was closed, but opposite was an ante-room, where dawn was breaking through a dormer window. There I sat reading the paper, for two and a half hours. At around nine, through the open door, I saw assorted clerks arrive and go into the Bill Office opposite. None glanced my way. A little before ten I walked across the hallway, knocked on the Office door and went in. The clerk sat behind his desk. He didn't look up. I coughed.

'Good morning,' I ventured, a little too cheerily.

No reply.

---

213 1932–95; a senior whip; MP for Staffordshire South East 1983–95.

'I've come with a Ten Minute Rule Bill.'

'I do not see you,' said the clerk.

'Sorry?'

'I do not see you, Mr Brandreth.'

'Then how do you know who I am?'

He didn't look at me. He simply glanced up at the clock on the wall. It was two minutes to ten.

I left the room, stood stupidly in the hall until I heard Big Ben striking, knocked on the Office door once more and went back in. The clerk couldn't have given me a more cordial welcome.

Teresa Gorman[214] tells me I'm lucky that I've only had to wait a couple of hours. 'In the good old days, you had to queue all night. Seriously. Take a camp bed up there and wait all night. It was rather fun.'

Not much fun at PMQs. John Smith returned to the assault on the Matrix-Churchill arms-to-Iraq affair. Major reiterated that the Scott inquiry will come up with the answers.[215] Until it does, of course, the questions hang in the air. Who knew what and when? Nick Lyell[216] vehemently denies any cover-up. F. E. Smith[217] he ain't, but he seems a decent cove in a lacklustre way and there's no reason not to believe him.

I am waiting for the ten o'clock vote (we're abolishing the wages' councils) and then I'm off to the Ivy to celebrate Simon's first night. It's been a long day.

....

TUESDAY 24 NOVEMBER 1992

....

We went to the lunch at Guildhall to mark the fortieth anniversary of the Queen's accession. She gave the most wonderful speech – wry, personal and very moving – and, best of all, she spoke before the meal not after it! The establishment was on parade: the Prime Minister, the Leader of the Opposition, the Foreign Secretary, old courtiers (Lord

---

214 MP for Billericay 1987–2001.

215 Sir Richard Scott's 'Report of the Inquiry into the Export of Defence Equipment and Dual-Use Goods to Iraq and Related Prosecutions' was eventually published on 15 February 1996. The key questions were: had ministers and officials connived with exporters to enable the export of defence-related material contrary to official government policy? Had ministers modified the policy on arms exports to Iraq and misled the House on the issue? In relation to the trial of the directors of the firm Matrix Churchill charged with contravening the export ban, had ministers signed Public Interest Immunity Certificates objecting to the disclosure of documents required in the case in an attempt either to cover-up government misdemeanour or avoid embarrassment, knowing that without access to the documents innocent defendants might suffer conviction and imprisonment?

216 1938–2010; MP for Hemel Hempstead 1979–83, Bedfordshire Mid since 1983; Solicitor-General 1987–92; Attorney-General 1992–7. Later Baron Lyell of Markyate.

217 1st Earl of Birkenhead, 1872–1930; Attorney-General in 1915; youngest Lord Chancellor in 1919.

Charteris),[218] old soldiers (Lord Bramall), old darlings (Lord St John of Fawsley) – the lot. We mingled, as one does on these occasions, feeling quietly smug that one is part of the party, and eventually, after the Guard of Honour had been inspected and the Marshal and the Remembrancer and the Commissioner and the Sheriffs and their Ladies had trooped this way and that, we were herded (most politely) into informal pens for 'informal presentations' as the royal party came past. The Queen has a filthy cold and was reduced to a whisper ('I'm not sure my voice will last') and consequently there was more nodding and smiling than small talk. Someone (the Lord Mayor? Sir Robert Fellowes?[219] the Queen herself?) had the bright idea of getting her to make her speech as soon as we were seated, before the meal was served and before her voice ran out. It's an idea that deserves to catch on. If the speaker does his turn before he eats, he's in with a chance of actually enjoying the meal. And if the speech is interesting then, as they eat, the guests have got something to talk about. The speech was interesting, as much for the manner as the matter. She talked about her *annus horribilis*, 'not a year I shall look back on with undiluted pleasure'. She didn't mention Anne's divorce, Andrew's separation, Charles' marriage on the rocks, but they were in her mind – and ours – and she talked about the weekend's fire at Windsor with a sense of pain and acute personal loss. She said, rather wistfully, that of course any institution must accept scrutiny and criticism but couldn't it be done with a touch of humour, gentleness and understanding? She commended loyalty and 'moderation in all things'.

We were seated with Peter Stothard, the curly-headed new editor of *The Times* (rather a likeable character, self-deprecating, odd-looking, not in a million years would his morning suit ever fit, hardly anyone's idea of a traditional establishment figure) and every time Her Majesty came up with a sideswipe at the press (and there were several, mostly done more in sorrow than in anger) we gleefully pointed at Peter and giggled. He took it in good part. And he was impressed by the speech. You couldn't not be.

All eyes glistening we gave Her Majesty a sustained standing ovation. Then Grace was said and we tucked into the turbot, partridge and ruby soufflé with gusto. The final treat of the outing was to turn round with our glasses of forty-year-old port in hand to find ourselves being caught on camera by Andrew Festing. He has been commissioned to paint the official portrait of the occasion. They picked the right man. Son of a Field Marshal, married a general's daughter, ex-Sotheby's, good shot, small house in Kensington, family seat in Northumberland, a gentle gentleman, gifted, civilised, amusing, moderate in all things. The Queen must love him.

---

218 1913–99; Private Secretary to Princess Elizabeth 1950–52; Assistant Private Secretary to the Queen 1952–72; Private Secretary to the Queen 1972–7; a Permanent Lord in Waiting to the Queen from 1978.

219 Private Secretary to the Queen 1990–99.

THURSDAY 26 NOVEMBER 1992

A perk of the place is a free medical check-up. The doctor (thirty-something, a touch insipid and a specialist in 'occupational medicine') comes in two or three times a week and is available in a small, airless makeshift surgery located off the Cromwell Lobby. He did all the usual tests and I was given the usual verdict. 'A little more exercise probably wouldn't do any harm. Most people put on a stone or so when they come here. You haven't done too badly. Moderation in all things.' My cholesterol is at the upper edge of the range. Why did I lie about my alcohol consumption? I said half a bottle of wine a day and it must be two-thirds. (I assume everyone lies and when you say half a bottle he puts down two-thirds.)

My young war widows did well giving their evidence to the National Heritage Select Committee enquiry on privacy and the press. I met them in Chester and felt their story was one worth telling: in the immediate aftermath of their husbands being killed in Northern Ireland, the grieving widows were plagued by the papers, local and national; and at the funeral of one of the soldiers, the photographers were climbing trees to get better shots.

The PM did well at PMQs. And at 3.30, when he went off to run the country, I stayed in my place for the statement on Sunday Trading (we're deregulating and getting a free vote); went to the Tea Room during the statement on the revenue support grant (Tea Room talk is of more trouble in store for the Chancellor); and then returned to the Chamber for a four hour stint: the 'Management of Public Service' debate. Not the sexiest of subjects. I was 'persuaded' (along with a couple of other saps: Edward Garnier,[220] Lady Olga Maitland)[221] to make a contribution and since the debate had to be kept going till ten o'clock (God knows why) we were encouraged to be as discursive as we felt inclined. My ramblings included a reference to Jeremiah Brandreth, noted Luddite and, in 1817, the last person to be beheaded for treason in England. He was known as 'the hopeless radical'. As I sat down William Waldegrave told me that it was his forebear, Edward Waldegrave, who led the brigade of hussars sent to suppress Brandreth's failed uprising.

William opened the debate. Robert Jackson[222] closed it. It was exactly like being back at the Union in the late '60s – except at the Union we played to full houses. During my speech tonight there were at most eight people in the Chamber. No one was really listening to what I had to say. No one will read it in Hansard tomorrow. It will go completely unreported. What there any point to it at all? Not really.

---

220 MP for Harborough since 1992.

221 MP for Sutton & Cheam 1992–7.

222 Parliamentary Secretary at the Office of Public Service 1992–3; MEP for Upper Thames 1979–84; MP for Wantage 1983–2005. Jackson, Waldegrave and GB were Presidents of the Oxford Union in 1967, 1968 and 1969.

WEDNESDAY 2 DECEMBER 1992

I have just come from drinks with the Princess of Wales in the Cholmondley Room. Everyone said how wonderful she was looking. I thought (ungallantly) that her skin had rather gone to pot: a sort of light pebble dash effect on her beaky nose. I thought the thing to do was try to make her laugh, so I talked about Norman Lamont. I don't quite know why. I'd just been looking at a cartoon of him in the paper – Norman as a collection of banana skins. Of course, before I opened my mouth I should have thought it through. Diana is sympathetic to poor Norman! The papers have been rotten to him. Just as they have to her. 'They make things up, you know.' In the case of the Chancellor, it seems it was the Thresher's shop assistant who made it up. Norman was not to be found prowling the back streets of Paddington in search of cheap fizz and fags: yes, he had visited Thresher's, but it was the Connaught Street branch, where he purchased Chateau Margaux at £9.49 the bottle.

In the Tea Room, unfair as it is, I'm afraid we do find the Chancellor's plight rather comical. 'Isn't it marvellous?' chortles Geoffrey Dickens, tucking into his toast and marmalade, leafing through the tabloids in search of more tasty titbits. Geoffrey Johnson-Smith is more circumspect. 'What was it Napoleon used to ask of his generals? "Is he lucky?" I think we've got to concede that Norman has been very unlucky. He's a decent fellow, but it's become a bit of a chapter of accidents.' If Geoffrey's saying this, then Marcus will be saying it too, and sooner rather than later they'll be handing poor Norman the dreaded black spot. There's genuine disquiet at the revelation that Norman's legal costs for evicting the 'sex therapist' from his house last year were covered in part by the Treasury, in part by Central Office. There's amazement that he allows his Access card to go over the limit and ignores the reminders. There's a general feeling he's too accident prone – and too cavalier – for our liking.

THURSDAY 3 DECEMBER 1992

Lunch with the Chancellor in the flat at No. 11. It's more duplex than flat, two floors, spacious but not specially gracious, faded English embassy feel. When I arrived William Hague was in the kitchen warming up the soup. I said I was sorry I hadn't brought a bottle, but Threshers was closed and my Access was over the limit. Norman laughed. In fact, we both laughed a lot. It was a very jolly little party. The only moment I misjudged it I think was when I stood looking out of the window, peering down onto Downing Street, and said 'Who'd have thought it? Isn't it amazing? I'm standing here and you're Chancellor of the Exchequer!' That was a touch of *lèse-majesté* too far. It isn't amazing to Norman that he's Chancellor. He believes he's the right man in the right job – and he's determined to stay. Inflation remains low, the recession's bottoming out, the autumn statement went well – 'the Prime Minister isn't going to give in to the press and a few disgruntled backbenchers.' He served a very acceptable wine (not the Margaux, but not at all bad) and couldn't have been a more relaxed or agreeable host. He does excellent impressions. His Heseltine's uncanny and his Brandreth's rather good.

At 5.00 I made my way to the Foreign Secretary's room at the House and sat with two or three other new boys while Douglas gave us a masterclass on international rela-tions. He offered an effortless world survey, moving easily from one continent to the next, from one war zone to the next, stopping off in countries I'd hardly heard of, but where Britain has interests, influence and friends. The message (if there was one) is that we shouldn't become obsessed with Europe: there's NATO, there's the UN, there's the Commonwealth. I got the feeling that he and the PM are cooking up some initiative to turn the spotlight on the Commonwealth … perhaps Her Majesty (in a hoarse whisper) put them up to it on Tuesday?

At 7.30 it was a masterclass of a different sort. Jonathan Aitken gave a supper party in honour of Richard Nixon.[223] We gathered in Lord North Street, in the long low-ceilinged, Aitken drawing-room (it's another house that's bigger than you'd think) and Jonathan introduced us to his 'friend, President Nixon, who has been so right so often'. This was Nixon as hero, elder statesman and freedom fighter, rather than Tricky Dicky, fiend of Watergate. Nixon then gave a wonderful address, a *tour d'horizon*, without notes, with surprising dry humour. And with great charm. He worked the room, he played the crowd. He's eighty, but, on a night like tonight, when there's an audience, the energy's still there. He said the energy's been drained from George Bush.[224] He's been sucked dry. He's got no more to give. 'The voters have sensed it and moved on. You can smell a winner. Clinton[225] is a formidable campaigner. I should know.' He was impressive. It was as Churchill said of his 'great contemporaries', 'one did feel after a talk with these men that things were simpler and easier.'

MONDAY 7 DECEMBER 1992

Christopher Hudson[226] came to lunch and asked me to produce the two from my intake

223 1913–94; US President 1969–74.

224 US President since 1989, he had just been defeated in the presidential election by Bill Clinton.

225 US President 1993–2001.

226 Leader page editor on the *Daily Telegraph* 1991–4.

that I thought destined to go the furthest. I chose Stephen Milligan and David Willetts.[227] And told them that's the reason they were invited.

I'd planned to spend the afternoon working on my speech for tomorrow, but walking along the corridor towards the Library I was ambushed by one of the whips.

'What are you doing tonight?'

'Um – er – '

'Good. Go straight to the Speaker's Office and apply for tonight's adjournment debate.'

'What? I don't understand.'

'The planned adjournment debate's fallen through. We can't let the opposition get it. You go now and apply for it.'

'What's it got to be about?'

'Anything you like. Neil Hamilton's the minister who's scheduled to answer the debate. Anything to do with the DTI. Inward investment in Chester, deregulation, anything you like. But go. Now. Before anyone else gets in.'

I trotted along obediently and found the Speaker's secretary and said I understood there might be an opportunity for an unexpected adjournment debate this very evening. 'Yes, as it happens, there is. What subject?' 'Deregulation and small businesses.' 'Very good.'

So, the afternoon ruined, frantically I tried to cobble together some thoughts for the debate. I did not do very well – but it didn't matter. At the right moment I was in the right place and got to my feet and burbled away and kept (loosely) to the theme and appeared to please the whips inordinately. When I'd said my piece, others joined in – including my neighbour from Ellesmere Port,[228] who is the dullest in Parliament and believes he's the brightest. Neil had no more notice of the debate than I had, but his reply was polished and to the point. (I say that and it's true, but several times while he was speaking he caught my eye and I thought we might both burst out laughing because we both knew how contrived and ridiculous the whole thing was. It's amazing really: middle-aged men, at the taxpayers' expense, playing pointless games in the mother of parliaments.)

TUESDAY 8 DECEMBER 1992

After PMQs I presented my Ten Minute Rule Bill. The speech went well. Good house, warm response. They like it when you're amusing and at the same time self-deprecatory. I had to have sponsors for the bill and I went for the cross-party approach:

---

227 MP for Havant since 1992.

228 Andrew Miller, Labour MP for Ellesmere Port since 1992.

Alan Howarth,[229] David Willetts, Angela Browning,[230] Liz Lynne,[231] Joe Ashton,[232] Glenda [Jackson].[233] (I cornered Glenda in the Smoking Room. She was sitting there alone, smoking a cheroot. She's often alone. She never looks happy.) When I'd done my turn (and it was a turn really),[234] Paul Flynn[235] (Labour, Newport West) did a quirky two-minute response, but didn't press for a division. I was then invited to 'present' my bill. This involved my moving from my place to the entrance of the Chamber, bowing once, moving forward five paces, bowing again, moving forward five more paces, by which time I was by the mace, and bowing a final time. Then I moved round the clerk's desk and handed the bill to the clerk who handed it to the Speaker who ordered the bill to be read a second time.

'What day?'

'Friday 22 January,' I said (as instructed). And that was that. The Second Reading is just a bit of flummery. The truth is: the bill will never be heard of again.

WEDNESDAY 9 DECEMBER 1992

I was closeted with Peter Brooke at the DNH, the meeting was about to begin, and a secretary sidled in, shimmied over to the Secretary of State and handed him a note. Peter read it and looked up. 'The Prime Minister is making an important statement to the House at 3.30. I think we should go.'

We arrived just as the PM got to his feet. 'It is announced from Buckingham Palace that, with regret, the Prince and Princess of Wales have decided to separate.' Suppressed gasps and a rumble of sympathy. 'Their Royal Highnesses have no plans to divorce and their constitutional positions are unaffected.' More murmurings. Major elaborated on this: the succession to the throne is unaffected; the Prince of Wales' succession as head

---

229 MP for Stratford-upon-Avon 1983–97.

230 MP for Tiverton 1992–2010; later Baroness Browning.

231 Liberal Democrat MP for Rochdale 1992–7.

232 Labour MP for Bassetlaw 1968–2001.

233 Labour MP for Hampstead & Highgate since 1992.

234 'Gyles Brandreth has decided to do within Parliament what he does best outside it. Mr Brandreth speaks after dinner. He believes in free speech but not free speeches. For decades he has been making rather good ones, for money. As dusk fell yesterday, the House enjoyed a rare treat: a top-class after-dinner Brandreth speech – but before dinner, and free. His subject was his proposed new bill (it will never, of course, become law) to encourage the use of "plain language" in consumer contracts ... If we were to judge his performance yesterday, we could do no better than quote Sir Noel Coward's impromptu response upon unexpectedly meeting the schmaltzy American pianist, Liberace, on the *Queen Mary*. "How do you do, Mr Liberace." (Embarrassed pause.) "I think you do" (pause) "*what* you do, very well."' Matthew Parris in *The Times*, 9 December 1992.

235 Labour MP for Newport West since 1987.

of the Church of England is unaffected; there is no reason why the Princess of Wales should not be crowned Queen one day! I find that a little hard to credit.

John Smith was commendably brief. Paddy Ashdown less so. Ted Heath went way over the top: 'It must be one of the saddest announcements made by any Prime Minister in modern times.' Willie Ross[236] and Ian Paisley[237] threw in their Celtic ha'porth and then (this was truly bizarre) Bob Cryer[238] was on his feet asking us to remember divorcees everywhere and telling us that it's poor housing and unemployment that puts marriages under strain and it's all the government's fault! Next up popped Dennis Skinner to tell us 'we don't need a monarchy any more and why should we swear an oath of allegiance to the Queen and her heirs and successors because it's now clear we don't know who they are.' He did not catch the mood of the House.

In the Tea Room William Hague was quite funny: 'At least this'll keep the Chancellor of the Exchequer off the front pages.'

---

236 Ulster Unionist MP for Londonderry 1974–83, Londonderry East 1983–5 and 1986–2001.

237 Leader of the Democratic Unionist Party; MEP since 1979; MP for Antrim North 1970–85 and 1986–2010.

238 1934–94; Labour MP for Keighley 1974–83; MEP for Sheffield 1984–9; MP for Bradford South 1987–94.

CHAPTER IV

1993

A thousand beacons blazed across the European Community at midnight to usher in the single market: one Europe of 340 million people. Mr Major (somewhat startlingly) sees 1993 as 'the year of charity and helping your neighbour'. This makes me a little ashamed to confess that I see 1993 as the year of looking after Number One!

What are my hopes/ambitions/resolutions for the year? Mundane.

1. I need to get the office organised. Jenny is a joy, always has been. She is my ideal PA – she does everything I ask of her and asks absolutely nothing of me. I couldn't tell you a thing about her private life, the date of her birthday, the colour of her eyes. All I know is that she's never late, she's never sick, she's brilliant on the telephone and she hoovers up the work. I have the perfect PA; what I now need is a good constituency secretary. I'm glad Angela moved on. I think I was seduced by the fact she was American and had once worked for Bob Dole! Joy looks the part: middle-aged, mousey, spinster-like and, at least this time, I got Michèle and Jenny to meet her too. We shall see.

2. I need to get on top of the correspondence. Sir Jack Temple told me that when he was the Chester MP he could manage a week's correspondence in a single morning in the Library, replying personally to each letter by hand. Now we all get hundreds of letters every week and I have discovered that it's not the quality of the reply that seems to count but its promptness. Fail to answer the letter within a fortnight and in week three there's a complaint in the local paper. 'I wrote to Mr Brandreth on 1 December. I still haven't even had the courtesy of a reply...' Bah. Peter Tapsell told me of the colleague of the old school who dealt with his correspondence on the terrace every morning at eleven with a massive G&T. As he opened the mail,

he filed it immediately – straight over the parapet into the Thames. I can't be that cavalier (though I sense several are), but I can aim to achieve what most of my colleagues achieve: let the secretary draft the bulk of the replies and only look at complicated cases myself.

3. I need to keep the constituency happy – that means keeping the Association activists happy (difficult, as they're insatiable) and ensuring I get sufficient local press coverage to give the broader constituency the impression I'm 'busy' on their behalf. (God knows, I am busy, but to how much real effect? 'Don't tell me how hard you work; tell me how much you get done.')

4. I need to become a PPS. I am embarrassed to confess that when Stephen [Milligan] became a PPS before Christmas I was irritated. Why should he be the first of our intake to get his foot on the ladder, and not me? The truth is because he's better at it: better informed, more intellectually focused, braver in the Chamber, more robust in debate. He deserves his success, he's earned it, he's my friend and I should be pleased ... and yet, and yet ... ('I must keep aiming higher and higher – even though I know how silly it is.' – Aristotle Onassis.)

5. I need to earn more money. Michèle says Grey Gowrie[239] was right: you can't lead a middle-class lifestyle on a parliamentary salary. We have a large house in London, we're buying somewhere in the constituency, we have three children in private education – it's a frigging nightmare! I know I shall never be seriously rich because, while I find money necessary I don't find it *interesting*. On the financial front in 1993 'something must be done'.

6. I need to be a better husband and father. Not easy, given 1 to 5 above!

SATURDAY 2 JANUARY 1993

Revised New Year message from the PM. Yesterday we were heralding the year of loving our neighbour. Today he's forecasting the dawning of a new era of Thatcherite prosperity.

Clearly, there's going to be something for everyone in 1993...

---

239 The 2nd Earl of Gowrie, Chancellor of the Duchy of Lancaster and Minister for the Arts 1984–5, had given up his political career to concentrate on business.

We're off to Kensal Green cemetery with Theo and Lee,[240] in search of Thackeray's and Trollope's graves. I am reading *Can You Forgive Her?*

> It is the highest and most legitimate pride of an Englishman to have the letters
> MP written after his name. No selection from the alphabet, no doctorship, no
> fellowship, be it of ever so learned or royal a society, no knightship – not though
> it be of the Garter – confers so fair an honour.

SUNDAY 3 JANUARY 1993

The benighted John Major and the newly knighted David Frost got together on the box this morning and the PM admitted that perhaps he hadn't offered sufficient clarity as to what his government is all about – and then proceeded to devote most of the interview to talking about the Prince of Wales' marriage and the Citizen's Charter! Maastricht, Mellor, the ERM, unemployment, the pits, we judder from shambles to catastrophe to disaster and *still* our leader speaks of the Citizen's Charter. This morning Gladstone was even prayed in aid: 'Gladstone said you make a candle by picking up candle ends. That's how you make proper public service, by dealing with people's small frustrations.' Um.

WEDNESDAY 13 JANUARY 1993

We're back and it's business as usual. On Monday night we were still voting at midnight. Last night I got away at half past twelve, and today we're resuming our line by line consideration of the European Communities (Amendment) Bill – and we all know what that means.

I have just dozed through the National Heritage Select Committee's grilling (well, gentle toasting) of Peter Brooke (amiable, courteous, concerned and waffly) because I was up at 5.30 a.m. to offer my two cents' worth on the breaking scandal from Down Under: tapes of an embarrassingly intimate telephone conversation between Prince Charles and his mistress, Camilla Parker-Bowles. Our papers have only hinted at the content. At GMTV they had faxed versions of the complete transcript, but because I'd been rather po-faced on air, condemning the monstrous invasion of privacy that these tapes represent, I didn't then have the nerve to sneak off with a copy of the offending material. It was a mixture of the lurid and the juvenile: goonish nicknames and HRH fantasising about life as one of Camilla's tampons…

---

240 Theo Richmond and Lee Langley, writers, friends of GB.

Coming up with a workable framework of legislation that won't infringe press freedom but will protect the privacy of the innocent isn't going to be easy. Peter Brooke seems ready to back a privacy law, but No. 10 is sending out the signal that Mr Major is set to reject Sir David Calcutt's proposal for a statutory press complaints tribunal, headed by a judge, with powers to impose hefty fines and impose full and proper corrections. Gerald [Kaufman] is determined that we come up with an answer that works and that everyone will accept. He wants his footnote in history – and who shall blame him?

THURSDAY 14 JANUARY 1993

Fiona Miller came to interview me for the *House* magazine and made me smile. She said, 'They say you're going to be the first of your intake to get a job.' I want to say, 'Wow! Who are "they"? And tell me more!' Instead, I say, 'Oh really, that's nice,' and burble on about the joys of the backbencher's lot and how my predecessor but three (Sir Basil Nield) remained on the backbenches throughout his career but changed the lives of tens of thousands of his fellow citizens with his private member's bill that became the 1950 Adoption Act.

I went to another of Jonathan Aitken's 'thinking people's soirées'. He made me smile too, told me a story of how Hilaire Belloc, when he was an MP, was asked by an old boy at his club what he did for a living. 'I'm a Member of Parliament,' said Belloc. 'Good God,' spluttered the old boy, 'is that still going on?'

MONDAY 18 JANUARY 1993

I returned from Chester (where the highlight of my weekend was a lengthy session with the Chester ME Group, all looking as listless as I felt) to find Simon [Cadell] in the Harley Street Clinic (which doesn't sound good, but he was very airy about it) and George Bush using his last weekend in the White House to fire off forty Cruise missiles in the direction of Baghdad's nuclear weapons sites. The Chancellor is equally gung-ho: as employment nears three million, the outlook, apparently, has rarely been rosier. I must tell him, that's not how it seems on the streets of Chester.

THURSDAY 21 JANUARY 1993

Audrey Hepburn has died. President Clinton has been inaugurated – and he looks good. And I have just come down from the committee corridor where, with colleagues from the National Heritage Select Committee, we have been taking evidence from Kelvin MacKenzie, bovver boy editor of *The Sun* – and we looked terrible. We *were* terrible. It was *The Sun* who won it. We may have thought we were going to give the terror of the tabloids a grilling. The truth is, from start to finish, Kelvin had us well and truly kebabed. It was very funny really.

This is the mother of parliaments. Gerald is one of Her Majesty's Privy Counsellors. When witnesses appear before us we expect a touch of deference, a bit of forelock-tugging, a certain becoming modesty. We don't expect what we got just now: a cocky Jack-the-lad, bruiser, joker, champion of the working man. He came on strong and walked off triumphant.

Customarily our witnesses are awed by the surroundings. Most look nervous: frequently they shake with nerves. Not Kelvin. He plonked himself down: 'Can I say what a pleasure this is?' he beamed. Working on the premise that attack is the best form of defence (and perhaps assuming, erroneously, that we were armed with a carefully crafted line of argument that we planned to deploy to devastating effect), he struck first: 'Frankly, I believe you are hostile to the press and hostile to ordinary people knowing what is going on in public life.' He rejected Calcutt's statutory tribunal out of hand. He told us we didn't know what we were talking about. 'All this stuff and nonsense about wanting US-style privacy laws – you guys must be nuts.' He taunted. He teased. It was crude but masterly. 'Now, Miss Lindi St Clair, a woman known – or not known – to some of you. She kept a little list. There are some extraordinary names on that list. If we had the American privacy laws here we could publish the name of every single MP named in the list, all their alleged sexual peccadilloes, and you couldn't claim a single penny.'

I said MPs were one thing, but what about Mrs Parker-Bowles? Wasn't she a private citizen? 'When you sleep with the next king of England you move into rather a different stratosphere.' He thought the British papers should be able to publish the Camillagate tapes in full. 'Prince Charles is the next defender of the faith and he's cuckolding someone else's husband.'

When Joe Ashton (who is usually quite good) got going, Kelvin turned the tables *effortlessly*: 'After many years of taking the tabloid shilling yourself, Joe…' Joe had given what we all thought was a good example of *The Sun* humiliating a private citizen when the paper reported the case of man who had glued his buttocks together, mistaking a tube of superglue for the ointment for his haemorrhoids. 'Our John's gone potty and glued up his botty' was the *Sun* headline. According to Kelvin, the man had approached the newspaper himself with the story. Collapse of argument.

When it was over, Kelvin left the conquering hero. John Gorst[241] (who is deaf) thought

---

241 MP for Hendon North 1970–97.

we had done rather well. Gerald knew the truth. We were lambs to the slaughter – and in large part it was our own fault. We hadn't prepared a considered line of argument. We hadn't done our homework. Complacency and laziness leading inexorably to humiliation.

MONDAY 25 JANUARY 1993

From 3.30 to 10.00 p.m. I sat patiently in the Chamber of the House of Commons, speech in hand, awaiting my turn. It never came. I wasn't called. It is so frustrating, but there we are. The National Lottery etc. Bill has achieved its second reading without benefit of Brandreth wisdom. The contributions we did have were pretty lacklustre. The only memorable diversion was Andrew Hargreaves,[242] sitting near me also waiting to get in, speculating as to the most fanciable Member of Parliament on the opposition benches. 'I'd say Jane Kennedy,[243] wouldn't you? Good figure. And she's nice.' From the whips' end of the front bench, we heard a low voice grunting, 'Nice be damned, what's she like as a lay?'

TUESDAY 26 JANUARY 1993

I have just been talking to Judith Chaplin, sharing with her this morning's experience. I went to Elvetham Hall in Fleet to take part in a 'Cabinet Office Top Management Seminar'. I was the token 'new MP'. My set piece seemed to go okay, but what was alarming was the discussion, both in the formal sessions and over coffee. These people were senior management, middle-ranking to senior civil servants, and their message was clear and uncompromising: this government's run out of steam. Worse, it's hit the buffers. It's come to the end of the line. It's got nothing to offer because it appears to have nothing it wants to offer. No ideas, no vision, no purpose.

Judith seemed personally affronted. 'Civil servants shouldn't be speaking like that.'

'But they are.'

'It's so unfair on John.'

'Is it?'

'Yes, it is. But you're right. We should do something about it.'

We have agreed to meet and talk it through. I like Judith. She knows her way around the system. She has the ear, and I imagine the trust, of the PM.

242 MP for Birmingham Hall Green 1987–97.

243 Labour MP for Liverpool Broadgreen 1992–7; Liverpool Wavertree 1997–2010. She was then thirty-four.

THURSDAY 28 JANUARY 1993

This place is a village. The corridors (there are two miles of them) are streets and alleys, Central Lobby is the market place, Members' Lobby the village green. Gossip travels from one watering hole to the next in moments. There was a buzz in the Library earlier, the crackle of electricity suggesting 'something' was in the air. I went in search of further and better particulars and the first person I came across was Emma Nicholson.

'What's up?'

'Haven't you heard?'

(How one hates admitting one hasn't heard!) 'No. What is it?'

'It's John. And his catering lady, Clare Latimer.'

'What? Having an affair?'

'So they say.'

'Is it true?'

Emma gives her barking laugh. 'John has always had an eye for the ladies. I know...'

Emma is deaf so regularly gets the wrong end of the stick. She's also vain. No doubt the PM has squeezed her hand in the way he does and Emma (poor deluded creature) has mistaken his naturally flirtatious way with women for a bad case of the hots. On the other hand, if the Clare Latimer story is true (and we know Michèle's line: 'Men – they're all the same'), what a field day Kelvin's going to have!

MONDAY 1 FEBRUARY 1993

Biddle & Co., the Prime Minister's solicitors, have descended from a great height and successfully killed the story. They've issued a disdainful denial on behalf of the PM and instant writs against the *New Statesman* and the *Scallywag*, the low-life perpetrators of the libel. That seems to be that. If there had been anything in it, the tabloids would have snuffled it out. I think one or two in the Tea Room are a mite disappointed to discover the story has no legs. They're making do with today's twist in the Downing Street soap opera: the PM and the Chancellor barely on speaking terms, Lamont sidelined, economic policy now being run from No. 10 rather than the Treasury. I go along to Drinks and Q thinking we might be given a line to take on all this, but no, the stories on all the front pages, the fact that the pound has just slumped to an all-time low (I've just read it on the tape outside the Smoking Room), none of this features on our agenda. Our theme for the week is the government's assault on unnecessary bureaucracy, how we're cutting through the red tape to help small businesses. That's what they want us to talk about, so (even if no one's listening) we will.

WEDNESDAY 3 FEBRUARY 1993

Good news. Malcolm [Rifkind] made a statement at 3.30: the army is getting an additional 5,000 men and the proposed amalgamation of the Cheshire and Staffordshire regiments will not now proceed. We've saved the Cheshires! The moment Malcolm sits down I beetle over the road to the office and fax the good news to the Chester media. I hail it as a great victory for our campaign – which it is. I do believe all the lobbying did make a difference. That's one of the real advantages of our absurd voting system. We are herded together in the division lobbies, government and backbenchers, from Monday to Thursday, for twenty minutes at a time, sometimes several times in a night. There is ample and regular opportunity for the ordinary backbencher to badger ministers – and, in this instance, it's paid off. Let's face it, Colonel Bob Stewart and the Cheshires' deployment in Bosnia haven't been unhelpful either. Anyway, whatever brought about the U-turn, it's what we wanted. Three cheers.

Rather less exciting is the fact that I've been dragooned onto the Standing Committee considering the Railways Bill. This means that from 10.00 a.m. onwards every Tuesday and Thursday for the next two months I'm going to be imprisoned on the committee room corridor going through a piece of legislation in which I have scant interest. I wanted to be on the Lotteries Bill. I volunteered to be on the Lotteries Bill. That was probably my mistake. Cecil Parkinson[244] put it so nicely: 'People here like to give you what they think you deserve and deny you what they think you want.'

My real mistake was letting slip to the whip that I knew quite a bit about the lottery and even had the managing director of Vernons Pools as a constituent. He wheeled me in to see the Deputy Chief Whip[245] where I compounded my error by showing off the extent of my knowledge of the bill, its strengths and its weaknesses.

'I don't think you'll find this government's legislation contains any weaknesses,' said the Deputy with a wintry smile and a slightly raised eyebrow.

I still didn't get it. I thought because I was keen and informed I'd be the man they wanted. Now I realise, it's *because* I'm keen and informed I'm the very last man they want. The upshot is I'm off Lotteries and onto Railways.

And I'm not going to New York either. Gerald and the Select Committee are off to the US at the weekend, gathering evidence for our enquiry into the cost of CDs. (Gerald buys a lot of CDs. They cost much more in the UK than in the US. Gerald wants to know why. Fair enough.) Lizard-like, skin glistening, eyes narrowed, tongue flicking, Gerald explained to us that if we all went, the Budget wouldn't stretch to us travelling

---

244 Lord Parkinson since 1992; MP for Enfield West 1970–74, Herts South 1974–83, Hertsmere 1983–92.

245 David Heathcoat-Amory, MP for Wells since 1983.

Business Class. He felt that those going would want to travel Business Class (murmurs of assent), so was anyone ready to volunteer not to go? I put my hand up. I've got a nightmare weekend in the constituency, things that to get out of would bring the house down; I'm committed to the wretched Winter Ball on Monday; there's the dinner with the PM on Tuesday; now there's the Railways Bill. I've been to New York – and in better company. It's less stressful staying put.

TUESDAY 9 FEBRUARY 1993

The Winter Ball could have been worse. I did my stuff. It turned out they asked me because they were weary of 'Jeffrey's hectoring tone'. I bet he raises more money though. I didn't do too badly, but it isn't much fun trying to raise £30,000 in under eight minutes flogging three items to four interested punters surrounded by 900 garrulous but non-bidding spectators. One good woman bought a bottle of champagne signed by the Prime Minister for £16,000. She deserves a peerage. (And I understand she may get one.)

I was warned off taking bids from punters at one particular table. Their dusky hue wasn't the problem; it was their 'slightly doubtful business reputation': 'they'll want a picture with the PM – we can't be too careful.'

The best bit of the evening was encountering David Cameron,[246] special adviser to the Chancellor.

'Well done,' he purred, pink cheeks glowing. 'I hear you'll soon be joining us at the Treasury.'

'Really?' I tried to look as if I knew exactly what he was talking about while being far too discreet to let on. 'Tell me more.'

'PPS to the Financial Secretary. Can't be bad.'

Wouldn't it be wonderful if it were true? In case it isn't, I've not mentioned it to Michèle. Let's wait and see.

This comes to you late on Tuesday morning, from Committee Room 12, where I am advised I shall be closeted every Tuesday and Thursday from now till the end of April. Three months locked in a room with John Prescott[247] and Glenda Jackson! Can you imagine? Prescott is pug-ugly, overweight, overbearing, but not, I imagine, over-promoted. He is brutish, but there's something rather brilliant about him as well. He's sharp, he's relentless, he has no way with words but he feels formidable, and he's openly

---

246 MP for Witney from 2001; Prime Minister from 2010. He was then twenty-six.

247 Shadow Transport Secretary; Labour MP for Hull East 1970–2010; MEP 1975–9; Deputy Prime Minister 1997–2007; later Baron Prescott of Kingston upon Hull.

contemptuous of our side. The contrast between him and our leading player could hardly be greater. Roger Freeman[248] is an old-fashioned smoothie. He's stepped straight out of the '50s: the posture, the manner, the pin-stripe suit, the Brylcreamed swept-back hair. When Prescott addresses the committee he leans forward in his place and simply belches out whatever he's got to say. Roger gets up and carefully stands behind his chair. He is punctilious with the courtesies, urbane, gracious, but businesslike not flowery, effortlessly reasonable, never crudely partisan. I'm impressed.

I'm also relieved to learn that this morning we just sit till lunchtime. From Thursday the routine is 10.30 a.m. till 1.00 p.m., 4.30 p.m. till whenever. It will be a long haul but it is, I suppose, what I'm paid for.

LATER

A day that's included tea with the editor of *Izvestia*, drinks at Buckingham Palace, and dinner with the Prime Minister, is almost worthy of Chips Channon. For tea in the Pugin Room with Oleg Golembiovsky I'm joined by Chips's son, Paul, the other non-jet-setting member of the National Heritage Select Committee. (I like to think Paul – 'his cheeks are pink, his hair is sleek' – urbane, amused, amusing, only flies *first* class.) The Foreign Office has set up the meeting and it's fascinating. Clearly nothing but uncertainty is certain in Russia now. Amiably chain-smoking, Igor tells us that *Izvestia*'s circulation has dropped from three million to one million since, now they rely solely on sales and advertising for revenue, the price of the paper has rocketed to fifteen roubles. The problems are no longer state control and government interference (you can print what you like), but the alarming cost of paper and distribution. Igor has been learning about how to become a capitalist from an American paperback: a do-it-yourself guide on how to start your own business that he picked up in an airport bookstall.

As Paul and I speak no Russian and Igor admits to little English we communicate through the good offices of the interpreter, who glories in the name of Aubone Pyke (you couldn't make it up) and appears to have no difficulty interpreting my story of the electronic translating device that was given the phrase 'out of sight, out of mind' and asked to translate it into Russian. The same machine was then asked to translate the phrase back into English and on retranslation 'out of sight, out of mind' came back as 'invisible lunatic'. I offer this to Aubone as reassurance that he's unlikely to be made redundant by a computer. He smiles at me indulgently. As we leave, *sotto voce* Paul cautions me against making jokes with interpreters. 'An awful lot of them are spies.'

---

248 Minister of State for Transport; MP for Kettering 1983–97; later Baron Freeman.

At Buckingham Palace we were launching the John Arlott Memorial Trust with the aim of raising funds to create low-cost rural housing and safeguarding recreational and play space to go with it. I'd said to the PM, as he was going to be in the same building at the same time, when he'd finished with the Queen why didn't he look in? I told him Mrs Arlott would be there, so he said he might, but he didn't. Because I was keeping my eye on the door in case he turned up, I fear I didn't work the room very effectively. The Princess Royal, of course, was a brick. That's the word for her. She's horsey, she's got an odd strangulated voice, a whinnying laugh, and yet there's something almost sexy about her – if you like that sort of thing. She made an excellent speech: crisp, clear, business-like. In my reply I was so busy trying to get away with a convoluted topical joke about Dolphin Square,[249] royal palaces and leasehold reform that I lost my way and forgot two or three of the key messages. Bah.

In my vote of thanks at the Marginals Club dinner I avoided convoluted jokes altogether and went straight for lay-it-on-with-a-trowel grovelling. The PM was in cracking form, relaxed, confident and discursive. He didn't say anything any of us hadn't heard before, but he said it in a way that made us feel that he's bigger, stronger, *better* that most of the press (and some of our colleagues) would have you believe. We presented him with our new club tie, made by the Chester Tie Company and designed by yours truly. (Diagonal stripes: dark blue, pale green, light blue. The dark blue and the light blue represent the *major* universities when your teacher is a *don*. The pale green is the colour of fresh *basil*. Basildon was the marginal constituency where the result last year showed us the way the election would go!) Peter Thurnham,[250] a well-meaning woolly sheep of a man, is the club founder and chairman. There are about thirty members, from all corners of the party but united in a common purpose: a determination to be ineligible for club membership after the next election.

It's 11.15 p.m. I'm in the Library, waiting for the last vote, which should be any minute now. An early night! At the table where I sit I have my back to a wonderful wall of books – plays, poetry, European literature. I am starting on *The Confessions of Felix Krull*.

No word of any PPS-ship at the Treasury. Heigh-ho.

WEDNESDAY 10 FEBRUARY 1993

This morning's tabloids are dominated by lurid tales of the dirty doings of Major Ronald

---

249 There had been press speculation that the Princess Royal might take an apartment in Dolphin Square, not far from the Palace of Westminster, where a number of MPs have flats.

250 MP for Bolton North East 1983–97.

Ferguson. Is this in the public interest? No. Is this even interesting to the public? Well, er, yes, sort of. Vying for front page space is a story about one of my constituents, a British 'mercenary' killed in Bosnia. The news of his death was brought to his parents by a local newspaper at 5.40 p.m. last night. They called me this morning. They are distraught and say they have nothing to say to the mass of press who are now besieging them. This is a tricky one. The story may well be in the public interest, but should grieving parents – even parents of a 'mercenary' – be obliged to submit to cross-questioning by the media? I have sent a fax to various papers asking them to leave the parents alone, but I don't expect it to make any difference.

··

LATER

··

I was invited to a preview of the new sex-and-politics movie *Damage* (aka 'Yes, yes, oh yes, yesss, Minister!) but because of the votes on the leasehold reform Bill couldn't go – which turned out to be fortuitous because, just as I was wandering off from the six o'clock vote, Stephen Dorrell,[251] Financial Secretary to the Treasury, tapped me on the shoulder. 'Have you got time for a drink?'

We went to the Smoking Room, happily deserted, and sat in one of the deep, uncomfortable leather sofas by the window. 'How would you feel about being my PPS?' He has an engaging way with him, shy, unconsciously charming. I said I'd be honoured. He grinned. He must be three or four years younger than me, taller, slimmer, brighter, better-looking. 'At Oxford,' he said, disarmingly, 'I used to sit at your feet at the Union. They told me I could have a PPS last year, but I didn't like the people they had on offer. I thought I'd wait for you.'

I don't really know him at all. He's been here since '79, a protégé of Peter Walker's, pro-European, dripping wet, and consequently not in the fast-track in Mrs T.'s time. He became a whip in '87, went to Health in 1990 and on to the Treasury after the election. They say he's a coming man, a certainty for the Cabinet, a possibility as leader. And now I'm his bag-carrier. I couldn't be more pleased.

I said, 'What's the job involve?'

'Not a lot. Odd meetings, a bit of bench duty, keeping me in touch with what's going on. Let's fix a time to talk it through.'

He is easy-going but I sense fundamentally serious. I heard myself saying, 'Well, if you're going to be a dogsbody you want to be one to a decent dog.' It sounded neither gracious nor right. As we parted (we drained our orange juices swiftly), I compounded the infelicity with my parting shot:

---

251   MP for Loughborough 1979–97; Charnwood since 1997.

'I'm sure we can have some fun.'

Stephen raised a dubious eyebrow: 'I'm not sure that *fun* is exactly what the Treasury has in mind.'

THURSDAY 11 FEBRUARY 1993

An unsatisfactory morning. While Gerald and the gang are winging their way to Washington DC, I'm struggling with the District Line. I make it to the committee room on time, but only just. And I make a couple of desultory contributions to our deliberations. It's silly point-scoring. Unattractive, unworthy, and I suppose I'm doing it because I haven't got anything of *substance* to offer. ('When in doubt, say nowt' is Michèle's rule. Oh my darling girl, why don't I listen? Why am I such a fool?) I got involved in some quite unnecessary banter with Glenda. She accused me (rightly) of patronising the committee by defining an oxymoron. I said something stupid about 'humble backbencher' being an oxymoron like 'military intelligence'. I should have brought in the one Richard Stilgoe[252] came up with last week: 'royal family'.

Lunch was more satisfactory. Sandwiches and mineral water with Peter Lilley. He's gathered a group of a dozen or so admirers. He chats through current social security issues with us, impresses us with his grasp of his brief, and, without coercion, ensures that we turn up when he has questions both to put in helpful ones and to cheer his robust replies. It's a good wheeze. More of them should try it.

At Home Office questions, I spoke up for the bingo clubs of Chester (who are not allowed to advertise their prizes) and was effortlessly upstaged by Teresa Gorman, so wonderfully vulgar and cocksure. She knows exactly what should be done with rapists: 'Cut off their goolies!'

In Members' Lobby afterwards several hacks descended on me together. I thought they might have got word of my appointment. No. They wanted to ask me if I knew the origin of the word 'goolie'. 'It's Hindustani for pill,' I said. I think they believed me.

MONDAY 15 FEBRUARY 1993

This morning's headlines told us: 'Major faces Maastricht constitutional crisis'.

I've just emerged from the Chamber and Douglas [Hurd] has defused the bomb – with such nonchalance that if you didn't know you'd never realise it's been another

---

252 Lyricist and broadcaster.

monstrous fuck-up. It seems the legal advice Tristan [Garel-Jones] shared with the House on 20 January was at fault. Regrettable, of course, but there we are. Fresh legal advice means that we'll have no problem ratifying the treaty regardless of the fate of the amendment dealing with the social chapter. So the rebels are outmanoeuvred. They can't defeat the bill by voting with the opposition on Amendment 27. As Tony Durrant said in the Tea Room, spluttering happily, 'He's shot their fox. Tee-hee.'

Good news: tonight we finish at ten and, better still, tomorrow night, when we probably won't finish till the early hours, I'm being slipped so that I can speak at a dinner at Guildhall with HRH. I've just called Michèle and she said, 'Your whips seem to have a warped sense of priorities. They'll give you an evening off to have dinner with Prince Philip, but a night off to have dinner with your wife? Forget it.'

FRIDAY 19 FEBRUARY 1993

Horrible news. Judith Chaplin has died.

She went into St Mary's Paddington for a routine operation and something went wrong, a suspected blood clot. She was fifty-four. I was with David Willetts when the news came through. He had been with Judith at No. 10 and possibly at the Treasury before that. The tears just streamed down his face. 'It's so terrible. She was so good, honest, decent. I can't believe it. It's so wrong.'

SATURDAY 20 FEBRUARY 1993

We went to St Anne's [College, Oxford] for the opening of the Clare Palley Library and, yet again, I marvelled at how Roy Jenkins[253] has got away with it for all these years. He's won every prize, secured every bauble, but, to me at least, every time I see him, he comes over as a complacent, self-regarding, bumbling toper. He is the Chancellor of the University of Oxford (on top of everything else), but his speech today was sloppy, uninspired, certainly uninspiring, frequently inaudible. I've not read his books and I didn't see him in action in his heyday, so let's put it down to envy – or, more precisely, irritation. I find it irritating that a shambling fat old fool should have us all fawning on him. (I love the famous line: 'The only thing that Roy Jenkins ever fought for was a table for two at the Mirabelle.')

---

253 1920–2003; Lord Jenkins of Hillhead from 1987; Labour MP for Southwark Central 1948–50, Birmingham Stechford 1950–76; SDP MP for Glasgow Hillhead 1982–7; Chancellor of Oxford University from 1987.

MONDAY 22 FEBRUARY 1993

I was told to present myself at the Chancellor's room at 10.30 a.m. for Treasury prayers. I arrived in good time, knowing there'd be a mix-up over my pass (there was), and fearing I'd get lost (I didn't). I climbed the great stone stairs, turned right, and made my way right round the vast rotunda, past the Chief Secretary's offices, past the Financial Secretary's office, through five sets of fire doors, past two stairwells. I met not a soul. The building has the air of a deserted Victorian hotel, the corridors clang, here and there the paint is peeling and some of the rooms still seem to have lino on the floor. The taxpayer's penny has not been wasted on refurbishments here. I reached the Chancellor's suite and decided that the grand doorway, with impressive oak surround, was not the way in for me. I was right. There's a humbler door to the right that leads to the Chancellor's 'outer office'. I was expected. The private secretary (I assume), shirtsleeves, braces, easy manner, introduced me to 'the team' (just two of them: his assistant and a diary secretary) and said 'They're just coming, go through.'

The outer office leads straight into the Chancellor's room: leather armchairs in a little group at one end, a small desk at the other, a mighty table that can seat twenty or more dominating the room. William Hague arrived.

'Welcome, welcome. That's your chair.'

I hesitated.

He laughed. 'Quite right. That's where the Chancellor sits. The ministers have the armchairs, we sit on the uprights.'

'What happens?'

He laughed again. 'Not a lot. You'll see.'

By 10.30 the team had assembled: Chief Secretary (Portillo), Financial Secretary (Stephen), Paymaster General (John Cope),[254] Economic Secretary (Tony Nelson).[255] The other PPSs: William (Chancellor), David Amess[256] (Portillo's man), Ian Twinn[257] (John Cope's). The Chancellor came in last. He was beetle-browed, preoccupied. He took his seat, folded his hands in his lap and closed his eyes. For a moment I thought, 'Goodness, we are going to say prayers', but no, Norman was simply collecting his thoughts. And his first thought was a kind one, a word of welcome to me. 'At least the jokes should improve.' This pleasantry over, an eerie silence fell. I didn't say anything. The PPSs contribute when invited, after the ministers have had their say. This morning

---

254 MP for South Gloucestershire 1974–83, Northavon 1983–97; later Baron Cope of Berkeley.

255 MP for Chichester 1974–97.

256 MP for Basildon 1983–97; Southend West since 1997.

257 MP for Edmonton 1983–97.

their 'say' didn't amount to much. Weak tea was brought in (with two sugar lumps in the saucer) and served in order of precedence. By the time I got mine and had burned my lip with the first sip, the meeting was over. Very odd.

This evening we're gathering in Stephen Milligan's room for the first get-together of our little group: the 'thoughtful' members of the 1992 intake. It's going to be fairly sombre, of course, because Judith was one of the lynchpins and we've lost her before we've even started. We're now six: me, Stephen, David [Willetts], Michael Trend,[258] David Faber,[259] Edward Garnier. Stephen wanted to include Iain Duncan Smith ('He's completely wrong on Europe, but he's very bright and he's going a long way') but David [Willetts] was wary of having a known rebel in our number.

THURSDAY 25 FEBRUARY 1993

A nice note from Gerald [Kaufman], acknowledging my resignation from the National Heritage Select Committee and wishing me well in my new job: 'I hope it is the first step on a ladder full of possibilities.' (I want to read his book, *How To Be A Minister*, but I don't feel one can be seen borrowing it from the Library.) An uncomfortable meeting with Joy.[260] It hasn't worked out. I'm not quite sure why.

SATURDAY 27 FEBRUARY 1993

Last night I spoke for Barry Porter[261] in Wirral South. He's a genial cove, but he's a drunk – an out-and-out alcoholic. Everyone knows it, no one denies, his Association members seem quite content. Indeed, pissed as a newt, they love the man! How can he get away with it? How has he got away with it? The mind boggles. It is all rather different in Chester where I shall remain resolutely sober through my surgery at 9.30 a.m., the Association quarterly meeting at 11.00 a.m., the lunch at Rowton Hall at 1.00 p.m., the trip to paperworks at 2.30 p.m., the tour of the Dukes Way housing project at 5.00 p.m. and the Dodleston School fund-raising evening at 8.00 p.m. But I have to confess that, come 10.30, when I return to my M&S microwaved curry, I shall be allowing myself a bottle of Oddbins best...

---

258   MP for Windsor 1992–2005.

259   MP for Westbury 1992–2001.

260   GB's short-lived constituency secretary.

261   MP for Bebington & Ellesmere Port 1978–83, Wirral South 1983–96.

I'm sitting in bed with tea and Marmite toast feeling surprisingly mellow considering *The Times* tells me that, according to MORI, eight out of ten people are dissatisfied with the way the government is running the country and half the population believes that, whatever the Chancellor says, the economy is going from bad to worse.

There's a lovely piece about Judith [Chaplin] by Simon Heffer in *The Spectator*. 'She was not just clever, she was politically clever.' He takes the view that if Judith rather than Sarah Hogg had been head of the No. 10 policy unit since last April, 'many of the humiliations of the post-election period might have been avoided.' He says Judith is a loss we can ill afford and calls the eight new MPs so far chosen as Parliamentary Private Secretaries a bunch of unprepossessing nonentities. 'There are one and a half exceptions to this list of nonentities. The only full-fledged entity is Mr Gyles Brandreth, MP for Chester. Mr Brandreth is famous for playing Scrabble and appearing on television in *fortissimo* pullovers. His political abilities are uncertain. However, he is a charming and decent sort who adds colour to this monochrome government, and therefore may be allowed to pass without further stricture. The semi-entity is Mr Stephen Milligan, who was briefly a BBC television news reporter. He has the manner and appearance of the sort that Lord Rees-Mogg might have deemed so alarming that he ought only to be allowed on screen once all the children are in bed.'

MONDAY 1 MARCH 1993

The Archbishop of York is blaming us – personally – for the upsurge in youth crime. Hugh Dykes[262] is foaming at the mouth, outraged that Portillo and Lilley have been breaking bread with Margaret Thatcher in the company of those twin princes of darkness, Norman Tebbit and Sir Alan Walters.[263]

The Tea Room is full of Welsh members self-consciously sporting daffodils in their buttonholes and, over in the Norman Shaw building, a wild-eyed colleague invites me into his office to discuss the Budget. He turns on his computer, the screen flickers, and up comes a rather jerky moving picture of someone having oral sex. I pretend not to notice. He is quite unabashed.

'Isn't it great?'

'Well, er, I'm not sure…'

'It's computer-generated. It's amazing what they can do now.'

'Yes. Of course. But…'

---

262 MP for Harrow East 1970–97; a fervent pro-European.

263 Monetarist guru and economic adviser to the Prime Minister 1981–4 and 1989.

'Look, we can get right close up.' He presses various keys to bring us closer to the action. 'Isn't she cute?'

He presses another key to lower the volume of background grunts and sighs, but leaves the pornographic pictures flickering away as he launches into our discussion. I find the image on the screen profoundly distracting. I am convinced someone is about to come in and catch us at it. I suddenly remember that I should have been somewhere else ten minutes ago. I decline the offer of coffee, make my excuses and leave.

There's no vote tonight. Michèle and I are off to *Turandot* at the Royal Opera House. The Arts Council Box. Natch.

THURSDAY 4 MARCH 1993

Treasury Questions. For the first time since my first day I sit in the second row, immediately behind the Chancellor and the PM. This time, of course, it's kosher. And it's wonderful: a ringside seat without responsibility. The Treasury team don't do at all badly: under the circumstances, Norman is impressively confident, neither too defensive nor unnecessarily combative. He is determined to survive. The PM gets a much rougher ride. He's clearly not happy, it doesn't go well, but he doesn't lose his grip even for a moment. As the questions are asked he sits on the edge of his seat, fingers inside his loose-leaf folder. With the planted questions on our side (good old Drinks and Q) he knows what's coming, so he can just flick the folder open at the appropriate spread and spout the pre-prepared answer. With the questions from the other side, and from the handful of our people who won't play ball (Marlow,[264] Cash and co.), it's trickier. Hearing the question is the first problem. The roar is tremendous. He is good at disregarding it completely. You can see him straining to hear the one word in the question that'll give him the clue which page to turn to – Europe, unemployment, the NHS, youth crime. He finds the page, neat paragraphs, in large type, in two columns, five words to a line, steps forward and, whatever the volume of cheering and jeering around him, delivers his answer in a reasoned tone, playing to the microphone rather than the House.

Today, the moment questions were over, he was up on his feet again, with a statement about the honours system. It's to be rewards on merit in future, no automatic knighthoods (suppressed cries of 'Shame!' from behind me), and the end of the British Empire Medal for 'other ranks'. It seems sensible and uncontentious. To my surprise, Stephen [Dorrell] was rather sniffy about it. 'It's hardly high politics, is it? I can't help feeling there are rather more pressing issues to which the Prime Minister should be turning his attention.'

---

264 Tony Marlow, MP for Northampton North 1979–97.

MONDAY 8 MARCH 1993

There's been a [No. 10] briefing that there'll only be a limited reshuffle this year. Lamont will go, to be replaced by either MacGregor[265] or Clarke, depending on whether you want a safe pair of hands or a swashbuckler. Next year, mid-term, the PM has major changes in mind. Douglas Hurd wants to step down. Norman Fowler could be Home or Foreign Secretary. Why this briefing now? Is it to distract the world from the calamity that may come our way tonight? The sceptics are holding the government to ransom. David Mellor is quite funny about them: 'When they started out they weren't even household names in their own homes.'

LATER

We've lost. And badly: 292 to 314. Twenty-six of our people voted with the opposition, eighteen more abstained. It's only a minor amendment, but the effect of the defeat is that we'll now have to have a Report stage which will delay ratification of the treaty for months and months. That's their aim, of course. The trouble is, they won't derail the bill (the opposition support the bill), but they could well derail the government.

There was uproar in the Chamber when the vote was announced. You can tell who has won or lost before the figures are read out because the tellers for the victorious side stand on the right facing the chair. When our whips, Lightbown and Chapman,[266] took up their places on the left, the opposition benches broke into a frenzy. They went berserk. We sat dumb-founded. The figures were read out. Cheering, counter-cheering, wild waving of order papers on their side, gasps of disbelief on ours. Then everyone got up to go. Skinner and co. began jumping up and down demanding the government's resignation. The PM, ashen-faced, set off for his room. Soames[267] pushed his way through the crowd, barking at the Wintertons,[268] 'You're cunts – and ugly ones to boot.'

It is not good news. Two minutes ago I was standing by the tape machine outside the Smoking Room (reading about the Bishop of Gloucester who has resigned after admitting an act of gross indecency with a novice monk) when Bill Cash wandered up and said to me, 'You lot will all be grateful to us in due course. We're doing what you want

---

265 John MacGregor, Secretary of State for Transport; MP for Norfolk South 1974–2001; later Baron MacGregor of Pulham Market.

266 Sydney Chapman, MP for Birmingham Handsworth 1970–74, Chipping Barnet 1979–2005; in the Whips' Office 1988–95.

267 Nicholas Soames, MP for Crawley 1983–97, Mid Sussex since 1997; son of Lord Soames, grandson of Sir Winston Churchill.

268 Nicholas and his wife Ann Winterton, MP for Congleton 1983–2010.

to do, but don't dare. We're saving the country.' Ian Taylor[269] came past, 'And destroying the government in the process. Thank you very much.'

10.30 p.m.: This has been my forty-fifth birthday and memorable in its way. We have just had another vote. I came through the lobby with the Foreign Secretary. 'What happens now?' He was philosophical. 'These things happen. We just plod on.' Wisely, I think, I didn't wish him many happy returns of the day.

WEDNESDAY 17 MARCH 1993

Treasury prayers. Incredibly, the view seems to be that the Budget's gone down fairly well. Well, yes, Norman's performance was fine, and the general message – taxes rises to support recovery and reduce debt – has been got across, but in the watering holes and the corridors of the Palace of Westminster the natives are rather more restive than the ministers seem to realise. They don't like VAT on domestic fuel. Nick Winterton is spluttering with indignation. Elizabeth Peacock's ample bosom is heaving in outrage. David Shaw[270] is beady-eyed and adamant – 'We won't wear it' – and when it comes to a campaign – and he's planning one – I imagine he's a terrier. Last night the Tea Room was working itself into a fine old lather about it. Lamont and Portillo both seem to think the 'brouhaha will blow over': 'we need the money and it's a green tax in line with our Rio commitments. End of matter.' I doubt it.

What was particularly fascinating to me was to discover that Peter Lilley knew nothing about the proposal till yesterday morning. It seems almost incredible that prior to taking the decision to increase pensioners' fuel bills by 8 per cent next year and 17.5 per cent the year after, there was no consultation with Lilley of any kind, but I suppose I've been here nearly a year so nothing should surprise me now.

TUESDAY 23 MARCH 1993

In the Kremlin Boris Yeltsin is struggling for survival. In Downing Street John Major is doing much the same. The headlines only feature the generals and the handful of foot soldiers who step out of line. What about the rest of us? There are 651 MPs, a hundred or so in government, fifty or so on the opposition front bench. That leaves around 500 backbenchers milling about Westminster, looking for something to do. Inevitably some

---

269 MP for Esher 1987–2010.
270 MP for Dover 1987–97.

of them get up to mischief. Broadly, on our side the colleagues fall into three groups: the old boys who've had their day and know it, some accepting it gracefully (Geoffrey Johnson-Smith, Terence Higgins),[271] others rather more grudgingly (John Biffen); the middle-aged ones who are going nowhere and either accept it (like the sweet man who shares the quiet room in the Library with me, whose name nobody knows and never will) or exploit it (Winterton) knowing they've got nothing to lose. Then there are those, like me, still burning with ambition, scurrying like dervishes round the bottom of the greasy pole. We're here every day, from breakfast till midnight (the *average* time of finishing has been midnight this session), darting from one committee to the next, signing letters, tabling questions, meeting constituents, being busy, busy, busy – but, frankly, to how much avail? Today I've done the Railways Bill, bench duty, a question to the Secretary of State for Health, a question to the PM, a Ten Minute Rule Bill ... I've not stopped ... I was pleased with my speech on children's play space: good points, well-made, coming from the heart. I went for cross-party support again and got some nice notes in my pigeon-hole later. But really, was there any point to it at all?

THURSDAY 25 MARCH 1993

Gerald's committee have produced their report. It's a compromise, but none the worse for that. They want a press ombudsman, empowered to impose fines, demand corrections etc.; a complaints hotline; a protection of privacy bill; and a 'privacy zone' to safeguard people like my war widows or the parents of my 'mercenary'.

Lunch with Tim Sainsbury[272] who is languid, owlish and amusing. He reveals that Heseltine's package to help the pits is going to cost £500 million. 'These rebellious backbenchers are very expensive people to keep happy.' I've gone to tell him what the business people of Chester are looking for from the DTI, but there's clearly not much point. I think Tim feels they've got all they can expect from government: 'Low inflation, deregulation, a flexible labour market – what more do they want?'

Later, on my way through the members' cloakroom, DD of the SS stops me. 'A word in your ear.' We huddle in a corner by the shoe-shine machine. 'There's something going round about you having financial difficulties.'

'What, me?'

'Yup. Business in trouble, that sort of thing. Anything in it?'

I am completely nonplussed. I can feel the blood draining away. 'No, no, of course not.'

---

271 MP for Worthing 1964–97.

272 Minister of State for Industry; MP for Hove 1973–97.

'Just thought I'd mention it. It's only a rumour. It's going round the secretaries' network. You know what they're like, jabbering women. Not to worry.' And he was off. And I'm now left, utterly thrown, wondering what on earth it's all about.

THURSDAY 1 APRIL 1993

There's a scratchy atmosphere in the Tea Room. When they're not grumbling about the Chancellor and VAT on fuel, they're muttering about John Patten's[273] classroom tests. They like the principle of testing; they don't like the high-handed Patten manner. Rightly or wrongly, when the PM walks in, the grumbling stops. I think there's a feeling the poor man needs a break. Let him eat his toasted teacake in peace.

I congratulated him on Questions. 'Yes, John Smith was a bit all over the place.' He patted the back of my hand. 'How's Chester?'

'Fine, thank you. I'm doing *Question Time* tonight.'

He brightened. 'Good, good. What do you think will come up? The train strike, I hope. Now this is what you need to say...'

He put it beautifully. I've noted it. I'll get it in. I'm well briefed, but ridiculously nervous all the same. Rachel [Whetstone] came over from Central Office and ran me through the questions she expects will come up. She says I can rely on her predictions: she always gets at least five out of seven right.

LATER

She got seven out of seven right. I think I did okay. No obvious gaffes. I played it straight down the line. It was nothing special, but I was perfectly happy with it, until the producer came up afterwards and said, 'You were very *reasonable*.' Clearly, they wanted me to be ridiculous – or outrageous. I toed the government line, I didn't produce any fireworks and I don't think I'll be asked again. (I think I also blotted my copybook by asking one of the production team what sort of rate David Dimbleby is on. I had to sign a piece of paper accepting a fee of £50. That's their standard apparently. I said, 'It's monstrous, you get four guests on the show for a total of £200. This is BBC1 prime time. We should be paid properly. What's Mr Dimbleby on – a thousand, two thousand? Look, I'll do it for a quarter of whatever he's getting.' They were not amused. They take themselves – and Mr Dimbleby – *very* seriously.)

---

273 Secretary of State for Education; MP for Oxford 1979–83, Oxford West & Abingdon 1983–97; later Baron Patten.

PALM SUNDAY, 4 APRIL 1993

No loud hosannas for the government as we approach our first anniversary. The Sunday papers can't recall another administration that has become so mired so quickly. Apparently, we won't be fielding senior ministers to talk up our year's achievements. According to Norman Fowler, 'it's going to be a low-key birthday'; we're producing a four-page pamphlet simply called *A Year's Work* (mostly about the Citizen's Charter I imagine!); Tony Newton (a lovely man but a mortician on the box) will be fielded if there are requests for a Cabinet minister, otherwise we're 'leaving it to David Amess'. I love David and, yes, it was Basildon that showed the world we'd turned the tide, but, but, but – we can't *seriously* be putting him forward as the Voice of the Conservatives One Year On, can we?

The 150th Grand National turned into a farce, with two false starts and the race declared void. Can't Mr Major get anything right?

(Yes – he can! Gin[274] has just called to congratulate me on *Question Time*. And she also heard bits of the PM's big speech on Friday. 'Daub,[275] Mr Major used several of your phrases. Did you give them to him or was he watching you on Thursday? Isn't it wonderful he's using your lines? You must be so proud.' I'm ashamed to say I didn't disabuse her.)

GOOD FRIDAY, 9 APRIL 1993

A deeply unpleasant thirty-six hours. I am writing this in our bedroom, at the back of the house. We're being staked out by the *Sunday Express*. There's a reporter and a photographer parked outside. They've been there for several hours. We're not answering the door or the telephone. Until they go, we're staying put. To see if they're still there, every hour or so I crawl across the spare bedroom floor and peek out of the bottom of the window. It's quite funny really.

Early on Wednesday evening I got a call at Westminster from an *Express* reporter. He said he wanted to talk to me about my interest in small businesses following my remarks last week on *Question Time*. Since I had absolutely no recollection of discussing any aspect of small businesses on *Question Time*, I knew at once something was up. I told the reporter I was just going to a meeting and suggested he call back at a more convenient time.

When I got home Michèle told me that the reporter had been on to our accountants enquiring about Complete Editions and the state of the business. Naturally the

---

274 One of GB's three sisters, Virginia.

275 Family nickname for GB, based on his middle name 'Daubeney'.

accountants told them they never commented on clients' affairs. Yesterday morning I was driven to Birmingham and back – a ludicrous five hours in the car to contribute five minutes to Anne and Nick's show on the death of Alfred Butts, inventor of Scrabble. (Anne's husband is the producer and I went having *squeezed* a fee of £200 out of him.)[276] While I was away the *Express* telephoned again. In the early evening I went over to Sky TV for another Scrabble interview and while I was out the reporter turned up at the house. He told Michèle there were 'allegations' about Complete Editions and 'facts' he wanted to check.

By the time I got back he'd gone. I telephoned Derek Sloane at Allen & Overy and, on his advice, we prepared a note to give to the reporter in the event that he turned up again: 'I have spoken to Gyles who I am sure you would not expect to respond to anonymous allegations … Our accountants are … Our solicitors are…'

This morning, first thing, the reporter rang the doorbell. Michèle opened the door and the reporter immediately placed his foot inside the door. He was holding a tape recorder. Michèle gave him the note, bent down, picked up his leg and forcibly moved his foot outside the door. She closed the door and double locked it. And here we are, holed up inside. And there they are, camped on our doorstep.

Why are we handling it this way? Mr Mellor would be marshalling his family for a photocall at the garden gate. Mary Archer would be serving them mugs of piping hot coffee and digestive biscuits. We are lying low, *hiding* in our own home. Why? Because this story hasn't got legs, it won't stand up. Complete Editions is in good shape and, now Michèle is running it, doing better than ever. (Michèle's business philosophy: 'Turnover is vanity, profit is sanity.') If I go out there now, give them their picture, make a comment, they've got their story: 'MP denies financial difficulties'. If I say nothing, if they don't see me, what have they got?

EASTER SUNDAY, 11 APRIL 1993

The tactic seems to have worked. There's nothing in the paper this morning. The *Express*'s ruthless investigative reporter and his sidekick lurked outside for most of the day and then disappeared. We stayed out of sight. At about eleven yesterday morning Michèle said, 'This is ridiculous, let's do something useful' and we vanished into the basement and did the most almighty clear-out: a real spring clean, what Michèle

276 Ann and Nick Owen (whom GB had known at TV-am) were now presenting *Good Morning* for the BBC at Pebble Mill, produced by Ann's then husband, Mike Hollingsworth. GB founded the National Scrabble Championships in 1972 and was a director Spear's Games, manufacturers of Scrabble.

has wanted us to do for months. So thank you *Sunday Express* – and fuck you *Sunday Express* because my stomach has been churning for three days. I feel guilty though I'm innocent. I've gone into hiding though I have nothing to hide. Who do these vermin think they are?

TUESDAY 20 APRIL 1993

There's a flouncing quality to John Patten that infuriates his enemies and disconcerts his friends. Everything he's saying about standards in schools and the need for these tests is spot on, but the way he does it is alienating people on all sides. He sat in the Tea Room today, ramrod back, head held high, being waspish and witty like a camp old thing, not realising that it's his manner not his policy that's driving his supporters away. We should be scoring in this area and we're not.

The Maastricht nightmare drags on – we finished at 1.13 a.m. yesterday. The Railways Bill drags on – Roger Freeman is a joy to watch, but I've fallen between two stools. You can either (like Sproat)[277] ignore the whole thing, sit in a far corner of the committee room, reading correspondence, signing letters, or (like Stephen [Milligan]) you can get stuck in and follow the bill line by line. I've been following it, but not with sufficient attention to detail to make either a worthwhile contribution or any impact. (My only 'moment' was when Prescott started muttering 'Woolly jumper! Woolly jumper!' while I was speaking. I came up with a reasonable riposte: 'The advantage of a woolly jumper is that you can take it off at will. The disadvantage of a woolly mind is that you are lumbered with it for life.')

I've just been for supper with Lord James.[278] I love him. He's straight out of *Jeeves and Wooster* – tall, slim, a little crumpled, slightly bent, blue-blooded, sandy-haired, sweet-natured, and can't be as bumbly and daffy as he pretends to be. Can he? Famously, he turned up for Colin Moynihan's charity boat race on the Thames wearing a pair of ancient gym shoes covered with filthy brown blotches. 'Filthy kit you've got there,' boomed Soames or some such. 'What are those horrible brown stains on your shoes?' 'Blood,' muttered James, 'my opponents' blood.' At Balliol he had five ambitions: to get a boxing blue, to become President of the Union, to be elected a Member of Parliament, to join the government, to become PM. Four down, one to go.

He said he thought we had time to go to his club. Pratt's, of course. I'd never been. His ministerial car drove us up St James' and dropped us at the corner. All the way, James

---

277 Iain Sproat, MP for Aberdeen South 1970–83, Harwich 1992–7.

278 Lord James Douglas-Hamilton, Under-Secretary of State for Scotland; MP for Edinburgh West 1974–97.

told me how much he liked Pratt's, 'my favourite club, my father was a member.' We got to the street, got out of the car, and James stood there, looking quite lost. 'Now where is it? I know it's along here somewhere. Let me see.' Like the White Rabbit searching for his gloves, he scurried up and down the street until eventually he hit upon the right one. 'Here we are!' It was like disappearing down the rabbit hole: another world, cosy, comfortable, safe; we shared the club table, 'the lamb looks excellent and I think you'll like the club claret.'

THURSDAY 22 APRIL 1993

This is a good place with good people. I have just been having dinner at the Chief Whip's table with the Deputy [David Heathcoat-Amory]), Tim Wood[279] and Tim Smith. They have been jolly and supportive and kind, and have taken the bitterness out of a beastly day.

I arrived at NPFA at lunchtime for my last council meeting as chairman. On the way over I bought the *Evening Standard* to read on the tube. Sitting in the meeting room waiting for the others to arrive I was flicking over the pages and, suddenly, my stomach lurched, my heart was in my mouth. The lead story in Londoner's Diary: 'Treasury man Gyles at a loss'. Six snide paragraphs, a picture of me looking bleary-eyed and sinister, an assertion that Complete Editions is going down the pan and speculation about what happens when an MP goes bankrupt.

I got on to Allen & Overy at once. At 1.48 p.m. Tim House [solicitor] got hold of a Mr Young in the legal department of the *Standard* and told him the piece is defamatory, it's clearly intended to mean that the business is in difficulties and I am facing a risk of personal bankruptcy, neither of which is remotely true. I faxed a letter simultaneously to Stewart Steven[280] – who I thought was a friend, but, of course, you can't have friends who are journalists. He turns out to be away but, come what may, we need a retraction, an apology, costs, damages – the lot.

I wrote a detailed note to my whip telling him there was nothing in it and went over to the Treasury to see Stephen [Dorrell] to apologise to him – because, of course, they've dragged his name in, included a picture of him. He couldn't have been sweeter, totally easy and relaxed about it. (He's fortunate – and wise. He doesn't let the papers impinge on him at all. I think he only reads *Der Spiegel* and the *Financial Times*.) I ended up looking in on the Upper Whips' Office (thinking I should be seen to be showing a face) and David [Heathcoat-Amory] said 'Join me for dinner', a kindness *much* appreciated.

---

279 In the Whips' Office 1990–97; MP for Stevenage 1983–97.

280 Editor of the *Evening Standard* 1992–5, formerly editor of the *Mail on Sunday* 1982–92.

MONDAY 26 APRIL 1993

A good day. On page 8 of the *Evening Standard*, Londoner's Diary: 'GYLES BRAN-DRETH – AN APOLOGY.

Last Thursday I suggested that Gyles Brandreth's company, Complete Editions Ltd, was facing financial problems. I am happy to report that I was wrong, and in fact the company is trading profitably. I apologise to both Mr Brandreth (pictured) and to Complete Editions director Michèle Brown for any embarrassment I have caused. I would also like to apologise unreservedly for any suggestion that Mr Brandreth is in personal financial difficulty. I had no basis whatsoever for any such suggestion, which I unequivocally retract.' And the photograph, I have to say, is one of the best I've seen. I look positively boyish.

They're bastards, they're vermin, but we got the retraction, we got the space, we got the photograph, we got the costs, we got the damages, *we won!*

FRIDAY 7 MAY 1993

We have lost the Newbury by-election [caused by the death of Judith Chaplin] to the Liberals by a margin of 22,000. It's devastating. And the local elections are not much better. Up here John Shanklin, Margaret Walker, Tony Llewellyn-Jones, all lost. A lot of local politicians are second-raters (some of the Labour people locally are third-rate), but these three are good: intelligent, sane, experienced – *normal*.

A real loss.

MONDAY 10 MAY 1993

No. 10 for lunch. There were ten of us in the small panelled dining room on the first floor; a delicious haddock pie (really delicious) and fresh green salad, followed by a splendid chocolate mousse. The PM was remarkably cool, calm and collected under the circumstances. He began by offering us his 'analysis of why we're in the doldrums'. He blamed a) the recession and b) the antics over Maastricht. I think there's more to it than that. My feeling is there's nothing in any of our policies or present programme that makes *anyone* feel good – let alone any of *our* people feel good.

My suggestion that John Smith's lamentable performance last Thursday might prove to be the beginning of the end for him prompted to PM to reveal that he has 'a fingertip feeling' that John Smith won't be the leader of the Labour Party come the next general election. 'It's just a fingertip thing, a pricking of my thumbs. I'm not sure why, but I just don't believe John will make it.'

'Who do you think it will be?'

'John Prescott or Bryan Gould.'

I sat one away from the PM, between the Chief Whip, who said nothing, and Alan Howarth,[281] who said a great deal. (Alan is eager for a return to government. Given that he is articulate and able, why do I feel this is unlikely? I imagine the whips think him longwinded, prissy and now rather wet. Perhaps they're right.) The PM made great play of the fact that he was here to 'listen', but I looked at him several times while the others were speaking and his eyes had glazed over. He was somewhere else, probably brooding over William Rees-Mogg's poisonous, patronising personal attack on him in today's *Times*. It's vile: 'the most over-promoted politician for a generation – at best suited for the role of Deputy Chief Whip'. The PM referred repeatedly to the coverage he's getting, 'the acid rain' that keeps pouring down on him, the 'war of attrition they're waging against me personally'. He asked for our advice and John Horam[282] came closest to offering a clear line to take: concentrate on the rhetoric of recovery, talk up our belief in manufacturing, maintain our position as the party of competitiveness; let social policy bed down, no more revolutions; play down Europe except as a means to improving the prospects of UK plc. The others rambled. The PM turned to his acting PPS (James Paice[283] who, bless him, has gone all serious and intense-looking since his appointment) just once to ask him to make a note – and that was to remind him to do some TV interviews in the West country ... Nigel Forman,[284] eyes gently popping, wiry and cerebral, lamented the fact that 'we don't seem to have a lot to say. It's a shame. The think tanks and the policy-making groups of the '80s seem to have lost their cutting edge.' 'Yes,' said the PM, 'all their knives are now buried in my back.'

As we wandered out of Downing Street, up Whitehall, leaving the Chief Whip and the PM's acting PPS behind us, we came to the conclusion that we were coming away feeling very much as we did when we went in. We like the man, we appreciate his clear head and his courteous manner, we know our victory a year and a month ago is down to him, but we're in desperate straits now and that's down to him as well – and he seems to have nothing to offer. Nigel said, 'He's drawing in the threads and we want him to be showing us the lead.'

---

281 MP for Stratford-on-Avon 1983–97, Newport East 1997–2005, later Baron Howarth of Newport.

282 Labour MP for Gateshead West 1970–81, SDP MP for Gateshead West 1981–3, Conservative MP for Orpington 1992–2010; later Baron Horam of Grimsargh.

283 MP for Cambridgeshire South East since 1987.

284 MP for Sutton Carshalton 1976–83, Carshalton & Wallington 1983–97.

LATER

Convivial drinks in John MacGregor's room to mark the successful conclusion of the Railways Bill. We have privatised the railways. 'Will it work?' I asked, innocently. John gave his Mr Pickwick's laugh: 'It had better.' Roger [Freeman] looked quite concerned: 'It most certainly will.' They are a formidable double-act, the government's unsung heroes. But curiously all talk of MacGregor going to the Treasury has stopped. I'd have thought he'd be ideal: a safe pair of hands, Dr Cameron's bedside manner, as sharp a political instinct as you could ask for, but, no, somehow his moment seems to have past. Norman [Lamont] is convinced he's going to survive, but he won't. My bet (seeing the way the PM works, sensing his insecurity) is Gillian Shephard as the 'big surprise' for Chancellor, David Hunt to Education, Stephen [Dorrell] to Employment. John Patten certainly goes. And what about my friend William Waldegrave who seems rather to have gone to waste/waist? The mind's still there, but the sparkle's all gone. Stephen Milligan tells me that John Kerr in Brussels reports that David Heathcoat-Amory is destined to replace Tristan as our Minister for Europe. How come the civil servants know all about it weeks before we do?

I did a couple of hours bench duty on the Finance Bill, sitting behind John Cope as he struggled with our fuel tax rebels. He was all over the place, but it didn't matter; if you're known to be a decent chap, if you make no pretensions to being a Big Beast, the House may jeer, may talk right through you, but everyone knows it doesn't really matter.

We survived the vote, but it was too close for comfort: 295 to 285. Technically, since Thursday, we have a majority of just nineteen, but tonight good people (like big-hearted Geoffrey Dickens) abstained and tossers (i.e. Nick Winterton) voted with the opposition. How on earth can we manage three or four more years like this?

TUESDAY 11 MAY 1993

The smack of firm government? The broadsheets tell us that the PM has sanctioned a full retreat on Patten's policy for testing in schools. The radio then tells us the opposite: the PM is four-square behind Patten, the tests proceed. I hear that the No. 10 briefing on the retreat was given last night, but that calls from the Patten camp *at 4.00 a.m.* ('Back me or sack me!') prompted this morning's revisionary announcement.

In the event at 3.30 p.m. Patten made his statement: this year's tests proceed, but for next year both the national curriculum and the tests are to be slimmed down and made more manageable. It's a half-retreat and he gets away with it, but he's subdued. The trouble with normally producing bravura despatch box performances, *con brio* and without notes, is that when you don't, it shows. He looked wounded and, unfortunately, a little absurd. Somehow his jacket wouldn't hang properly. Fabricant, sitting next to me, wondered if his back's gone and he's wearing a truss and the back of his jacket had got caught up in it.

WEDNESDAY 12 MAY 1993

William [Hague] and I spent two hours alone with the beleaguered Chancellor this morning working on his 'fighting speech' to the party's Scottish Conference. He was tired and twitchy, puffing on his cigars, hell-bent on knocking the press. As drafted, the speech sounded bitter and embattled. He had one good joke (about being born in the Shetlands and consequently being the only member of the government who could genuinely look down on a Scottish audience) and I did my best to add a bit more humour, more confidence, a lightness of touch. He wanted to go to town on how the press had misrepresented his '*Non, je ne regrette rien*' remark and eventually we slimmed his media-bashing diatribe down to a single line: 'As usual, the press did it their way.' I also put into the section on unemployment: 'My job is unimportant. What counts are *your* jobs.' He'll be fiddling with it all the way to Edinburgh. Poor man. I like him. I think he still thinks he can hang on.

Michèle and I gave the Lord Mayor of Chester and his wife lunch in the Strangers' Dining Room. They are nice people, traditional Labour but genuinely friendly towards us. I followed Patrick Cormack's advice and allowed them to see me paying for the meal. 'If you just sign for it, they think that somehow the taxpayer is picking up the tab.' Andrew Miller joined us for coffee. He's so boring it's unbelievable. What makes it quite funny is that he has no idea: he thinks he's quite fascinating. (At the Lord Mayor's dinner in the town hall Michèle sat next to him and followed her usual formula when seated next to middle-aged men at functions: ask them what they do and tell them how wonderful they are. The more tedious Andrew became the more wonderful Michèle told him he was. By the end of the meal, she was virtually asleep and he was in a state of ecstasy.)

At 3.30 p.m. all the PPSs gathered in the large ministerial conference room for a session with the Chief Whip. He looked a little peaky (as well he might) and his performance was as wan as his appearance. If his plan had been to rally the troops (or even to reassure them) I'm afraid he failed. He protested that he and the PM are 'very much in touch'; they 'recognise all the concerns', but we have got to recognise the special problems that come when you are operating with a majority of nineteen. It came over as routine stuff, predictable and undynamic. The responses from around the table were equally predictable, ranging from 'Don't worry, Chief, we've been here before, we'll come though' to 'Look here Chief, it's more serious than you think.' We went round in circles and emerged,

I imagine, just a fraction more despondent than when we went in. It interests me that no one seemed to want to make any *practical* suggestions about what we might do to improve morale and performance – e.g. find ways of involving the backbenchers more, test out proposed legislation before forging ahead with it, coordinate lines between government departments etc.

John Birt[285] came to address the media group. He looks like Daddy Woodentop, but, as his hour with us wore on, he impressed more and more. There's clearly more to him than mere management-speak and he seemed to have a firm grasp of the breadth and depth of the challenge he faces. Perhaps we should have him in the government?

THURSDAY 13 MAY 1993

It's fascinating the way the Chamber sometimes can make a difference. When John Patten came to announce his partial retreat on testing, he came away a broken reed. I've just witnessed Kenneth Clarke perform an equally spectacular U-turn and emerge a hero. We're scrapping the system of income-related fines we introduced only a matter of months ago, we're rethinking the whole of the 1991 Criminal Justice Act, we're reversing great chunks of our own policy under pressure … it should have been a humiliating climb-down. Instead, the way Clarke played it, breezy, bluff, commonsensical, he came out triumphant. Blair[286] helped. Blair's dangerous. He could be one of us: public school, Oxford, decent, amiable, well-groomed, no known convictions, he's been scoring on law and order. Not today. Today he got it all wrong. And Ken knocked him for six, dismissed him as 'a tabloid politician' obsessed with side-issues, incapable of dealing with substance. Our Sumo wrestler flattened Labour's flyweight. It was a pleasure to watch and fascinating to see how the mood here can change in a matter of minutes. When it was over we set off for the Tea Room with a spring in our strides. We felt good about ourselves again.

MONDAY 17 MAY 1993

The PM rallied the troops at the Scottish Conference on Friday. 'Give up? Give over.' Not quite in the Churchill league ('Some chicken! Some neck!'), but not bad for a damp Friday in Carnoustie. Could I do any better? We shall see.

---

285 Director General of the BBC 1992–2000; later Baron Birt.

286 Tony Blair, shadow Home Secretary; MP for Sedgefield 1983–2007; Prime Minister 1997–2007.

I got a call just now from No. 10, Alex Allen [Principal Private Secretary] in the PM's office. 'The Prime Minister is due to make a big speech to the business community. We've done a draft, but the Prime Minister feels it needs a bit of brightening up, a touch of humour, a few jokes, you know the sort of thing. He wondered if you might be able to help.' I said I'd be delighted to try (of course) but that it isn't easy conjuring up phrases, lines, jokes in a vacuum. You need to know the context. 'Yes, of course. But if you can send anything across the Prime Minister would be much obliged.'

This is a bugger because while it's nice to be wanted (it's *wonderful* to be wanted) my schedule today is a nightmare and I'm going to have to spend the rest of the day juggling the diary while trying to cobble together anecdotes and turns of phrase for the PM – most of which I know will go straight from the fax machine to the shredder.

....
LATER
....

I sent over two pages of lines, quips, asides. There was some quite funny stuff about the Chancellor which they binned at once. I said that making jokes about an issue shows you are relaxed about it. Clearly No. 10 is not relaxed about the Chancellor. There were a couple of lines I think they liked and one story that seemed bland enough to fit the bill:

> Nobody likes paying taxes. When I first went to the Treasury I was shown a let-
> ter from someone who had just arrived in Britain from the Commonwealth and
> set up business. He had written to his Inspector of Taxes, 'I am unable to com-
> plete the tax form you have sent me. Moreover, I am not interested in the income
> service. Could you please cancel out my name in your books as this system has
> upset my mind and I do not know who registered me as one of your customers.'

I have just left a very convivial group in the Smoking Room: David Lightbown, a gentle giant, Sydney Chapman (who reminds me of Arthur Howard, Leslie Howard's brother who played Jimmy Edwards' sidekick in *Whacko!*), John Taylor,[287] former whip now the Lord Chancellor's man in the Commons, and Jeremy Hanley. We have been having rather a lot to drink and rather liking it! High politics was not on our agenda. John Taylor asked if we'd heard about the American university where, in the interests of political correct-ness, they are alternating seminars with ovulars. David banged his glass on the table, 'Sod political correctness!' Jeremy said that if we were to be politically correct we shouldn't call Sydney Chapman 'Chapman' we should call him Sydney Personperson. (It seemed very

---

287 MEP for Midlands East 1979–84; MP for Solihull 1983–2005.

funny twenty minutes ago.) John Taylor then got the hiccups and I began telling the group how excellent Kenneth Carlisle[288] had been this afternoon when I took my deputation to see him about the A51 and the bypass. Carlisle said virtually nothing at the meeting, but listened with real concern and impressed the local councillors considerably. Jeremy said what a decent chap Kenneth Carlisle is: suddenly the whips fell ominously silent. I imagine Mr Carlisle is not long for the ministerial corridor … poor man, he probably has no idea.

THURSDAY 20 MAY 1993

The end of the Maastricht road is nigh. The Danes have voted 'yes' in their second referendum and the PM has called for unity. Fat chance. We have the Third Reading tonight and I have just spent a very jolly hour closeted with the Chancellor working on his speech. He was in high spirits. 'We end the Maastricht debate tonight,' he chortled, 'and I shall have the last word. It's as it should be.' We trimmed the draft drastically and added a number of robust touches: 'We put Britain first. Always have. Always will.'

Norman seemed pleased with our endeavours. 'I think we've got the balance right, don't you?' Mischievous grin. 'At least it isn't too Hurdy.' Much chuckling over Norman's exchange with the Foreign Secretary:

'What should I say in my speech, Douglas?'

'I think you have your own distinctive line, Norman.'

We toyed with the idea of a section mocking Gordon Brown for fumbling his way round Europe declaring '*Je regrette beaucoup!*' As I left, Norman walked me to the door half-singing half-laughing, '*Non, non de non. Je ne regrette rien. C'etait seulement les chansons du bain.*'

LATER

Norman did well. He battled through the mayhem and came out on top. Gordon Brown had plenty of bark, but no bite. The Labour Party abstained so, inevitably, we won the vote, but it was a hollow victory. At least fifty of our side either voted against or abstained. It's taken almost a year to secure this Third Reading, hundreds of hours of debate, dozens of futile divisions, endless late nights, and, beyond these walls, no one seems to have much of an idea of what any of it's about! In the Smoking Room the champagne is flowing. The Bill now goes to the Lords, but at least for the time being we're shot of it. Hooray!

---

288 Under-Secretary of State for Transport; MP for Lincoln 79–97.

I said to DD of the SS, 'I'm not sure that we should be celebrating yet. The headlines aren't going to say "Maastricht Bill Achieved", they're going to trumpet "Tories' Biggest Ever Revolt".'

'I think not,' he said, with a sly grin.

'Why not?'

'Why not? Because the Queen Mother has just been rushed to hospital. Haven't you heard? It's touch and go. We're not sure if she'll last the night…' 'Wolfish leer followed by conspiratorial chuckle. 'Yes, the arm of the Whips' Office has a lengthy reach.'[289]

TUESDAY 25 MAY 1993

Day 3 of the Finance Bill Committee. I shall be confined to Room 10 every Tuesday and Thursday till the end of June, but as a PPS I don't speak, I simply sit behind the minister passing him notes from the civil servants as and when required. It is not taxing and should leave me time enough to think of lines for our beleaguered Prime Minister – from whom I have just received a very civil letter thanking me for my contributions to his speech for the CBI dinner: 'in future I will try to get you more notice and see the context in advance. I have a speech to the Women's Conference in around ten days – text unwritten as yet … if anything strikes you!' It is gratifying to get handwritten notes from the PM, but I am a little alarmed to think of him finding the time – or feeling he has to find the time – to send these billets-doux.

I have just come from a meeting with Michael Howard. Half a dozen of us gathered in his tiny room on the ministerial corridor to discuss the aftermath of Rio.[290] There's only a small sofa and a couple of chairs, so two of us sit on the floor, arms clasped around our knees. We are all middle-aged men, but you'd think we were schoolboys gathering round the housemaster for hot chocolate and a late-night reading of John Buchan. Michael has hardly launched into his spiel (he knows his stuff, he's impressive) when the phone goes. It's No. 10. He's wanted. Urgently. It can't wait. He must go. He leaves us and, at once, we all think the same thought. The reshuffle has begun.

In fact, it hasn't, but reshuffle fever is definitely in the air. Who's up, who's down, who's in and who's out? It's the life-blood of the place. According to Portillo (I'm sitting right behind him as I write: his hair really is impressive at close quarters, a high sheen and not a touch of dandruff), since the Whitsun Recess begins on Friday, the reshuffle will happen on Thursday. That way, if you get the sack you can slink off home to lick your

---

289 In fact, the Queen Mother had suffered a minor injury to her foot. She was only in hospital briefly as a precaution.
290 The international summit conference on the future of the global environment.

wounds and don't have to face your apparently sympathetic (secretly gleeful) colleagues for a week or two.

THURSDAY 27 MAY 1993

Well, well, Norman [Lamont] has gone and John Patten has survived. David Hunt moves up the Cabinet pecking order (to Employment) which is good; John Gummer ditto (to Environment) which is surprising. Michael Howard is Home Secretary and Ken Clarke Chancellor. The Cabinet newcomer is John Redwood,[291] about whom I know nothing.

Wanting to see the action I skipped the Voluntary Arts Network meeting and went into a deserted House for lunch. On the way in, my first encounter was with Jeremy Hanley who had just emerged from No. 10 and was bubbling with justifiable excitement: Minister of State at Defence. I lunched with Michael Ancram[292] and teased him about his reshuffle haircut. He was looking very spruce – and eager. He treated me to a large Bloody Mary on the strength of an intimation that he should not wander too far from his telephone. Before lunch was over the call had come though. He's going to Northern Ireland to replace Jeremy. He'll be superb. We were halfway through the meal when Tristan [Gard-Jones] sauntered in and announced – to general astonishment and barely concealed flickers of dismay – that the PM had asked him to stay on – and that he'd agreed. He gave a three beat pause and then said, 'He asked me to stay on – for a week – to chair a meeting – so I agreed.' David Heathcoat-Amory replaces Tristan [as Minister for Europe] and DD of the SS replaces Robert Jackson who gets the boot. I like Robert, but he is an oddity. He sits in the Library translating obscure Greek texts into Latin or vice versa. Kenneth Carlisle goes too: I could have told him: too lacklustre. Edward Leigh[293] also gets the push: too pushy and too openly disloyal.

It's a good day for loyalists: my friend William Hague goes to the DSS and there are jobs for three of the Drinks brigade: John Bowis,[294] Derek Conway[295] and Michael Brown.[296] Who says grovelling doesn't pay?

---

291 He became Secretary of State for Wales in place of David Hunt.

292 MP for Berwick & East Lothian 1974, Edinburgh South 1979–87, Devizes 1992–2010. He succeeded as 13th Marquess of Lothian in 2004, by which time hereditary peers no longer had an automatic right to sit in the House of Lords. In 2010 he was created Baron Kerr of Monteviot.

293 Under-Secretary of State for Industry and Consumer Affairs 1990–93; MP for Gainsborough & Horncastle since 1983.

294 Became Under-Secretary of State at the Department of Health; MP for Battersea 1987–97.

295 Joined the Whips' Office; MP for Shrewsbury & Atcham 1983–97.

296 Joined the Whips' Office; MP for Brigg & Scunthorpe 1979–83, Brigg & Cleethorpes 1983–97.

I saw Stephen [Dorrell] at six. Bless him, he'd had an optimistic haircut too. He was disappointed, but sanguine. During the day he'd heard, and I'd heard, rumours that he was going to go to Wales, but if Lamont was the only one to be dropped he knew the newcomer would have to come from the right, so there we go. His time will come. Meanwhile, we have the interesting prospect of ringside seats at the court of King Ken…

FRIDAY 28 MAY 1993

I'm sitting in bed in Chester, befuddled and bemused. Bemused because I've a feeling that – already – within twenty-four hours – the reshuffle hasn't worked. Everyone said: Norman must go. Norman goes. But no one seems any the happier – except for Ken Clarke who is pictured on the front page of half the papers, standing on the steps of the Treasury, beaming inanely, beer belly and Garrick Club tie to the fore. I'm befuddled because I've spent the evening enjoying the excellent hospitality of the Cheshire Regiment. I was much honoured by being invited to take the salute at Beating Retreat in the Castle Square. If I'd known what was expected I might have declined. I turned up on time, but without a hat.

'Where's your hat?' gasped Colonel Ropes, red-faced, perspiring with anxiety.

'I haven't got a hat.'

'Haven't got a hat? You must have a hat. You can't take the salute without a hat.'

'I didn't know one needed a hat. No one said anything about a hat.'

The Lord Lieutenant came to the rescue. He opened the boot of his limousine. It was stuffed with hats – top hats, bowlers, berets, hats with plumes. Colonel Ropes selected a brown trilby which made me look at best like a bookie, at worst like a spiv. He's a sweetheart, as anxious and well-meaning as they come, but his briefing was useless. I didn't understand a word. He said, 'Don't worry. You'll be driven to the podium. Climb the steps and stand to attention. I'll be on the ground beside you and I'll tell what to do and when to do it. The main thing to remember is that when you salute you take the hat off your head with your right hand, put it to your chest, and then put it back on your head again.'

I was driven onto the parade ground. I climbed the steps and stood there. Alone. Ropes was 6 feet away at least and inaudible. If he'd been my officer at the front I'd never have gone over the top because I wouldn't have heard any of his orders. Every now and then I could hear the wretched man *muttering*, but of what he was saying I heard not a word. The massed bands marched to and fro and I doffed and donned my trilby with gay abandon. When the regimental goat came forward and bowed, I glanced towards my Colonel and caught him looking at his knees. I decided to salute the goat on the grounds that it was wearing the regimental colours.

The ordeal over I vowed never to wear a hat again and retired to the mess and drank a great deal – as you can probably tell.

THURSDAY 3 JUNE 1993

A week after the reshuffle and already it seems as bad as ever – if not worse. Indeed, from the PM's standpoint it is worse. There's a poll today showing him to be the least popular Prime Minister on record – less loved even than Neville Chamberlain in 1940. The shuffle itself now seems a one-day wonder, its impact already evaporated and colleagues wondering why it didn't go further. People are even feeling sorry for Norman. He is feeling sorry for himself, understandably: he did the government's bidding within the ERM and then delivered clever packages in both the Autumn Statement and the Budget, quelling the disquiet from business, raising taxes without damaging prospects for recovery. What more can you ask? More bounce, better PR – attributes Ken Clarke may well bring to the job. Who knows? What we all know is that things don't look good for the PM. People are openly giving him 'a year to sort things out'. The general verdict seems to be: if things haven't improved by next summer, it's curtains for nice Mr Major. As David Willetts put it on his return from Michael Portillo's fortieth birthday bash: 'Let's go for Ken Clarke – better to have strong leadership you disagree with than no leadership at all.'

We're just in from Jeremy Hanley's farewell bash at the Northern Ireland Office. Drinks, nibbles and a window view of Beating Retreat on Horse Guards Parade – a slightly grander affair than last Friday's effort in Chester. The Prince of Wales was on the podium (no sign of Colonel Ropes) but as the massed bands were floodlit and Charles wasn't, we cannot be certain whether or not the heir to the throne saluted better than I did. (We can guess…) At lunch Michèle sat next to his father and made him laugh a lot. Afterwards I made the rather po-faced gathering laugh a little by saying the Queen hadn't put a foot wrong in forty years – and nor had Prince Philip. He'd put his foot *in* it now and again, but that was different … The event was my swansong as NPFA chairman and HRH presented me with a hideous framed caricature that looked nothing like me but seemed to delight everyone else. NPFA Scotland presented me with a gold medallion inscribed to 'Giles'.

This keeps it all in perspective.

MONDAY 7 JUNE 1993

At 6.30 p.m. I made my way to Downing Street. I am not blasé. It is very thrilling to walk up Whitehall in the early evening sunshine, to smile at the policemen who swing open the gates for you, to stroll to the door of No. 10 and have it opened before you've even knocked. It is thrilling and extraordinary to be me walking alone along the corridor that leads from the front door straight to the Cabinet room.

What is alarming is to get there, to turn left at the end of the corridor and walk into the small study that is the office of the Prime Minister's political and parliamentary secretaries and suddenly think, 'Oh dear, is this it?' The room is impressive enough (the customary panelling and leather), it's the people. There's nothing wrong with them – they're decent, loyal, determined. It's just that they don't seem special. They seem ordinary and I think I want to feel that the Prime Minister of the United Kingdom is surrounded by people who are *exceptional*. It reminds me of the moment in *The Wizard of Oz* when Dorothy, awed and trembling, goes to see the Mighty Oz, all-knowing, all-powerful, and her little dog pulls back the curtain to reveal the great wizard for what he is: a sweet old bumbler pushing buttons and pulling levers to very little effect.

Graham Bright is Tweedledum. I'm not sure what to make of Jonathan Hill.[297] He's personable, intelligent, articulate, but extraordinarily laid back under the circumstances, and so young.

We were meeting to discuss Wednesday night's big speech – a debate on the economy with John Smith opening. I said I thought Friday's rallying call at the Women's Conference had worked well. I liked 'I'm fit, I'm well, I'm here, and I'm staying.'

'A bit defensive?'

'A bit.'

'On Wednesday we've got to come out fighting and end up on top.'

'Agreed.'

Jonathan is working up a draft. I said I'd fax through some ideas. I left feeling that these well-intentioned, reasonable, responsible, relatively inexperienced guys recognise there's a problem, want to do something about it but aren't quite sure what.

In the Whips' Office they seem to have a firmer grip on what needs to be done. I arrived for Drinks (now, for some reason, rechristened A and under the command of Bob Hughes) to be asked, 'What do you know about Gordon Brown?'

'What do you mean?'

'Is he gay? We need to nail the bugger. If there's dirt to dish this is the week to dish it.'

After several minutes of fairly disgusting banter the mood of the meeting was that Gordon ought to be gay, could indeed be gay and should in fact be gay, but maddeningly we have no evidence of any kind to suggest that he *is* gay!

---

297 Political Secretary to the Prime Minister 1992–4. He was thirty-two. Later, Baron Hill of Oareford; Leader of the House of Lords since 2013.

I suggested too that, given the Michael Mates[298] affair, this was perhaps not the ideal week for highlighting buggery in high places. Colonel Mates, of course, is as straight as they come (ramrod back, black bushy eyebrows, slightly preposterous military bearing), but the watch he presented to Asil Nadir bore the unfortunate inscription, 'Don't let the buggers get you down'. (The whips view on Mates seems to be that he may be an idiot, but he isn't a crook. He interceded on Nadir's behalf because he took a sympathetic interest in his case. One of Nadir's advisers was one of his constituents. The Serious Fraud Office confiscated Nadir's own watch in one of their raids. Mates replaced it as an act of friendship and solidarity. He had no idea Nadir was going to jump bail of £3.5 million a few days later...)

TUESDAY 8 JUNE 1993

This is Michèle's and my twentieth wedding anniversary. I love my wife very much and the only thing I don't like about being an MP is that I'm always here – and she isn't. We had a celebratory lunch on Sunday with Simon [Cadell] and Veronica Hodges,[299] but the Finance Bill Committee has kiboshed the dinner I'd planned for tonight. Heigh ho. I'm not sure what the answer is.

Life could be worse. I could be Michael Mates. He looked pretty strained last night. The Tea Room view this afternoon is that we can't afford another fuck-up, so, fair or not, he ought to go now. The SFO are investigating Nadir for fraud amounting to tens of millions. You can't have ministers of the crown appearing to side with a crook. At Questions the PM took a more generous line: 'It was a misjudgement, but it is not a hanging offence.' Tony Marlow's verdict: 'The Prime Minister just can't get anything right, can he?'

WEDNESDAY 9 JUNE 1993

This morning, our first prayers with the new Chancellor. It is going to be very different. And rather fun. This afternoon, the old Chancellor had some fun of his own. At 3.30 p.m., to a packed house, he made his resignation statement. It was fairly devastating stuff. 'Since the war only two Conservative Chancellors have succeeded in bringing inflation down to below 2 per cent. Both of them were sacked ... I am delighted to hear from the Prime Minister that policy will not alter ... I now wish to say one thing to him: there is

---

298 Minister of State, Northern Ireland Office, 1992–3; MP for Petersfield 1974–83, Hampshire East 1983–2010.

299 The sole witnesses at GB and his wife's marriage at Marylebone Register Office in 1973.

something wrong with the way in which we make our decisions. The government listens too much to the pollsters and the party managers … There is too much short-termism, too much reacting to events. We give the impression of being in office but not in power.'

I sat behind the poor PM. He didn't flinch. For twenty minutes he hardly moved. Others turned to look towards Norman; the PM, with studied neutrality, gazed steadfastly ahead. Norman's statement left our side numb, shell-shocked, silent, and the opposition benches cock-a-hoop. John Smith could hardly have asked for a sweeter curtain-raiser. He took full advantage of it. And when he got to his peroration – 'the stark reality of a discredited government presided over by a discredited Prime Minister' – how they roared. We cheered our man, of course, but our hearts weren't entirely in it and while the PM did valiantly, in truth he survived, he didn't triumph.

THURSDAY 10 JUNE 1993

At around midnight, just after the second vote, Stephen [Dorrell] found me in the Smoking Room. He was in state of high excitement. 'The PM wants me to draft his speech for Friday – the Welsh Conference. We need to get the government back on track. Shall we go to my room?'

I was ready for bed. I was ready for bed partly because I'd had several glasses of wine and partly because I have a wife to go to bed with. Stephen, I imagine, had had several glasses of orange juice and his wife is at home in Worcester. He had no incentives for bed. We set off for his tiny room and I perched on the edge of an armchair while he began bashing out a speech. Soon after one I threw in the towel and left him to it.

He has just faxed me the material he is sending round to No. 10. The covering note is good:

> Graham –
>
> I would *strongly* urge him to concentrate this weekend on a measured statement of what we are about. Ignore the alarums and excursions. The most damaging line is that the government doesn't know its own mind. If we can begin to answer that – by showing clearly that we do – much of the rest will lose its sting. If we are distracted into answering the latest barbs, the damaging charge will go unanswered. Furthermore this line plays to our *strengths*. It is not true that the government doesn't know its own mind. What is true is that we haven't succeeded in articulating it. *Please* press this line on him as hard as you can.

The advice is sound, but the speech (six pages, single spacing) will go the way of most of my contributions. It's solid stuff – sound money, the role of government, managing the public finances, improving public services, jobs, education, nationhood – it is indeed what we're about – but it won't set the valleys alight, it won't do the trick.

LATER

I don't see how the poor PM can take much more of this. He's battered from dawn till dusk. PMQs were chaos. Some Labour chap got in with a very funny opening dig suggesting that the government was beginning to look like the seaside hotel that's just collapsed and crumbled down the cliff face, and John Smith followed up with a triple whammy exploiting Norman's barbs from yesterday. The PM did his best, but he played straight into Smith's hand:

PM: As one of my predecessors might have said, we've had a little local difficulty. We shall get over it. I am going on with the work in hand.

Smith: Doesn't the Prime Minister understand that when he announced business as usual this morning he caused apprehension throughout the land?

The only good moment in the Chamber came later when Archie Hamilton gave a little gem of a four-minute resignation statement.[300] It was wry, funny and self-deprecatory; the antithesis of what Norman gave us yesterday. Archie told us he was looking forward 'to spending more time with – pause – my constituents.'

Word has just reached us from No. 10. Stephen's speech has been gratefully received and will form a substantial part of the PM's Welsh oration. Well, yes, perhaps this is a weekend for being dull-but-worthy. Let's get back to basics.

MONDAY 14 JUNE 1993

The full complement of Q gathered at No. 10 for a splendid lunch in the state dining room. A drained and rather blotchy-looking PM presided. The gathering was arranged a while ago to celebrate our achievements. Tony Durrant, as chairman, made a little speech, rather sweet and bumbly, reminding the PM that we're his secret weapon – good men (plus one woman, Angela Knight)[301] ready to go over the top at a moment's notice. He said it as if he believed it – and, in truth, there is a value in what we do. We meet once a week and a little bit of bonding is no bad thing; we can be briefed on what to say; we can be relied on to ask whatever questions the whips provide; those

---

300 Unlike Lamont, Archie Hamilton had stepped down as a Defence Minister at his own request.

301 MP for Erewash 1992–7.

of us with the requisite courage/foolhardiness/ambition turn up in the Chamber and do our best to bate the opposition. No doubt it could be much more effective, but it's better than nothing.

There were thirty-four of us in all, eight already in government, the rest lusting to be. I sat between DD of the SS, as happy as a sandboy now he's a minister, and Roger Evans, whose elevation to office can't be far off. (He's round and rather Dickensian, a lawyer, Welsh and sharp, so that something in the Welsh Office is as good as guaranteed. If you are Welsh or Scots and not a total halfwit eventual preferment is a certainty. Rod Richards[302] was there. I think he *speaks* Welsh so his future is doubly assured.) When the PM gave his response he did his best to summon up some energy, but it simply wasn't there. He fell back on a few clichés and, unfortunately, he was still speaking when half a dozen of us had to make our excuses and leave. I had to be in the Chamber by 2.30 p.m. as mine was the very first question (urging the Secretary of State for National Heritage to give support to Chester Cathedral) so I sort of bobbed backwards out of the state dining room muttering apologies under my breath while the Prime Minister chuntered on. I paced back to the House with Stephen Milligan. It's a pleasure to be with him. He is enjoying life here so much even the disasters seem to delight him. He's a loyalist through and through, but he expatiated on the complete failure of the reshuffle with gusto. 'It's simply blown up in the PM's face. Too little too late.'

TUESDAY 15 JUNE 1993

It's 9.30 on Tuesday night. I'm in Committee Room 10 where we are on Day 6 of our weary trudge through the fetid swamp of the 1993 Finance Bill. The crone of Cambridge[303] is on her feet droning on about the costs of relocation while poor Michael Portillo, bored out of his elegant skull, is immediately in front of me, head in hands, wishing he was at the Mansion House listening to the new Chancellor of the Exchequer making his debut there. Michael *bought* white tie and tails for the occasion and then found that Harriet Hopeless[304] wouldn't pair. She's a cow. (She's also an inexplicable half-inch away from being wonderfully attractive. In the right light and when she's facing you – so you don't notice the incipient widow's hump – she's almost gorgeous, but then she opens her mouth and suddenly you realise she's not that pretty, she's not that bright and – worst sin of all – she has no sense of humour.)

302 MP for Clwyd North West 1992–7.

303 Anne Campbell, Labour MP for Cambridge 1992–2005.

304 Harriet Harman, shadow Chief Secretary to the Treasury, Labour MP for Peckham since 1982.

LATER

It's twenty past midnight and we're still here. Apparently all-night sittings are part of the macho tradition of the Finance Bill. At 11.30 p.m. we took a half-hour break, agreed between the committee chairman and the whips on each side. We descended to the Smoking Room and I began by buying Michael a drink and ended up buying a bottle of champagne for the gang: MP, Stephen [Dorrell], John Cope, David Amess and my new whip, Michael Brown. He's delightful, full of Tiggerish bounce, but I'd have thought a surprising choice for the Whips' Office. He doesn't seem particularly discreet (or bright) and I imagine he's gay. (I don't know, of course. Unless one has actually witnessed the act of darkness taking place, how can one know? The rumours persist about Portillo and Lilley, and about Alan Duncan[305] and William Hague, but is there any truth in them? Almost certainly not, but we don't like to discount them totally because we do enjoy the frisson of possible scandal.) David Amess is another wholly likeable fellow, a complete quainty whose chief delight in life (I am not exaggerating) seems to be to go off with Ann Widdecombe to say prayers.

MP said that the Chancellor's Mansion House speech, at least in draft, had been quite ordinary. Stephen told me that David Cameron has been sacked as a special adviser. This is a mistake. He may come from the right, but he has astute political antennae and a fabulous turn of phrase. I suppose Bill Robinson [another of Lamont's special advisers] will be on the way out too. I'm having a drink with him tomorrow. They were good people, funny and companionable. I'll be sorry to see them go.

In Committee we are allowed to write, read correspondence, do paperwork, but books and newspapers are not allowed. I want to read the obituaries of Les Dawson and Bernard Bresslaw. I've got the papers with me, but I don't dare produce them. Old hands *photocopy* whole books in the Library, and read their novels in committee page by photocopied page.

I'm shattered because I was here by seven this morning, up in the turret, guarding my place in the Ten Minute Rule Bill queue. At the Equity reception in the Jubilee Room I was telling Denis Norden[306] about it and he simply didn't believe me. He simply couldn't, wouldn't, didn't believe that I had had to sit alone in a windowless room for nearly three hours simply waiting to knock on a door and present a piece of paper to a clerk in the hope of securing an opportunity to address the House of Commons in a fortnight's time on a proposed piece of legislation that will never materialise … He said, 'Is this democracy?' We moved from democracy to civilisation and he said that,

---

305 MP for Rutland Melton since 1992.
306 Comedy writer and television presenter.

for him, Radio 4 epitomises true civilisation – not just the plays and the documentaries, but the oddities: 'the sound of people squelching up the Andes...'

EVEN LATER

It is five in the morning. Dawn is breaking across the Thames. The Chief Secretary to the Treasury has laid his head in his arm to sleep. Harriet Hopeless is sitting immediately opposite me, slumbering gently. (I can say I have slept with Harriet Harman, and I shall.) Looking around it seems most of the committee is dozing fitfully. This is democracy in action. Would that Dennis could see us now!

This is a *daft* way to carry on.

THURSDAY 17 JUNE 1993

Tony Marlow is telling anyone who'll listen that John Major has outlived his usefulness and should now do the decent thing and *go*. Mrs T. has emerged from the undergrowth to endorse her successor. She'll stand by her man. When I suggest at prayers that they're both barking in their different ways, the Chancellor leans back in his chair so he's out of Portillo's eye-line and pulls a very funny face, implying he fully agrees with my analysis but had it occurred to me that possibly the Chief Secretary mightn't.

Thursday prayers is now a leisurely lunchtime gathering in the Chancellor's room at the Treasury. A generous spread of sandwiches, some take-away Indian bibs and bobs, and a bottle or three of wine. (We have Treasury Questions today, so Portillo, Cope, Dorrell and Nelson stick to orange juice and water. The Chancellor is more relaxed.) It's a jolly occasion, easy, informal and pleasantly gossipy. No officials, just the new special advisers (a rather serious-looking lady and a tousled-top boy, I've got neither their names nor the measure of them yet),[307] the ministers and the PPSs. The Clarke and Lamont styles could hardly be more different. The manner of their PPSs could hardly be more different either. William Hague was quiet, conscientious, courteous and attentive, ever at his master's beck and call. Phillip Oppenheim[308] is extraordinary. He turns up late, leans nonchalantly across his boss to collect his glass and his plate of sandwiches and then lounges at the end of the table leafing through the *Financial Times*. He's self-assured, self-absorbed, self-indulgent and apparently fearless. He's charming. I rather like him. I

---

307 Tessa Keswick, later Director of the Centre for Policy Studies, and David Ruffley, MP for Bury St Edmunds from 1997.

308 Kenneth Clarke's PPS; MP for Amber Valley 1983–97.

imagine he's clever too, so he can afford to be lazy. He's seen at once that I'm the eager-beaver naive new boy and he's going to leave all the work to me.

TUESDAY 22 JUNE 1993

Michael Heseltine has had a heart attack in Venice. The pictures of him being carted off to hospital, his spindly legs exposed to the world, were certainly an invasion of his privacy. Interestingly, the Tea Room reaction has been one of shock rather than sympathy, concern for the government's dwindling majority rather than concern for Michael's health. People here admire him, respect him. They don't appear to love – or even like – him very much.

By uncanny coincidence, Heseltine's henchman, Colonel Mates, the man who led Heseltine's campaign to oust Thatcher in 1990, is also swinging in the wind. He's hanging on (just) but he's doomed. It turns out that even after Nadir had jumped bail, Colonel Bonehead let one of Nadir's PR people lend him a car for his wife to use! Can you believe it? It turns out too that the party accepted at least £440,000 from Nadir, so now we're all tarred with the same brush. Naturally, and quite skilfully (Margaret Beckett[309] is ugly but effective), the Labour Party is milking it for all its worth. They're going to use their opposition Day debate this afternoon to rake up every disreputable ne'er-do-well who has contributed to our cause in recent years – and there seem to be dozens of them – and all we can throw back at them is Robert Maxwell.

LATER

Committee Room 10: I trust we're not going for another all-nighter. I was here at 7.30 a.m. because the BBC came to film me for the *Bookmark* programme on Trollope. They turned up at 8.00 and I took them off to the deserted Chamber where they set up their lights and the camera and I did my stuff. We were in the middle of the third or fourth take when a posse of doorkeepers burst in: 'Stop! You can't film in here. No one has filmed inside the Chamber of the House of Commons – ever!' Well, I thought, they have now.

I tried to persuade Portillo to take part in the programme, but he wouldn't. 'Trollope is the PM's territory. I wouldn't presume.'

I'm going through the post. It never ends. I have had an amusing letter from Norman [Lamont]. When he was sacked I sent a note of commiseration, but somehow it got

---

309 Deputy Leader of the Opposition and shadow Leader of the House; Labour MP for Lincoln 1974–9, Derby South since 1983.

snarled up in the system. I saw him at the end of last week and he said, 'Are you ignoring me?' I said 'No, of course not.' He said, 'Maybe you shouldn't be seen talking to me. Consorting with the enemy … If you want to get on you need to watch the company you keep. The eyes and the ears of the whips are everywhere…'

Anyway, my note eventually reached him:

> It has arrived! And I was glad not to miss it!
> 'Oh you forgive my little jokes on thee
> And I'll forgive thy great big joke on me.'

FRIDAY 25 JUNE 1993

Michael Mates has gone and not before time. I'm on my way to Chester where my weekend promises visits to three schools, two factories, the Volunteer Stroke Service, the Muir Housing Association, the Lache Carnival, and the cub scouts at Pulford, plus four hours of surgery and a 'working breakfast' with the Association officers. How come this is how I spend my weekends when the President of the Board of Trade manages to spend his enjoying the Venetian high life? While I'm flogging the streets of Chester he's quaffing and sluicing in the Cipriani. Still, we must count our blessings. At least I've not had a heart attack. (Richard Ottaway[310] says the heart attack was serious, but not dangerous and 'Michael will bounce back'. Even so, the Tea Room view is that this finally puts paid to his leadership prospects.)

TUESDAY 29 JUNE 1993

9.00 a.m.: With the Home Secretary [Michael Howard] to discuss funding for the fire service. He's needle sharp, briefed to the eyeballs, tough as they come, but there's an almost imperceptible twinkle there too.

11.00 a.m.: With Roger Freeman and the delegation from Chester City Transport. He sweet-talks them to perfection. Even I fall for his schmooze. At PMQs I put my question (on the Manchester bid for the Olympics) as agreed, and the PM gives a full and fulsome answer as planned. Even though it's all set up I marvel at how nervous I still feel when I ask a question. I can address an audience of 2,000 after dinner without a note and without a worry. Stand up in the Chamber, with 600

---

310 Michael Heseltine's PPS; MP for Nottingham North 1983–7, Croydon South since 1992.

baying colleagues all around, and getting through an anodyne five lines suddenly becomes a stomach-churning ordeal. But my moment of anxiety (which you would not have noticed had you been watching) was as nothing compared with what was to follow.

As I sat down, Michael Mates got up. 'Madam Speaker, This is the third and I trust final resignation statement the House will hear during this session. I did not want to make it. I did not want to resign…' He got off to a predictable start, telling us how much he'd loved his time in Northern Ireland, how grateful he had been to the PM for his support, how he had never sought to plead Asil Nadir's innocence or establish it – then, suddenly, the genial ramble took a more sinister turn as Mates launched himself on what appeared to be a detailed, highly damaging full-scale attack on the Serious Fraud Office. Madam Speaker intervened, warning him off matters that might be sub judice. Mates persisted, accusing the SFO of shady dealings, of underhand operations, of putting 'quite improper pressure' on the trial judge, Mr Justice Tucker. The clerk kept swivelling round in his seat urging the Speaker to get Mates to stop. She tried and tried and tried again. She must have interrupted him eight, nine times. She was angry, she was flustered and she was confused. I don't think she was listening to what he had to say. She was just deter-mined to stop him. But he wouldn't be stopped. On he went. It was agony. I didn't follow everything he was saying – I don't think anyone did – but we got the gist of it: the SFO had been up to no good and someone, somewhere along the line, was intent on per-verting the course of justice. It was a truly bizarre, uncomfortable half-hour.

THURSDAY 15 JULY 1993

It's four o'clock. In the Chamber it's the Welsh Language Bill. At Buckingham Palace there's a garden party. I am bidden to both, but I am going to neither. I've decided instead to spend a couple of hours here in the Silent Room in the Library, catching up. This is my favourite place. When I am no longer an MP being in this room is what I'll miss.

I hardly ever go to my office. It's bright, fresh, modern, equipped with comfy arm-chair and TV, but what's the point of being a member of the House of Commons if you're going to have to base yourself halfway down Millbank? I like to be here and I've got the secretarial set-up sorted now. Jenny [Noll] and Di [Sabin][311] come over to see me here: we sit at a table in the Cromwell Lobby and do the correspondence there.

311   GB's constituency secretary.

The other disadvantage of 7 Millbank is getting from there to here for unexpected votes. There's six minutes from the moment the division bell goes to the moment they slam the doors and unless you move sharpish you're cutting it fine. Last night I cut it fine anyway. I was at the Blue Ball to conduct the auction (they think I love doing it – I *hate* it) and we had to dash back for the vote at ten, setting off from the top of Park Lane at about three minutes to the hour. William Waldegrave gave me a lift, which was good of him, except that he was completely laid back, indifferent as to whether we did or didn't make it in time, while I was having a minor heart attack. He was being very amiable and gossipy (such a pity I wasn't his PPS, poor John Patten is clearly having a complete breakdown etc.) but I couldn't concentrate. All I could think was 'We're going to miss the vote!' In the event, of course, we made it with a couple of minutes to spare.

It turns out John Patten is now in hospital – 'viral gastroenteritis'. As we all know, the PM should have fired him when he had the chance – or, as Stephen says, 'possibly not have appointed him in the first place'. The PM had another rough ride at PMQs. John Smith skewered him fairly comprehensively on Maastricht and the Social Chapter. Norman [Lamont] teased him beautifully with a question congratulating the new Chancellor on 'the rapid success of his policies'. Instead of a gracious and good-humoured response, the PM was curt – giving the impression that Norman had got to him. He looked pretty ashen again. His nerves must be as raw as they come. We're in for another nightmare week.

MONDAY 19 JULY 1993

At 12.15, encouraged by Toby Jessel,[312] who is *so* eccentric I'd have thought him unelectable, I clambered aboard a coach in Speaker's Yard for the ten-minute ride to Victoria. Along with eighty or so fellow parliamentarians of all parties I was on my way to a rather swish Indian restaurant for the annual Indo-British Parliamentary Lunch. Why on earth did I go? The food was splendid, but what was the point? The speeches were inaudible and the room was too crowded. I suppose I went because I was badgered by Toby (whom I like: his loopiness is engaging) and because I have this sentimental feeling about India. But there really wasn't any value to it and it confirmed me in my view that, as a rule, freebies are to be avoided.

I spent the afternoon with the Financial Secretary receiving 'Budget representations' from backbenchers. It's both a relief and a disappointment to find that most of them have as little grip on the detail of the mechanics of managing the economy as I do.

312 MP for Twickenham 1970–97.

There are people who do know their stuff (John Townend,[313] Nigel Forman, Quentin Davies),[314] but most turn up for the meeting wholly unprepared, with nothing thought through, and simply mouth whatever banalities are uppermost in their minds. 'We must do more for manufacturing,' barks Winterton, but precisely what and how (and with what consequential effects) is not addressed.

At A and Q the message is clear: this is the week we back our beleaguered leader to the hilt. Whatever he says, whatever he does, we're here to roar our approval. At Questions we must all get to our feet ready to ask a question even if we know none of us will be called. If only a few get up it makes the PM look isolated. Graham Bright says, 'It makes a real difference to John. He needs to hear people cheering behind him. If John Smith gets a bigger cheer when he comes into the Chamber than John does, he notices. It throws him.'

It is 1.00 a.m. We have just finished a string of votes on the Education Bill. The hapless Education Secretary was not with us, but on Thursday he'll be dragged in from his sickbed. When not voting I've been in the Smoking Room, drinking steadily (yes, and fairly heavily) with Lightbown and Chapman. They are both delightful: one is a hippopotamus, the other a bedraggled secretary bird. Lightbown's loyalty is *fierce* and consequently both impressive and rather moving. Chapman has a real sweetness: he is gentle and funny and frequently tells you the same story twice in the same evening and then realises and apologises most charmingly. His chief task in the Whips' Office seems to be to write the daily 'message' to Her Majesty. He takes this very seriously. Every day, without fail, he writes to the Queen – I think in longhand – a two- or three-page report of our proceedings and it is driven over to the Palace or flown to Balmoral so that the monarch has 'a proper flavour of what's happening here.' Whenever I make a little joke in the Chamber, Sydney comes up afterwards and says, 'I've told the Queen that story of yours. I think she'll like it.'

TUESDAY 20 JULY 1993

I'm just back from the PM's end-of-term party at No. 10. It was one of those disconcerting occasions where everyone seemed to be muttering about the host behind his back. In fact, he was pretty chirpy, almost bouncy. He says he's going to win on Thursday. He's no longer saying that if he loses he goes. That's the line we were getting over the weekend.

313   Chairman of the Conservative Backbench Finance Committee 1992–7; MP for Bridlington 1979–97, East Yorkshire 1997–2001.

314   Member of the Treasury Select Committee since 1972; MP for Stamford & Spalding 1987–97, Grantham & Stamford 1997–2010; he defected to Labour in 2007 and became Baron Davies of Stamford in 2010.

He's now saying – no, not saying, *implying* – that if he loses on Thursday we all go. 'Back me – or I'll call a general election. And then we'll see who survives.'

THURSDAY 22 JULY 1993

This has been an extraordinary day. The PM opened the debate quite brilliantly. He has never been better. He was simple, direct and passionate. We took the decision to join the Community over twenty years ago. It was the right decision. We must make the Community work in Britain's interests. 'I believe the ratification of the Maastricht treaty is in the interests of our country. That is why I signed it.' He built his argument gradually, reasonably, with clarity and conviction. It was a forty-minute tour de force with some happy knockabout along the way. He flattened Ashdown, who was at his most pompous (that's saying something) and who made the mistake of losing his temper. The PM never lost his. He was wonderfully, amazingly relaxed, and, of course, the better it went the better he got. When he sat down at the finish he looked so happy. And we roared our approval and waved our order papers in the air.

At teatime in the Tea Room the feeling was that we'd win. 'If the Unionists come on board we'll be all right.' At 6.30 I had a rendezvous with Phillip Oppenheim. The Chancellor had gone off to an emergency Cabinet meeting, ready to urge the PM to call a confidence vote in the event that we lose tonight. 'Ken just can't believe the party's tearing itself apart like this.'

I went for dinner with petite and elegant Alan Duncan in his petite and elegant house in Gayfere Street. I was sorry to be going because I wanted to eat at the House and keep tabs on developments, but it turned out to be rather jolly. The guest of honour was Lord King,[315] a self-indulgent old monster but good value as these old rogues often are. I asked him what single quality a leader needed most and he twinkled, 'Luck – and energy. His own and other people's.'

We got back to the House for the end of the wind-ups. David Hunt was struggling, but it didn't matter because no one was listening. The place was packed. Everyone was talking at full pitch. You couldn't hear a word – except in the dying moments of his speech we caught David speaking of 'the principles that unite us as members of the Conservative and Unionist Party' – and we thought, '*Yess*, the UUs are on board!'

The first vote was on the opposition amendment – don't ratify the Treaty until we've agreed to accept the Social Chapter. This was the one we expected to win. Why on earth should any Conservative vote with the opposition on this?

---

315 Lord King of Wartnaby from 1983; chairman of British Airways 1981–93.

The lobbies were packed. It was rush hour on the Northern Line. As soon as I'd voted I returned to the Chamber. The PM looked mighty calm. The Chief Whip looked almost relaxed. Other whips wove their way in and out of the throng. Andrew 'snake hips' Mackay[316] was very funny to watch: tan-coloured suit (not quite a gentleman), tanned face (not quite ringing true), he glided smoothly among us, bringing word from the doors of the lobbies back to the front bench. One thing I've learnt: the calmer the whips appear, the more leisurely their stride, the deeper the crisis. And so it proved.

After what seemed an eternity, the result came through, read out by Sydney Chapman (who looked to me as if he hadn't had a drink all evening in recognition of the importance of the occasion): 'Ayes to the Right 317, Noes to the Left 317.' A tie! In accordance with precedent, the Speaker backed the government with her casting vote. Scenting blood – and pints of it – the opposition benches went berserk: cheering, shouting, waving their order papers, slapping one another on the back. There was an eerie silence our side. Immediately we returned to the lobbies for the second vote, this time knowing we were doomed.

Twenty-three of our people voted against us. We lost by eight votes: 316 to 324. The PM was prepared. The moment the result was declared, he was on his feet telling us, quite calmly, that he's tabling a motion of confidence for tomorrow. We start all over again at 9.30 a.m.

What happens now? The good news is that I don't have to go to Chester in the morning; the bad news is that we're really on the ropes. The mood here is mixed. Some (like me perhaps) have secretly rather enjoyed the high drama, can't quite believe it's actually happening. Others, decent, civilised old boys (Terence Higgins, Michael Jopling)[317] are going round shaking their heads in mournful disbelief. A few (Gummer, Fowler, Soames) are telling the rebels what they think of them in no uncertain terms. But you can't reach these people – they're true believers. Cash is demented: he's a monomaniac. Trevor Skeet[318] is a creature from outer space. They believe in what they've done. They think we should be *grateful* to them!

FRIDAY 23 JULY 1993

At breakfast there was much amusement at the discovery that last night the Wintertons were in different lobbies. Ann voted against the government. Nicholas was with us. How come? 'Nick is frantic for a knighthood,' chortled Geoffrey Dickens, 'and our excellent

---

316 In the Whips' Office 1992–7; MP for Birmingham Stetchford 1977–9, Berkshire East 1983–97, Bracknell 1997–2010.

317 MP for Westmorland 1964–83, Westmorland & Lonsdale 1983–97.

318 MP for Willesden East 1959–64, Bedford 1970–83, Bedfordshire North 1983–97.

whips probably promised him one.' The two whips at the table studied their grapefruit and said nothing.

Later, during the debate, Winterton intervened with some fawning observation about the PM's unparalleled commitment to manufacturing and deregulation. I do believe a bauble may indeed have been dangled in front of him. How very funny.

The debate itself was a bit of an anti-climax. It was clear before we started that the rebels were going to come back on side. Norma and James Major [in the gallery] looked on anxiously as the PM set out his stall. He was tired and it showed. The speech was workmanlike, but lacklustre. John Smith, by contrast, sparkled. He was stylish, sarcastic and effective. I intervened on him to no good purpose. (The only point of intervening is either to score a direct hit or to throw the other side off track. I did neither.) Douglas Hurd was good. He did the wind-up: mellow, emollient, patrician, persuasive. 'This is a turning point. We can put behind us the roughness and misfortune of the past year.' He was the genial archdeacon bringing balm and solace to a scratchy congregation. 'The political mood of the country often starts in this House. It takes time to percolate and prevail, but this afternoon we have a chance to change the tone. We have cultivated the land well, despite much rough weather. We have sown good seed. We can now work together to bring in a good harvest.'

With a full turnout on our side, with the lame and the halt on parade, with the rebels back in line and the Unionists sticking with us, we coasted home with a majority of forty. And that's parliament done and dusted till October.

·MONDAY 26 JULY 1993

I don't see how the Prime Minister can struggle on for four more years like this – lurching from shambles to disaster to catastrophe. If it weren't so heartbreaking, it would be very funny.

On Friday, in the afternoon, after the vote, the PM gave a series of television interviews at No. 10, drawing a line under the rancour and divisions of the past year, looking forward to a fresh start and united future. Michael Brunson was interviewing him for ITN. When the interview was over, the lights went down, and the PM and Brunson continued to chat. Unfortunately, the tape was still running … Brunson asked Major about the three Cabinet ministers who threatened to resign if we had ratified the Maastricht Treaty incorporating the Social Chapter.

Major: 'Just think of it from my perspective. You are the Prime Minister with a majority of eighteen, a party that is still harking back to a golden age that never was, and is now invented. You have three right-wing members of the Cabinet who actually resign. What happens in the parliamentary party? … I could bring in replacements, but where do you think most of this poison is coming from? From the dispossessed and the never-possessed. You can think of all sorts of ex-ministers who are going round causing all sorts of trouble. We don't want another three more of the bastards out there. What's Lyndon Johnson's maxim?' Better to have them inside the tent pissing out than outside pissing in…'

What is incredible to me is that the PM should talk like this to any journalist. Of course, Brunson didn't leak it. Brunson's a gent, but even so, isn't the rule *'never* trust a journalist'? The inevitable has happened. The tape has found its way into the public domain and all hell has broken loose. The truce achieved at such cost on Friday is now shattered. And who are the bastards? Portillo, Lilley and Redwood, I suppose. Except that Redwood has only been in the Cabinet five minutes. Could it be Howard? I hope not. Ken Clarke says Howard supported him 100 per cent in urging Major to take the 'thermo-nuclear' option and risk the confidence vote last week.

Anyway, the point is that the only person who can be blamed for this particular gaffe is the PM himself. The nation already knew he led a divided party. Now he has advertised the fact that he heads a divided government. And on Thursday we have a by-election. Oh dear, oh dear, oh dear.

THURSDAY 29 JULY 1993

I was at Downing Street at 9.00 a.m. for the photo call for the World Transplant Games. The PM was in cracking form! We took the pictures on the front doorstep – the PM, me, and assorted folk from the north-west who have survived a variety of transplants and gone on to become athletes – and then, just as we were gushing our thanks and making to leave, the PM said, 'Come on in.' 'Have you got time?' I burbled. 'Of course. Let's see if we can't fix tea or coffee for you all. Would you like to look around?' He took us on a conducted tour, showed us the Cabinet room and took us upstairs for tea. He was easy and charming and simply wowed them. They couldn't believe their good fortune (nor could I) and afterwards kept saying, 'Isn't he nice?' Yes, he is very nice – and that makes me all the more ashamed for thinking some of the things I do about him.

On the way out I stopped and chatted with Tony Newton and Norman Fowler who were on the way in.

'How's it looking for tonight?'[319]

'We're not holding our breath,' said Norman with a nervous giggle. Tony lit another cigarette. He manages to laugh and look dreadfully anxious at the same time.

---

319 A by-election was taking place in Chistchurch, caused by the recent death of Robert Adley, aged fifty-eight, who had been the local MP since 1974.

'The PM's in great shape,' I said.

Tony shook his head, 'He's going to need to be.'

FRIDAY 30 JULY 1993

We have lost Christchurch to the Liberals. Robert Adley's majority of 23,000 has been transformed into a Lib Dem majority of 16,400 – a swing against us of 35 per cent, the biggest anti-government swing since the war.

SUNDAY 1 AUGUST 1993

I am on the train coming back from Cornwall. I went to Falmouth to speak to Seb [Coe]'s people (the usual crowd in the usual school hall – and the usual jokes from me) and stayed the night in Seb and Nicky's tumble-down tucked-away constituency cottage. Seb is truly delightful, so decent, so straight and so loyal. I'd forgotten what it was like to have a baby in the house. I dandled their eleventh-month old girl on my knee and, suddenly, felt happier than I have in weeks. She is perfect, sleeps all night, gurgles all day. We struck up an excellent relationship, blowing bubbles and kisses at one another at bath time, and waving our toast fingers at each other over breakfast.

The papers are full of the PM's woes. The latest MORI poll tells us the public see him as weak, out of touch and poor in a crisis. Teresa Gorman tells us the post-Maastricht truce won't last the month. An anonymous 'senior MP on the right of the party' (Budgen? Tapsell?) is convinced the PM's on the way out: 'I have a feeling he will go suddenly. He has not got the stomach for a sustained fight.'

Tomorrow I begin my book.[320] Tomorrow evening, we're with Pat Hodge[321] at Pizza on the Park. It's going to be a good August, a 'working holiday', at the word processor all day, lots of treats in the evening: plays, films and friends. Four weeks away from politics; four weeks away from the constituency. Heaven.

FRIDAY 20 AUGUST 1993

A good news day. Benet has secured his place at Cambridge, Magdalene College – Pepys'

---

320 *Under the Jumper*, published in November 1993.

321 Actress, friend of GB, appearing in cabaret singing songs by Noel Coward.

college. His parents are very pleased and proud. We celebrated at Tootsies (the young scholar feasted on a double double burger with a fried egg, cheese, bacon and tomato on top) and we're off to *Les Enfants du Paradis*. (Pepys, 330 years ago today, 20 August 1663: 'Up betimes and to my office, having first been angry with my brother John and in the heat of my sudden passion called him Asse and coxcomb, for which I am sorry, it being but for leaving the key of his Chamber within-side of the door ...' When we first got the complete diary I began reading it to Michèle in bed. I never got through more than half a page before she was fast asleep.)

The Chester papers have arrived full of the good news about MBNA [the Maryland Bank of North America]: a £43 million investment at Chester Business Park, promising a thousand new jobs. My hastily faxed press releases – claiming a fair share of the credit for GB and the PM – have paid off. We get good coverage – and deservedly. The taxpayer has coughed up some £7 million in assorted inward investment incentives. I reckon MBNA would have come if the sweetener had only been half as much, but I got a near-hysterical call from Paul Durham [chief executive, Chester City Council] spitting and spluttering that if '*your* government doesn't come up with the money' the whole deal would fall through. Paul's tone needled me. I wanted to say, 'Fuck off, you silly little man', but I didn't. I said, rather petulantly, 'It's not *my* government; whether you like it or not it's *our* government' and added, rather pompously, 'I shall speak to the Prime Minister.' I called Alex Allen at No. 10, and put the case and asked the PM both to take a personal interest and to write a personal letter to MBNA saying how Britain in general, and Chester in particular, wanted – really wanted – MBNA. The PM obliged. (That is the joy of our system. Every member of the government is a Member of Parliament. Every MP has ready access to every minister. Time it right, pitch it right, don't try it too often, and you can cut through the bureaucracy and go straight to the top.)

The Chester press for the PM is good. The national press is less encouraging. Cecil Parkinson has gone into print with an energetic denunciation of a 'terrible twelve months' of drift and dither. The voters 'feel let down, even betrayed.' Thank you, Cecil.

SATURDAY 11 SEPTEMBER 1993

This is so terrible I don't want to write it down. I don't want to see the words on the page. Simon [Cadell] is going to die.

We were in the kitchen having lunch. The phone went. Michèle answered. It was Simon. 'You're going to have to be brave, darling. I'm in the Harley Street clinic. It's not good news. I'm riddled with cancer. It could be just a matter of days. Of course, I'll want Gyles to do the address at the service. We must talk about that.' He was so matter-of-fact and brave and several times he tried to be funny. When we had both talked to him (and been wonderfully British and brave too) we put down the phone and stood in the kitchen clinging onto one another, sobbing uncontrollably. It is so awful. I don't know what to say.

TUESDAY 14 SEPTEMBER 1993

I am on the 8.30 a.m. flight from Manchester to Heathrow. I flew up yesterday afternoon for the Bingo Evening at the Sealand Deaf Centre. The flying trip to play bingo with around thirty-five frail folk of riper years will have cost the taxpayer several hundred pounds, but there we are.

Simon's got it into his head that the press vultures are circling and word is going to get out. We are drafting a press statement to pre-empt them.

He is being so brave and funny. A nurse whipped back the bedclothes to give him an injection. 'Just a little prick,' she said. Simon looked at her indignantly: 'There's no need to be insulting.'

FRIDAY 17 SEPTEMBER 1993

The Harley Street Clinic put out the statement yesterday. Simon is the lead story on several front pages. 'I am dying says Hi-de-Hi star Simon' is the main headline in the *Mirror*, reducing the political story of the hour to a single column:

> Major knifes Lamont as No. 10 crisis deepens. John Major came close to calling
> Norman Lamont a liar last night as the Premier's leadership crisis deepened. He
> hit back at his former friend's claim that only bad leadership was holding Britain
> back by labelling him 'disingenuous' – parliamentary language for lying.

It is so strange to see pictures of my best friend staring out at me like this, stills of his funny, lovely, lopsided face, alongside these stark headlines. It's an odd (macabre) thing to say, but I think he'll be quite pleased with the coverage.

I wonder who Mr Major's best friend is? It was never Lamont. Norman managed his leadership campaign, but I don't believe they were ever especially close. They were colleagues and allies, but it was a friendship of convenience. Norman is bitter because he feels betrayed. This time last year he offered to resign. Major said 'I'm not going to, you shouldn't either'. Norman believed he was safe because the PM told him he was safe. That's why he feels betrayed. He *was* betrayed. That's politics.

And I'm going to lose Simon. That's life. And I can't bear it.

SUNDAY 19 SEPTEMBER 1993

I'm on the 8.30 flight to Heathrow. I came up for the Cheshire Regiment officers' association dinner, a generous spread and good people. I sat next to Lt Col Bob Stewart,[322] hero of Bosnia. He's attractive but strange, a little overweight, possibly a little too ready to believe his own publicity. I liked him, but I can see why the MoD is wary of him. He has all the qualities to take him to the top – energy, intelligence, courage, achievement – but there's something there that isn't quite right. A perversity, a devil, something. His speech was a bit all over the place, which surprised me, but I liked his line: 'Gentlemen, my rule is this. If there's a battle, go towards it.'

Michèle is meeting me at Heathrow. We are going straight to the Harley Street Clinic and then on to lunch with Stevie and Jo.

FRIDAY 1 OCTOBER 1993

According to the latest opinion poll, 92 per cent of the population oppose the imposition of VAT on domestic fuel. We do not seem *quite* to be marching in step with the people. The Labour Party on the other hand ... Tony Benn has just been voted off Labour's national executive after thirty-four years and, largely thanks to a wonderfully passionate speech by John Prescott, John Smith has won his battle to reform Labour's links with the trade unions. They've discovered the will to win while we don't seem to be able to get our sticky fingers off the button marked 'self-destruct'.

I am on my way to Liverpool to address the Merseyside Conservative Ladies at the Adelphi. I have the draft of the Chancellor's conference speech with me, and as whatever I say will go completely unreported, I'm going to try it out on the good women of Merseyside. (I've got a couple of extra gags for him and I'm going to be going more softly on the VAT on fuel section. He wants to bang on about 'why we must carry it through'. This could provoke jeers on the day and be a hostage to fortune. Whether the policy is right or wrong, if we can't muster the support for it in the House a retreat will become inevitable.)

An earthquake in India has killed 10,000, which should put the Chancellor's troubles in perspective.

---

322 Commander, 1st Battalion, Cheshire Regiment, 1991–6; MP for Beckenham since 2010.

WEDNESDAY 6 OCTOBER 1993

At 6.30 I turned up at the conference hotel 'autocue room' to rehearse the Chancellor's speech with him. Ken knows this sort of thing is necessary, but he can't bring himself to take it seriously. Just as he gets to the podium and is set to start, in comes Jeffrey Archer. It seems that *he* is expecting to rehearse the Chancellor. Ken reads the script. He isn't a natural orator and he isn't any good at reading a script either. He manages to emphasise all the wrong words and he puts over the jokes in a curious one-note sing-song without any inflexion at the finish so the audience has no idea if this is the point at which to laugh. I don't say any of this – or indeed anything – because Jeffrey is saying all that needs to be said, and more. KC reads a chunk and pauses. Jeffrey offers his critique. He's so joyously bombastic, so cocksure it's terribly funny. KC turns to me, 'What do you think, Gyles?' 'I think Jeffrey's spot on and you are quite brilliant, Chancellor.' There's no point in saying anything else.

When our time was up, Jeffrey sailed off, very pleased with his endeavours, the Chancellor, chuckling, rolled away in search of a pint, and I made my way to some South Ribble backwater called Grimsargh where I was doing a turn for Nigel Evans.[323] It went rather well: they liked the jokes and the answers to the questions came easily. For what it's worth (which isn't much in the wastes of Lancashire on a wet Wednesday night), I felt I'd hit my stride.

THURSDAY 7 OCTOBER 1993

A long day. I drove up to Blackpool in time to be on the platform for the Chancellor's speech. He is *such* a nice guy, chuckling nervously in the wings as we waited to go on, chortling with relief when it was over. He paid absolutely no regard to anything that Jeffrey or I had said at the rehearsal. He just did it as he'd have done it anyway, and it worked. The troops rose to his rallying cry: 'Any enemy of John Major is my enemy. Any enemy of John Major is no friend of the Conservative Party.' And, despite my misgivings, he got through the passage on VAT and fuel without interruption.

Even more remarkable was that I got through my lunchtime address to the Ulster Conservatives without embarrassment. I don't quite know how I came to let myself in for it. I simply hadn't thought it through. The invitation came and I said yes and it wasn't until I arrived at St John's Church and saw it surrounded by police that I began to register that Northern Ireland is one of those delicate issues that require deft handling and

---

323 MP for Ribble Valley since 1992.

a sure touch! Anyway, I nailed my Unionist colours to the mast, hoped I was taking the government line, and appeared to get away with it.

Michèle arrived for our party at the Savoy (the *Blackpool* Savoy) – nuts, crisps, an open bar and a motley crew of activists from Cheshire, Kent and Kingston, with GB, Alastair Goodlad, Jonathan Aitken and Norman Lamont as an equally motley crew of co-hosts. Norman feels he's had a good week. He's certainly had plenty of coverage. He wants to see a further £5 billion cut in public expenditure. KC said to me, 'Do ask Norman where we're going to find it.' I think he feels we could make cuts in health and education. That's a political impossibility. Indeed, much of what we might like to do is a political impossibility.

We then went on to the Conference Ball where I conducted a knockabout auction and the PM spoke informally to the troops. I think he's at his best off the cuff. He was surprisingly relaxed and fresh. We talked about tomorrow's speech. Stephen [Dorrell] has produced reams of ideas, none of which are going to be used. Clearly they're still dithering as to whether or not to mount a full-scale assault on the 'fringe lunatics'. I said, 'If you attack the people causing the divisions you make them the focus of the headlines. The Chancellor has done the call for unity.'

'Yes, wasn't he good? Isn't he good?' The PM trusts KC. He is right to.

'Mrs T. has called for unity,' I added.

The PM gave me one of his blank stares, with the hint of a raised eyebrow. 'If you do another call for unity, that'll end up as the story. "Prime Minister pleads for unity". What we want from you is the core message. "What I believe. Here I stand".' I think that's what we're going to get.

FRIDAY 8 OCTOBER 1993

'Let me tell you what I believe … It is time to return to the old core values. Time to get back to basics. To self-discipline and respect for the law. To consideration for others. To accepting responsibility for yourself and your family, and not shuffling it off on the State. Madam President, I believe that what this country needs is not less Conservatism. It is more Conservatism… It is time to return to our roots.'

It went down wonderfully well. He did it wonderfully well. I watched it cocooned inside the Channel 4 commentary box, surrounded by professional cynics, but even they had to concede that he'd touched a chord with the faithful. They don't adore him as they adored Thatcher, but they love him and they share his nostalgic longing for Miss Marple's England.

When it was over we met up with Peter Lilley and drove him to Chester for the reception at the International. Clearly, the right feel they've had a good week. Portillo has told the PM he mustn't appear to be all things to all men. Peter has called for the return of 'conviction politics'. The espousal of 'core values' is just what Mrs T. wants to hear. The mood music certainly suggests a shift to the right, but Clarke and Hurd and Heseltine aren't worried. They have nothing to fear: they know that, whatever the rhetoric, Major shares their instincts.

In his dry/shy way Peter did us proud at our gathering of the local business community and then raced off with Michèle to catch the train from Crewe. Because he was on party, not government, business there was no ministerial car, and she said he cut rather a pathetic figure struggling up the lane to the station, lead-lined ministerial box in one hand, overnight bags in the other. It was the last train, so no buffet, and he made it with only seconds to spare. He'll get in to London after midnight. He's due on the *Today* programme at 7.00 a.m. It's a punishing life.

The Chester troops are in high spirits, not just a good conference but, better still, a full spread featuring our 'Summer Soirée' in the 'Mr Society' pages of *Cheshire Life*! This is what they want and what, on the whole, I fail to deliver. (My only recollection of the evening is of how we all stared frantically into our coffee cups as Cecil Parkinson told a never-ending story about a serial adulterer and a bicycle. Lady P. maintained a brave grimace throughout.)

MONDAY 18 OCTOBER 1993

As Mrs T. launches her memoirs, she tells us the PM is now back on 'the true path' and rejoices. At Drinks in the Lower Whips' Office, we turn our minds to lower things: Steve Norris[324] and his *five* mistresses. We are full of admiration. It is amazing – and amusing – apparently Mrs Norris knew what was going on, it was the mistresses who were unaware of one another – but utterly maddening for No. 10. 'Back to basics' was never supposed to be about sexual morality. Jonathan Hill tells me, 'It hasn't backfired. We're sticking with it. This Norris nonsense will blow over. It's a nine-day wonder. People wanted the PM to have a theme. Returning to our core values is his theme and he's sticking with it. It's working for us.'

Iain Sproat wants me to meet with him and officials at the DNH to talk about violence on TV. 'The PM believes there's too much violence on TV. It desensitises people. We must do something about it.'

Agreed. But what?

---

324 MP for Oxford East 1983–7, Epping Forest 1988–97.

FRIDAY 22 OCTOBER 1993

I'm on the train from Derby to Crewe. I travelled to Derby with Edwina [Currie]. I like her, but I'm not sure that anybody else does. In the Tea Room, she's the easy butt of every joke. In the Chamber, she speaks well, with conviction and authority, but no one seems to rate her. Perhaps it's because she behaves like a man – she interrupts, she's loud, she's opinionated. I asked her why she turned down the chance to be in government again. 'Who'd want to be Prisons Minister? And I couldn't stand working for Ken Clarke again. He's impossible.' (I wonder how she'd have done as Prisons Minister. In the Tea Room queue, lining up for our lunchtime salads, David Maclean[325] told me that drugs are now endemic in our prisons – in every prison – and there's nothing we can do about it. Try to clear out the drugs and you'd have riots in every gaol in the land. With Edwina as Prisons Minister we might well have had riots in every gaol in the land...)

At Westminster, the right despise her, the old buffers regard her as a vulgar parvenu, and her natural allies, the Euro-enthusiasts, don't love her as they might because she steals their limelight, treads on their toes. Happily, in South Derbyshire, where I've been doing my turn on her behalf, she seems genuinely quite popular. I'd half thought of trying to get out of going because today's the day Mrs T. is in Chester, talking about her book at the Gateway Theatre, and they'd asked me to chair the session. In the event, I decided I'd better stick by Edwina and they've got Nick Winterton fawning on Mrs T. instead.

THURSDAY 28 OCTOBER 1993

At lunch the Chancellor is in expansive mood – literally. Glass of wine in one hand, cheroot in the other, he tells us he's ruling out early independence for the Bank of England, leans back with a contented sigh and a button bursts from his overstretched shirtfront, wings its way past Portillo's ear and gently pings against a Treasury chandelier. Silence falls. We're not sure whether to laugh. This is the Chancellor of the Exchequer after all. The team look down at the table, the Chancellor giggles, and we carry on as if nothing has happened.

He has given the Bank greater operational independence – they can publish their inflation report without Treasury approval now – and he may go further in due course, but clearly complete independence is a way down the road. Lamont is advocating it now

---

325 MP for Penrith & the Border 1983–2010; later Baron Blencathra.

(as is Lawson), but I imagine KC sees merit in the final say on interest rates remaining in the hands of the elected politician who can take his own instincts as well as the statistics into account ... especially, of course, when KC is the elected politician in question.

What nonsense it all is. Yesterday we were here till two in the morning struggling through the Lords' amendments to the Railways Bill. Since it took five hours to get through barely fifty out of a total of 500, Tony Newton moved a guillotine motion to put a timetable to the proceedings. Uproar followed and tonight Labour mavericks have been seeking their revenge by lurking in the lavatories in the division lobbies so as to delay/obstruct/derail the votes. At about half past nine we were plodding through our lobby during the fifth division of the night when Greg Knight[326] suddenly pounced on me.

'Get back in there.'

'What?'

'Get back into the Chamber now.'

'Why?'

'You've got to make a point of order. Complain about the delaying tactics. Get the Speaker to order the Serjeant At Arms to clear the lobbies. *Now.*'

When the whip speaks, you move. I stumbled into the Chamber, where all was chaos, several hundred people milling all over the shop. I said to the whip on the front bench, 'I've been told to make a point of order.'

'You'll need the hat.'

'What?'

'Get him the hat.'

A collapsible black silk opera hat was produced from the clerk's table.

'Put it on, stay seated and catch the Speaker's eye.'

During a division the rule is that you can only speak when 'seated and covered'. Don't ask me why. I suppose it's so you can be easily spotted. I donned the ludicrous top hat, feeling quite as foolish as I must have looked, and made my protest. Would the Deputy Speaker call the Serjeant At Arms to clear the lobbies and note the names of those members who were causing the obstruction? No, he would not.

Immensely relieved, I sat back and took off the hat. The whip on the front bench whisked round and hissed. 'Put it back on. Try again. Go on. *Go on.* Now, man, *now.*'

On went the hat once more. I made a further protest, again to no effect. I passed the

---

326   In the Whips' Office 1989–96, Deputy Chief Whip 1993–6; MP for Derby North 1983–97, East Yorkshire since 2001.

hat back to the whip. Someone called for it from the other side of the Chamber. It was flung over to Ernie Ross,[327] tossed like a Frisbee. Then back it came to James Paice. Then it went shooting over to Mark Robinson.[328] It whizzed here and there around the Chamber like a ludicrous flying saucer. Suddenly it disappeared and John Marshall[329] was calling for attention. We turned to look at him and there he was, the Honourable Member for Hendon, Parliamentary Private Secretary to the Lord President of the Council, seated in the Chamber of the House of Commons with a knotted hanky on his head.

It's nearly two in the morning and I'm going home, but I just wanted posterity to know how we conduct our business here.

THURSDAY 11 NOVEMBER 1993

Lunch with Jeffrey [Archer] and half a dozen new boys at Jeffrey's flat. The view is fabulous. The host is generous. His great strength is his loyalty. He is gung-ho for the PM without equivocation. He thinks the PM's initiative on Northern Ireland could transform his premiership. Others are more cynical. 'You can't go wrong with a peace initiative. If it succeeds, you're a hero. If it fails, at least you were brave enough to try...'

Under the Jumper is published today. The House of Commons Librarian has sent me a note explaining that it is a custom of the House for members to present a signed copy for the Library's 'special collection'. Clearly knowing nothing about my wild and woolly past, she assumes the title is based on a line of T. S. Eliot and calls the book *Under the Juniper* ... I enjoyed writing it, but I don't think it's going to enjoy quite the success of *The Downing Street Years*. (Evidently I was right to avoid Mrs T. in Chester. The locals are up in arms about the cost of the visit and the disruption caused. The Police Authority is considering sending her publishers a bill for £26,000 to cover the security costs involved and today's postbag contains a hoity-toity letter from one of my activists: 'I would have been very sorry to see you with even a walk-on role in the Thatcher circus. Lord Home of the Hirsel is the proper role model for all former Prime Ministers.')

A sobering letter today too from Sir John Page:[330]

> We met at the Harrow West lunch where I much enjoyed meeting you and listening to your speech. May an elder nobody put a, no, two thoughts in your mind?

---

327 Labour MP for Dundee West 1979–2005.

328 MP for Newport West 1983–87, Somerton & Frome 1992–97.

329 MEP for London North 1979–89; MP for Hendon South 1987–97.

330 MP for Harrow 1960–87.

John Peyton once said to me: 'The reason you never became a minister is that you make people laugh and then they don't take you seriously.' And, in about 1962, Harold Macmillan said to Bill Van Straubenzee and me, after a wind-up speech by Harold Wilson:

'What did you think of Wilson's speech?'

'Brilliant. Marvellous. So witty,' we said.

'No good,' said he, 'Make more than two jokes and you become a turn.'

So … work hard at trying to be dull! What awful advice – but well-meant by a new well-wisher.

MONDAY 15 NOVEMBER 1993

John Major will relaunch his faltering 'back to basics' initiative tonight by distancing himself from calls to cut back on welfare payments to single mothers. Amid signs that senior ministers are becoming alarmed that the Prime Minister's social agenda is in danger of being bogged down in a political quagmire, Mr Major will turn the spotlight to his policies on education and law and order. We're promised a new Criminal Justice Bill (the fifth in eight years), a Police Bill, and another Education Bill (the seventh in eight years). A full, fat legislative programme is going to be unveiled on Thursday and, according to Sarah Hogg[331] and Jonathan Hill, every element of it will 'go with the grain of our people'.

I suggested to the PM that less-legislation-not-more could be part of the back to basics programme. People are suffering from change-fatigue. We are going to have a Deregulation Bill essentially to undo all the unnecessary regulations *we* have introduced! Why not revisit the good old Tory adage, 'When it is not necessary to change, it is necessary not to change'? His eyes glazed over. A government that isn't busy-busy-busy is perceived to have run out of steam.

The truth is there's too much legislation, inadequately prepared, pushed through in too great haste. There was a good piece on all this by Anthony King[332] last week. He noted that on John Patten's last Education Bill there were 278 government amendments introduced during the Commons committee stage, 78 more on report, 258 more during the Lords committee stage, 296 more on report and 71 at third reading. King reckons this mania for legislation began with Thatcher. Action, revolution, change, never let up, never stop. 'I tinker, therefore I am.' King quotes Bagehot[333] with approval: 'If you are

---

331 Head of the Policy Unit at No. 10 1990–95; later Baroness Hogg.

332 Author and commentator, Professor of Government at the University of Essex.

333 Walter Bagehot, 1829–77, author of *The English Constitution*, 1867.

always altering your house, it is a sign either that you have a bad house or that you have an excessively restless disposition – there is something wrong somewhere.'

WEDNESDAY 24 NOVEMBER 1993

Last night I spoke in the debate on the Queen's Speech. I was called at 8.20 p.m. when all sensible people should be (and were) elsewhere, feeding their faces. Janet Fookes,[334] bird-like and motherly, was gently clucking in the chair, John Patten flounced and bounced on the front bench, and I think I counted a total of six other lonely souls dotted about the Chamber. They weren't there to hear my words of wisdom, of course: they were simply waiting to offer their own. Why did I speak? Because I had something to say? Yes, oddly enough. Was anyone listening? No. Will anyone read it in Hansard? No. Was there any point to it? None at all – except that someone's got to speak because the whips believe they've got to keep the whole thing going till 10.00 p.m. regardless – even on a night like last night when there isn't going to be a vote. Naturally, I can – and have – done a press release based on what I said, but you don't have to go through the rigmarole of putting in to speak and hanging around for hours to make your ten-minute contribution to get a paragraph in the *Chester Chronicle*. Regularly I do press releases beginning, 'Gyles Brandreth said in the House of Commons today…' meaning that I dictated the words to my secretary in the purlieus of the House of Commons.

At prayers this morning I told the Chancellor that I'd been advocating a brief Budget statement. 'The recovery is coming along nicely, we've had some encouraging figures, we had a very full Budget earlier in the year, steady as she goes – thank you very much.'

He laughed. 'I think you're going to be disappointed. It could be the fattest Finance Bill on record. You and Stephen [Dorrell] are going to enjoy that.'

'As long as it doesn't include VAT on reading.'

He disappeared inside a cloud of cigar smoke. 'What about newspapers?'

Oppenheim looked up from the *Financial Times*. 'You could hardly describe VAT on *The Sun* as a tax on knowledge.'

SATURDAY 27 NOVEMBER 1993

Last night I went to Enfield to speak for Michael Portillo. They treat him like a god. He

---

334 Second deputy chairman of Ways and Means (one of the Deputy Speakers) 1992–97; MP for Merton & Morden 1970–74, Plymouth Drake 1974–97. Later Baroness Fookes.

comes into the room and the crowds part like the Red Sea. He walks among them without *hauteur* but with a complete assurance, an absolute acceptance of the fact that they are the worshippers and he is the worshipped one. All this – in Enfield!

I've just come from doing *Loose Ends*.[335] Without warning Ned [Sherrin] got me to tell the Queen Mary story and I stumbled through it because I couldn't remember the pay-off. (As Kenneth [Williams] used to say, 'For gawd's sake, don't tell a story unless you can get the bloody tag right. It's all in the *tag*.') The story starts with George V out walking in the garden of Buckingham Palace and asking why his customary equerry was not in attendance. He is told the man is unwell. 'What's wrong with him?' asks the king. 'Oh, you know, sir, the universal complaint…' Next day, Queen Mary remarks to someone, 'I hear His Majesty's equerry is ill. What is the matter with him?' 'A bad attack of haemorrhoids, I'm afraid, ma'am.' 'Oh,' says the queen, 'Why did the king tell me it was the clap?'

As I write I'm in the plane flying to Manchester. Because we signed our wills this week, because the insurance means that I'm worth a lot more dead than alive, because the children are virtually grown up, because I've ticked off my little list of footling ambitions, because Simon is dying, I suddenly realise I've lost my fear of flying. If the plane falls out of the sky, so be it. I don't want to die, but I'm not frightened in the way I used to be. I used to be *terrified*. Now, here I am, drinking my British Airways coffee, feeling childishly pleased because I've secured my favourite front row seat, feeling (dare I say it) *happy*. (Michèle says I dare not say it. She never lets herself feel happy because she knows the moment she lets her guard down, the moment she allows herself fleetingly to feel relaxed, the moment she thinks for a second 'Well, things aren't too bad', *disaster* strikes.) I am even ready for what Chester has to offer this weekend: the dinner dance at Upton Golf Club, my quarterly meeting with the farmers tomorrow, Sunday lunch with Anne, Duchess of Westminster as guest of honour. (She's wonderful value: a game old bird, with a deep-deep voice, a low-slung bosom and a big heart. She has no idea who I am, but so long as she's got a fag on the go and there's plenty of G in the G&T, she's the easiest company in the world.)

....

WEDNESDAY 1 DECEMBER 1993
....

A long forty-eight hours. To secure my rightful place behind the Chancellor for the Budget, I turned up at the Commons at 7.00 a.m. yesterday morning to join the queue. The Chamber opens at eight, when we fools rush in, armed with our little green prayer cards and bag our favourite places. By tradition Dame Elaine Kellett-Bowman[336] (knocking seventy)

---

335 GB was appearing on Ned Sherrin's BBC Radio 4 programme to promote his new book.
336 MP for Lancaster 1970–97; MEP for Cumbria 1979–84.

is always at the front of the line. She brings a sleeping bag and a portable bed which she parks outside the door to the Chamber and she spends the night there, sleeping in the shadow of the statues of Churchill and Lloyd George. By the time I arrived there were about forty ahead of me, some standing, some squatting, quite a few with chairs they'd brought from nearby offices, and the line stretched back from the Chamber across member's lobby through the swing door towards Central Lobby.

The Budget itself was a triumph for KC. It was a delicious, teasing, playful performance. He is a wonderful operator and such a likeable man. He's had a superb press: 'A Budget for economic and political recovery' says *The Times*. 'No smoke, no mirrors, just loads of chutzpah' says Anatole Kaletsky. And so say all of us – though the Chancellor said to me last night, 'It's a golden rule – a Budget that's acclaimed on the day doesn't fare so well in retrospect. Let's not get too cheerful too soon. Wait till they've read the small print.'

I think I'm weary through a surfeit of duchesses. I was on the bench till gone ten, not in bed till gone midnight, then up at dawn to fly to Manchester for the Waterstones's Literary Lunch. The line-up was Trevor McDonald,[337] Lt Col Bob Stewart, Fergie and me. Fergie[338] spoke surprisingly well: she'd worked on her material, had several pages of notes written out in a large and loopy hand. She rather overdid her undying devotion to the present Queen and her grovelling gratitude for Her Majesty's sustained and unstinting kindness to her, and I imagine her claims to have some sort of spiritual connection with Queen Victoria has the widow of Windsor spinning in her grave (and the likes of Lord Charteris positively spitting), but she was eager and good-hearted and nicely flirtatious in a gosh-golly-girls-in-the-dorm kind of way, and I liked her – especially because she gave me a copy of her book and bought three copies of mine.

'What's the worst thing about being royal?'

'When you meet them, people remember what you say. And when you meet them for the second time, years later, they say, "You don't remember me, do you?" I *hate* that.'

I was planning to come back by train because it was going to be easier for me from Euston. 'No,' she said, 'Come on the plane.'

'I haven't got a ticket.'

'I've got two tickets.'

'Why?'

'Just in case! I always get two … you never know.'

I imagine the money's pouring away. She bought several copies of everybody's books. She gushed and gladhanded and *yearned* to be wanted and liked and loved. Colonel Bob

---

337 Newsreader and journalist.

338 The Duchess of York was promoting her book based on the journals and travels of Queen Victoria.

did his best to imply an established intimacy. ('Yes, Sarah, I'll call you.' It *has* all gone to his head.) Trevor and I settled for a new friendship and, while I imagine our hoots and giggles and guffaws will have been immensely irritating to our fellow passengers, we rather enjoyed the flight home.

As a consequence of being seduced onto the plane, I arrived late for the charity do at St James's Palace. They were already *à table*. I went to apologise to our hostess, the Duchess of Gloucester, knelt at her side and said 'I'm so sorry I'm late.' She was not amused. I compounded my *lèse-majesté*, by telling her (as Fergie insisted I should, absolutely insisted, 'You must, please, please. I don't see any of them now and I don't want to be frozen out') that I'd spent the day with the Duchess of York and 'Sarah particularly asked to be remembered to you.' The Danish duchess said nothing, nothing at all, frowned ever-so-slightly to get her 'Who do you think you are?' message across, and returned her attention to her plate.

I should have remembered that she's not an easy ride. At the Roy Miles Gallery, at a private view, somehow we'd been left alone in the middle of a quite small room. I'd struggled with the small talk long enough. She was saying nothing: I had nothing more to say. I moved slightly closer to her and, while I burbled some inanity in her ear, behind her back I frantically gestured to Michèle to come and rescue me. Suddenly I realised that Her Royal Highness was gazing over my left shoulder into the mirror that was facing her. She was staring at the awful reflection of me frantically waving – and drowning.

WEDNESDAY 8 DECEMBER 1993

Last night at the Foreign Office party, in the newly refurbished and quite splendid Durbar Room, I met up with Liza Manningham-Buller, whom I last saw when she played the Fairy Queen in my production of *Cinderella* at Oxford twenty-six years ago. She seemed remarkably unchanged, except that I gather she's now one of our most senior spies, destined to be, if not already, the head of MI6.[339] Extraordinary.

Tonight we're voting on Sunday trading. I'm voting for total deregulation. I like these free votes. It is a relief now and again to be able to make up one's own mind – even if, as in this case, my vote is going to upset the churches, M&S, and the small shopkeepers in Chester. Never mind. For once I shall do what I believe to be right and hang the consequences. There's got to be *some* point to being an MP. (People are quite shocked when you admit that most of the time most MPs have no idea what they're voting about. They just walk into the lobby where they see one of their whips standing and that's that.)

---

339 In fact, she became Director General of MI5, 2002–7; later Baroness Manningham-Buller of Northampton.

TUESDAY 14 DECEMBER 1993

The Treasury Christmas lunch was a fairly hard slog. The Financial Secretary entertained his team at Joe Allen's, which was an ideal venue because the din and clatter were so great no one could hear anybody and the fact that nobody seemed to have much to say to anybody consequently didn't matter. Stephen [Dorrell] is delightful, I like him more and more, but slumming it with the troops, small talk with the secretaries, seasonal banter with the lower ranks – these are not his forte. They are the sort of thing Mr Major does better than anybody. He (the PM) came to mingle with his men in the Tea Room this afternoon and did well. He's engrossed in the Northern Ireland business and both his commitment and grasp of detail are impressive. He was busy sending out signals to reassure the UUs, he reiterated his line that having to deal with Gerry Adams[340] would 'make his stomach turn', but he concedes there's been a 'chain of communication' between the government and the IRA for years and there's no doubt, before too long, we'll be talking to the terrorists face to face. What happens to our fragile majority then?

MONDAY 27 DECEMBER 1993

We are in Framlingham with Simon and Beckie [Cadell]. Simon seems to be in much better shape. Beckie is a saint. The boys [their young sons] are amazing. They do their own thing, watch TV, play with the computer, scamper about outside, leaving us to get on with the serious business of working our way through Simon's cellar. 'We don't know how long I've got,' says Simon, in his best Ralph Richardson voice, dropping a splash or two of *pêche* into our mid-morning champagne, 'so we'd better get on with it, eh cockie?'

We've had a merry Christmas. I imagine the PM was feeling relatively festive too – until yesterday when the *News of the World* brought us its latest world exclusive. Tim Yeo,[341] our Minister for the Environment and the Countryside, has a love child! Michèle has been against him since she saw him lolling on the front bench with his feet up against the despatch box. 'Arrogant sod.' I tried to explain that they all sit like that. 'No they don't. Mr Major doesn't. I tell you: Tim Yeo's an arrogant bastard. The sooner he goes the better.'

According to today's papers, the Prime Minister is taking a more charitable view. He is standing by his man. 'Minister with love child wins Major support.' 'This is a purely private matter,' says PM. Oh yes?

---

340 President of Sinn Fein since 1983; Sinn Fein MP for Belfast West 1983–92 and 1997–2011.

341 MP for Suffolk South since 1983.

THURSDAY 30 DECEMBER 1993

Yesterday: lunch with the Hanleys. Jeremy told a funny story. Pretty young diary secretary comes in to see her minister.

Secretary: Well, Minister, there's good news and bad news.

Minister: Give me the good news.

Secretary: You're not infertile.

Jeremy is loving the MoD. He rates Rifkind highly, he's wary of Aitken. They're both (Jeremy & Verna) quite seduced by the PM. People who get close to him invariably are. We went to John Schlesinger's new flat last night. He thinks Major is quite wonderful too. Close up, the PM has a charm that disarms, that positively seduces. The flat is fabulous (an unexpectedly spacious duplex perched at the top of a single mansion block on the Gloucester Road) and the evening was very jolly. Eileen [Atkins] & Bill [Shepherd], Twiggy, Albert Finney and co. Noel[342] was so funny. The stories just keep tumbling out – the old favourites and always one or two someone hasn't heard before. The Gurkha story, which I love, seemed new to one and all.[343]

I doubt there'll be much of that kind of humour *here*. We're in Ablemont, in Normandy, staying in what I'm choosing to call 'the valley of the Lilleys'. It's a bourgeois house, not grand but solid, surrounded by farm buildings in the middle of nowhere. Peter and Gail escape here whenever they can. They say they just 'hop over'. It took us rather longer to reach than that. We got to Folkestone to find the crossing cancelled. We moved on to Dover where they warned us the Channel was fairly choppy. This turned out to be something of an understatement. (Already we are dreading the return journey on Sunday.) It's an odd party – Michael Brown, the Chopes,[344] Peter Oborne[345] (I am always wary when there's a hack in the house) – but we're promised plenty of wine, candles when the lights go (which apparently they will – they always do), no party hats but civilised parlour games. On the sideboard in the dining room there's an elegant glass bowl engraved with a playful inscription to 'The Bastards'. We arrived as night was falling, to see Peter through the window, sitting at his laptop, engrossed. What was he doing? 'Looking for ways to reduce the social security bill.' It is good to be spending New Year with the most *thoughtful* member of the government.

---

342 Noel Davis, casting director, friend of GB.

343 It's the story of the flighty lady at the military cocktail party who was introduced to a colonel in the Gurkhas and burst out, 'Oh, goodness, Colonel, you've quite taken me aback. You're *white*. I thought all you Gurkhas were black.' 'No,' said the colonel, 'only our privates are black.' 'Oh,' gasped the lady, 'how thrilling!'

344 Christopher Chope, MP for Southampton Itchen 1983–92, Christchurch since 1997, and his wife Christine.

345 Journalist.

CHAPTER V

1994

Back with a vengeance! The 7.25 a.m. train from Euston. This morning: the Unicef photocall, followed by a session at Birch Cullimore, local solicitors, to be told how we've got it all wrong – we're alienating the lawyers, Mackay's a disaster (and, worse, a Scot),[346] the Crown Prosecution Service is packed with second-raters and the country is being asphyxiated by pettifogging regulation. This afternoon: a briefing from the Chester Greens (I am their friend), a visit to the British Heart Foundation shop in Frodsham Street (I am their friend too), a session with the Chief Executive at County Hall – I am even ready to be his friend. (He's an easier ride than his counterpart at the Town Hall. He's a smoother, more effective operator. Of course, they both know that at Westminster no one is interested in local government, no one at all.) This evening: the 'Younger Women's Supper Club at the Chester Rows. They are adamant: 'Tim Yeo must go. Pass it on.'

THURSDAY 6 JANUARY 1994

Sometimes I feel I lead a double life. Not quite like Mr Yeo. I have no secret love child. But a double life in the sense that who I am in Chester, what I am, where I go, who I meet, how I spend my time, is so different there from here. I don't have the contempt for my constituents and party activists Alan Clark[347] clearly had for his. On the whole, I rather like them, and I want them to like me, but the truth is, while Tuesday evening with the Younger Women was fine, it wasn't very *interesting*. And we only pass this way once. Let's face it, last night was more my idea of a good time. We went to *She Stoops to Conquer*. Donald Sinden was

---

346 James Mackay, Lord Mackay of Clashfern since 1979; Lord Chancellor 1987–97.

347 1928–1999; MP for Plymouth Sutton 1974–92, Kensington & Chelsea 1997–9; GB had been reading Clark's *Diaries*.

magnificent: outrageous but still real (just) with a fantastic bit of business that had him forever glancing back at his heel because he'd caught something unpleasant on his shoe. It was a joy. We went on to supper at the Ivy: Donald, Diana [Mrs Sinden], Simon, Beckie [Cadell], Joanna [Lumley]. We were joined by Richard Gere who walked across the tables – on top of the tables – to reach us. Simon looked so happy and Don was so funny, saying:

> A young actor, playing his first Hamlet, wanting to understand the relationship between the moody Dane and poor Ophelia, consulted an older actor who had played the part many times in the past. 'What do you think, sir? Do you think Hamlet sleeps with Ophelia?'
> 'I don't know about the West End, laddie, but we always did on tour.'

The news is that Tim Yeo has gone. His wife was ready to stand by him, but his officers weren't. Of course, if he'd gone on Boxing Day we'd have been spared a fortnight of nonsense.

From the PM's viewpoint the sadder news, I imagine, will be the death of Brian Johnston – who was indeed quite as delightful as everyone says and who epitomised everything that the PM holds dear – cricket, warm beer, old English values, *Conservative* values.

SATURDAY 8 JANUARY 1994

Little Alan Duncan has fallen on his sword.[348] He did it swiftly and with a good grace. He is in Switzerland on the parliamentary skiing trip. I've just been watching him on the box and he couldn't have handled it better. We all know that a Parliamentary Private Secretary is a nobody, a nothing, just an ambitious little tyke with a tentative toe-hold on the very bottom rung of the ladder – but the media know better. This is another 'government resignation' set to 'rock Westminster'. The nature of Alan's offence is not entirely clear to me. The gist of it seems to be that he 'exploited' the right-to-buy scheme by coming to an arrangement with his neighbour in Gayfere Street, whereby his neighbour, a council tenant, acquired the property he was living in with a £50,000 discount, on the understanding that Alan would fund the acquisition and eventually have the property. There's no suggestion that Alan's done anything in any way illegal, but who cares about that? The feeling seems to be that he's done something a bit fly and those of our colleagues who have always regarded him as a spiv (too well-dressed, with an untrustworthy tan) will be pleased to feel their suspicions have been confirmed.

---

348 Duncan resigned as PPS to the Minister of State at the Department of Health. He had only been appointed in December.

SUNDAY 9 JANUARY 1994

Another resignation – but this is horrific. Malcolm Caithness,[349] our aviation and shipping minister, has resigned following his wife's suicide last night, the eve of their nineteenth wedding anniversary. According to John MacGregor, Caithness is more substantial than the goggle-eyed chinless wonder he appears to be. He is 'a good man and this is a real loss to the government'. According to Stephen [Milligan], the word is that, in the true tradition of the rutting aristo, Caithness has been having an affair with Mrs Jan Fitzalan-Howard, sometime confidante of the Princess Royal.

Either way, it's a tragedy. But happily we've had farce on the menu too today. It turns out that Tim Yeo has a *second* love child! (So it was a lifetime ago, when Yeo was at Cambridge, and the baby was put up for adoption – but who cares about the small print? This is the Back to Basics roadshow and we're going to have some *fun*.) And, yes, there's more. And if it weren't so pathetic this would be funny. Mrs David Ashby has denounced her husband – the mild-mannered member for Leicestershire NW – because of his unnatural friendship with 'another man'.

LATER

The Press Association have just called. They want my reaction to a story in tomorrow's *Guardian*.

'What story?'

'About the government loan to your business being written off.'

I stayed calm. 'There can't be any story.'

'Shall I read it to you?'

'No, no. I'll see it in the morning. I'll comment then. Thanks.'

I can't believe what's happening.

MONDAY 10 JANUARY 1994

I am so angry.

'The government has written off a £200,000 debt to the taxpayer owed by a company set up by the Conservative MP Gyles Brandreth, who is Parliamentary Private Secretary to Stephen Dorrell, Financial Secretary to the Treasury. Peter Brooke, the

---

349 20th Earl of Caithness, a government minister in the House of Lords 1984–94.

National Heritage Secretary, has instructed recovery agents at the English Tourist Board to stop pursuing Mr Brandreth, the broadcaster and MP for Chester, and his fellow directors for the return of a venture capital grant.'

Yes, when we set up Royal Britain we applied for a grant and got it. When, two years later, we had to close because we weren't attracting the numbers we needed, everyone lost their investment – me, the shareholders, the ETB, everybody. I assumed the grant was written off then – and had every reason to do so. From that day to this, I have had no communication of any kind from either the ETB or the DNH or the Treasury or anybody. It is so fucking annoying. I am so angry.

I have spent the whole day on it. It has been an unadulterated nightmare.

My stomach already churning, I went out to buy the paper at about seven. I tried to stay calm and, as soon as I got back, began to draft a rebuttal statement. By eight the phone was ringing. It rang all day. I called the whips. I called Stephen [Dorrell]. I called all the Chester papers. I got Jenny to do letters to all the activists on the mailing list and she brought them over for me to top and tail. I am not going to be beaten by this.

When IRN [Independent Radio News] called and said Mo Mowlam[350] was calling for my resignation I went berserk. I still cannot believe it. God, how naive I am. I thought she was my friend. Aren't I pathetic? Because we chat, because we're friendly, because we've had a drink and a laugh, I thought I could trust her. She is the enemy. Of course she is.

Anyway, I thought, 'What do I do? I'm not going to take this. It is so fucking unfair!'

I called her. I got through. I said, 'Mo, I can't believe this. We're friends, aren't we?' She said, 'But the story in *The Guardian* … Shouldn't you be considering your position.' 'But *The Guardian*'s got it wrong. I haven't been pursued by anybody for anything. You must believe me. Yes, the ETB put money into the exhibition. It ran for two years and then it folded. It's like the Arts Council investing in a production at the National. If the audiences don't show up, the money's lost. It's a bad investment, that's all. There is nothing underhand in any of this. You must believe me.'

I think she was taken aback. I've a feeling she won't do anything more now. But she's done enough.

'Don't worry,' said Michèle, 'you'll get your revenge. You always do. She's a fat bitch and Peter Preston[351] is a deformed dwarf and I think we can take it for granted that David Hencke[352] is as ugly as sin. God will not be mocked.'

---

350 1949–2005; shadow National Heritage Secretary, 1992–94; later Secretary of State for Northern Ireland; Labour MP for Redcar 1987–2001.

351 Editor of *The Guardian* 1975–95.

352 *Guardian* journalist.

She is so wonderful. She has been fantastic today. She's handled all the press calls and kept a log – who I've spoken to personally, who has been faxed with what. She's masterminded it quite brilliantly. I've done no on-the-record interviews and we decided that I shouldn't be on the sofa at GMTV tomorrow to 'look at the whole back-to-basics issue'. Michèle put them onto Stephen Milligan – who's been wonderful. All the colleagues I've talked to have been wonderful. I'm utterly drained.

Fuck you, *Guardian*. Fuck you, Mo Mowlam.

Thank you and goodnight.

TUESDAY 11 JANUARY 1994

'Scandals have Tories reeling – Major faces worst week of premiership'. 'John Major was fighting a desperate battle tonight to keep his battered government on course…' 'Tory MPs and ministers were in a state of stupor…' 'Minister's wife shot herself with husband's gun…' 'I shared a bed with a man just to save money, says MP'. It's all too fantastic. I'm there too, but only a paragraph or so tagged onto the end. There are no quotes from Mo Mowlam.

I want to survive. Yesterday I thought I couldn't. Today I think, *perhaps*, I can. Today's calls have all been from local press. I'm doing an article for the *Chronicle* setting out my side of the story. I agreed to have my picture taken for *The Independent* – I thought better to let them do it properly than have a shot of me on the run looking furtive.

LATER

Tony Newton was standing in for the PM at Questions. Skinner got in with the last question. Because I'm always in the Chamber, because I use the Chamber, he tends to treat me fairly gently, but this was too good to resist. He got it in – with that nasty sneer of his, 'How can the government justify bailing out the Honourable Member for Chester at £200,000 when thousands of firms have gone to the wall and millions been made redundant?' – and I sat there, trying so hard to look so cool, and thinking this is the worst moment of my life – and then Tony came back, easy, matter of fact, *fabulous:* 'Neither the company nor my Honourable Friend has been treated differently from any other company or any other individual in similar circumstances.'

I brave the Tea Room and one or two mutter something sympathetic, but most haven't noticed my story – or, at any rate, don't let on. There's much sympathy for Malcolm

Caithness, who it seems is a person of real quality (and a close friend of Douglas Hurd), but not a lot for the PM. 'Of course, Yeo's a fool and Norris is an idiot, but the boss should have seen this coming.' Sir Richard Body[353] is quoted with approval: 'John Major has no great philosophy of his own and is surrounded by people of the same calibre … They merely present views they think will go down well with the public.'

Back-to-basics is going down like a lead balloon at Westminster – but Graham Bright says the PM's determined to stick with it. Yes, I suppose it is a little difficult to ditch it now…

I had a cup of tea and the consolation of a teacake with the comic hero of the hour, the hapless David Ashby.

'Haven't you ever shared a bed with a bloke?'

'Well, er –'

'It happens all the time. I've shared a bed with a man on any number of occasions. It makes sense. There's nothing in it. Of course, my wife's mad.'

'I've met her. She seemed very nice.'

'Oh yes. I love her very much. It's just that we can't stand living with each other.' He suddenly burst out laughing and laughed so much his whole body shook, his tea sloshed out of his cup into his saucer. 'It's so bloody ridiculous.'

WEDNESDAY 12 JANUARY 1994

There is a vast picture of yours truly on the front page of *The Independent*. The story that goes with it could be worse. It shows that the decision to write-off the ETB grant was taken by a Treasury official. It never reached any minister. *The Times* says 'Brandreth backed by Minister'. Bless you, Mr Newton. I will not forget. The *Telegraph* headline reads: 'Gyles Brandreth is cleared of blame by whips'. I pray it may be over. I want it to go away. Absurdly, I toured the Library and the Tea Room and the Smoking Room removing copies of *The Independent* – not only so that others mightn't see it, but so that I didn't have to see it either. I couldn't bear to see the picture staring up at me – though, Michèle says, as a picture it's not bad!

I have had the most wonderful telemessage from Paul and Betty Le Rougetel. I'm not sure who they are, but I love them: 'Take no notice of the envy, spite and malice of inferior red shadow. You and your wife are the most able and well-liked representation we have had for many years. The whole country could do with people of your quality in Parliament.'

---

353 MP for Billericay 1955–9, Holland with Boston 1966–97. Boston & Skegness 1997–2001.

LATER

Andrew Mackay (who has been wonderful in all this) sought me out and took me in to dinner. We sat with Peter Tapsell who was in heroic anecdotal form – stories of kings and princes, premiers and potentates, of empires lost and fortunes won. From Haile Selassie to Benazir Bhutto he's known them all – intimately! It was fantastic. And fun. This is a good place to be when you're on the ropes.

There is kindness here.

THURSDAY 13 JANUARY 1994

I met up with Stephen [Dorrell] for our usual pre-prayers pow-wow. I apologised once more. He was sweet. 'It was nothing and it's over.' He really doesn't read the papers. Every minister's office gets every daily newspaper every day. They are laid out on a side table. I have only ever seen Stephen looking at the *Financial Times*. I glanced up at his portrait of Oliver Cromwell. 'What do you think he'd have made of all this?' 'I don't think he'd have got us into this mess in the first place.'

At one we trooped along the corridor to the Chancellor's room. KC, in his shirt-sleeves, glass of wine in one hand, sandwich in the other, belly to the fore, chuckled when I came in, 'I'm glad to see you've ridden the storm.'

At Cabinet this morning they weren't going to talk about Back to Basics, but they did – for over an hour. The upshot is that the theme remains central to the government's purpose – and ministers are charged with promoting the policies that flow from it, remembering, of course, that it's all about core values, 'it isn't a moral crusade'. KC explained all this with a humorous twist to his mouth and a slightly raised eyebrow to make it quite clear what a lot of nonsense he thinks the whole thing is. 'And I shall be going on the telly later in a valiant attempt to dampen down the general hysteria.'

LATER

It's getting worse. The district auditor has just published his report accusing Westminster Council of a 'disgraceful, unlawful and improper' £21 million vote-rigging scam – 'gerrymandering' to lure Conservative voters into marginal wards. Shirley Porter, Barry Legg,[354] and an assortment of other councillors and officials are charged with

---

354 A former Westminster City councillor; MP for Milton Keynes South West 1992–7.

'wilful misconduct'. It's a nightmare. Poor Shirley. I can see her riding roughshod over mealy-mouthed wishy-washy fainthearted nobodies to achieve her ends, but she would not knowingly break the law. I'm sure of that.

Sir Marcus and his chums [the Executive of the 1922 Committee] have had an hour-long session with the PM. 'I think you know me well enough by now, Gyles. I don't pull my punches. We were very frank with the Prime Minister. At times like this you have to be.'

Apparently they told him the party rank and file are all for Back to Basics and, yes, it is a moral crusade!

LATER

I have just returned from the Smoking Room. The right think it's a shambles, the left think it's a pantomime. Edward Leigh wants the PM to play Back to Basics for all its worth. 'This is our chance to tackle the permissive society. Let's speak up for family values. Let's be fearless. The trouble is, the moment anyone says "Boo" to the Prime Minister, he runs away. We've got to stick with this. It's our only chance.' Ian Taylor: 'That way madness lies.'

I have dinner with a completely civilised trio: Nick Baker,[355] Michael Ancram, Sebastian [Coe]. Because of Northern Ireland Ancram is now very close to the PM and full of praise for what he's achieving. 'Margaret would have wanted to solve it all at a stroke. The PM is ready for the long, slow haul, the patient painstaking inching along the road, three steps forward, two steps back, for as long as it takes.'

FRIDAY 14 JANUARY 1994

The headlines are terrible. 'Vote-rigging scandal stuns Tories'. 'Wilful, disgraceful, improper, unlawful, unauthorised'. Even Sarah Keays[356] has crept out of the woodwork to dismiss Back to Basics as 'a sick joke'.

I'm on my way to Chester – the Autistic Society coffee morning, the BT Pensioners Club lunch, the Blacon Ladies Guild – ready to put on my 'business as usual' face at the end of what the *Chester Chronicle* is pleased to call 'the toughest week of my political career'. I have to say it hasn't been that pleasant – but I have survived!

---

355   1938–97; in the Whips' Office from 1989; MP for Dorset North 1979–97.

356   Sometime mistress of Cecil Parkinson and mother of their daughter Flora.

SATURDAY 15 JANUARY 1994

The local press hasn't been at all bad – and the local people have been good, kind and supportive. There's been some hate mail, but not much. The local Labour people have tried to fire a few squibs, but they would, wouldn't they?

Nationally, it doesn't look so good. Heath and Hurd are saying it isn't a moral crusade; Redwood and Portillo seem to be saying it is. Portillo's speech to the Way Forward group laments 'the self-destructive sickness of national cynicism' and is full of stirring (if self-evident) platitudes – 'Social disorder follows when respect breaks down' – but is somehow being written up as 'Portillo's bid to hijack the agenda.' 'The speech ran well away from the reassertion of the Back to Basics theme that ministers were supposed to be coordinating after one of the most disastrous weeks for a government in modern times.' According to the *Mirror*, at the farewell dinner for Gus O'Donnell[357] on Thursday night, the PM said, 'I will fucking crucify the right for what they have done, and this time I will have the party behind me.'

There's consolation of sorts in the news from Rome. When it comes to moral confusion we are not alone. A respected Vatican theorist has published an official manual for Catholic youth and, according to *The Guardian*, 'Masturbation no longer a sin' was the gleeful headline in several Italian papers yesterday. But Cardinal Biffi of Bologna is outraged. 'It *is* a sin,' he insists. Sensibly, Cardinal Hume has no comment. His mind is on higher things. Last night, at the Archbishop's House in Westminster, he received the Duchess of Kent into the Roman Catholic Church.

LATER

I have just had a bizarre – and unpleasant – experience.

I had a ninety-minute surgery scheduled for 11.00 a.m. It was the usual mix – a couple of CSA cases, a housing problem, a neighbour problem, somebody's grandmother's heating problem and – booked in for 12 noon – a Miss Ann Rogers of 25 Bridges Street. When she phoned to make the appointment she told Gwyn her problem was 'palaver' with her landlord.

The 11.45 appointment failed to show, so I was alone in the office when Miss Rogers arrived. She was a young woman, with short dark hair and a common little face caked in heavy make-up. I said, 'Come in, sit down; what can I do for you?'

As she came through the door she seemed nervous, flustered, even frightened.

---

357   The Prime Minister's Press Secretary, 1990–94, was leaving No. 10 and returning to the Treasury.

I said, 'Now, what's your full address and phone number?'

She didn't reply. She leant towards me and started talking about her 'employers': 'They're giving me a lot of aggro about you...'

'About me?'

'Yeah, you know. About you and me.'

I protested, 'But we've never met.'

'We have,' she said, 'You know we have. At Pinkies.'

My stomach lurched. I have heard of Pinkies, a local massage parlour, only because it featured in the Chester press when a murder took place there. Immediately I realised this woman was trying in some way to set me up.

I stood up. I repeated that we had never met and she knew it; I told her I had never visited Pinkies, I didn't even know where it was located; I said that if she was having 'aggro' from her employers she should go straight to the police.

I showed her the door as she continued to protest that we knew one another, that we'd met at Pinkies. The interview can't have lasted more than a couple of minutes. As soon as I had seen her out, I locked the office and walked immediately down the road and into the headquarters of the Cheshire Constabulary. I asked to see the senior officer on duty. I reported the entire episode to him. He took a photocopy of the appointment sheet and told me he would make out an incident report. He expressed the view that the woman was 'probably trying it on' having read about me in the papers this week, but he would send an officer to the address given by her 'if it exists'. I've now checked. It doesn't.

What is going on? Am I to be blackmailed for something I haven't done?

MONDAY 17 JANUARY 1994

First victim of the week: Gary Waller[358] – of all people. Yes, Gary who? Inoffensive, mild-mannered, chubby, pint-sized, potters round the Library with beetle-brows ... turns out he's a demon between the sheets. Outed by *The People* the poor bugger has had to confess that he has fathered an illegitimate son by a House of Commons secretary *and* he has a separate girlfriend who had no idea. What next? It has all got completely out of hand.

The PM's alleged line about crucifying the right is being comprehensively denied. No. 10 has contacted every one of the thirty-two guests at the dinner: no one heard the PM say any such thing – or anything like it.

---

358 MP for Brighouse & Spenborough 1979–83, Keighley 1983–97.

At A and Q it's business as usual. We must talk up the economy and cheer the PM. In the Tea Room there's open debate as to who is going to be his successor. The view is that Clarke would beat Portillo, but the Eurosceptics have a horror of Clarke so has Heseltine's moment come at last? That the clearly weird – Gardiner, Body, Skeet etc. – have lost faith in Major is hardly news. That Sir Marcus is shaking his head, and Geoffrey Dickens is huffing and puffing, and Geoffrey Johnson-Smith is tut-tutting – all that bodes ill for the boss.

WEDNESDAY 19 JANUARY 1994

On Monday night we finished voting at 2.00 a.m. Last night it was nearer 3.00 a.m. Stephen [Milligan] drove me home. He so loves the gossip and intrigue. He's predicting a leadership election in July. Sir George [Gardiner] and the 92 Group are going to lead a delegation to the PM demanding a clear rightward lurch and Cabinet posts for Jonathan Aitken, Michael Forsyth and Neil Hamilton. If they don't get their way they'll 'force the issue'. 'What do we do?' I asked. Stephen snickered: 'Enjoy the show!'

Brian Redhead[359] is on his last legs.

SUNDAY 30 JANUARY 1994

The *Sunday Times* speaks for Chester: 'John Major's prime ministership appears to be in terminal trouble.' That, alas, was the verdict at the Chester Rotary Club dinner at the Town Hall last night. Perhaps the PM's new press secretary, Christopher Meyer, will help him turn the tide. Meyer has produced a list of Ten Commandments – how to handle the hacks and come out on top. Be accessible. Be helpful. Be friendly, but not over-friendly. Do not waffle. Do not lie. Do not have favourites. Take journalists seriously. Make news. Save complaints for serious matters. Assume that everything you say will be reported.

TUESDAY 1 FEBRUARY 1994

9.00 a.m.: Gathering at No. 11. The Chancellor merry as a grig. Last night, when Sir George [Gardiner] and his ramshackle crew turned up with their list of 'demands', the

---

359 1929–1994; journalist and broadcaster; when he was Editor of the *Manchester Evening News*, 1969–75, he gave GB his first job.

PM showed them the door. The Chancellor approves: 'You can't have the Prime Minister of the United Kingdom being dictated to by a bunch of backbench dinosaurs. All this nonsense has just got to stop. We must get on with the serious business of government.'

In the Tea Room all they want to get on with is the serious business of discussing the leadership. That's the only thing anyone is talking about. Lamont is saying the PM is 'weak and hopeless' and, privately, all too many are ready to agree. As Tony Marlow bleats 'Where does he stand on anything? Does anybody know?' junior ministers shuffle in their seats, staring into their coffee cups, pretending not to hear.

THURSDAY 3 FEBRUARY 1994

Last night I had the Chester President's Club up for their annual dinner. This is the highlight of their year. They pay £100 to belong. This is the big night out. Because we had the Chancellor of the Exchequer as our guest of honour we were blessed with a full house.

At 7.00 p.m. I got a message from the Chancellor's office. 'He's running a bit late, he's had to look in on the PM.'

At 7.45 p.m.: 'I'm afraid he's still with the Prime Minister. He should be on his way shortly.'

At 8.45 p.m.: 'I'm afraid I don't think he's going to make it. Sorry.'

Sorry! I managed to locate Stephen [Dorrell]. He was in his room at the Treasury. Yes, of course, he'd come over and do a turn. He came, bless him, and gave an excellent off-the-cuff speech on the state of the economy. He saved the day – but he wasn't the Chancellor and my hundred-pound-a-throw punters sat there looking at him glumly. What was worst is that I got the impression that most of them reckoned the Chancellor was never going to turn up, that I'd boasted that I could get him when really I couldn't, that my running in and out of the dining room for 7 p.m. onwards bring reports from No. 11 was just a charade. At times I hate this job.

LATER

At lunch the Chancellor was his twinkling self. 'Sorry I got tied up with the boss last night. It just sort of ran on and on.' It seems the Chancellor was steeling the PM to address the troops: tell the backbenchers to stop feuding, tell the ministers that if they don't behave themselves and toe the line they're out. Give us the smack of firm government. Well, it's worth a try.

FRIDAY 4 FEBRUARY 1994

A good day. I'm just in from darling Saethryd's birthday supper at Riva[360] and full of the joys of chilled Frascati. I spent the morning at the Commons in a fairly deserted Chamber taking part in the debate on the Energy Conservation Bill – not knowing a great deal about it, but rather enjoying the sound of my own contributions! At noon I popped over to Millbank to do a turn on Channel 4's *House to House* programme – and didn't cock it up. Then I returned to the House and had a quick lunch in the Tea Room with Stephen [Milligan]. He spoke in the debate. He is *very* good. I imagine he'll be the first of our intake to become a minister. He wolfed his sandwich and disappeared to talk to his whip about his prospects: 'I'm going to ask him where I'm going wrong.' 'But you're not going wrong.' Stephen shook with delight, 'I know, but I want him to tell me!' He has the singleness of purpose of the properly ambitious, but it doesn't grate because he is so open about it. When we arrived and *The House* magazine asked us about our aspirations, creeps like me talked piously about the fulfilment to be had as a good constituency member. Stephen came clean: 'I would like to be Foreign Secretary.'

SATURDAY 5 FEBRUARY 1994

Not such a happy day for poor Portillo. I had supper with him on Thursday night and he told me he was going to Southampton to address the students. He did not tell me he was going to say to them, 'If any of you have got A levels it's because you worked for them. Go to any other country and when you've got an A level you've bought it.' He appears to have told his impressionable young audience that nepotism and bribery are rife across Europe. 'If you're in business in Britain and you secure a contract it's because you've worked for it. In other countries you've got the contract because your uncle's a minister and you've lined the pocket of some public official.' Poor bugger, he realised his gaffe almost as soon as the words were out of his mouth and scurried after the journalists who were there in an attempt to retract what he'd said – but too late. Now the poor sod is all over the papers and the airwaves giving grovelling apologies, eating humble pie.

MONDAY 7 FEBRUARY 1994

This is truly appalling. Stephen [Milligan] has been found dead. He may have been

---

360 GB's elder daughter was seventeen.

murdered. I know it can't have been suicide. I have just come from the Smoking Room where Bill Cash told me there's a rumour going round that it was some sort of sex killing. 'I don't think you'll like the details.'

I cannot believe this has happened. I am going home.

TUESDAY 8 FEBRUARY 1994

When I saw Stephen on Friday he was in cracking form. I think he said he was going to play golf on Saturday. Anyway, yesterday, when he failed to show up for various appointments in the morning, and wasn't answering his phone, Vera, his secretary, grew concerned and, after lunch, she decided to go to Black Lion Lane to find out if he was all right. When she arrived, the milk was still on the doorstep and there was no reply when she rang the bell. She let herself in with her spare set of keys and she found him dead, lying on the floor in the kitchen, naked apart from a pair of stockings and a suspender belt, with a flex tied round his neck and a black plastic bag over his head.

She called the police at about 4.20. She called Gerry Malone[361] and Gerry and Norman Fowler went together to Hammersmith Police Station. Incredibly, by five, or soon after, we'd got word at the House that an MP had been found murdered. Immediately I thought it was Stephen. Then I thought 'it can't be'. I called him at home. The machine answered. I didn't leave a message. Somehow I knew it was him.

It seems that, either alone or with a companion, he was playing some sort of bizarre sex game. A piece of orange was found in his mouth. Some kind of drug could have been in the orange. The bag was over his head and the flex was around his neck to restrict the amount of oxygen getting to his brain and so increase the sexual thrill.

This doesn't seem like Stephen at all. It is so horrible – and pointless. And, of course, – and, for once, understandably – the press is having a field day. There are pictures of us together at the Oxford Union in several of the papers. He was my friend. He was my best friend here. And now he's gone. It is so maddening – and so stupid. He was so happy with his life here, so fulfilled. And he was loyal. He would have been mortified by the effect of all this on the party in general and the PM in particular.

I wrote to his parents this morning, simply saying how wonderful he was. I wrote to Jonathan Aitken too because I wanted Jonathan to know how much Stephen *loved* being his PPS. When he got the job, I said to Stephen, 'What do you actually do?' 'I've no idea,' he said, 'but it's wonderful!'

At 2.35, after prayers, the Speaker made the formal announcement to the House:

---

361 Deputy chairman of the Conservative Party; MP for Aberdeen South 1983–7, Winchester 1992–7.

'I regret to have to inform the House of the death of Stephen David Wyatt Milligan, esquire, Member for Eastleigh, and I desire, on behalf of the House, to express our sense of the loss we have sustained and our sympathy with the relatives of the Honourable Member.' We murmured our 'hear-hears', then we had Defence questions. I had one about Bosnia. And, afterwards, as we trooped out, Jonathan gave me a note in response to mine:

> Poor Stephen! How cruel it seems that such venial sins of the flesh should have had such catastrophic consequences. He was such a good and decent man that I feel confident that the celestial trumpets will be sounding for him despite his temporary bad press on earth. I have written to his father and stepmother. When the pain recedes I feel sure they will recognise how much they have to be proud of in Stephen's life and good works. But oh the pain, the tears and the *waste* of it! *Requiescat in Pace.* Thanks for writing. Perhaps to correspond is to heal for both of us.

WEDNESDAY 9 FEBRUARY 1994

It's rolling on. The Ministry of Defence has to assert, 'There are no security implications in the death of Stephen Milligan.' The *Sun* has 'gay soccer star Justin Fashanu' claiming that Stephen introduced him to 'two high-flying Tory MPs for three-in-a-bed sex romps'. I don't believe it. That he subscribed to a dating agency called 'Drawing Down the Moon' is quite possible. I think he wanted a family life. He sat in our kitchen only a few Sundays ago saying how he envied us our marriage and our children. There are now pictures of Julie[362] in all the papers. He was quite open (at least to me) about how he had used her at the time he applied for Eastleigh. The Associations prefer a married man, so Julie tagged along as Stephen's girlfriend/fiancée. They both knew what they were doing – even if the Association officers didn't. The games we have to play, the white lies we have to tell…

Norman Fowler has just told me that when he and Gerry [Malone] arrived at Hammersmith Police Station on Monday night they had to join the queue at the desk, lining up with a prostitute, a vagrant and a busker – who favoured them with a song. Peter Luff[363] is saying it's like living in a Michael Dobbs novel. It's more like a Joe Orton farce. Paul Channon says there's a dangerous feeling in the air that reminds him of 1963, the time of Profumo, the end of Macmillan. I've just been listening to the poor PM on the radio dismissing the latest wave of leadership speculation as 'empty chatterings' (it's just

---

362 Julie Kirkbride, *Daily Telegraph* political correspondent; MP for Bromsgrove 1997–2010.

363 MP for Worcester 1992–7, Mid Worcestershire since 1997.

his sort of phrase, isn't it?) and getting the line on Stephen quite wrong. He said Stephen must have been 'pretty unhappy, pretty miserable'. I know he'll have meant well, I know it was off the cuff, but it's completely wrong. Stephen was gloriously happy. He'd had another good week in Parliament. He was looking forward to promotion. I imagine he went for his round of golf and came home and thought he'd play his little sex game as a weekend celebration – as a treat.

FRIDAY 11 FEBRUARY 1994

At 2.00 p.m. yesterday I was summoned to a meeting in the Lower Ministerial Conference Room. Jeremy Hanley and Douglas Hogg[364] gave a briefing on Bosnia and the NATO decision to use bombing to secure Sarajevo. They put it over well, involved us and took questions, but there was something unreal about the session. It is serious – and they are serious – but somehow I find it difficult to take them seriously. Sitting there, watching the presentation, I felt like an extra in a '50s comedy, with Jeremy as a tall Kenneth More and Douglas as a squat Richard Wattis. That said it was a worthwhile exercise. Giving the backbenchers advance warning of announcements, keeping them in the loop, always pays off. I am encouraging Stephen D. and Portillo to do much more of it. Michael [Portillo] shares my view of the special advisers: lack of focus, poor follow-through and slow turn-around.

At dinner David Amess did sterling work paying court to Lord Hailsham,[365] who joined our table. (Their Lordships who were previously MPs have free access to the Members' Dining Room, Smoking Room and Tea Room, but we see them rarely.) Said QH: 'The government is doing well in truth, and in the sight of God, but not, alas, in the view of the public.'

At the ten o'clock vote Patrick Cormack rumbled towards me and asked me to do the obituary of Stephen for *The House* magazine. The whips seem to dismiss Cormack as a puffed-up pompous self-regarding old fart, but I have to say he has never been anything but amiable to me. Anyway, I'm pleased to have been asked. I have been reading Churchill's *Great Contemporaries* again and I want somehow to incorporate Churchill's brilliant description of F. E. Smith: 'In every affair, public or personal, if he was with you on the Monday, you would find the same on the Wednesday, and on

---

364 MP for Grantham 1979–97, Sleaford & North Hykeham 1997–2010. Hogg was then Minister of State at the Foreign Office, Hanley Minister of State at Defence.

365 1907–2001; Quintin Hogg, father of Douglas Hogg; Lord Hailsham of St Marylebone from 1970; MP for Oxford City 1938–50, St Marylebone 1963–70.

the Friday when things looked blue, he would still be marching forward with strong reinforcements. The opposite type of comrade or ally is so very common that I single this out as a magnificent characteristic. He loved pleasure; he was grateful for the gift of existence; he loved every day of his life. But no one could work harder. From his youth he worked with might and main. He had a singular power of concentration and five or six hours of thought upon a particular matter was always within his compass. He possessed what Napoleon praised, the mental power *de fixer les objets longtemps sans être fatigué.*'

It's absurd to make comparisons between two such different animals from two such different eras, especially when one reached the summit at about the age the other was just starting out, but several of the qualities Churchill found in F. E. were there in Stephen too: a delight in life, loyalty, persistence, perseverance and the power of concentration.

And speaking of loyalty, I'm scribbling this on the 8.50 to Preston, whither I'm bent to do my bit for Robert Atkins[366] and the South Ribble Ladies. Robert's a bit of a boom-boom merchant, but I imagine if he's with you on Monday he's with you on Friday too. I'm not sure he's as much of a bosom-buddy of the PM's as everyone says (he fans the myth a bit – 'I call John every Sunday – we have a bit of a jaw – I tell him how it's looking') but I am always careful to treat him as if he is…

MONDAY 14 FEBRUARY 1994

The roller-coaster continues. Last week's tragedy is followed by this week's farce – or, as it turns out, this week's light romantic comedy. Hartley Booth, Mrs T.'s soft-lipped wouldn't-say-boo-to-a-goose successor in Finchley, has resigned as Douglas Hogg's PPS following the revelations of his infatuation with a 22-year-old art college model turned political researcher. Apparently there was no affair, merely a *tendresse.*

Graham Riddick[367] (admiring the newspaper photograph of the fair Emily): I'd have given her one, wouldn't you?

Bob Hughes: Hartley Booth is a gentleman.

John Sykes:[368] He's a wanker.

The Tea Room is not taking this latest calamity very seriously. Poor Hartley is a kindly, good-hearted fellow, never destined to go very far and now destined to go absolutely nowhere. He turns out to be forty-seven, a happily married father of three, a Methodist lay preacher, and – wait for it – a minor poet. On Saturday night he was denying any

---

366 MP for Preston North 1979–83, South Ribble 1983–97.

367 MP for Colne Valley 1987–97.

368 MP for Scarborough 1992–7.

improper relationship, but then he was confronted with copies of poems he had sent to his inamorata – sentimental love poems to make the cheeks burn and the flesh creep. Poor sod. He is a nice man – and ridiculous. (He's one of dozens here that I marvel at. How could he secure a safe seat? I realise now that I could have walked in anywhere. No wonder Seb and I were parcelled off to the marginals: they needed the rock-solid seats for the loons, goons and no-hopers. There are scores of colleagues, in every part of the House, which I would consider unelectable. Sitting ten feet away from me here in the Library is a Labour member who is, without question, completely gaga.)

Never mind this latest bit of nonsense – never mind the *Sunday Telegraph* poll telling us 64 per cent of the electorate consider us 'very sleazy and disreputable' – the PM is letting it be known that he will be ploughing on with Back to Basics.

Michèle is joining me for a Valentine's Day supper in the Churchill Room. The harp music can be a bit lugubrious, but the food is surprisingly good and, as we're on a running whip, there doesn't seem much alternative.

MONDAY 21 FEBRUARY 1994

O joy, o rapture! Dennis Skinner has been caught with his trousers down and his muffler up. It turns out the Beast of Bolsover has a wife at home and a mistress in London. The lucky lady is his 47-year-old researcher Lois and the Beast of Legover (as we must now think of him) has been photographed, cap down over his eyes, woolly scarf up to his nose, in the bushes near their love-nest. The delight this has engendered at both ends of the Tea Room is palpable. Phillip Oppenheim was very funny: 'It's comforting to know that Dennis is human after all, but this does not reflect well on his researcher's tastes.'

I never knock him when I'm away from here, because the public admire him. He's like Madam Speaker – you can't knock her. The punters see them on the box and like their style – barmaid and barrow-boy. Yes, Dennis can be funny and effective, but his reputation as an outstanding House of Commons man is overdone. He is certainly in the Chamber all the time, but I've never seen him on any committees, serving on bills, doing the drudgery, and while once in a while he hits a bull's-eye there's a whining sourness to most of his rants. I admit I'm prejudiced. He – and Bob Cryer and, worst of all, Derek Enright[369] – chip away at me, with nasty, narky jibes about the ETB grant – oh, it's all part of the game I know, part of the rough and tumble – and there's nothing I can do about it except patiently wait and watch for them to take a tumble. The whirligig of time … one down, two to go.

---

369 1935–95; Labour MEP for Leeds 1979–84; MP for Hemsworth 1991–5.

TUESDAY 22 FEBRUARY 1994

Extraordinary goings-on last night. We were besieged. The Palace of Westminster was surrounded by a marauding mob of gay rights protesters outraged at the failure of Edwina's attempt to introduce an equal age of consent in homosexual relationships. The amendment would have legalised consenting sex at sixteen. It was defeated by 307 to 280. There were only a couple of dozen from our side who voted for sixteen – a mixture of libertarians and liberals and (who knows?) one or two (or three or four?) closet queens encouraged by the whips to vote with us and reduce the risk of being outed by Tatchell[370] and his merry men. I missed the beginning of the debate – the living members of the Wednesday Club were raising their glasses in memory of Stephen [Milligan] and Judith [Chaplin] – but caught Tristan [Garel-Jones] who was wholly convincing (by all accounts the speech of the night) and Chris Smith[371] who was overly sentimental. Choice quote of the night came from Sir Nicholas Fairbairn who probably scored a parliamentary first of some sort with his assertion, 'Putting your penis into another man's arsehole is a perverse act...' When I saw him later he could barely stand. 'I hear you were fairly forthright tonight,' I said. His eyes were closed, his head was lolling, but he managed to hiss, 'I thought getting back to basics was part of our policy.'

When the result of the vote on consent at sixteen was announced – my 'friend' Mo Mowlam and my true friend Andrew Rowe[372] (a really good man: why isn't he in the government?) telling on our side; Bill Walker[373] and Richard Page[374] telling on theirs – there was pandemonium in the gallery and, within moments, word had reached the streets and there was a near-riot at the St Stephen's entrance with protestors attempting to storm the building. We then went on to vote for the compromise: reducing the age from twenty-one to eighteen. That secured an easy passage, 427 to 162, and that was that. Hearing the place was surrounded and escape impossible, I adjourned to the Smoking Room for a drink. At about 11.30 I made my way out into Whitehall, calling 'I voted for sixteen! I voted for sixteen!' as the police let me through the gate. The rumble of the crowd turned instantly from jeers to cheers – loud and generous. They cleared a path for me. If they'd had them, I felt rose petals would have been strewn before me. It was very funny.

---

370 Peter Tatchell, gay rights activist.

371 Labour MP for Islington South & Finsbury 1983–2005; later Baron Smith of Finsbury; Westminster's first openly gay MP.

372 1935–2008; MP for Faversham & Mid-Kent 1983–2001.

373 MP for Perth & East Perthshire 1979–83, Tayside North 1983–97.

374 MP for Workington 1976–9, Hertfordshire South West 1979–2005.

The gays who have been to see me in Chester will be happy. Quite a few of the activists will feel 'let down'. (That's the way they always put it when I do something they hate.) I've tried to explain that I'm not advocating sex at sixteen for anyone. I want to decriminalise it, not promote it. Michèle thinks the age of consent should be fixed at sixty for all.

THURSDAY 24 FEBRUARY 1994

Went down to Woodmancote for Stephen's funeral. Just a small party from Westminster: me and Michèle, Jonathan Aitken, Andrew Mackay (Stephen's whip), Julie. It was a lovely service – 'The Lord's my shepherd, I'll not want', 'He who would valiant be', an extraordinary address by Stephen's vicar from Hammersmith – and then we had to troop out into the graveyard for the interment. We were only a matter of thirty or forty feet from the hedge surrounding the churchyard and right along the lane, standing on stepladders to get a better view, were the press – photographers, cameramen by the dozen. All they wanted was a shot of Julie with a tear in her eye. They snapped away ferociously until they got it. Stephen was laid to rest to the sound of clicking cameras.

At the eats afterwards Stephen's father was so brave. He's deaf so we shouted our condolences and he barked back. He played the perfect host and insisted that we be *celebratory* – thanking God for Stephen's life and achievement. I can think of nothing worse than losing your child in your own lifetime – nothing.

TUESDAY 1 MARCH 1994

The advent of women priests has driven John Gummer to Rome.

Peter Bottomley[375] has just driven yours truly to Eltham – and back. We set off the moment the seven o'clock vote was through. We arrived at the hall about eight. I walked through the door, onto the platform, was introduced at once, spoke for half an hour, waved at the applauding crowd and retreated to Peter's car. We sped straight back. I've really no idea where I've been or what I said, but as Virginia's coming all the way to Chester on Friday I didn't feel I could duck out. I had to get back by nine because, as ever, I'm on the Finance Bill and, as ever, divisions are 'imminent'. Peter is likeable but definitely in some difficult-to-specify-way *odd*. He has bees in his bonnet. We all care

---

375 MP for Greenwich Woolwich West 1975–83, Eltham 1983–97, Worthing West since 1997; married to Virginia Bottomley since 1967.

about road safety, but he can talk about it for *hours* without pause. He said he'd asked Mrs T. to bring his ministerial career to an end because you cannot have two high-fliers in one family and it had to be Virginia.

I am struggling with a paper the Treasury has prepared for No. 10. The PM asked us to come up with a rebuttal of Harriet Harpie's assertion that the 1993 Budgets had put up the average tax bill by £22.32 a week. The excellent Mridul Hegde has produced ten pages of paperwork, blessed by Sir T. Burns, Culpin et al,[376] that does exactly that – I think. That's the problem. Mridul says £22.32 is misleading and offers several alternatives – £9.45, £11, £15.65 – each of which can be justified in different ways, if you read, understand and absorb the small print. The challenge is to settle on one figure that the PM can use and justify in a couple of phrases, and that the Chancellor can ram home every time he opens his mouth. Aye, there's the rub. KC sees all this 'presentational nonsense' as a waste of time. Getting him to agree a coordinated line, getting him to marshal his ministers to go out and preach it, simply isn't his style. Meanwhile, out there in voter-land, the punters think taxes have gone up by £22 a week and the poor are getting poorer simply because that's what Harriet and Gordon Brown tell them morning, noon and night.

TUESDAY 8 MARCH 1994

The PM has had rather a frustrating time with Jimmy Young [on BBC Radio 2]: 'I shall fight on as leader whatever the outcome of the European elections. I was elected with the largest vote any party or any leader has ever had...' I have had rather a frustrating morning at the Treasury. I began by sitting in on Alan Howarth's delegation to see Sir John Cope about tax breaks for charities. I think John had forgotten we were coming. He was genial (as ever) but you felt he hadn't the least grasp of the detail of the subject and he certainly had no plans to do anything very much about it. Perhaps there is nothing he can do, but come away from a comparable meeting with any number of other ministers – Widdecombe, Hanley, Burt,[377] Freeman, Maclean, Norris – and they give the delegation the impression that you have been galvanised by them, that this is an issue of as much burning importance to you as to them, and that, thanks to this very meeting, it's going to be Action this Day – and, in Ann's case, invariably it *is* action this day.

---

376 Treasury officials: Sir Terence Burns, Permanent Secretary to the Treasury 1991–8, later Barons Burns; Robert Culpin, Director of Budget and Public Financial Directorate 1994–2003.

377 Alistair Burt, MP for Bury North 1983–97, North East Bedfordshire from 2001; then Under-Secretary of State for Social Security.

John, bless him, seemed to think the meeting had gone rather well and together we toddled along to the Chancellor who, when I told him the backroom boys at No. 10 were keen to get the Treasury team 'out there' putting our message across, gave me very short shrift. 'We never stop. I spend half my life lunching for England. You tell 'em.'

I am forty-six today and weighing in at thirteen stone. I can live with the former, but I should do something about the latter. (I asked Michèle what she'd like for her birthday – 'You to be the weight you were the day we met.' If I really loved her I would deliver, wouldn't I? Well, I do really love her, so what's stopping me? a) Exercise doesn't interest me at all and b) when the Committee breaks tonight I shall be in the Smoking Room having a glass or three. Resolution: from tomorrow, no from tonight, no spirits and a salad every lunch.)

TUESDAY 15 MARCH 1994

Bad news for the PM. Sir George Gardiner, death's-head at any feast, has been re-elected chairman of the 92 Group – which now boasts 107 members, all too many of them openly hostile to Major. 'Our' man, Sir Anthony Durant, chairman of Q, good-hearted buffer, to the right (sort of) but wouldn't rock the boat, got nowhere. And I shall get nowhere with the memo I've drafted to give to the Chancellor:

> Talking widely – here, outside, with the press, in the city – I get the impression that there is a feeling that, as yet, *this Chancellorship has no theme.*
>
> Does it matter? Yes:
>
> a) Because it isn't true
>
> b) Because No. 10 rightly want key departments to develop the substance of the 'core values' that underpin the government's philosophy
>
> c) Because if our central purpose is not understood we will get no credit for our part in the recovery, and when we respond to events/figures we will appear to be doing so defensively
>
> What do we do?
>
> Agree the themes and then set them out fully, repeatedly, persistently over the coming months.
>
> This won't happen by chance. There needs to be a proper programme – an agreed plan – of who says what to who and when.
>
> As well as speeches and interviews, we need to work with the appropriate press and with the business/financial communities. It is not a matter of aimless 'lunching for England', but a concerted campaign to get the underlying purpose of the

government's economic strategy understood and consequently to allow the press
and business to share in the ownership of that strategy.

Even though this is the approach the Labour Party takes, even though this is what No.
10 wants, even though Portillo and Tony Nelson certainly agree, and David Ruffley is
bouncing about with enthusiasm, I know it's a waste of time. KC has been in government so long,[378] and is so comfortable in government, so easy with the way he handles
it himself, he simply can't see the necessity. If he's himself, and simply talks good sense,
he assumes the message will get across.

Anyway, it's worth a try. Oppenheim clearly thinks it's laughable.

THURSDAY 17 MARCH 1994

The twenty-five calls made a day to the Citizen's Charter Helpline cost £68 each. This
unhappy bit of intelligence is not something we want raised at PMQs. One of the roles
of A and Q is to ensure that all the questions coming from our side give the PM an
opportunity either to shine or to bash the opposition or, preferably, to do both. Unfortunately, our leader doesn't make it any easier for us to the recruit helpful questioners
by the way in which he regularly appears to 'put down' those that have been 'put up' to
ask him planted questions. Some poor sap – Olga [Maitland], Nick Hawkins,[379] anyone,
me – is given a question, gets up, asks it precisely as drafted and agreed with No. 10, and
instead of getting a warm and winning reply, is given a sort of patronising brush-off by
the boss who appears to snicker in collusion with the opposition implying 'Who are
these children coming up with these creepy questions?'

Today I sought out Seb [Coe] and gave him a soft-ball question on the Missing Persons
Helpline. It was topical, it was safe and it was what No. 10 wanted. It was not a success.
Seb struggled to get it out, lost his way, stumbled and dried. (The Chamber is a bear-
pit.) The PM gave him fairly short shrift.

Last night, in the large ministerial conference room, Douglas Hurd held a pow-wow
on QMV and 'enlargement'.[380] He was smooth, emollient, 'Hurdy', but there's going to be
trouble, no doubt about it. I reported this to the Chancellor at lunch. He just can't see it.

'I don't know what all the fuss is about.'

---

378 Kenneth Clarke first became a frontbench spokesman under Edward Heath in 1974; he had been a Minister since
1979. He was still a minister in 2014.

379 MP for Blackpool South 1992–7, Surrey Heath 1997–2005.

380 The proposed enlargement of the European Union would mean adjustment to the rules on Qualified Majority Voting,
reducing the ability of a minority to block proposals supported by the majority.

'Perhaps you should spend some time in the Tea Room,' I ventured.

'How can I when I've got to make all these speeches you keep urging on me?' He laughed. He's irresistible. But, increasingly, he's out of touch. Howard, Portillo, Lilley, they work the Tea Room. Howard told me he eats in the Dining Room at least once a week 'without fail – you must'. KC simply assumes good sense will win the day. It isn't necessarily so.

I'm writing this in the Finance Bill Committee. Alistair Darling[381] (not a wholly attractive specimen but needle-sharp) is droning on. When we break I'm going over to Jonathan Aitken's for another soirée with Richard Nixon. As Bernard Jenkin[382] put it, 'The Great Host and the Great Liar with the great and the good at their feet.'

TUESDAY 22 MARCH 1994

At PMQs I asked a question on inward investment – that was the brief. As I got to my feet, the jeering from the other side was extraordinary. Purple-faced Enright with a jabbing finger, yelling 'Give back the money!' I ploughed into my question, but the roar grew. Madam Speaker called the House to order and I started again. I got through it and the PM's reply was fine. It was an unpleasant experience, but one, I suppose, that I'll have to get used to. Several years ago, in the last parliament, Quentin Davies had some problem with sheep on his farm – a critical report from the farming inspectorate or some such – and, to this day, whenever he gets to his feet in the Chamber there are sustained braying choruses of 'Baa! Baa!' from the opposition benches. It is all very silly.

The serious news is that the PM is standing firm on QMV. And he thinks he can do it without delaying the enlargement process. The nub of the issue is that when we joined the Community the way QMV worked meant that the representatives of about 30 per cent of the Community's population could be voted down by the remaining 70 per cent. Now the ratio is about 40 per cent: 60 per cent. That's a trend that's going to be perpetuated on enlargement. There are ninety votes on the council of ministers. Delors and the Commission are proposing that the blocking minority be extended to twenty-seven. We want it to stick at twenty-three – and, according to the PM, at his rabble-rousing best, 'We will not be moved by phoney threats to delay enlargement.' He had our sceptics whooping with delight as he derided John Smith as 'the man who likes to say yes in Europe – Monsieur Oui, the poodle of Brussels.' (Yes, it is rather a cringe-making turn of phrase – produced, I imagine, by Jonathan Hill – and one the poor PM may come to

381 Labour MP for Edinburgh Central 1987–2005, Edinburgh Central since 1987; later Chancellor of the Exchequer.
382 MP for Colchester North 1992–7, North Essex since 1997.

regret. But it prompted a roar and, at least for this afternoon, it did the trick. The problem is, the way Douglas Hurd tells it, without bringing down the whole pack of cards the PM won't be able to deliver.)

THURSDAY 24 MARCH 1994

A bumpy ride for the boss at PMQs. He had to sweet-talk Teddy Taylor on the European Court, shore up the Attorney-General on the muddle over public interest immunity orders, and rebuff John Smith who (frankly) got it spot on when he accused the PM of trying to face two ways simultaneously, appeasing the sceptics one day, reassuring the rest of us the next. We did our yobbish best to barrack Smith, boorishly shouting him down as best we could (with Oppenheim fearlessly to the fore), but he wasn't thrown. He's impressive. And the PM was valiant. He was standing firm. Twenty-seven isn't on. He won't have it.

MONDAY 28 MARCH 1994

We had the Lilleys to dinner last night. Joanna [Lumley], bless her, kept the table on a roar and Stevie [Barlow] was funny and delightful. Gail [Lilley] was alternately skittish and daffy; Peter was subdued, weary, washed-out, no doubt wondering why he'd let himself in for an evening of tiresome banter when at home he's got three red boxes overflowing with unfinished paperwork. And, of course, he's brooding about the QMV debacle. The PM, having said 'No surrender', is now suing for peace. Hurd is going to come back with a compromise and Peter and Portillo and Michael Howard and Redwood will huff and puff, but they'll be outgunned by Hurd and Heseltine and Clarke. Is it customary to have a Cabinet so fundamentally – and openly – divided? Did Ted and Sir Alec and Macmillan have to put up with all this?

TUESDAY 29 MARCH 1994

A horrible afternoon. Last week the PM marched us up to the top of the hill and today he marched us down again – and at PMQs he paid the price. It was the worst it's ever been. We heard him in stony silence. It was the silence that made it so eerie and uncomfortable.

I am afraid A and Q failed to deliver. We didn't have the stomach for it, we lacked the courage. Our man was alone out there and we did nothing to help him. We sat on our hands, we averted our eyes. John Smith asked simply, 'Does the Prime Minister agree with the Foreign Secretary that the blocking minority in the enlarged community will be twenty-seven?' The PM flannelled. John Smith repeated the question. The PM flannelled some more. For the third time, Smith repeated the question: 'The blocking majority will be twenty-seven? Yes or no?' The PM was quite white, his mouth was dry and his hands shook as he held his folder. The other side jeered and we all sat in complete silence looking at our knees. It was desperate. He was so alone – and I suppose we left him there to swing in the wind because this particular nightmare was of his making, his and his alone.

Normally, between twenty or thirty, maybe more, stand up on our side looking to be called. Today, nobody. We reached the last question and the Speaker turned to our side of the House and there was no one standing – no one at all. Not one of us ready to put his head above the parapet. She scanned our benches – an eternity seemed to pass (this not an exaggeration) – and then, just as she was going to give the opposition an unprecedented extra question, at the far end of our side of the Chamber, Simon Burns[383] slowly got to his feet and asked a question about the road-building programme in his constituency.

It saved the moment – and from Simon's point of view it will have made his career. I know now how the system works here. It may seem absurd, but I guarantee that – regardless of his capacity or qualifications – that moment of courage will guarantee Simon a job. I told him so. Well done him. He stood up when it counted, when no one else would.

From Questions we went straight on to the PM's formal statement. He did his best to dress it up as a reasonable compromise, but it was hopeless. Smith made mincemeat of him, even Ashdown scored. The whips had orchestrated interventions from the loyalist knights of the shires – Dame Jill,[384] Cranley [Onslow], Archie Hamilton, Peter Emery[385] – 'We'll bring on the big beasts' is what the Chief Whip will have said – but they made no difference. The PM had promised us a triumph: he brought us a humiliating climb-down. That was all there was to it. Unctuous praise from demented Euro-enthusiasts (Ian Taylor, Hugh Dykes) hardly helped, and probably encouraged Tony Marlow to deliver what he clearly felt was the coup de grâce:

'As my Right Honourable Friend has no authority, credibility or identifiable policy in this area, why does he not stand aside and make way for somebody else who can provide the party and the country with direction and leadership?'

The Labour benches rocked with excitement. 'Resign! Resign!' they brayed. On our side there was an intake of breath, heads were shaken, there were desultory cries of shame – and when the PM came back with a jibe at Marlow's expense – 'It might be a

383 MP for Chelmsford since 1987.

384 Dame Jill Knight, MP for Birmingham Edgbaston 1966–97; later Baroness Knight of Collingtree.

385 Sir Peter Emery, 1926–2004, MP for Reading 1959–66, Honiton 1967–97, East Devon 1997–2001.

useful novelty if, now and again, he was prepared to support the government he was elected to support' – we managed a bit of a cheer and Skinner punctured the tension with a nice aside: 'Who's going to clean up the blood?'

All in all it was a hateful hour and, as I write this, around six o'clock, in the Finance Bill Committee, the feeling is that the PM may survive the week but, after today, he can't survive the summer.

I get the impression that at the Cabinet meeting this morning, Howard led the way urging a rejection of the compromise, with Portillo and Lilley weighing in, and John Redwood returning to the attack a second time. But Hurd had to win, not just because he's got Heseltine and Clarke with him, but because the second tier – Gummer, Hunt, MacGregor, Waldegrave, Mayhew, Bottomley – are with him too.

This is the PM's fifty-first birthday. For a moment, just before he went into the Chamber, I came face to face with him behind the Speaker's chair. I smiled weakly and muttered 'Good luck'. He squeezed my arm.

WEDNESDAY 30 MARCH 1994

Tomorrow we're off to Framlingham, to Simon and Beckie for Easter. I'm just in from supper with Stephen D. We went to his favourite Italian, Pasta Prego in Beauchamp Place. We had the same food and came to the same and fairly obvious conclusion: it's looking pretty dire for the PM.

'How did he get to become leader?'

'Nobody knew who he was. Thatcher thought he was "one of us". We thought he was one of us.'

'Which he is?'

'Yes, I suppose so.'

That's the crux of the matter. No one's *quite* sure. Major's a natural charmer, a pastmaster at listening to what you have to say, absorbing it and then playing it back to you. Clearly Stephen feels he should never have got beyond the rank of Chief Secretary, but he did and he has and now, three and a half years down the road, his number is up. Sir Peter Tapsell's verdict is gaining sway: 'Nice chap, just not up to snuff.'

Who next? It's too soon for Portillo. It's too soon for Stephen. Heseltine's pitching it just right: wooing the right with his plans to sell-off the Post Office (while letting us know that it's Douglas Hurd and Tony Newton who are urging caution), soft-pedalling on his Euro-enthusiasm, looking fit again, looking like a grown-up. Ken Clarke remains my candidate, but he's missing the moment – and, oddly, for such an instinctive political animal, he doesn't seem to realise.

TUESDAY 12 APRIL 1994

I invited John Gielgud to lunch to celebrate his ninetieth birthday. There was just the four of us: Sir John, Michèle, me and Glenda [Jackson]. (Glenda was Michèle's idea – and inspired. She looks so sour, but she was sweet and gossipy and exactly right for the occasion.) He arrived in Central Lobby at one, on the dot, twinkling and cherubic, amazingly upright and steady.

'It's a great honour that you should join us, Sir John,' I said.

'Oh, I'm delighted to have been asked. All my real friends are dead, you know.'

The stories just poured out of him. 'Marlene [Dietrich] invited me to hear her new record. We were in New York. We all went and gathered round the gramophone, and when we were settled the record was put on. It was simply an audience applauding her! We sat through the entire first side and then we listened to the other side: more of the same!'

He asked after Simon and said he remembered his grandmother, Jean Cadell, 'so well. She was a fine actress: she did *what she did* so well. She played Prism with me in New York, when Margaret moved up to play Lady Bracknell instead of Edith.'[386]

'Why didn't Dame Edith play the part in America?'

> She was introduced to a blind devotee of the theatre who heard her speak and said to her, 'You are much too beautiful to play Lady Bracknell', and that was that. Edith was very much concerned about her beauty, you know. Margaret agreed to move up from Miss Prism to play Lady Bracknell on condition she could model her performance entirely on Edith's. It was typically modest of her. [Pause. Sip of wine. Twinkle.] Of course, Margaret's Lady Bracknell was very much the Lady Mayoress to Edith's Queen Mary.

That prompted Queen Mary stories:

> Queen Mary herself enjoyed the theatre. King George enjoyed his play-going at the back of the box, chatting about racing with Sir Edward Elgar. They went to a matinee of *Hamlet* at the Haymarket and the Queen enquired at what time the performance was due to end. 'You see, the King always has to have his tea punctually, and he is so anxious not to miss the girl with straws in her hair.'

The conversational cast list included Orson Welles, Micheál MacLiammoir (was it

---

386 Gielgud's celebrated wartime production of Oscar Wilde's *The Importance of Being Earnest*, in which he played John Worthing, and, in London, Edith Evans played Lady Bracknell and Margaret Rutherford played Miss Prism.

MacLiammoir or Orson who kept a flashlight up his sleeve so he could illuminate his face on the darkened stage?), Sir Ralph ('dear Ralph'), Mrs Pat, Kenneth Branagh ('so clever and so delightful'), Peter Brook ('so very clever – but oh dear…'), Binkie, Donald Wolfit ('He hated me, *hated* me. The feeling was entirely mutual').

He was extraordinary – and he's ninety. I said, 'After lunch, would you like to come to Prime Minister's Questions? I know the Prime Minister is hoping to pay a small tribute to you.'

'Oh, no, no,' he looked quite alarmed. 'I think I might find that a little embarrassing. So kind of him. He is so nice. I think I'll just slip away quietly, if you don't mind.' As we were walking him across Central Lobby back to the St Stephen's entrance, he paused and smiled and fluted gently, 'This has been great fun. You know, the last time I was here Mr Bonar Law was answering the questions.'

We waved him into the street and I went into the Chamber and, on cue, as arranged with No. 10, asked the question prompting the PM's little tribute to Sir John. At 3.30 I followed the PM out and went with him to him room.

'Sir John decided to slip away,' I said. 'He didn't want any fuss.'

'I wanted to give him a cup of tea. And say thank you.'

'He's amazing.'

'Yes. During one of our recent bouts of bad publicity, he sent Norma some beautiful flowers. That was kind.'

'Yes.'

His face clouded over. 'How do you think it's going?'

'Better,' I said. What should I have said?

'Do you think so? Have you heard the latest? The Liberals are publishing a document with disloyal quotes from sixty Conservatives – *sixty* colleagues. Can you believe it?'

'They're a minority.'

'Are they? Are they?'

'Yes.' I thought perhaps it was my turn to squeeze his arm. 'Onward and upward.'

I left him looking pretty dejected. He's disappointed in us and too many of us are disappointed in him.

WEDNESDAY 13 APRIL 1994

It is 1.32 a.m. and all's quiet in the Silent Room at the end of the Commons Library – or relatively quiet. Raymond Robertson[387] is snoring gently. The other seven are sleeping

---

387 MP for Aberdeen South 1992–7.

peacefully. Matthew Carrington[388] and Peter Luff are reading, and I am reflecting on the absurdity of it all. In the Chamber they're grinding slowly through the final stages of the Criminal Justice Bill. With a bit of luck, the last vote will be about an hour from now.

Bob Cryer has died, killed in a car crash. I'm not sure what to say.

MONDAY 25 APRIL 1994

The word is that Douglas Hurd is not going to step down at the reshuffle after all. He is planning to stay on to 'shore up' the PM. John Carlisle[389] is saying in public what in the Tea Room we already know: if the Euro-elections are a disaster the avalanche could bury Major.

The only President in the history of the US to be forced to resign in order to avoid impeachment has died. He certainly impressed me. Jonathan has written an affecting tribute in *The Times* – not whitewashing the dark side, the vindictiveness, the paranoia, the 'sordid and shameful mess' of Watergate, but checking off the achievements too – desegregating the Southern schools, ending the Vietnam war, ending the draft, saving Israel from annihilation, detente with the Soviet Union, opening the door to China. He tells a fascinating story of a conversation he had with Nixon about his mother – who never kissed him. 'My mother,' said Nixon, 'could communicate far more than others could with a lot of sloppy talk and even more sloppy kissing and hugging. I can never remember her saying to any of us, "I love you" – she didn't have to.' During his wilderness years in the '60s he said the real reason he continued to want the presidency was to honour his mother's ideals. She was a Quaker. Last month when we stood on the pavement in Lord North Street and waved him off his last words to Jonathan were, 'Keep on fighting!'

We've just returned from Raymond and Caroline Seitz's farewell party at the ambassador's residence in Regent's Park. Michèle says it's the best party of its kind she's ever been to. Certainly, Ray has been the most successful – and popular – US ambassador anybody can remember. He exemplifies 'discreet charm'. He's wooed and won the entire British establishment, and they all seemed to be on parade tonight. A. N. Wilson and I shared high church memories: smells and bells at St Stephen's, Gloucester Road. Peter Ackroyd was fruity and very funny – and quite won me over: he said he'd loved my biography of Dan Leno. Michèle said, 'You could see he was drunk.' There was a lovely moment at the end, when we were lining up to take our leave. We were standing in the queue, just behind the Frosts – (David: 'Gyles, a *joy*, an absolute *joy!*') – and up strode the Heseltines, saw the length of the line, stalked grandly past us and went straight to

---

388 MP for Fulham 1987–97; later Baron Carrington of Fulham.

389 MP for Luton West 1979–83, Luton North 1983–97.

the front. 'No line-jumping,' said Ray with a smile and back the humbled Heseltines came. Democracy in action. Michèle said, 'That man mustn't become Prime Minister.'

TUESDAY 3 MAY 1994

Douglas Hurd has been offering us 'a few home truths'. The 200 or so MPs *The Times* claims would support moves to loosen links with Brussels are 'out of touch with reality', according to the Foreign Secretary. Unfortunately their number appears to include the Chief Secretary to the Treasury who – without consulting either KC or the PM – has unilaterally ruled out the single currency claiming it will lead 'inevitably' to a united Europe which 'people don't want'. Gillian Shephard has helped keep the pot boiling nicely by offering a school-marmish rebuke to 'the contenders'. It certainly is extraordinary that members of the Cabinet seem to be openly jockeying for pole position.

David Evans[390] is adding to the general sense of *degringolade* by demanding a clear-out of the Cabinet. He wants at least six of them sacked – with Fowler, Patten, Gummer and Waldegrave heading the list. (I think Fowler's wanting out anyway and Patten should have gone last time round. We're not overstocked with talent and experience so I imagine Gummer will stay and I've now changed my mind about Waldegrave's prospects. Watching the PM's body language when he's with William, I am *certain* that so long as JM is PM Waldegrave will be in the Cabinet.) Amazingly, the Evans outburst is the front page splash. Of course, we know Evans is simply a music-hall turn who likes to play the loutish loud-mouthed Essex man for a laugh. The press know it too, but that's not the way they're writing it up. Evans is a member of the 1922 executive, 'an influential senior figure in the party'. In truth, he's a tosspot. In the papers he's a 'Top Tory'.

John Smith had fun with all this at PMQs, but given his impossible wicket the PM didn't do too badly. He wasn't cowed. He hit back: 'Unlike the right hon. gentleman, at least I am not faced with senior ministers emigrating to New Zealand.'[391] Energy, attack, humour – deploy all three at once and both sides of the House give you credit.

After PMQs the Chamber emptied and we proceeded to the second reading of our new Education Bill – with only dedicated education nuts (Jim Pawsey,[392] Harry Greenway,[393] Rhodes Boyson[394] etc.) and professional toadies (Brandreth, step forward) in attendance.

---

390 MP for Welwyn Hatfield 1987–97.

391 Bryan Gould had announced he was returning to his native New Zealand.

392 MP for Rugby 1979–83, Rugby & Kenilworth 1983–97; chairman of the Conservative Backbench Education Committee 1985–97.

393 MP for Ealing North 1979–97; former Deputy Headmaster.

394 MP for Brent North 1974–97; former Headmaster.

As far as I can see this is a completely unnecessary piece of legislation – a perfect example of 'I tinker therefore I am.' No doubt teacher training can and should be improved, but this Bill isn't going to make any real difference on the ground. And bashing the student unions is harking back to an agenda that was looking pretty tired ten years ago, isn't it? (My friend Graham Riddick thinks not. He thinks there's still mileage in it. I'm sure he's wrong and I sense there's increasingly a problem for Conservatives of his ilk: what are they going to do when we've slain all the dragons?)

In the Chamber, of course, I cheered on the government. In the Tea Room I raised one or two reservations with the Secretary of State [John Patten], who was looking more than ever like an oddly corsetted Regency fop. Tea cup in one hand, pinkie extended, other hand held close to chest, palm outwards, waving my concerns away, he closed his eyes, 'Not to worry, my dear. Not to worry. Trust me, *trust me.*'

Word in the lobby is that No. 10 is briefing that the PM has rapped Portillo over the knuckles. A decision on the single European currency is a long way down the road...

THURSDAY 5 MAY 1994

We had a 9.00 a.m. meeting at the Treasury to discuss how the government can take more credit for the recovery. Stephen kicked off by identifying the problems: a) the absence of a feel-good factor, b) the extent to which any sense of recovery is believed to be despite the government not because of it! Tessa Keswick was least forthcoming. Culpin was the star – amusing, eccentric, spot-on. It was a good hour, less rambly than many and we at least emerged with some specific proposals – which Sarah Hogg should like, which Christopher Meyer will welcome, and which the Chancellor will certainly ignore!

We're on the 11.35 train to Chester, steeling ourselves for a long afternoon and evening touring the committee rooms and polling stations.

FRIDAY 6 MAY 1994

'A night of catastrophe for the Tories.' Lib Dems have been trouncing us everywhere. Rotherham has a new MP, swept in on a landslide. He's calling himself Denis Mac-Shane[395] ... Can this be the Denis Matijasek I knew at Oxford? It will be rather amusing to see him again.

---

395 Labour MP for Rotherham 1994–2012.

M has gone back to London, leaving me to spend the day visiting the Cheshire Fire Brigade, the West Cheshire College and the Chester Mobility Centre – all done on automatic pilot. At Michèle's insistence, I now have a helper in attendance at every surgery – not in the room, but within shouting distance.

I'm just in from Upton High School and a gala gathering of girl guides – yes, hundreds of teenage girls in uniform – and I realise, while I have many weaknesses, the wrong kind of interest in seventeen-year-olds is not among them.

SUNDAY 8 MAY 1994

Here we go again. Poor Michael Brown has been outed by the *News of the World*. They are bastards. And he is a fool. He took a young man on a Caribbean holiday. There's some dispute as to the boy's age, but he's certainly under twenty-one – and the eighteen-plus legislation doesn't come onto the statute book before the autumn. He's leaving the government. Under the circumstances (everybody realises he's gay, don't they?) I'm not sure how he got in. He will be very sad because he loved being a whip, relished it. When he took me to sit on the Chief Whip's table he said to me, 'This is the happiest dinner of my life. We shall have champagne and I shall pay. When you sit on this table, the senior whip present always pays for the wine. I never thought I could be sitting here like this.' And now it's over.

You've got to pity the poor PM too. As Michèle says, 'That's Back to Basics gone to buggery.' (My wife is very funny. When Lord Caithness stepped down, M looked at a picture of him in the paper and said, 'Well, you can't say "Chin up!" to him, can you?')

THURSDAY 12 MAY 1994

Ascension Day. We were in Committee Room 10, just getting into our second session on the Education Bill, it wasn't long after ten-thirty. There was a sudden subdued flurry of people slipping into the room – someone went up and whispered to the chairman, a Labour whip passed a note along their front bench. The chairman got to his feet, 'Order. I am afraid there has been some terrible news. John Smith has died. I believe we would want to adjourn the committee.' There was silence. We were stunned: there was a sense of profound shock. The poor Labour people looked so bewildered: they all had tears in their eyes. We went out into the corridor: there was a complete hush. The word spread round the whole Palace in minutes, moments. The people who sit at the tables outside the committee rooms dictating to their secretaries were packing up their papers. People really did not know what to say, where to go, what to do. The Labour people stood around in twos and threes, the women hugged one another, and I noticed that every time one of our people passed one of theirs we instinctively touched a shoulder or an arm and said 'I'm so sorry', and I felt we meant it.

The Tea Room was packed the rest of the morning. At their end they sat and stood, shaking their heads, some crying openly. At ours we were subdued, but once we had got the details – a heart attack this morning, around breakfast time; he'd seemed fine last night at some fund-raising dinner; Margaret Beckett will be their acting leader; there'll be tributes in the Chamber this afternoon – *immediately* we agreed on two things: this could save Major and it's all over for Michael Heseltine.

The PM opened the tributes and pitched it perfectly: it was simple, sincere, colloquial not oratorical – what he does best. There were nice Major touches: 'We would share a drink – sometimes tea, sometimes not tea...' You recognised the man he was talking about. I can't imagine anyone on our side who could have done it better. Margaret Beckett followed. I thought she was brilliant – moving and very brave. She was sitting next to the poor man at dinner only eighteen hours ago. She kept her tears at bay with a Herculean effort. Kinnock was good, passionate, strong; Ashdown just missed it, too wordy, too much about himself; I wasn't sure about Kaufman either. The best in a way was Tony Benn – there was old-fashioned eloquence and two messages put across in under a minute: 'Inside John Smith burned the flame of anger against injustice, and the flame of hope that we can build a better world ... He was a man who always said the same wherever he was. For that reason, he was trusted.'

....
LATER
....

I think I'm going to have a heart attack. No joke. When the tributes finished, around 4.15, the House adjourned and I went over to 7 Millbank to take advantage of the unexpected 'window' to have a catch-up session with Jenny. There was a message waiting. Would I call Maz Mahmood on 'a personal matter'. Because I'd known him at TV-am I called. I was cheery, 'Hi, how are things?'

'I'm at the *News of the World* now.'

'Sorry to hear that.'

He didn't laugh. He said, 'We've had a tip-off that *The People* are going to run a story about you on Sunday.'

'What?'

'A story of a sexual nature.'

My heart was thumping. I said, 'I can't believe what I'm hearing.'

'We wondered if you'd like to talk to us first, put your side of the story.'

My mouth was dry. 'I don't know what to say.'

'It's about the girl who came to see you, the girl from the massage parlour, the girl from Pinkies.'

I think the number I called him on must have been his mobile: 0860-109876. He asked if he could call me back 'on a better line' – I presume so he could tape our conversation. I told him the line was quite good enough and that, yes, a woman had visited my surgery and that I'd reported the incident immediately to the police. I told him that I simply didn't believe any newspaper would run a story about me 'visiting a massage parlour' because I had never done so – in Chester or anywhere else. I said, 'This is a non-story that shouldn't be dignified with comment of any kind. No one will run with it, Maz, because there's nothing to run with.' He then said that he'd heard that *The People* have 'three signed affidavits from women who saw you at Pinkies.'

I told him that I didn't believe anyone could or would run with it, expressed my sadness that he was using his talents in this ghastly way ('I've got a mortgage' he said), thanked him for calling and rang off.

I rang Tim House at Allen & Overy. His view was that it's a 'fishing expedition': 'they haven't caught anything because there's nothing to catch'. I then went straight over to the House. The place was deserted. I went to the Upper Whips' Office and found Tim Wood and Irvine Patnick.[396] I told them the story. (That's one thing I have learnt: if there's trouble brewing, *never* keep it under your hat, tell the whips.) They asked me to give them a written narrative of the whole incident – which I've now done and taken to them. It's 8.00 p.m. I'm going home. I'm drained.

SUNDAY 15 MAY 1994

Last night I got back from Chester around 8.00, having spent the afternoon wandering round the Festival of Transport gladhanding and chitchatting mindlessly while all the time my stomach was churning and inside my head I kept thinking, 'Will they dredge up something? What will they run? God, how I hate all this.'

The moment I got in Michèle said:

> I've made a decision. We're not going to put up with this. Fuck them. We have nothing to hide. I have led a totally blameless life. I have done nothing wrong,

396 1929–2012, MP for Sheffield Hallam 1987–97; in the Whips' Office 1989–95.

illegal, illicit, questionable, ever. EVER! I am not going to let these bastards ruin my life. We're going to have a new policy. If anyone calls with any allegation of any kind, we're simply going to say, 'Publish whatever you want – and fuck off'.

Needless to say, I do not feature in either *The People* or the *News of the World* – where my place is taken by poor Nick Scott[397] under the headline: 'Lying MP and the disabled bisexual'! To achieve this ludicrous headline they've conflated two stories: Nick, the 56-year-old minister, 'lying' to the House over the Disability Bill, and Nick, the young lothario, 'cuddling and kissing' a 'bisexual disabled woman'/judge's daughter on occasions unspecified but around about a quarter of a century ago! Nick shares the front page with a royal exclusive: 'Lusty Linley made me go wild in bed … Six-foot blonde Laura Horton shared nights of passion with Viscount David Linley. "David's a truly wonderful lover with a terrific body – and such an erotic kisser". Full story: page 30.'

Week in, week out, these tawdry papers trample over the lives of the famous, the not-so-famous and the ever-so-slightly well-known. It's horrendous. Footballers, actors, politicians, we're all game. If this is the price of life in the public eye, it shouldn't have to be. I told M – which I hadn't told her before – that sometime last year the *Mail on Sunday* called. They spoke to one of the children, wouldn't leave a message; it was 'a personal matter and very urgent', would I call back? I did – 'We're sorry to trouble you, but there's a story going round that you've got an illegitimate child. Do you deny it?' I do, I do, but why should I have to? Why should I have to pay for legal advice when I've done nothing wrong? Why should Michèle dread answering the phone in case it's another poxy 'investigative journalist' with fresh tittle-tattle to relay? Why should we let ourselves become the victims of the gutter press?

I have spent the day writing all this up for the *Telegraph*. This was Michèle's brainwave. 'Let's not have another week waiting and wondering and worrying what they're going to try and dredge up for next Sunday. Let's stop the madness now. If you write up the whole story, it'll kill it.'

WEDNESDAY 18 MAY 1994

The *Telegraph* has run my piece. It looks good. The picture of me is a bit quaint (soft-lipped and fey), but never mind that. For some reason – I suppose to confirm that Maz really was calling from the *News of the World* – the *Telegraph* wanted me to telephone

397 1933–2005, MP for Paddington 1966–74, Chelsea 1974–97; Minister of State for Social Security and Disabled People 1987–94.

Piers Morgan[398] to tell him what I was writing. I called, got through at once (perhaps he thought I was going to offer to 'confess' after all?), and explained what I was up to. As they requested, I taped the call – holding my little dictating machine up to the earpiece (!) and accidentally dropping it so that it made a terrible clattering noise as it hit the desk!! Morgan said his policy is always and only to publish the truth. That I don't dispute. The headlines can mislead, but on the whole I'm sure they do try to check the 'facts'. My complaint is that sections of the press have created – and sections of the public have accepted – a climate in which prurience and sensationalism reign supreme and discretion has gone by the board.

Anyway the piece is in and the phone hasn't stopped ringing. First on the line was Jonathan Aitken: 'It's absolutely brilliant. It needed to be said. Bravo!' He told me he's involved in some protracted dispute with *The Guardian* which has been using forged faxes in their desperation to dig up evidence against him. Just now I passed the Chief Whip in Members' Lobby. I got the *impression* that the piece itself was 'fine' but he rather hoped I wouldn't be milking the subject…

Ken Livingstone[399] (an amusing cove, easy, friendly, pleasantly absurd) is going to stand in the Labour leadership race, but won't declare until after John Smith's funeral on Friday. Blair is way out front. We want Beckett or Prescott, of course. Brown might be best for them long-term: he's the one I find most approachable, most human, and he still seems blessed with a touch of socialist zeal. However, they seem to be setting their hearts on the Young Conservative … We're being briefed that Hezza is set to sell off Royal Mail. This isn't news, this has been in the pipeline for months. Could it be that this briefing has been timed to remind us that, *pace* poor John Smith and his dicky heart, the President of the Board of Trade has never been fitter and – look! – here he is firing on every cylinder?

SUNDAY 5 JUNE 1994

A Whitsun week of cultural treats. *King Lear* with Robert Stephens at the Barbican (*almost* as good as it gets); *Crazy for You* at Drury Lane (my kind of show!); Beating Retreat from Michael Ancram's window at the Northern Ireland Office; Kiri te Kanawa – on song and in the rain – at Hampton Court. Stevie [Barlow] was conducting and introduced us to the diva – who is a Big Girl. Jo [Lumley] took us and Simon and Beckie and went to *so much* trouble with the picnic: dripping, shivering we huddled

---

398 Editor of *The News of the World*, 1994–95.

399 Labour MP for Brent East 1987–2001; first Mayor of London 2000–08.

together in our *impermiabili* pretending it was the golden summer evening it ought to have been. Bowen Wells[400] happened to be there and the highlight of the night for Michèle was when I went across to his wife as she emerged from the loo and gushed one of my unctuous and effusive greetings only to be dismissed by Mrs Wells with a brisk, 'I'm so sorry, I haven't got time for new relationships.'

Today we've had Seb and Nicky [Coe] over for lunch in the kitchen with Simon and Beckie. Shall we all buy a house in the south of France? Tomorrow, as guests of Manweb, we're joining Neil and Christine [Hamilton] at Glyndebourne – *Marriage of Figaro*. Then, Tuesday, Chester and the last gasps of the Euro campaign CANNOT BE AVOIDED! The PM's new line – 'a multi-speed Europe', with the UK, by implication in the slow lane – doesn't mean a lot, isn't really realistic, but it's gone down well with the troops.

WEDNESDAY 8 JUNE 1994

I'm on the 4.47 from Chester getting into Euston at 7.19, on my way to a twenty-first anniversary supper in the kitchen with my darling girl. I've had a very funny day on the campaign trail with our Euro-candidate, the diminutive, dapper, delightful, banjo-playing David Senior. From a platform he speaks rather well – an old-fashioned Oxford Union tub-thumping style, but he is so small, bald and strange-looking that I'm afraid the troops aren't taking him very seriously. What was most hilarious was that he clearly didn't want to emerge from the battle-bus. We sat in the camper van and were driven from Hoylake to West Kirby to Heswall and back. Whenever the vehicle was moving David was happily blaring away on the loud-hailer, 'This Thursday vote for David Senior, your Conservative Euro candidate', but the moment the vehicle stopped and there was the prospect of having to get out and meet the electorate, the little fellow giggled, fell silent and stayed put.

FRIDAY 10 JUNE 1994

'Tories face crisis of confidence'. Yes, it's a disaster, but it could have been worse. I'd say we won the campaign. At least we *had* a campaign. I went up at the crack of dawn to spend the day touring the committee rooms. Our people were fine: they don't take

400 MP for Hertford & Stevenage 1979–83, Hertford & Stortford 1983–2001; newly appointed to the Whips' Office in succession to Michael Brown.

Euro elections seriously. They know MEPs don't actually do anything (apart from collect the salary and handsome expenses), they knew our little man wasn't going to win, they were simply going through the motions. I raced back to be at the Albert Hall for 7.30: Brian Conley and Bob Hope. Brian was the warm-up and brilliant. Bob Hope, alas, is gaga. He's ninety. We expected a miracle. Instead we got a confused old man shuffling around the stage, with no idea quite where he was or why. The musical director kept him just about pointed in the right direction and, whenever the poor old boy started tottering towards the wings or, worse, the edge of the stage, went off to retrieve him. It was a sad sight. The surprise was Dolores Hope: great presence, glorious voice, kept under wraps for forty years she emerged from the shadows and the stole the show.

I'm speaking for Michael Forsyth at Strathblane. Back first thing for a matinee of *Love's Labours Lost* at the Barbican. 'The words of Mercury are harsh after the songs of Apollo.'

MONDAY 13 JUNE 1994

We're back. In the Tea Room, it's all doom and gloom. Apparently it was our worst performance in a national election this century. In Downing Street, Christopher Meyer has had a bright idea. Get the PM to give a presidential press conference *in the garden*. We can't change the play, but we can change the set! By several accounts, the PM was on form: sharp, rested, resilient. He's staying and he's going to lead from the front. That's the message. Oh, and yes, there'll be a reshuffle, but only when he's ready.

For collectors of the truly ludicrous there's a treat in the pages of *The Times* today: Sir Antony Buck,[401] looking like a terminally ill scarecrow, presents his new wife to the world. 'Tamara saw my picture in a Moscow newspaper and arrived at my doorstep unannounced.' Happily, the paper reminds us that Sir Antony's second marriage was to Bienvenida Perez-Blanco whose subsequent dalliance with the Chief of the Defence Staff brought his distinguished career to a rapid close. (Cue Michèle: 'Men! They're all the same...') When Tony and Bienvenida flew off on Concorde for a few days' honeymoon in Barbados, the happy groom was in prophetic vein: 'It's a long way to go for such a short time,' he said, 'but you only get married two or three times in a lifetime.'

When I first met him, years ago, I couldn't believe that such a complete tosser could find a place in the government. But now I see how the system works.

---

401 1928–2003, MP for Colchester 1961–83, Colchester North 1983–92; Minister for the Navy 1972–74.

WEDNESDAY 15 JUNE 1994

Up at dawn to make my way to the turret off Members' Lobby to sit in an empty room for upwards of two hours waiting to secure my next Ten Minute Rule Bill ... This afternoon I present my Marriage Bill for first reading. The aim is to deregulate civil weddings, enable them to take place in venues other than register offices. I have all-party support, and high hopes.

Long letter from HRH. He's sent me a photocopy of the serialisation of a book that's being published in Australia: 'Prince Philip's torrid sex life – famous lovers named.' It's utterly ludicrous – they've thrown in everybody – Fergie's mum, Merle Oberon, Katie Boyle, Princess Alexandra, Patti Kluge – but what does he do? His only defence is to sue for libel, but as he says, never mind the cost, think of the additional publicity it then gives the book. His idea is a sort of tribunal to which material like this could be referred. The author would then have to satisfy the tribunal that there was sufficient acceptable evidence to prove the truth of the statements.

When we know who our new Secretary of State for National Heritage is going to be I might float the idea past him. Certainly it's maddening for the likes of HRH and Joanna [Lumley] that absolute fantasies, utter rubbish, can appear in the press and be repeated endlessly and, short of litigation, there's nothing they can do about it. And, of course, people believe it. If it's in the papers, it must be true. No smoke without fire. People want to believe the worst. (I was at a party and, *within earshot of the Queen*, someone was muttering to me that Prince Andrew was really the son of Lord Carnarvon. Lord Carnarvon's actual son was also in the room at the time. I said, in a sort of desperate hushed whisper, 'Don't be so stupid.' The fellow continued, 'No, it's true. I swear. I read it somewhere.' I know that almost anything is possible in this world, but that the Queen has committed adultery is not.)

THURSDAY 16 JUNE 1994

It's going to be Blair. The remaining question: who gets the second spot. I'm backing Chester's son, John Prescott,[402] but Margaret Beckett has been quite impressive as acting leader these past few weeks.

Seb and I had dinner with the Chief Whip [Richard Ryder]. He was going to take us to Bucks, but there was the threat of a maverick vote on the incomprehensible Local Government (Wales) Bill (Lords), so we had a corner table in the Strangers' Dining

---

402 John Prescott's parents were constituents of GB's.

Room instead. We initiated the dinner: Seb wanted to feed in his concerns that the government is doing nothing (nothing at all, at all, at all) that is likely to interest/attract/appeal to the younger voter; I wanted to remind the Chief of my charming presence, easy manner, natural eloquence, commitment and intelligence in the run-up to the reshuffle...

I'm not sure either of us had much luck. Richard is quietly charming and the evening wasn't unenjoyable, but a) he wasn't interested in Seb's ideas, b) he's the Chief Whip so with the likes of us he only gossips guardedly, c) I was so busy being careful what I said I didn't say anything worth saying.

MONDAY 20 JUNE 1994

I've just come from the All-Party Media Group reception in the Jubilee Room. Unbearably crowded, stuffy, sweaty, and largely (no, entirely) pointless! Amiable if desultory small talk with Michael Grade,[403] John Birt, Prince Edward. Grade asks, 'Who will be party chairman now that Heseltine's ruled himself out? Jeffrey Archer?' I pull a naughty face, 'I think *not*.' (The activists out in the Styx may want him, *do* want him, but there'd be a riot in the Tea Room.) I said, 'I think it'll be David Hunt.' 'Is he your candidate?' 'No, my candidate is Jeremy Hanley.'

FRIDAY 24 JUNE 1994

A congenial morning in the Chamber. The whips have a list of the willing and ambitious ready to idle away a Friday talking about nothing very much to nobody in particular in the hope of earning a couple of brownie points and a brief mention on the Saturday morning edition of *Yesterday in Parliament*. It was a debate on the leisure industry with plenty of scope for platitudes and legitimate references to the touristic charms of Chester. I also needed to be on parade at 2.30 for the formal Second Reading of the Marriage Bill.

On my way to the Tea Room just before one I encountered Kenneth Baker who said, 'I'm having lunch with the Foreign Minister of Panama, come and join me.' I went. There were half a dozen colleagues in Strangers' Dining Room waiting to be dined (I presume at the Foreign Office's expense) with our South American guest – whose name I never caught but who has invited me and Michèle to visit him as soon as we

---

403 Chief Executive of Channel 4 1988–97.

can! I shared with the Foreign Minister my favourite palindrome – 'A man, a plan, a canal – Panama!' – and he revealed to me that the Panama hat comes not from Panama at all, but from Ecuador. As the Master said, you live and learn ... then you die and forget it all.

John Patten has agreed to pay 'substantial damages' to the chief education officer he called 'a nutter'. I imagine he'll be gone within the month. How about Stephen [Dorrell] for Education?

I am on my way to Luton to speak for Graham Bright. In the Tea Room he is blamed for a lot of the PM's woes: he's not bright enough to pick up the signals, he's not brave enough to relay them to the boss.

WEDNESDAY 29 JUNE 1994

I've just returned from lunch with Tony Newton at 68 Whitehall. He is so lovely, but what a worrier! The Chancellor's declaring that the single currency is a long-term goal. 'True, but do we need to hear it?' Blair's pledge that, if elected, he will keep our education reforms couldn't be more unhelpful: 'It's the sort of thing that'll simply do for us'. Yes, Tony, but there's not a lot we can do about it. He spent most of lunch shaking his head and lighting up. I tried to cheer him up by telling him about the file I've unearthed at the Treasury. I wished I'd taken it to show him. It's wonderful: File EO 223/02 – 'Treasury cat – subsistence allowance of'.

The first memorandum dates from October 1930:

> Rufus is unwell and should be seen by a vet. He has mange or ear-canker, I think. Authority is requested for the expenditure of a small sum on medical fees.

> 9.x.30
> Chief Clerk
> Authorised conditionally upon

> (i) every effort, consistent with a speedy recovery to health, being made to keep the expenditure to a minimum;

> (ii) further authority being obtained should total expenditure be likely to exceed £1;

> (iii) any savings on subsistence during the period of incapacity being applied towards meeting the medical fees;

   (iv) no supplementary estimate being required;

   (v) a total prohibition on night wanderings during incapacity and convalescence and a partial prohibition afterwards.

20.xii.30

Following our recent talk about Rufus' subsistence I have spoken to the office keeper and to Mrs Andrews, the Supervisor of Chairwomen. The latter has made herself responsible for the cat's feeding and brings up cooked fish, meat etc., for him. She says that the official allowance does not cover her expenditure.

The allowance was raised from 1d to 2d a day in January 1921. The office keeper says that Rufus fully justifies his existence as a mouser: there are plenty of mice, he states, to be found from time to time in the basement parts of the office…

The allowance was raised from twopence to threepence a day.

19.i.37

Accountant

Please note that the cat, Rufus, died in the night of 18/19 January 1937.

6.iii.37

Chief Clerk

I regret that I have omitted until now to notify you officially of the appointment of the new Cat to HM Treasury to succeed the well known and much lamented Rufus. The new cat 'Bob' is black and I hope he will prove to be as good a mouser and custodian as his predecessor. Bob commenced his official duties on 10 February 1937.

31.xii.37

The white cat 'Heather' was officially appointed on 9 November 1937 as assistant to Bob.

24.ii.43

Bob refused to leave the Treasury after the building was damaged by enemy action, and is now apparently being looked after by the Staff at No. 10 who draw no ration allowance. He is a wild independent animal anyway.

> Heather, unfortunately, was injured ratting or mousing in the Home Guard Store in the New Public Offices, and after treatment at the Animals Dispensary had failed to effect a cure, was destroyed.

By the early '50s the subsistence rate had gone up to 2 shillings. On 7 July 1952, Mr Tinkler (a *Carry On* name if ever there was one) makes a successful pitch for a whopping increase – to 5 shillings:

> We are told that 2 lb of horsemeat is provided at 2/- a lb in addition to cat food and milk. The cat is very efficient at its job and provision of this food in no way reduces its hunting activities. It is a born hunter and does not devour the rodents it catches.

The last entry is dated 16 September:

> The Treasury no longer employs a cat in this building.

TUESDAY 5 JULY 1994

Blair, not formally elected yet, is letting it be known that he is an admirer of Mrs Thatcher's leadership qualities. At least we can now be sure he isn't going to get Ted's vote.

At Health Questions I ask about suicide and, shortly after, find myself contemplating it. Well, not quite. But I got snared in one of those meaningless whip games. Antony Steen[404] had a Ten Minute Rule Bill: 'The French Language Prohibition Bill', a riposte to some French parliamentarian who is seriously hoping to introduce legislation to outlaw English words in France. Antony suggested I might be amused to oppose the bill. I said I might. He relayed this to the whips. I then thought better of it: I have my own Ten Minute Rule Bill tomorrow – a proper one (School Leavers Community Service) where I've got something sensible to say. I told the whips that I wouldn't be replying to Antony's bill. 'Good,' they said, 'We were going to stop you anyway. We need to get on with the Police and Magistrates' Courts Bill.'

At 2.20 p.m., I'm in the Library, pondering the suicide rates, when Bob Hughes scurries up: 'You're on!'

'What?'

'You must reply to Antony's bill—'

---

404 MP for Liverpool Wavertree 1974–83, South Ham 1983–1997, Totnes 1983–2010.

'But I don't want to.'

'You must, but don't force a division.'

'What?'

'Make your speech, but don't call for a vote.'

'Why?'

'Because we've heard Jeremy Corbyn[405] wants to speak. Because if you put in first, you'll be called instead of him. If he speaks he'll go on for ten minutes and then we'll have a division and we'll lose half an hour. If you just do two or three minutes, he can't be called and we can make progress. It's a double bonus: thwart Corbyn and save time. Okay?'

'Okay,' I said with a heavy heart.

The inevitable happened. Steen (who is gloriously eccentric) made a very funny speech – it was a little work of art. I got up and gabbled lamely (hating what I was doing, knowing I was offering dross after gold), and sat down. The question was put. Steen shouted Aye. I kept stumm, as instructed. From the opposition benches Corbyn and co. chorused 'No, no, no!' and the House divided. Another whip scam down the pan and I ended up with a rich helping of *omelette sur le visage*. Of course, it doesn't matter at all. It's all a lot of nonsense. But, all the same, how I hate it.

FRIDAY 8 JULY 1994

'The millionaire novelist and Conservative peer Jeffrey Archer is at the centre of an official investigation into alleged insider share dealings in Anglia Television, of which his wife is a non-executive director.' O Jeffrey! Jeffrey! Jeffrey! 'Insider dealing is a criminal offence which, if proven, carries a maximum prison sentence of seven years.' Apparently, the DTI investigation was launched in February, so how come it leaks six months later and in the run-up to the reshuffle? Can this be Heseltine's doing? No. He may not have much time for Jeffrey, he may not want to see him as party chairman, but Hezza doesn't make mistakes, doesn't break the rules. This'll be the work of an official with an understandable grudge against multi-millionaire Conservative peers with fragrant wives.

SUNDAY 10 JULY 1994

This is bad. The *Sunday Times* (bastards) and their 'Insight Team' (sanctimonious bastards)

---

405 Labour MP for Islington North since 1983.

have successfully hanged, drawn and quartered Riddick and Tredinnick[406] – naive fools. Tredinnick I hardly know – he seems a bit friendless, wanders the corridors looking rather wan and lost. Riddick is a friend – and a good man in his funny right-wing way – with a sweet wife and courage and ambition – one of the best of the A team – and before the end of the month he would have been in the government, without doubt. And now this. I have tried calling him, but the line's constantly engaged. Natch.

The essence of it is this: an Insight journalist, masquerading as a businessman of some kind, contacted twenty MPs – ten of ours, ten Labour – and asked them to put down a parliamentary question on his behalf, offering them each a payment of £1,000 for their pains. Almost all who were approached gave variations of the response you'd expect: 'No thank you – I can't help – contact your own MP – this doesn't need a parliamentary question, get your MP simply to write to the relevant ministry etc.' Bill Walker said 'give the money to charity', John Gorst declined payment but was content to discuss a future 'arrangement'. Only two of the twenty – it had to be our two, of course – rose to the bait. '£1,000? That'll do nicely.'

It's entrapment posing as 'ruthless investigative journalism'; it's unfair; it's outrageous; but what does the *Sunday Times* care? It's a great story for them and another nightmare for us.

MONDAY 11 JULY 1994

Graham [Riddick] is here, facing the music. He's a funny-looking creature at the best of times, a touch of the Munsters with a gangly, loping walk. But funny-looking, baggy-eyed, washed-out, he's doing absolutely the right thing: being seen, apologising to everyone he meets but, at the same time, fighting his corner. Yes, he'd tabled the question – about a company called Githins Business Resources (Githins being an anagram of Insight, ho ho) – he'd received the cheque – but then he'd had immediate misgivings and, *before he had any idea he was the victim of a set-up*, by return post he sent back the cheque.

Tredinnick I've not seen. Yesterday, apparently he denied it all, said he'd refused to accept any money. Today, alas, the *Sunday Times* have released the tape of the telephone call in which we can all hear him asking for the cheque to be sent to his home. (The man really must be a fool: once he'd discovered he'd been set up he could have guessed that the call had been taped.)

In the Tea Room there's some sympathy for Graham ('There but for the grace of

---

406 David Tredinnick, MP for Bosworth since 1987.

God etc.') and lots of righteous indignation at the *Sunday Times*. There's also a feeling of 'how much more of this can we take?'

There was a barrage of points of order for the Speaker. Bill Walker (highland terrier on high horse) indignantly asking the Speaker what she intends to do about the 'confidence trickster', the *'agent provocateur'* from the *Sunday Times*. Dale Campbell-Savours[407] (arthritic bloodhound) telling us that, since 1695, it's been 'a high crime and misdemeanour' to offer money to any Member of Parliament 'for promoting any matter whatsoever' in Parliament. It seems she's going to make a statement and we'll have no alternative but to concede a debate.

So yet again the PM's 'fight-back' is thrown off course. He came to give us his report on the economic summit in Naples – but was anybody listening? Of course, not. Forget international diplomacy, forget high politics. On radio, TV, in tomorrow's papers, the headlines will all be the same: it's cash for questions.

WEDNESDAY 13 JULY 1994

Trollope says somewhere that there's nothing pleases the House of Commons so much 'as a graceful apology sincerely meant'. I've just come from the Chamber. Graham pitched it exactly right: a fulsome apology to one and all – to colleagues, to friends, to the PM, 'but most of all, I wish to apologise to you, Madam Speaker, for undermining – to whatever degree – the standing of the House.' He did well. From, Tredinnick: silence. A terrible mistake.

Patrick Nicholls[408] made a good point. The Insight team claim to have started their entrapment procedure because a genuine businessman told them he was in the habit of giving MPs money to table questions. Where is he?

Tony Benn gave us one of his engaging history lessons, took us right back to 1066, to Runnymede, to Magna Carta, to the Chartists, to Jim Callaghan, but made the perfectly valid point that ministers undertake not to accept gifts, hospitality, services etc. that might, or might appear, to place them under an obligation – why not MPs?

The tragedy of all this is that out there in voter-land people will now be thinking that MPs do accept money for performing their everyday duties. The truth is they don't. I don't believe any Member of Parliament has accepted cash for asking a question. And I doubt that anybody would be daft enough to offer it. If you have a question that needs a ministerial answer, write to your MP, he'll forward your letter to the ministry and a reply will be yours – *gratis*.

---

407 Labour MP for Workington 1979–2001; later Baron Campbell-Savours.

408 MP for Teinbridge 1983–2001.

LATER

I have just come from Nick Scott's room on the lower ministerial corridor. He had eight of us in to 'clear the air' on the Disability Bill. Another fine mess. At one extreme you have Alan 'Mr Piety' Howarth and friends, who would like to see proper disability discrimination legislation with an agreed timetable for implementation and, if necessary, funding to follow. At the other extreme you have the likes of Jim Cooper,[409] truly disabled, who think it's a lot of PC nonsense, more red tape, more uncalled-for costs for small businesses etc. In the middle, sits (or, more accurately, shambles) Nick – pulled one way by the ferocious disability lobby (not a pretty crowd), pulled the other by the Treasury, the planning people, the instinctive deregulators. The handling of it has been horrendous, but it's not entirely his fault. The government, as a government, should have thought it through. Anyway, we're going for a compromise that'll end up pleasing nobody: a Bill of sorts so we can say we're doing something, but sufficiently toothless that in fact we're doing nothing. Nick – grey-faced and weary, puffy bags under watery eyes – knows all this; knows too, I imagine, that this time next week he'll be out of a job.

THURSDAY 14 JULY 1994

I'm just in from the Blue Ball. Another night, another auction – and, yes, I managed to get through it without saying, 'And what am I bid for a parliamentary question? Any advance on £1,000?' I did my stuff. It was fine. The PM did his stuff (including a paragraph or two of mine) and it was fine too – but much too long, as always. He feels he's got to cover the ground, say *everything*, when what the punters really want is ten minutes not half an hour: a couple of jokes, keep it personal, then a single, simple moving message – and sit down. Instead of speechifying for the next twenty minutes use that time to work the room, tour the tables – that's what they'll remember: touch their hands and you touch their hearts.

I sat with Norman Fowler and Angela Rumbold[410] and it was very jolly. Norman is demob happy, but declined to be drawn on who he thinks his successor [as party chairman] should be. Angela and I were less reticent. I volunteered my idea that there are two jobs to be done: 1) coordinating the government line and handling the press – give that to David Hunt – and 2) chairman of the party, rallying the troops, gladhanding the

---

409 Chairman of the Chester Conservative Association who had lost his legs while serving in the RAF.

410 MP for Mitcham & Morden 1982–97; deputy chairman of the Conservative Party 1992–7.

faithful – give that to Jeremy Hanley. Norman looked dubious. Angela squealed with delight: 'Oh, yes, yes, yes, let's have Jeremy!'

The PM came up to our end of the table, very relaxed, very amiable: 'What are you three gossiping about?'

'We're discussing who should replace Norman as party chairman.'

'He's irreplaceable.' The PM gave Norman his customary squeeze.

'Exactly!' shrieked Angela, nostrils flaring. 'We think we've got the answer.'

'Oh yes?' said the PM.

'Yes. You tell him, Gyles.'

I ran through my spiel and, as I spoke, I watched the PM's grin broaden. 'Well, well, well,' he said. He looked positively impish.

Jeremy's got the job. That's certain.

....
FRIDAY 15 JULY 1994
....

The House is deserted. It is a very quiet Friday, just as I like it. Mid-morning, walking from Members' Lobby to Central Lobby, who should I bump into but Jeremy Hanley? We exchanged a cheery 'Hi', I was going to let him pass, and then I couldn't resist it. 'You're going to be the next chairman of the Conservative Party.'

'What?'

'I know it. I was with the PM last night. I'm sure of it.'

'No. No.'

'Yes, yes. It's in the bag.'

'I don't think I can do it. It's not for me. Really. I don't think I'm right.'

'You are. You'll be brilliant. I must go.'

I left him looking truly perturbed.

In the Chamber we had the third reading of my Marriage Bill. For some reason – the late night, no lunch, the excitement of getting a piece of legislation onto the statute book – I felt absurdly light-headed. I trundled happily through my speech, took a range of interventions, and got to a bit where I was trying to explain why a civil wedding could possibly take place on a moored ship at a fixed site like the Thames embankment but not on a free-floating vessel, when I caught sight of Anthony Coombs[411] laughing – and he set me off on a fit of the giggles. I tried to pull myself together, I tried to carry on, but every time I began a sentence I burst out laughing. I was in paroxysms, guffawing, giggling, thinking through my tears, 'What is this madness? I can't go on.' Mercifully, Tony

---

411 MP for Wyre Forest 1987–97.

Banks came to my aid: 'I intervene to assist the honourable gentleman while he convulses.' He blathered for a minute or so while I recovered my composure, and though there was an inane grin on my face for the rest of the debate and hysteria was only ever a bat's squeak away, I got through it. It was a strange, heady experience, but not unpleasant.

LATER

I talked to Jeremy on the phone. I apologised for disconcerting him, told him that I might have got it wrong, but that I didn't think so.

'I'm not sure that I'm right for it,' he persisted.

'You are. You're ideal. And at least now you can think what to say when you're asked. Make sure you get a seat in the Cabinet. Right?'

'Right.'

WEDNESDAY 2O JULY 1994

Reshuffle Day. This is a day that makes a handful of people very happy and leaves several hundred others thoroughly fed up.

I didn't really expect anything (thanks to others I've had too much of the wrong kind of publicity and that's not what the government needs now, I know) but I hoped, I hoped.

At 10.30 I walked over to the Treasury. Stephen was in his room, alone, scrubbed, boyish, eager, pretending to read some document on the private finance initiative. He'd been 'summoned' for around 11.15. He looked up, 'What's the news?'

'Jeremy Hanley as party chairman,' I said.

'That's terrible. I like him and all that, but really…'

'And you're going to National Heritage.'

'No.' He looked utterly appalled. 'Are you sure?'

'No, it's just a guess.' (I now know how the PM thinks. He thinks exactly as I do. What I think today, he thinks tomorrow – and Peter Riddell[412] comes up with a week later. The PM is completely predictable.)

'You know, don't you?'

'No, it's my hunch, that's all.'

He didn't believe me. He looked profoundly distressed. 'I'd rather stay here. I'd rather carry on as Financial Secretary.'

---

412 Political commentator for *The Times* 1991–2010.

'Just be ready for it, that's all.' I wanted to add, 'And remember who would be ideal as your junior minister' – and half did, but he wasn't listening. I said, 'I'll be back in an hour. Good luck.'

I then went off to have coffee in the Pugin Room with a constituent (son of the rector of Handbridge) and a second coffee with the folk from the Missing Persons Helpline, pathetically checking with Jenny (virtually between sips) to see if there were 'any messages' for me.

At 11.45 I returned to the Treasury. Stephen was in his room – surrounded by the team, the officials, John K.,[413] Culpin – champagne glasses in hand.

'Congratulations Secretary of State,' I said. 'What is it?'

'I'm not allowed to disclose it for the time being – but it's the Cabinet.'

'Yes,' sighed Culpin. 'Yet another Financial Secretary moves on without reforming CGT.'

Glasses drained, the crowd departed. Stephen closed the door. 'You were right.'

'Well done.'

'It's ghastly. What on earth can he have been thinking about? I know nothing about the arts. Anything would have been better. Agriculture. Anything.'

'The PM takes the view that this is the department that helps us deliver a nation at ease with itself.'

'Oh God!' He laughed.

'Did you discuss junior ministers?' I already knew the answer.

'No, no. He just said I'd like you become a Privy Counsellor, join the Cabinet and it's the DNH. And I just said, "Thank you very much". What else could I say?'

I had to go back to the House, to be in attendance upon V. Bottomley at the official opening of the Samaritans exhibition I've sponsored (!), but then I met up with Stephen again and, with John K., in the ministerial car we drove over to Beauchamp Place. Over the pasta, he simply kept repeating how he couldn't understand how the PM could have given him the job – 'it's a non-job'. He's clearly of the view that the concept of the department is pretty laughable and he can't bear the thought that he'll be away from 'real politics'. When I returned from the telephone (again) and reported that there was no summons for me, he sweetly said, 'But I'm going to need you more than ever. I know nothing about it, absolutely nothing.' It's true.

THURSDAY 21 JULY 1994

The reshuffle gets a good press. And I have to say that, apart from one lapse in judgement

---

413 John Kingman, Principal Private Secretary to the Financial Secretary.

and good taste at the lowest echelon (the inexplicable exclusion of yours truly), the PM hasn't done a bad job. The upper reaches of the Cabinet are unchanged. Patten goes (of course), Wakeham goes (past his sell-by date),[414] Brooke goes (ditto), MacGregor goes – which is the one surprise: a year ago he was going to be Chancellor, now it's all over. I thought him impressive and, *pace* some of the buffeting on rail privatisation, a safe pair of hands. (Round here that's almost the highest accolade one fellow can bestow on another: 'a safe pair of hands'.) David Hunt (my friend) moves up to be Chancellor of the Duchy, Cabinet Office spokesman and behind-the-scenes Mr Fix-It; Gillian goes to Education (exactly right); William to Agriculture (I've not seen mud on his boots, but then I wouldn't have thought he often gets out of the Range Rover); and Portillo gets Employment. The newcomers: Stephen; Brian Mawhinney[415] at Transport (well…); Jonathan Aitken as Chief Secretary (excellent); Robert Cranborne[416] as Lord Privy Seal (the Cecils are back – all's well with the world); and, of course, Jeremy as Minister without Portfolio and party chairman. *The Times* looks forward to 'a period of competent and confident government at last'.

At 9.00 a.m. Stephen and I arrived at the DNH. It's next to Canada House, just off Trafalgar Square, a vast modern interior like a Manhattan bank. The Secretary of State's suite is impressive: a spacious office (light wood furniture, comfy sofas), an airy outer office, a proper bathroom and even (if I want it) a reasonable sized office for me. The private office team were welcoming – young, fresh-faced, friendly, the private secretary unaware that Stephen is already planning to replace him with John K. The Permanent Secretary[417] was shorter, smoother, less-Mandarin-like than I'd expected. He greeted me with excessive effusion: 'I have heard *so* much about you!' I realised that how he appeared to me must be how I appear to many people – which is depressing.

The junior ministers are Iain Sproat, whom I like enormously (but I'm told is 'impossible'), and William Astor,[418] whom I don't know at all, who was very charming but in whose manner there was something that made us (Stephen and me) think (doubtless irrationally) 'Is he lightweight and lazy?'

Photographs were taken, coffee was had, we agreed that the ministerial team should meet up on Monday to decide 'who does what'.

It's an extraordinary system. Twenty-four hours ago Stephen was Financial Secretary,

414   John Wakeham had been in the government since 1979; MP for Maldon 1974–83, Colchester South and Maldon 1983–92; as Baron Wakeham Lord Privy Seal and Leader of the House of Lords 1992–4.

415   MP for Peterborough 1979–97, Cambridgeshire North West 1997–2005; later Baron Mawhinney.

416   Viscount Cranborne, 13th Baron Cecil of Essendon, son and heir of the 6th Marquess of Salisbury; MP for Dorset South 1979–87.

417   Hayden Phillips, Permanent Secretary at the Department of National Heritage 1992–8.

418   4th Viscount Astor.

doing a job he understood, for which he had a feeling, where he felt he could make a difference. He is summoned by the PM and, without discussion, without briefing, without even a line about why he's been given the new job or what the PM hopes he may achieve, he's translated from one end of Whitehall to the other, or as Stephen sees it, from one world to another, from the centre of the universe to the realms of outer darkness. The moment you get promotion, the moment you get the sack, that's it. You don't sign the letter you were about to sign, you don't complete the paper you were reading, you clear your desk and you go.

LATER

We're just in from dinner at Quaglino's, crowded, clattery, like eating on the refurbished concourse at Waterloo Station, so noisy we just shouted at one another. Stephen generously took us to celebrate his elevation to the Cabinet: he is very generous, very sweet, but his dismay at his predicament is rather disconcerting. It was us, Annette [Dorrell], the Luffs, Tom and Jane Strathclyde (Tom[419] is the newly appointed roly-poly Captain of the Gentleman-at-Arms, aka as Chief Whip in the Lords. He's about fourteen but I guess will be rather effective.) We'd come on from the Buckingham Palace garden party (the usual form, two hours going round in circles nodding at bishops) and the PM's reception at No. 10 – a peculiar affair: the promoted trying not to look smug, the demoted looking brave (I thought John MacGregor, though, looked bruised – he can't have been sacked, can he?), the regularly overlooked looking resigned (and drinking steadily), the freshly ignored (*moi*) attempting to appear devil-may-care and perky. The PM was relaxed, friendly. 'What do you think?'

'Looks good. Jeremy's going to be excellent.'

'Yes. And Stephen?'

I didn't say, 'You tosser – Stephen's in the wrong job – and what about *me* mate?' I said, 'I think Stephen sees the DNH as the department that can help deliver a nation at ease with itself.' The PM grinned and patted me on the shoulder.

Tony Blair is the new leader of the Labour Party.

THURSDAY 28 JULY 1994

A week in and Stephen is no happier. He can't see what it's 'about'. I've suggested he leaves

---

419 2nd Baron Strathclyde; he was thirty-four.

sport entirely to Sproat, let's Astor (a Viscount, a proper lord, a chap with a castle) look after 'the heritage' in all its glory, so that Stephen can concentrate on three or four areas where there's 'profile' and where he can make an impact: tourism, the arts, the lottery, broadcasting. He just doesn't see it. And because the whole vocabulary of this world is foreign to him he feels insecure. That's why he's frantic to get John K. over here – even though he knows, if John comes (and he will), he's sacrificing the certainty of life in the fast-track at the Treasury for the uncertainty of life in a cul-de-sac here.

But there's good news too: Stephen has taken his first decision – he's going to save [Canova's sculpture] *The Three Graces* for the nation (or at least delay the export licence for three months more while Mr Getty junior coughs up) and Jeffrey [Archer] has been cleared of 'insider dealing'. The DTI will take no further action.

TUESDAY 2 AUGUST 1994

Benet has set off for China, Saethryd is in Venice (en route for Florence, Sienna and Pisa), we have just seen Aphra off for her holiday on Cape Cod, Rhode Island and Manhattan.[420] It certainly beats a week in Broadstairs. (Michèle claims she only had one holiday as a child. I say, 'The world has changed'. She says, 'That's the one thing to be said for money. It keeps you in touch with your children.')

Long letter from Portillo: 'I loved the work at the Treasury. But already I feel few regrets other than for missed colleagues and staff. It does make a difference having your own command and the interest of leading a team will compensate for a loss of influence which does undoubtedly result from leaving the Treasury. My new department is very welcoming and they welcome being told what I want. That is quite demanding but I shall try always to know it!' Even longer letter from the Chancellor (a good and kind man): 'If I was starting with a clean slate I would invite you to be my PPS, but Stephen is a friend of mine! I have no doubt you are disappointed not to be a minister and I think he is a little unhappy with National Heritage. Both of you are rather impatient but your time will come! … Let us both ensure that we keep Stephen an ally in our duty of cheering the country up! He has every other talent and he needs to be good at that.'

Given that in my experience the Chancellor's PPS sweeps into government (Hague, Oppenheim), I recommended Seb, Garnier, Hendry[421] or Trend to Ken – but, on advice from the whips, he's gone for Angela Knight. ('I hope that you do not now produce some killing reasons against A. Knight – you will be too late!')

---

420 GB's three children were now nineteen, seventeen and sixteen.

421 Charles Hendry, MP for High Peak 1992–7, Wealden since 2001.

These handwritten letters make a difference. I've said this to Stephen time and again. He knows I'm right, but because he thinks it's fundamentally absurd he can't bring himself to do it. I replayed to him a story he'd told me about Helmut Kohl. Apparently, the German Chancellor has a list of the thousand most influential people in the country, and whenever he has an idle moment, being driven from A to B, he picks up the telephone and speaks to one of them, just touching base, just letting them know that the Chancellor knows who they are and values them. I suggested to Stephen that he might try the same trick with some of the DNH constituents – call the director of Opera North, introduce yourself, say you're new to the job, ask his advice ... Stephen agrees with the theory, but I know it won't happen. He's conceded that I can organise some sandwich lunches so he can meet 'key players' in assorted fields. 'Oh God,' he shook his head despairingly, 'lunch with the luvvies!'

....

SUNDAY 7 AUGUST 1994

....

We're on our way to Toulouse. We're meeting up with Simon and Beckie and going on to Jill [Simon Cadell's mother] at Le Vigan. Fatty Mowlam has put her pudgy foot in it. She is suggesting the royal family move out of Buck House and that we build an ultra-modern 'People's Palace' for them, with a 'designer kitchen'. I trust Stephen will have some fun with that – though I'm not sure he'll want to make the effort. He's still sulking. Michèle is not impressed. We had lunch yesterday with the Hanleys. Jeremy, by contrast, is exultant! 'I blame you entirely,' he boomed happily, 'and I'm having my revenge. At the party conference, I want you to do the financial appeal and speak on the Friday, just before the PM. Okay?' Okay, of course – but I'm not going to think about that now, I'm forgetting Westminster, I'm forgetting Whitehall, I'm forgetting Chester. I am going to drink some fine French wine and read *Mrs Palfrey at the Claremont*.

....

THURSDAY 1 SEPTEMBER 1994

....

We are going for a strawberry tea at Strawberry Hill House, the home of Horace Walpole. The news is that the IRA has declared a 'ceasefire'. If this can be made to last, if we can inch our way towards some sort of constitutional settlement, this will be the PM's great achievement. For over a quarter of a century, there has been bloodshed and terror within the United Kingdom. Over 3,000 have died, tens of thousands have been wounded ... and now it's stopping.

I am returning to the Chester fray at the weekend (it's the Pimm's party on Sunday!) and pulling together my new stump speech: with the PM in Northern Ireland, with Douglas Hurd 'a uniquely respected figure on the world stage', with a Chancellor who is delivering sustained growth with low inflation, with a Home Secretary whose instincts go with the grain of our supporters ... I am even convincing myself we're getting it right!

MONDAY 12 SEPTEMBER 1994

Suddenly it's all going wrong again. 'Hanley gaffe knocks Tory fightback bid'. Last week the PM told us he wants to root out Britain's 'yob culture'. Shown a clip of it in action on *Frost on Sunday* – film of a near-riot at a boxing match in Birmingham on Saturday night – poor Jeremy dismissed the scenes as mere 'exuberance'. Within the hour he realised his mistake and started frantically backtracking and in the process made matters worse, a) by overdoing the apology ('I'm new in this game. I was caught on the hop. I've made a mistake. I apologise. It's entirely my fault.') and b) by describing his answer as 'incompetent'. Now it's Jeremy 'by his own admission "incompetent"' Hanley.

We had our first weekly planning meeting at the DNH. I tried not to chip in *too* often – but when I think I know all the answers and the Secretary of State knows none it is a little bit *difficile!!*

TUESDAY 13 SEPTEMBER 1994

Breakfast with Stephen at the Ritz. He is in much happier form. He likes Hayden [Phillips, the Permanent Secretary] (entirely *trusting* Hayden of course is quite another matter – the Treasury was never quite *Yes, Minister*: the DNH under Hayden in *Yes, Minister* in spades), he likes his private office, he's got John K., he's got me. We are going to do without a Special Adviser. I'm going to have his office.

Over properly poached eggs and mushrooms and *brilliantly* grilled bacon, we agreed that the summer hadn't been too bad – 'But' – Stephen grinned from ear to ear – 'your friend Mr Hanley...'

It's got worse for Jeremy. The papers are producing full fat features listing the litany of gaffes – being in Scotland and muddling up which party thinks what on devolution; inviting Jeffrey [Archer] to make a full statement on the Anglia shares business just when we'd all forgotten about it; telling the Chancellor he's had his last interest rate hike; telling the PM that's he's got the job as party chairman for at least two and a half years … They're all tiny, trivial trip-ups – exactly the kind I know I'd make (admittedly the kind Ken Clarke wouldn't) – but coming like this, one on top of another, and what do you end up with?

Headline: 'Hanley fulfils deep foreboding.'

LATER

When I got to the department, John K. handed me a letter: 'Hayden Phillips mentioned that there were rules set out in *Questions of Procedure for Ministers* governing the activities of Parliamentary Private Secretaries. He thought you might want to see them, and they are attached.' It's three pages of closely typed blah. I am clearly to be kept in my place.

WEDNESDAY 12 OCTOBER 1994

I am commuting to Bournemouth for the party conference. I saw Margaret Thatcher. She looks quite terrible: gaunt, pale, shrunken. She's lost at least a stone, and the mad glint in her eye had gone. She just looked sad. I saw Norman Lamont who has never looked happier! He's been making mischief on the fringe, telling us to reject a European superstate, and dismissing the PM's approach as 'simplistic'. Douglas Hurd is being magisterial, Geoffrey Howe is huffing and puffing in the wings, Norman Tebbit (now looking like a moth-eaten polecat) is adding his own touch of bile to the brew.

The news from the conference platform is that the Michaels did well – Heseltine did his usual stuff and they stood and cheered; Portillo wrapped himself in the Union Jack, denounced Europe's 'crackpot schemes' and demanded 'clear blue water' between us and the opposition, and they stood and they stamped and they *roared*. And Stephen's debut passed off well enough. Rousing the conference crowd at the fag-end of the day when National Heritage is your brief isn't easy – isn't possible, actually – but Stephen's speech was sensible, thoughtful, and well-received. The really good news is that Jeremy's speech was a triumph – all is forgiven, gaffe-man is forgotten. Verna [Hanley] is beaming and Jeremy is greeting and gladhanding and backslapping to the manner born. They took us to their 'suite': they've got a pair of tiny interconnecting bedrooms. We went in and closed the door and hugged them long and hard. 'It's been one hell of a summer.' They're shattered. They both had tears in their eyes.

BREAKING THE CODE

FRIDAY 14 OCTOBER 1994

The speech is behind me. I was going to say it was a triumph, but now I'm wondering. It certainly felt like a triumph at the time.

After our drinks 'do' for the activists last night (the usual: us, the Goodlads, the Sackvilles,[422] Jonathan Aitken) we murmured something about 'getting on to the next "do", climbed into the car under cover of darkness and raced home. (For sentimental reasons I was almost tempted to stay: we were at the Palace Court Hotel where, aged twenty-one, I treated Michèle – more than once – to a slap-up dinner of lobster Thermidor and chilled Sauternes!) This morning I drove back down again – alone. Sometimes, on a difficult day, I prefer to go it alone – I can concentrate on the task in hand, not worry about M – and then, if it's a success, I can report back, and, if it's a disaster, I can pretend it never happened.

I found my way to the makeshift greenroom behind the stage. The Cabinet was gathering, lots of bonhomous banter, Gummer giggling, clanking of coffee cups, genuine pleasure – and relief – that Jeremy has survived the week and come out on top. I huddled in a corner with the PM. They were fiddling with his tie, which was fine, but what was absurd was they were still fiddling with his speech. (The essence of a conference speech is that it is full of bravura banality and uplifting clichés – you could write it several years in advance! But, no…) Anyway, at 2.00 p.m. the moment was upon us. The party apparatchiks lined us up behind the stage, the martial music played and on we trooped – the party hierarchy, me, the Cabinet: only the PM stayed behind. I was introduced, nice applause, full house, over the top. I did my stuff: a couple of jokes; praise for the activists (laid on with a trowel); knock the opposition (compare/contrast our team with theirs: mocking Prescott, Cook,[423] Beckett – looking at Hezza, 'Who needs Bambi when we've got the Lion King?' – line kindly provided by Peter Shepherd[424] who I bumped into on my way to the platform – it worked a treat); encapsulate the policies they love best in three sentences; throw in a touch of sentiment ('You do this not just for love of party, but for love of country'); then rack up the pace and the emotional charge for the peroration: 'Ours is the only party that believes, that truly believes, in the United Kingdom. Ours is the only party that understands … Ours is the only party etc. etc. … Onward and upward!' Cue: sustained standing ovation – which, let's face it, is very nice.

Thinking of Michèle, I tried not to milk it and after a wave or two (well, three – possibly four) I returned modestly to my place. Lots of back-slapping from all round and

---

422 Tom Sackville, MP for Bolton West 1983–97, and his wife Katie.

423 1946–2005, Robin Cook, Labour MP for Edinburgh Central 1974–83, Livingston 1983–2005.

424 City of Chester Conservative Association Treasurer.

then, as we were settling down for the PM's entrance, a party man (I don't know who he was) leant over and said, 'Brilliant, well done.' I nodded gratefully. 'Of course, you know what W. G. Grace said to the young fellow who bowled him out with his first ball?' (I raised an eyebrow.) '"I think you'll find, lad, that the crowd came to see me bat, not to see you bowl."'

In fact, both the PM and I did exactly what was required of us. I offered fifteen minutes of rousing knockabout and he gave us an hour of what he is – intelligent, thoughtful, middle-of-the-road, determined, honest. He has no oratorical flourishes to offer, but there is always something quite moving about his manner. The crowd loved him – they want to love their leader.

Afterwards we returned to the green room for tea. I congratulated him on a triumph. He said, 'I hope yours went well. I'm afraid I didn't catch it.'

I drove straight back to London. The traffic getting onto the motorway was impossible. I realised there was a car next to mine with its horn honking. I looked across. It was Portillo, leaning forward, with both thumbs up, mouthing, 'You were brilliant, you were brilliant.'

TUESDAY 18 OCTOBER 1994

7.45 a.m.: Breakfast with Stephen at the Ritz.

9.00 a.m.: DNH prayers. Timothy Kirkhope[425] is our whip. Droll.

9.30 a.m.: Lottery planning meeting. Who will buy the first lottery ticket? Stephen? The PM? What happens to the money if they win?

11.00 a.m–1.00 p.m.: Good catch-up session with Di. Lunch in the Tea Room: smoked mackerel, salad, lots of tomato and grated carrot, no dressing, cup of tea. Much chuntering about the royals: Sir Marcus and co. think Charles and Diana should divorce – 'otherwise she'll end up on the throne – God, can you imagine!' I point out that the Queen Mother is set to live to a hundred and the Queen will probably do the same which means that Prince Charles will be about eighty if and when he becomes king. Do we really need to worry about this now? James Hill[426] is *very* worried: he really is: red-faced, anxious, he feels Charles has done irreparable harm to the monarchy

---

425 MP for Leeds North East 1987–97.

426 Chairman of the Conservative Backbench Constitutional Committee; MP for Southampton Test 1970–74, 1979–97.

by talking to Jonathan Dimbleby.[427] I got the impression James has actually been losing sleep over it.

At 3.15 p.m. it was Blair's first outing at PMQs – not at all bad. He paid tribute to the PM's achievements in Northern Ireland and then went for our divisions over the single currency: Portillo wants to rule it out (true), the PM is contemplating a referendum on the issue (true), the Chancellor has tried to rule out a referendum (also true) – where are we? The PM walked the tightrope well. There were lots more warm guff about Ireland and just two tricky moments: did Mark Thatcher make £12 million from the Al-Yamamah arms negotiations? And doesn't Lord Archer owe the public an explanation on his Anglia share dealings? The PM, on song, brushed both effortlessly aside.

WEDNESDAY 19 OCTOBER 1994

11.10 p.m.: High drama. I was with John Redwood, thanking him for his oh-so-smooth handling of the Raytheon Jets meeting,[428] when [David] Willetts appeared, I thought/hoped to offer me a lift home. But no. 'Haven't you heard?' We hadn't. (Maddening. What you know and when you know it is everything here: intelligence is power.) He tried to look solemn: 'A story in tomorrow's *Guardian* that could prove profoundly damaging.' He was quite excited. Perhaps we're all hooked on disaster? In which case, we may be in for one hell of a high. I've just come from the Chamber where Stuart Bell, out of the blue, on a point of order, got up and told the House that *The Guardian* is accusing Neil Hamilton and Tim Smith of taking £2,000 a time to ask questions on behalf of Harrods. It beggars belief. There's a buzz in the building that makes me feel people believe it. I am now off to the Smoking Room to see if the first editions are in yet.

THURSDAY 20 OCTOBER 1994

It is extraordinary.

What Mohammed Al-Fayed[429] says is this:

---

427 The Prince of Wales had cooperated with the broadcaster Jonathan Dimbleby on a book and television series about his life and, for the first time, had admitted his own adultery.

428 The Welsh Secretary had seen a delegation including some of GB's constituents about a local employment issue.

429 Egyptian entrepreneur who acquired Harrods, the Knightsbridge department store, in 1984. The acquisition was controversial, opposed, among others, by 'Tiny' Rowland, founder of Lonhro, and the subject of a DTI inquiry in 1987. Fayed, anxious both to retain his ownership of Harrods and to be granted British citizenship, sought support from Members of Parliament and did so by retaining the services of Ian Greer Associates, parliamentary lobbyists.

I was approached by Ian Greer who offered to run a campaign. He came to see me at my home and offered his services. He told me he could deliver but I would need to pay. A fee of about £50,000 was mentioned. But then he said he would have to pay the MPs, Neil Hamilton and Tim Smith, who would ask the questions. Mr Greer said: 'You need to rent an MP just like you need to rent a London taxi.' I couldn't believe that in Britain, where Parliament has such a big reputation, you had to pay MPs. I was shattered by it. I asked how much and he said it would be £2,000 a question. Every month we got a bill for parliamentary services and it would vary from £8,000 to £10,000 depending on the number of questions. Then Mr Hamilton rang up and requested to stay at the Ritz Hotel in Paris with his wife. I agreed. I am a generous man, but he ran up such a big bill, even coming back for afternoon tea.

This is truly horrendous. Tim I have known since Oxford. We might have gone into business together. I don't know him well, he's a dry stick, difficult to know well, but I like him. He's got a ramrod back, a City background. This doesn't make sense. And Neil and Christine are real friends. I can't believe it – and yet – I almost don't want to put this in writing – I know they did go to Paris at Fayed's expense. They revelled in it. They relish these treats. But a Paris freebie is one thing: 2,000 quid a question quite another.

LATER

Tim Smith has resigned. Yes, he did have a 'business relationship' with Fayed and, yes, he failed to register it. Curtains. Another career bites the dust. But Neil denies it all. Well, not quite all. Yes, he stayed at the Ritz, in Fayed's 'private rooms' and the bill topped £3,000, but he is adamant he accepted no fees, no 'cash for questions' of any kind.

At Questions the PM was as robust as circumstances allowed. He first got to hear the allegations three weeks ago. They were brought to him by an unnamed emissary, but, said the PM, 'I was not prepared to come to any arrangements with Mr Al-Fayed'. What? We all gasped. Was the gyppo trying to bribe the PM? Skinner called out, 'How much did he offer?' The PM repeated his line, plainly implying that the king of the kasbah was attempting to sort out some sort of deal with the Prime Minister of the United Kingdom – 'give me citizenship and we'll say no more about it, Johnnie.' The PM was doing no deals and put the Cabinet Secretary on the case. As a result of Sir Robin's discreet enquiries, Tim was forced to put his hands in the air, 'It's a fair cop, guv.' Amazing. The Tea Room buzz is he took thousands, in cash. Neil, on the other hand, stoutly maintains his innocence: he has written to the PM explicitly denying the charges, he has issued a writ against *The Guardian*, he keeps his job. The Tea Room is not happy: 'no smoke without fire', 'Neil's a greedy bugger, we all know that', 'let him fight his libel action from the backbenches, then come back in glory.' The last line (from Sir Fergus) is the right one, isn't it?

Lunch with Michael Grade in his office at Channel 4. He is Mr Schmooze: if he doesn't get the rebate from ITV, the beautiful C4 movies are going to be in jeopardy … I don't think he realises the Secretary of State has probably never seen a Channel 4 movie – in truth, has probably never seen Channel 4! Dinner with Bill Deedes[430] in Dining Room C. This is what we want: an evening of claret and anecdote – tales of the Smoking Room from the golden age of Supermac. He sees distinct parallels between now and 1963. And suggests we underestimate Blair at our peril. (I don't think we do underestimate Blair, but we don't *rate* him. Deep down, he's shallow. On our side, it's Cook we most respect. The Tea Room line: if he didn't look like a garden gnome he'd be their leader – no question.)

Ulrika[431] has had her baby: 9 lbs. 11 oz. Michèle: 'Poor girl.'

SATURDAY 22 OCTOBER 1994

I have just left a 'chin-up' message on Neil's answering machine, but he's an idiot. He emerged from a school he was visiting in his constituency yesterday brandishing a biscuit that one of the children had baked and given him. 'Shall I declare it?' he inquired of the photographers at the gate. He just can't resist it. The inevitable has happened: the picture of Neil and his biscuit (a grinning Christine in the background) adorns the front pages. The PM will not be amused.

Alex Carlile[432] (smug bugger, nasty piece of work) is successfully making matters worse. The trip to Paris now appears to have cost £4,000 plus. Carlile wants an investigation by the Committee on Members' Interests. Neil will have to step down. That seems self-evident to all – except apparently to Neil and Christine. Yesterday I went to Boothferry for David Davis and Morecambe and Lunesdale for Mark Lennox-Boyd: the activists were all of a mind – Hamilton must go. Mark gave me two rather distinguished-looking bottles of claret. Nice man.

430 1913–2007; Lord Deedes from 1986; MP for Ashford 1950–74; Editor of the *Daily Telegraph* 1974–86.

431 Ulrika Jonsson, television presenter, a colleague of GB from TV-am days.

432 Liberal Democrat MP for Montgomery 1983–97.

MONDAY 24 OCTOBER 1994

Arts & Heritage Advisory Committee: wind and waffle (wind courtesy of Patrick Cormack who I'm afraid does seem somewhat puffed up without cause). Positive European Group: more wind and waffle (I don't think I'm going to go any more meetings. There really isn't any point). Douglas Hurd at the FCO: what a class act! How does he manage it? Jocelyn Stevens[433] at English Heritage: seems a bit of a self-indulgent, self-regarding piss-artist to me (and certainly not Stephen's type), but what do I know? Apparently he's unassailable. The same cannot be said for Neil who is clinging on by his fingernails. He has upset all and sundry (and most critically the PM) by protesting that if the PM could stay in office and pursue a libel action against the publications that suggested he had had an affair with his caterer, Neil should be afforded the same opportunity.

TUESDAY 25 OCTOBER 1994

Neil has gone, protesting his innocence. The PM is setting up a 'committee on standards in public life' to be chaired by a judge, Lord Nolan. There's a lot of huffing and puffing in the Tea Room. An outside body scrutinising our behaviour? We don't like it.

THURSDAY 27 OCTOBER 1994

Jonathan [Aitken] has been magnificent. *The Guardian* splashed their story about his weekend in Paris (the bloody Ritz again!), Gordon Brown picked it up at Treasury Questions and Jonathan knocked him for six – the Cabinet Secretary has investigated and fully accepts Jonathan's version of events: he paid his own bill in full. Can we now have an end to this 'hysterical atmosphere of sleaze journalism'?

He did well.

SATURDAY 29 OCTOBER 1994

It's 7.00 a.m. and I don't want to get out of bed. But I have to. In fifty-five minutes from now I'm on parade at the Moat House for one of my 'business breakfasts' – taking the temperature of local business opinion so that I can relay it to the Chancellor. We had a

---

433 Chairman of English Heritage 1992–2000.

good night last night. Tim Rice[434] came for the inaugural gathering of the Friday Supper Club. He was a delight. He has a relaxed approach to life I envy. I suppose the money helps.

The Aitken saga is rumbling on, but Jonathan is in the clear. Mrs Aitken paid the bill at the time, but didn't pay quite enough. When Jonathan discovered the under-payment, he paid the balance – albeit four months later. His Association is standing by him. His chairman, Major John Thomas (there's a name to reckon with) is offer-ing Jonathan 'unconditional support': 'As we all know, his integrity and his moral and Christian standards are above reproach.'

SUNDAY 30 NOVEMBER 1994

Hosanna! Now it can be told. In their attempt to secure a copy of Jonathan's bill from the Paris Ritz *The Guardian* used House of Commons notepaper to forge a fax, ostensi-bly from him but actually from Peter Preston and his crew. Preston is blathering that it's 'all a bit of a red herring', but the truth is it shows the criminal lengths to which they'll go in their desperation to discredit us. It's rather reassuring to find they are as vermin-ous as we always thought they were.

TUESDAY 1 NOVEMBER 1994

It is nearly four in the morning and we are still here, struggling through the last, dire stages of the Deregulation and Contracting Out Bill (God save the mark!). The way we conduct our business is quite farcical. There are half a dozen clowns in the Chamber and the rest of us – hundreds of us! – are scattered about the palace, propped up in cor-ners, curled up on sofas, slumped in armchairs. The old guard and the whips seem to feel there's some sort of *machismo* merit in all this. Cobblers. It's simply silly.

The entire day has had a weird Alice in Wonderland feel to it. We want to conduct the enquiry into 'cash for questions' in private, simply publishing the report at the end. Labour says the hearings should be held in public. Tony Benn (the Mad Hatter) is defy-ing the Speaker (The Cook? the Duchess?), taking his little tape recorder into the sessions and producing his own minutes for distribution to the press. Tony Newton (the White Rabbit) is scurrying hither and yon trying to keep everybody happy and falling between all the stools. It's a shambles. And there's real trouble ahead. We're backtracking on Post Office privatisation. It is exactly 4.00 a.m. and the division bell is going.

---

434 Lyricist, friend and neighbour of GB in Barnes.

MONDAY 7 NOVEMBER 1994

David Martin[435] has stepped down as Douglas Hurd's PPS. Incredibly, this is front page news: 'Top Tory aide quits over PO sell-off failure'. No doubt, David is disgruntled that we've neither the bottle nor the majority to do as we might like, but the truth is he's also miffed that he's been bag-carrying for Douglas for four long years without a whiff of preferment. We all want to climb the greasy pole and when, time and again, we're overlooked we don't like it.

We're just in from a jolly dinner with the Lamonts. Norman is enjoying making mischief. Major is weak-kneed, lily-livered, pusillanimous. The case for privatising the Post Office is overwhelming: it's absurd that the government is being held to ransom by a rag, tag and bobtail of nonentities. He's also anticipating a Eurosceptic revolt on the forthcoming Bill to increase our EU contributions. 'Surely the government isn't going to be held to ransom by a rag, tag and bobtail of sceptics, is it?' I ask. 'This is different,' says Norman. 'These are men of principle!'

I like him. He has a happy piggy face and raffish charm and he likes a laugh – hence the presence at the table of Woodrow Wyatt who was in typically impish form. 'Gadfly in bowtie with bad breath' was M's verdict. (The bad breath is due to the cigars. There is a lot of bad breath at the Palace of Westminster. This is because some of us are there from breakfast till midnight, don't brush our teeth during the day and drink too much coffee and too much alcohol. Michèle has equipped me with breath fresheners and suggests I also take a change of shirt when a late-night sitting is anticipated. There is quite a civilised 'gentleman's club' style washroom in the basement, with fresh linen etc. supplied at the taxpayers' expense, so there's really no excuse.)

WEDNESDAY 23 NOVEMBER 1994

Chaos. We are dancing the rumba on the foredeck of the *Titanic*. In the hope of bringing the rebels into line the entire Cabinet has agreed to resign en masse if Monday's vote on the European Finance Bill is lost. The Chancellor tells me 'It's a fuss about nothing – £75 million this year rising to around £250 million in five years' time. The party's got to pull itself together.' The party seems to prefer to pull itself apart. Gill[436] and co. are standing firm. My friend Patrick Nicholls (bravest of the A team) has tonight been obliged to resign as party vice-chairman having told his constituents that he doesn't like the EU

---

435 MP for Portsmouth South 1987–97.

436 Christopher Gill, MP for Ludlow 1987–2001 and determined Eurosceptic.

because it's dominated by two profoundly unpleasant countries, one of which embroiled us in two world wars and the other of which boasts about its resistance fighters when in truth it is a nation of collaborators!

In the Tea Room Edward Leigh is telling us that Major hasn't lost his way because it's apparent he never had a way and we really do need to come up with some sort of vision and a few policies to go with it. In the Smoking Room Ted [Heath] is harrumphing that it's high time the whips got to grips with the right-wing riff-raff and that we got ourselves a party chairman who knows what he's doing. 'Maples[437] is a simpleton.'

'He's deputy chairman.'

'And an absolute simpleton. How could he have been appointed? These days if you put something on paper sooner or later it'll be leaked. Any fool knows that. It was different in my day. In my government nobody leaked. I wouldn't have it.'

MONDAY 28 NOVEMBER 1994

We survived. Thanks to the Ulster Unionists, fairly comfortably. Ken gave a robust speech, the PM sitting glumly at his side. When it came to the vote, eight of our people rebelled and apparently they are to lose the whip, in which case Sir Richard Body (who voted with us) will give up the whip as well by way of protest. Body is seriously strange. He's the one whose very name conjures up the sound of the flapping of white coats.

Hero of the hour: Lord James Douglas Hamilton. On Thursday night he succeeded to the Earldom of Selkirk. The Serjeant At Arms came to drag him from the Chamber. This morning James did the decent thing and renounced the title so that he would be able to vote with us tonight. Soames: 'Lord James is a perfect gentleman. Gill is a perfect cunt.'

Technically we are now a minority government and the feeling in the Tea Room is that we are in terminal decline.

TUESDAY 29 NOVEMBER 1994

The Budget's been and gone. Ken was upbeat, 'a Budget for jobs', but the House dozed. I often find I've sat through a whole debate and not absorbed a thing. (The other day Sir Peter Emery was fast asleep on the front bench below the gangway. He had propped

---

437 John Maples, the deputy chairman of the Conservative Party, had written a memorandum anatomising some of the party's weaknesses and proposing remedies. The document had found its way into the national press.

himself in Ted's corner seat. Ted arrived, Peter slumbered on. Ted prodded him; Peter stirred and then settled back again. Ted stood glowering at the sleeping figure. From across the way Skinner barked, 'Wake up, Ted's here.' Sir Peter roused himself and shifted along the bench to make way for the Father of the House.)

George Walden's[438] line is good: 'The Budget was better than exciting. It was sensible.' The excitement will come next Tuesday. Will we have a new set of rebels on VAT on fuel? The word from the PM is that this time it won't be a matter of confidence, but I'd have thought a defeat pretty catastrophic. When did a Chancellor last have a major plank of his Budget voted down?

SUNDAY 4 DECEMBER

A bizarre few days. The press has been very little interested in the Budget. For them the story of the week has been Michael Portillo's party on Friday night.

Michael's over-eager agent had the bright idea of marking our young hero's first decade at Westminster with a gigantic bash at Alexandra Palace – a thousand guests, fireworks, the Band of the Grenadier Guards, a *This Is Your Life* tribute, Margaret Thatcher, Norman Tebbit – the works. When word of this got out, the mockers in the media scented blood and set to work. Though the damage was done, Michael decided he'd better backtrack. Gradually he scaled the whole thing down – no video portrait; no military band, just a string quartet; no Margaret, no Tebbit, just me.

We turned up at Alexandra Palace at seven to find the place surrounded by police, Criminal Justice Act protestors, and an assortment of television crews and youthful radio reporters who ran alongside us as we marched in. 'What sort of evening are you expecting, Mr Brandreth?' 'A good one.' 'Why is Mr Portillo holding this party?' 'To thank his constituents for ten years of support and hard work.' 'Is it true that you used to do this sort of thing for Robert Maxwell?' 'No, but I know a lot of Socialists who did.'

Inside we were ushered to the VIP reception where a desperately over-anxious chairman's wife talked at us to such an extent that, literally, she backed us from one end of the room to the other. Harvey Thomas [Portillo's agent] had produced a forty-eight point battle plan for the entire evening ('1700 Michael Portillo's dinner jacket to be delivered to Palm Court Office: Roger Vince to organise') and at 1945 on the dot he lined us up for our walk from the reception onto the stage, with Michèle, poor girl, leading the way. So ruined had the occasion been by the pre-publicity, so subdued was the mood, the poor punters (about 600 of them in the event) didn't know whether or

---

438 MP for Buckingham 1983–97.

not to applaud. When they came, my speech was a non-event and Michael's as safe and non-triumphalist as he could make it. The hall was like an aircraft hangar, the acoustics a nightmare, the sound system a disaster, the lighting nil, and the atmosphere at best flat, at worst apprehensive. I could tell from the way his voice was wobbling and his leg was shaking that Michael hated every second of it and when he finished the applause was as restrained as the speech. Poor fellow, he didn't even get a standing ovation at his tenth birthday party!

There were hacks disguised as punters at every other table and a couple of them, masquerading as enthusiastic constituents wanting souvenir snapshots, came onto the stage to get their close-ups. It was all very silly and rather unpleasant. We slipped away as soon as we could. As we emerged, arc lights came on and a girl ran alongside us calling out, 'Channel 4, *A Week in Politics*, what was the party like?' I blathered on about how it had been a great constituency party for a great constituency MP until we reached the end of the cordoned off pathway when it appeared that our exit was blocked. For a ghastly moment, it looked as if we were either going to have to retrace our steps or attempt to climb over the barricade – still on camera whichever course of action we took. In the event, Michèle found tiny gap and we slipped through and away. It was 11.30-ish and in the car park a couple of coaches were disgorging extra Criminal Justice Act protestors.

At lunchtime we had been to Worcester where we all wore paper hats and I entertained Peter Luff's Ladies (a mature group) to my usual knockabout. It was a much jollier affair.

Last night we went for supper at Clive and Sarah's[439] where Michael Cockerell[440] was a guest and he and his third wife seemed quite surprised by the contempt in which we seem to hold the press. He seemed genuinely shocked when I told him that I had counselled Ken Clarke strongly against letting him make a TV portrait of him. But wasn't it sympathetic? Didn't it do him more good than harm? Didn't it show the human side of the man? I said that I didn't believe it had done much harm, that it had probably reinforced the 'good bloke' image of KC, but it didn't add anything to his standing. He didn't need it. Cockerell seemed an odd mixture of vanity and naivety – proud of his work (fine), but overrating its significance quite ludicrously and thinking that he was in some way a key part in the political process, getting to grips with the politicians themselves, probing behind the mask etc. Sally Burton,[441] who was sitting next to me, said later that she finds now that you daren't trust any journalist and consequently most of the time – and certainly in any vaguely public place – you're on your guard. On Thursday night we were at the Elton John Aids Benefit at the Albert

439 Clive Syddall, television producer, and Sarah Stacey, writer, friends of GB.

440 Television producer, specialising in political profiles.

441 Widow of the actor Richard Burton.

Hall and when Elton said, 'Let's line up all the press and machine gun them' the audience cheered and cheered.

Paul Gambaccini[442] told us that next year there are going to be 'Elton John condoms' – 'that's the nearest you and I are likely to get to star-fucking'. We were at the Albert Hall as guests of the ever-generous Clelands.[443] John told us that Meatloaf had just given a concert in aid of the Prince's Trust. Prince Charles arrived, not looking forward to it. John hadn't been looking forward to it either, but it turned out to be sensational. Said John, 'All of Charles's people were there, all ages, all types, a true cross-section of the British public, having a great time in aid of the Prince's Trust. And what did HRH do? He put in his earplugs and looked sad. As he left he said, "Dreadful, wasn't it?"'

We have just been over to Tim and Alison Heald and had the literary encounter of the year – with the lady who has written the novel based on the Gold Blend TV commercial! *Love Over Gold* has sold 177,000 copies to date. (She is now working on a sequel to *The Secret Garden*.) Wendy Perriam[444] revealed that the man Sir Kenneth Dover tells us he wanted to push into suicide[445] was not only her tutor but one of her first lovers – 'and he was suicidal then, and a hopeless lover, but he had a nice prick. I can see it now.'

TUESDAY 6 DECEMBER 1994

At 12.45 I was standing on the steps of No. 1 Parliament Street waiting for the Chancellor of the Exchequer. His office had said he would be coming by car, even though the Treasury is literally only across the street. In the event, it might have been better if he had. He came over on foot, pursued by a Father Christmas carrying an anti-VAT-on-fuel placard and a small posse of photographers. I got him up to the Astor Suite and he did his stuff like an old pro – ten minutes of mingling with the Chester faithful, a bullish ten-minute speech, a couple of questions and then we were off. Anti-VAT Santa was still at the door and the posse of photographers had grown to a crowd. We made our way into the basement and after scurrying along assorted corridors eventually found the Derby Gate exit. Ken chuckled happily at the nonsense of it. He said

---

442 Writer and broadcaster, one of the hosts at the Aids Benefit.

443 John Cleland, chairman of the Albert Hall, and his wife Annie, friends of GB.

444 Novelist, friend of GB.

445 In his memoirs, currently being serialised, the classical scholar and Professor of Greek at the University of St Andrews revealed his dislike of a fellow academic who took his own life.

he wasn't sure how the vote would go tonight ('our party seems to have taken leave of its senses') so he has been preparing for 'all contingencies'.

Heseltine gave a gloriously rumbustious performance opening the debate. He has a standard technique: he begins slowly, head down, reading, and gradually works himself up into a frenzy so that he ends with a real barnstormer. It worked surprisingly well, given there was such a thin house. By the time KC rose for his wind-up at the end of the evening the place was packed and there was much gallows bonhomie on the front bench – to the extent that the hacks in the press gallery seeing the relaxed demeanour of the PM and the Chancellor assumed we'd won. In fact, Ken arrived ready for defeat, a three-page contingency statement tucked in his pocket. During his speech he threw £10 million in additional insulation grants to Harry Greenway and £110,000 to Andrew Bowden[446] which made everyone think that had done it. In the event, we went down by eight votes. It isn't good. For the last vote I found myself crouching next to Richard Ryder [the Chief Whip], all pasty-faced and puffy. He saw Neil Kinnock come into the Chamber. 'Is he still a member?' he yelped. Talk about clutching at straws.[447]

WEDNESDAY 7 DECEMBER 1994

I spent the morning at the BBC while the Chancellor and the Governor met and decided to put up interest rates. I had my hair cut at Simpsons and emerged into Jermyn Street to see Malcolm Rifkind climbing into his car. I cadged a lift and asked Malcolm how he is getting on with the new US ambassador. He says Admiral Crowe has far less acumen and clout than Ray Seitz, but far greater direct access to Clinton. Crowe's best line to date: 'In my experience as an admiral I have only come across one kind of ship that leaks from the top and that is the ship of state.'

Judge Tumim[448] came to the Penal Affairs Group and described himself as an old buffer – a civilised and shrewd old buffer I'd have thought. Of those now in prison 75/80 per cent are under thirty, uneducated and from broken homes. The majority of offences involve drinks, drugs and cars and the offenders will be inside for twelve to twenty-four months. What we should be doing while we've got them is offer intensive education – from basic hygiene and civic values to training. His manner was a caricature of the good-hearted, slightly dotty Englishman. I warmed to him, but I could see how he was irritating one or two of my colleagues.

---

446 MP for Brighton Kemptown 1970–97.

447 Neil Kinnock was about to step down as an MP to take up his post as European Union Transport Commissioner.

448 Stephen Tumim, Circuit Judge 1978–96, and HM Chief Inspector of Prisons for England and Wales 1987–95.

Hartley Booth approached me. Incredibly, he is planning to produce an anthology of love poetry and wondered if I had any suggestions. I did not know what to say. Matthew Corbett came to lunch and fell foul of the security people. 'What have you got in this case, sir?' 'Sooty,' said Matthew. 'Now, don't try and be clever with us, sir.'

Dinner with Stephen D. and John Kingman with 'How to improve perceptions of the Secretary of State' as the main agenda item.

We did not get very far.

THURSDAY 8 DECEMBER 1994

We had a late night. Because it was the European Finance Bill the whips were taking no risks. At the final division, at about 1.00 a.m., there were twenty-three of them and 295 of us! As a consequence I failed to make it to Harold Elletson's[449] birthday breakfast at the Carlton Club (kidneys and claret at 8.00 a.m.) but (to oblige Nick Winterton) I managed lunch with the CanWest Global Communications Corp – where our host was called Israel and at which I heard his son say twice: 'And Moses said to Israel…'

KC was magnificent in the presentation of his mini-Budget restoring the lost billion from the negated VAT on fuel. (Clobber the motorist, drinker, smoker.) It wasn't the matter but the manner that swung it his way. It was a perfect example of how the right approach in the Chamber can make all the difference. Gordon Brown failed to score. More chattering in the Tea Room: 'Why oh why isn't Ken Clarke our leader?' 'Because he's a Euro-nut. Otherwise he'd walk it.'

FRIDAY 16 DECEMBER 1994

I'm on the train travelling to Chester, my last constituency weekend of the year. When I get to the other end I will step off the train and unveil a plaque marking the refurbishment of the station. It's shaming to confess it, but I like unveiling these plaques, feeling I've left my little mark here and there. I'm particularly chuffed at the thought of the one in the old folks home in Blacon. It was once council run, then taken over and revamped by a delightful Indian family who invited me to perform the reopening ceremony. I pulled the little rope, the curtains parted and I read the words: 'This plague was unveiled by Gyles Brandreth MP…' True.

---

449 MP for Blackpool North 1992–7.

The news is that we lost Dudley West by a margin of 20,000![450] We are now the most unpopular government on record. The Labour Party is standing by for an early election.

The first day of the Christmas recess. I am on my way to Sir Jack Temple's funeral in Chester Cathedral. Is this the final perk for a member representing a city seat – a cathedral send-off?

Rod Richards, impetuous boy, has hit the headlines. The junior Welsh Office minister tells us the people of the Valleys 'have no sense of self-worth' and the Welsh in general suffer from an inferiority complex. Best of all, Labour councillors in the principality are 'short, fat, slimy and fundamentally corrupt'.

At last, a minister not frightened of the truth. I imagine he'll be gone by Christmas.[451]

---

450 Until his death, John Blackburn, the MP since 1979, had held this seat for the Conservatives with a majority of 5,789.

451 In fact, he survived as a Welsh Office minister until June 1996 when allegations in the *News of the World* that he was having a relationship with a public relations officer twenty years his junior and not his wife prompted his resignation.

CHAPTER VI

1995

···

FRIDAY 6 JANUARY 1995

···

Lord, spare me from becoming a silly old buffer. Lord Charteris of Amisfield, former private secretary to Her Majesty, was interviewed by *The Spectator*. He thought he was giving an off-the-record briefing as background for a profile and is now aghast that his remarks have been reproduced. He's a vain old fool. He simply couldn't resist. His verdict on Fergie: 'She is vulgar, vulgar, vulgar, and that is that.' Charles' marriage was doomed from the start: 'The pity is that the Prince of Wales had to marry a virgin.' He expects a divorce 'sooner rather than later', Camilla is 'the love of the Prince's life'. 'When the dear, sweet Queen dies, although I wish she could go on forever, a council of succession will appoint Charles as head of state. I know Charles, know the man, and believe he will be a good king, a king for his time.'

When Charteris came to Chester (for which I was grateful, very grateful) my people loved him. Hobnobbing with an establishment grandee of the old school (and a royal confidant to boot) is their idea of heaven. It was mine too, I suppose, once upon a time. But the novelty's worn off. This year I want to spend less time with complacent old farts who know it all and more with the likes of my new young friend Finkelstein.[452] Danny (thirty-something, bright as a button, easy, funny, funny-looking) belongs to a breed I'd not encountered before I arrived at Westminster: people who write pamphlets. There are scores of them, earnest young men (they're mostly men), producing earnest papers that nobody (other than other earnest pamphleteers) reads. But I think Danny is special. He was once an SDP groupie, now runs the Social Market Foundation (a think tank, funded by David Sainsbury, chaired by Will's dad)[453] and though he takes his work

---

452 Daniel Finkelstein, later executive editor of *The Times* and Baron Finkelstein of Pinner since 2013.

453 GB's daughter Saethryd was a friend of Will, the son of Robert Skidelsky, Lord Skidelsky since 1991, author and academic, chairman of the Social Market Foundation since 1991.

seriously he seems to take himself less so. Anyway, we get on well (he laughs at my jokes), he has ambitions to get onto the candidates list (the name Finkelstein may prove a bit of a downer there), and he's going to come on board as an informal adviser.

TUESDAY 10 JANUARY 1995

Breakfast with Stephen and Danny at 20 Queen Anne's Gate. It's a small office right at the top of the building – flight after flight. The exercise will do me good. Danny supplied coffee, croissants and diet coke (that's all he drinks). He is very engaging – and just what Stephen needs. He can help draft speeches (which I hate doing) and he can keep S in touch with ideas/life beyond the DNH. (Ministers have so much departmental bumf to get through they have little opportunity to meet with other members of the government outside their department and no time at all to *think* about anything. Stephen's mentor was Peter Walker who made it a rule to have half an hour written into the diary for daily contemplation. Stephen does not follow his example, but Stephen, of course, doesn't want to think about the DNH!) We've agreed to meet every Tuesday morning like this. I'm delighted.

I had my postponed meeting with Hayden Phillips to discuss Honours. It was very funny. Hayden, of course, didn't want the meeting to happen in the first place. Indeed, after he'd ushered me to a corner of his office and tea had been served and the door securely closed, he murmured, 'This meeting isn't taking place, you understand.' 'Of course,' I murmured back.

Of the great mysteries of British society – how to get a table at The Ivy, who decides who features in *Who's Who* – none is more shrouded in secrecy than the detail of the workings of the honours system. Honours are only to be discussed by the Permanent Secretary and the Secretary of State – nobody else (not the junior ministers and certainly not the Parliamentary Private Secretary) is to know what's going on. Unfortunately this Secretary of State simply isn't interested. He thinks it's a lot of nonsense. It's not why he came into politics and he's not going to give it any time, but if it amuses me, that's fine by him. It *does* amuse me. I don't take it too seriously, but I go along with the Anthony Sampson[454] line: 'honours make people happier, and sometimes nicer.' And, of course, if you don't like them you can always turn them down. ('To be Bernard Shaw is honour enough.')

I think Hayden does take it seriously. He enjoys the power of patronage. He also likes playing at being conspiratorial. For much of the meeting he held his notes close to his chest – literally – and when I mentioned a name he would glance slyly down at his papers and then purr at me, 'Mmm – something for Alan Bates? Mmm, yes, I think we can help you

---

454 Journalist, author of *The Anatomy of Britain*, first published 1962.

there.' He played a funny cat-and-mouse game with a document which he flashed in front of me, then half showed me, then pulled away from me, then gave me, murmuring silkily 'I shouldn't, I really shouldn't … but why not?' I presume he had intended to give me the paper – 'Honours in Confidence' – all along, but by going through the little arabesque he heightened the drama and made me feel I was getting more out of him than actually I was.

Anyway, this is what I now know. Twice a year (around 1 May for the New Year's honours, around 1 November for the Birthday list) the department submits its recommendations to No. 10. They end up with around twenty-four successful candidates, perhaps one Companion of Honour, a couple of knights, a dame, three or four Commanders of the Order of the British Empire, five or six Officers, six to ten MBEs. The final list is drawn from recommendations from different desks within the department, from outside suggestions, and from bright ideas conjured up by the Permanent Secretary. The department's list is seen by the Secretary of State, who can comment, make suggestions, even tinker with the order of priorities, but it goes to No. 10 from the Permanent Secretary, not from the SoS. The essence of it is: it's Hayden's list.

'I felt the K for Robert Stephens was right, didn't you? I saw his *Lear* and thought, "Yes, yes."'

'Isn't Donald Sinden on the list?'

He glanced down at his crib-sheet. 'Mmm, doesn't seem to be.'

'He should be.'

'It works on the escalator principle. You can be on the escalator for a year or two before you reach the top. I don't think Donald Sinden's been on the escalator in my time.'

'I think he's one for the escalator, don't you?'

(Before he dies, Simon wants to see Don achieve his K and, if it can be done, it will be.) I threw out one or two other ideas – children's writers and illustrators, Cliff, Elton, Cameron Mackintosh, George Speaight – and we agreed that I would return in a week or two for a further 'meeting that isn't' equipped with a considered list of potential nominees. There will be nothing in writing, of course. Rule No. 1:

> Honours are dealt with on an 'in confidence' and personal basis. Individuals must in no circumstances be informed (or get to know) that they are being considered for an honour and this information must therefore be restricted to the smallest possible circle. Absolutely no correspondence about the potential or actual success, or otherwise, of nominated candidates can be entered into.

According to the 'confidential' paper I have before me, honours are given for 'outstanding service (not for merely successfully filling a job for a long period)'; 'it is unusual for a person with less than twenty years' overall service to receive an honour'; 'there should be very strong reasons for putting forward people in their thirties or early forties; if they are good enough at that age for an honour it is possible they will subsequently reach a position eligible for a higher honour'. You are unlikely to get a knighthood before you are fifty; you won't be offered a second honour within five years of receiving your first; and if you are expecting your gong on retirement, if you don't get it in the list *immediately* following your retirement, you've missed the boat. And keep your nose clean: 'It is important that those recommended for awards have a private character which reflects the high standard expected of recipients of honours. Nor should there be anything in their past history which would make the person unsuitable to receive an honour.'

Marginals Club dinner with Jeremy Hanley. Everyone likes him (you couldn't not), but the verdict of his peers is damning: he's punch-drunk and he's blown it.

MONDAY 16 JANUARY 1995

Small lunch with the PM at No. 10. I sat immediately opposite him. He was in good form, feels the year's got off to the right start, sensed he'd scored a few points in his *Frost* interview. He thinks we've got Labour on the ropes over devolution. And Blair is vowing to renationalise the railways which could be useful. The PM has high hopes of Norman Blackwell.[455] 'He's fizzing with ideas.' And he's asked key departments to set up policy groups to develop radical new thinking 'right across the whole range of government'. By the summer he wants to have the makings of 'a new manifesto for the new millennium'. 'And, as well as general themes, I want some bite-sized chunks of policy voters can get their teeth into.'

When I report the PM's turn of phrase to Stephen he winces. 'We're forty points behind in the polls! It's going to take more than "bite-sized chunks of policy" to turn the tide.' It is going to fall to me to organise the national heritage 'policy' group. (Yes, it's that unimportant.)

WEDNESDAY 1 FEBRUARY 1995

High drama in the middle of the night. I'd had a pleasantly liquid and gossipy supper with Seb and was gently wending my way along the Library corridor when around the bend swept Jeremy Hanley.

'Go to the Prime Minister's room at once.'

'What's up?'

---

455 Successor to Sarah Hogg as Head of the Prime Minister's No. 10 Policy Unit 1995–7; formerly of McKinsey & Co.; since 1997 Lord Blackwell of Woodcote.

'Just go. Now. I'll see you there.'

I beetled round the corner and down the corridor to the PM's room. It was packed. There were thirty or forty of us, crowded round the table. I squeezed my way in and perched myself directly behind the PM's chair. He looked calm but anxious. 'If everyone's here, let me tell you what's happened. *The Times* have got hold of a paper they claim is the Anglo-Irish joint framework document and they're publishing it in the morning. It isn't what they say it is and what they are doing is grossly irresponsible. I don't know what they think they're playing at. There are black works going on at the crossroads of peace.' He was angry, frustrated, desperate that this premature publication of an incomplete, unfinished draft could derail the peace process. He took us through what he's achieved to date, told us not to take what's in *The Times* at face value ('It's like the first chapter of an Agatha Christie mystery, it doesn't tell the whole story'), and repeated that there would be, could be no betrayal of the Unionists. When he'd said his piece, he invited questions and for half an hour self-important colleagues made fairly obvious points in urgent and hushed tones to show that they understood the gravity of the situation. While one vain old goat was droning on, I caught Jeremy's eye and, fearing I was suddenly going to get an attack of nervous giggles, leant back against the wood panelling – only to have the wall suddenly swing away behind me. It turned out I was leaning against a disguised door that opened onto the PM's private loo. (I didn't know he had one.) I caught myself halfway to the floor and for the rest of the meeting stood, half-crouching, frozen to spot.

This morning *The Times* is saying there's going to be a joint North–South authority with executive powers and a declaration of 'the birthright of everyone born in either jurisdiction to be part as of right of the Irish nation.' Molyneux,[456] Trimble,[457] John Taylor[458] – they're all crying 'betrayal'. We're getting a statement this afternoon and the PM's going to broadcast to the nation tonight.

LATER

Paddy Mayhew did well. He was sombre, *sotto voce*, convincing. 'Consent is the very foundation of everything we are seeking to achieve.' The UUs are incandescent, but overall in the Tea Room on this one the troops are content.

----

456 James Molyneaux, Ulster Unionist MP for Antrim South 1970–83, Lagan Valley 1983–97; Leader of the Ulster Unionist Party 1979–95; later Baron Molyneux of Killead.

457 David Trimble, Ulster Unionist MP for Upper Bann 1990–2005; Leader of the Ulster Unionist Party 1995–2005; First Minister of Northern Ireland 1998–2002; later Baron Trimble of Lisnagarvey.

458 John D. Taylor, MEP for Northern Ireland 1979–89; Ulster Unionist MP for Strangford 1983–2001; later Baron Kilclooney of Armagh.

I've just returned from dinner with the European Commission at 8 Storey's Gate. They seem bemused by our goings-on. Quentin Davies (who is wildly pro-Euro) reassured them that we'll be in EMU in 1999. I said I reckoned we wouldn't join in the first wave, but we'd be there two or three years later. What does the Cabinet want? Half want in, half want out, and the sceptics are gaining ground. What does the party want? Fisticuffs in the street. Tim Renton[459] is calling Portillo 'a flat-earther'. Teddy Taylor is dancing in the lobby because Douglas Hurd has had his 'position paper' on the IGC [Inter-Governmental Conference] negotiations stuffed up his jacksie. 'We're all bastards now.'

And down at the shallow end of the pool, at the Department of National Heritage, things aren't much better. I accompanied Stephen to the Heritage Select Committee this morning and, faced with fairly hostile questioning (Kaufman is so pleased with himself; Gorst is such an ass) my man didn't do too badly – but on the way in one of the hacks hovering at the door asked him (I think quite innocently) what films he'd recently seen and enjoyed. Stephen couldn't think what to say. He hasn't been to the cinema in years. Films do not feature on his radar screen. His mind went blank. He said he couldn't remember. That's what's going to make the headlines.

We must do something about it, both because it's doing him harm and because we're wasting an opportunity. At six I went to the Arts Council for a drink with Mary Allen[460] and she asked, 'How's he getting on? Is he enjoying it?' 'He's beginning to enjoy it,' I lied, 'sorting out the priorities.'

'Now tell me, Gyles, what does he want from us?' What on earth could I say? I simply blathered.

TUESDAY 7 FEBRUARY 1995

'If Mr Dorrell does, as is rumoured, see himself as a future leader, he had better sharpen up his performance.' This morning we agreed that if *The Times* is actually giving over a whole leader to Stephen's 'studied disdain' of his portfolio, we need to take action fairly urgently. The trouble is, in this business, once you get a certain reputation it's difficult to shift. Look at poor Jeremy. Michael Grade has sent over a batch of Channel 4 movies on video. John K. is putting *Four Weddings and a Funeral* in the Secretary of State's box this weekend.

The news of the hour is that Allan Stewart[461] has resigned from the government. The likeable mutton-chopped junior Scottish Office minister, who has always seemed rather

---

459 MP for Sussex Mid 1974–97; later Baron Renton of Mount Harry.

460 Secretary-General of the Arts Council 1994–7.

461 MP for East Renfrewshire 1979–83, Eastwood 1983–97; Under-Secretary of State for Scotland 1981–6, 1992–5.

a mild man to me, appears to have taken a pick-axe to some of his constituents! You couldn't make it up. Allan, unhappy at the disruptive antics of a group of anti-motorway protestors in his patch, decided to confront them, and sometime on Sunday turned up at their encampment with half a dozen like-minded souls all set for a confrontation. Things got out of hand. Allan says he picked up the pick-axe for self-defence. The eco-warriors tell a different story. Whether the unfortunate minister was breathalised we've not been told. Anyway he's gone and he's being replaced by George Kynoch.[462] I've just been with Raymond Robertson who is incensed. He cannot see why *he* hasn't been chosen. He's hurt, upset, angry. I know the feeling. I didn't tell him that the problem is that George *looks* ministerial (he has the suit, the posture, the slightly pompous know-all manner) while Raymond, who is really sweet, giggles too much, drinks too much, is unmarried and overweight.

While the Scottish Under-Secretary of State was brandishing his axe in Glasgow, the Chief Secretary to the Treasury was in Oxford saying his prayers. Jonathan Aitken preached at evensong at Hertford College Chapel on Sunday and he's sent me a copy of his address: 'My thesis to you tonight is that the gap between the Christian teachings and the honourable profession of politics is a narrow one, bridgeable by prayer.' It's exactly a year ago today that Stephen Milligan died and the springboard for Jonathan's address was the quite wonderful sermon the Vicar of Hammersmith gave us at Stephen's funeral. Jonathan quotes from it: 'Let us affirm today the possibility of grace in political life, the marriage of vision with pragmatism, and be thankful that Stephen recognised it … Stephen would not have been ashamed to acknowledge the half forgotten truth that politics can be one way in which the Kingdom of God is advanced.'

I like Jonathan more all the time. Stephen D. doesn't trust him.

MONDAY 13 FEBRUARY 1995

We've lost another minister, but this is bizarre. Charles Wardle[463] has resigned because Britain's 'quality of life is jeopardised by European immigration laws'. It doesn't make sense. The PM and Michael Howard are leading a counter-offensive. Tebbit is doing his best to mix it. In the Tea Room the other ranks are confused. The whips are busy spreading the word that Wardle (an odd fish) is in the throes of some sort of mid-life crisis and he's disaffected because his talents haven't been fully recognised. Here, Wardle doesn't

---

462 MP for Kincardine & Deeside 1992–7. Both George Kynoch and Raymond Robertson were elected for the first time in 1992.

463 MP for Bexhill & Battle since 1983; Under-Secretary of State at the Home Office 1992–4, at the DTI 1994–5.

count for much (actually, I don't think he counts for anything), but out there this will just add to the general sense of disarray.

<hr>

WEDNESDAY 15 FEBRUARY 1995

Newt Gingrich's 'pollster' is in town.[464] We've just had supper with him and he's a joy. He's called Frank Lemt, an unlikely-looking specimen, in his twenties, sneakers, jeans, backpack. We picked him up in Central Lobby, squeezed into the ministerial car (Stephen in front, me, Danny, Frank squashed in the back) and sped across to Pasta Prego in Beauchamp Place. As we went, Frank offered his thumbnail analysis of our position: 'You are in a fast car driving towards a brick wall. You can either stop and get out or you can continue as you are, heading for that wall, foot on the gas. If you stop and get out you might have a chance. If you don't, then take my word for it: you're heading for (theatrical pause) *o-bli-vion!*'

Over the meal he talked non-stop and the essence of his message is we're doomed because a) we're a shambles, b) we're divided, c) nobody knows what we're about, d) we've been in power for seventeen years. Because the electorate is ungrateful, our only hope is to find a way of wiping out the past. We need to create a clean slate and make ourselves credible again. As one of the authors/architects of Newt's 'Contract with America', he proposed that we should come up with a UK equivalent:

> On 1 March your Prime Minister gets up in the House of Commons and says, 'On 1 March next year there will be a general election. Between now and then, this is what my government will deliver.' Make the goals deliverable – inflation at a certain level, x more policeman on the beat, y more nurses, z more teachers in schools. Because you have set out specific targets everyone will focus on what you deliver during the year. Your past record will become irrelevant. At the end of the 365 days you have the election. Your Prime Minister says, 'This year I promised you so and so and I delivered. Next year I'm promising you and such and I can deliver again. Trust me.'

We were enchanted by his manner and there's more than something in what he's saying. 'Look, it worked for Newt.'

Stephen grinned, 'I'm not sure it's a very British way of doing things.'

'Have you got another way out?' enquired Frank. We hadn't. 'Remember the alternative,' he said cheerily. 'It's *o-bli-vion!*'

<hr>

464 Newton Gingrich, the Republican from Georgia and Speaker of the House of Representatives, credited with the success of the electorally popular 'Contract with America'. Gingrich made extensive use of polling and focus group discussion in developing policy.

THURSDAY 16 FEBRUARY 1995

The Prime Minister is telling ministers to pull themselves together and 'toe the line'. Over breakfast Stephen, Danny and I worked up a draft memo to send to the PM. It's Frank's 'Contract with Britain', but knowing the PM's commitment to his charters (aaargh!) we've called our paper 'The Charter for Government':

1. The problem: we've been in power for seventeen years; dissatisfactions have accumulated; there's a perception we've not kept our promises.

2. The solution: draw a line under both past failures and past successes (the electorate isn't grateful) and only talk about the future; make ourselves accountable for the promises we make.

3. The proposition: a Charter for Government – a one-year programme of deliverable promises on which we are prepared to be judged.

4. Stage One: announce the preparation of the Charter at Central Council; launch a period of consultation: 'listening to Britain', letting the nation decide the priorities. Do this by means of a) formal polling using focus groups; b) open meetings around the country with ministers, MPs etc., where they don't speak, they *listen*; c) policy panels based on the manifesto groups now being set up which would also take evidence from public and experts.

5. Stage Two: the consultation period lasts three months; the outcomes are translated into the Charter for Government unveiled on Day One of the party conference in October – a programme of specific deliverable promises with the promise that we will be accountable for the success of our delivery at the end of the year. Each minister's conference speech centres on what their department has to deliver.

6. The idea is to look to the future and make us seem responsive and accountable.

The alternative ... *o-bli-vion!*

MONDAY 20 FEBRUARY 1995

Michael Foot[465] (still wearing that same donkey jacket) has reassured us, 'I was never a Soviet agent.' Nicholas Fairbairn has died 'from liver complications', aged sixty-one. 'Nicky

---

465 1913–2010; Labour MP for Devonport 1945–55, Ebbw Vale 1960–83, Blaenau Gwent 1983–92; Leader of the Labour Party 1980–83.

liked his dram' is how the obituarists are putting it. The poor man was a sot, watching him stumbling about the corridors here, pitiable. People like Ancram and Lord James say, 'Ah, you should have known Nicky in his prime.' Even knowing him in his decrepitude there were still flashes of brilliance that managed to fight their way through the alcoholic haze. He listed his recreations in *Who's Who*: 'making love, ends meet and people laugh.'

Excellent session with Stephen and John K. at the DNH. We've actually got a credible (and creditable) programme of policy announcements/initiatives to set out over the next three months. March: the tourism document on the 1st; the big heritage speech on the 8th (opening up the listing system); sponsorship and the arts on the 29th. April: privacy, film and the future of the BBC. May: the Fundamental Expenditure Review, working title, 'Growing the Audience' (could be worse, could be better), and the big Youth and Sport launch on the 23rd. Plus some odds and sods: Stonehenge and the private finance initiative, the glories of Greenwich, the first dollops of lottery distribution.

Yes, we should have got to grips with this months ago, but at least it's happening now. *And* Stephen has agreed to a series of set-piece speeches on key areas, speeches that will contain both commitment and (wait for it) passion!

WEDNESDAY 22 FEBRUARY 1995

The PM was on a roll tonight, exhilarated by the triumph of the London-Dublin framework document. There's going to be a Northern Ireland assembly (with PR); a North–South body with members from both the assembly and the Irish Parliament; an end to the Irish constitutional claim to NI and changes to our legislation to give the people of NI the option of staying part of the UK or voting for a united Ireland. Paisley is ranting that Major has 'sold out the Union', Willie Ross says it's 'unworkable', but in the Chamber and the Tea Room it went down well.

The PM began the day in Belfast, then did his statement to the House, then ended up at No. 10 for our reception for the London arts community. We were fearful that with all the Irish excitement he might have to give us short shrift. In the event, though he was late, when he arrived the adrenalin was overflowing and he was at his absolute best: there was energy, easy charm, a sense of purpose. I said to him, 'This is one of those days when you realise why you came into this, isn't it?' He grinned: 'Yes.' Then he checked himself, 'There's a long way to go, but at the end … just think of the prize.'

He stood in front of the fireplace on a little footstool and gave a gem of a speech. He talked about the artists who have made Downing Street what it is – he talked about the craftsmen, the furniture makers, the painters. He thanked and celebrated the artists in the room, buttered them up like nobody's business. But they sensed he really meant it

– and I think he did. It was exactly the kind of speech Stephen should have been making for months. It was wonderful – impressive and moving. He spoke without notes (I imagine the stuff about the pictures etc. is part of his set-piece Welcome to Downing Street routine) and the effect was everything we could have wanted. I wheeled Hugh Grant over to meet Norma and the light flirtation (on both sides) was charming to behold.

At the ridiculous end of the spectrum I found myself in a corner of the green drawing room with a moist-eyed Andrew Lloyd Webber who, not having any idea who I was, said 'Are you coming to Antigua for the weekend?' Lady Lloyd Webber turned to Nicholas Lloyd and Eve Pollard and cooed, 'Oh do. It's just the Lloyd Webbers and the Frosts and the Saatchis – the home team.'

Donald Sinden was funny – as always. He asked Richard Eyre[466] if it's true that Harriet Walter is to play Hamlet at the National. Before Eyre could answer, Don went on: 'I understand you approached Paul Scofield to play Claudius, but he said, "No – have you tried Miriam Margolyes?"'

Supper with David Willetts. I don't think he's enjoying the Whips' Office. I think he thinks a lot of it's very silly and he may be insufficiently clubable for their taste.

Under cover of the framework document, we've slipped out an announcement on prescription charges. They're going up 50p to £5.25.

MONDAY 27 FEBRUARY 1995

I took Stephen to Buckingham Palace to see Prince Philip. Not much was achieved. HRH was running late. We waited in his study – it's very Peter Scott, long shelves of books, furniture with a distinct '50s Erkalion feel. Just before HRH appeared, the young equerry (who I didn't know) came in and got us to stand side by side at a certain angle at a specific point (yes, a precise spot) a third of the way into the room. He marshalled us into this awkward receiving line and we stood there like Tweedledum and Tweedledee awaiting the arrival of the King of Hearts. The whole set-up is ludicrous – but the D of E is a good man and he never stops wanting to make a positive contribution. We didn't get very far on privacy. Stephen was fairly frank and said there isn't much the government can do – 'or will do' I chirruped. HRH then set out his stall on competitive sport. It's a hobby-horse and he rides it well and convincingly. What he says about the value of team games is exactly right and exactly what Sproatie and the PM want to see in the White Paper. In fact, it would probably have been better to take Sproat. Heigh-ho. Anyway, HRH promised to send us all sorts of thoughts and to

---

466 Director of the Royal National Theatre 1988–97.

introduce Stephen to anyone he'd like to meet and Stephen mumbled the right sort of responses and nodded charmingly until the equerry, who had popped his head nervously around the door a couple of times, returned wide-eyed with anxiety: 'I'm sorry Sir, but Her Majesty is waiting.'

I've just returned from No. 11. The Chancellor was late. He'd been in a huddle with Eddie George[467] in the wake of the Barings collapse. Ken's line: 'It's bad, but I'm not sure it's as bad as Eddie seems to think.'

I said, 'What exactly happened?'

Ken laughed, 'I'm not entirely sure.'

It seems a Barings trader, aged twenty-six, managed to lose around £600 million trading in derivatives without anybody knowing. 'It's beyond belief.' 'You'd have thought so.' I love the way Ken chuckles in the face of adversity. Ever-ready Eddie and his boys spent the weekend feverishly trying to put together a rescue package, but without success – so bang goes Britain's oldest bank, 4,000 employees have lost their jobs, the pound's got the jitters, an international banking crisis is on the cards, but our admirable Chancellor is still chortling. He's irresistible.

WEDNESDAY 1 MARCH 1995

The roller-coaster ride continues. Tonight we survived – with a majority of five. We knew the UUs and the Paisley boys would exact their revenge by voting with Labour. What we didn't expect was that Norman Lamont would vote against us. I suspect his plan was to abstain, but he was tipped into voting the way he did by Douglas Hurd. I saw it happen. During Douglas's smooth-as-alabaster wind-up Norman intervened to ask if the government believes monetary union will lead to political union. Douglas side-stepped the question, but couldn't resist a little jesting at Norman's expense: 'My RHF is one of the great experts on the subject because, with the Prime Minister, it was he who negotiated our opt-out. I have always admired the skill with which they did that. I was sitting in admiration in an adjacent room at the time.' As the laughter rolled round him, Norman's face turned to thunder. He thought, 'I will not be mocked. I will be revenged on the whole pack of you.'

And indeed he might have been had not five of the whipless wonders voted with us and five abstained. We wheeled in our sick, including Geoffrey Dickens, who has lost so much weight and looks like death. He is a lovely man and, quite rightly, the PM sought him out to give him a grateful squeeze.

---

467 Governor of the Bank of England 1993–2003.

MONDAY 13 MARCH 1995

Benet's twentieth birthday. Our little celebration lunch in Cambridge yesterday was really good. Blair has replaced Clause IV with a new creed that promises to put 'power, wealth and opportunity into the hands of the many not the few.' So that's all right then. I think *my* new creed may be 'communitarianism'. I've just emerged from a session with Amitai Etzioni, Harvard lawyer and father of the concept. Given the collapse of the family network, urbanisation and the disappearance of the street as a real community, what do we do? And how do we do it without creating a paternalistic nanny state? Amitai is experimenting with practical ways of reinventing communities, doing it locally, from the bottom up. Alan Howarth is organising a small group to have dinner with him tomorrow night.

As if he didn't have enough to do, the Prime Minister obliges colleagues by generously autographing bottles that can then be auctioned off at party functions. I am about to take two bottles of House of Commons Wickham Fumé to his room in the hope that they can be signed after PMQs tomorrow. On a bad day there are *dozens* of bottles clanking on John Ward's[468] desk awaiting prime ministerial attention. Colleagues of the old school (and a more generous disposition) get brandy or malt whisky for the great man to sign. I'm opting for the Wickham Fumé at a fiver a bottle, despite the lordly reprimand I received from Sir Peter Tapsell: 'You cannot ask the British Prime Minister to autograph a bottle of *table* wine. You really cannot.'

'It is English,' I bleated.

'Non-vintage?'

'Er … yes.'

'Good God, what is the party coming to?'

THURSDAY 16 MARCH 1995

Inadvertently I appear to have landed poor Fergie in the soup. She called. 'Children in Crisis' was in a crisis. They had a fund-raising dinner in the City and needed a speaker. Could I? Would I? *Please.* Yes, of course, but I have to be back at the Commons to vote at ten. Fine. So along I go last night and all is hunky-dory. Sarah is in very jolly form, I sit on her right, we are cosy, gossipy, giggly (*slightly* excessively so: I imagine we rather irritate the rest of the table whom we appear to ignore). Sarah tells me how she's made nothing out of Budgie the Helicopter, but *she's* got a new idea for a children's story that

---

468 MP for Poole 1979–97; he succeeded Graham Bright as the Prime Minister's PPS 1994–7.

turns out to be just like *my* new idea, so why don't we do it together? Nine-thirty comes and I say I've got to speak now because I've got to go and vote at ten. 'No, no, no!' 'Yes, yes, yes!' I get up and do my speech, going right over the top about the Mountain Haven Centre and Sarah's commitment, achievement, beauty, brilliance, pizzazz. I've got tears in my eyes. She's got tears in hers. I say I've *got* to go now. 'No, no, no!' 'Yes, yes, yes!' Lots of huggy-kissy goodbyes and then, just as I'm slipping out, I have a bright idea.

'Look, why don't we find the richest man in the room and get him to take my place?'

'What?'

'He can sit next to you for coffee and you can seduce him. Before the brandy's arrived he'll have promised a nice fat donation for the cause.'

'I'm not sure.'

'Go on, go for it.'

And poor girl, she did. I've just had a call from the *Daily Mail* and, after I'd departed what happened, it seems, was this: the rich stranger was found and placed next to Fergie; to everyone's surprise a Beadle-style prankster's auction then ensued, in which people were somehow persuaded to raise money by removing their clothing. The long and the short of it is that the man who filled my seat was encouraged to drop his trousers in aid of the cause – and just as he did so photographers appeared from the shadows and flash, bang, wallop caught candid snaps of dear old Fergie with a fellow she's never met before with his trousers round his ankles.

....

LATER

....

I was going to say none of us can choose how we are going to be remembered, but I've just come from sharing a cup of tea with the Prime Minister and I think he is *actively* engaged in securing his future reputation. He was talking about his trip to Israel, Jordan, Arafat etc. and let slip that Martin Gilbert[469] had come along. I said, 'The historian?' 'Yes, he's an authority on the Holocaust.' 'Of course, but did you get him to keep a record of your meetings?'

The PM quickly changed the subject.

Very evidently he wasn't going to let himself be drawn. But it's clear: he's got Gilbert on board as his personal chronicler.

Five years down the line, we'll have Churchill's authorised biographer producing the definitive insider's take on 'the Major years'.

---

469 Historian, fellow of Merton College, Oxford, since 1962; official biographer of Sir Winston Churchill since 1968; knighted 1995.

WEDNESDAY 22 MARCH 1995

A funny letter from Fergie – 'Life might have been easier if I had had to leave for a vote at 10.00 – alternatively had you remained at my right hand I would not have been on the front page of *The Sun* this morning!' – but I'm afraid the notepaper confirms Lord Charteris's worst fears: a huge swan-like S (at least 50 point font) surmounted by a coronet. 'Where are your children's books? I would love to hear more about your writing…' Michèle says: steer clear – 'the woman's a disaster waiting to happen'.

I have just returned from taking a delegation to the Department of Employment to see a woman who can only be described as a triumph. She may look like a death-watch beetle, but Ann Widdecombe is quite simply the best woman we've got. She had my Chester people eating out of her hand. She understood exactly what they were after, told them precisely what she could and couldn't do, and when she makes a commitment you know she'll deliver.

I gave the city council people a copy of yesterday's Hansard. I wanted them to see that I had been badgering Gummer on the local government review. I should be ashamed of my own hypocrisy (because Gummer has done exactly what I wanted and the badgering was merely for show), but I don't quite see how else I could have played it. Our people on the city council wanted unitary status, wanted it *passionately*, but our people on the county council naturally wanted the status quo. I don't think the man in the street really gives a toss. If we'd gone for unitary status, my city people would have been overjoyed, but the county would have been dismayed, the county headquarters might have moved out of Chester, we'd have had disruption, additional unemployment and no guarantee of improved services. Despite being harangued by the city councillors (it was a horrible scene – they were spitting blood), privately I opted for the status quo. I think I was swayed by the fact that I find the officers on the county council more impressive than those on the city council. Irritated at being shouted at by Paul Durham over the millions we coughed up for MBNA, I fear there may even have been a smidgeon of vengefulness in the way I decided to go. Formally, I did everything as I should: I conveyed all the views I had received to the Department of the Environment. Informally, in the lobby, I tipped J. Gummer the wink that I felt the status quo would 'probably be best'. Now every other historic city, every vaguely comparable city in fact, is going to get unitary status. Chester is the lone exception. Was I right? It's a close call.

LATER

The Marginals Club dinner with Michael Dobbs[470] was poorly attended and not encouraging.

---

470 Novelist; deputy chairman of the Conservative Party 1994–5; later Baron Dobbs of Wylye.

The PM can't wait to get shot of poor Jeremy and I imagine Michael (another truly nice guy) will join him on the way to the knackers' yard. But never mind Smith Square: Stephen and I began the evening at No. 10. We went to see Norman Blackwell, Head of the No. 10 Policy Unit, the 'thinker' at the right-hand of the leader of our great nation, the man who is fizzing with those ideas and bite-sized chunks of policy that are going to sweep us back to power and give Martin Gilbert something to write home about. It was truly appalling.

We climbed the stairs to a garret-like office, small and Spartan, where Norman, courteous, self-effacing, smiling quietly behind the owlish giglamps, shared with us the fruit of his pensive nights and laborious days. He has spent months on this and had it all set out neatly on display sheets. As he turned each page our hearts sank lower. You couldn't argue with any of it, but it was all so horrifyingly obvious and banal. He's identified our weaknesses (correctly) and he listed what we need to offer under five 'policy themes', each subdivided into various strands: 1) delivering economic security; 2) creating a society of opportunity, choice and reward; 3) support for law, order and justice; 4) a commitment to first class public services; 5) reflecting national pride in the UK and our role in the world. It was very worthy – you wouldn't want to disagree – but the average well-informed activist could have cobbled it together in an afternoon. And the Big Ideas ranged from 'creating a good news package on information technology' to – wait for it! – 'relaunching the Citizen's Charter'. I said almost nothing. Stephen probed a bit, tried out one or two of the thoughts we'd gained from Newt Gingrich's man, but Norman Blackwell is what he is: a decent dull dog. And we are doomed. Forget the Charter for Government. Here comes *o-bli-vion*!

MONDAY 27 MARCH 1995

I found Jeremy alone in the Tea Room. He was gazing at the front page of *The Times*: 'Major ready to get rid of Hanley'. He looked up, all puffy-eyed. 'I blame you,' he said, 'personally.' He laughed and shook his head. 'You just can't win.' He remains fiercely loyal to the PM – while around the knives are out. Everyone is agreed that Jeremy must go, preferably sooner than later. The likely scenario is that he'll be sacrificed on 5 May in the aftermath of our local election bloodbath. The real question is: can the PM survive? Open speculation is rife again. Today's most popular prediction: a leadership challenge in the autumn, with Lamont as the stalking-horse, pre-empted by Major stepping down to be replaced by a so-called 'dream team': Heseltine as PM, Portillo as deputy.

The Wednesday Club gathered for our occasional Monday night of gossip, wine and sandwiches. We met in the Home Secretary's room behind the Speaker's chair. (Only the holders of the great offices of state – plus the Leader of the House – have decent-sized rooms here. The rest of the Cabinet have fairly poky rooms, sub-Pugin, a desk and a couple of chairs, off a long narrow corridor upstairs.) In theory the setting was exactly right for half a dozen of the more upwardly-mobile members of the government's team to meet and put the world to rights. In practice, it didn't work at all. The room was inhibiting. We felt guilty about our gossip. We talked conspiratorially, in hushed tones, as if the room might be bugged. (Perhaps it is?) And when I suggested we might each give a sketch of our boss, strengths/weaknesses/prospects, Lidington[471] [Michael Howard's PPS] looked really alarmed. 'I don't that would be quite proper,' he squeaked primly. I was irritated at the time, but I think he was probably right.

I am in the Library, leafing through a long screed that has arrived from Sandringham. HRH hopes I will 'persuade the SoS to read, at least, bits of it'. Look what he has to say about team games: 'It is the coordination of individual skills and team tactics and the sublimation of individual ambitions for the good of the team that brings success.' Exactly.

We've just been voting on the Disability Discrimination Bill. Hague is very, very good, but Alan Howarth voted with Labour. He gets wobblier by the hour.

THURSDAY 30 MARCH 1995

I am sitting alone on the PPSs bench as the three-hour tourism debate trudges towards its close. Around me, assorted good-hearted oddities (Toby Jessel has been speaking with his mouth full and his Garrick Club tie poking out through his flies); facing me, empty Labour benches and a pretty desultory opposition double act: Chris Smith, thin and worthy, Tom Pendry, fat and worthy.[472] It's interesting how little they've got to offer.

It's been another long DNH day. To get to breakfast with Stephen and Danny by 8.00 I leave home at 7.00 and tonight I'll be back by 11.00 p.m. which will be my earliest night this week. Sometimes I creep out of bed and M's still fast asleep and when I get back it's gone midnight and she's already asleep again. I don't like it. But we're making progress. Stephen is infinitely more engaged. I'm making real headway on the funding of dance and drama students, largely by scurrying from Stephen to Gillian [Shephard, Education Secretary] and talking up the issue, saying that 'No. 10 are anxious for us to find a solution' when I've no idea whether or not No. 10 is interested at all. (In fact, they would be.) Sproatie is irritating Stephen by running off to No. 10 whenever he senses the DNH and the DfE are diluting the school sport policy – but he's doing the right thing. The only

---

471 David Lidington, MP for Aylesbury since 1992.

472 Chris Smith was the shadow Heritage Secretary; Tom Pendry, Labour MP for Stalybridge & Hyde 1970–2001, his junior.

way to make progress here is to take ownership of what you believe in and, come hell or high water, drive your policy through.

I had another meeting with Hayden on honours. Between us Danny and I had cobbled together a little list (literally on the back of an envelope) and as well as the legit end of the business (Richard Curtis, John Cleland, Martin Jarvis, Eileen Atkins, Alec McCowen etc.) we threw in some populist suggestions of the 'Arise Dame Cilla' variety: Norman Widsom, Bruce Forsyth, Julie Goodyear, Peggy Mount, Michael Elphick, Delia Smith. Danny (off the top of his head) conjured up a raft of names for the sports list and, knowing I wouldn't have heard of half of them, supplied thumbnail portraits: Ian Rush ('Liverpool soccer legend. This is his testimonial season'), Fred Street ('for many years the England football team's physiotherapist'), Martin Edwards ('chairman of Manchester United. A go-ahead sporting entrepreneur of the sort we are trying to encourage'), Len Martin ('The best-known voice in Britain. He reads the football results on BBC1. He is getting on a bit and presumably will soon retire').

MONDAY 3 APRIL 1995

We went to the Olivier Awards last night *in loco* the Secretary of State. It was *quite* fun (we saw a number of chums, we sat with Sally Greene[473] and Diana Quick – in my mind's eye still in that leather mini-skirt[474] – and Bill Nighy[475] – whose half-hesitant self-consciously sexy style M and I love and Simon [Cadell] *loathes*) – but it doesn't work. If Stephen can't go/won't go (and these events are often on a Sunday night, his one certain night at home in Worcester), then it's better to send no one. My turning up just advertises the fact he's failed to show – again. In the speeches there was the customary mocking of Stephen and sneering at the government.

Good old Sproatie. John K. has just shown me a minute from Sproat's office to the SoS, cc Lord Astor and the Permanent Secretary:

APPOINTMENTS TO THE THEATRE TRUST

Mr Sproat has read Mrs Walker's submission of 28 March and your minute of 29 March asking for views by 31 March.

The Minister does not agree with the recommendations put forward including,

---

473 Theatre owner and producer.

474 GB first met the actress Diana Quick at university when she was President of the Oxford University Dramatic Society.

475 Actor.

specifically, the proposed reappointment of John Drummond and Yvonne Brewster. The Minister also objects to the shortage of time given to him to consider the recommendations and queries whether Mr Brandreth's views have been sought. Mr Sproat points out that it was agreed at 'prayers' that he would discuss appointments with Mr Brandreth before submitting views to the Secretary of State. There has not been sufficient time to do this in this case.

The Minister also objects to the cosy, incestuous and 'mutually flatterous' source of 'outside' advice.

SUNDAY 9 APRIL 1995

Palm Sunday. No hosannas. The *News of the World* strikes again. Last month, my friend Bob Hughes.[476] Today, my friend Richard Spring.[477] 'Tory MP, the Tycoon and the Sunday School Teacher. We expose three-in-a-bed sex session. Exclusive.' Richard, tall, likeable, languid, elegant in a Bertie Woosterish-Newmarket Races sort of a way, appears to have invited an acquaintance (a pensions company executive) and his girlfriend (Odette Nightingale, occasional Sunday school teacher – you couldn't make it up) to dinner last Sunday. The hospitality was generous, the conversation lively (it seems Richard thinks Portillo's quite fanciable, doesn't rate the PM but is ready to give Norma one anytime), and, evidently, *chez* Spring the post-prandial treats go well beyond *crème de menthe frappé* and a Bendicks Bittermint. Poor bugger. I talked to him during the week. He was positively chirpy – off on Friday on a freebie fact-finding jaunt to the Canary Islands. No doubt the vermin from the *News of the World* will have taken particular delight in dragging him from his Lanzarote poolside to confront him with their 'allegations'. Anyway, though he's divorced, though presumably what consenting adults do in private is still nominally their own affair, he's a goner. He's done the right thing: he's resigned as Paddy Mayhew's PPS and he's flying back to face the music. The pity of it is that because the PM has been concentrating so much on Ireland in recent weeks he's seen a lot of Richard and I get the impression (indeed, I know) he liked what he saw: promotion was on the way. Being a hidden genius in an obscure backwater (i.e. yours truly at the DNH) is neither here nor there: in this place being seen to be good by the right people in the right places is what counts. And now he's blown it – and for what?

476 Twice-married Hughes resigned as Parliamentary Secretary at the Office of Public Service and Science on 4 March 1995 in anticipation of the *News of the World*'s report of his extra-marital relationship with his House of Commons secretary, Janet Oates. The paper carried the story under the headline: 'Minister Got His Oates Morning Noon and Night'.

477 MP for Bury St Edmunds 1992–7, Suffolk West 1997–2010; later Baron Risby of Haverhill.

TUESDAY 18 APRIL 1995

Progress on assorted fronts:

Appointments. Stephen is not interested so Sproatie, Tim Kirkhope and I are now having a weekly meeting to vet the department's candidates and feed in our own ideas. We know Hayden will always have the last word (we're just the poor elected), but as Sproatie says, 'Let's see if we can't get the occasional right-thinking bloke with a bit of experience in there alongside the disabled black lesbians – excellent though they no doubt are.' Today's inspiration: my friend Richard Whiteley[478] for the board of the Royal Armouries in Leeds. (Says TK, who is a Leeds MP, 'We must make sure he knows who he's got to thank for this.')

Libraries. I believe there's mileage, purpose and value in rediscovering/reinventing the library service. (An author and communitarian speaks!) Danny agrees and we're developing ideas for a pilot project, involving private finance. Stephen's eyes glaze over ('Let's get the film policy out of the way first') but I'm going to persist.

Film.

SD: 'Gyles, have you got anything to do over the next three weeks?'

GB: 'Er...'

SD: 'Clear your desk – completely. Write the film policy.'

GB: 'Er ... fine.'

The truth is we've got little time, little scope, little room for manoeuvre. What the industry wants are Irish-type tax breaks which the Chancellor can deliver, but we can't. But we can at least put our best foot forward – and raid the lottery. I am seeing David Puttnam[479] at 7.00 p.m. Sproatie would not approve.

Trafalgar Square plinth. Months ago, doing a photocall for the lottery launch in Trafalgar Square, I noticed the empty plinth in the top left-hand corner of the square, by the Sainsbury Wing of the National Gallery. As a joke, making small talk at prayers, I suggested we put a statue on it. And everyone said, why not? My idea was to make it 'the people's statue' – recruit suggestions through a TV show. Naturally, it's not that easy. It seems all sorts, from Lord Pisspot of Fawsley upwards and downwards, have to have a say, but we're making progress. Tomorrow we're meeting Prue Leith[480] and we're going to get the RSA to handle the nominations. The Queen Mother is out because she's alive. Ditto Mrs T. in the tank. Stephen favours the Duke of Wellington on horseback. Sproat says Shakespeare. I have floated the notion of Britain's leading children's characters: Alice, the Mad Hatter, Peter Pan, Rupert, Paddington, Winnie-the-Pooh.

---

478 Reporter and presenter with Yorkshire Television since 1968; host of *Countdown* on Channel 4 since 1982.

479 Film producer; knighted in 1995; Lord Puttnam since 1997.

480 Restaurateur, caterer; chairman of the Royal Society of Arts 1995–7.

LATER

The drink with David Puttnam was very funny. He's diminutive, friendly, eager and has the perfect solution to each and every problem on the planet. He has *all* the answers and has written papers outlining most of them. I rather hoped he'd be turning my children's books into movies. Dream on. He clearly can't wait to get out of movies into politics. Anyway, he's on board. I'm wheeling him in to Stephen on Monday. Because of his Luvvies-for-Labour connections, we shall keep his involvement hush-hush, but at least our policy will be written with a practitioner to hand.

FRIDAY 21 APRIL 1995

I'm Chester bound. A day of local election canvassing beckons. The chairman of the party is on his way to Derbyshire on the same mission – but unfortunately the local Conservatives don't want him! He was due to walk the streets in Erewash, but he's not welcome. The council candidates there say my friend is 'so gaffe-prone' he's bound to bring up 'smutty' national issues when what they want to do is emphasise their local achievements. Poor Jeremy.

And poor Graham Riddick. Last night we 'censured' him, 'suspended' him from the House for ten working days, docked his pay and watched him make another grovelling apology and slink away. I had a cup of tea with him before the debate. He's still kicking himself at his own stupidity. He has handled the aftermath impeccably, but thanks to being set up by the *Sunday Times* and a moment of folly his career has been ruined and he knows it. Nice man.

TUESDAY 25 APRIL 1995

Good breakfast: Stephen, Danny, Andrew Lansley,[481] Michael McManus.[482] Afterwards, we agreed that we'll have Stephen as the new chairman of the party and Danny as director of the Research Department. Now, to make it happen...

The whipless wonders have been invited to return to the fold – but the mischief will go on. At PMQs Blair played a blinder. He taunted the PM on the returning Euro-rebels. The PM countered with Blair's Clause IV rebels. What was he going to do

---

481 Director of the Conservative Research Department 1990–95; MP for South Cambridgeshire since 1997.

482 Former special adviser; Head of Sir Edward Heath's private office from 1996.

about them? Blair came back: 'There is one very big difference – I lead my party, he follows his.' The Labour benches went berserk. We sat sullenly, knowing it was true.

The PM was unhappy. John Ward was unhappy. 'The boss needs the support behind him – he needs to *hear* it.' And where were the planted questions, where were A and Q? What were we playing at? Jim Spicer[483] asked about homosexuals in the armed forces. This is not what the PM needs. He did his best to show he understands the concern of the defence chiefs while keeping sweet with Ian McKellen.[484] Alan Howarth invited the PM to abandon the quest for a national identity card scheme. The PM couldn't oblige him. (This is another fine mess we're getting into quite unnecessarily. We advertised our enthusiasm for identity cards ('a bite-sized chunk of policy') before thinking it through. Privately Michael Howard acknowledges it isn't practical and it won't happen. Publicly we're still flirting with it, there's to be a Green Paper, but we're rousing the rabble *knowing* that in due course we're going to have to disappoint them. Madness.)

Unhappy bunnies everywhere. I've just opened a note from Michael Morris,[485] Deputy Speaker: 'I am just a little surprised and disappointed that I never seem to get invited to functions in my own right ... It may be too late now but I would have hoped that my wife and I might have been included in the VIPs for the VE concerts either on the Monday or the Saturday. While the honour of being Deputy Speaker is very nice, it would be equally nice to enjoy some of the fruits of government.' Stephen is not impressed.

LATER

I am in wine – and why not? I have just come from the Churchill Room where I have been embraced by Franco Zeffirelli![486] He does what I do: pretends to know everybody he meets so he doesn't give offence by failing to recognise someone he met in Padua thirty years ago who recalls the encounter vividly while Franco naturally can't remember it at all. We talked about (I raved about) his John Stride/Judi Dench *Romeo* and the Maggie Smith/Robert Stephens *Much Ado* which made him think we must have worked together at the Old Vic in the '60s! He pressed me to come and stay in Amalfi. I presented him to Stephen.

---

483 MP for Dorset West 1974–97; MEP for Wessex 1979–84.

484 The actor, knighted in 1991, had met with John Major to discuss gay rights issues and received a sympathetic hearing.

485 MP for Northampton South 1974–97.

486 Italian director of opera, theatre, film; a member of the Italian Senate.

I *dragged* Stephen down there to meet him. I said, 'Stephen, you must meet him. This is a great man – theatre, opera, movies.'

Stephen looked bemused.

'And politics,' I said, 'He's a senator now.'

'Let's go,' said Stephen, grinning.

WEDNESDAY 26 APRIL 1995

DNH breakfast (coffee, cold croissants, warm orange juice): Grey Gowrie, Mary Allen, Peter Gummer,[487] David Puttnam. I do envy GG's civilised patrician manner. You can't fake it and you can't beat it. P. Gummer is so like J. Gummer it's disconcerting. Mary Allen, I'm still figuring out. But the news is: we've lottery money for film all sewn up.

We also have lottery money, of course, for the Churchill papers – and, alarmingly, what we naively thought of as a timely triumph is turning out to be a colossal balls-up. The fact is that these are private papers, not state papers, and they've been acquired for the nation at a good deal less than the open market price. A fifth of the lottery money is ear-marked for 'the heritage' and these papers are indisputably part of our heritage and, in the run-up to the VE day anniversary, we thought 'saving them for the nation' would have been greeted with loud hurrahs. Instead, it's loud raspberries all round. Young Winston is being pilloried as a greedy bastard and the government is being accused of slipping millions into one of its own backbenchers pockets. The horror of it is, we didn't just walk into this blindly: we ran towards it eyes wide open, arms outstretched. The PM is not amused.

I took part in the debate on children. Andrew Rowe is a good man, thoughtful, with ideas. Why isn't he in the government? Too soft, too woolly for the whips? Lunch at the Sony Radio Awards. I sat with Duke Hussey[488] and John Birt, old school and new, both doing rather well in the eyes of the government, both seemingly unaware of the depth of despair felt by their ground troops.

Afternoon at the DNH closeted with Puttnam and Carolyn Lambert.[489] The content will be workmanlike, but it's going to *look* great. We are engaging a flash design house to design a flash report – each page presented like a giant screen, stills from British films from *In Which We Serve* to *Shallow Grave*. I guarantee this will be the

---

487 Chairman of the Arts Council Lottery Board until 1996; Lord Chadlington since 1996; younger brother of John Gummer.

488 Chairman of the BBC Board of Governors 1986–96; Baron Hussey of North Bradley from 1996.

489 The Department of National Heritage official in charge of film policy.

first-ever government command paper to feature a spread from *Carry On Up the Khyber*. ('What did you do in government, Daddy?')

....

MONDAY 1 MAY 1995

....

'Tory leadership tries to quell poll panic on back benches'. Sir Marcus is tottering round the watering holes saying 'Now lads, steady the buffs.' In fact, it isn't panic. It's a mixture of despair and resignation. That nice, mild man from Norwich who has been here for years but whose name nobody knows[490] – he's sitting in the Tea Room staring bleakly into his empty cup. We have seen the future – but we haven't a clue what to do!

The manifesto policy panels are a complete waste of time. [Patrick] Cormack, Simon Coombs,[491] Basil Feldman,[492] they chunter on, the hour passes, but nobody has any fresh ideas to offer – not one.

Alan Howarth is profoundly unhappy. Stephen and I are taking him to Pasta Prego on Wednesday.

Norman Blackwell and Howell James[493] came to the Marginals Club dinner. Norman gave edited highlights of his 'five themes for a nation of opportunity' and was respectfully received. Howell (whom I know from TV-am days) surprised them by not being what you expect a Prime Minister's political secretary to be: jokey, camp, quirky, shrewd. I think he's going to be very good news. He's been talking with Nicholas O'Shaughnessy[494] about ways to 'present' the PM. N. O'S sees Major as a modern Baldwin – I think Major sees Major as a modern Baldwin. I told Howell Frank Longford's story about the time in the thirties when Frank was just starting out as a Conservative Party researcher and found himself at a country house party where Baldwin was the guest of honour. The Prime Minister invited the young Longford to join him for a stroll. The conversation didn't exactly flow, but eventually Longford asked the great man, 'Tell me, Prime Minister, who would you say has most influenced your political ideas?'

After an interminable pause, Baldwin replies: 'Sir Henry Maine.'

'And what did he say?'

---

490 Patrick Thompson, MP for Norwich North 1983–97.

491 MP for Swindon 1983–97; chairman of the Conservative Tourism Committee 1992–7.

492 Conservative activist, former chairman of the National Union of Conservative and Unionist Associations; member of the English Tourist Board 1986–96; Baron Feldman of Frognal since 1995.

493 Jonathan Hill's successor as Political Secretary to the Prime Minister 1995–7.

494 From the Judge Institute of Management Studies at Cambridge University.

'That whereas Rousseau argued all human progress was from contract to status, the real movement was from status to contract.'

Baldwin halted in his tracks. His face darkened. 'Or was it the other way around?'

FRIDAY 5 MAY 1995

'The Tory Party is today reeling from a night of unprecedented electoral disaster.' The local elections have not gone our way. I'm off to the Cenotaph at Blacon Crematorium.

LATER

I am sitting in bed with a bottle of Oddbins finest and a plate of Boots long-life chicken Madras curry (it's actually v. tasty). I have just returned from *Ruddigore* at the King's School (the children play the minor parts, the headmaster plays the lead!). My wife (whom I love) is in London, there is nothing on the box, so I am reading O'Shaughnessy's thoughts on Major and oratory. Howell sent N. O'S the text of the PM's speech at Central Council and N. O'S makes all the points I've tried to make but much more tellingly: the PM aims at too many targets in his speeches, tries to persuade too many disparate groups, says too much. Baldwin's speeches were very short. He invented the sound bite. He used simple language, a simple message, short sentences, easy vocabulary.

'In this speech the PM recounts many important facts about our record. But the speech is too much of a mere recitation and needs to be enlivened by various literary devices.' Story-telling, anecdote, the odd joke, 'the odd reference to popular culture/soap opera etc. since this is the only shared cultural vocabulary we possess.' More imagery and metaphor – 'when he does use them the choice is too mundane to be memorable.' 'The devices I have discussed are not icing on the cake: they have been the core of all persuasion for several thousand years. Communication is an emotive event and not a reasoned process. Finally, the PM needs to paint a vision – currently he is positioned in popular perception as a fabric maintainer. He needs both a policy and a communications strategy ... Painting a bright future is an old political trick but an effective one.'

He's also fascinating on what he calls 'visual rhetoric'. He sent Howell a photo of Blair kneeling to lay a wreath at the spot where a policeman had been murdered. The picture does all the work: Blair's suit, the way he's kneeling, the look, the association with a fallen policeman – it delivers *everything*. 'A visual strategy is essential but must be orchestrated with great care.'

If Howell can deliver even some of this it could make a spectacular difference. We might even return to the vexed issue of *wunt* ... the PM thinks it doesn't matter the way he pronounces a word. The truth is that his positively weird pronunciation of want – *nobody* says 'wunt' – gets in the way of what he's trying to say. It's obvious. However, when I said that Simon [Cadell] had volunteered to come in and offer some discreet professional advice ... Thank you and goodnight.

WEDNESDAY 17 MAY 1995

Geoffrey Dickens has died and I am surprised by how distressed I am. He was a lovely man. At the Marginals Club dinner we raised our glasses to him and there were tears in most eyes. Richard Ryder was the guest: his discretion did him credit, but did not make for a lively evening.

The talk of the Tea Room is the crass stupidity of Jerry Wiggin.[495] 'Greedy tosser' seems to be the general verdict. Incredibly, he tabled an amendment to the Gas Bill in Seb's name without consulting Seb. It's something to do with supplying gas to mobile homes and Sir Jerry is, of course, a *paid adviser* to the British Holiday and Home Parks Association. We move from cash-for-questions to cash-for-amendments ... There is no word yet from Wiggin on the subject. He is in South Africa on a fact-finding jaunt with the Agriculture Committee. Natch.

I talked with Jeremy [Hanley] in the corridor behind the Speaker's chair. He looks punch-drunk. I wanted to discuss Danny [Finkelstein] and the [Director of the Research Department] job at Smith Square, but he couldn't concentrate. He accepts he's moving on. He hopes he'll be offered National Heritage. 'And if I am, I want you as my junior minister.' Indeed.

MONDAY 22 MAY 1995

Poor Stephen has bombed in Cannes. He has been received by British film-makers with a predictable mixture of derision and contempt and he has not enhanced his reputation as a man of culture and self-confessed born-again *cineaste* by assuming that the head of the festival jury, one Jeanne Moreau, is a man.

The PM has sent us all a 'Dear Colleague' letter setting out Norman [Blackwell]'s 'five themes' and explaining the process of consultation with us and with the grass roots that 'will release ideas and energy across the party'. In the Tea Room Alistair Burt alone gives

---

495 MP for Weston-super-Mare 1969–97

an endorsement that sounds sincere, 'This is just what we need.' Alan Duncan suppresses giggles. John Sykes splutters into his tea. Soames bangs the table, 'For God's sake, men, show some fucking respect.'

WEDNESDAY 24 MAY 1995

The House adjourned after we had listened to the tributes to Harold Wilson.[496] The best stories – and the most touching speeches – came from Tony Benn and Gerald Kaufman. Gerald told a story from the time when he was a junior minister at the department of the Environment in charge of the government car service – 'possibly the most powerful position in any government apart from that of Prime Minister.' Gerald received a minute from Wilson – a rare thing for a junior minister to receive a minute from a Prime Minister – instructing him to write to all former Prime Ministers still living offering them a car and a chauffeur. 'I realised then that Harold had definitely decided to retire. He liked to plan ahead.'

Gerald said that Wilson wrote all his own speeches, dictating them, striding up and down smoking his pipe, correcting them later in green ink. And yes, his love of HP Sauce was genuine.

Benn: 'Like all Prime Ministers, Harold Wilson worried about plots. I asked him once, when the plots were thickening, "Harold what shall we do if you are knocked down by a bus?" Harold said, "Find out who was driving the bus."'

Benn is a wonderful speaker. He even managed to work in some New Labour baiting: 'Harold believed in close links with the unions. "Every bird needs a left wing and a right wing and it can't fly with its right wing alone."'

Wilson had been gaga for years. To have been so brilliant, so razor sharp, and to become aware of your failing powers must be terrible. When I first met him, fifteen years ago, he seemed fine. I sat next to him and at the beginning of the meal he was due to say grace. I watched him take out his pen and begin writing something on the back of his name-place card. I leant over to see what he was doing. He was writing out the grace. He smiled sadly, 'Lest we forget.'

TUESDAY 6 JUNE 1995

I have spent the evening engaged in the Waldegrave counter-offensive. I watched the

---

496 Lord Wilson of Rievaulx had died aged seventy-nine; Labour MP for Ormskirk 1945–50, Huyton 1950–83; Prime Minister 1964–70, 1974–6.

PM and William together. The PM was ashen-faced. I have never seen him look so pale and drawn. Poor William was shaking.

The essence of it is this: William was at the FCO as a junior minister from August 1988. There were existing guidelines on the exporting of arms to Iraq and elsewhere. The guidelines were applied with flexibility on a case by case basis. Last night the BBC leaked chunks from a draft of the wretched Scott Arms-to-Iraq enquiry report which appear to suggest that Scott is going to find William guilty of misleading the House – telling the House the policy on the guidelines hadn't been changed when it had been. William has produced a piece of paper asserting his innocence and we've been scurrying around giving it to all and sundry. We have tried to reach every colleague in the building – and William is ready to go through it all line by line for those who still have doubts.

Labour has scented blood. Prescott attempted to go for the jugular at PMQs. The headlines all suggest William's a goner – but, here, most of our people quite like him and even those who can't abide an egg-head and a wet know this one's fundamentally as honest as the day is long. As he says in his note, he wouldn't 'consciously mislead Parliament for no personal or political gain'. (When I read that I wondered if he had crafted it quite carefully. For a political gain, might one deceive Parliament?) 'There is no plausible reason why my officials should have encouraged or permitted me to mislead Parliament. I did not.'

The Smoking Room view is that William may hang on awhile, but come the reshuffle he'll discreetly dropped. I think not. Having observed the body language between them today, there's an alliance there that's out of the ordinary. As long as John Major is PM, William will be in his government.

At 3.30 p.m. our film report came and went. It does look stunning and Stephen launched it well – but nobody was listening. The Chamber was four-fifths empty and around the watering holes the talk is entirely of the Scotts – Sir Richard Scott and his leaky report and poor Nicholas Scott (no relation) – breathalysed, arrested, released on bail and now destined to be dropped by the sour-faced old sobersides of Kensington & Chelsea. (Apparently Nick had a minor collision with a parked car and the parked car was shunted forward and unfortunately trapped a small Swiss child in a baby buggy. It seems Nick did not linger at the scene of the accident, and his female companion declined to exchange names and addresses, allegedly declaring, 'What are you worried about? The child's not dead – he's not even English.' Nick did not appear in the division lobby just now. Said Seb, 'He's probably drowning his sorrows. At Mothercare.')

WEDNESDAY 7 JUNE 1995

This is very funny. 'Sir David Puttnam dismisses package as "one shoe of a pair to keep us hopping along". That's the headline. If you read all the papers you get the distinct impression that the man leading the attack on the report is not Chris Smith, not Gerald Kaufman, but the saintly Sir D. Puttnam – who, did they but know it, has been closeted with me and Stephen and Carolyn these past two months *writing* the frigging report! Of course we haven't gone as far as he would have liked, but he knows the tax breaks are not in our gift, he knows Stephen's working on the Treasury, he can see we have produced £84 million plus ... He could have been a *mite* more generous. Heigh-ho.

MONDAY 12 JUNE 1995

Mrs T. is rocking the boat. The Baroness has been on the radio, telling us how much she admires Mr Blair, how she's 'absolutely against' the single currency, how she's glad Major is going more sceptic, how what we really need is more Thatcherism – 'we must get back to Conservative policies'. The Tea Room is fairly deserted because the whips seem to have organised a week of 'light business' and fairly early nights. Willetts tells me this is calculated: they don't want the lads sitting around the watering holes grumbling and plotting.

Michael Grade came to plead his cause. He is a smooth and attractive operator – and he *is* Channel 4 in the way that Branson *is* Virgin and Mrs T. *was* the government. (That's something Major hasn't achieved: what is the 'brand' of the present government? Nobody quite knows.) I like Grade. Our small talk is always the same: our shared birthday.[497] Stephen likes him too, but he's not going to get the rebate. Nor, it seems, is he going to get the consolation knighthood. Jocelyn Stevens is ahead in the queue.

The arts policy meeting went nowhere – slowly. And after the vote Richard Spring came up to Stephen's little room to tell his tale. The room is so small you feel you're in a cabin on a cross-Channel ferry. There's just a tiny sofa and a couple of upright chairs. I brought some wine from the Smoking Room. We sat in the gloom, looking at our knees, while Richard took us through the embarrassing details of how he had been set up by the trollop and the *News of the World*. 'It was just what my father would have called "a bit of horse-play", bit of rough 'n' tumble.' Stephen looked particularly uncomfortable. I don't think his father went in for quite that kind of horse-play. Richard was perfectly reasonable: he said he wasn't looking for sympathy, but his career has been ruined and his seat is in doubt because his privacy was invaded – he was bugged in his own home indulging in a perfectly legal and 'perfectly harmless' bit of horse-play. When he went, Stephen was surprisingly unsympathetic. 'The man's an ass.'

---

497 8 March. Grade was born in 1943, GB in 1948. Other Westminster 8 March birthdays included: Douglas Hurd 1930, the Prime Minister's PPS John Ward 1925, the Speaker's Secretary Nicolas Bevan 1942. Michael Grade received a CBE in 1998 and became Baron Grade of Yarmouth in 2011.

TUESDAY 13 JUNE 1995

I have just come from a convivial drink with the Chancellor of the Exchequer. While we were downing the Rioja, it seems the PM has been being harangued by a unruly mob of right-wingers. This isn't an exaggeration. The PM agreed to meet up with members of the Fresh Start group. Fifty or sixty of them turned up and instead of listening to the PM they started barracking him. He stuck to his line that we've got an opt-out so there's no need to rule the single currency in or out at this stage, but they wouldn't have it. It seems it was a ghastly one-sided shouting match.

Ken's view is that the PM shouldn't have let himself in for it. It's humiliating and demeaning – it undermines his authority – and 'the more you concede to these mad xenophobes' the more they'll want. 'He's got to make it clear where he stands.' That's the problem: he's flirted with these people to keep them sweet and now he won't deliver they're turning ugly. And none of them is very pretty at the best of times.

LATER

I have just seen the PM. He looks quite ghastly, poor man. He's going to Canada for the G7 summit. And while he's away the plotting will start in earnest. We all know what mad Marlow and his ilk want, but even the Bill Walkers are now saying 'We've got to get this leadership issue sorted'. Sir Marcus, at his bibulous best, thinks it can all be fixed – 'Eee lad, he's got to get a grip' – and a fresh agenda, a bit more sceptical on Europe, toughen up on law and order, cut taxes and public spending, 'Bingo!' But it won't happen – because Heseltine and Clarke won't wear it. And it's not that simple. Sir Marcus: 'You can shave a billion off social security, easy like.' Peter Lilley: 'That means taking £1,000 each from the million least well-off people in the country. Is that really what we want to do?'

THURSDAY 22 JUNE 1995

He's outflanked them all. It's quite extraordinary. The PM has resigned as leader of the Conservative Party. Rather than wait for the inevitable challenge in November, he has forced the issue. The election will be on Tuesday week. We were given the news at five o'clock. We shuffled in for the regular 1922 Committee meeting, Sir Marcus got up and made a bald announcement. The PM is stepping down as leader, he continues as Prime Minister; nominations for the position of leader should be handed to Sir Marcus by noon next Thursday. The PM will be a candidate and expects his opponents to 'put up or shut up'. We all sat there, speechless, wide-eyed and amazed, taken by complete surprise. Bemused, not initially knowing how to react, we stumbled out of the committee room and made our way to the Chamber. There we discovered Stephen, a solitary figure on our front bench, thinking he'd come to give a dozy reply to Graham Allen's[498] adjournment debate on digital television, and suddenly finding himself in the middle of a maelstrom. Assorted Labour rabble were hopping up and down, hysterically claiming the PM was perpetrating a constitutional outrage, furiously demanding to know what was going on. How could the Prime Minister resign as leader of the party and continue as PM? How dare the Prime Minister treat the House in this cavalier fashion? When were we going to get a statement? Dame Janet [Fookes, Deputy Speaker] clucked and flannelled, we had a couple of pointless divisions ('I spy strangers'),[499] Stephen threw in his 2 cents' worth (he was enjoying the excitement), I threw in a farthing, Banks and Mackinlay[500] and Spearing[501] and Skinner did their best to keep the pot boiling, but after an hour or so the fever subsided, the Chamber emptied, and we turned our attention to the delights of digitalisation. I have left Stephen to it. I am ditching Hayden's drinks at the DNH and going in search of 'further and better particulars'.

LATER

It seems the PM decided on this in Canada at the weekend. Douglas Hurd was with him. Douglas is now definitely standing down as Foreign Secretary. Last night the PM called in a handful of trusties – Lang,[502] Cranborne, Newton, Mawhinney (no potential rivals, you notice) – and told them the plan. He said nothing at Cabinet this morning. Not a hint. And it was business as usual at PMQs. He was very relaxed, at his best. He is certainly a cool customer. Around 3.30 p.m. he had Sir Marcus and the 1922 executive into his room here and broke the news to them; then he drove straight back to Downing Street for a press conference in the garden.

The initial feeling here is that he's scored a brilliant coup. If he trounces any stalking-horse, and he will, then the sniping has to stop. And will there be a stalking-horse? Undoubtedly. The sceptics will certainly seize the moment. Incredibly, Barry Field[503]

---

498 Labour MP for Nottingham North since 1987.

499 An MP calls out 'I spy strangers' as a procedural device for forcing a division.

500 Andrew Mackinlay, Labour MP for Thurrock 1992–2010.

501 Nigel Spearing, Labour MP for Acton 1970–74, Newham South 1974–97.

502 Ian Lang, Secretary of State for Scotland; MP for Galloway 1979–83, Galloway and Upper Nithsdale 1983–97.

503 MP for the Isle of Wight 1987–97.

may be a contender. I've seen Teresa Gorman, 'I'm ready to stand if no one else will. It's about time we had another woman at the helm.' I saw Lamont in the division. 'What do you think?' I said. He just gave a wolfish leer.

FRIDAY 23 JUNE 1995

The PM's team (Robert Cranborne i/c) have set up shop at 13 Cowley Street. I have just telephoned. An over-excited Bunterish voice answered. 'John Major's campaign headquarters.' It was Oliver Heald.[504] How on earth has he managed to get his chubby knees under the table so quickly? I said, 'It's Gyles.' He said, 'Can we count on your support for John Major?' I said, 'Of course. That's why I'm calling. Who else did you think I was going to support? Is there anything I could or should be doing to help?' 'Thank you for your support. We'll let you know.' God almighty! To be patronised by that bumptious fat ass.

LATER

The word is that Lamont is about to declare. The entire Cabinet (including Portillo) have given the PM a rousing endorsement – except for John Redwood who is at Lord's watching the cricket and 'won't be saying anything until Monday'. The view now seems to be that it isn't going to be the walk-over we thought last night. The stalking-horse might only get thirty or forty votes, but if there are a hundred or more abstentions what happens to the PM's credibility then?

We're driving to Stratford. We're seeing Anne Wood at Ragdoll[505] and then Allied-Domecq are entertaining us to *The Taming of the Shrew*. I'm scribbling this in the car which is a mistake because now I'm feeling sick. (Or is it post-Heald nausea?)

MONDAY 26 JUNE 1995

Redwood is the challenger. I've just witnessed his extraordinary press conference. JR was quite impressive in his funny Daddy Woodentop way, but his supporters – ye gods! I've a feeling they may have kiboshed his campaign before it's even started. It wasn't what they said: it was how they looked – Teresa to the right of him in a hideous day-glo green and

---

504 MP for Hertfordshire North 1992–7, North East Hertfordshire since 1997.

505 Television producer, creator of the *Teletubbies*, former colleague of GB.

Marlow to left in a quite ludicrous striped blazer. Every picture tells a story: this one said, 'Here's a truly barmy army.'

He has some more credible backers as well – Lamont and Edward Leigh were on parade – and in the Tea Room suddenly everybody is much more tight-lipped. There's a sense now that anything could happen. According to Willetts, who was keeping his counsel at our Wednesday Club cabal, Richard Ryder has apparently upset the Major camp by insisting that the whips remain totally neutral and above the fray. 'We have to be ready to serve the Prime Minister of the day – whoever he may be.'

I was standing behind the Speaker's chair just now, when a gangly Labour MP sidled up to me. I thought he was going to offer me some dirty postcards. I don't know his name, but he was at the Allied-Domecq do on Friday. 'Are you going to declare it in the register?' he asked, all *sotto voce*. 'If you don't, we won't.' There are some pretty tawdry types round here.

TUESDAY 27 JUNE 1995

Breakfast with Stephen, Danny and Tim Bell[506] – who volunteered his services to 'advise' the Major campaign. Afterwards I said to Stephen, 'I think we should drop in on Cowley Street, don't you? Take them the message from Tim Bell, nail our colours firmly to the mast, see and be seen.' In brilliant sunshine we sauntered over and were gratified to be filmed going in and coming out. The house itself is tiny and the 'campaign HQ' is packed into a couple of rooms on the ground floor and the kitchen in the basement. We squeezed past various smug young men wearing striped shirts and red braces and found Ian Lang. He was fairly distracted, took Tim Bell's number, thanked us for our interest but made it abundantly clear that he's got more helpers than he knows what to do with. At least we showed a face.

Major, Hurd and Clarke are at an EU gathering in Cannes – echoes of Mrs T. in Paris in November 1990?

WEDNESDAY 28 JUNE 1995

Heseltine has been on the radio this morning telling us that Major will win 'convincingly' on the first ballot. But what if he doesn't? Hezza would not be drawn.

Talking to Richard Ottaway, it's clear that if Major stumbles Heseltine is ready. Talking to David Amess, it's equally clear that Portillo is standing by and is convinced he could

---

506 Advertising and public relations entrepreneur; adviser to Mrs Thatcher as Prime Minister; knighted 1990; Baron Bell of Belgravia since 1998.

make it too. The Tea Room fantasists (Fabricant, Greenway, Uncle Tom Cobley) are conjuring up a Heseltine–Portillo pact, Hezza as PM, Portillo as Foreign Secretary, with Peter Lilley as Chancellor, and the promise of a referendum on EMU.

Out on the terrace we are gathering in twos and threes, enjoying the gorgeous sunshine, revelling in the sense that 'something is happening'. The banter is genial, but no one really trusts anybody at all. Nigel Evans is adamant he'll vote for Major, but do we believe him? David Davis, who has wheedled his way into the heart of Cowley Street, said to me, 'I don't trust anyone, but I trust some even less than others.' Of course, DD likes to play up his Machiavellian credentials. The official Cowley Street line is that a majority of one will be enough, but they know that isn't true. If Major only squeaks to victory, he's fatally wounded – then anything can happen. I've spotted Gillian Shephard in a couple of cosy corners. She's as loyal to the PM as they come, but if it goes to a second ballot … ah, that's different. She'll be there, offering an alternative for those who can't stomach Hezza. John Major in skirts – and she believes she could make it. I reported this to Stephen. His jaw fell, '*Please* – spare us.'

And talking of falling jaws, here's the real news of the day: Hugh Grant has been arrested in Hollywood and charged with 'lewd conduct'. 'At last,' said Michèle, 'something interesting to read in the paper.' Cruising along Sunset Boulevard in the early hours yesterday Hugh picked up one Divine Marie Brown and offered her ready money for oral sex. 'Vice officers walked up on the car and observed the act.' Funny old world.

SATURDAY I JULY 1995

'I am bewildered and alone,' says Liz Hurley. If Major wins, we can picture *la belle* Bottomley saying something similar. Poor Virginia has put her foot in it by declaring that she could and would serve in a Redwood Cabinet. The official line, of course, is that such a possibility won't arise. Norman Tebbit has clambered out of his coffin to urge us to vote for JR, praising his 'brains, courage and humour'. Norman Lamont has just left a message on my answering machine saying he'd be 'very grateful for a chat'. The Redwood camp has produced a telling flyer that may well concentrate the minds of some of the waverers: 'No change = No chance. The choice is stark. To save your seat, your party, and your country, vote for John Redwood.'

MONDAY 3 JULY 1995

Ottoway is adamant: Heseltine is whole-hearted in his support for the PM. Ken Clarke is very funny: 'The party can't seriously be considering voting for this Martian.' 'I think he's supposed to be a Venusian, Ken. Or a Vulcan.' 'It's another planet, that's for sure.' But the man with green blood has fought a good campaign. Sir George Gardiner (Pluto's representative on earth) is rallying the 92 Group behind him. Even if he doesn't make it tomorrow (and he won't) in the longer term he's positioned himself to overtake Portillo as the champion of the right. Tom Arnold: 'John Redwood had the courage to do it. In politics you need courage more than almost anything else.' JR is certainly inspiring devotion among his followers. I saw Walter Sweeney[507] (a huge, overweight walrus in a rather shabby suit) and there were tears in his eyes. He'd just been listening to JR: 'He has greatness. He has the qualities of Margaret Thatcher.' Portillo has been very quiet in recent days.

Later I wandered along to the Smoking Room in search of company and a glass of wine. (John Taylor/Sydney Chapman can usually be relied on – kind hearts, familiar stories, another round.) The place was deserted. Just as I'd ordered my drink and ensconced myself in a corner behind the *Evening Standard*, in came Archie Hamilton, from the little chess room no one uses, between the Smoking Room and the Dining Room. He lighted on me.

'Aah. Are you eating?'

'Er –'

'Good. Go through now. Keep the PM company. He's on his own.'

'But he's got my vote. There are people he *needs* to talk to.'

'Go on. He's on the Irish table. I'm going to drum up a few more.'

I did as I was bid. Archie is my dark horse candidate for Chief Whip. But my heart sank. Making small talk with the PM is never easy. On such a night as this…

I found him gazing blankly into the middle distance. He looked pasty-faced and weary. 'I think it's going pretty well,' I said.

'Do you? Do you?' He shook his head. 'I just don't know. I just don't know.'

He thinks the *Daily Mail* is going to come out against him in the morning. *The Sun*, *The Times*, the *Telegraph*, they're all saying he should go. 'But the *Mail*? There you go … This time tomorrow, who knows?'

Silence fell. He looked at his plate. I burbled stupidly. He was monosyllabic. I burbled some more. Silence fell again. I thought, 'Poor sod, this could be his last night as Prime Minister and he's spending it with me, *like this!*' And then a gallant knight rode to the rescue. In came the Rt. Hon Peter Brooke CH and sat down beside me. He looked across at the PM and said he had just finished reading an article about a certain Surrey cricketer whose heyday was in the 1930s. The name meant nothing to me, but the PM

507 MP for Vale of Glamorgan 1992–7.

brightened at once. Peter continued, describing some particularly memorable match from the glorious summer of '37, and within a minute the pall that had engulfed the table lifted and Peter and the PM talked cricket – talked '30s cricket! – in extraordinary, animated, fascinated, happy detail. For half an hour or more, until the division bell went at around 9.30, Peter distracted the PM with an absorbing conversation he truly enjoyed. I had no idea what they were talking about, but tonight, no question, Peter served his Prime Minister well. I knew I'd been useless. I sat silent in admiration.

TUESDAY 4 JULY 1995

He's done it:

> Major, 218
> Redwood, 89
> Abstentions, 22

I've just been on the radio hailing it as a 'resounding victory', a 'personal triumph' for the PM and the 'defining moment' when we put our divisions behind us. The truth is it's good enough, just. It allows the PM to carry on, but it shows the world that at least 111 of his foot-soldiers – a third of the parliamentary party – don't support him.

The voting was in Committee Room 12. I went first thing. It was just like the mock elections at school, rows of brown wooden desks and Sir Marcus as Mr Chips at the front of the class, collecting the ballot papers. Given all the talk of people saying they would vote one way, then voting another, rather ostentatiously I displayed my ballot paper as I handed it in. Outside hordes of hacks were gathered in the corridor hoping to pick up droppings from the electorate. Steve Norris duly obliged with something along the lines of, 'I'm voting for Major. He's the least bad option. Besides I owe him one.' The feeling is this may be a quip too far.

We've just had a division. The PM looked suitably relaxed and cheery. As we trooped through the No lobby there was much jostling to pat the victor's back. I murmured 'Well done' and had my shoulder squeezed. I saw Redwood who looked quite buoyant too – I told him what he knew, that he'd had a good fight and put himself in serious contention for next time. He was clear that he now plans to 'row in firmly behind the Prime Minister'.

Stephen, of course, is hoping to be released from the bonds of the DNH, but he's not counting chickens. He accepts that he didn't manage/wasn't asked to get in on the inner circle of the PM's campaign team so the spoils will go to others. Stephen sees himself as party chairman, but that'll go to Mawhinney for certain – notwithstanding the fact that Mawhinney isn't that good on the box and lacks some of the emollient interpersonal skills that make for a happy ship. But there's a momentum going for him – and around here that's everything. I huddled in a corner with poor Jeremy [Hanley]. Through oyster eyes he was expressing his 'sheer joy' at the PM's success. He knows he's doomed. 'I did my best.' He's hoping for Heritage – 'with you as my junior'. That would be nice, but it won't happen. I know because *about three weeks ago* Jenny Shaw[508] told me that Sproat is staying in the department and being moved up a rank from Parliamentary Secretary to Minister of State. The civil servants were groaning at the prospect.

LATER

Jonathan Aitken is resigning … to spend more time with his lawyers. He says he is leaving the Cabinet at his own request to concentrate on his libel actions against *The Guardian* and *World in Action*. Who comes in as Chief Secretary? Roger Freeman? Hague? Heseltine was closeted at No. 10 for most of the morning and the buzz now is that he's going to become Deputy Prime Minister in return for having committed his men to the PM's cause. The first part of the rumour I can believe; I have my doubts about the second. But if Hezza is promoted and Rifkind or Lang gets the Foreign Office rather than Howard, the Redwoodites will be spitting blood. I have already heard Wilkinson, Sweeney, Walker, Jenkin grumbling, grunting, grinding their teeth – and this within a matter of four hours of the election designed to resolve all our differences!

WEDNESDAY 5 JULY 1995

Stephen is the new Secretary of State for Health and he is so pleased it's almost comical. He can't stop grinning; he's rushing from here to there in a state of happy excitement. I, on the other hand…

I began the day by making the pilgrimage to the stately home of the Heseltines. It is magnificent, not at all as vulgar and *arriviste* as Alan Clark had led me to expect.[509] The pictures, wall hangings, furnishings, all in the best possible taste. A little clangy, a touch of the uncomfortable French salon about the public rooms, but unquestionably a home fit for a *grand seigneur*. While Hezza himself was strutting into Downing

---

508 Assistant Private Secretary in the Secretary of State's office at the Department of National Heritage.

509 See Alan Clark's *Diaries*, 17 November 1990.

Street as our new Deputy Prime Minister, I was doing my turn for the benefit of his Association ladies. Once a year they're given this treat – bussed over from Henley for a peep inside the great man's mansion, followed by lunch down in the garden by the lily ponds. I gave my talk in the hallway with the ladies sitting on spindly gilded chairs. Anne was very gracious and rather sweet. 'Don't slim like Nigel Lawson. He looks so old and tired. You'd slip through the floorboards.' If only.

I got back mid-afternoon and found Stephen already ensconced at the Department of Health, gurgling with delight. I said, 'Who are the ministers going to be?'

He said, 'I'm not sure. Gerry's staying,[510] which is good. He's an ally. They want to move Julia Cumberlege.[511] What do you think?'

'She knows the nurses and the midwives. I don't think you're going to want to spend a lot of time sweet-talking the midwives.'

'You're right. Let's hang onto her. I'll call Alastair.' Alastair is the new Chief Whip.[512] (He has a Chief Whip's gift for oratory.) Stephen called No. 10. He got through to Alastair. 'Look, Chief, on second thoughts, could I keep Julia Cumberlege ... No ... Who else have you got? ... Could I have Willetts? No... '

In the corner of the room rather pathetically I mouthed, 'What about Gyles?'

'If you can manage it then, I'd like to keep Julia ... She knows the midwives ... Thanks.'

Crossing Members' Lobby just now I was stopped by a scurrying, breathless Greg Knight [Deputy Chief Whip],[513] busy, busy, it's all happening. 'Could we have a word – tomorrow?' he said. 'Come and find me around 2.15 p.m.'

This means I'm not getting anything, but I'm going to be let down lightly with a kindly word. I imagine it's part of a concerted exercise to keep the disappointed 'on side'.
Bah.

THURSDAY 6 JULY 1995

The dust has settled. Rifkind, Foreign Office. Lang, Board of Trade (in 'an expanded role' – the bollocks they do talk.) Portillo, Defence (that's clever). And the surprises: Waldegrave as Chief Secretary, Gillian Shephard combines Education with Employment,

510 Gerry Malone had been Minister of State under Virginia Bottomley since 1994; he remained at the department until 1997.

511 Baroness Cumberlege since 1990; Parliamentary Under-Secretary of State for Health 1992–7.

512 Alastair Goodlad had been Minister of State at the Foreign Office 1992–95; he had three spells in the Whips' Office: as an Assistant Whip and Lord Commissioner of the Treasury 1981–84, as Comptroller of Her Majesty's Household and then Treasurer of HM Household and Deputy Chief Whip 1989–92, as Parliamentary Secretary to the Treasury and Chief Whip 1995–7.

513 MP for Derby North 1983–97, East Yorkshire since 2001; in the Whips' Office 1989–96, 2012–13; Deputy Chief Whip 1993–6.

and Virginia gets Heritage. She went in and was offered Transport, but she said 'No, thank you Prime Minister. There's only one job I want, National Heritage. *Please.*' And she got it – instead of Jeremy for whom it had been destined. Reshuffles are in large part made up as they go along. It's extraordinary. She does feel a twinge of conscience, just a pang. But Jeremy, wisely (and because he is a good man) has accepted Minister of State rank at the Foreign Office – demotion but a real job. Other than Jeremy the one involuntary departure is poor, dear David Hunt – his moment passed (it does), as the year went by somehow he faded. So the great Hanley-Hunt double act, that for which I led the cheering just a year ago bites the dust … (Michèle said to me this morning, 'Let's face it, you've got absolutely no judgement – and no sense of timing. To be endorsed by you is the kiss of death.' A loyal wife speaks!)

Newcomers: George Young[514] at Transport ('Virginia won't do it – bring on the bicycling baronet!'), Douglas Hogg at Agriculture, Forsyth to Scotland (which is amazing – when I was there for the Fairbairn by-election I was told time and again 'the party in Scotland hates Forsyth – he can never be Secretary of State' – but actually he's a tough cookie, a sharp operator and who else was there?), Roger Freeman replacing Hunt (Roger will be superb), and for Wales, the baby of the party, young Master Hague, age thirty-four, the youngest Cabinet minister this century. The boy done well. And he's decent, and nice.

All in all, it's not a bad line-up and the rest of the shuffle looks okay – except for one thing: it doesn't include me! I went to see Greg as instructed. He came out of the Upper Whips' Office and we huddled in a corner. 'I'm afraid it didn't work out for you this time. The PM had to look after the Cowley Street lot – and you've got testicles which is a big disadvantage. He wants to reward his team and promote the women.' So Oliver Heald goes to Social Security and Cheryl Gillan (!!!!!) to Education.[515] And naturally Ken Clarke's PPS gets something nice: Angela Knight is Economic Secretary. It beggars belief. I should have ditched Stephen last year and gone with Ken when I had the chance.

At lunchtime, I said to Stephen that I thought he should get a new PPS, that I'd done enough. He was very sweet (he is very sweet) and said 'No, no, no. I need you. I'd be heartbroken.' But the truth is Health is of no interest to me – at Heritage he *did* need me and I could actually make a modest impact on this and that. I know it's only a game, a stupid merry-go-round, nothing matters very much etc., and this time next week I'll be as happy as Larry – but here and now, this minute, I do find it *very* galling.

---

514 Sir George Young, 6th Baronet; MP for Ealing Acton 1974–97, Hampshire North West since 1997; he had succeeded Stephen Dorrell as Financial Secretary to the Treasury 1994–5.

515 Cheryl Gillan, MP for Chesham & Amersham since 1992, became Parliamentary Under-Secretary of State at the Department for Education and Employment 1995–7; later Secretary of State for Wales 2010–12.

WEDNESDAY 12 JULY 1995

The Chancellor is magnificent. We're halfway through the debate on the economy, I'm sitting just behind him, 'helping out on the bench', and he's at his chuckling, combative, blokeish best. He's been knocking Gordon Brown all over the shop. Gordon's a good guy, always friendly in the Tea Room, infinitely more *real* than Blair, but what a windbag! The waffle and the gobbledygook, they just come tumbling out. He's been at it twenty minutes and there are clearly masses more to come – he's got reams of handwritten notes perched on top of a foot-high stack of bound copies of Hansard balanced on top of the despatch box – presumably so he can read his never-ending speech without resorting to the indignity of spectacles. Inflation target, borrowing limit, base rate – he daren't commit himself to anything, so all he can offer is rant and wind.

Ken has just leant back and 'wondered' whether I'd be interested in being his PPS. He's a good, kind fellow, and the surest-footed political animal we've got, but somehow I think I've done my eager-beaver PPS-ing, the moment has passed.

William [Waldegrave] is looking very chirrupy. It's a strange business this: a week ago he was our expert on agriculture, tonight he makes his debut as Chief Secretary with all the Treasury answers at his fingertips. As it turns out, Jonathan's departure may have been timely. The poor man is now contending with a prostitute who knew him fifteen years ago and has suddenly surfaced with the promise of a book of torrid revelations. Sadomasochism is her bag, Jonathan was her lover.

In the Tea Room they're saying there's more to come. 'Some aspects of Jonathan's love-life are very dark indeed.'

SATURDAY 15 JULY 1995

I'm in bed. Tea and Marmite toast, and I don't have to get up for an hour. If living in the moment is what we should be doing this is a good moment in which to live. M is looking very beautiful and last night, at the Chester French Circle fifteenth anniversary dinner (!), she was quite wonderful. She plays the constituency wife to perfection. I am very lucky and I know it.

Poor Peter Morrison has died and the obituaries (*Times*, *Telegraph* anyway) are pretty uncharitable, concentrating on his time as Mrs T's PPS ('His part in her downfall') with a definite unpleasant nudge and wink in the direction of his 'bachelor' status and interest in 'young people'. Rumours abound, but I don't think anyone knows the truth of the matter. What we do know is that he smoked and drank himself to death. He was found dead at the foot of the stairs. He was only fifty-one. He looked seventy.

LATER

The 'Chester Jobs Summit' went well – good press turnout and some useful contri-butions. Yes, it was my initiative, inspired by Stuart's[516] anxiety that my local profile wasn't high enough, and designed to outflank the Labour group on the council, but it isn't quite as cynical as it sounds. We can do more to attract investment and I believe I can help.

This afternoon's surgery was alarming. A fellow was booked in for 4.00 p.m. Yesterday his 'care worker' called to say he was dangerous and on no account should I see him. Unfortunately we didn't have a number for him so we couldn't cancel. I suggested to the care worker that he might like to come along and help hold my hand. He said, 'Oh no, that'll only make him worse. He can be very violent.' On the care worker's advice, I rearranged the office, so that the man would have to sit right inside the room and I could sit behind my desk right by the door 'which should remain open at all times.' The care worker said, 'Whatever you do, when he's speaking don't interrupt him and look straight in his eye. Never look away. And if he makes one false move, get out as fast as you can, lock the door and call the police. I'm deadly serious.' At four o'clock, when the poor unfortunate arrived, my stomach was churning. I manoeuvred him into the chair in the far corner of the room and hovered nervously by the open door. I gazed steadfastly at him as, very politely, his voice hardly above a whisper, he told me his problem: 'It's my care worker. He doesn't understand me.'

The *Chronicle* piece about Peter is fine. They've used my tribute and a nice quote from Mrs T. Given what Peter thought of the *Chronicle* I think he'd feel they've done him proud.

TUESDAY 18 JULY 1995

I have mastered the art of arriving at a Buckingham Palace garden party. The hordes turn up between three and half-past. The real time to reach the main gates is exactly 3.53 p.m. The riff-raff are already inside, so all alone you have the pleasure of scrunch-ing your way across the gravel, past the guardsmen, under the arch, across the deserted square, up the red-carpeted stairs and through. Proceeding at a leisurely pace, taking in the pictures, pausing to admire the porcelain, you will arrive at the bay windows leading out onto the garden at 3.59 on the dot. It's too late for the flunkies to push you out onto the lawn to join the crowds. You've got to stay where you are, in pole posi-tion, for Her Majesty's arrival under your very nose as the clock strikes four.

---

516 Stuart Begbie, a Chester City councillor and chairman of the Chester Conservative Association.

We took Aphra and Saethryd, it's Aphra's seventeenth birthday, and then we went on to the end-of-term drinks at No. 10 and the PM was mellow, relaxed, almost playful. I talked publishers with Norma[517] and the PM (good man) took the girls off to see the Cabinet room. I said to Aphra, 'The Prime Minister has wished you a happy birthday – that's one for the diary.' She gave me one of her 'Oh-dad-how-can-you-be-so-embarrassing' looks. They take it all for granted. And why not? So long as they're happy...

WEDNESDAY 26 JULY 1995

Lunch with Richard Ottaway. This was the united-in-sorrow lunch we fixed in the immediate aftermath of the reshuffle when RO was feeling even sorer than I was – and with greater cause. He first arrived in '83 and he's Heseltine's PPS. Apparently, the DPM lobbied on his behalf, but couldn't pull it off ... Sounds a bit unlikely. If the Deputy Prime Minister can't get his man preferment ... Never mind. RO is bullish once more – and his loyalty to Hezza is absolute. He says that Major and Heseltine are going to be 'as one' between now and the election: 'you won't be able to put a cigarette paper between them'. The real joy from the PM's point of view is that Hezza is going to take on chairing most of the Cabinet committees which will free hours of the PM's time, release him from mountains of paperwork, enable him to concentrate on the key objectives. It could work. Longer term, *bien sûr*, the Heseltine ambition remains undiminished. Says RO: 'Michael will *never* give up.'

And speaking of those who never give up, we had dinner with the Portillos *chez* Hamilton. Neil was quite quickly in his cups, Michael was abstemious. He is chuffed with the new job and taking it *very* seriously. He won't be wearing Hezzalike flap-jackets, but we all agreed he'd look so dashing in full-dress mess-kit. He's a happy bunny. Carolyn [Portillo] seemed fairly remote from it all. Christine [Hamilton], a touch more manic.

I've just come from a long session with Stephen at the DoH [Department of Health]. I advised him that he could probably get away with having Oliver Cromwell on the wall, but it would be a mistake to get rid of the drawing of Florence Nightingale. He is so glad to be where he is doing what he's doing. And, of course, he's another one with the 'longer-term ambition'. And I'm backing him. (Michèle: 'God, poor man, he's doomed. You're the kiss of death. You know it.')

Stephen asked, 'What are you going to do in the summer?'

I said, 'Write a novel.'

He looked alarmed, 'What – like Edwina?'

---

517 Norma Major had published a biography of Joan Sutherland and was writing a history of Chequers.

I said, 'No – why write about your own life with added sex? My novel is going to be a romantic mystery set in America, nothing to do with politics.'[518]

And that's what I'm going to do, starting tomorrow. 'Beginning. You're never finished if you forever keep beginning.' [519]

MONDAY 25 SEPTEMBER 1995

Chapter Five completed – despite interruptions. At 9.15 a.m. Gillian Shephard telephoned. Would I call Trevor McDonald, reassure him that the Better English Campaign is above party politics, keep him happy? I said 'Yes, of course'. But who are we kidding? Yes, the campaign is in the national interest, but it's a political exercise as well. Gillian wants to announce it in her speech at the party conference! Trevor is very good to come on board. I hope he gets a K. He deserves it.

We're just in from seeing Joanna [Lumley] and Tim Pigott-Smith in *The Letter*. The piece is dated, but Jo and Tim are good and the house was full. Simon [Cadell] came. He's so gaunt and frail and brave – but he loved seeing Jo and Tim.We managed lots of *laughs* – that's all we want.

SUNDAY 8 OCTOBER 1995

Alan Howarth has defected to Labour. On the eve of our conference. The man is a traitor and a shit. Yes, I liked him, he was a sort of friend I suppose, but changing your views is one thing, timing your betrayal to maximise the damage to your erstwhile friends quite another. When Stephen and I had supper with him in the summer we knew he was unhappy, but he gave no hint of this. I'm not wholly unsympathetic to some of his gripes, but he's so bloody prissy and precious and high-minded. Derek Conway[520] called. I said I thought we should take the line that Alan's an eccentric loner, a disappointed man with bees in his bonnet and a mid-life crisis (how's his marriage, eh?). Derek wanted to know if I felt there might be others similarly inclined. Peter Temple-Morris?[521]

---

518 The novel, *Who is Nick Saint?*, was published in October 1996.

519 When GB was appearing on television in the '80s, Clifford Warren, a clergyman from Gwent, sent him a postcard that read: 'Beginning. The word "begin" is full of energy. The best way to get something done is to *begin*. It's truly amazing what tasks we can accomplish if only we begin. You're never finished if you forever keep beginning.'

520 Now GB's whip; in the Whips' Office 1993–7.

521 MP for Leominster 1974–2001; he left the Conservative Party in November 1997 and became a Labour peer in 2001 as Baron Temple-Morris of Llandaff and Leominster.

Ray Whitney?[522] Andrew Rowe? They may not be happy with the rightward lurch, but I can't see them kicking the colleagues of a lifetime in the teeth.

This means our majority is down to seven – five if you count another of the oddballs, the pointy-headed Sir Richard Body who has 'freed' himself from the Conservative whip but still seems to vote with us … except, of course, when there's a full moon.

WEDNESDAY 11 OCTOBER 1995

I'm sitting in bed, a rather comfy fold-me-down, in Nick Hawkins' front room. It's gone midnight. It has been a long day. I reached Blackpool in time to hear Hezza's end-of-the-pier knockabout (all the old tricks, it creaks but it works) and sat on the platform for Stephen's speech. Stephen did well, but he probably lacks the vulgarity required to make a truly acclaimed conference speech. The talk of the town is Portillo's effort yesterday. It was clearly as crude as they come – awful mock heroics, cheap Brussels-bashing, wrapping himself in the Union Jack – but the activists stood and cheered and roared for more. He was shameless. Dishonest really. He conjured up the spectre of a European army only so he could say it would only happen over his dead body. He made us believe Brussels are about to launch a EU foreign and defence policy simply so he could reassure us that he'd have none of it. Don't mess with Britain – don't mess with Portillo. Having paraded Nelson, Wellington and Churchill as his heroes/role models, he coasted to his climax on the coat-tails of the SAS. 'Who dares wins!' The PM was on the platform so had no alternative but to lead the ovation – and I presume No. 10 cleared the speech in advance. Rifkind was not impressed. I think Hurd wouldn't have let it happen. I saw Michael at the Imperial. I said, 'How about you then!' He gave a wan smile. He knows he went too far. He's had a good summer, been taken seriously, impressed and surprised the brass hats. This devalues the currency.

THURSDAY 12 OCTOBER 1995

Highlight of the conference to date: lunchtime with the ladies of Blackpool South. In return for my room for the night I went along to speak to Nick Hawkins' Association Ladies. As Nick's car swept us into the car park, we were suddenly confronted by a little demonstration, a couple of ugly women holding placards and a seven-foot tall chicken.

'What's that?' I squeaked.

---

522   1930–2012; MP for Wycombe 1978–2001; chairman of the Positive European Group.

'It's the chicken,' said Nick as if it were the most ordinary thing in the world. 'Ignore it.'

'The chicken?'

'Yes,' he said, without a flicker, 'It follows me everywhere. Ignore it.'

He jumped out of the car and, together, Nick and I, dutiful wives in tow, marched briskly into the Conservative Club pursued to the door by the giant chicken squawking and flapping its wings. As we went in, Nick waved a dismissive and rather lordly hand towards the local hack who was covering the visit, 'No comment, no comment, it's just the chicken.'

Inside the club, Nick made no reference to the man-sized fowl, and, sensing it was a sensitive topic, I made no further enquiries. But when I came to make my speech it was agony. Michèle was biting her fist to suppress the giggles. As I stood there singing the Prime Minister's and the local member's praises, Nick standing po-faced and statesmanlike at my side, I kept catching sight of the wretched chicken, bobbing up and down outside.

The explanation? Nick has told Blackpool South, where he has a majority of 1,600 and boundary changes that will make him even more vulnerable, that he is looking for a safer seat.[523] The Labour party are accusing him of being on the 'chicken run' and they've hired this costume to provide him with regular, and seemingly effective, embarrassment.

....

TUESDAY 17 OCTOBER 1995
....

We've only been back twenty-four hours and it's all going wrong again. Michael Howard is in real trouble over his sacking of Derek Lewis.[524] The PM put up a so-so defence at PMQs, but Lewis is very plausible and there's the scent of blood in the air. David Lidington (who is devoted to his man) says MH considered resignation, but 'was persuaded it would be the wrong course to take'. The way it feels tonight he may find he has no choice in the matter ... I don't sense that his junior ministers are as supportive as they might be.

So, Howard's on the ropes and Portillo's digging in. Michael P is standing by his conference speech – '*Je ne regrette rien*' – saying that he and the PM are singing from the same sheet while conceding he's singing *fortissimo*. Meanwhile the PM, poor bugger, has to backtrack: he knew the general line the speech would take, he hadn't seen the wording.

---

523 He found one. From 1997 to 2005 he was MP for Surrey Heath, one of the Conservatives' safest seats. He was dese-
     lected as the Surrey Heath Association's candidate in 2004 following a postal ballot of members. His difficulties began
     soon after he left his wife for a Conservative county councillor in 1999 when a first attempt to deselect him was suc-
     cessfully defused.

524 The Home Secretary dismissed the Director General of the Prison Service in the light of General Sir John Learmont's
     report into escapes from Parkhurst Prison in January 1995. The Home Secretary drew a distinction between 'policy
     matters' for which he had ultimate responsibility and 'operational matters' which were the responsibility of the Prison
     Service.

With noises off from Geoffrey Howe and Jacques Santer [President of the European Commission], with Hugh Dykes hopping up and down in the Tea Room and on Palace Green denouncing the defence secretary's 'grotesque and foolish antics', we're back to the same old story. *O-bli-vion* here we come!

But there's good news for someone: Douglas Hurd is to get £250,000 a year working a two-day week as deputy chairman of NatWest Markets.

I'm just in from St James's Palace, the Chester Cathedral fund-raising reception. My chat with the Prince of Wales consisted largely of manic barking laughter on both sides. Evidently we both felt that was the best way to get through it.

THURSDAY 19 OCTOBER 1995

A unique day. It began with the Home Secretary on the ropes, probably a goner. It's ended with him triumphant, as good as unassailable. This is the first time since I arrived here that I have seen a performance in the Chamber – by itself – transform a situation.

It was an opposition motion – 'That this House deplores the unwillingness of the Secretary of State for the Home Department to accept responsibility for serious operational failures of the Prison Service' – and Jack Straw led the charge. He had a powerful case to deploy, but right from the outset he was woolly and plodding, easily confused, thrown by the interventions and virtually sunk only five minutes in by a beautifully judged question from Bernard Jenkin: 'Under the circumstances, would *he* have dismissed the Director General of the Prison Service?' It was a little hand-grenade lightly lobbed, but its effect was devastating. Straw hesitated. For a second the wretched creature couldn't think what to say. He didn't have an answer. And as he began to flannel we began to jeer. He never recovered and, as soon as Howard started intervening on him – urgent, attacking, determined, but not for a moment losing his cool – we knew we'd won. Straw was a mangy old sheepdog, and toothless, our man a thoroughbred panther, fangs bared.

By the time Michael got to his feet Straw was already in retreat and Michael pushed home his advantage mercilessly. He had wonderful venomous fun at Alan Howarth's expense – how we loved it! – and he scored again and again both because he was so unrelenting – chillingly so – and because his mastery of the brief was absolute.

Blair sat next to Straw looking increasingly grumpy and uncomfortable. He was hating the hash Straw was making of it. He kept nudging him, telling him what to say. Howard saw what was happening – the despatch boxes are only six feet apart – and began goading Blair, taunting him – so that eventually Blair made the fatal mistake of getting to his feet, humiliating his man in the process, but completely failing to deliver any kind of blinding strike. It was an electric ninety minutes and when Michael finished and sat back, triumphant, the roar from our side was incredible. We cheered and cheered, we waved our order papers, those of us sitting right behind him leant forward to pat him – to touch his garb. At lunchtime in the Tea Room there was a general acceptance that Michael's number was almost certainly up. Thanks to Straw's ineptitude and Michael's nerveless bravura performance, whatever the rights and wrongs of the case, Michael has set himself free. Amazing.

Walking along the corridor between Members' Lobby and the Tea Room I came face to face with Alan Howarth. He said, 'I feel bad about you and Stephen.'

I said, 'But you let the Labour Party use you. They've simply exploited you.'

'It wasn't supposed to happen like that.'

I said, 'Never mind. It's done now.' I think I was trying to sound scornful, dismissive, but it came out wrong. I just walked away. It's probably childish, but I really don't want to talk to him any more.

WEDNESDAY 25 OCTOBER 1995

A happy day, much of it (about eight hours) spent in the Chamber. This morning I initiated a ninety-minute debate on community service – raised an issue that I care about, even put forward a couple of practical ideas. This afternoon, from 3.30 p.m., we've been debating the national lottery. I chipped in merrily here and there and, for once, I was called to speak at a relatively civilised hour – 7.00 p.m. I spoke for about half an hour, easily and well. At least, I made myself laugh.

I've had an excellent dinner with congenial coves and I'm on my way to a nightcap with Willetts and Coe – intelligent, attractive, interesting achievers. It's not a bad life. I can see how easily one could turn into a Tufton Bufton – a settled backbencher, making the odd speech, writing the occasional article, opening fetes and bazaars and hostels for single mothers in the constituency at the weekend (bit of a bore, but there we are), being wined and dined by all and sundry, having access to anyone – the life of Patrick Cormack or Geoffrey Johnson-Smith, or Gerald Kaufman, comfortable, complacent, not entirely without achievement (a useful campaign now and again, a constituent's intractable problem actually solved once in a while) ... but it's not what I want, is it?

TUESDAY 7 NOVEMBER 1995

8.00 a.m.: Breakfast with Stephen, followed by DoH prayers at 9.00. Stephen's in his element. He knows his way around the department,[525] he rates the officials, he's happy with his ministers – especially Gerry. The others I think he doesn't notice. Tom[526] loves to be ignored. 'God, you should have seen Virginia!' Clearly Virginia was busy-busy-busy morning, noon, and night, on the line all the time – daybreak and weekends a speciality. Stephen doesn't refer to the ministers unless he needs them. Julia finds this disconcerting. I said to Stephen, 'She hasn't had one proper conversation with you since you arrived.' He said, not unkindly, 'That's the junior minister's lot. What does she want to say anyway?' He sounded genuinely puzzled. Because he is self-contained and certain of what he's doing, he doesn't realise that others may want the occasional pat on the back. 'You can tell her how wonderful she is.' 'I do. Actually, I tell her how wonderful *you* think she is.'

10.30 a.m.: Coffee in the Pugin Room[527] with Ned Cavendish. It's one of the good places here, the one room we share with the Lords, hence their red carpet underfoot but our green leather to sit upon, Mr and Mrs Pugin gazing down at us, the friendly Filipino waitress (who is always so sweet to Michèle) who always arrives with the coffee before she's even asked. Ned is some sort of descendant of the Marquis of Hartington[528] – Harty-Tarty – my favourite nineteenth century politician since I heard the story of how, invariably, he would dismiss the bright new schemes and bold initiatives brought to him by ambitious eager-beavers with the same refrain, 'Far better not!' Ned is droll, foppish and has hopes for the candidates list. He is destined to be disappointed. I think he knows it.

11.30 a.m.: As instructed, I presented myself at 12 Downing Street. I arrived with Michael Jopling. We were ushered into the Chief Whip's little study. We have been singled out for a signal honour: next Wednesday, when the Queen opens Parliament, we are to propose and second the Loyal Address. Alastair mumbled that he was sure we knew the form, Murdo Maclean[529] crept forward like Uriah Heep with photocopies of the choicest speeches of recent years, I said 'Thank you very much, I'll do my best', and Jopling sighed and shook his head and snorted and whinnied like an old cart-horse. 'I'm not sure, Alastair, that I'm the right man, I'm really not. With all the stuff about

---

525 Stephen Dorrell had been Parliamentary Under-Secretary of State at the Department of Health 1990–92.

526 Tom Sackville was PUSS at the department 1992–5.

527 The Chamber of the House of Commons and much of the Palace of Westminster were destroyed by fire in 1834. Charles Barry (1795–1860) won the competition to design the new Houses of Parliament and Barry employed Augustus Welby Pugin (1812–52) to make detailed drawings for the restored Palace and to design and model much of the interior decoration.

528 Spencer Compton, Marquis of Hartington, later 8th Duke of Cavendish, 1833–1908.

529 Private Secretary to the Chief Whip 1979–2000.

my outside interests, there'll be barracking. Could spoil what should be a special occasion.' Alastair protested that thanks to his reforms Michael is admired across the House. True. Still, the old Eeyore hemmed and hawed. He'd think about it. All the way back to the House, he chuntered to me about how he really didn't think he could, it would backfire, it would prove embarrassing. He's going to bottle out. I'm sure of it. I'm not unsympathetic, but if anyone's going to be barracked it's me. (It is awful to admit it, but it's a relief to feel my tormentor-in-chief[530] won't be here. I didn't want him to die. I just wanted him to go away.)

I've got to do this speech and, *come what may*, I've got to do it well. They say it is only given to those for whom advancement is imminent. Get it right – and up you go. Get it wrong and that's that. (It's absurd, but so often this place *is* absurd. Outside, no one has heard about this bizarre tradition, but inside, here, especially on our side, especially among the old guard, this sort of nonsense still counts. I've got to take it seriously and I've got to deliver. David Sumberg[531] told me he did it several years ago and blew it completely. That was the end of him.)

MONDAY 13 NOVEMBER 1995

I'm glad Jopling bottled out. It's now to be Douglas Hurd, which is so much better, more distinguished. He commands respect, he'll settle the house, he'll be good to follow and I can make something of the shared birthdays – his, mine, John Ward's and the Speaker's secretary. I have finished the speech. I've done what's expected: some self-deprecating jokes, a paean to one's constituency (the honour is Chester's not mine), a few minutes on the contents of the Queen's Speech. Quite early on I've also put in a bit of buttery stuff about the values of the House – 'a good place where – for the most part and in all parts of the House – good people of good faith are doing their best to do a good job for their constituents' – both because it's true but principally to defuse hostility. Greg Knight was very funny: 'Remember, there'll be 300 people in there all wanting you to fail. (Pause) And the opposition won't want you to do that brilliantly either.'

I was feeling *relatively* easy about it till last night when I thought, for fun, I'd look up accounts of past State Openings. Look what I found: Chips Channon on 3 November 1936:

---

530 Derek Enright, Labour MP for Hemsworth, died on 31 October 1995.

531 MP for Bury South 1983–97.

I heard the Address moved and seconded. The mover was Miss Florence Hors-brugh, Member for Dundee, an extremely likeable and able woman. She used simple, but magnificent prose, and scored a great success; she was wearing a dark-brown, flowing dress and fawn gloves. She was followed by Harold Nicol-son, from whom so much was expected. He was in diplomatic uniform, and somehow looked ridiculous ... He rose, and immediately 'lost' and annoyed the House. Indeed, his speech was one of the saddest I have ever heard, so well meant and so well phrased, but meaningless to the point of absurdity. He began with a tribute to Ramsay MacDonald, which irritated both sides of the House, then he stumbled, and at one moment I feared he was breaking down. I felt sick for him ... He sat down, at long last, in complete silence.

And Harold Nicolson himself, 7 November 1936:

Many press cuttings come in which suggest to me that my speech on the Address was really more of a floater than I had imagined. It is most unfortunate, as I gather that they really did mean to give me a job in the government when the reshuffle comes in the Spring and I may now lose the chance for ever. Three minutes of blindness and a ruined career![532]

Oh God!

TUESDAY 14 NOVEMBER 1995

At 6.20 p.m. I presented myself at No. 12. Douglas was already there. Drinks were handed round (the Chief is a generous host), banter exchanged. Were we happy? 'No,' smiled Douglas, 'but what has happiness got to do with it.' Alastair ran through the form. Murdo ran through the form. Douglas mentioned a school song that he might refer to. Alastair spluttered, 'Good God, you're not going to sing!' Douglas murmured reassurance. Greg Knight was perched on the edge of the sofa next to me. I passed him my speech. He read it through. I was glad. I wanted *someone* to have seen it, to share in the responsibility. 'Looks fine,' he said.

The Chief heaved himself to his feet and led the way to No. 10. There are intercon-necting doors that take you from No. 12, through the hallway at No. 11, straight into the entrance hall at No. 10. I trooped alongside Douglas. 'Well,' I said rather stupidly

---

532 Nicolson, 1886–1968, MP for West Leicester 1935–45, never achieved office.

(why do I always have to fill the air with sound?), 'I suppose it's something for us to say we've done.' 'Yes,' he said, 'another of those curious little cul-de-sacs life throws in one's way.'

Upstairs, in the main drawing room, the entire government had assembled. This was the 'Eve of Session Reception'. Once upon a time there was a dinner, but when ministers were asked to pay for their own meals the mean and the impoverished grumbled and the tradition lapsed. Now we get drinks (plenty of them) on the taxpayer. The PM, in good humour, welcomed us, told us what a challenging and exciting session it's going to be and then asked for the doors to be shut and invited the Cabinet secretary to step forward and read the Queen's Speech. He read it out, word for word, as Her Majesty will read it tomorrow. Then Madam Speaker spoke – graciously and well, wishing us all the best in the coming session and doing so with sincerity and style. She paid a lovely tribute to Tony Newton – 'he is a golden man, golden'. And he is.

We quaffed, we sluiced, we made our way into the street. As we stepped out into Downing Street, Andrew Mitchell (who did it so well in the year I arrived) caught up with me and put an arm around my shoulder, 'I know exactly how you're feeling. It's hell. But it'll be all right.'

WEDNESDAY 15 NOVEMBER 1995

And it was! Joe Ashton saved the day.

The butterflies were terrible. I must have gone for a pee at least three times between lunch and 2.30 p.m. I have spoken thousands of times (for thousands of pounds!) – I am an old hand, but I've never known anything like this.

Madam Speaker: 'I shall now call on Mr Douglas Hurd to move the Address, and Mr Gyles Brandreth will second it.'

Douglas got up – and almost at once it went wrong, not badly awry but just enough for us all to feel instantly uncomfortable. It must have been the first time he had spoken from the back benches in twenty years. He made an immediate mistake saying when he leaves the House it'll be his constituents not us he'll miss the most. And then he went all dewy-eyed and lyrical as he took us on a rural ride through Oxfordshire – we had the local school song, verse after verse of it – and while on our side we listened with respect, on their side they lost interest, the murmuring and shuffling began. As he got away from the sentiment and onto the substance of the Queen's Speech he began to recover and by the end – not that I was really listening – it seemed fine, not a triumph but by no means a disaster.

But as I stood up and heard the groans and jeers from the benches opposite, I thought to myself, 'This is going to be a disaster. And there's nothing I can do.' My mouth was so dry I thought I might not be able to utter a sound. I started. I was struggling, but I knew all I could do was plough on. Madam Speaker, bless her, was sitting forward on the edge of her seat looking directly at me. I looked directly at her, concentrated entirely on her, she was willing me to keep my nerve – the rumbling opposite was subsiding, they were beginning to listen, and then, about three minutes in, I began my passage extolling the virtues of the matchless city of Chester. 'It has 2,000 years of history,' I said, and from the far end of the second row of the Labour benches Joe Ashton cried, 'And a one thousand majority!' The House roared. I rallied, and suddenly they were on my side. And from there on in there were no problems – even a couple of blissful moments. A joke at the expense of the Liberals united all but thirty members; a joke at Paddy Ashdown's expense united all but one.

It's done. And it went well. For this relief, much thanks.

THURSDAY 16 NOVEMBER 1995

Lots of nice notes about the speech. Good notices too. Matthew Parris: 'one of the best of recent years'. Hooray. Now draw a line and move on.

The Queen's Speech itself gets a so-so press, probably much as it deserves.

Hero of the hour: little Alan Duncan who performed 'a citizen's arrest' on one of a gaggle of Asylum Bill protestors who threw paint and flour at Brian Mawhinney as he and Alan were crossing College Green. He is cooler and more courageous than I would have been. (I like Alan. He is amusing, and effective, but within the system here they're suspicious of him. They don't *quite* trust him.)

Joke of the hour: Sir Julian Critchley[533] has declared that he would not vote Conservative next time. The papers are playing this up as 'a serious blow' as though Critchley were a serious figure. He is an entertaining writer and, for all I know, may have been an effective MP, but since I have been here I think I've seen him on the premises five times.

In the Tea Room this morning there was considerable resentment at the coverage he's getting – and 'the salary he is drawing given that he does bugger all' (Simon Burns). He's never here and while his illness is debilitating (I last saw him in a wheelchair) he's clearly fit enough to write, broadcast and kick the party in the shins when it suits.

---

533 1930–2000; MP for Rochester & Chatham 1959–64, Aldershot 1970–97.

TUESDAY 21 NOVEMBER 1995

I breakfasted with the only other person in the country who didn't watch the Princess of Wales being interviewed last night on *Panorama*. Stephen didn't watch because he really isn't interested. I didn't watch because I was in the Chamber waiting for my adjournment debate on 'employment in Chester'. (For most adjournment debates there are just two MPs in the Chamber – the backbencher and the minister replying. Last night, we had a grand total of three – the dullard of Ellesmere Port joined us to be seen to be 'in on the act'.) Diana had clearly worked hard at her sound bites and tragi-pathetic look. But I think we already knew that she and James Hewitt had been lovers, didn't we? In the Tea Room Fabricant was disappointed when I told him that I was pretty sure she met Hewitt nine months *after* Harry was born, not nine months before. Soames (Charles' fat-man at Westminster) went over the top and is being sent a 'cool it' message from No. 10. However, I think we can take it that Soames' line that Diana's behaviour shows 'advanced stages of paranoia' reflects the true feelings of the Prince of Wales.

I spent the morning at a Better English Campaign meeting. Trevor [McDonald] is a good chairman, courteous, well-briefed, keeps the show moving, but I wonder if anything is to be *achieved*? Yes, we'll get coverage, picture stories, fleeting awareness, possibly one or two pilot schemes to help youngsters with 'interview skills', but will the campaign make any sort of lasting difference? I think we know the answer to that.

I'm just in from the Chester Association President's Club lunch at the Carlton Club. Our guest of honour: the Deputy Prime Minister. (It's done on a quid pro quo basis. You go to their constituency; it's difficult for them to refuse to come to yours.) Hezza arrived late. I couldn't face the small talk while we were waiting, so went outside and paced the pavement, heart sinking, stomach churning, glumly anticipating the 'well-he-can't-really-deliver-the-big-names-can-he?' looks I got last year when the Chancellor failed to show. Happily, and actually only about fifteen minutes behind schedule, the DPM swept in. He went straight into his turn: 'We'll win the election because people vote with their wallets not with their hearts. It's the economy that decides it and on the economy middle-Britain trusts us more than Labour.' He shook hands, posed for photos and swept off again. I was grateful, but whenever I see him at close quarters I notice how he impresses but he doesn't seduce.

TUESDAY 28 NOVEMBER 1995

The Budget's been and gone.

A penny off income tax, steady-as-she-goes, I'm-a-prudent-Chancellor. Two-fifths of the roads programme is to be cut, which will have one or two jumping up and down in certain parts of the constituency, but on the whole it's all very reasonable (MIRAS untouched), very Ken, easy enough to defend on the doorstep. As the Chancellor sat down, from below the gangway Skinner called out, 'Is that it?' I suspect that may be the general verdict.

Public spending is currently running at 42 per cent of national income. Equally alarming (possibly more so) is the news that I've put on a stone since I arrived here. I had my 'medical' in the little room off the Cromwell lobby: cholesterol improvement (all those salads, all that grated carrot!) but 'a little regular exercise wouldn't come amiss'. Potentially more exciting is news of the virtually unnoticed mini-mini-shuffle. John Taylor is swapping with Jonathan Evans. Because John is frayed at the edges, looks as if he has lived a little and is divorced, the view is that clean-cut Evans is our boyo for the matrimonial legislation. Horam is coming to Health and Willetts replaces him as Roger Freeman's sidekick. There was confusion for a time when it dawned on somebody that moving Horam to Health made Sackville surplus to requirements. Poor Tom hung in limbo for an hour or two until a berth was found for him at the Home Office. They are going to have five ministers there, instead of four. It's only a game. Why not?

The upshot of the musical chairs is this: there's a vacancy in the Whips' Office. Once the panic over Tom had been resolved, I said to Stephen, 'This means there'll be a new whip.'

He looked at me blankly, 'Yes.'

I said, 'Well?'

The penny dropped. 'I'll speak to Alastair,' he said.

We'll see.

WEDNESDAY 29 NOVEMBER 1995

Memorable day. President Clinton came to address both Houses of Parliament. At 12 noon we trooped into the royal gallery and took our places. We had the usual flummery: Black Rod, the Lord Chancellor, Madam Speaker, all in full fig, figures straight out of Gilbert & Sullivan. The fanfare sounded, trumpets from on high. In came the Clintons and the Majors. The PM, Norma and Hillary sat in the front row; only the President sat on the stage. In the middle of the stalls we'd come because we thought we should. He may be a Democrat, but he's still President. 'Be not too proud to be there.' This is a collector's item, we said to ourselves. But if we'd come to mock, we stayed to praise. He was sensational.

He looks good – tall, slim, handsome, his eye meets your eye – but the way he talks … His speech was just perfect. It was measured, easy, elegant; he touched all the right buttons. He saluted the PM's quest for peace in Northern Ireland, he affirmed the special relationship, he even announced that the US navy's latest vessel is to be named the *Winston Churchill* (gasps around me, 'First he wins the lottery, now this!'). He said all the things you'd expect him to say, but in such a way that they seemed neither predictable nor clichéd. There was a grandeur about it, yet his language was simple and the manner almost conversational. He brought us towards him. It did what oratory should, it stirred and lifted, but he made it personal and intimate. There was none of the phoney theatrics you'd have got from Heseltine or Hague (or even me) – no dated Oxford Union nonsense about this. This was modern oratory, the best speech of its kind I've ever heard. If we walked in wondering how he ever got to the White House, by the time we shuffled out we knew.

Moments before the President made his entry, Greg Knight bustled down the central aisle. He saw me, stopped, pointed at me – I was halfway down the row – and said in an alarmingly loud stage whisper, 'The minute this is over the Chief needs to see you in his room.' 'Who's been a naughty boy then?' said my neighbour. I said nothing. Once we'd cheered the President on his way, I ankled round to the Chief's office. There are two ways in. One through the Upper Whips' Office, the other, a back way, down a corridor through an ante-room. I took the back way.

'Ah,' said Alastair, getting up from behind his tiny desk, 'Good, good.' He perched on one sofa. I perched on the other. He gobbled gently and then, as though suddenly remembering why he'd summoned me, 'The Prime Minister hopes you will accept your first ministerial appointment by joining the Whips' Office. Yes?'

'Yes.'

'It's the one job in government that you can only get with the full approval of your peers – so you're here because we wanted you.'

'Thank you.'

'Lunch?'

He got up and rolled through the Upper Whips' Office, me in tow. We went down to his car and drove to Downing Street. 'You'll have to give up your outside interests. That's the way it goes. The Deputy will explain the form. And you'll get a security briefing. We're lunching their lordships by the way.'

Their lordships turned out to be Tom Strathclyde and the other whips from the Lords, only about two of whom I recognised. This lunch is an annual event, 'a tradition'. 'There are lots of traditions here,' giggled Liam Fox. 'It's very old-fashioned. And hierarchical. As you'll discover. For the time being, if I were you, I'd keep my mouth shut.'

And, so far, I have. As I write, it's gone midnight and I'm just in from my first whips' dinner – an Italian meal in an upstairs room in a little restaurant off Victoria. Copious drinking, banter, and schoolboy games. When it came to nominating my 'shit of the year' I came up with John Gorst. Other than that I have hardly uttered a word all day. 'You got it just right,' said Liam, still giggling, 'a certain modesty is becoming in a new boy.'

I am the most junior member of Her Majesty's government and now I am going to bed, tipsy but content. Goodnight.

THURSDAY 30 NOVEMBER 1995

They do take the hierarchy very seriously indeed. The pecking order is as follows:

Chief Whip (formally Parliamentary Secretary to the Treasury): Alastair Goodlad, to be referred to henceforward as 'Chief'.

Deputy Chief Whip (formally Treasurer of Her Majesty's Household): Greg Knight, to be referred to henceforward as 'Deputy'. (According to Patrick McLoughlin,[534] who is offering plenty of avuncular advice for which I am duly grateful: 'You really must call them Chief and Deputy and if you've got a problem you take it to the Deputy. You never go direct to the Chief. Keep in with the Deputy and he'll protect you.')

Comptroller of Her Majesty's Household: Tim Wood.

Vice-Chamberlain of Her Majesty's Household and pairing whip: Andrew Mackay.

Senior whips (Lord Commissioners): Derek Conway, Bowen Wells (also social and carriage whip), Simon Burns, Michael Bates[535] and Liam Fox.

Junior whips: Patrick McLoughlin (Head of the Lower Office!), Roger Knapman,[536] Gary Streeter,[537] Richard Ottaway and GB.

We meet every day at 2.30 p.m. in the Upper Whips' Office. Crowded, cluttered, untidy, mounds of paperwork piled high on every desk, unwashed wine glasses, yesterday's newspapers; it has the feeling of the staffroom of a minor public school, circa 1950. For the meeting the senior whips sit at their desks around the walls of the room, the juniors sit in designated places on sofas in the middle. The junior whip (yours truly) sits in a low armchair immediately in front of the Deputy and consequently can't see him – or be seen by him. If the junior wishes to speak he raises his right hand. The

534 MP for Derbyshire West 1986–2010, Derbyshire Dales since 2010; PUSS at Transport, Employment and DTI 1989–94; in the Whips' Office from 1995; Chief Whip 2010–12.

535 MP for Lanbaurgh 1992–7; Baron Bates of Lanbaurgh since 2008.

536 MP for Stroud 1987–97; later Nigel Farage's predecessor as Leader of the United Kingdom Independence Party 2002–6.

537 MP for Plymouth Sutton 1992–7, Devon South West since 1997.

junior's duties at the meeting seem to be to ensure that the 'Do Not Disturb' notice is in position and to hand out any paperwork – distributing it strictly according to hierarchical ranking.

The Deputy chairs the first half of the meeting, 'the housekeeping':

1. Bench changes. At all times when the House is sitting there has to be a whip on the government front bench. There's a rota, but you can swap if you need to.

2. Business of the day. Each whip looks after the business of one or more departments (mine is to be Environment) so if it's your department's 'business' that day you're supposed to know all about it and tell the team what to expect.

3. Committees. There are a dozen (and more) backbench committees every day. One of us is supposed to be in attendance at each of them. (Most of these committees are a disgrace – attended by the chairman, secretary and a couple of loners with nowhere else to go. A distinguished visitor turns up expecting to address a House of Commons committee and finds himself exchanging pleasantries with half a dozen nonentities. The system is dying on its feet. When I first attended the Backbench Treasury Committee there were twenty or so in regular attendance. I went last week and three turned up. Simon Coombs had some bigwig from British Airways or the BTA on parade at the Tourism Committee and, apart from Simon and the whip, nobody showed.)

4. Voting lists. The pairing whip tells us who failed to vote in yesterday's divisions without being slipped or registering a pair and if it's one of ours we have to seek them out and find out what happened. (Each whip has a card listing his charges. It's done on a regional basis. I'm looking after the north-west.)

About twenty minutes into the meeting, the Chief arrives. He clambers over the outstretched legs of the junior whips and makes his way to his 'chair', facing the Deputy. In his hand he has the 'whips' notes' which he proceeds to read out loud. This, I understand, is as close as we get to the fabled Black Book. There's a huge old-fashioned safe in the corner of the office. Inside the safe are a couple of notebooks. Whips are expected to use them to record any 'intelligence' that may be of interest as concisely as possible. There's a top copy which is torn out for the Chief to read out. The carbon remains in the notebook. I get the impression (early days) that the notes are to gauge general mood (tittle-tattle from the Tea Room): any *significant* information should be taken to the Deputy in the first instance. He will then decide whither it goes...

SATURDAY 2 DECEMBER 1995

Clinton has had a remarkable week. The crowds in Ireland, north and south, Protestant and Catholic, they love him. He's delivered five major speeches in three days, by all accounts each one as powerful as the first. He must have a core of writers – real writers – who don't simply have a fine way with words but who understand the vocabulary and the *rhythm* he requires. That's what Major needs. In this country our senior politicians' speeches are simply cobbled together, usually at the last minute, invariably by young men in red braces.

And Brandreth hasn't had too bad a week either.

Michèle said to me, 'I hope you're happy now?'

I said, 'I *am*.'

She knows that we're going to lose the election, that's why she's content for me to stand again. She knows we could be out for ten years or more – if PR comes in, who knows, forever? This could be my one and only chance to be in government. If it hadn't happened I would have been disappointed *always*. And I've a feeling the Whips' Office is going to suit me – and I may even suit it.

The upside: I get a salary, a car, a phonecard, a ministerial black box (Shana[538] explained, 'It'll take a few weeks to arrive – it's hand-made by prisoners') and, best of all, no more speeches. Whips mouth various procedural mantras in the Chamber and on committee, but they don't ask questions, they don't make speeches, they don't have views. (Greg Knight: 'We're here to support the government in general and the Prime Minister in particular. Our job is to secure the government's business – not think about it.')

The downside: I now have a pager strapped to my waist. I am at someone else's beck and call. And from Monday to Thursday I will be a prisoner at the Commons – but I've been that anyway.

And, of course, the constituency round continues – remorselessly. Last night we had Norman Lamont to the Friday Supper Club. He's searching for a seat, so he's trawling the circuit, and if he's making speeches as good as last night's he'll find one. He was funny (which surprised them) and loyal (which amazed them) – he peddled his Eurosceptic line, but quite gently. There wasn't a word against Major. He got a standing ovation. He'll have gone off feeling good. I'm glad.

I'm now off to the Newtown residents (they want better central heating, more double glazing, more police on the beat), the World Development Group (they want action on aid, debt and East Timor), and the Association of Wrens (who want nothing except a few laughs – bless them. Their modest wants I can supply.)

---

538 Shana Hole, Special Adviser to the Chief Whip.

MONDAY 4 DECEMBER 1995

I have just done my first hour of bench duty – not very stimulating. Three worthy contributions to the Budget debate: David Mitchell,[539] decent, humane, old-fashioned; Jeremy Bray,[540] boring for science; Nigel Forman, wiry and customarily sharp, getting off to an appalling start with a ghastly joke. Prompted, he said, by seeing me on the front bench he wanted to liven things up and asked, 'What is the difference between O. J. Simpson, Rosemary West and the Leader of the Opposition? The answer is that only Rosemary West has convictions.' The few who were there groaned and shook their heads. What made him do it?

The whip on duty sits on the front bench, book on lap, recording not the details of what's said – that is available in Hansard – but his *impression* of the tone, content, attitude, thought processes of each of the speakers. The idea is to get a handle on where so-and-so may be coming from, to spot early signs of wobble, disaffection, disloyalty. Marks are not given, there are no hieroglyphics, it's simply an instant subjective digest of what's happening in the Chamber. You report on ministers as much as backbenchers – good speech, bad speech, insensitive, well-briefed, all over the shop, drunk again! – and *no one* outside the Whips' Office is permitted to look at the book, other than the PM.

I was also introduced to the emergency button. Secreted in the panelling of the clerks' desk is a hidden button. Press it and a bell rings in the Upper Whips' Office. Reinforcements come scurrying into the Chamber at once. At least, that's the theory.

When I'd completed my hour I joined Stephen in the Tea Room.

'Are we still going to have our breakfasts?' he asked.

'Oh, I hope so,' I said.

'Good.'

How do we square this with our consciences? Fairly easily, I think. We are totally loyal to the present administration. We work for its success. But we know it's doomed. We are looking over the hill.

WEDNESDAY 6 DECEMBER 1995

On a Wednesday, instead of our 2.30 p.m. meeting, we meet at No. 12 for a marathon session from 10.30 a.m. to lunch. We sit around the large table, the Deputy at one end,

---

539 MP for Basingstoke 1964–83, Hampshire North West 1983–97; father of Andrew Mitchell MP.
540 1930–2002; Labour MP for Middlesborough West 1962–70, Motherwell & Wishaw 1970–83, Motherwell South 1983–97.

his back facing the window onto St James's Park, the Chief at the other end, near the door to his study. The rest of us are arranged in a precise pecking order on either side, the more junior you are the nearer you are to the centre of the table.

The agenda is as per the 2.30 p.m. meetings, except for 'extras' and refreshments. The extras include detailed discussion of the next two weeks' business – what needs to go where, when and why – and a weekly assessment of the state of our sick and our troubled. The 'troubled' feature on a list marked U (for Unstable); the sick merely have their names read out. There is much banter, most of it directed at Liam as our resident doctor.[541]

'I thought you said George Gardiner was going to be dead by Christmas. He's never looked fitter.'

'What do you make of Ted's ankles? They've swollen terribly.'

'It's fluid retention, not a good sign.'

'They look like elephants' feet.'

'They *are* elephants' feet. Ted never forgets.'

When we arrive there's coffee and biscuits. During the meeting the coffee is topped up by Doris, who seems to be the No. 12 housekeeper, a jolly lady of riper years, with a heart of gold and an ample bosom. The bosom is quite disconcerting. It's low slung and pressed very firmly against you as the coffee is served.

At 12 noon champagne is served – in silver goblets. The goblets are rather fine pieces, all shapes and sizes, donated to the office down the years. Each whip has his own goblet and it is the junior whip's task to carry the tray of goblets round the table, moving from one end to the other, from one side to the other – fourteen separate moves all told – to ensure that the tray is proffered in the correct pecking order. Bowen Wells, as social and carriage whip, opens the champagne (with difficulty – his inability to perform the task without squirting the stuff all over the place is evidently a running joke) and pours it, partly onto the table, with luck into the goblets. The junior whip follows him, altar boy behind the celebrant, offering orange juice to those who like their champagne diluted. (The Chief does not.) To go with the champagne there are rather good, thick, scrunchy cheese straws. (The Chief likes these kept within reach.)

As far as I can tell the junior whip's duties are as follows:

1. At 10.30 a.m. on the dot, to close the double doors.

2. Before the meeting, to distribute the paperwork. After the meeting, to clear it away and destroy it. We keep no record of our deliberations.

---

541   Liam Fox was a GP before entering Parliament.

1995

3. At 11.59 a.m. to catch Bowen's eye, so that as the clock strikes twelve I can begin my perambulations with the silver goblets and he can begin faffing about with the champagne.

Extraordinary.

TUESDAY 12 DECEMBER 1995

David Lightbown has died. He collapsed at the Varsity match at Twickenham. He was sixty-three and hopelessly overweight – though not on Liam's list of the vulnerable. The atmosphere in the office is very subdued. Those who knew him well really loved him. He cultivated the myth of the whip as burly bully boy and there was certainly something alarming about the sight of him rumbling slowly down the corridor towards you like a menacing hippo. In truth he was a gentle giant. This brings our majority down to five – three when Labour holds Hemsworth and we lose David's seat, as we will.

I saw the PM tonight. He looked quite chipper. The progress on Northern Ireland gives him a real (and justified) sense of achievement. Heseltine chairing all those Cabinet committees frees so much time. He was relatively sanguine about the shrinking majority: 'Perhaps it will concentrate the minds of some of our loose cannons.' Then he laughed, 'On second thoughts, perhaps it'll just encourage them.' He is extraordinarily normal, easy, rational. He has been Prime Minister for five years. It may have hardened, but it hasn't spoilt him. Old hands say that after five years Mrs T. was well on the way to lift-off. He asked how I was enjoying the Whips' Office. He patted my arm: 'There's nothing like it. A year as a whip and you'll learn more about how government works than in five years as a departmental minister.'

TUESDAY 19 DECEMBER 1995

Last night: the whips' Christmas party at No. 12. Quite jolly. Aphra said, 'Actually, dad, quite strange.' And it was an odd mix, from the lordly (the Heseltines) to the lowly (assorted secretaries, drivers, Doris, et al), wrinklies (the Wakehams, the Onslows), teenagers, toddlers. Greg had persuaded Ray Alan to provide a cabaret with Lord Charles (which made Greg and me laugh, even if it left others bemused) and Tim Wood appeared as a mildly gauche Father Christmas. A lot of pre-planning went into ensuring that the business of the House couldn't possibly disturb the revelry – one year it did, necessitating David Lightbown's appearance in the division lobbies in a Santa suit.

This morning, breakfast at Claridges with Stephen and the gang. This afternoon, tea with David Ashby. The poor man has lost his case against the *Sunday Times*.[542] I am ashamed to say that in the Tea Room over the past four weeks we have followed it in all its unhappy detail: the tears, the tantrums, the marriage from hell, the wife who routinely called him a poofter, the evidence of his impotence (which he called), the extraordinary elephantine device that he wore to ease his snoring (which he produced and put on in court), it was ludicrous and pathetic – and riveting. He endured the humiliation convinced he would win. He said that his wife, having given evidence against him, tried to console him after the hearing. He pushed her away. He said he'd broken down and wept when the verdict came in. Now he's wearing a sort of fixed beatific smile. Bravely he asked a question in the Chamber just now and was touched by the nice reception he got. He is certainly odd, but there is something about him that is endearing.

At seven o'clock the potential for high drama. There is a series of EU documents relating to fishing quotas and regulations that somehow the House is obliged to 'take note of' before Tony Baldry[543] turns up at the EU Fisheries Council on Thursday. Sceptics and colleagues with fishing interests in their constituencies object because the council wants to further restrict the catches of the British fleet. The manic Euro-enthusiasts (Dykes, Heath) are equally unhappy because they believe we're not embracing the European ideal with sufficient enthusiasm. I don't understand a word of it, but I do know we're hauling in the lame and the halt and those who thought they might have been getting away for an early Christmas – and Baldry has £12 million by way of sweeteners ('restored grants to harbours') ready to throw in the way of recalcitrant colleagues. Even so, it's going to be touch and go.

....

LATER

....

A personal disaster. I am angry and upset, but I have no time to do more than record what happened as I was due downstairs in Dining Room B ten minutes ago to address a frigging dinner for John Watts.[544] We won the first vote by a margin of eight. We

---

542 In January 1994 the *Sunday Times* alleged that Ashby had left his wife because of 'a friendship with another man'. Ashby admitted sharing a bed with a man in a French hotel while on holiday, but denied any impropriety. The paper later alleged Ashby had shared another bed with a man on holiday in Goa. This was untrue and the *Sunday Times* apologised for the Goa story, but refused to withdraw the allegation that Ashby was a hypocrite and a liar because in his election address he claimed to be 'a man of integrity who believes in traditional moral values' while his private life suggested otherwise.

543 Minister of State at Agriculture 1995–7; MP for Banbury since 1983.

544 Minister of State at Department of Transport 1994–97; MP for Slough 1983–97.

came to the main vote, the 'take note' motion – and we lost it by two. Cash and Cart-tiss[545] voted against us and we had eleven abstentions – including one of mine, Peter Thurnham. I was 100 per cent convinced all mine were sound – I'd checked with Winterton, I'd checked with Barry Porter, they were 'unhappy' but with us. I'd said to the Deputy, 'You can count on my lot.'

In the first division, Thurnham came up to me with his Eeyore face and said, 'I'm not at all happy, not at all happy.'

'But you're doing the right thing,' I said glibly. 'Keep it up.'

He went back to his place in the Chamber and when the second vote came, he just sat there. As the doors were about to shut, the Deputy barked at me, 'Where's Thurnham?'

I said, 'I don't know. Hasn't he voted?'

It was too late to fetch him. The door slammed shut. That was that. Immediately the vote was announced, I ran up to him. He wouldn't look at me. I crouched down and pushed my face into his: 'How could you do this to me, Peter. How *could* you?' I was distraught.

'I told you I wasn't happy,' he said, still not looking at me. 'You didn't listen.'

At least we lost by a margin of two. If it had just been one, I'd have been suicidal. Greg was so decent about it. 'Welcome to the Whips' Office. When it's going well, it's fun. And when it goes wrong, it's hell. The lesson is "Don't trust Thurnham."' Then he chortled, shoulders heaving, 'Don't trust *anybody*!'

THURSDAY 21 DECEMBER 1995

The Christmas recess starts here. Eighteen days of freedom. I want to finish the novel (I need to finish the novel), so it's the desk every day 9.00 to 6.00 but treats (movies and meals) in the evening – starting with Jo and Stevie and *In the Bleak Midwinter*.

The Queen has written to Charles and Diana telling them to stop squabbling and get divorced. She cleared the letter with the Archbishops of Canterbury and York and told the PM about it on Tuesday.

FRIDAY 29 DECEMBER 1995

Emma Nicholson has defected to the Lib Dems. We had no idea this was coming. She did not feature on the list of the Unstable. We know that she's self-serving, self-regarding,

---

545 Michael Cartiss, MP for Great Yarmouth 1983–97.

regularly misses the point not only because she's hard of hearing but also because she's not as bright as she thinks she is. None of this can we use to rubbish her. We *can* say – and Heseltine is going to – that twice in recent months she went to see him pleading for promotion. She's a disappointed lady whose talents have been rudely overlooked. So what's our majority now? Three, two? And who's next? Thurnham? Happy New Year.

CHAPTER VII

1996

Parliament reassembles tomorrow. We had a whips' meeting today at No. 12 at 3.30 p.m. We agreed that Thurnham heads the list of the Unstable. I said that he's prim, prissy, prickly, self-pitying and unpredictable. He wants love and a safe seat. The root of the problem is that he announced that he was retiring (because he didn't fancy defending Bolton North East, majority 185!) and then decided to put in for Westmorland (majority 16,000 plus) and didn't even get an interview. He feels 'let down' by the party. The party should at least have secured him an interview. That could and should have been achieved and wasn't. Now he's bitter – and his resentment is being fuelled by his wife who feels that neither her contribution nor Peter's great gifts have been properly recognised. I explain that I'm the wrong person to woo Peter because I've only been here five minutes and he's been here twelve years. The Chief agrees to ask the PM if he will entertain Mr and Mrs Thurnham to tea. Unbeknownst to Peter I have established an excellent telephone relationship with his association chairman (Norman Critchley, good man) who is keeping me posted with news of Peter's behaviour in his patch.

Andrew Rowe is reported as saying he would 'owe it to his constituents' to resign the whip if the party lurched further to the right, but we agree this isn't a serious threat. Emma's 'a cow', Thurnham's 'sad', but Andrew's fundamentally sound and 'a gent'.

Ashby has to stay high on the list, not because he's about to go overboard, but because his failed libel action has left him with a bill of around £500,000. According to Derek Conway, we don't need to search for funds to bail him out, because his admirable daughter has money and is coming to the rescue. We know his prospects are bleak, we assume his constituency will ditch him, we imagine he can't be getting much work at the Bar, we agree we need to keep a close eye on him, 'keep him busy' and lard him with tlc [tender loving care].

FRIDAY 12 JANUARY 1996

I'm on the 9.45 a.m. flight from Heathrow. Mrs T. is on the rampage – and the front page – big time. 'I am not sure what is meant by those who say that the party should return to something called One Nation Conservatism. As far as I can tell by their views on European federalism, such people's creed would better be described as no-nation Conservatism.' To say we don't need to move to the right is 'baloney'. She knows exactly what the party and the country need: more Thatcherism, pronto.

The crafty little garden gnome [Robin Cook] is already exploiting the situation: 'John Major has to decide whether he sees himself in the tradition of Thatcher or Keith Joseph or the One Nation tradition of Disraeli and Iain Macleod.' The potential for grief is considerable.

In the departure lounge my pager went: 'Call the Chief at once.' I called from one of the payphones, surrounded by eavesdroppers.

'Where are you?'

'Heathrow.'

'Good God, are you leaving the country?' Banter over, he got to the point: 'Contact all the ministers on your card. Tell them we want no reaction to the Thatcher speech. The Prime Minister is handling it. We want no other comment of any kind.'

MONDAY 15 JANUARY 1996

This is really bad. I have cocked up. I've survived, but it's not good. I failed to speak to Alistair Burt on Friday and he's written a letter to *The Times* taking issue with Lady Thatcher. I left a message on one of his numbers, but I didn't chase him and I should have done. By the time I got hold of him this morning, it was too late. He sent the letter on Saturday, they're publishing it tomorrow. If we try to retrieve the letter it will just fuel the row. Alistair admits he was a fool to send it, but, of course, if I had done as instructed he wouldn't have done. When the Chief heard about the letter, he was *incandescent*: 'He'll have to be sacked.' I have not seen the Chief angry before. It is a truly terrifying sight.

'He expressly disobeyed the Prime Minister's instruction. He'll have to go.' The Chief was raging, red-faced, raving. He looked at me, 'You spoke to him, didn't you?'

I am ashamed to say I answered ambiguously. 'Yes, he knows he shouldn't have sent the letter. He's full of regrets.'

'Fuck his regrets. Get him over here.'

I scuttled down to the Lower Whips' Office. It was empty. I called Alistair at the DSS. He was remarkably calm – and very sweet: 'I don't want to drop you in it,' he said, 'but somehow they have to know I didn't get the message.' The Deputy arrived in the room. We were alone. He said, 'Look at me. Now tell me the truth. It's just between us. No one else will ever know. You didn't speak to him did you?'

'No,' I said, 'I didn't.'

'Okay, if ever anything like this happens again come straight to me. Now forget it. I'll sort it.'

And somehow he has. Alistair has had his knuckles rapped, but nothing more. I saw the Chief a few moments ago. He made no mention of it.

TUESDAY 30 JANUARY 1996

Our voting procedure is absurd. This is what happens. A division is called. Two government whips and two opposition whips volunteer as tellers and give their names to the Speaker. Then one of our whips and one of their whips go and station themselves by the exit door of each of the voting lobbies. The members vote by filing past a clerk sitting at a desk on a raised stool (he ticks their name off on the register) and then exit, one by one. As they pass through the doors, the government whip counts them through, counting out loud, 'One – two – three – four – etc.' doing his best not to be distracted by the nudges, banter and asides of colleagues as they come shuffling through. The numbers counted, the whips return to the Chamber and hand the figures in to one of the clerks. The clerks then write the figures out on a form: 'Ayes to the right, so and so; Noes to the left, such and such.' The senior whip on the winning side then reads out the result of the vote to the House.

What I didn't realise until half an hour ago is this: the figure the whip gives to the clerk is the figure that counts – and if he gets it wrong, too bad. Never mind what it says on the register, never mind how many people actually voted, what the whip says goes. And last night it seems I miscounted by six! Fortunately, the Labour Party was not out in force and we had a comfortable majority, but had it been one of our tight ones we'd have lost – *thanks to me*.

I am being gently joshed in the office about this. The error was discovered when they were going through the voting lists for broken pairs and absentees. Yes, you would have thought counting from one to 300 relatively easy, but it isn't. I fear that on nights when I'm on telling duty I shall have to lay off the vino.

I'm in the Chamber virtually full-time this week. Yesterday, the Housing Bill Second Reading. Today, opposition Day: privatised water companies debate. Tomorrow, local government finance. Gummer is leading every day and *pace* all the jokes about him ('The weak are a long time in politics') the reason he has survived in government so long is because he is just so good. I endorse the David Curry[546] line: if Gummer had been six inches taller and had a voice half an octave lower he'd have held one of the great offices of state. As it is, he comes across like a pixie on Benzedrine. He loves to attack, he's wonderfully combative, but he knows his brief, he knows what he wants and he gets it.

I've just come from prayers. Invariably he arrives late (just as the meeting is due to start he phones from the car to say he's reached Marble Arch), but he's worth waiting for because when he arrives he wants to be larky, he wants to have fun. He sits enthroned in the corner, flicks his tie over his shoulder, sips his coffee and says, 'What scandal has the whip brought us?' And before I can answer (and I do try to come up with titbits to keep him amused) he's continuing: 'Gentlemen, I think you will want to know that I have decided to cull the ruddy duck. The white-headed duck must be conserved, and the ruddy ducks must pay the price. We must ready ourselves for the ruddy duck flak.'

I am going to see Michael Forsyth. He is speaking at the bicentennial Burns Night dinner at Guildhall or the Mansion House or somewhere. The PM and the cream of the establishment will be there. Michael wants some laughs, some poetry, some high emotion and a sustained standing ovation. I am to assist.

MONDAY 5 FEBRUARY 1996

Edward Leigh has sent Alastair [Goodlad] a very interesting letter:

> It is fairly clear that these defections that have caused us so much grief are not so much fundamental differences of principle or policy as a cry for help or frustrated ambition … The difficulty is that Parliament and the role of MPs assumes that we are still nineteenth-century gentlemen of independent means with a part-time interest in politics. The truth is that most MPs are career politicians who want to have some sort of role in government or of monitoring it effectively.

His analysis is spot on: 'The Select Committees are powerless debating shops based on lowest-common-denominator consensus-making and backbenchers' speeches are hardly reported and responded to only in passing by ministers.' Too many backbenchers have too little to do, so they end up craving attention and can only get it by making dissenting contributions on radio and TV. Edward understands the problem and has come up with five pages of specific proposals – e.g.:

---

546 Minister of State at the Department of the Environment 1993–7; MEP for NE Essex 1979–89; MP for Skipton & Ripon 1987–2010.

1. Expand the number of MPs who can work in government. There are about 95 ministers and whips, but there are 109 government agencies employing over 300,000
   people. Edward suggests these agencies have chairmen appointed who are Members
   of Parliament. The advantages would include meeting the 'democratic deficit' argument that the agencies are drifting away from the control of Parliament.

2. Beef up the Select Committees by giving the chairmen the status (and salary) of a
   Minister of State and the deputy chairman (from a different party) the rank of an
   Under-Secretary.

3. Standing Committees at the moment perform little useful function. Backbenchers
   are put on them as a chosen government supporter and encouraged to say little or
   nothing and opposition members to filibuster. Could we not make all Standing Committees into much smaller temporary Select Committees with a government majority
   working to a timetabled schedule taking evidence and making technical improve-
   ments, with partisan amendments reserved to the Report Stage?

4. 'Debates on the floor of the House are increasingly avoided by members.' They are
   too long, you won't be called at a reasonable hour, you won't be reported, even the
   ministers' aren't listening. Edward suggests shorter debates, timed speeches, proper
   ministerial responses – and, best of all, votes grouped together at 7.00 p.m. and 10.00
   p.m. so we don't keep up this farce of padding out debates with meaningless speeches
   from obliging stooges who are just standing up and spouting to fill the time and do
   the whips a favour.

He's come up with about thirty specific suggestions – all of them seem to have something
to commend them. He's sent a copy of the paper to the PM and the DPM as well as the
Chief. It's superb stuff which we should certainly be developing. Why am I certain then
that it is going to be comprehensively ignored?

TUESDAY 6 FEBRUARY 1996

Our tails are up. The PM is in cracking form. At PMQs he's outscoring Blair every time.
Today he was outstanding. We're having fun with the Harriet Harpie hypocrisy charge[547]

---

547 Harriet Harman had chosen to send one of her children to a selective grammar school and had been openly criticised
     by her shadow Cabinet colleague Clare Short, among others.

– and making it stick. Even the opinion polls are moving a point or two our way. In the Tea Room we seem to have rediscovered the will to win. For about three weeks we've been on an almost even keel. Is this a record? Of course, it's fragile. Next week, the Scott Report. Who knows what happens then?

Meanwhile, this morning we embarked on the Housing Bill. This is the first major piece of legislation I have taken through committee. We only have a majority of one, but I'm hopeful that I've got a reliable, pliable crowd. I've included Ashby as part of our policy of keeping him usefully employed. (The joy of the system is that the whips select who serves on the committee: genial coves are in, trouble-makers are out.) It's going to run at least till Easter and my aim is to have happy bunnies all the way.

THURSDAY 15 FEBRUARY 1996

Round One to us. The Scott Report was published at 3.30 p.m. The House was adjourned for ten minutes while several hundred members descended on the little window in Members' Lobby to collect their copies. It comes in five volumes, running to 2,000 pages – and that's what's saved us. There's so much in it that by selective quotation you can come to what conclusion you please. Sir Richard Scott has not brought in a verdict: he has simply presented his findings so that we can decide. We have: not guilty! Ian Lang was formidable. He got up and asserted categorically that the report clears Waldegrave, Lyell and the rest and there's an end on it. He turned on Cook: all his accusations were without foundation, he should apologise to the House and the ministers forthwith – or resign. When Cook got up, we all cried, 'Resign!' Cook fought back with counter-quotations, but it was too late. Lang had told us that the report 'wholly vindicated' our lads so that was that. The truth is the report is fairly damning – the ministers *did* give misleading answers, there was 'a failure by ministers to meet the obligations of ministerial account-ability' – but he accepts there was no 'duplicitous' intent and in one bound we're free. William is now touring the TV studios proclaiming his innocence and his gratitude to Sir Richard: 'The inquiry has cleared my name and my honour.' Nick Lyell is not so obvi-ously off the hook, but because of Scott's footling double negatives – he does not accept that Lyell was not personally at fault – and because he doesn't question Lyell's good faith, the Tea Room conclusion is that we've got away with it – Scott-free!

FRIDAY 23 FEBRUARY 1996

The papers do not make comforting reading. Thurnham is the lead story: 'Majority cut to two as Tory resigns whip.' Michèle said, 'He's one of yours, isn't he? Bit careless.' We tried to woo him every which way, but if someone is determined to be unhappy what can you do? We wheeled in Michael Howard (his old friend from Cambridge), he saw Waldegrave, he saw Lyell, the PM saw his entire family! Indeed, when I left last night, the PM thought he might have done the trick. Peter had agreed to 'think it over'. He appears to have thought it over on his way to the *Newsnight* studio. He's calling himself an 'independent Conservative' so we're going to be as friendly to him as possible in the hope that we can somehow win him back. Meanwhile, we won't have his vote on Monday – and if we lose on Monday (which we well might) there will be a confidence vote on Tuesday.

Other cheery news: 'Scott accuses ministers of distorting his report.' Well, what do you know? He claims to have been quoted selectively... Bless him, what did he expect? And there's more: 'Tory feud on single currency reopens.' Tony Nelson is telling us that business is clamouring for the single currency. Redwood begs to differ and wants Nelson slapped down. I am on my way to the local mental hospital and then the Cheshire Mediation Service. Sounds about right.

MONDAY 26 FEBRUARY 1996

11.00 p.m.: I am waiting for my car. It's chaos in New Palace Yard so I've retreated here [to the Library] to write this. We won the vote – by one. The PM looked so happy. It was 320 to 319. Quentin Davies, Richard Shepherd,[548] Thurnham voted against us. There was nothing we could do. Shepherd was immoveable. And we had no hold over him. We surrounded Quentin with persuasive 'friends' in the hope of cajoling him into the right lobby at the last minute, but he had a bee in his bonnet (and the bees in his bonnet buzz relentlessly), he'd made up his mind to play the 'integrity' card and that was that. At the eleventh hour, Rupert Allason relented – he knows his position is wobbly in his constituency: this would have been one rebellion too far. He huffed and puffed during the debate and then did the decent thing. It was his vote saved the day.

The PM and Paddy Mayhew spent the afternoon trying to persuade Trimble and co. to stay on side, without success. Trimble was looking for assorted assurances on the talks, but the PM was adamant that while he made all sorts of soothing noises he wasn't up for any kind of deal. We had a complete turn-out. I saw faces tonight I've never seen before. The lame, the halt, the gaga, the dying, we hauled them all in. Those that are too sick to stagger through the lobbies are allowed to sit in their ambulances in Speaker's Yard. Just before the vote whips from each side go to inspect them and report their presence

---

548 MP for Aldridge-Brownhills since 1979.

within the precincts to the tellers. At 9.30 p.m., with one of the Labour whips, I set off to carry out the identifications. I do now know everyone on our side by face and name, but there are still dozens of Labour members I couldn't name with certainty. We peered inside one ambulance (it had come all the way from Yorkshire) and gazed at the poor unfortunate within. I had no idea who he was, but I nodded as knowingly as I could and said, 'Yes, that's him.' What a farce.

THURSDAY 29 FEBRUARY 1996

On my way in I went to see Simon [Cadell] at the Harley Street Clinic. It can only be a matter of days now. He is beginning to look like my father looked, gaunt and beaky, unnaturally wide-eyed. When I arrived he was sitting propped up, gazing into the middle distance. He is ready to go. He's done enough fighting. He has been so brave. I would want to die at home, but I think he thinks it will be easier for Beckie and the boys if he's here. He was too tired to talk, so I just burbled on about what's happening at Westminster, and hugged him and kissed his funny bristly lopsided face and came away.

LATER

What larks! Sandra Howard has written to Sarah Thurnham: 'It's not an easy thing to write and Michael has no idea that I'm writing (and trying to defend the government and the party!), but he and I have such a bottomless well of admiration for you both and feel so desolate that you should have felt so badly as to not be able to stay loyal to a great and good party – and an honest and caring party at heart.' This letter, sent on Saturday, has come to light because Thurnham's secretary 'inadvertently' faxed it to the local newspaper!

The Chief's initial reaction was a spluttering 'Good God! What next?' but the office view now seems to be that once we've weathered the embarrassing headlines – 'Home Secretary's "admiration" for defecting MP' etc. – overtures like this may help bring Peter back into the fold. We all know that Peter is a self-indulgent tosser, but the policy is to treat him quite normally, as though he is very much still 'one of us'.

SUNDAY 3 MARCH 1996

M says Simon is much weaker, sleeping most of the time, can't really talk but gives a wan little smile when you peer into his face. It is so wretched.

I had a two-and-a-half-hour surgery. I had to keep shifting in my chair and jabbing my fingernails into the palm of my hand to stay awake. It's like going to the cinema or the theatre now – just suddenly sitting still in one warm place and I begin to nod off. It was the usual mixture: housing, CSA, difficult neighbours, 'The school won't do anything for Darren – they think he's thick, but it's dyslexia.' The only diversion was to have two transvestites on the trot – except they were both so pathetic. One of them has been hoping for a sex-change operation for nearly thirty years. He/she comes to see me every six weeks or so, looking like a tragic drag queen, awful white make-up over his stubble. This time he brought his mum with him. She must have been seventy, tiny, dotty, wearing a little fur hat, loaded down with carrier bags. She kept repeating, 'If that's what he wants, let him have it, let him have it.'

The only bit of light relief on the radar screen is moon-faced Ron Davies,[549] shadow Secretary of State for Wales, who has marked St David's Day with a delightfully loopy attack on Prince Charles. Ron says that a man who talks to vegetables, kills animals for pleasure and betrays his wife isn't fit to be king. We're jumping up and down, calling for Ron's resignation, but of course we don't really want him to go. We want him to hang around as long as possible: we can have a lot more fun with this boyo before we're through.

TUESDAY 5 MARCH 1996

I am, of course, an idiot. We know that. I thought I could 'contain' David Ashby. I thought that he liked and trusted me and that I had the measure of the man. Apparently not. We suffered our first defeat on the Housing Bill today because Ashby voted with the opposition. I should have seen it coming. Glenda [Jackson], looking more sour-faced than ever, tabled an amendment that would give homosexuals living in council or housing association property the right to remain in the property if their partner dies. I'm quite sympathetic to the amendment, so is David Curry, but Gummer is dead against it so there we are. Ashby told me last night that he felt he would have to vote with Glenda. I told him that I didn't expect us to reach the amendment till Thursday (a lie) and that I hoped he'd think it over (true). I also said, quite casually, that I had a spare 'pair' to offer him today (another lie) so that if he wanted to have the day off he could. He said he would. I thought my scheme had worked, but this morning, just as we were reaching the amendment, in he toddled.

'The amendment's come up earlier than you expected,' he whispered to me as he sat down behind me.

---

549 Labour MP for Caerphilly 1983–2001.

'Yes,' I said, pathetically, 'we're rattling along nicely now.'

'I'm going to have to vote with Glenda, you know.'

I pleaded with him to abstain. I said, 'You're meeting with your Association on Friday. You want their support. This isn't the week to vote against the government.'

He wouldn't be persuaded. He made a long, rambling, emotional speech about a gay friend of his who had lost his partner. He told the story with tears in his eyes, voice quavering. He was doing this for him. The moment the damage was done, from the booth just outside the committee room I paged the Deputy, then I telephoned Gummer. He wants us to reverse it on the floor of the House. I'm not sure we can. Or should.

Gentle ribbing in the office followed: 'Your friend Mr Ashby seems to have let you down. It was your idea to have him on the committee, wasn't it?'

I had to put a report in the book, but I couldn't get into the wretched safe to get a book to write in. The safe is vast and ancient. We can all remember the combination – the digits from the date of the PM's birthday – but only Tim Wood seems to have the knack of turning the dial, so if he isn't around we can't get into the bloody thing.

THURSDAY 7 MARCH 1996

Simon died last night. He was my oldest and best friend.

FRIDAY 8 MARCH 1996

Simon gets a wonderful press. He claimed he never read his notices, but I think he'd have been pleased with these. It is my forty-eighth birthday. Ma and Gin joined me and Michèle for lunch in the Stranger's Dining Room. It was a bit bleak. I couldn't concentrate. Last night we had the whips' dinner. I wasn't in the mood, but I felt obliged to go. Actually, I was probably pleased to have the distraction and, at least, by being subdued I managed to avoid saying anything I might live to regret. It's rather an odd lads' night out really. Because we're male, because this is the whips' letting their hair down, we somehow deliberately coarsen ourselves for the evening, use bad language when we wouldn't normally, give the gathering an artificial 'stag night' feel. It was the mixture as before: Italian food, much wine, banter and silly games, plus Greg's video – a curate's egg of a home movie, Greg's Guide to How to Be a Whip into which (incredibly) he'd managed to incorporate a clip from my Birdseye Waffle commercial of six years ago. He works hard – and successfully – at forging us into a cohesive and contented group. We do feel bonded. There is a freemasonry between us.

SUNDAY 10 MARCH 1996

Drove to Honington for Simon's funeral. We arrived at the same time as the Sindens. They were outside the church reading the cards on the flowers. Jeremy is dying too.[550] He was so brave and jolly and sweet about Simon it was quite heartbreaking. I read the lesson without tears or a crack in my voice – which is really all I wanted to achieve. The church is small and the nave quite narrow and when I walked back to my pew I somehow brushed the coffin – and thought immediately of Pa. When he died I remember my mother stroking his coffin as it was carried into the church. She stroked it so tenderly. I've had that picture in my head all day.

MONDAY 11 MARCH 1996

Lunch with the PM at No. 10. We're back in shambles-ville. He was shaking his head wearily and muttering about the sceptics being 'up to their tricks again', but if he lacks the authority to command his own Cabinet it's not altogether surprising he can't control the lower ranks. There's no doubt the PM wants to promise a referendum on monetary union, but because Ken won't wear it he daren't. Listening to him hemming and hawing (oh so reasonably) it's clear as crystal we're going to have weeks of debilitating shilly-shallying on this, weeks of weak government, and then, when the damage is done, we'll concede that we're going to have a referendum after all.

Of course, the poor man, who was having one of his looking grey-as-slate days, feels boxed in whichever way he turns. We had some deregulating measure in the pipeline – to take 'the burdens of red tape off small businesses' by taking away a raft of employment rights from the workers – but he says we're going to have to abandon it because we now realise we won't be able to push it through. As usual, we've had the worst of both worlds. We've floated the idea, seen the row looming and retreated.

We're back to the old Tea Room talk: the leadership is decent but weak, roll on defeat and let's get a new leader. Chris Patten is this week's pick of the left – but, as Stephen points out, it won't be him since he won't be an MP. The new flavour of the hour on the right is Michael Forsyth, but, given his majority, post-election he won't be an MP either.

The above I did not discuss with the PM. I assume he knows it, though this is an area where (so far as I can tell) the Whips' Office let him down. If Ottoway knows what Heseltine is really thinking about his medium-term prospects he's not reporting it in the

550 Jeremy Sinden, the actor son of Donald and Diana Sinden, died of cancer on 29 May, aged forty-five. The Sindens and the Cadells had been friends since the '40s: their eldest sons, born in the same year, died in the same year.

book. If Portillo is plotting and one of our number knows it, he's not saying. I certainly don't relay the full tenor of my weekly meetings with Dorrell and Finkelstein. The PM believes we're onto a winner with the notion of a grammar school in every town. It's his current 'Big Idea'. He thinks Gillian [Shephard] is dragging her feet on it – which she is, and understandably, because in principle the idea may be appealing, but it's fraught with difficulties. There's certainly no lusting for a grammar school in Chester – from anyone. I did not say this to the boss because I felt this wasn't a day for negative contributions. I kept my small talk to Will Carling who is stepping down as the England captain for 'rugby reasons', 'nothing to do' with his personal life.

I said, 'Carling says he's going "on his own terms".'

The PM grinned (for about the only time today), 'Yes, that's the way to do it.'

WEDNESDAY 13 MARCH 1996

We were halfway through the morning meeting when Murdo came into the room, 'We're getting reports, Chief, of a terrible tragedy in Scotland. A gunman appears to have got into a school and murdered a large number of children.' We didn't know how to react, so we murmured, tut-tutted, shook our heads for a moment and then carried on. At 12 noon Bowen got up to open the champagne and I trooped round the table with the silver goblets. Somebody should have said, 'Under the circumstances I'm not sure this is appropriate', but nobody did, so it was the ritual as usual, champagne on the carpet and all.

THURSDAY 14 MARCH 1996

We have just had the statement on Dunblane. The horror of what happened is unbearable: sixteen children and their teacher murdered in cold blood by a man called Thomas Hamilton, a former Scout leader who had some sort of grudge against the parents at the school. Michael Forsyth went up yesterday with George Robertson.[551] It's in Michael's constituency; he'd actually met the man, he'd been to see him at his surgery. Michael said there was nothing about him that would have given you an inkling that he was capable of so terrible an act. Michael's statement was perfectly judged. It was clear, simply expressed, softly spoken, *exactly* right. He was deeply impressive – as was Robertson.

---

551 Shadow Scottish Secretary; Labour MP for Hamilton since 1978.

As, indeed, in a quite different way, was Ian Paisley. He rose, like an Old Testament prophet, and his voice rumbled round the Chamber. Customarily, when we hear him he's ranting. Today it was Paisley the preacher (biblical texts and all) and you could see how he has built up his following. Everyone got it right really, except – dare I say it? – poor Nicholas Winterton. The sentiment was fine – 'Isn't it wonderful how the love of little children has brought the House together? I pray that it will do so more often' – but there's something about the jerky way he barks out the words – getting all the emphases wrong – that always ruins it. And there's a sense too that he says what he says not just because he cares, but because he wants to be in the spotlight. Today wasn't a day for wanting to be in the spotlight.

FRIDAY 15 MARCH 1996

We're flying to Manchester. Last night we had M's birthday supper at San Remo, a little Italian restaurant at the top of Castelnau by the Bridge. It was just the two of us, a tiny candle-lit table in the corner. It was like going back twenty-five years. The candle should really have been stuck in a basket-clad Chianti bottle. We had *moules* in a cream and white wine sauce and I don't think I have enjoyed a meal more *ever*. The whole meal cost less than half a starter at *Le Manoir*. 'This is what we like, isn't it?' said M. It is.

What she doesn't like is what we're embarking on now – a full 'constituency weekend', lunch with the bishop, the Ellesmere Port Conservative Association dinner, the Cheshire Yeomanry *en fete* at the Town Hall. She doesn't dislike it – she says all the individual elements are fine (and she's brilliant at them) – it's just not what she wants to be doing for the next twenty years. Politics is a way of life and not one she enjoys. 'You're out five nights a week, sometimes six. The only night we know we'll have together is Sunday and then you're so shattered all you do is fall asleep in front of the box.' It's true. And it's one of the reasons why I'm reconciled to losing my seat. The other, of course, is that while government is exciting (I am loving the Whips' Office), being a backbencher is a pretty thankless occupation – the status has been tarnished, the money's derisory, the potential for influence pitifully slight. We have our AGM tonight and I'm going to be readopted as our candidate, nem. con. I shall fight the good fight with complete commitment, but when I lose I shall be able to do so with a good grace because it's certainly what M wants and it's sort-of what I want. I shall miss the thrill of government and the camaraderie of the House. Clearly what I need is the House of Lords!

M is very funny. Driving to the airport (we get a free parking space, courtesy BAA) I said, 'But you've got to admit we've met some interesting people.'

'*You've* met some interesting people,' she squawked, 'What have I met? Boring men who only want to hear how wonderful they are and ghastly women who ask, "What's he really like? Do you knit his jumpers?"'

I think she should write a novel about constituency life. You could have the Bishop and the Dean at the heart of the story. They're both good people (we really like them, admire them, enjoy their company) but they are ripe for literary exploitation. The Bishop[552] is tall, thin, balding, set to retire, ready to retire, slightly disappointed. A hymn-composing evangelical who kindly gave us a copy of his sex manual (dedicated to his wife Myrtle), he and the Dean (stocky, golden head of hair, port-coloured face) do not see eye to eye. At all. I suspect the Dean is at fault here, but, poor man, he has had quite a cross to bear: a brilliant, mad, alcoholic wife. We used to see her fairly regularly, but the 'embarrassing moments' became ever more frequent. When the Queen came to the Cathedral, the Dean's wife circled round her muttering like a demented witch.

It was agony.

MONDAY 18 MARCH 1996

Something's up. I'm not sure what. I've just seen the unflappable Roger Knapman[553] looking almost wild-eyed. I said, 'How are you?' He mumbled and began gathering up papers from his desk. I said, 'Anything serious?' He looked at me and said, 'Deadly serious. For the government, for all of us. It could be devastating.'

WEDNESDAY 20 MARCH 1996

Stephen cancelled breakfast and, last night, I stood in for him at the United & Cecil Club dinner. All yesterday, all this morning he worked on his BSE statement.[554] He was excited in anticipation of it and exhilarated at the way it went. He did well: he was clear, moderate, totally on top of the brief, and managed to walk the wire, getting the facts out into the open asap while trying hard not to sound alarmist. But I was a little alarmed to see the adrenalin flowing at quite such a pace. Clearly he

---

552 Michael Baughen, Bishop of Chester 1982–96.

553 The whip with responsibility for the Ministry of Agriculture Fisheries and Food.

554 The government was advised for the first time that there was a possibility that Bovine Spongiform Encephalopathy ('mad cow disease') could be transmitted from beef to humans. Stephen Dorrell and Douglas Hogg came to the House with statements outlining the government's proposed course of action in the light of the new scientific advice.

feels this is going to do him a lot of good, plenty of exposure, leading from the front, proof that he can handle a delicate issue with a sure touch. He wants to do all the broadcasts, be seen in the front line. When I said, 'Are you sure?' he looked at me as though I was quite barmy. I persisted, 'I just don't see this as a winner. You've done the responsible thing today, getting it out into the open. Now lie low. Let Hoggie get the flak from the farmers.'

He wasn't listening. 'No, no, no, I've got to run with this one. It's important.'

Harriet [Harman, shadow Health Secretary] was at her worst. Whining, whinge-ing, scare-mongering. I imagine she'll have done herself a lot of harm. If ever she gets into government she'll be a disaster.

We finished early. I was home by nine. Supper in the kitchen with M and Jo [Lum-ley]. Pasta and peppers – of course. M doesn't eat meat and Jo's virtually a vegan. *They* think we've known about the dangers of BSE for years and we've been keeping quiet because we don't want to upset the farmers.

WEDNESDAY 27 MARCH 1996

This morning we trooped through from No. 12 to No. 10 to have our picture taken with the PM. He was at his twitchiest. And with cause. The handling of the beef cri-sis is going from bad to worse. Our beef is now banned around the world. The British beef market has collapsed. And no one in government – least of all the Agriculture Minister – seems to have a clear idea what to do.

According to Roger [Knapman], last week we were considering slaughtering all eleven million cattle in the country; this week it's four million. We're saying 'beef is safe' but because nobody believes us we're going to have to slaughter half the cattle in the kingdom at a cost to the taxpayer of something around £6 billion! This could be announced any minute now – except we're not sure how practical it is. Who will do the slaughtering? How many years will it take? How do we dispose of the carcasses? Nobody knows! The PM is 'impatient'. Hogg is evidently all over the place. Roger describes the ministerial meetings quite dispassionately, he adds no 'colour', but his unvarnished literal account makes it plain it's *chaos*. Hogg hasn't got a grip, Angela Browning (the PUSS) appears to be the best of the bunch, but the back-up from the civil servants is woeful. Stephen (who is still high on it all) was so eager to rush out his statement they clearly hadn't had time to think through the consequences. And they had no contingency plans. It's beyond belief. Now we're simply reacting to events, making it up as we go along.

This is incompetent government.

More news of mad cows ... Neil and Christine [Hamilton] invited their friend Dame Barbara Cartland[555] to dinner and asked Michèle and me to join the party. Ten of us, Members' Dining Room, her son at one end of the table, Dame Barbara at the other. I sat on her left. She was as ridiculous and glorious as ever: the white-powdered face, the giraffe's eyelashes, the eight remaining strands of hair spun into an extraordinary candy-floss confection, flowing pink tulle everywhere, she seemed to have come dressed as the fairy queen in a Victorian pantomime. She didn't draw breath. Out the stories tumbled: Noel Coward, Beaverbrook, Churchill, 'darling Dickie'. 'No one knew him as I did, he was quite extraordinary. He was the most fascinating man in the world, so ahead of his time.'

According to Dame Barbara, Mountbatten pioneered the zip fastener instead of fly buttons – and persuaded the then Prince of Wales to follow suit. 'But it all went terribly wrong one evening at a very smart supper in Biarritz. The Prince went to the cloak-room, but, poor lamb, didn't dare emerge because the zip got stuck! He had to slip out by the back door. He was furious, had all the zips taken out of his trousers.' She was full of concern for the plight of the present Prince and Princess of Wales. 'It's so sad for them both. It's heart-breaking. Of course, you know where it all went wrong? She wouldn't do oral sex, she just wouldn't. It's as simple as that. Of *course* it all went wrong.'

SATURDAY 30 MARCH 1996

I flew up to Chester yesterday morning and had a really good session with the farmers on BSE. They are profoundly worried, but remarkably calm. I've scored with them not because I have any of the answers but because almost every day since this broke I have sent them the relevant pages from Hansard. They think I'm listening and that I care – and I am and I do. While they offered their solutions, I scribbled away furiously. I didn't say much, other than voice sympathy. I pulled appropriate faces, but I was careful not to *say* anything overtly critical of Hogg in case one of them might repeat it to the press. Then I did our local election press conference and photo call. Then I spent four hours on a variety of dismal trains getting from Chester to Harrogate via Leeds arriving in the nick of time for the Central Council conference dinner at which I was the after-dinner turn. I sat with Brian Mawhinney [party chairman] who seems permanently grumpy. I am clearly not his cup of tea. I imagine he finds me

---

555 1901–2000, novelist; her only daughter Raine married the 8th Earl Spencer, father of Diana, Princess of Wales, in 1976.

bumptious, egregious, too fruity by half. I'm not sure what to make of him. He's not an easy ride. He's frustrated that the PM can't/won't announce a referendum on the Euro this weekend. He can't understand why Ken won't concede when there's really nothing to be lost and everything to be gained. (Ken, of course, believes these things should be settled by Parliament. That's what parliamentary democracy is all about. He's worried too that a simplistic, jingoistic referendum campaign would a) split the party and b) bring about the wrong result.)

In my speech I lavished mountains of praise on Stephen, only because he was sitting there with Annette and I thought it would please/amuse her. I think it did. Afterwards, we went up to their bedroom and Danny [Finkelstein] joined us and Stephen kindly ordered a bottle of wine and I drank most of it. He clearly believes the last ten days have been to his advantage. I said, 'They've raised your profile, that's for sure.'

WEDNESDAY 3 APRIL 1996

A jolly whips' meeting. I do my best to keep in with the Chief by at all times ensuring he is within reach of the cheese straws. He is in mellow mood today – except, it seems, when Roger is speaking. Roger appears to irritate him. I have a feeling that when he presents his weekly report on the Lloyds' Names he *intends* to irritate him! (Roger is guardian of the list of colleagues who are Names and is supposed to update us on the state of their fortune – or misfortune as the case may be. Roger is a Name who has lost a great deal. The Chief is a Name who may have lost rather less. Roger talks knowledgeably about the vagaries of the various syndicates, but what Roger knows doesn't always tally with what the Chief believes. Roger speaks, the Chief twitches. Roger continues, the Chief snaps a cheese straw. Roger won't stop; the Chief leaves the room to make an urgent phone call. I don't understand the ins and outs of any of it, but it's quite funny to watch.)

I can't work out if Roger in his account of life at the Min. of Ag. is intending to alarm us or amuse us – or simply inform us. Probably the latter, because he seems a totally straightforward guy. (I like him a lot, but I don't really know him. I don't think I had spoken to him more than once before I joined the office). Hogg is ready to resign. My feeling is he should. That's not what I say. What I say is, 'If he stays, that hat must go.' We all agree: the wide-rimmed fedora is ludicrous. If he gets rid of the hat, he may be perceived as less of a joke. We charge Roger with stealing and *shredding* the hat.

The Chancellor is not resigning either. I don't believe he ever was. He is 'reluctantly' accepting the proposed referendum 'for the sake of the party'.

THURSDAY 4 APRIL 1996

We're having Easter at home, the Hanleys for lunch on Saturday, Benet's organising a boat race party, and then we're off to Venice for five nights. I am taking Elizabeth Taylor. She is now my favourite author.

Is Ann Widdecombe now my favourite female politician? Possibly. She came up to Chester with me this morning. We travelled together on the train, second class (Ann insisted). The hair, the teeth, the vast low-slung lopsided bosom, she's certainly an oddity, but the integrity, the commitment, the ambition make her quite special. She's like Ken: she can never really go wrong because she only says what she believes. You can't fault her. I asked her why she always sits on her own in the Aye lobby on days when she's got Questions. 'I'm there for forty-five minutes in case colleagues have any queries. All ministers are supposed to do it.' She is the only one who does.

She came to address the President's Club. Of course, they were disappointed not to have a Cabinet minister. When I told Stuart [the association chairman] who I'd secured his face fell. I said, 'We've already had the Deputy Prime Minister, the Chancellor, the Home Secretary, Portillo, Virginia... '

'Yes,' he said, 'I know it isn't easy,' (meaning, of course, you haven't got the clout to get us anyone decent) 'but she's not much of an attraction.'

I said rather petulantly, 'She could very well end up leading the party one day.'

In the event there was a *reasonable* crowd and they *were* impressed. She was good on the collapse of the 'moral consensus'. In the '50s there was an agreed standard – everyone – politicians, teachers, church leaders, judges, newspaper editors, everyone – subscribed to the same standard. Of course, people fell below it, but they knew what it was, they accepted it and life was easier. Now there are no agreed standards and life is a lot more troublesome. She told us about her first election campaign, in the run-up to which she had published a pamphlet called *Christian Principles*. She was going to do an open-air meeting. She'd set up her soapbox in the market square and then suddenly remembered she had left her pamphlets in the boot of her agent's car. She was to be seen running down Maidstone High Street shouting, 'Stop, stop! I've lost my *Christian Principles*!'

TUESDAY 16 APRIL 1996

Our majority of one[556] is now threatened by Sir George Gardiner. Well-intentioned loyalists in Reigate want to deselect him, but Sir George says if he isn't readopted he'll resign

---

556   On 11 April the government lost the Staffordshire South East by-election, its thirty-fifth successive by-election defeat.

and force a by-election. The view in the office is that this is 'probably but not certainly' an idle threat. We look to Liam to explain how it is that Sir George is still alive when we understood he should have died months ago. Liam cannot help us. We look to the chairman of his association (a retired Major-General and by all accounts 'thoroughly sound') to keep Sir George on board at least until we're within shouting distance of the election – and *then* dump him.

Lord Archer is wandering the corridors of Westminster urging us to take Sir James Goldsmith and his ludicrous Referendum Party seriously. Sir James (bronzed, rich, mad) is putting £20 million into his campaign and threatening a candidate in every seat where the Conservative is not committed to a referendum – not *our* referendum on the Euro, *his* referendum on the whole future of our relationship with the Union. Jeffrey has produced a list of the seats most vulnerable to Goldsmith interference. Chester, naturally, is high on it. Jeffrey has lost about a stone and, in his breast pocket, alongside his Goldsmith list he has a card with the details of his diet. He has promised to send me a copy. (I could do with losing two stone. In photographs, face forward, if I push my head towards the camera the chins disappear and I don't look too bad – but caught at the wrong angle and I recognise the awful truth.)

The good news is that Alastair Campbell[557] and co. are going into overdrive in their desperation to gag Clare Short. She said on the box on Sunday that she favoured a fair tax system where 'people like me would pay a little bit more'. She's been yanked off the airwaves by the spin doctors and locked in a darkened, airless room. With luck, the way she's been gagged will provoke further outbursts. We want her making mischief, but we don't want her sacked. (The truth is we should be as ruthless and determined to succeed as they are. But we aren't. We're flabby and weary and only seem to have energy sufficient to pull ourselves apart. I said to Jack Straw in the Tea Room, 'Why are you looking so cheerful?' 'Because I've been here for seventeen years. It's a long time. We've been in opposition for all the time I've been here. And soon we're going to be in government.')

SUNDAY 21 APRIL 1996

I'm just in and pleasantly squiffy. M's asleep. Felix[558] is climbing all over the desk, bumping his head up against mine. We've just had the whips' dinner with the PM, preceded by our annual 'assessment' of the government. This is an interesting ritual. We all turned up at No. 12 at 2.30 p.m. Dress was casual. I wore a suit without a tie, but the others came

---

557 Former journalist; Press Secretary to Tony Blair as Leader of the Labour Party 1994–7, as Prime Minister 1997–2003.
558 The Brandreth cat.

kitted out in the assorted versions of what a Tory MP wears on a Sunday afternoon, ranging from cravat, blazer and slacks to cavalry twills, hacking jacket and knitted yellow tie. I admired Roger Knapman's highly polished brown shoes. I said, 'I don't think I've got any brown shoes.'

Roger looked bemused. 'What do you wear on Sundays?'

I looked down at my ordinary, everyday, workaday footwear. Roger said smoothly, 'The rule is "brown shoes on Sunday" because it's the servants' day off.'

I tried to rally, 'But does a gentleman wear brown shoes in London?'

'As a rule,' said Roger, 'a gentleman is not seen in London on a Sunday.'

Banter behind us, we took our places. Shana had prepared a dossier for each of us, like an exam script, a page for each department of state, arranged alphabetically, from Agriculture through to Wales, with each of the departmental Ministers and PPSs listed according to rank, with a space below their names for comments. The idea, the Deputy explained, was for the whip for the relevant department to give his assessment of the performance of his Ministers, concentrating not so much on the Cabinet members – as the PM gets to see them in action anyway – as on the rest. Who merits promotion? Who needs a rest?

The exercise took three solid hours. There was joshing now and again ('If you could put Ann Widdecombe's brain inside Virginia Bottomley's body – think of it!' 'Yes, but what if it all went wrong and you got Virginia's brain inside Ann's body …'), but on the whole the assessments seemed to me to be carefully made and well-judged. There were no revelations and no excoriations. We seemed to bend over backwards to be fair (Roger was unduly circumspect re Hogg) and it was evident that former members of the office are reviewed with a specially light touch – e.g. we all know that David Davis[559] is unhappy, already difficult, potentially more troublesome, feeling overworked and undervalued, and believes he should be in the Cabinet *now, now, now* – but that's not quite how it came across. And perhaps it didn't need to because we know it – just as we know that Arbuthnot[560] is rising effortlessly (the Ian Lang of his generation?), that Andrew Mitchell is almost crazy with ambition, that we will continue to keep faith with John Taylor for all his endearing frailty because he is 'one of us'. The only exception to this rule that I noticed was in the case of Willetts. It's not just envy of his intelligence: I think they feel when he was in the office he didn't *quite* 'fit in'. The truth is he couldn't wait to get out.

As usual, the Chief said nothing but his grunts said it all. When I was talking up Douglas

---

559   He was now Minister of State for Europe.

560   James Arbuthnot, MP for Wanstead & Woodford 1987–97, Hampshire North East since 1987; he was now Minister of State for Defence Procurement; he had been in the Whips' Office 1990–92; Conservative opposition Chief Whip 1997–2001.

French,[561] impatient clearing of the throat on my right made it evident I should move on and that poor Douglas's prospects are poor. When I was talking up Seb, there was a gentle, encouraging gobbling noise from the Chief's end of the table. Clearly Piers Merchant[562] has done something to upset somebody. His name produced splenetic spluttering all round. Overall my interpretation of the Chief's guttural emanations of the afternoon leads me to believe that David Curry and Michael Ancram are both comfortably ahead of David Davis in the Cabinet queue.

We broke to change for dinner. I went with Richard Ottaway to his house in Victoria, put on my tie, read the papers, returned for 7.30 p.m. The Chief served his lethal Martinis, the PM was himself – friendly, decent, unstuffy, collegiate. He is encouraged by the Clare Short row ('If we give them enough time, they'll begin to unravel…'), depressed by the latest from Norman Lamont ('How and why he thinks Goldsmith can do us anything but harm, I just don't know…') I was alarmed to find myself sitting next to him for dinner (junior's perk), but it wasn't a problem: he talked to the table as a whole. The only ghastly moment came after we'd raised an informal glass to Her Majesty on her seventieth birthday and I embarked on my story about the Queen and the recession and her nine Prime Ministers not having a clue – and, suddenly, in full flight realised that the story as told by me on automatic pilot is both *lèse-majesté* and patronising to the PM. In desperation and through an alcoholic haze I tried to edit/adapt/improve the tale as I told it and ended up rambling *hopelessly*. Sniggering giggles from Liam: 'Aren't funny stories supposed to have a punchline, Gyles? Oo, that was it, was it?' Fortunately my blushes were quickly obliterated by an extraordinary, lengthy, impassioned outburst from Simon Burns at the end of the table – ten minutes of inane burbling on behalf of the Chelmsford fire brigade! As ever, the wise ones kept their mouths shut. The idiots were on song.

MONDAY 22 APRIL 1996

For the second or third time, I cancelled my lunch with Robin Oakley[563] at Simply Nico. We'd said we ought to have lunch after the Queen's Speech when I'd made my joke about being mistaken for him by one of Blair's spin doctors. But the truth is I'm not comfortable with journalists. Because I'm watching what I say, I can't relax. Because I'm not giving them what they want, I feel I'm lunching under false pretences. So here I am, alone in

---

561 MP for Gloucester 1987–97; PPS to John Gummer; further advancement was not to be his.

562 1951–2009; MP for Newcastle Central 1983–7, Beckenham 1992–7; PPS to Peter Lilley; further advancement was not to be his either.

563 Political Editor of the BBC 1992–2000.

the Library. It's 1.15 p.m. I've had my smoked mackerel, tomato salad and shredded carrot and I shall return to the Tea Room for a coffee at 2.00. This afternoon's excitements include the whips' meeting at 2.30 p.m., William Hague's Rotary Club tea at 4.00 p.m. and a curious encounter with the Deputy in his den at 4.30 p.m. When he said 'Can I have a word?' and pulled me out into the corridor my heart began to pound. I thought, 'What have I done now?' It turned out that he wanted to suggest we put our heads together to see if we can't come up with an idea for a television sitcom!!

5.30 p.m.: Jenny/Di. I never go over to 7 Millbank now. I get them to come over here and we sit at the table off the Cromwell lobby, at the foot of the stairs with the Spencer Perceval bust.[564] 6.30 p.m. Raymond Robertson – to work on his speech for the Scottish Conference. 7.30 p.m. Letter-signing in here. 8.00 p.m. Dinner. 9.00 p.m. Bench duty. The Northern Ireland (Entry to Negotiations etc.) Bill may well be keeping us here late into the night. (It transpires that Mo Mowlam has a research assistant paid for by Mirror Group Newspapers – a fact that doesn't feature in the Register of Members' Interests. We're hoping to have some fun with that…)

Christopher Milne has died. He was a good man, gentle and amusing.[565] The obituaries all play up his resentment of his parents and Pooh and the whole Christopher Robin phenomenon, quoting his line that he believed 'my father had got where he was by climbing on my infant shoulders, that he had filched from me my good name and had left me with nothing but the empty fame of being his son.' But that was how he felt in the '40s. In the end he felt quite differently. His marriage, the bookshop in Dartmouth, his own success as a writer, changed all that. He wasn't reconciled to his parents, but he came to terms with who he was. I liked him. It was a privilege to know him. I shook the hand that held the paw of Winnie-the-Pooh.

TUESDAY 30 APRIL 1996

The Housing Bill is behind us! We concluded the Third Reading fifteen minutes ago. During the course of the day we had five divisions and I am proud to report that we managed each one of these within two to three minutes of the times I predicted. As far as the office is concerned, that's all that counts. They don't give a toss about the quality of the legislation or the content of the debate. I was determined to deliver it all on schedule

---

564 The only British Prime Minister to be assassinated, Perceval (1762–1812) was shot as he entered the lobby of the Commons by a bankrupt Liverpool broker, John Bellingham, who was subsequently hanged for the murder.

565 GB got to know him in the early '80s when, with Julian Slade, he was writing a play based on the life and work of A. A. Milne.

and that I did is thanks entirely to Gummer, Curry and Clappison[566] who all played ball. They *rattled* through it. When I said 'You've only got two minutes on this clause' that's all they took – and when they strayed I yanked the back of their jackets and down they came. It's a complete game – but today it was a fun one.

We survived the vote on the extension of leaseholders' rights with a majority of two. And, yes, we even kept David Ashby on side! Gumdrops had been reluctant to move on the equal rights for homosexual couples ('Gyles, you and I move in sophisticated circles, some of our best friends really are gay, but to validate homosexual partnerships in *legislation* will send out the wrong signal to the majority of our electors who do not move in the sort of theatrical *millieu* to which we are accustomed' – he has a way with words) but he accepted that if it came to a vote we'd lose so he agreed to a compromise: a beefed-up guidance note putting the principle of equal rights on paper but not on the statute book.

The bigger picture is less rosy: beef, Europe, the leadership – it's all as bad as ever. Chancellor Kohl lunched at No. 10 and was served Aberdeen Angus. I said to the PM, 'Did he eat it?' The PM looked at me and half raised an eyebrow – which makes me think he didn't! The prospects for Thursday [the local government elections] are dire and there's a rumour swirling round the lobby that Hezza and the PM have done a deal that if we see meltdown on Thursday Major will step aside and Heseltine will take the helm. It's cobblers. It makes no sense, it isn't true, but the leadership is a sore that won't heal because we just keep picking at it.

THURSDAY 2 MAY 1996

A bad night. Richard Short, Neil Fitton, Joan Price, Sue Rowlandson, John Ebo,[567] all lost their seats. These are five of our best people. Richard is the Lord Mayor. He is devastated, poor man. I went to the count and told them this was an opinion poll on the government not a reflection on them. They know it's true, but it doesn't make it any better. All afternoon with Stuart I toured the committee rooms. Our activists are getting ever older, thinner on the ground and more demoralised.

Tomorrow the PM will issue his rallying cry – 'We fight on, we fight to win. The election's a year away. The economy will turn it round for us, just you wait and see' – and we are charged with ringing round our cards, 'steadying the nerves, taking the temperature'.

---

566 James Clappison, Parliamentary Under-Secretary of State at the Department of the Environment 1995–97; MP for Hertsmere since 1992.

567 Chester City councillors.

I talked to Neil [Hamilton] who was in excellent spirits. He didn't appear to have registered that there were local elections going on. He is obsessed with his case to the exclusion of all else. He is hopeful that a Lords amendment to the Defamation Bill is going to enable him to pursue his case against *The Guardian* after all. Essentially we are having to revise the 300-year-old Bill of Rights to accommodate Mr Hamilton – and we're doing so a) because it's probably right (i.e. the original Act was created to protect parliamentary privilege and *The Guardian* is now using it to deny Neil access to justice) and b) because if we're to survive for another twelve months we can't afford to have a single colleague going wobbly. We need them all – the good, the bad, and the ugly. (Speaking of which, Sir George is still with us – just.)

....

THURSDAY 9 MAY 1996

....

In the division lobby last night, during the ten o'clock vote, the Chief padded over to me.

'Play Bridge?' He didn't wait for a reply. It was a question expecting the answer yes. A government whip plays Bridge – by definition. 'The Prime Minister needs us.'

'What?' I suddenly had an awful vision of having to sit down to play cards with the PM. 'I er—'

'I don't know how long I'll be. I've left you a good hand. See you there.' And that was that.

I ankled it back to the Pugin Room where I'd left Michèle and her brother and sister-in-law.

'I'm awfully sorry, but I've got to go and play a hand of Bridge on behalf of the Chief Whip who has been called in to see the Prime Minister.'

'Oh,' said Mike, 'so that's how the country's run.'

I left them to finish their coffee and scuttled over to Lord North Street. It must be twenty years since I played Bridge, but last night, though I didn't have the first idea what I was doing, the cards were kind and my partner turned out to be Tim Sainsbury (I imagine a veteran of the green baize table) and it was really rather *fun*.

The District Auditor (a po-faced Mr Magill who comes across as self-regarding and peculiarly unpleasant) has produced his report on the Westminster City Council so-called homes-for-votes scandal. The bad news is that he finds Shirley Porter and five of her colleagues guilty of 'wilful misconduct' and is demanding they repay £31.6 million. The good news is that Barry Legg[568] is off the hook and Shirley is going

---

568 MP for Milton Keynes South West 1992–7, formerly a Westminster city councillor. The Auditor's final report, while clearing him of misconduct, concluded that he had been aware of the 'party electoral reasons' behind the council's housing policy.

to go for a judicial review which won't be heard until next year – almost certainly *after* the election. Our strategy is to adopt a high moral tone (step forward J. Gummer) and refuse point blank to condemn or condone until all the judicial processes have been exhausted while throwing as much mud at the opposition as we can muster.

Shirley no longer seems to have many friends here. Perhaps she never did. This is still very much a gentleman's club. We tolerate these loud, brash, ambitious women when they're riding high, but once they take a fall … I feel sorry for her. Sorrier still for Leslie [Porter], who is a decent man and has been a good friend.

MONDAY 20 MAY 1996

I am sitting on the front bench apparently listening to and noting the progress of the Commonwealth Development Corporation Bill. The fact that I'm writing the diary instead is not because I am negligent in my duties, it's because there is nothing for me to do. All the speakers lined up for the next hour are from the opposition benches – the cow Nicholson, Diane Abbott,[569] George Foulkes,[570] Ted Rowlands.[571] Unless they come up with something unexpected (and these four will be painfully predictable) we don't make a detailed note of opposition speeches in the whips' book. It's our side's performance we're monitoring – but, other than the minister (J. Hanley), there's no one from our side here. This is because dear Bowen [Wells, the Foreign Office whip] has cocked up and failed to press-gang any speakers on our side. One of our responsibilities is to ensure that we always have sufficient speakers a) to sustain the debate, and b) to match the other side. The reasons: a) to prevent the opposition from getting extra airtime, b) to send out a positive signal to any outside observers, c) to ensure that we get a fair share of the coverage in the unlikely event of the debate featuring on *Yesterday in Parliament.*

Finding colleagues to press into service is becoming increasingly difficult – for several reasons: a) nobody's listening, so what's the point? b) the Speaker's office keeps a note of how many times you speak in a year, so if you speak in an unpopular debate in which you have no interest just to do the whips a favour you may be reducing your chances of speaking in a sought-after debate in which you actually have something you want to say; c) as the parliament progresses we have an ever-weaker hold on colleagues:

---

569 Labour MP for Hackney North & Stoke Newington since 1987.

570 Labour MP for South Ayrshire 1979–83, Carrick Cumnock & Doon Valley 1983–2005; later Baron Foulkes of Cumnock.

571 Labour MP for Cardiff North 1966–70, Merthyr Tydfil 1972–83, Merthyr Tydfil & Rhymney 1983–2001; later Baron Rowlands.

between now and the election the possibilities for advancement are virtually nil, so what's to be gained by earning brownie points from the whips?

As a rule, Lady Olga [Maitland] can be pressed into service for a debate like this, but maybe even she's had enough. We have exploited her mercilessly. When the air needs to be filled with empty sound, the cry goes up, 'Send for Olga!' We sent her over the top on the Disability Bill, promising we'd look after her, knowing we wouldn't. She's a PPS and that's as far as she's going. And where is Nirj?[572] He's from Sri Lanka, he's eager to please, why isn't he on parade?

Of course, I may be doing Bowen an injustice. I wasn't at the 2.30 p.m. meeting. It could be that the Deputy took the view that nobody (other than Her Majesty) gives a toss about the Commonwealth, so we're 'letting the debate find its own level' (Whips' Office euphemism for 'nobody gives a monkey's, chaps, so you can all bugger off home').

The reason I wasn't on parade at 2.30 p.m. is that I was at Chequers for the junior ministers' brainstorming session with the PM. The setting is wonderful, the house is a joy (exactly my idea of a weekend hideaway – a Tudor mansion in the Chilterns, not too large, not too far out of town, civilised, civilising), but the occasion was dispiriting. This wasn't the PM's fault. We arrived at ten and there he was, in his jumper, all easy smiles, ready to greet us, hoping he'd found us 'fizzing with ideas'. We had coffee in the hall (Tom Sackville took to the grand piano, uninvited – a mistake) and then the PM led us upstairs 'to get down to work'. A two-/three-hour discussion followed – education, law and order, rethinking the social security system, reinventing local government – all valid themes, but we got nowhere because the PM was inviting a 'blue skies' approach ('think the unthinkable') but there were thirty of us each desperate to get his two minutes in the spotlight. There was no scope for developing a line of thought or argument – it was just a motley collection of variously ambitious people throwing their assorted two cents' worth into the ring. There wasn't an original idea (not one) and it was clear that the only way to stand out from the crowd would be either to make a sparklingly original contribution or say nothing. Because I knew I didn't have the former at my disposal, I opted for the latter. I was the only one not to say a word.

It was a buffet lunch and my heart sank when the PM ushered me to his table – not because he isn't a nice guy (he is), but because nobody behaves naturally with him, silences always fall and then I feel compelled to fill the air with noise. In the event, it was fine. I got him to talk about the house and its treasures, and, over coffee, upstairs, I persuaded him to unlock the drawer of Chequers treasures and show me Oliver Cromwell's death mask.

---

572 Nirj Deva, MP for Brentford & Isleworth 1992–7.

TUESDAY 21 MAY 1996

The PM has had a triumphant afternoon. Learning last night that the EU veterinary experts had declined to sanction any easing of the beef ban, he decided this morning, as a matter of policy, to go berserk. 'I've gone through merry hell to keep this show on the road, but enough's enough. We've been let down by our partners once too often.' He has just made a statement to the House saying that until the ban on beef by-products is lifted and there's a framework in place for lifting the rest of the embargo, we are going paralyse the Union – vetoing EU decisions, disrupting the Florence summit, halting progress on preparations for the IGC.[573] We roared, we cheered, we rocked in our seats with delight. Cash, Tapsell, Jenkin (the usual suspects) got to their feet to salute our leader for taking this 'bold and necessary stand'. The PM is the hero of the hour.

But, but … over at the Department of the Environment (Gummer, Curry, yours truly) we have our doubts. It's not just that our instincts are more Euro-friendly (which they are), it's that this is one of those moves that provides forty-eight hours of gung-ho glory to be followed by eventual disappointment leading to resentment and anger when the policy fails to deliver. The PM is marching us up the hill again – 'we're taking on Brussels, boys' – but what happens when he has to march us down again?

The plan has been on the table for a couple of weeks. The Chancellor and the Foreign Secretary gave it their blessing this morning. Ken went along with it because he's read the small-print. (Well, he hasn't read it, but he's got the gist of it.) We're frustrating the EU until we've got the ban on by-products lifted and a 'framework' for the lifting of the wider ban. The 'by-products' are tallow, gelatin and bull semen – we're pretty sure that getting the ban on them lifted is achievable – but their contribution to the economy of the industry is minimal so the 'victory' when it comes won't amount to much. It's the ban on beef that counts and all we're asking for here is a 'framework' for lifting it – a 'framework' can be anything: what it isn't is a *timetable*.

Anyway, however the new policy pans out, there is good news not yet in the public domain. Roger Freeman is being brought in as 'beef war supremo'. Hogg is being side-lined and Roger will oversee the implementation of the slaughtering policy. He's a 'grown-up' (as we like to say), he'll 'get a grip' (ditto), it has to be an improvement. Hogg wanders into the office quite regularly (former members of the office tend to), lisping, 'I'm quite content to be culled myself. I could be earning a great deal more at the Bar.' He may be highly gifted, and he's certainly quite congenial, but as a political animal he's more flawed than most – and he's still wearing that hat!

---

573   The inter-governmental conference on the future of the European Union scheduled for 1997.

SUNDAY 26 MAY 1996

A few nights ago Brian Mawhinney sought me out in the lobby during the ten o'clock vote. He was quite abrupt: 'Need to have a word. Met your chairman the other day. Says you're never in the constituency.'

'But I protest – '

'I don't mind what you do with your time, I'm just telling you.'

Brian did not linger to hear my protestations, but I was so bloody angry. I wanted to go and ring Stuart [Begbie] up that minute, I wanted to ram my wretched constituency diary down his throat, but I didn't – of course I didn't. I simply simmered, bubbled, internalised my anger as (on the whole) I do. And now I'm glad. Last night Stuart and David Pickering[574] gave me dinner at the Arkle, the formal, pretentious, overpriced restaurant at the Grosvenor – chilling atmosphere, silver tureens lifted from nouvelle cuisine in unison, the sort of thing Michèle absolutely *hates* but now and again I quite like. Anyway, Stuart could not have been more mellow and positive and generous. He ordered a wine, a Margaux – at, I think, £300 the bottle. We glugged it down. He ordered another! I did not mention my conversation with Mawhinney, but over the course of the dinner I ran through my programme for the weekend in harrowing detail: the architects' conference at the Town Hall, the Training Into Jobs launch, the visit to the Regimental Museum, the Samaritans charity walk, my official opening of the Save the Family offices etc. etc. – and what I realised, of course, as I described these activities, is that there wasn't a known Conservative at any of them and if the activists don't see what you're doing they don't know what you're doing … So, from now on in I'm going to do a monthly newsletter listing everywhere I've been, everyone I've seen, everything I've done. (It's pathetic really, since I expect to lose the seat, I'm ready to lose the seat, but I *kill* myself here every weekend, and I want to be appreciated, I want to be loved.)

More seriously, I have just been watching the box and George Walden (who is not standing at the election) has been pleased to tell us that he's ready to resign the whip and wipe out our majority! His line is that he won't be party to a government of pettyminded Little Englanders. The PM's beef-war policy is 'silly and cynical' and George (from his great height) wants us to know he'll have none of it. He is so self-righteous. At Westminster no one (no one at all) takes him seriously any longer – he's a column in the *Evening Standard*, amusing enough to flick through, that's all – but (this is the hell of it), rate him or despise him, *we need him.*

The papers report that David Hunt is launching a pro-European counter-offensive. As his whip, shouldn't I know about this? Yes, I should but I don't. I phone David. He's

---

574 Cheshire county councillor and generous supporter of the Chester Conservative Association.

alarmed – but only gently. David's responses are always measured. He has no desire to rock the boat. He only gave the *Sunday Times* a sentence or two. It's been misconstrued. His new group, Mainstream, is simply a loose umbrella for One Nation Conservatives. It's not going to be doing any campaigning, just quietly supporting the PM and reminding the world outside that the majority of the party believe in the centre ground. David is, as ever, *l'homme raisonable*. But is he right? Like it or not, the sceptics are in the ascendant.

SUNDAY 2 JUNE 1996

The good news is that there are *five* photographs of me in the *Chester Standard* this week. The bad news is that the national press are proving less helpful. Rod Richards has been fingered by the *News of the World*. Our swaggering, fiery-tempered junior Welsh Office minister, champion of family values, husband of twenty-one years, father of three, has been caught with his trousers down in the company of a fetching PR lady twenty years his junior. I imagine he'll have gone by lunchtime.

I'd say 'poor bugger' (and I do say 'poor bugger' – I loathe the *News of the World*) but this one we did see coming – he was warned, he knew what he was doing, he took the risk. What more could we, should we have done? I heard, via a journalist, that one of my charges – Nigel Evans – had been seen more than once in a gay bar in Manchester. I asked the Deputy, 'What should I do?'

'Tell him.'

I took Nigel to the Smoking Room, bought him a drink, and told him. He was outraged, angry, indignant. He denied it – furiously. I said, 'Good God, I believe you – and I don't care one way or the other. I'm simply telling you…'[575]

WEDNESDAY 5 JUNE 1996

Good news. My friend Sebastian Coe has joined the Whips' Office. It was to be another of the new intake but as we'd had word that he's also been engaged in an extra-marital dalliance (strenuously denied by him when I took him to dinner in the Churchill Room to 'sound him out') he was passed over 'this time round' and the cards fell Seb's way. He is delighted and so am I. He is a proper friend. I like almost all my colleagues here, but this is a closed community: we are close when we're here, but we know that when we

---

575 Fourteen years later, in 2010, Nigel Evans acknowledged that he was gay. In 2014 he was found not guilty of series of sex offences involving young men.

leave the place we'll rarely see one another. There are a handful of exceptions. When I'm no longer here, I know I'll still see Seb.

Jonathan Evans has replaced Rod at the Welsh Office. He moved with a bad grace. He was happy where he was, but as he's now the only credible Welshman we've got (other than Sir Wyn who is a darling but 107)[576] there wasn't much choice. He was harrumphing about it last night. I said, 'Go with a will and you're doing them a favour. Next time, they'll be obliged to make you a minister of state.' He grunted. He is not a happy bunny. Gary Streeter (God-fearing solicitor and general good egg) leaves the office to replace Jonathan [Evans] in the Lord Chancellor's Department, hence the vacancy for Seb. I am no longer the junior whip. My days of hanging out the 'Do Not Disturb' sign and circulating the silver goblets are over.

SUNDAY 9 JUNE 1996

Yesterday was our 23rd wedding anniversary. The sun shone and we had a happy day. We took Aphra and Julian Slade to The Ivy for lunch and then went to the matinee of *Salad Days*. It still works. I said to Aphra, 'Julian is the Andrew Lloyd Webber of his generation.' She didn't believe me, but it's true.

The *News of the World* have got Rod's moll to kiss and tell. He is in a very bad way. And the rest of the press (more legitimately) are having fun with Portillo. He hosted a party in Admiralty House on Thursday night (to which we were invited but didn't go) and, as happens at these parties, the guests talked and drank and then talked more loudly and paid no attention at all to the Beating Retreat taking place on Horse Guards Parade below. The noise of raucous revelry from the Defence Secretary's open windows was such that 'complaints were made' and poor Michael has been obliged to issue a grovelling apology.

THURSDAY 13 JUNE 1996

My 'shit of the year' has lived up to his billing. Sir John Gorst of the poisonous breath has teamed up with another unfathomable soul, Hugh Dykes, in an attempt to blackmail Stephen into saving the casualty unit at Edgware Hospital. This has been bubbling up for months, but it came to a head on Monday when they sent Stephen a letter saying that, as of last night, they wouldn't vote with the government unless they got their

---

576 Sir Wyn Roberts, MP for Conway 1970–83, for Conwy 1983–1997, Welsh Office minister 1979–94, was actually sixty-five; later Baron Roberts of Conwy, he died in 2013, aged eighty-three.

way. Stephen had come up with a compromise on the hospital that predated their threat, but Gorst and Dykes proceeded to go public and claim the compromise as a personal victory – leaving the government open to the charge that it's now so enfeebled that any two-bit threat and the PM instantly succumbs. Blair put it alarmingly well at PMQs: the PM's policies are now 'determined solely by the imprint of the last person who sat on him.'

The Chief (in his crimson-with-anger mode) hauled them in and gave them a bollocking – a terrifying experience for most normal mortals, but as Gorst is arrogant and deaf and Dykes is strange the effect on them may not have been as harrowing as it would have been for your average colleague. That said, their post-meeting demeanour suggests they got the message – more or less. The Chief, of course, is frantic that everyone else gets the message too – which is why two things have happened: we discreetly 'inspired' denunciations of the would-be blackmailers at this afternoon's 1922 Committee and an account of the Chief's 'unpleasant encounter' with them has been fed to the press. (This is very unusual. The Chief believes absolutely in the golden rule that Chief Whips are silent and invisible, neither heard nor seen, never photographed, never quoted. And even in an emergency like this he won't have talked directly to the press. What will have happened is that either the Deputy or Andrew [Mackay] will have slipped into Members' Lobby and whispered what we want to say into the selected correspondent's ear. It's an extraordinary system: the licensed tip-off. It can be on the record or off, as you please. And it's a service that's available round the clock. In Members' Lobby, immediately outside the Upper Whips' Office, there are lobby correspondents loitering hopefully at all times of day and night. When there's a division on they're shifted from the lobby itself to the corridor that runs past the Tea Room to the Library and there they line the walls, lounging up against the panelling likes tarts beneath the lamppost plying for trade.)

LATER

The PM is 'incandescent'. Yesterday the Chief hauled in Bill Cash to tell him that his ludicrous 'European Foundation' should either stop accepting funding from Sir James Goldsmith or Bill should step down as the Foundation's chairman. Bill agreed 'on reflection' that it was probably 'inappropriate' to be taking money from a man who will be putting up candidates against Conservatives in the election – and we thought that was that. But no. It turns out that Mrs T. has now called Bill to offer him some of her money. She is going to make 'a substantial donation'. Of course, the official line is that it's up to her how she spends her money, but the PM is white with anger.

....

SATURDAY 15 JUNE 1996

....

Sometimes, like yesterday, when I get in I'm simply too weary for the diary. I should be more disciplined, do it at the same time each day, like Douglas Hurd. Fifteen minutes in the dressing room, every night, before saying one's prayers. But Douglas is more organised, more certain, (more impressive) than I am. I imagine he wears a wine-coloured dressing gown, and striped pyjamas with a cord like we had at prep school. On Friday nights as a rule I stumble back to the flat around eleven, half-past, and have half a bottle of wine collapsed in front of the box (if there isn't *The Word* I make do with Jools Holland). Last night I crawled straight into bed and curled up with comfort reading (the Sherlock Holmes that Saethryd gave me). Between twelve and one, I say 'goodnight' to Michèle's picture (out loud), turn on the World Service and switch out the light. I'm asleep in less than ten minutes.

Yesterday: another 'listening session' with the farmers. The scheme isn't working. There's queue-jumping, the renderers can't cope, it's chaos out there. I gave them copies of the latest letter from Tony Baldry.[577] It contains his home number. They won't use it, but I wanted them to know I'm on their side. I ended the day at Chester Castle – Beating Retreat, generous hospitality to follow. (Never mind Options for Change – the mess budgets seem happily unaffected.) I took the salute – and this time I had a hat and knew what to do with it.

The papers tell us that the PM has had 'a bellyful' of Euro-rows. (Who comes up with these phrases? Howell, I suppose. 'Bellyful' is a perfect Major word.) Hilariously, Hugh Dykes is on the rampage: 'The Whips' Office behave like hysterical children and if they try any dirty tricks over the weekend I will be having strong words with them on Monday.' We're quivering in our boots to be sure. What a tosspot. (And the Chief was right. He didn't over-react. If every disobliging backbencher with a grudge thinks he can to hold us up to ransom, we're doomed.)

The Birthday Honours are really dreary. The knighthood for George Martin is spot-on, but that's about it. There are Ks too for some of our harmless old boys (Roger Sims,[578] Robert Hicks),[579] but nothing for Nick Winterton, who will not be amused. In the office we've taken Nicholas's recent egregious grovellings at PMQs as a sure sign that the poor man thought his overdue recognition was imminent. Certainly he's served more than his time (a quarter of a century, as he regularly reminds me) but I've a feeling (fair or unfair) he won't be getting his knighthood under the present dispensation. He *claims* he was as

---

577 Minister of State at the Ministry of Agriculture.

578 MP for Chislehurst 1974–97.

579 MP for Bodmin 1970–74, 1974–83, Cornwall South East 1983–97.

good as promised it a year or two back. The prospect may have been wafted loosely in the air, but I can't believe anything was said 'in terms'. When colleagues come to see the Chief, as they do, 'to discuss the workings of the honours system' as he puts it (he's very funny), he may twitch and gobble at them in such a way as to give them hope, but I'm sure he never *says* anything. He's a brilliant operator. (And *his* knighthood is assured.)[580]

WEDNESDAY 3 JULY 1996

We discovered at this morning's meeting that the PM planned to announce this afternoon that the Stone of Scone is to be returned to Scotland. After 700 years, it is to be yanked out of Westminster Abbey and carted off to Edinburgh – swirling bagpipes and wee Michael Forsyth in his tartan trews doubtless leading the parade. This is a Forsyth scam, a brilliant coup from his point of view, but the news of it provoked ruffled feathers and a fair degree of tut-tutting at the meeting a) because we're not sure how well this will go down in England and b) because we knew nothing about it. The office *hates* not being in the know. Clearly Forsyth thought this up and nobbled the PM direct. He's kept it entirely under wraps. I don't know how much advance notice the Chief got. The Deputy, Mackay, Conway, looked distinctly miffed. Michael Bates, as ever, played the *faux naïf*.

We're also not too happy with the PM because of his proposed Holy-Joe response to the recommendations of the Senior Salaries Review Body. It looks as if the SSRB are wisely suggesting a £9,000 hike for backbenchers (up to £43,000 from £34,000) and what amounts to a sweet £17,000 more for Ministers. This is 26 per cent plus-plus. The PM wants us to settle for 3 per cent. We say 'give us the money'. We want the money – we particularly want it *now* because it'll mean enhanced pensions when we all lose our seats. It'll be a free vote, but the payroll [Ministers and PPPs] will be whipped to support the government's line and Blair and his acolytes will vote for restraint, so it's touch and go.

LATER

Nothing has been said, but smirks and nudges from Conway and the Deputy in the upper office just now suggest that we needn't worry too much about the salaries' vote.

---

580 Nicholas Winterton was knighted eventually, in 2002. He retired as an MP in 2010, following criticism of expenses claims described by David Cameron as 'indefensible'. Alastair Goodlad was appointed KCMG in 1997 in John Major's resignation honours. In 2005, following five years as British High Commissioner to Australia, he became Baron Goodlad of Lincoln.

Forsyth has had a triumph. Townend and his ilk are in the Tea Room touting him as leader-in-waiting.

I've been over at 7 Millbank recording my contribution to Prince Philip's obituary. I wasn't nearly as good as I would have liked to be. I am cross with myself because I should have thought it through more carefully, prepared the right sound bites. He is a remarkable man and I would have liked to do him full justice. I may phone them and ask if I can do it again.

THURSDAY 11 JULY 1996

At around ten past midnight the deed was done. Five divisions, each one going the way we wanted. I am now £17,000 better off. There's a feeling in the office that Derek may have over-egged the pudding. The government lost the main vote by 168 to 317. It says in *The Times*: 'Around fifteen of the government's 126-strong "payroll vote", who had been told to support 3 per cent, did not register a vote, but the whips insisted they had good reasons for being away.' According to my reckoning, the figure's nearer forty than fifteen. The PM is seriously displeased. He's been undermined by the office and he knows it. But now we've got what we wanted, the Deputy is sending out the signal: no grinning, no hurrahs, straight faces, don't refer to it, move on. (I wonder if this would have happened under Thatcher or Churchill. Under Thatcher, possibly. Under Churchill, probably not. They all had private incomes in those days.)

This morning's other excitement has been the visit by Nelson Mandela. Westminster Hall was decked in all its glory: red carpets, gilded thrones, state trumpeters, Yeoman of the Guard, gentlemen at arms (none too steady on their feet). The hall was packed: Lords, Commons, the great and the good – even Jeremy Thorpe,[581] bent and pathetic. The sun filtered through the west window. There was a palpable sense of expectation, and when the trumpets sounded and the great man made his entrance I doubt there was a completely dry eye in the house. He is tall and handsome, but he's frail. He tottered down the steps. The Speaker had to hold his hand. I imagine it was the proudest moment of her life – and why not? In her speech – just a touch too much me-me-me for my taste – we learnt that Betty in her day had been at the heart of the anti-apartheid movement, one of the white sisters of Black Sash protesting in Trafalgar Square. But, in fairness, if she said too much, she did at least say all the right things. Mandela said too much, too. His speech was rather long, rather ponderous and, from where we were sitting (about halfway back) difficult to hear. But it didn't matter. It was the presence we

581   Liberal MP for North Devon 1959–70; Leader of the Liberal Party 1967–76.

had come for – and the presence we got. And when he'd finished and we stood to cheer, he teetered down the steps and made his way out along the central aisle. Curiously, close to he looked less frail. His smile is enchanting. As he passed he shook hands on either side. I was on the end of the aisle and he came right up to me – and then clasped the hand of the bugger behind. It was General de Gaulle all over again.[582]

TUESDAY 16 JULY 1996

We had the full cast for prayers at the DoE: Gummer, Curry, Robert Jones,[583] Robin Ferrers[584] (it really is like having Osbert Lancaster in the government), Beresford,[585] Clappison, Douglas French, Matthew Banks.[586] It's not a bad team. In fact, it's quite impressive. Gumdrops is outstanding – he has defused the green lobby, indeed he's claimed ownership over a range of the green issues – unthinkable five years ago. Curry is on tenterhooks hoping that the reshuffle will see him into the Cabinet. I now think it won't. Any changes will be minor – not just because we know that 'refreshing' the look of the government only has a twenty-four-hour effect, but mainly because reshuffles leave bruised souls and we daren't risk any more unhappy bunnies. This means Beresford is safe – though in fairness he has been trying quite hard to be more emollient. He has learnt at last that when one of our side introduces an adjournment debate, the minister is not supposed to duff him up and put him straight: he's supposed to butter him up, woo him, praise him to the skies. And Douglas French is a decent guy. He's been here ten years and deserves a break. But he won't get it. He's one of those: always in the frame, never in the picture.

Speaking of which … I was saying in the office how jolly Jeffrey Archer has been being in recent days – and there was a lot of chortling from Conway and Tim Wood: 'There couldn't be a reshuffle coming up by any chance, could there?' Anyway, I met up with Jeffrey for coffee in the Pugin Room (I was three minutes late, Jeffrey was tapping his watch when I arrived, 'I am *never* late!' he barked) and he took me through the key ingredients for making a successful novel – the shape of the book, the number of pages,

---

582 In 1960 President Charles de Gaulle of France paid a state visit to Britain, during which he addressed Members of Parliament in Westminster Hall and visited the French Lycée in South Kensington. GB was a pupil at the Lycée and one of those lined up for presentation to the President. When de Gaulle passed down the line, he patted or shook hands with every child but one – GB.

583 1950–2007; PUSS at Environment 1994–5, Minister of State 1995–7; MP for Herts West 1983–97.

584 1929–2012; 13th Earl Ferrers; on the Conservative front bench in the House of Lords from 1962; Deputy Leader of the Lords 1979–83, 1988–97; Minister of State at Environment 1995–7.

585 Sir Paul Beresford, PUSS at Environment 1994–7; MP for Croydon Central 1992–7, Mole Valley since 1997.

586 PPS to the Ministers of State at Environment; MP for Southport 1992–97.

the quality of paper, the type size, the number of lines on a page. It was both ludicrous and compelling – and he's done it, damn him, he's a world-class best seller.

But that's not what he wants. He wants to be in the government – Minister of State, nothing more junior, and actually as Arts Minister or Sports Minister he'd give it energy, commitment, brio. But it won't happen. The activists would welcome it; the parliamentary party wouldn't wear it. The office would regard it as 'a risk' and risks are not what we're taking this year.

LATER

An amusing cock-up. One of my SIs[587] this morning. I take a pride in rattling through them. When I joined the office it was explained to me that you'll get reliable people to serve on your SIs if they know they're going to be brief and you send them a note to thank them for coming. My record to date is thirty seconds. Beresford played ball and simply got up and said, 'I recommend the measure to the committee' and sat down. We voted and that was that. Well, this morning we rattled through it – whatever it was – some nonsense to do with rating – voted – the committee members duly thanked me for a three-minute session and we all toddled on our way. Now I learn from one of the clerks that the Instrument was riddled with misprints. We are going to have to reconvene the committee next week and go through the whole rigmarole again. So much for parliamentary scrutiny.

MONDAY 22 JULY 1996

Housing Bill, Lords' amendments. At the 2.30 p.m. meeting I promised to deliver the votes at 5.30 p.m., 6.15 p.m. and 8.15 p.m. In the event, the first was six minutes late, but the other two were spot on. Curry and Clappison were magnificent. James [Clappison] kept protesting, 'I must put this on the record.' I kept hissing, 'No you don't – no one cares', then barked out loud, 'Beg to move!' For three hours I was bobbing up and down like a yoyo. We *rattled* through it. I told Michèle that we'd be in the Strangers' Dining Room by 8.30 p.m. – and we were! It was Jo, Beckie, Seb, and a good time was had by all. (I am still mildly in my cups as you can tell. The news I should be reporting at greater length is that David Heathcoat-Amory's resignation is now out in the open. He's going

---

587 A Statutory Instrument is a piece of secondary legislation that introduces schemes, schedules, rules usually related to, but too detailed or time-specific to be part of, primary legislation. SIs are considered and voted on upstairs in Committee, not on the floor of the House.

because 'our European policy isn't working'. Of course, he may also be going because he knows there's no place for him in the Cabinet, so he can afford to take this principled stand. Is that unfair? Probably not. David Davis is staying put – and keeping mum. I sense he's to be placated with a PC in the not too distant future.[588] The mini-reshuffle is now a muddle and scheduled for tomorrow. The joy of the Whips' Office is that I know I will not be featuring. I am very content where I am.)

TUESDAY 23 JULY 1996

'Minister's resignation over Europe reopens Tory wounds'. Redwood, Tebbit, Lamont are hopping up and down hailing Heathcoat-Amory as the hero of the hour. Joe Public is saying, 'Who? What?' The rest of the reshuffle will also pass the great world by. Willetts becomes Paymaster-General (excellent), but at the Cabinet Office (under Roger Freeman) not at the Treasury. Oppenheim goes to fill the gap at the Treasury with a splendid title they've dusted down from somewhere: Exchequer Secretary. Steve Norris and Tim Eggar[589] are stepping down at their own request with a view to making boodles of dosh. John Bowis (good man) goes from Health to Transport and *three* members of the office move on: 1) Liam Fox goes to the Foreign Office to ease their workload. (David Davis whinges that's he's got too much to do – and won't do it. Jeremy [Hanley] obliges and is exhausted. Enter Liam to help share the burden.) 2) Simon Burns replaces Bowis at Health (did the Chief feel he'd heard enough about the Essex Fire Service?) 3) The Deputy becomes Minister for Industry at the DTI. (This is a just reward. His seat is none too safe and out of the office he can raise his profile. Also, if it all goes wrong, there are going to be more jobs going for a former Industry Minister than a former Deputy Chief Whip.)

The office will miss Greg. I think he has been outstanding. I've just sent him a long note saying that I don't think I've ever come across a person better suited to their job or one who did it so well. And I meant it. His handling of the team has been perfect: he made it fun and he covered our backs, so when he whistled we *jumped*. His successor as Deputy is Andrew Mackay. This will disappoint Derek [Conway], but it was inevitable. By rights, by seniority it should have been Tim Wood, but that was never going to be. Perhaps a consoling K is in the pipeline? Given that he's bound to lose his seat it ought to be.[590]

I slid into the meeting at 2.31 p.m. to find Andrew firmly ensconced at the Deputy's desk – Greg's mountains of debris already cleared away. As I flopped into my chair, all of

---

588 David Davis became a Privy Counsellor in 1997.

589 He had been Energy Minister since 1992; MP for Enfield North 1979–97.

590 It wasn't.

sixty seconds late, he curled his lip and said, 'I shouldn't need to remind the office, the meeting begins at 2.30 sharp.' Faintly silly. (I like him – I like him a lot – but he *is* faintly ridiculous – the impeccably tailored suits, the perma-tan, the self-consciously smooth gliding through the corridors of power...)

For what it's worth (not much – not anything actually) I'm now head of the Lower Office, and we have three new whips: Peter Ainsworth,[591] Anthony Coombs, Jacqui Lait. Jacqui is the first female Conservative whip in the history of the office. This is quite a departure, unthinkable, I imagine, until *very* recently. The office is run entirely like a gentleman's club (that's part of its charm) and, nominally, potential whips come up for election. The Chief certainly goes through the motions of leading a discussion, out of which names emerge, but the names that emerge are the ones that he had in mind and the PM has blessed. He tells us, in terms, we can blackball any candidate, and he says it with conviction, but he slips into the chat that the PM rather feels it's time for a woman whip – and he rather agrees – and Jacqui seems 'a decent sort of chap' (ho ho) – and immediately we all murmur our assent. Thus a little bit of history is made.

FRIDAY 23 AUGUST 1996

It is quite funny. We have had to agree: this is our worst holiday *ever*. I wasn't going to keep the diary this week, but I want to record the essential horror of it.

North Wales is *death*. Beaumaris was bad enough. We arrived on the night the circus left town. Our little attic room at Ye Olde Bull overlooked the main street and into the small hours, as we tossed and turned, the caravans, the lorries, the transporters rumbled, trundled, thundered pass. Michèle said, 'I can't stay here another night.' We did the castle, we did the Museum of Childhood Memories (!!!), we buggered off. Snowdon was *invisible*. It wasn't half-hidden in a romantic mist, it was unseeable in a grey-green fog. And last night, as we drove into Abersoch, through the swishing windscreen wipers and wash of hailstones I saw the huge sign by the bridge: WELCOME TO THE WELSH RIVIERA! We put the car in the hotel car park, opened the door and stepped out – the puddle was so deep my feet *disappeared*. After dinner (which was fine – circa 1956 fine, but fine all the same) we retreated to our garret. The bed is one of those that has given way in the middle: we spent the night rolling into one another and then clambering back towards the sides. At two in the morning I went to the loo and, returning, pulled the bathroom door shut after me. As I pulled it (this is true, I promise) the door came off its hinges and fell onto the bed. We lay there through the night gazing at the

591   MP for Surrey East 1992–2010.

lavatory bowl that was intermittently illuminated by the flashing neon side in the street outside.

We are abandoning ship.No doubt Llandudno is lovely – and we'd get the pick of the shelters – but we're going home. We are driving to Chester, then to Birmingham (for the pre-Raphaelites – something *civilised*), then to *Barnes*. O joy, o rapture! Michèle said at about four in the morning, 'Perhaps we should have tried Benidorm.'[592] Yes, it's been that bad.

SATURDAY 7 SEPTEMBER 1996

I'm on the 8.30 a.m. flight from Manchester. I began the new novel yesterday morning.[593] I flew up last night for the Aldford evening. I'm up again on Monday for the Rotary lunch, a surgery and Bingo night at the Deaf Centre. It's all happening!

I did a ring round the card[594] and the troops are quite mellow. The polls are improving and the general line is what I was getting from my people in Aldford: 'it doesn't feel too bad on the patch'. Several who didn't like Blair's demon eyes think we're mad to be using them again.[595] Den Dover: 'Why can't we be more positive?' (Answer, according to Finkelstein: Because positive campaigning doesn't work.)

Neil [Hamilton] is bubbly. His libel action begins on the eve of the party conference. He knows this has not made him popular with the powers that be, but he had to 'seize the moment'. *The Guardian* (crafty buggers) are planning to subpoena the PM, the DPM, the Cabinet secretary and Richard Ryder. Publicly, the PM is treating the possibility of having to appear in court with a light touch. Privately, he is not amused. This is a distraction he could do without.

THURSDAY 26 SEPTEMBER 1996

'John Major was struggling to prevent open warfare within his government last night after a Foreign Office minister publicly attacked Kenneth Clarke over his stance on a single European currency.' Bonsor[596] has backed down, apologised, eaten humble pie

---

592 The week before the Labour Party had sent Glenda Jackson to Benidorm to canvas for support among British voters living and holidaying on the Costa del Sol.

593 *Venice Midnight*, published in September 1998.

594 The card is the list of MPs for which each whip is responsible. A 'card operation' means speaking to each one of those MPs.

595 The Advertising Standards Authority had criticised a poster from M & C Saatchi depicting Tony Blair with 'demon eyes'. At the beginning of September a new poster was launched featuring the eyes on their own, lurking inside an open purse, with the slogan: 'New Labour, New Taxes'.

596 Sir Nicholas Bonsor, MP for Nantwich 1979–83, Upminster 1983–97; Minister of State at the Foreign Office.

– but on it goes, relentlessly. What hope is there? *Some*. Today we learn that Gordon Brown may be proposing a 50p top rate tax for high earners – and Blair has to slap down Jeremy Corbyn for inviting Gerry Adams to Westminster. It also seems that Tony Blair has also been asking my old friend Geoff Atkinson[597] for some funny one-liners for his conference speeches – quips on the defections, Maurice Saatchi's peerage, Portillo, fat cats and the beef crisis preferred. Geoff has declined, somewhat indignantly – but while they may have handled it ineptly, the principle is right. If you want jokes in your speech, get in a professional.

I'm at the Ramada, Manchester. Saeths[598] is coming over for supper. I've done the Waterstone's lunch. Also on the bill: Humphrey Carpenter, Peter Stringfellow. Humphrey's book is becoming a bestseller.[599] Of course, Runcie was naive to gabble away to him as he did, and on tape, but I sensed (though he denied it) that Humphrey does feel a *bit* sheepish – as I would if ever I published my diary. I might do it, but I'd feel those pangs of guilt. What I would *not* do is emulate the amazing Stringfellow. 'Hello, ladies. You've read about me, haven't you? It was in the paper. It said I'd slept with 400 women. (Pause) That was *last* year! (Nervous tittering from audience.) Mind you, I've had some good times in Manchester. Have I slept with any of you ladies? (He shades his eyes, scans the room.) Come on, ladies, own up.' At the back of the room a middle-aged matron raises a tentative arm. Throaty laugh from the platform.

I kid you not.

TUESDAY 1 OCTOBER 1996

Neil's case has collapsed. I don't understand the ins and outs of it, but the essence is that last night Neil and Ian Greer decided they had no choice but to abandon their action. They have agreed to pay some of *The Guardian*'s costs, they've their own costs of £300,000 plus, and today's *Guardian* headline reads: 'A liar and a cheat: official'.

The paper claims that Neil collected tens of thousands of pounds from Fayed, the money in £50 notes stuffed into envelopes. It's got three of Fayed's staff ready to swear to it, claiming that Neil turned up at Fayed's offices demanding his envelopes. Neil continues to deny it all. He now wants it investigated by the Standards and Privileges Committee. He says he and Greer have abandoned the case simply because the costs have proved

---

597 Scriptwriter and producer of *The Rory Bremner Show*.

598 Saethryd, GB's elder daughter, was at Manchester University.

599 Humphrey Carpenter had published a biography of the former Archbishop of Canterbury containing indiscreet remarks about the royal family, among others. Lord Runcie said, 'I have done my best to die before this book is published.'

prohibitive, but reading between the lines it seems he and Greer have fallen out. *The Guardian* forced the disclosure of a minute taken by Robin Butler[600] of Heseltine's conversation with Neil. Heseltine asked Neil, in terms, if he'd had a financial arrangement with Greer. Neil denied it. Now it turns out he had – and this minute is being described as 'exposing a conflict of interest' between Neil and Greer. (Minutes of ministerial telephone calls are not unusual. The outer office can listen in on any call and be taking a note, unbeknownst to the caller.)

I've been ringing Neil's flat. It's permanently engaged. I don't know what to say. I believe him, but millions won't. Not now. I began the day at the Department of Health.[601] Prayers. Not many friends for Neil to be found there. I then went (incredibly) to Harrods because they'd prearranged a signing session in the book department. I didn't linger. Clearly when Fayed stalks the store the staff are terrified. When Saethryd did a holiday job in the cosmetics department she said the girls used to hide under the counters and round the back to avoid catching the owner's eye … Michèle, bless her, has cut up her Harrods account card to show solidarity. (It's the right gesture, but we have to be honest. I don't think we've used the account in years.)

MONDAY 7 OCTOBER 1996

I'm on the train to Bournemouth. I'm staying at the Highcliff. Damn the expense, it could be my last conference ever. I've just done the John Dunn Show, Radio 2. John is so nice, so good (he is the best interviewer in the business) – but he's not happy. It's become a miserable place, the BBC. Perhaps we should have privatised it? At least at the commercial stations they've got some *bounce*.

The serious news is 'the Willetts memorandum'. It's now in the public domain because it was subpoenaed by *The Guardian*. It's just a whip's note recording a conversation David had with Geoffrey Johnson-Smith when Geoffrey was chairman of the Committee on Members' Interests and the Committee was investigating Neil's undeclared sojourn at the Paris Ritz. The memo said Geoffrey 'wants our advice' and then explored the possibilities: either encourage the Committee to investigate the matter quickly or, 'exploiting the good Tory majority', get them to defer the investigation, citing Neil's pending libel action, saying it was going to be sub judice. Geoffrey recalls the conversation, but naturally denies that he sought advice or that he could or would for a moment have been

---

600 Cabinet Secretary 1988–98.

601 As a rule whips change departmental responsibilities each year. At the reshuffle GB was moved from the Department of the Environment to two other departments: Health and Transport.

influenced by it. (Geoffrey is indeed Mr Probity, loyal and decent. He still looks quite amazing, a handsome fifty. In fact he's seventy-two, getting deafer, not necessarily the safe pair of hands he once might have been.) Of course, it's all a lot of nonsense. David was simply doing his job. Part and parcel of a whip's job is to seek ways of ensuring that the government is seen in the best light. Of course, the Hamilton enquiry was an embarrassment and we wanted it to go away, but there was no sinister or corrupt intent. But never mind the reality: it's going to be played up as the government in general and David in particular, attempting to subvert the independence and integrity of the Committee.

TUESDAY 8 OCTOBER 1996

Every morning at 8.45 a.m. we are to meet in the Poole Room. There really isn't anything to be done here: the MPs who come to the conference come on flying visits. Caballing in corners is not taking place. Where there is some action, however, is on the box. On Sky they're running and rerunning an amazing video of Princess Di and James Hewitt. It is extraordinary, a monstrous invasion of their privacy but gripping. She's in a leotard riding around on his back. I think this must be what Richard Spring's father would have called 'a bit of horseplay'. It's in fuzzy long shot, but it's certainly them.[602]

I went along to Stephen [Dorrell]'s room to collect him to go over to the hall. When I arrived, I thought he had someone with him. I waited outside the door. It turned out he was rehearsing his speech. We do lead funny lives ... middle-aged men in solitary rooms in seaside hotels mouthing clichés and platitudes hoping to wow a crowd we need but secretly disparage.

THURSDAY 10 OCTOBER 1996

Last night, without seeking clearance (for fear I wouldn't get it) I snuck up to London by train to speak at the Ernst & Young dinner at 1 Whitehall Place. *Inevitably* as the train pulled out of Southampton, my pager went. (I hate the pager. I hate the sensation. I'm convinced it's giving me liver cancer. I wear it on my belt because if I have it in my pocket I can't feel it when it vibrates.) It was Shana. 'Call at once.' I ranged up and down the train looking for a friendly face with a mobile phone. I found one, called, heart thumping, thinking I was about to be summoned back. It turned out to be nothing.

After the speech, I went home, picked up the car and drove back to Bournemouth.

---

602 It wasn't. It turned out to be an elaborate hoax.

I got in by 2.00 a.m. Not bad. This morning's meeting was only enlivened by the news that poor Nick Scott was found flat on his face in the street outside the hotel. 'According to the police,' said the Chief (chuckling, but not unkindly), 'Sir Nicholas was found "kissing the pavement".'

The PM's had a good press for his shirtsleeves question-and-answer session. This is what he does so well. And today is 'unity day'. Portillo has called for 'unity, unity, unity'. The Chancellor has wooed and won the faithful. And Hezza was at his ridiculous barnstorming best. It all feels quite good again. But it always does by the end of the conference. And then we go back into the real world and discover out there it's as bleak as ever.

MONDAY 14 OCTOBER 1996

Thurnham has gone over to the Liberals. This isn't a total surprise, but it's still nasty. He's claiming Mawhinney offered him a knighthood which is just not credible. Ashdown is looking suitably smug. Heseltine has been leading our response: 'I thought he'd gone months ago...'

We returned for the 'overspill'[603] at 2.30 p.m. Madam Speaker got us off to a nice start by declaring that she wants *The Guardian*'s range of allegations investigated as soon as possible. She's looking for an enquiry that's broad, speedy and 'as transparent as possible'. That means it will include the Willetts memorandum. In the office we've been instructed to say nothing about it to anyone. This will not be a problem as there's nowt to say.

At 4.30 p.m. I descended into the bowels of the building to find Canon Donald Gray.[604] The Speaker's Chaplain has a shoe-box of an office deep underground at the far, far end of a series of ever-narrowing subterranean corridors. He is a good and kindly man, twinkly, friendly, always happy to chat. It was Andrew's idea that I seek his advice. (Andrew got to value him in the aftermath of Stephen [Milligan]'s death. That's also, I imagine, when Andrew got to value Julie. They are now definitely an item.[605] What happened to that nice Mrs Mackay I met when I went to speak in his constituency? Well, there you go. Julie is certainly younger and prettier. Distant echoes from Michèle: 'Men ... *bastards*.')

Anyway, the point is: a couple of our charges are in a bad way, one especially so – bit of a breakdown – nowhere to go – what to do? Donald thinks there may be a monastery that could take him – provide space, solace, peace, a chance to recuperate, and he'd be within reach for critical votes. He has given me numbers and I'm to investigate.

This is good. This is part and parcel of the whips' service. We do care. We do try to

---

603 The remaining business of the 1995–6 session. The new session would begin with the State Opening on 23 October.

604 Rector of St Margaret's, Westminster Abbey, and Chaplain to the Speaker since 1987.

605 Andrew Mackay and Julie Kirkbride married in 1997.

help. We do say, 'Here's a doctor who can help,' 'Have you thought of AA?' 'Here's a lawyer/accountant/shrink who can sort you out.' When bankruptcy looms, we do look for ways to help bail them out. I'm going to see one of our friendly solicitors on Thursday on this very score. Yes, we're doing it to safeguard the majority, secure the government's business, but we're also doing it because it's good man-management. I don't know why we can't be more open about our role, our function, how we operate. We're not freemasons. We're Members of Parliament trying to make the system work in the best interests of party, government and country. It's all the hush-hush hugger-mugger secrecy nonsense that gets us into the sort of mess we're landed in with the wretched Willetts memo.

TUESDAY 15 OCTOBER 1996

The F. E. Smith dinner. Another damn fool little 'project' in which I should not have got myself involved. It seemed a good idea at the time ... Sproat, who had once known/gone out with (?) F. E.'s daughter (granddaughter?), had the idea that the great man deserved a memorial of some kind within the precincts – not a full-length statue (reserved for former premiers) but a bust or a painting ... Excellent idea ... Greg Knight comes on board ... Let's set the ball rolling with a dinner ... and who volunteers to 'organise' the dinner? Yes. First we plan it for the spring, then some crisis vote forces postponement. Then we go for the summer. Another crisis. Then we realise that we'd better get on with it because if we don't the election will be upon us and it's too late. So we opt for tonight, the ninetieth anniversary of F. E.'s celebrated maiden speech.

We (I) secure the guests of honour – the only three living parliamentarians who remember F. E.: Lords Longford, Boyd-Carpenter[606] and Hailsham. Hailsham is the key catch. Greg is adamant we must have Hailsham. Hailsham knew F. E., Hailsham was also Lord Chancellor, Hailsham is an orator, Hailsham will give it the sense of 'occasion'. But Hailsham, as I discover, plays hard to catch. I approach him in the Dining Room one lunchtime. 'Yes,' he says, 'I knew F. E., knew him well as a matter of fact. But I don't get out much in the evenings.' I ask Douglas if he'll work on his dad. He says 'No, I am not my father's keeper, and if you get him I'd rather not come.' I decide to write. I write at length, persuasively. 'This is to be a memorable night – we need you.' No reply. I write again, at greater length, more seductively still. 'We need you. No one else will do.' Eventually, the letter comes: 'Yes, I knew F. E., knew him well. Weather permitting, I'll come. I'll need a car.'

The cast complete, we set about choosing the guests. The dinner is taking place at

---

606 John Boyd-Carpenter, 1908–98; Baron Boyd-Carpenter from 1972; MP for Kingston-upon-Thames 1945–72; father of Sarah Hogg, later Baroness Hogg, married to Douglas Hogg, son of Lord Hailsham.

No. 12 so space is limited, around forty. We opt for whips, former whips, lawyers, chums. The Chief agrees to say a word of welcome – and, indeed, his introduction turns out to be a little gem: droll, carefully researched, hitting the right note precisely. Shana, bless her, sorts out the caterers, hiring of the silver, waitresses, wine, the diplomatic niceties of the *placements*. (Michael Howard calls me yesterday, '*Please* don't seat me next to Frank Longford. I don't think I could face a whole evening talking about Myra Hindley.')

6.30 p.m.: I arrive at No. 12. Everything is under control. 7.00 p.m. The guests begin to arrive. We're dining early so there'll be plenty of time for the speeches before the ten o'clock vote.·

7.15 p.m.: Lord Longford arrives, John Boyd-Carpenter arrives, F. E.'s son-in-law arrives.

7.30 p.m.: Lord Hailsham arrives. Hooray! (I had sent Jenny in a taxi to Putney to fetch him. I told her to bring him whether he'd remembered or not, whether he was willing or not. In fact, he was ready and waiting.) The dinner was fine (rather tasty), I didn't drink, and when I have responsibility for an event I never really enjoy it. I don't relax, I can't concentrate on the conversation I'm having.

At last, we reached the speeches – in good time, it was around 9.00 p.m.

I'd asked Sproat to set the scene and introduce the guests of honour. I thought he'd be rather good. He can be very good. In the event, he didn't appear to have prepared anything, simply chuntered briefly and said 'Here they are.' Longford was up first. He didn't tell us much, but he burbled with a certain eccentric charm. He was followed by John Boyd-Carpenter who didn't tell us much either, but was commendably concise. He told us we wouldn't want to hear a lot of old men rambling so he'd written what he had to say on a postcard. He read it out – with energy – and sat down. Then came F. E.'s son-in-law who explained that though he was indeed the son-in-law he'd never known his father-in-law who, of course, had died in 1930, so he really couldn't tell us anything and was here under false pretences, but thank you very much for such a nice meal in such elegant surroundings.

We passed the port and, at long last, Sproat introduced Lord Hailsham. Greg handed me a note written on the back of his place card: 'And now for the vintage stuff …' Hailsham was looking at his most twinkly and cherubic. He stood. We banged the table. He began: 'Gentlemen, I knew F. E., knew him well as a matter of fact. Let me take you back to the Oxford Union. Pause. There were these three Liberals…' Pause. 'There were these three Liberals…' FURTHER pause. Then he sat down. We gazed at our glasses and wondered, 'What next?' Suddenly, he was on his feet again. 'I knew F. E., knew him well. At the Oxford Union.' pause. 'There were these three Liberals…' He looked around, he chuckled, he sat down. He got up. 'Gentlemen, I *knew* F. E., knew him well, as a matter of fact. Have I told you? … There were these three Liberals …' pause. And he sat down once more.

It was 9.15 p.m. Sproat looked frantically around him. And a knight of the garter came to the rescue. The Earl of Longford slowly got to his feet and said, 'Let me tell you some of the other things I remember about F. E. ...' And for five minutes or more that great and good man burbled. When he sat, how gratefully we banged the table. But, suddenly, spurred by Frank, Hailsham was on his feet again. 'Gentlemen. There were these three Liberals ...' But still that was as far as he got. Dorrell to my right was stifling a fit of giggles. The Home Secretary to my left had left the room to take an urgent call. Sproat looked towards Boyd-Carpenter who waved his post-card triumphantly in the air and sat smugly in his seat. For the third time, Frank Longford struggled to his feet. He did well and we were grateful and by the time he sat down it was almost 9.25 p.m.

Silence fell, we looked into our glasses, a gentle murmuring began. I looked towards Lord Hailsham. He was getting to his feet. 'There were these three Liberals ...'

As he sat down, I called out to Sproat, 'Iain, I wonder if we don't each have a favour-ite F. E. story.'

There was a small chorus of 'Yes, yes' erupting round the room. 'Michael,' I said (but I was desperate), 'what was that one you were telling me over dinner?'

The Home Secretary (now cursing the fact that he'd returned from taking his phone call) gallantly struggled through the anecdote (Judge: What do you suppose I'm on the bench for, Mr Smith? F. E.: It is not for me, your honour, to attempt to fathom the inscrutable workings of Providence); John Taylor (bless him) got to his feet and did one (Judge: I have read your case, Mr Smith, and I am no wiser now than when I started. F. E.: Possibly not m'lud, but far better informed.')

Then someone said, 'Let's hear from Gyles,' and there was a gentle banging on the table. My heart, already at my knees, sank to the floor. Last night I had photocopied three pages of good F. E. material, the old chestnuts, plus a couple of other bits, but today I decided *deliberately* not to bring them. I thought 'If I don't take the notes, if I don't have a drink' I won't make a fool of myself. If only... Anyway, lamely, I struggled to paraphrase Churchill's marvellous description of F. E. from *Great Contemporaries* and, as I finished, or rather as my burbling dribbled to a standstill, I looked desperately towards Sproat and the Chief who did nothing (what could they do?) as Lord Hailsham emphatically rose to his feet once more: 'Gentlemen. I knew F. E.' pause. 'Knew him well.' pause. 'There was an occasion at the Oxford Union.' pause. 'These three Liberals...'

The Home Secretary leant towards me, 'It's a cracking good start to a story.'

Stephen spluttered, 'Yes, and one we're not likely to forget.'

When his lordship resumed his seat, we banged the table one last time, the Chief got up and thanked our guests for giving us such a memorable evening. 'A division is expected in ten minutes' time. Your continuing support for Her Majesty's govern-ment is much appreciated.'

We scuttled off to vote, leaving their lordships to await their cars. I thanked Boyd-Carpenter who seemed to have had a happy evening. I embraced Lord Longford.

'It's been marvellous,' he said, 'I hope I didn't say too much.'

'Not at all, not at all.'

'The best part for me has been meeting the Home Secretary. I believe he is a good man, compassionate, much misunderstood. I am sorry it's not more widely known. He is a truly *good* man. I shall have to write to the newspapers.'

I said goodbye to Lord Hailsham. He winked at me, 'Went rather well, don't you think?'

SATURDAY 26 OCTOBER 1996

It is 7.00 a.m. I am sitting up in bed with a mug of tea gazing at myself in the cupboard mirror opposite. At this distance I think I look quite boyish. (In a moment I shall put in my lenses and then, suddenly, the full horror will be revealed. The jowls, the bags under the eyes, the thinning, receding hairline ... Bah.) I have got an hour to sit in bed. My first appointment is at 8.30 a.m.: 'The Safer Chester Breakfast'. This is a Brandreth initiative: get a range of people – police, the crime prevention groups, retailers, residents associations etc. – to pool ideas. What can be done, in a practical way, by us as a community? What are our priorities for government, national and local? Yes, of course, there's a photo call at the end of it, but it's not entirely cynical. And yesterday wasn't entirely cynical either.

On Thursday night I'd gone to Birmingham for the *Birmingham Post* Literary Dinner. Kenneth Baker, Jane Asher, Peter Stringfellow ('200? That was last year. Hands up any of you ladies who've had the pleasure?'), me. The speeches started late, went on too long. I didn't mind as I wasn't due to do the local radio at Pebble Mill till midnight. That done, I got back to the hotel at one. I turned on the light in my dismal room and the lights fused. Every one. Pitch darkness, in the room, in the corridor. I stumbled about. I tried the bedside light. Nothing. I tried the TV. Joy. It crackled to life. The hotel porn channel: I began to undress in the flickering glow of two young women soaping one another in the shower. Suddenly, crackle, crackle, rain across the screen. 'If you want to see the rest of the movie dial X.' I got dressed, stumbled to the door, felt my way along the corridor, got to the landing. Lights! I went down to reception. *Eventually* a night porter was produced, who accompanied me back to my room, found the fuse box outside, flicked the switch and all was well. 'This happens most nights,' he said cheerily as I fumbled in my pocket to find him a tip.

I was asleep by two, awake at 6.30 a.m., and turning on the radio as I dressed suddenly found myself hearing about 'a serious fire in Chester'. I called Brian Bailey, I called Neil Fitton [Chester City councillors]. I got on to the *Chronicle*. A major fire in Lightfoot Street, several houses still ablaze, casualties unknown. I cancelled the Birmingham book signings and set off for the constituency. I got to Lightfoot Street by lunchtime. The police, the fire services, the WRVS, everyone had done a superb job. No life lost, but several houses destroyed, families made homeless. The city council had come up trumps – at once. Refuge found, food laid on. Martin Seed [the local manager] from M&S rolled up with supplies and blankets and fresh underwear for all. Truly impressive.

I asked the Superintendent if he could show me what had happened and, accompanied by two television crews, we walked the course of the devastation. The stench of the smoke was terrible. I showed my concern because I was concerned, but I am troubled because I know as I walked through the debris I was glad that I was on camera and (in my head) as I listened to the police and the firemen I began phrasing and rehearsing my thoughtful sound bite. It was worth it, I'm afraid, because when I got to the Eddisbury Patrons' Club Dinner at Rowton Hall at 8.00 *everybody* had seen me on the early evening news. My admiration for what the rescue services achieved is heartfelt, the congratulations I offered was richly deserved, it was right that the Member of Parliament should be there showing interest and concern and offering (genuinely) to help. But when I volunteered to be the one to take the pet rabbit that had been saved from the fire over to the refuge to restore him to his young owner, I knew that my motive was not entirely worthy.

MONDAY 28 OCTOBER 1996

Marginals' Club dinner with the PM. He's remarkably chipper, considering. On education, law and order, the reform of the welfare state – 'there's clear water between us and Labour.' He thinks Blair is beginning to come over as too holier-than-thou, evangelical, 'preachy'. 'People don't want the "nanny state".' And the economy's coming our way. He managed to be upbeat and relatively relaxed. He's in no hurry to go to the polls – 'no hurry at all.'

'We've got a working majority and the whips tell me everything's nicely under control. Isn't that right, Gyles?' I *assume* the Chief has told him about Barry Porter. If Barry dies, our majority falls to one. If we lose Barry's seat in the by-election we then become a minority government. And Barry, poor man, is going to die any day now. I speak to his wife and his mistress on alternate days. His wife (plus four, five children) are up in the constituency. His mistress, Angela, is nursing him in the flat down here. They are both coping remarkably.

THURSDAY 31 OCTOBER 1996

Breakfast at Claridges with David Puttnam. He has some deal with the hotel (is/was a non-exec director or some-such) whereby he gets the breakfast at a fiver a head. This is the sort of arrangement I could usefully use. He's full of his schemes, plans, committees, initiatives. I imagine he is hoping to be one of Mr Blair's first peers and a minister of state in the new administration. He is certainly busy-busy-busy. He floats the idea that within a year of the election Blair will have dropped Ken Livingstone and the hard left and that Ken Clarke and co. will somehow have come on board. He's convinced of it. He deploys the argument persuasively and implies (but doesn't state) that he's as good as heard the plan from his leader's lips ... Is this why we still have breakfast? Because David thinks I may be a conduit to Clarke, Gummer, Curry, Stephen D.?

It won't happen – even if Portillo or Redwood becomes leader. He misunderstands why we are Conservatives. But the left (or, as we like to think of ourselves, 'the moderate middle ground') are not enamoured of the rightwards shift. One of the advantages of where I'm sitting now (in the quiet room in the Library) is that it used to be part of the Speaker's apartments and the corridor leading from the House itself to the internal entrance to the Speaker's house is actually part of this room – the 'wall' is simply a glass and wood panel divide. As people come and go to and from the Speaker's house, I prick up my ears. Betty as she sweeps through is invariably chatty, but usually discreet. But now and again I do hear something worthwhile – most recently Douglas Hurd plotting with someone (it might have been Kenneth Baker, but possibly not, the other voice was quite low – Peter Brooke? Peter Lloyd?)[607] to find ways to undermine Michael Howard's plans to introduce mandatory sentences for repeat offenders ...

And have I recorded our latest wheeze for tackling our vanishing majority? It came up when we were trawling through names, wondering who might be next to follow Thurnham, Howarth, Nicholson across the floor. Why don't we find someone to defect to us?! We decided Kate Hoey[608] was our prime target. We like her, she seems sensible, she isn't valued by New Labour – let's have her! It's laughable, of course, a daydream, but you never know. We're going to put out the gentle, gentle feelers. Seb is going to seek her out and have lunch.

MONDAY 11 NOVEMBER 1996

I caught the 8.05 for Liverpool for Barry Porter's funeral. It was at St Xavier's, Oxton. The

---

607 MP for Fareham 1979–2001; Minister of State at the Home Office 1992–4.
608 Labour MP for Vauxhall since 1989.

wake was across the road from the church, at a pub called The Bowler Hat. I travelled up with John Ward, who was representing the PM. John arrived at Euston, grey, puffing, looking unusually anxious. He'd got the funeral details faxed to him from No. 10 yesterday, had seen mention of the Bowler Hat on the briefing note and, knowing Barry's Unionist sympathies, spent the entire night worrying where he was going to find one.

John is exactly what the PM needs: he's good, decent, dogged, loyal, no axes to grind. He's quite a bit older than the PM too, which may help. He doesn't look it, but he's coming up for seventy-two. We chatted all the way. It's clear the PM feels beleaguered on all sides, fed up with the factions, infuriated by the infighting. He no longer trusts anyone. Norma, John, Howell, Norman Blackwell, the inner circle excepted, can he completely trust his most senior colleagues? Not really, and he knows it.

The train arrived late. We shared a taxi with Frank Field. Fortunately he knew where we were going. He spent most of the journey leaning across me giving instructions to the driver. Right close up, nostrils flaring, Frank looks *exactly* like Kenneth Williams.

I am writing this on the front bench. We got back from Liverpool at 5.30 p.m. It is now after nine. The Second Reading of the Education Bill is drawing to a close. Rather to my surprise, Lady Olga is telling us she is against caning. We have done her an injustice. In the office, we'd put her down for a lash 'em and thrash 'em woman. (This may, of course, have been wishful thinking on some of my colleagues' parts.) What is incredible, of course, (and what, justifiably, has had the PM hopping with anger), is that the education debate has been hijacked by all this rubbish on corporal punishment. It's not going to be reintroduced, so why discuss it? We can only disappoint the diehards out there who want it, while reinforcing the view of everyone else that most Tories are heartless brutes.

THURSDAY 14 NOVEMBER 1996

Breakfast with Tim Rice at Claridge's. He is late, but we don't mind because when he arrives he readily agrees to be our 'Luvvies for John Major' front man. I wanted Charles Lewington[609] to hear it from his own lips. We're drawing up a long list of potential celeb supporters and Tim is going to top and tail letters to them. I told him his peerage is now in the post. (I assume he's too sensible to believe me.)

Back at the Palace of Varieties it's all gone wrong again and I think it's probably worse than it's ever been. The caning nonsense is just a side-show. The main event this week is the Firearms Bill. The shooting lobby (step forward Prince Philip) think we're going too far (it's gesture politics, won't change a thing), Mellor and co. want a total ban and

609 Director of Communications at Conservative Central Office.

are going to back Labour because we're not going far enough. The boys want a free vote. That would get us off the hook, but the PM won't have it. This is *government* policy. It must be backed by a three-line whip.

And coming up on the radar screen: more Euro trouble, major Euro trouble. The PM's standing by with a confidence motion. 'Do turkeys vote for Christmas?' he asks plaintively. 'Some of our colleagues have got to decide if they want me or Mr Blair.' The truth is a great swathe of his colleagues have decided it's going to be Mr Blair come what may.

....

THURSDAY 21 NOVEMBER 1996

....

It's a shambles. We are six months away from a general election at most and the Prime Minister is being barracked by his own backbenchers. In the Tea Room he's being openly derided. The poor man, of course, is caught between a rock and a hard place. What the troops want is a debate on the floor of the House on the latest range of EU documents relating to EMU. They want the debate before ECOFIN.[610] And 'they' is everyone from Hugh Dykes to Bill Cash! But the PM won't have it, both because the Chancellor says it isn't necessary, and because it could prove impossible to avoid a division on it and we might lose the vote – and why go to the country as a broken-backed government in the aftermath of a lost vote in the Commons if there's a chance of struggling on till the Spring and finding calmer waters?

At PMQs the PM resisted demands for a debate – to open cries of 'Shame!', 'This is a constitutional outrage!' etc. He then made the mistake of saying that the European reports on the single currency had been subject to 'detailed scrutiny' in the Standing Committee. This was met with hoots of derision. The scrutiny at European Standing Committee B yesterday was cursory at best – and in any event Whitto[611] voted with the other side so it's not clear whether the documents have been formally 'taken note of' or not. Heathcoat-Amory got up and flatly contradicted the PM. When the poor man persisted, there were shouts of 'No! No! You're wrong!' At 3.30 p.m. the PM stomped off, looking ashen, and angry, leaving Tony Newton to pick up the pieces. For the forty minutes of Business Questions the demands rained down on him. Cartiss, Marlow, Wilkinson, Heathcoat-Amory, but not just the usual suspects. John Townend: 'May I *implore* my RHF to think again?' Even Sir John Stanley (who I don't think I've ever

---

610 The meeting of EU Economic and Finance Ministers scheduled for early December.

611 John Whittingdale, MP for Colchester South & Maldon 1992–7, Maldon & Chelsmford East since 1997; Political Secretary to Margaret Thatcher as Prime Minister 1988–90.

heard speak before) threw in his two cents' worth from a great height. I sat right next to Tony. (I'm afraid I moved myself into the doughnut. If your constituents see you sitting there amazingly they think you're *doing* something.) His hands were shaking violently throughout. He voice trembled too, but his content was measured, courteous. He did his best, he held the line. Every time he sat down, he muttered, 'Was that all right?' 'It's fine,' I said, 'It's the wicket that's impossible.'

MONDAY 25 NOVEMBER 1996

Not that we are describing it quite like this, but we have capitulated. The Chancellor is making a statement at 3.30 p.m. and we're going to find time for a debate after all. (This is how we play it: five days of digging-in, mayhem and bloodshed all around, followed by total cave-in. Evidently we have a death-wish.)

LATER

Ken was brilliant. He is extraordinary. He defused all the hostility. He even had Lamont on his feet saying he'd got it right! He was conciliatory, he was good-humoured, he was so reasonable. It's all been a misunderstanding. The press are guilty: a lot of 'farcical misrepresentation'. Of course, there's to be a full debate. Of course, we must have proper scrutiny. There will be no binding decisions made at ECOFIN on 2 December. That's guaranteed, copper-bottomed. Make no mistake, the government isn't frightened of debate. The government welcomes debate, hungers for it. And, remember, everything is subject to parliamentary approval anyway. The man is a master.

WEDNESDAY 27 NOVEMBER 1996

I've taken to turning up for Transport prayers ten minutes ahead of time in order to have a while *à deux* with the Secretary of State [Sir George Young]. I like him, but I don't really know him. For example, this morning we agreed that Ken is brilliant, that he rescued the fat from the fire on Monday, that his Budget performance yesterday was a model of bonhomie and shrewd politics, but we *didn't* then go on to discuss what happens after we've lost the election. With colleagues one doesn't know that well one still goes through the charade of pretending victory is possible.

Transport prayers are oddly formal. At nine we troop into a conference room. The

Permanent Secretary and heads of department – about a dozen in all – line up on one side of the table, and we sit facing them on the other. George then goes down the line, inviting news and views from each area – rail, shipping, road, air, the press office etc. It's a curious ritual, but I suppose it keeps everyone roughly up to speed. (Ken or Stephen would regard it as a complete waste of time.) Sometimes, but not always, the ministers then troop back to George's room for a coffee and chat. The chat is fairly stilted. John Watts[612] is pretty leaden. Giles Goschen[613] looks like an elongated version of Jiminy Cricket and can be quite fun, but somehow *fun* is out of place at the Department of Transport. (At the DoE when Robin Ferrers returned to prayers after he'd been off with his bad leg, at 9.00 a.m. Gummer arrived with a tray of glasses and a bottle of chilled champagne. That's the way to do it.) At Transport, the issue of the hour is the proposed ministerial photocall: to celebrate the sixtieth anniversary of the zebra crossing (or some-such) the four ministers will be pictured crossing Abbey Road (or equivalent) in the manner of the Beatles. Given their unusual figures, two bean poles and a brace of Bunters, I urge caution. But I think they want to do it.

TUESDAY 3 DECEMBER 1996

No votes last night (Budget debates continuing) so M and I went with the Willetts to *Le Bonheur* at the Curzon. It was quaint and lovely. We then had supper at L'Odeon, which wasn't quite so jolly, only because poor David is fixated with the outcome of the hearings on the wretched memorandum and not optimistic. While we were reflecting on David's future, the Conservatives of Kensington & Chelsea were dissecting Nick Scott's past. In the end, despite our good efforts (possibly because of them – Associations hate attempted interference from on high) he lost the vote: 509 to 439. He had pleaded with them, paraded his track record, told them he'd as good as given up the bottle, but to no avail. It turned out that what really turned them against the poor man wasn't his being found kissing the pavement in Bournemouth, it was the fact that the day before he failed to turn up at his own activists' conference reception … So the great white hope, who thirty years ago was featured in *Time* as 'the man most likely to', ends up in the gutter and without a seat. Drink is a demon. The other day coming down the steps towards the members' cloakroom, we found one of our colleagues spreadeagled on the stone floor. And Iain Mills is now in such a bad way that when votes are coming up we provide him with a minder to help him stagger into the right lobby.

---

612 Minister of State at Transport 1994–7.

613 4th Viscount Goschen PUSS at Transport 1994–7.

There's trouble looming on every front. When Labour wins the Barnsley by-election next week, we lose our majority. We may lose it before, of course, because Gorst is playing up again. The Chief is right: 'What justice is there, when decent men like Nick Scott go down and shits like Gorst can hold the government to ransom?'

We're bracing ourselves for a major rebellion tomorrow on the Firearms Bill. There could be fifty or more who defy the whip[614] – so many there's nowt we can do, except accept it, pretend it hasn't happened and move on. Since we'll secure the business with opposition support, we're hoping no one will notice.

....

THURSDAY 5 DECEMBER 1996

....

If it weren't so heart-breaking, it would be very funny. We are disintegrating. We are in a massive hold and we can't stop digging! Today's Gallup poll puts Labour on 59 per cent and us on 22. We're heading for wipe-out – and we seem DETERMINED to make it worse.

Yesterday Jon Sopel [BBC journalist] had lunch with Ken – and got the impression from the Chancellor that the Chancellor believes 'someone close to the Prime Minister' is trying to modify the agreed line on EMU. Said Ken (of course, he didn't *say* it, but he could have implied it) if there's any shift on our 'wait and see' policy on EMU, then I'm off and a good chunk of the government will be coming with me. Sopel ran the story – and all hell has broken loose. I *hope* I am not the cause of this mayhem. I *have* said to Ken that Finkelstein is now thinking maybe we should rule ourselves out of the first wave and is sharing his more sceptical thoughts with No. 10 – but Ken won't be taking what I've said as his sole source of intelligence, will he? Danny seems amused. Ken has said to Mawhinney, 'Tell your kids to get their scooters off my lawn.' Danny is rather flattered and excited.

Anyway, denials have been rushed out on all sides. 'No one is threatening to resign. The PM and the Chancellor are in perfect harmony.' Meanwhile, up in Committee Room 10, the 1922 Committee have been gathering – and shouting the odds. 'Clarke must go!' 'Clarke must stay!' 'We can't go into a general election like this.' I was the whip on duty, so I sat on the platform, between Sir Marcus and Dame Jill (combined age 140), gazing out at the feuding fray, thinking this is totally *bizarre*. The most successful political party in the history of democracy is committing hara-kiri and here I am with a ringside seat.

Being 'whip on duty' at the 1922 is oddly daunting. There's really nothing it: your only job is to read out the next week's business and the proposed whipping for it and be

---

614 In the event, it was sixty-three. The rebels wanted improved compensation for those affected by the proposed legislation banning handguns. Sir Jerry Wiggin, one of the leaders of the revolt, said, 'I am deeply ashamed of my government.'

ready to answer questions on it. It's made to seem daunting by virtue of having the rest of the Whips' Office sitting in judgement at the far end of the room and because, prior to the Committee meeting, there's a rehearsal in the Chief's office. It's the rehearsal that's alarming. Shana has typed out the script and you read it out loud to a trio comprising the Chief, the Deputy and Murdo – who then fire sample questions at you. The sample questions are invariably more taxing than the real ones. At the meeting itself, the rule is say as little as possible and when some tosspot from the floor makes an outrageous demand, give the traditional 'you might say that, I couldn't possibly comment' look and promise to convey the message to the Chief Whip.

WEDNESDAY 11 DECEMBER 1996

David Willetts has resigned. The view is that he had no alternative because the criticism in the Standards and Privileges Committee report is harsher than expected. They accuse him of 'dissembling' and say that in future they propose to 'take evidence on oath' – suggesting, without stating, that had David been on oath he'd have answered their charges other than he did. It's unfair – actually, it's ridiculous: a career blighted for no good reason – but in the office the feeling is that it went more badly wrong for David than it need have done for two reasons: a) David handled his defence badly. He should have played the apologetic innocent, not tried to justify himself. The Trollope line: 'A graceful apology etc.' That non-sense of saying that 'wants our advice' means 'lacks our advice' because David was using the verb in the eighteenth-century way was *disastrous*. (I don't think it was David's idea. I think it was a ruse dreamt up by one of the civil servants.) b) He was unlucky in having Quentin Davies on the committee. QD is a prim, prissy, priggish *disappointed* man, clever but flawed, who, by siding with Labour, was able to successfully shaft his cleverer more successful colleague – and feel good/holier-than-thou about it at the same time.

The Chief's view is the office view. This is monstrously unfair. Davies is a shit. David is a good man and he will be back in the fold sooner rather than later. The PM has told him as much 'in terms'.

I haven't spoken to David yet. He's gone home. He will be devastated and will see this as more terminal than it is. His only weakness as a person (and I love him) is that he takes himself and his career *so* seriously. That, of course, is also the secret of his success. I have written him a long note, not saying the above, but saying (because it's true) that he has 'done the decent thing' and he will be back at the centre almost instantly – and for the long term – because he is, quite simply, indispensable. (This is true and, in many ways, alarming. We do not have that many thinking people actively engaged in the practice of Conservative politics. That's how Danny has managed to come from nowhere – a top-floor office at the Social Market Foundation – to the heart of government inside a year. He has walked right into Downing Street – and been welcomed with open arms – not just because he is so good (and has the knack of making bright ideas accessible to politicians), but also because there was no one else there. You would have thought that the Prime Minister of the United Kingdom would be surrounded by the brightest and best minds in the land. He isn't. There is an intellectual vacuum at the heart of government – so we have to be thankful there are the likes of David and Danny on hand, ready, willing and able to fill it. And I have to be thankful that these chaps are my chums.

LATER

Fall-out from David's resignation:

1. A new policy on whips' notes. David only ended up in this mess because his note to the Chief was kept on file. There seems to be a dispute as to who has legitimate claim on messages sent to the Chief Whip. Are they his personal property to be kept by him and disposed of as he sees fit? Or are they, as whips are all government ministers, government property, to be treated accordingly? Some blame R. Ryder for not destroying the evidence… The question is: what to do in the future? The Chief's conclusion is: keep writing the notes – he needs the information, so does the PM. But, sleep easy, boys, from now on the notes will be shredded on a regular basis.

2. Michael Bates becomes the new Paymaster-General (he has been sulky since the summer: now he is a *very* happy bunny) and I move from the Lower Office to the Upper Office and become a Lord Commissioner of Her Majesty's Treasury[615] and – better still – assume the mantle of the whip responsible for the First Secretary (aka Deputy Prime Minister), for the Chancellor of the Duchy of Lancaster, and for HM Treasury. (And, yes, I have noticed. My advancement is due entirely to someone else's misfortune. And the someone else is a proper friend at that.)

MONDAY 16 DECEMBER 1996

10.40 p.m.: We have survived the Fisheries vote. This is the one we lost last year and, had the UUs been against us, feared we might lose again. We summoned the lame and the halt (I was on the ambulance run), we brought ministers back from hither and yon

---

615 Constitutionally, the Treasury is governed by a Board of seven Lords Commissioners. The First Lord is the Prime Minister, the Second Lord is the Chancellor of the Exchequer and the remaining five are government whips.

(Brussels and Belfast mainly), the UUs were persuaded to abstain, likewise the poison-ous Gorst, and it turned out fine: we coasted home with a majority of eleven. The PM is delighted. And relieved.

The evening began with the Christmas party at No. 12. It felt busier, fuller, jollier, more relaxed than last year. (Or is it just that I am more at ease in the office?) There was much embracing of the Willetts. David is going to be given a 'thinking' role at Central Office. He'd like to be chairman of the Research Department, and if Danny is happy (and he is), why not?

Heseltine stood by the doors gazing imperiously across the room. I told him that I'm now the whip designated to his domain. He glanced down at me briefly, uncompre-hending, nodded a wintry smile and immediately resumed his lofty survey of the sea of quaffing, sluicing heads. Ann was rather more giving. I embraced her and introduced her to Michèle. Ann managed a good forty-five seconds of tinkly charm before moving on. (M said to me later, 'Don't bother, *really* don't bother. They're not interested in you, and they're *certainly* not interested in me.')

Contrasting Heseltine's common touch with Major's is fascinating. The PM arrived and the first person he saw was Sarah Box.[616] He clapped his hands with genuine delight. She giggled and was thrilled. He took her hands in his, they spun round together – I thought for a moment, he was going to pick her up and swing her round by the arms. He kissed her. It was warm, it was affectionate, there was a *frisson* on either side. It was real. The PM is attractive to women. The PM is attractive in a way Heseltine (superfi-cially more handsome, a self-styled hero) could never be.

Howell [James], like a slightly camp royal equerry, kept a few paces behind the boss. I said to him, 'I think we should stop saying our policy on EMU is "wait and see". It sounds weak, indecisive, as if we don't know where we're going. Why don't we replace "wait and see" with "negotiate and decide"?'

'Excellent!' He called the PM back. 'Have you heard Gyles's idea?' The PM, beaming his nice beam, listened, laughed, agreed and moved on – in search (very sensibly) of something younger and prettier.

TUESDAY 17 DECEMBER 1996

It seems we over-egged the pudding. To assist us in securing last night's majority Derek paired three of our people with three Labour people *and* with three Liberals. All hell is breaking out. We're being accused of cheating, double-dealing, 'subverting the democratic

616 The Chief Whip's assistant secretary, a civil servant, not a political appointee.

process'. We can't very well deny it, but, within the office and outside it, we're saying nothing. Discussion is *verboten*. It seems this is a ploy we may have tried before. When silencing us, the Deputy said, 'We've had next to no majority for months. How do you think we've done it? Just be grateful.'

The scam was discovered only because last night's majority was surprisingly handsome under the circumstances and Archie Kirkwood (Liberal whip) and George Mudie (Labour's pairing whip) decided to double-check names and numbers. If we hadn't done the double-dealing and the UUs had voted against us (as they might well have done) we'd have lost by one vote. Now, of course, Dewar has climbed onto his Scottish Presbyterian high horse and declared that all pairing, all cooperation, all communication via the 'usual channels' is off.

I am on my way to the Treasury: Finance Bill Planning Meeting in the Financial Secretary's office. It seems we will have no majority on the committee. I think it's all going to be rather fun.

WEDNESDAY 18 DECEMBER 1996

There's a wonderfully pompous first leader in *The Times*: 'WHIPPED SENSELESS – A stupid piece of double-dealing does yet more damage.' The Chief will not like this. He does not like us to get press of any kind – never mind press like this. The Tea Room is equally unimpressed. As is Michèle.

'Did you know this was going on?'

'No.'

'Were you a party to this?'

'No.'

'Would you have been?'

'Er—'

'It's utterly wrong, utterly indefensible, isn't it?'

'Er—'

Breakfast at the Ritz. Stephen, Danny, John K[ingman], Tim [Rycroft]. I have poached egg, bacon, mushrooms. My one complaint here is that the tea gets cold. It is still the prettiest dining room in London. And it is good to be a Lord Commissioner of the Treasury breakfasting with the Secretary of State for Health and the director of the Conservative Research Department and talking of the great figures of our time as if we knew them – because we do know them! We raise our glasses of freshly squeezed orange juice to the excitements that lie ahead. Within the year Stephen sees himself as Leader of the Party – and why not? Of course, as I don't remind him (because I don't need to), he is not alone. Heseltine, Clarke, Howard, Portillo, Rifkind, Forsyth, even Master Hague and Mrs Shepard are no doubt all harbouring the same fantasy – and, for all we know, hosting comparable breakfasts in other parts of town.

CHAPTER VIII

1997

Where will it all end?

When will it all end?

That's easier. 20 March, 10 April, 1 May are the obvious election dates. And I'm going for 10 April, a) because it won't be quite the last gasp, and b) because we can then avoid the humiliation of the Wirral South by-election. At Barry [Porter]'s funeral the activists were confident of victory, but even with a majority of 8,000 I'd have thought there's no hope. There's certainly no hope for me in Chester. I have mixed feelings about it. Michèle has none.

We're snowed in here [in Suffolk, staying with Simon Cadell's widow, Beckie, and their two sons] so we can't go back to London as planned. We're sitting by the fire drinking Simon's special peach and champagne cocktail instead. I'm reading Richard E. Grant's film diaries (my Christmas present from M – 'fucking fantastic – yeeeesssss!' Never mind the language, feel the verve) and the new novel by Michael Dobbs (cosy and quite comforting: Dobbs does for Westminster skulduggery what Agatha Christie did for the country house murder). Beckie's done just the right lunch to go with the weather (roast chicken, roast potatoes, roast parsnips, glorious gravy, mellowing Burgundy), we've watched *Babe* on video with the boys (it's odd and sentimental, but eventually it works) and we've pondered the mysteries of the New Year's Honours. If an OBE for Joan Collins, why a CBE for Ned Sherrin? Are these the fruits of feasting with panthers? Still no knighthood for Donald Sinden. Virginia is on side, Murdo is on side, the PM is supportive. I took it up with him again before Christmas.

I said, 'When everyone thinks it's right and richly deserved and wants it to happen and it doesn't, it's so frustrating.'

'I know,' he said, 'I've been trying to get a knighthood for Alec Bedser. It isn't easy.' But it can be done. Today Bedser has his K and the PM has a happy start to his year.

THURSDAY 2 JANUARY 1997

Or does he? The lead headline in today's *Telegraph*: 'Dorrell urges Europe rethink'. The PM will not be amused. I call Stephen. He's delighted. Of course. For him to succeed we need support from the centre and the centre-right, and the centre today is Euro-sceptic. This isn't mere positioning. Stephen's view on the EU has changed markedly over the last three years, but the message has only filtered out fitfully. I speak to Tim [Rycroft] who says: 'Well, we agreed before Christmas the time for subtlety was over.'

Back to London. We shared a taxi to Ipswich with a garrulous lady who was on her way to a funeral in York and talked non-stop in the manner of Hyacinth Bucket scripted by Alan Bennett. The icy roads were a nightmare too.

As we got in the phone was ringing. Little Michael Jack,[617] eager-beaver Financial Secretary, was on the line. 'You know today's the day we publish the Finance Bill. I'm supposed to be on the media spreading the good news on the economy and what happens? I'm pulled from every programme and the whole thing is hijacked by the Secretary of State for Health banging on about Europe. It is so bloody frustrating.' He is right to be angry. I call Stephen and give him Michael's number.

FRIDAY 3 JANUARY 1997

Stephen calls. The Prime Minister has been on the line, 'seriously dischuffed'. The poor PM has his New Year 'relaunch' all set up – *Frost on Sunday*, ad campaign on Monday, press conference on Tuesday – and what is today's helpful headline? 'Dorrell sparks Tory feud over leadership'. The PM wants to know what Stephen proposes to do about it. The PM favours a statement from Stephen via PA asserting that Stephen and the government are as one. Stephen prefers a single briefing of one Sunday lobby correspondent along the lines of 'this isn't about the single currency – it's about ambitious change within the EU – it's in line with the government's own White Paper – I've said all this in public before (true) – I didn't time it as a New Year bombshell (also true: Stephen gave the interview early in December) – this isn't about the leadership of the Tory party (ho-ho), it's about the clear difference between us and Labour (and it is that too).'

The PM also wants to know why Stephen hadn't cleared his pronouncements on the future of the European Union with the Foreign Secretary. 'Er … er…' Stephen had at least got clearance from Tony Newton to do yesterday's round of radio and TV interviews.

---

617 MP for Fylde 1987–2010; Financial Secretary to the Treasury 1995–7.

(Tony is chairing EDCP[618] in the absence of the Deputy Prime Minister who is in East Africa bird-watching. The Chancellor of the Exchequer, who is being 'kept in close touch', is in Mexico, also bird-watching.) Unless health is the subject under discussion, the PM does not want or expect to hear Stephen on the airwaves for the foreseeable future.

SUNDAY 5 JANUARY 1997

Today's headline beggars belief: 'TORY MP: MY LOVE FOR GAY TEENAGER'. You can only pity the poor PM! He turns up for his New Year *Frost* interview, armed with his Dorrell answers, ready to lay into Labour, happy to assert that ours is the party of the Family, and what does he find? The *News of the World* – and every other paper – packed with choice extracts from Jerry Hayes' passionate notes to an eighteen-year-old 'Young Conservative and Commons researcher': 'I've just been crying my eyes out. I can't help it. I love you with every fibre of my body.' Yup, it does make you want to weep.

Despite this, the PM does rather well. He usually does. Before Christmas Howell told me that he favoured 'a presidential campaign, distancing the boss from the rest of the rabble' and this, clearly, is what we're going to get. Of course, it won't work – both because EMU is a real issue that isn't going to go away and because the public made up their mind about a year ago and nothing we can do will persuade them to change it now.

Not a bad press for Stephen. Gerald Scarfe's cartoon has him as a vulture perched on the end of the PM's sick-bed.

Last night we had Noel [Davis], Harry [Audley], Joanna [Lumley] and Stevie [Barlow] for supper in the kitchen. Noel was frighteningly wheezy, but as funny as ever. He offered an old Ralph Richardson story he claims he hadn't heard until recently. Sir Ralph, on stage, mid-scene, suddenly staggers towards the footlights. The rest of the cast is alarmed. The audience holds its breath. 'Is there a doctor in the house?' asks Sir Ralph. A voice from the rear of the stalls calls out. Richardson peers out towards the voice and says, 'Terrible play this, eh doctor?'

As my chestnut-I'd-only-just-picked-up I offered Bernard Shaw being set the poser: 'You are in the National Gallery and it catches fire. Which one painting would you try to save?' GBS: 'The one nearest the door.' This prompted Joanna to give us her story of a private dinner at the V&A at which, before dinner is served, the distinguished guests are invited to examine some of the museum's choicest treasures – exquisite boxes of ivory, silver and gold, designs by William Morris, sketches by Leonardo, the Thomas-a-Becket reliquary. At table, Joanna finds herself seated next to John Paul Getty Jr and asks him,

---

618 Ministerial Committee on Economic and Domestic Policy: the Cabinet Committee coordinating policy presentation.

'If the lights had gone out when we'd been looking at all those fabulous treasures, what would you have been tempted to slip into your pocket?'

'I'd take the da Vinci notebooks,' says Getty.

'Why?' asks Jo.

'Oh,' says Getty, 'I could buy the rest.'

WEDNESDAY 8 JANUARY 1997

Went to the Caprice last night with Ros and Mart [Jarvis] and so missed The Great Debate on the monarchy – clearly a collector's item of a fiasco. Poor Trevor![619] Until last night he belonged to that select band who Can Do No Wrong. Robin Day is huffing and puffing with due pomposity: 'The programme consisted of two hours of ignorance, distortion, prejudice, half-truths, crude assertion, bad temper and cheap personal abuse.' The old fart makes it sound quite watchable.

Talk to Danny who reports that the PM did well at his first presidential press conference – except that he didn't say any of the things they'd briefed him to say so that the press are writing it up as a bit of a non-event. Happily, today Kevin Keegan has resigned from Newcastle and Richard Branson is lifting off in his balloon so Blair's New Year launch is nicely sidelined.

Harold Elletson calls. Tony Benn has written to the PM to enquire if it's true that Harold is in the pay of MI6 and, if it is, isn't that 'an office of profit under the Crown' incompatible with his membership of the House? It can't be true – can it? 'TORY MP IS A SPY' – that's all we need!

Talking of all we need, speak to Christine and Neil [Hamilton]. They seem brighter, but still in limbo, waiting, hoping, praying that Gordon Downey [the Parliamentary Commissioner for Standards] will produce a report that lifts the clouds. 'Our life has been ruined, utterly ruined. Until Neil is exonerated we can't start living again.'

THURSDAY 9 JANUARY 1997

Jolly lunch with Laurie Mansfield, who is off to Hollywood tomorrow. Laurie (who is a Major fan and whose agency represents Jim Davidson, Paul Merton, Julian Clary, Hale & Pace etc.) advises strongly against the PM appearing on showbiz-type shows. 'It takes an entertainer to be entertaining on an entertainment programme.' Blair at the Brits or with

---

619   Trevor McDonald, the presenter of the programme.

Des O'Connor was embarrassing – also Blair was tempted (one would be) into elaborating an incident in his childhood to turn it into a full-blown anecdote ('How I became an airline stowaway') only to find it blowing up in his face when his dad emerged from the woodwork to tell us he has no recollection of any of it…

Mihir Bose[620] points out that this is an established British political tradition. F. E. Smith's father went on several holidays to Egypt and F. E. claimed to have travelled with him, regaling audiences with tales of how he sailed through the Med, stayed at Shepherd's Hotel in Cairo, even rode a primitive bicycle from the city to the pyramids – to the wonderment of the Egyptians. However, when John Campbell came to write F. E.'s biography he thoroughly investigated these favourite stories in the F. E. repertoire and found them to be complete fiction. F. E. never left Birkenhead as a boy.

SATURDAY 11 JANUARY 1997

To Chester for the enthronisation (sic) of the new bishop – a contemporary from Oxford. Never mind the police looking younger: when the bishops start to be contemporaries…[621] The ninety-minute service was an odd hotchpotch of familiar and unfamiliar ritual, ancient tradition, ecumenical moments and evangelical flourishes. There was the one customary embarrassment we all dread: making the sign of the peace – assorted Lord Lieutenants, High Sheriffs, Mayors, aldermen, military personnel and the lone MP (the only one without uniform or vestments) turning awkwardly to one another, shaking hands with as few people as possible, resolutely refusing to catch anybody's eye. All the processing is splendid – but absurd. The most moving moment came when the new bishop's wife and three of their children led the prayers and did it with wonderful certainty and simplicity. The bishop ended his sermon with a prayer from Dag Hammarskjold: 'For what has been: thanks. For what is to come: yes!'

At lunch I sat between the Bishop of Blackburn[622] and Lady Temple[623] and thought to myself, 'This is provincial society and I'm part of it. It's quite fun, but I can't take it seriously and it's not what I want.' I learnt something useful from the Bishop of Blackburn (who was very convivial): a Very Reverend is a dean or a provost, a Right Reverend is a bishop, and a Most Reverend is an archbishop.

I'm just in from the King's School Old Scholars' annual dinner at which I was seated

620 Journalist.

621 In fact, Peter Forster, born in 1950, is two years younger than GB

622 Alan Chesters, Bishop of Blackburn 1989–2003.

623 Widow of the former MP for the City of Chester, Sir Jack Temple.

next to the dean (the Very Reverend). We drank a *great deal* of port and pretended to be a couple of minor characters from Trollope. He volunteered to bring me home. I assumed he'd have a driver, but no. He drove me himself, very slowly, very steadily, right in the centre on the road. He is a good thing.

MONDAY 13 JANUARY 1997

Back to school. The atmosphere in the Tea Room is surprisingly buoyant. Jerry Hayes does well by being evidently present, self-deprecating and yet his curly-headed self.

'You're looking fit, Jerry.'

'I've been on the *News of the World* diet. It's a *very* fast way to lose weight.'

Last night we had the Wednesday Club to dinner. Willetts, Michael Trend (deputy chairman of the party), Charles Hendry (vice-chairman), Edward Garnier (PPS to the Attorney-General), David Lidington (PPS to the Home Secretary), David Faber (Stephen's PPS), plus wives, or, in Faber's case, plus girlfriend. In the early hours of this morning, she was my worry: the girlfriend – tall, slim, and, yes, she was called Sophie and worked for *Vogue*. Was it a dangerous mistake to play indiscreet games with an outsider in our midst? Were we going to be set up like the hapless Richard Spring? But David wouldn't have brought her if he didn't trust her, would he? And we weren't that indiscreet – except we went round the table collecting predictions of the election result and only David and Sarah [Willetts] thought we could still win. And if we lose, who will be leader this time next year? It was a close-run thing: Dorrell one ahead of Howard with Portillo bringing up the rear. Michael Trend and his wife were joint but emphatic voices declaring that William Hague would slip through in the final round. 'He's the Cabinet minister constituency associations most frequently ask for.'

TUESDAY 14 JANUARY 1997

Breakfast with Stephen. He arrived late and (unusual for him) grouchy. He'd been on the *Today* programme with prissy Chris Smith, and perhaps Chris got the better of him? He missed Danny who came and went and left us with the message: 'We need Peter Lilley. If we could secure Lilley, we'd have it sewn up. He knows he'll never be the king, but he can be the kingmaker.'

Today, for the first time in three years I went back to the Treasury for prayers. When I first went, in 1993, when Norman [Lamont] was Chancellor (and Hague was his PPS and I was Stephen's) I didn't know what prayers involved or meant. Norman was quite formal in the way he ran the meeting: the ministers (in armchairs) were invited to contribute in the correct pecking order while the PPSs sat behind (in upright chairs) and had to signal if they wanted to throw in their two cents' worth. It's all very different now … There's a giddy atmosphere of *carnivale*. We all sit round the Chancellor's table: there's no pecking order: no agenda: and a general free-for-all ensues in which people speak over one another and the loudest voices seem to be those of the PPSs – notably Peter Butler[624] (who has the sort of suspect moustache that goes with yellow string-backed driving gloves) and madcap Michael Fabricant (he of the straw-coloured wig, complete with pink highlights). The Chancellor looks on, benign but bleary-eyed.

At 3.30 the Treasury team is on the front bench to support William [Waldegrave, Chief Secretary] as he moves the Second Reading of the Finance Bill. Listening to William isn't easy because I'm distracted by the fact that the Chancellor keeps falling asleep. Every time Ken nods off too obviously I give him a gentle prod and attempt a little small talk. 'Normally jetlag doesn't get to me like this. It's very odd.'

WEDNESDAY 15 JANUARY 1997

I had my first sighting of the Deputy Prime Minister's celebrated office today. 'It isn't a tennis court, is it?' said Lady Strathnaver[625] proudly, 'It's a football pitch!' Actually, it isn't that large. What are big are the sofas – big and ridiculous. It's impossible to sit on them: either you perch right on the edge or you sit back and disappear. (We can assume this is where John Gummer has got to – he's slipped down the back.)

Sandwich lunch with Roger Freeman, Chancellor of the Duchy, minister responsible for the civil service, the Citizen's Charter and anything else the PM lands on his desk (i.e. mopping up after Hoggie on BSE). Roger's room is on the same floor as the DPM's, much, much smaller, but with wonderful views – one way over Horseguards Parade, the other over the Downing Street garden.

'I can see into the Prime Minister's bedroom.' Roger presses his nose to the window. He gives a little wave. 'Hello John!'

I've never known Roger as unbuttoned as this. Customarily he's a caricature of a minister from a '50s Ealing comedy, all pinstripes, Brylcream and punctilious correctness. But today he's Mr Mischief. With a twinkle he produces the scorecard on which he has marked the ministerial teams who are best and worst at getting the government's message across. The Treasury team score particularly poorly…

624 MP for Milton Keynes North East 1992–7; PPS to the Chancellor 1995–7.

625 Eileen Strathnaver, Michael Heseltine's Special Adviser.

One of Roger's jobs is to monitor the cost-effectiveness of government PR. He reveals that the press conference to unveil the age of electronic government – No. 10 on the Internet! – cost £250,000 and resulted in just one small paragraph in the *Evening Standard*. We laugh that we may not weep.

We laugh too when Michael McManus (formerly David Hunt's special adviser and now 'Head of Edward Heath's Private Office' and, intriguingly, apparently a regular at these lunches) tells us that Ted is contemplating suing the odious James Goldsmith over the slur that Heath 'lied to the people' when persuading the nation to sign up to the Common Market. We agree that it's terribly unfair on poor old Ted, but when it comes to litigation, 'Far better not.' Ted is eighty but determined to stand again at the election. 'Why does his Association let him get away with it?' 'Because they're *terrified* of him.'

A typical Freeman touch (unique in Whitehall, I'd say): as we leave, his special adviser collects £3 from each of us to pay for the refreshments.

Dinner (at his suggestion) with Bowen Wells in the Churchill Room. He volunteers for the Dorrell campaign. Heseltine's over the hill, Clarke won't make it, so what else have the centre ground got? Bowen supported Hezza in 1990 and has names to offer. Paddy Ashdown is at the next table being severely reprimanded by his wife for leaving his unwashed shirts all over the house.

Willetts catches me in the division lobby. While we're chatting ('I haven't been approached to join any of the campaigns yet and I wouldn't want to at this stage') Quentin Davies sidles up awkwardly. 'David, I just wanted to say that your speech yesterday provided the best argument I've heard against the windfall tax. It was quite excellent.' Brow moist, face red, olive branch extended, the assassin withdrew. David muttered, 'Thank you, Quentin.'

THURSDAY 16 JANUARY 1997

Breakfast at the Ritz. David Mellor is at the adjacent table negotiating a fat fee to chair some international conference. The first time I lunched here (more than thirty years ago) I remember Reginald Maudling[626] was seated at the selfsame table – fast asleep. *Plus ça change.*

The Chancellor was wide awake at lunch today. He was brilliant on the *Today* programme this morning – genial, sharp, on top of his brief, and they managed EIGHT WHOLE MINUTES without touching on Europe once!

Before Ken arrived, William [Waldegrave] was attempting to impose some order on

---

626 1917–79; MP for Barnet 1950–79; Chancellor of the Exchequer 1962–4; Home Secretary 1970–72.

the meeting. Should we sacrifice our proposed hike in airport duty to keep the Ulster Unionists on side? We don't come up with an answer because the moment Ken appears the usual brouhaha breaks out. William shakes his head, the Chancellor winks at me, and the rest of the team all talk at once. They want to agree lines to take at Treasury questions. 'We're going to say we've created two jobs a minute, aren't we?' 'Since when?' 'Since last year.' 'No, since '92.' 'Is that two jobs for every minute? Or for every working minute?' 'Are we using the European forty-eight hour week?' 'I think it's better to say 10,000 jobs a week.' 'What's our line on Halewood?' 'Isn't it 15,000 jobs a week anyway?' Calculators are produced, banter is exchanged, but a definitive answer comes there none.

We've found Iain Mills dead in his flat, surrounded by bottles. We're now a minority government. Suddenly 20 March looks more likely.

FRIDAY 17 JANUARY 1997

Watched *Dispatches* on Channel 4 last night: a hatchet job that rehashes all the worst slurs about Neil – the trips to the Paris Ritz, which he admits, and the brown envelopes stuffed with used notes, which he strenuously denies. Shots of Neil and Christine are intercut with shots of money being counted and champagne being poured. It's TV crucifixion and what's alarming is this: I know and like Neil and if he says he never took the money I'm ready to believe him – and yet, as the slanders are repeated and repeated, even their best friends begin to wonder...

MONDAY 20 JANUARY 1997

Christine has just been on the line, inarticulate with sobbing. 'We don't know what to do. They're killing us. We're alive, but only just. They keep on repeating these lies and what can we do? We've been found guilty without a trial. They've ruined us. I don't know how we can go on.'

In the division lobby we make sympathetic noises at Angela Knight whose ex-husband has been assisted by Max Clifford[627] to vilify Angela in the *Daily Mail*. Waldegrave comes up with a comforting arm and a gentle joke: 'The last time I said to a colleague "Don't let the buggers get you down" I was talking to Jerry Hayes...' Poor Angela looks wan and whispers, 'I don't find I can take it very easily.'

627 Publicist whose client list had included Antonia de Sancha (David Mellor's friend) and Paul Stone (Jerry Hayes' admirer). In 2014 Clifford was found guilty on a series of charges of indecent assault and imprisoned.

At 6.00 p.m. in the Chancellor's room in the House the red wine flows and blue smoke fills the air. Senior backbenchers have come bearing advice. Nigel Forman, eyes gently popping, leans forward: 'We're on the defensive, Ken. We talk about the Labour government as a fact: we use the future tense, not the conditional. We need to reintroduce the subjunctive – and we need two or three big speeches, Ken, from you and the PM, on the key issues: the economy, education, law and order. We want to hear from you on law and order. Michael Howard may go down well with the constituency associations, but he's a mixed blessing with a wider audience.'

Robert Atkins proposes – apparently in all seriousness – an immediate referendum on Europe, not just EMU, but the EU itself, in or out. The Chancellor is unconvinced: 'If we keep arguing about Europe it just shows up our divisions. We no longer look like a natural party of government and that's Blair's opportunity: to offer Tory measures with new faces. If we go all anti-European we'll go glug-glug down the plughole.'

While we're quaffing and sluicing with the Chancellor, the Deputy Prime Minister is meeting the 92 Group. He tells them the European issue is settled and nothing will be gained by reopening it. They beg to differ. Later, Nicholas Winterton, red face glistening with excitement, tells me proudly how he led the assault on Hezza: 'Michael, I believe the PM would like to rule out EMU for the whole of the next parliament, but he's being held back by two or three Cabinet colleagues. Michael, just as we toed the line when we were in a minority, isn't it right that the new minority accept what the majority now want?' Nick was clearly delighted with his self-styled bravura performance, but Heseltine 'put the shutters down – he wasn't even listening.'

Sitting next to young Raymond Robertson on the front bench we play the leadership game and he offers a novel scenario: 'Portillo knows he can't make it this time, so he does a deal with Heseltine. Hezza as leader, Portillo as deputy.' Sounds a bit unlikely to me.

Martin Redmond[628] has died, so we're back to level-pegging. Even so, there's a vote tonight that we expect to win comfortably, but we scrape home with a margin of one. In the Whips' Office nerves are a little frayed.

TUESDAY 21 JANUARY 1997

In Washington, Bill Clinton has been inaugurated for a second term. At Westminster, Gordon Brown has promised a public spending freeze, no income tax increases and no extension of VAT. In Kensington & Chelsea, Alan Clark has reached the shortlist. We live in an age of miracles.

---

628   1937–97; Labour MP for Don Valley 1983–1997.

At Treasury prayers the Chancellor confesses that excessive indulgence with his PPS last night has left him feeling a little fragile – and no doubt lunch in half an hour with his brother-in-law will leave him feeling worse. Ken closes his eyes and the Chief Secretary looks pained as three or four simultaneous discussions ensue. Later in the day I remark to Ken that prayers appears to have changed since I was last at the Treasury: 'Everyone seems to speak together and all at once these days.'

'Oh yes,' chortles Ken. 'That's deliberate. It saves so much time.'

Today is our first real parliamentary test of the New Year. Each year the opposition has around eighteen 'opposition days' when they can choose the subject for debate. Today they've gone for the NHS. If we win or draw we survive and live to fight another day. If we lose, Labour have promised a confidence vote – which we'd probably win, but in doing so we'd look beleaguered and reinforce the impression of a government 'clinging to office'. It's going to be tight. The basic arithmetic looks like this:

There are 651 MPs. Four don't vote (the Speaker and her three deputies). Three are dead. And this is the balance:

Conservatives – 322

Labour – 271

Liberal Democrats – 26

Scottish Nationalists – 4

Plaid Cymru – 4 Ulster Unionists – 9

Democratic Unionists – 3

SDLP – 4

United Kingdom Unionist – 1

opposition parties total – 322

If all of the opposition vote against us and any of our troops fail to show, we're in trouble.

LATER

We're in trouble. Julian Critchley (self-indulgent *flâneur* of this parish) maintains he's too ill to turn up, but we're bringing in the rest of our sick and we're praying that some of the UUs will abstain. (They don't want an election yet, surely?)

At 9.30 p.m. I meet up with a desiccated hamster from the ranks of the Labour whips[629] and together we set off on our rounds. We have two walking wounded to check and two lying in ambulances in New Palace Yard. (Sheila Gunn – formerly of

---

629   Clive Betts, Labour MP for Sheffield Attercliffe 1992–2010, Sheffield South East since 2010.

Steve Norris and *The Times*, now a friendly spin nurse at Central Office – rather hoped we could sneak the ambulances through the House of Lords entrance and avoid the cameras at our end of the building, but this isn't on because the archways aren't high and wide enough.) Griffiths[630] and Grylls[631] look quite perky. Tom Arnold appears shrunken and sad. Goodson-Wickes[632] is distinctly woozy – he had a general anaesthetic only a few hours ago. Having agreed with Betts that they're alive (and that the system is barbaric and absurd) we go back up for the vote itself. There's tension in the air. The Chief mutters, 'Lose this and it's big potatoes.'

We win – by a margin of five. Four Labour members are missing, three UUs abstain and, bar Critchley, every living Tory turns up. Perhaps we can get to 1 May after all?

Before the vote the Marginals Club entertains the Foreign Secretary in Dining Room D. We swop stories about our appalling opponents. Someone mentions that his Labour PPC [prospective parliamentary candidate] (chosen in a women-only shortlist, natch) is rumoured to be a witch and he's wondering how best to give the rumour wider currency. This prompts William Powell[633] to tell the story of Melford Stevenson (later Mr Justice Melford Stevenson) standing against Tom Driberg[634] just after the war. Driberg, of course, was a notoriously promiscuous homosexual. At a public meeting at the start of the campaign, Melford-Stevenson declared, 'I have heard the terrible rumours that are circulating about my opponent, Mr Driberg. I want to deny these scandalous and scurrilous rumours here and now. There is no truth in them whatsoever. Indeed I say that with confidence as I was at the Old Bailey on the very day Mr Driberg was found Not Guilty.'

Malcolm [Rifkind], with a beady twinkle in his eye, offered an engaging pep talk and encouragement from Scotland. Apparently we're up to 19 per cent in the polls. Sounds pretty dire to me, but Malcolm says that's a point ahead of where we were at the start of the '92 campaign. The discussion – inevitably – centres on Europe. In vain, Malcolm urges the company to toe the government line in their election addresses.

They won't.

After the vote I make my way up to Stephen's room at the far end of the ministerial corridor. As so often at the start of one of our conspiratorial chats, we agree that the best option – by far – is for the Conservatives to win the election under John Major. We do this both because it is self-evidently true and to salve our consciences. We then

---

630 1928–2013; Peter Griffiths, MP for Smethwick 1964–6, Portsmouth North 1979–97.

631 1934–2001; Michael Grylls, MP for Chertsey 1970–74, Surrey North West 1974–97.

632 Charles Goodson-Wickes, MP for Wimbledon 1987–97.

633 MP for Corby 1983–97.

634 1905–1976; Independent MP for Maldon 1942–5, Labour MP for Maldon 1945–55, Barking 1959–74; later Baron Bradwell.

review the prospects. Who'll enter the ring? From left to right: Clarke, Heseltine, Lang, Rifkind, Hague, Howard, Portillo, Redwood. If he's still around, Forsyth. And what about Gillian? It's absurd to think it, but people do think the absurd. Stephen says, 'Don't discount Major. He could stand.' But would he want to?

Even though we know he'll prove unelectable, Clarke has to be the centre's front-runner by a mile. I tell Stephen the Chancellor is entertaining our candidates in winnable seats at No. 11. 'That's a bit blatant isn't it?' 'It's legitimate – the economy will be central to the campaign. You need to see them to talk about health.'

WEDNESDAY 22 JANUARY 1997

The Committee Stage of the Finance Bill. We have two days on the floor of the House, then we go upstairs to a committee room. After protracted negotiations with Labour, we have agreed a loose timetable in return for parity on the committee – seventeen of them, seventeen of us.

Today we've agreed to have a possible division at around 7.00 p.m. and a definite one at 10.00 p.m. This seems sensible because it means people can go out to dinner between votes. In fact, while it may convenience the diners, it makes a nonsense of the legislative process. To achieve the agreed timetable the Financial Secretary has to reply to one full debate in under forty seconds and then be ready to expatiate on another (more minor) subject for anything up to three hours!

There has to be a better way.

I sit on the bench all evening marvelling at my colleagues' capacity for blather. Generously three of them have volunteered to talk and talk and talk to ensure that the business doesn't collapse and we're not forced into a vote at an unexpected and vulnerable moment.

At regular intervals my infernal pager throbs with playful messages from fellows in the Whips' Office: IS EVERYTHING UNDER CONTROL? HOW LONG IS THIS OLD FOOL GOING ON FOR? ARE WE BEING AMBUSHED? (The pager is helping make the game ever more unreal. There's a story going round that ITN paged Gordon Brown *at the despatch box* because they missed his sound bite first time round – or he fluffed it – and they needed him to say it all over again.)

The bastards don't force a vote at seven after all, but because they might have done they've achieved their object: inconveniencing us. The Foreign Secretary, who I last saw here late last night, has just come in to report that he's back.

'Where have you been?' I asked.

'Madrid. It went well.'

THURSDAY 23 JANUARY 1997

Cabinet meets to discuss the Chancellor's paper on EMU.

At one o'clock at the Treasury we gather round the television to watch Ken emerging from No. 10 brandishing a piece of paper and telling us our European policy is quite unchanged. William arrives and leads us to the sandwiches at the Chancellor's table. His lips are pursed.

'The Chancellor appears to be on television telling us that nothing has changed and this may cause a leetle un'apiness in certain quarters.'

This is a deliberate understatement, intended to be mischievous and droll, but it goes entirely unnoticed because the rabble is standing around chatting, chuntering, chuckling, grabbing sandwiches, pouring wine. William raises his voice.

'If we can have some order, I can tell you what has been decided.'

Still they go on burbling. Eventually, William is heard.

'There has been a *change of emphasis*,' he says with satisfaction and authority – at which precise point Ken strides through the door: 'What are you saying, William? There has *not* been a change of emphasis.'

'Well,' says William, with a smile, 'Time has passed and we can come to a clearer judgement.'

Ken is not amused. He repeats, 'Nothing has changed. I've said before that EMU by January 1999 is unlikely, but when I say it nobody listens.'

An hour later when the PM spells it out at Prime Minister's Questions it goes down exceedingly well with our troops. Blair is lame. Whatever Ken says, the PM has given a clear, personal, sceptical spin to the policy and our boys and girls lap it up.

Later I'm on the bench and the PM comes in and sits himself down next to me. This is always disconcerting. He covers my hand with his and gives a little squeeze. As ever, I marvel at the amount of luxuriant dark hair sprouting out of his cuffs.

'How's it gone down?' he asks.

'Nicely,' I say (which is true). 'People are taking from the statement exactly what they want – the antis love the brave new scepticism and the Euro-enthusiasts are saying nothing's changed.'

The PM gives me another squeeze. He's pleased. This is Ur-Major. The policy hasn't changed, but he's been able to give it a gloss that makes it much more evidently sceptical, will please the majority in the party but won't do much more than unsettle Ken and the DPM.

'This is it though,' he says, eyes narrowing. 'We're not going to move from this.'

When the PM goes, Michael Jack summons me to his end of the bench to ask what the boss was after. I tell him and add how unnatural I always feel when I'm talking to him. 'I'm so glad you say that. I find it impossible to be normal with him. He telephoned me at home early this morning and I was in the shower. I didn't dare tell him. I was stark naked and dripping, but because it was the PM I felt I had to stand to attention.'

The Finance Bill clauses under discussion this afternoon merited fifty minutes at most, but for some reason Labour didn't want a vote before 6.45 p.m. so they padded it out for two and a half interminable hours. After the vote we moved on to an environment bill or some-such and I retreated to the Whips' Office. In the corner we have a drinks cupboard (we each pay a share) but there's only a tiny fridge and that's tucked away in the Chief's room. I poured out some glasses of tepid white wine and recalled the Duke of Wellington's remark to the flustered hostess who apologised for the fact that the food was lukewarm because the kitchens were so far away from the dining room: 'No matter, dear lady. At least the champagne was warm.'

This prompted the Chief to offer his Wellington story – the Iron Duke's diary entry soon after becoming Prime Minister: 'Held my first Cabinet meeting today. Rum do. They all turned up. I gave them their marching orders. Then they sat around for two hours discussing them!'

FRIDAY 24 JANUARY 1997

Kensington & Chelsea have chosen Alan Clark. The mind boggles. Oh, he writes like an angel, but he's the very devil … Never mind his age, his philandering, his intoxication at the despatch box (at least Nick Scott was only discovered drunk in the street!) I was sure the way he'd described his old constituency association – 'petty, malign, clumsily conspiratorial and parochial' – would have sealed his fate. Wrong again. Clearly, you can't beat star quality.

The PM will be irritated – not so much by AC as the fact that 'Kensington Comeback for Clark' is getting more coverage than 'Major rules out Euro in 1999'. The boss notices these things. Last night he said to me, 'You know I spoke to 400 businessmen last week and only Andrew Marr in *The Independent* wrote it up.' I imagine the PM is the only person still reading *The Independent*.

I'm writing this on the bench where the week's business is drawing to a bizarre close. One day we're trawling for speakers to talk about nothing for hours on end: the next we're rattling through nine separate bits of legislation (all stages!) in less than six minutes. The mumbo-jumbo is amazing, with me bobbing up and down moving various stages of each Bill and the Deputy Speaker commuting between the Speaker's chair and the committee chairman's chair (two feet away, on a lower dais) as we move in and out of committee stage in a matter of seconds. In the space of six minutes the

Serjeant At Arms, in full fig, has advanced and retreated nine times to move the mace from position A (House sitting) to position B (Committee sitting). There's one Bill we have to postpone because it requires the Queen's Consent and a Privy Counsellor is needed to 'nod briefly' at the appropriate moment. It's Friday and all the PCs are out of town. Last night, the Queen's Consent was required on the Environment Bill, but because the PC was at the WC at the critical moment there was panic in the ranks and the House was suspended pending his return…

SUNDAY 26 JANUARY 1997

Chester. Friday night, after the TA do, I took part in Christian Question Time, much enlivened by a Paisleyite in the body of the church who lambasted us for failing to mention the scriptures in our answers and by my opponent from the 1992 election who, purple-faced with indignation, stormed down the aisles to protest hysterically at the insufferable smugness of my answers. The Labour people on the ground are clearly driven mad by Brown's edicts on public spending. It's very helpful.

MONDAY 27 JANUARY 1997

The sun rises on a Prime Minister at ease with himself welcoming his Cabinet to Chequers for a session 'fine-tuning the manifesto', and sets a few hours later on a government in disarray and on the ropes. A disaster of a day. Through a straightforward cock-up – we should have kept speakers speaking and simply didn't – Labour managed to force a vote an hour earlier than expected and consequently we LOST the division by one vote. The PM was incandescent. Not a pretty sight. While he'd spent the day confidently telling the world that we were planning to play it long and go for 1 May, we kiboshed the whole exercise by failing even to survive the evening.

Over dinner Portillo looked bleak. Scrubbed and polished, the hair up and at it, but something mournful in the eye that said 'I'm not a happy bunny.' I suspect it wasn't so much the lost vote as the way the royal yacht decision has backfired. Soames was booming. He appears to have a new baby: 'I like it to be handed to me like a machine gun, lightly oiled. There's a crisis back at base though "cawse Nanny Caroline's gawn and the new gal doesn't arrive till Thursday. Cue for me to decamp on manoeuvres, don't ya think? Four nights at the Dorchester, eh? Eh? Ha-ha! Ho-ho!'

Verdict on the day at Chequers from three sources: 'Quite unreal, a complete waste of time.'

TUESDAY 28 JANUARY 1997

The PM's worst fears are realised. The fiasco of the lost vote on the Education Bill has eclipsed the Chequers story.

I go in to the office in a state of suppressed trepidation because I've spent most of the night hoping, praying I'd counted the numbers right. As I arrive my throat goes dry as I discover we cocked-up the cock-up. We didn't lose the vote: we were tied. I counted our side correctly. It was poor Anthony Coombs who got the Labour numbers wrong. Anthony is grey with dismay. It is a nightmare. Hezza, who is beginning to look more like his *Spitting Image* puppet daily, wearily shakes his mane: 'John has had extraordinary bad luck. I've never known anything like it.'

LATER

Dinner with Ted Heath, the old boy at his most curmudgeonly. 'The Whips' Office is a disgrace. Wouldn't have happened in my day.' Everything was better in his day; everything is dreadful now. RAB[635] was a proper Home Secretary, 'with vision, decent, humane, not like this fellow now'. Ted was specially scathing about the royal yacht, called Portillo 'Porthole' and couldn't believe that Major hadn't consulted Blair. 'When I was Leader of the Opposition Harold Wilson had me in two or three times a week.' (Really?)

He was contemptuous – of course – of the plans for the Millennium Exhibition at Greenwich and when he warmed briefly to my suggestion that the elimination of Third World debt should be an international millennium project it became quickly apparent this was because, when he was on the Brandt Commission, they'd thought of it first. Eventually we got round to the point of the dinner – keeping Ted on side during the election – and Roger Freeman who, having contained BSE for us has now been given the rather greater challenge of containing Ted, purred: 'We need you to see John, Ted, spend some time with him – he's so nice.'

'So I'm told,' said the old monster, shoulders heaving.

'He needs your advice,' urged Roger.

'Would he take it?' harrumphed Ted.

Later, I pass another Grand Old Man in the corridor. Tony Benn is telling a young colleague: 'I don't understand what Blair thinks he's up to. You know, Clem would never have done it like this ...'

---

635   1902–82; R. A. Butler, MP for Saffron Walden 1929–65; held every senior office other than that of Prime Minister; Home Secretary 1957–62.

Incredibly, in the light of last night, one of our ministers has just missed a vote! I think we can guess where he is. A little earlier I heard him boasting: 'I've got some right high-class shank tonight. I'm going to take her home and knob her rigid.'

When I got home just now I found that Michèle had left a sweet note and a consoling bottle of wine open on the kitchen table. She's heard about the miscounting of the vote on the news and assumed it must have been me.

WEDNESDAY 29 JANUARY 1997

Last night David Willetts was summoned to No. 10 to work through the draft manifesto with Norman Blackwell. The Willetts verdict: 'It's terrible – dreadful, truly dreadful. There's nothing there. It's like a Research Department brief – lots of bullet points, a few new ideas – very few – but no theme. You'd think we had a year to go till the election, not a few weeks. It's like being an understudy and finding you're in a play that hasn't yet been written, let alone rehearsed and blocked.'

It's because there's nothing there that all we could spin on Monday was the line that the PM's going for 1 May. Today No. 10 is spinning that the PM has NEVER committed himself to 1 May! Speculation on dates is all we have to offer. Perhaps we should be publishing a calendar instead of a manifesto…

THURSDAY 30 JANUARY 1997

At Prime Minister's Questions the boss was in sensational form. There was some splendid knockabout at Blair's expense, followed by two solid statesmanlike answers on Northern Ireland that brought a lump to the throat and a tear to the eye. None of this will come over on TV, but it does our side good.

The Chancellor was equally sensational at lunch! So off-message on Europe that all you could do was gasp and laugh. William wanted to concentrate on ways of skewering Labour, but Ken, in swaggering mood, wanted to toast the chairman of Toyota whose line this morning is that there'll be no new Toyota investment in the UK if we're not part of the single currency.

'That's what he told me weeks ago. That's what they all think. That's why virtually every businessman I meet wants us to join!'

Fortunately Ken's on the three-thirty to Geneva (world bankers – say it carefully – are gathering at Davos) and it'll be good to have him out of the way. He's managed to antagonise all and sundry today with an interview in the *FT*. He sticks to the letter of the agreed line in public, but gives it *his* spin not the PM's. And he's also shared again with journalists his continuing ambition one day to lead the party. If it weren't for Europe, he might. As Chancellor, he's a domestic triumph. As a performer, he's a class act. As a person, he's irresistible. But if he stands, he'll get forty votes.

MONDAY 3 FEBRUARY 1997

The Chancellor has behaved well in Davos. The same cannot be said of Sir George Gardiner in Reigate. He has been deselected. The Whips' Office view: it couldn't have happened to a nicer fellow. He promised his Association he would be unequivocally loyal to the PM. He hasn't been and now he's paying the price. His lugubrious face peered out from most of the front pages on Friday, taking the shine off the PM's second 'presidential' press conference – of course. It's clear poor old George isn't going to go without a fight: he's digging in (the Chief has nicknamed him 'Swampy'), he's threatening legal action and the wags are saying 'Oh dear, it looks as if George is turning ugly' – a nice variation on the classic line about D. Mellor: 'What *will* David do once his looks go?'

We have moved the writ for the Wirral South by-election, now scheduled for 27 February. With a world-weary smile, David Hunt (Wirral South) tells me our prospects are dire (I might have guessed!) which is why the press today is thick with speculation that, come 22 February, the PM may be tempted to call the general election for 20 March. If that happens we avoid a by-election – and a humiliation – but instead we march towards the gunfire six weeks earlier than necessary and face a certain rout.

My instinct is we'll attempt to shrug off a defeat in Wirral South ('This is what you expect at a by-election') and hang on for 1 May. It is what the boys and girls want here and very much what our troops in the field believe would be best. (A major consideration, of course, is that if we wait till 1 May we move into another financial year and our pensions and redundancy packages will all be quite nicely enhanced.)

The *Sunday Times* featured the troubled love life of Dudley Moore, the secret love life of Lord Snowdon, and – another scoop! – speculation that John Major has told Stephen Dorrell he'll have his blessing as his successor on the understanding that when Stephen becomes PM John can be his Foreign Secretary!

Back in the real world, Blair has played another 'blinder' by telling us (via the *Telegraph*, God save the mark!) that *defence* is his issue and the armed forces face a certain future under New Labour. Should we have anticipated this? Danny told me that, before Christmas, he'd set up what he called the 'Red Group': a weekly gathering that put itself into Labour's shoes for an hour or so of fantasy politics in an attempt to be ready for what Labour might do next – so we can either pre-empt them or produce an immediate counter-offensive. I suspect the Red Group will turn out to be another bright idea – borrowed from the US – that could work if executed professionally by grown-ups … but isn't quite delivering the way we're making it happen this time round.

Today we launched our tearful lion poster as part of our Eurosceptic tilt – and Robin Cook has helped considerably with his timely suggestion that we'll be part of EMU by 2002 come what may. The campaign's a victory for Danny and Maurice Saatchi and the PM and Malcolm Rifkind. What will the Chancellor make of it? Was he consulted?

TUESDAY 4 FEBRUARY 1997

At breakfast, Danny, increasingly pear-shaped, croissant in one hand, Coke in the other, is firmly of the view that if we can't comfortably survive till 1 May we should go for 20 March and avoid the Wirral holocaust. He also reports that the manifesto is looking a lot better. It was never as bad as David made out, but, yes, it was drafted in Norman Blackwell's plodding prose and didn't have much sense of theme or purpose. David's now closeted at No. 10 working on the prose and, between what the PM likes to call 'bite-sized chunks of policy', there's a kind of core message emerging: stability v. risk.

Ludicrous fun and games on the Finance Bill. Because David Hunt was entertaining the President of the Law Society to lunch today and Angela Knight, Economic Secretary, wants to be away on Thursday afternoon, I suggested to my opposite number – a perfectly amiable shop steward from Coventry[636] – that he might like to offer a couple of pairs. He declined. I then suggested that tonight, to make progress, we might need to keep the committee going till 10.00 p.m. – knowing full well he wants to be away from 7.00 p.m. He said he'd think about it and, a few moments later, flexed his muscles by pulling all but one of his side out of the committee room so that, suddenly, the committee became inquorate. We need at least thirteen in the room at all times and half a dozen of ours were out in the corridor having coffee, on the telephone, dictating correspondence, gossiping, going to the loo etc. Fearful that the chairman would suspend the committee, I got up on a point of order and began to blather: 'Sir James, I can't believe that we are inquorate given the eloquence of the Honourable Member who has the floor. It is simply that colleagues have gone to fetch others to come and hear his eloquence, to marvel at the power of his presentation, to take note of his unique way with words …' by which time we'd got two or three of our chaps back and the committee resumed.

It was a narrow escape. Happily James Hill is a benevolent chairman: a splendid old combustion engine, good-humoured and good-hearted. Had his alternate, Gwyneth

---

636 Bob Ainsworth, Labour MP for Coventry North East since 1992.

Dunwoody[637] (Hattie Jacques with attitude) been in the chair, we would have had at least a twenty-minute suspension and I'd have ended up with egg on my face. This charade over, the Labour whip and I then agreed that we would pull stumps today at seven (which he wanted) if we could also agree to reach Clause 30 by lunchtime on Thursday (which I wanted). So I didn't manage to release Hunt early for his lunch, but at least Knight is sorted for Thursday. It's just a silly game.

The high-jinks continued during the afternoon when we were interrupted three times by votes on the floor of the House – after one of which Peter Butler, the Chancellor's PPS, failed to return. With a vote in the committee now imminent I got assorted members of the team to filibuster while frantically I telephoned and paged all and sundry – the Deputy Chief Whip, the Tea Room, Butler's office, Central Lobby. I thought he might have been closeted with the Chancellor – but his line was engaged so I had to get the switchboard to break in on his call to discover if Butler was in with him. He wasn't. Mouth dry, heart pounding, I paced the committee corridor until, all of a sudden, I sighted him: nonchalantly sauntering towards me, as cool and complacent as Mr Toad on his way to order a new motor. He hadn't appreciated a vote was in the air. So sorry. Poop-poop.

....

WEDNESDAY 5 FEBRUARY 1997

....

Walking to Downing Street I bump into the BBC's John Sergeant.

'If you wait too long,' he beams, 'the public will get fed up.'

'Isn't it you lot who'll get fed up? And what about the Lazarus factor? Aren't we all hanging on for our man to work his miracle?'

John giggles: 'Not any more. Unless you leap ten points in the polls it's all over.'

Clearly, this morning the PM feels it's far from all over. He's very perky, hopping from one foot to the other, hands deep in pockets, flashing his engaging grin.

'Have you seen it? Have you seen it?' he asks, nodding towards a copy of the *Daily Express* lying open on the coffee table.

An NBC reporter, one Daphne Barak, has been to interview Tony Blair and her verdict is damning: 'Never have I come across anybody quite as frightened, quite as uncertain, quite as eager to please.'

The PM already seems to have some of Ms Barak's phrases by heart: '"Nervous, boring, empty, at a loss" – that's more like it, isn't it?' He goes off to greet the Children of Achievement looking positively *jaunty*.

Leaving No. 10 I paused for a moment in front of the wonderful picture of Ellen Terry

637 1930–2008; MP for Exeter 1966–70, Crewe 1974–83, Crewe & Nantwich 1983–2008; MEP 1975–9.

and allowed myself a self-conscious, wistful moment. 20 March looks more likely now. The PM doesn't want us to go to the country because we've lost a confidence vote – and after Wirral South there's a danger of that. Charles Lewington has just called to get me to call Tim Rice to activate our Celebs for Major programme, 'just in case we do go for 20 March'. In the Tea Room at lunch Michael Bates is adamant: 'On 20 March I will lose my seat. On 1 May I can win.' Ian Lang is looking very spruce in what he describes as his 'election haircut'. If we were a plc rather than a party Ian would certainly be our next leader.

In the papers Elizabeth Taylor has had a stroke and Melinda Messenger ('Page 3 Girl for the Thrillennium') is alleged to have implants. In the Lords we have had a series of defeats on the Firearms Bill. No doubt we shall have severe problems if we attempt to reverse what their lordships have done.

In the Commons we're in for a tight vote tonight. Winston is in Paris where his mother[638] is dying. (Someone describes her as a remarkable lady who got where she did admiring rich and powerful men's ceilings.) We're bringing in our sick and keeping our fingers crossed. Ted said, shoulders heaving, mischievous grin, 'You've got it completely wrong. It's Liberal business today and there are no votes tomorrow. Keep us here and you'll have a majority of 153.'

I said, 'As a former Chief Whip, wouldn't your policy be "Better safe than sorry"?'

'No,' he harrumphed and padded softly away.

....

LATER

....

I've just emerged from the Cabinet committee on science and technology. The Deputy Prime Minister took the chair. 'It is now 3.30 p.m.,' he began. 'When Sir Maurice Bowra was Vice-Chancellor of Oxford University and chaired meetings of convocation, they started as the clock began to strike twelve. It was always Sir Maurice's aim to conclude the entire meeting, minutes, apologies, any other business and all, before the final stroke of twelve. I propose to conduct today's proceedings upon similar lines. I have read the papers prepared for us and they seem to me to be entirely satisfactory. Unless colleagues have something material to contribute, I suggest we accept the proposals—'

'— keeping within current spending limits,' chirruped the Chief Secretary.

'— and consider the results at our next meeting.'

From the far end of the table a hapless civil servant was heard to bleat, 'Can we publish the reports?'

---

638 Pamela Harriman, US ambassador to Paris, third wife of Averell Harriman, and mother of Winston by her first husband Randolph Churchill.

'After we've considered the results – at our next meeting. This concludes the present meeting. Thank you.'

The clock on the TV monitor changed to 3.31 as we gathered our papers and, murmuring complacently 'Now this is the way to do business', made for the door. Poor Ian Taylor, our Science Minister, sat in his place, crestfallen, like a deflated balloon. He had a twenty-minute presentation all rehearsed and ready. Nobody in the room had wanted to hear what he had to say anyway. Now nobody was going to.

On the way out, I gave Roger Freeman the cash I owed him for the Heath dinner and, taking my £10 note, he told me that the cricket match depicted on the back of it is a scene from *Pickwick Papers* set in Dingly Dell – and Dingly Dell now forms part of Roger's back garden. When the Chancellor of the Exchequer told Cabinet not to get their knickers in a twist about the design of the new Euro because nobody in their right mind ever looks at their money, the PM piped up, 'There's a cricket match on the back of the £10 note.'

'The PM', said Roger, 'has a wonderful eye for detail.'

THURSDAY 6 FEBRUARY 1997

As I write this, Dawn Primarolo[639] is grinding her way through the iniquities of the Insurance Premium Tax while the two Old Labour lags sitting immediately behind her – ruddy, sweaty, beer-bellied, one has a face that looks exactly like a fat old man's bottom with a moustache clipped to it – gaze intently at her rear end. Angela Knight has just drawn this phenomenon to my attention: 'Their instincts are entirely healthy – her backside is so much more appealing than her mind.'

We've had a fair bit of banter in this vein on the committee to date – and not merely as whispered asides. Discussing the economic advantages of motor cycles Phillip Oppenheim told us, 'There is a saying about people with big cars: BCSD. I don't know whether that also applies to motorbikes, but I can assure the committee I only have a small car.' Much ribald chuckling ensued. His jest at Michael Fabricant's expense was less flavoursome. Recalling how the Hon Member for Mid-Staffs had ridden a Yamaha to Gallipoli, Phillip said, 'He informed me he had a sore backside at the end of the journey. I sincerely hope it was as a result of riding the bike and not any other action.'

I sat talking with the Deputy Prime Minister in his room at the Commons last night. I was in a low leather armchair: he was behind his desk, on a high-backed throne, as if presiding over a banquet in the guise of a medieval king played by Errol Flynn. He is

639 Shadow Financial Secretary; Labour MP for Bristol South since 1987.

very like an ancient matinee idol in an MGM movie: the performance is stagey and the colour isn't quite true, but there's still something rather compelling about it.

We talked about our revised Euro stance: 'Our sceptics are real monkeys, aren't they? But we've given the monkeys something they can fall in behind, haven't we? Of course, some of the monkeys will never be satisfied. They're real *monkeys*, the lot of them!' When he moved on admiringly to the tearful lion in our campaign poster it suddenly occurred to me that maybe he takes the Tarzan thing seriously and all his metaphors are drawn from the jungle…

He wasn't amused to hear that colleagues would like us to accept the Lords' reverses on the Firearms Bill. He was taken with the idea of highlighting the elimination of Third World debt as an international millennium project. He accepts all the arguments for playing it long on the election date, but understands the PM's fear of losing a No Confidence motion after a defeat in Wirral South. 'I remain convinced that, when it comes to it, it's the pound in your pocket that determines the way you vote. Always has done, always will.'

In the Members' Dining Room seven of us played the 'Who-would-you-like-to-have-lead-your-platoon-into-the-jungle?' game. Hezza didn't feature. 'Too old.' Major? 'Too soft.' Clarke? 'Too fat.' The consensus was that Michael Howard might well survive but his men mightn't; that George Young would be good for morale ('and at least he's tall so they'd shoot him first'); but that our front-runners were Roger Freeman and Tom King.

When it came to the vote, we were right and Ted was wrong. Officially Labour was on a one-line whip. In the event, all but twelve of them turned up.

LATER

Lunch at the Treasury these days is like an informal family picnic. While the Chancellor – nonchalantly lighting his cigar with EU matches – flicks through the *Express* – enjoying Mandelson's response to yesterday's hatchet job on Blair – others chat to one another, pick over the sandwiches, pour out more wine. You'd never think a general election was only a matter of weeks away … Ken says he's discussed dates with the boss and knows he hasn't made up his mind yet. Phillip Oppenheim says: 'The Conservative Party is united on only two issues. We all loathe Edwina and we all want the election on 1 May.' Plenty of chuckles. I mention the idea of highlighting our targets on Third World debt as a potential international millennium project. General guffaws. 'We might get votes in Uganda, but not many here.' Around the table there's genial banter, much mocking of Central Office, but no sense of urgency – or impending doom.

Later I meet up with Howell James and tell him I sense that only the PM and the DPM are still wholly committed to victory. Howell has an attractive, infectious laugh.

He blinks behind his owlish giglamps: 'Don't we just know it, my dear!' I tell him that everyone wants to go on 1 May and not before and try a line I believe to be true: 'If the PM goes on 20 March against the better judgement of the party and we lose, they'll blame him personally.'

'They'll blame him anyway,' says Howell. 'They always do.'

SATURDAY 8 FEBRUARY 1997

Spend a couple of hours on the campaign trail in Wirral South where our candidate is impressive and the local troops quite buoyant. They were pleased to see me because the expected 'star' for the day – J. Gummer – failed to show. He has gone to Kenya for the weekend. Critical international environmental business, no doubt.

On the cold and windy streets of Heswall we thrust our faces and our leaflets into the paths of shoppers scurrying by. The reception we get is predictable: some greet you quite cheerfully ('You'll be all right with me'); some shake your hand but refuse to catch your eye; only one or two manifest open hostility. Most, needless to say, come from outside the constituency.

At my surgery yesterday a man came to see me about a contested planning application and said, leaning meaningfully across my desk, 'I'd rather give £5,000 to the Conservative Party than see this go the wrong way.' For an awful moment I thought he was going to wink, touch the side of his nose and mutter, 'Nudge, nudge, know what I mean?' Thinking it might be a set-up and wondering where he was hiding his tape recorder I said, rather loudly, enunciating every word, 'No donations are required here. As your Member of Parliament it is my duty as well my privilege to investigate every case that its brought to me with due care and attention.' The poor man looked utterly bemused.

MONDAY 10 FEBRUARY 1997

Is this the moment to be considering modifications to the quarantine regulations for pets? Chris Patten thinks it is. Our Kent colleagues beg to differ. And Norman Tebbit is of the opinion that we should allow in *quadrupeds* from Hong Kong, but impose strict restrictions on *bipeds* … This has to be one for the long grass, doesn't it?

Virginia stops me on the stairs leading up to the Cabinet ministers' corridor. She perches on the third step, knees tucked under her chin. She is wearing trousers – a fashion unknown when I arrived, but successfully pioneered by Margaret Beckett. (Virginia, of course, looks good in trousers. This cannot be said of one and all – e.g.

I have just passed Mo Mowlam in a day-glo boiler suit.) Virginia reports that the PM is to host another reception at No. 10 for the arts community and Sproatie has seen the plans and gone berserk. I'm not surprised, first, because the event is to be called 'Cool Britannia' (Ye gods, can you believe it?) and, second, because the guest list reads like a Luvvies for Labour Who's Who. The TV section features Harry Enfield, Martin Clunes, Neil Morissey, Angus Deayton, Richard Wilson, Stephen Fry and someone billed as 'Andy Coulson, *Sun* journalist.' I agree to try to find some additional names to help leaven the list. Clearly the Department of National Heritage (along with the rest of Whitehall) is readying itself for the new administration. Wouldn't it be *glorious* if we managed to win after all!

TUESDAY 11 FEBRUARY 1997

The press have had fun with Stephen's gaffe on devolution. Interviewed by *The Scotsman*, Stephen said he couldn't envisage a future Conservative government leaving a Labour-created Scottish Parliament 'unchanged'. Fair enough – except that canny wee Michael Forsyth's line is that devolution is an omelette that canny be unscrambled and that's why it canny be risked. Stephen was wrong. Forsyth is right. And all the papers are having a field day: leaders, cartoons, headlines, 'Dorrell drops a clanger.' Over breakfast we agree: if the press decide to make Stephen the government's new 'gaffe-man' he's in trouble. Danny counsels against going on the offensive: 'The press are never wrong. They never admit mistakes. They never see anybody else's joke. They never lose.'

LATER

The PM's third 'presidential' press conference is thrown off-message. Of course. The theme was to be education, but the focus was Stephen and devolution. The PM was asked, twice, who had responsibility for this area of policy and, twice, he replied 'The Scottish and Welsh Secretaries'. No. 10's background briefing later gave the line that Stephen had been asked to campaign on the constitution last summer, but that had simply been a short-term arrangement. Not true, of course. Stephen was, until today, and with the full authority of No. 10 and Central Office, very much a key spokesman on matters constitutional – and was planning something on proportional representation for later this week – but No. 10 and Central Office are now sending out the signal: Dorrell rebuked – Dorrell loses campaign role – Dorrell demoted. Stephen asked Hezza what he should do. 'Nothing. This is part and parcel of being one of the big boys.'

LATER *STILL*

The PM has Stephen in for a whisky. This is pure Major! At the press conference, in the briefing, at PMQs, the boss dumps his man; privately, he immediately rebuilds the fence and offers the consoling, reassuring hand of friendship. He's quite an operator.

During the afternoon I managed to get lost in the House of Lords. Turning an unexpected corner, who should I encounter but George Bridges from No. 10 scurrying along like the White Rabbit. We exchanged pleasantries and off he scampered. I turned another corner and found myself face to face with Howell James, clearly on his way to the same tea party. Odd, I thought. What is the PM's political secretariat doing pacing the red-carpeted corridors of their Lordships' House? Then it dawned on me. The PM is setting up his own command centre – and Lord Cranborne is commander-in-chief. Does the party chairman know?

WEDNESDAY 12 FEBRUARY 1997

The Chancellor was on the *Today* programme this morning and utterly brilliant. This afternoon he was prowling round looking for a 'pair' so he could go to the England/Italy match. Labour, by several accounts, is prowling around looking for an old boy ready to accept a peerage so that they can gerrymander a safe seat for Alan Howarth.

Last night I had dinner with Michael Fabricant. This came about because during the Finance Bill committee he passed me a copy of a letter he had just sent to the PM's PPS: 'Although Prime Minister's Questions went well for the Prime Minister today, I do believe that this was an opportunity wasted. For the first time in ages we dominated the Order Paper with questions 2 to 5 inclusive from Conservative members. Yet did we use this opportunity to express a common theme as the Labour Party has done so successfully in the past?' In fact, we do try to orchestrate PMQs. At 8.30 every Tuesday and Thursday morning Seb and Peter Ainsworth meet up with George Bridges at No. 10 to work out what we want. They then do their best to persuade colleagues to ask what's wanted. Unhappily not all of our colleagues are persuadable.

Michael then sent me a further note – this one in green ink – suggesting dinner *à deux*. This means that we can't eat in the Members' Dining Room because the tables there are for four or eight and the form is you sit wherever there's a space. There's a waiting list for the Churchill Room (West End food at West End prices) so we make our way to the Strangers' Dining Room where MF is confident we'll be properly looked after. He's right. Clearly he's a regular and generous tipper. (When I arrived here I had difficulty securing a table and endured surly service when I did. Then, one evening, Michèle noticed Soames sign the bill and tuck a tenner underneath it. Yes, of course, *that's* how it's done.) Over our roast beef and Yorkshire pudding and our second bottle of Fleurie, MF confided that he isn't gay, it isn't a wig exactly ('it's more complicated than that') and he knows he allowed himself to become a figure of fun in his first couple of years – but no one offered him any guidance. 'No one tells you anything here. This place thrives on secrecy and mystery. If you're not in the loop you're nowhere.'

LATER

A desultory meeting of EDCP. The Minister without Portfolio [Brian Mawhinney] is in the chair: the Lord President, the Chancellor of the Duchy, Norman Blackwell from No. 10, Charles Lewington and Sheila Gunn from Central Office, subdued but in attendance. Michael Bates [Paymaster-General] outlines the 'themes' for next week – all pretty meaningless, of course, since we're not commanding the agenda, but it does at least allow the key players to know what's in the air and spot potential pitfalls and opportunities in advance. The meeting catches fire briefly when Michael mentions the Department of Health's forthcoming announcement on adoption.

'Ah, yes,' says Mawhinney with authority. 'This is important. Now that abortion is going up the political agenda we must certainly make something of that.'

'Adoption, Brian.'

'We may not like the fact that abortion's now a political issue, but there's no escaping it.'

'Adoption, Brian, *adoption*.'

'Adoption, abortion, it's all the same … er, no, well…' He has a cold and he's tired. The Lord President is yawning noisily. The DPM has gone home with 'flu.

Over dinner Jeremy [Hanley] was looking profoundly pug-eyed: he is still recovering from his nightmare year as party chairman: none of it's as much fun as it used to be. But I love him and he still makes me laugh. He reported that on his last visit to the People's Republic he was presented with a magnificent stallion from Mongolia. Of course, you can't bring it home, but you accept it graciously and ask them to look after it for you – and they do, sending you the bills for its fodder. Malcolm Rifkind was presented with a beautifully wrapped goodbye gift from the Sultan of Brunei. The moment he boarded the plane to come home, Malcolm ripped open the package to discover what the world's wealthiest monarch had given him. It turned out to be a short video of the Sultan's recent birthday party.

At the 1922 Committee it was clear as crystal that almost everybody wants us to kick the Firearms Bill into the long grass. The PM won't.

More trouble ahead.

Over lunch at the Treasury – Prêt-a-Manger sandwiches and treacle tart – we discuss the price of baked beans. The Chancellor joined the Wirral South by-election campaign yesterday and Central Office fixed him up with a photo opportunity in a local super-market. Inevitably – certainly, predictably – the press asked him what the items in his shopping basket cost. Equally predictably, Ken didn't have a clue! We should have seen it coming. (When Mrs T. did this sort of thing she had an equerry in attendance armed will a full list of current prices.) All the papers today are running pictures of a grinning Chancellor with matching quips about half-baked Ken who doesn't know the price of beans. So how much *is* a tin of baked beans? We go round the table – Chief Secretary, Financial Secretary, Exchequer Secretary, Economic Secretary, Lord Commissioner to the Treasury ... not one of us knows. It's bound to come up in Treasury Questions this afternoon. Should the PPS go out and buy some beans? Possibly not: that would be too good a story. Eventually we settle on the line to take: 'The price of beans? A lot less than it would be under Labour!'

That's about the only line we can agree on. Tentatively, I suggest that, if we can, we should come up with a theme and a phrase for the day – but get nowhere. Actually, there's no point trying. It simply isn't Ken's style. Inevitably – predictably – when we get to Questions, Labour *does* have a theme – VAT on food – and they hammer it home relentlessly. They bring it up in every single question. It's risible, but it works. Ken's a bit all over the place. He's done fourteen separate radio and TV interviews in the past twenty-four hours (a couple of them quite brilliantly) and he's talked himself out. Now he's going to drive himself all the way to Leeds to take part in the BBC's *Question Time*.

Two sittings for tea today. When constituents call and tell you they're coming it's very difficult to say 'no'. They were so good-hearted and sat in the Pugin Room soaking it up and scoffing away. First they had the sandwiches, then the scones – they scooped every bit of cream and every last dollop of jam onto the scones, they weren't going to miss a bit – and *then*, mouth still stuffed to overflowing, one of them sighted the tray of cakes passing by. Spraying crumbs and cream *everywhere*, she gasped, 'We must have some of those!'

Winston is back from his mother's funeral in Washington. He was purring:

> The two Presidents have been extraordinary. Chirac awarded her the highest rank
> of the *Légion d'Honneur* – the only civilian ever to receive it posthumously. *On a*

rien de plus! Clinton sent Air Force 2 to bring the body home. We had the Vice-President to meet us and Bill gave the oration. What a woman!

The *Evening Standard* seems to concur, describing her as 'the greatest courtesan of the twentieth century'.

At around six the Deputy [Andrew Mackay] and I nipped over to Sarah Willetts' private view somewhere off Sloane Square. The pictures are wonderful, Mediterranean and classy, but Sarah was a touch unreal and David quite twitchy. Why became apparent when the man from Special Branch appeared, flashed his badge and started casing the joint.

David whispered, 'The PM's due at seven – and look who's here.' A hack from the *Evening Standard* (looking like a refugee from *The Munsters*) was monopolising Sarah – 'and we told No. 10 there'd be no press. What do we do?'

'Nothing,' I said, helpfully.

Andrew took me by the arm and said, 'If the Prime Minister is coming, I think we'll just slip away. With a close vote tonight I wouldn't like him to see two members of the office out socialising. Just in case it goes wrong.'

TUESDAY 18 FEBRUARY 1997

It didn't go wrong. It went rather well. 'Censure Vote Backfires on Labour' is the headline. *And* we won the Test against New Zealand. The PM will wake a happy bunny.

Dewar deserves the rotten press he gets this morning. He played it badly. Because the issue was Hogg's handling of BSE, he took the support of the minority parties for granted, which they resented, and then hyped it up as an attempt to bring down the government. The media played along – BBC2 cleared the decks to bring you the entire debate live and in colour, schedules were disrupted to rush you the result as it comes through – so the effect of our victory – a majority of thirteen, with three Labour members missing – has been to exaggerate our triumph, give Labour a bloody nose, and make us look and feel safe for 1 May.

It's particularly gratifying to have come through it unscathed because, in truth, on the issues involved there is quite a case to answer! Roger Freeman gets – and deserves – much of the credit for establishing confidence that we had some idea what needed doing and some commitment to doing it. That one Cabinet minister has to be brought in to make up for the inadequacies of another Cabinet minister is simply extraordinary, but actually we got away with it. We've also got away with spending £3.3 billion tackling the crisis without resolving it!

I stood at the bar of the House to listen to Roger's wind-up and he did a marvellous job: hubbub all around, intemperate catcalls from the opposition benches, but on he rolled imperturbably, while beside me a colleague muttered, 'This is the night manager at the Ritz stepping forward to sort out the double booking.'

At breakfast Stephen was buoyant and delightful. 'Last week was a setback, there's no use denying it'. We readily agree that the upside is that he's now universally recognised as one of The Contenders (with cartoons galore to prove it). The downside is the damage to his reputation as a safe pair of hands. Of course, it's wholly unfair. As Stephen pointed out, if you want a good example of a safe pair of hands you should consider his handling of the paedophiles at Ashworth Hospital – 'Whitemoor Prison with knobs on' – but successfully defused last week in under twenty-four hours. There are few prizes for keeping the dogs quiet in the night, but when the barking starts the fall from grace can be swift and merciless. Remember John Moore?[640] Danny's private verdict (whispered on the way to the lift): 'If we get anything like it again and soon, the press will link last week's gaffe back to the early days at Heritage and he's doomed.'

Overall, Danny was more positive: 'Our tracking surveys are moving the way we need them to, slowly. And the press have changed since we shifted on Europe. It may not be enough, but at least it makes you feel what you're doing is worthwhile.' There's another nice embarrassment for Labour today: their plan to privatise the Tote, floated on Saturday, running on Sunday, denied on Monday. Seb has spotted a horse called 'Pause for Thought' running this afternoon and is constructing an amusing question for PMQs this afternoon. (Is this the way they did it in Disraeli's day?)

I told Stephen about my encounter with the No. 10 team in the hinterland of the House of Lords. Stephen shook his head. 'That's JM's trouble. He's paranoid.'

I smiled. 'Perhaps he has good cause. Look at us.'

WEDNESDAY 19 FEBRUARY 1997

Ninety-five Conservatives voted against the government on the Firearms Bill last night. It's bad, but there's worse to come. In the bath, I have just heard Malcolm Rifkind say to John Humphreys [on BBC Radio 4's *Today* programme]: 'No, we are not neutral. We are actually on balance hostile to a single currency, but we accept that you have to think very carefully about these matters before you rule it out completely.'

Oh dear, oh dear.

---

640 Once tipped as a future leader, and saviour, of the Conservative Party; MP for Croydon Central 1974–92; Secretary of State for Transport 1986–7; Secretary of State for Health and Social Services 1987–9; Lord Moore of Lower March since 1992.

LATER

At 12.30 I went to see the Chancellor. He was sitting alone in the middle of his vast table, puffing at his cigar, signing constituency letters. He laughed, but he was angry. 'I heard Malcolm. I went into the kitchen to listen to it properly. The Foreign Secretary did not take the government line, Gyles, so when I was doorstepped I said it must have been a slip of the tongue. We are *not* hostile to EMU. Government policy remains unchanged.'

I asked if perhaps he thought he should agree a full response with No. 10 or the DPM or Central Office.

> No. Absolutely not. We've got a line. Let's stick to it. Malcolm's the one who needs to explain himself, not me. I know what John Humphreys was up to. I'm on *On the Record* on Sunday and, now, instead of talking about the economy it's going to be Europe, Europe all the way. Sometimes I despair of this party. If we think we can win the election by running an anti-Europe campaign we must be mad. Have you seen our new posters? They're dishonest. 'Labour's Euro policies will cost £2,300.' It's plainly untrue. It's a lie. We shouldn't be running them.

He got up and gazed out of the window. Through a cloud of smoke, almost in a whisper he said, 'The truth is, Gyles, that, privately, John has changed his mind. He's changed sides. It happened last summer. That's the problem.'

The *Evening Standard* has the headline: 'RIFKIND v. KEN: NOW IT'S WAR'. The party chairman, on the stump in Wirral South, has backed Malcolm and declared he was speaking 'for the full Cabinet'. 'Downing Street, floundering, repeatedly refused to say whether Mr Major supported his Foreign Secretary or not.' When I talk to Alex Allen at No. 10 he sums it up with commendable economy: 'I think we have an inherent problem here.'

At five o'clock the Chancellor addresses the 1922 Committee. He speaks on automatic pilot and manages to get through it without mentioning Europe once. Questions are not invited. Afterwards, he is chased down the corridor by lobby correspondents, but his lips remain sealed. We take refuge in his room at the Commons and find his desk piled high with tins of baked beans. (Heinz has sent him a case of forty-eight with a note: 'We sense that not enough of our product has passed through the Clarke household.') We sit in front of the TV, sipping whisky and white wine. Ken shakes his head: 'I'm not going to Ronnie Scott's tonight. I know what Malcolm's up to. And he must be stopped.'

John Gummer, pop-eyed and incandescent, puts his head around the door: 'Can I have a word? All I want to say is this: they can go more sceptical if they like, but they'll do it without me.'

A messenger arrives from the Treasury: 'The Foreign Secretary is having dinner with a Mrs Allright (*sic*),[641] but he could be free to see you at Carlton House Terrace around 10.00 p.m.' On the television we see Norman Lamont opining: 'Oh, yes, the party on the whole is hostile to EMU.' John Gummer: 'If anyone asks me if I am hostile I shall tell them I am not. And if the government says it is hostile I shall resign. And I shan't be alone. And if it brings down the government, so be it. I am going to telephone the PM now. The leadership we have had on this has been appalling – and I've never said that before.'

Over dinner Hezza tells me how once – and only once – a solution to a problem came to him in a dream. It was at the time of Greenham Common, when he was Defence Secretary, and the Greenham women and the flower children were planning to surround the place, just holding hands. To move against them would be a PR nightmare. In his dream Hezza saw the solution: leave the country! The next day he flew to Germany, visited our troops, and flew straight back – with a message to broadcast to the waiting media: 'I've been in Germany today, talking to our service people, young men and women who are risking their lives to defend our freedoms, to defend the freedom of the protestors at Greenham Common. It did the trick.'

At about 10.20 p.m. the Chief Whip phones Carlton House Terrace. Ken and Malcolm are already there. 'Shall we go?' A policeman shows us into a tiny lift and we make our way to the Foreign Secretary's flat. In the small wood-panelled sitting room, beneath the little print of Saint George, Glenfiddich is being taken and peace is breaking out. Malcolm is nursing a bishop's mace. Ken is nursing a whisky. Malcolm has apologised for the word 'hostile'. Ken has apologised for the phrase 'slip of the tongue'. A compromise statement is agreed and the No. 10 press officer called. He's at home and we've woken his baby. Nevertheless, he'll get the statement out in the early hours. Mission accomplished. Bomb defused. The Chief and I teeter down the stairs into the night, the Chief reminiscing: 'The first time I came here, I met RAB on these stairs. He had a withered hand, y'know.'

FRIDAY 21 FEBRUARY 1997

The *Times* headline: 'Major–Blair clash electrifies MPs'. Not quite, but last night's debate on the constitution was certainly a Big Occasion, with a full house and a strong showing from the boss. William [Hague] skewered Blair with a couple of fearless interventions. Several around me sensed it as a defining moment. 'William's now the one to watch.'

When it was over half a dozen of us had a drink with the PM. He was pleased with the way it had gone. And rightly. He had a beer. And then a second. And lots of peanuts.

---

641 Madeleine Albright, the US Secretary of State, was in London.

As always, long silences fell. For once, I resisted the temptation to try to fill them. As he left (dragged away by the invaluable John Ward – 'I know what he'll be like in the morning') someone murmured, 'A little touch of Harry in the night.' So, for at least one of our number, the magic holds.

MONDAY 24 FEBRUARY 1997

Derek Lewis has published an account of his brief time as head of the Prison Service. He gets Michael Howard completely wrong: 'He is a dark, closed-up person, who rarely relaxes and seldom shows a warmth in his political capacity.' In fact, Michael is warm, generous, sunny, sometimes funny. His capacity for work is extraordinary and his efforts at the Home Office have been Herculean – going every inch of the way against the grain of the Queen Anne's Gate culture. Michael Forsyth told me that he and Howard used to pass papers to one another personally to keep the diluting-influence of the civil servants at bay. Clearly Howard doesn't come across on TV. Lewis (who comes over as both plausible and pleasant on the box) concedes that Michael was 'brilliant in the debate'. It was an extraordinary afternoon, one of those rare occasions when what happens in the chamber of the House of Commons actually makes a difference.

Ted [Heath] has gone to town. He's been on the box telling us that Labour's got it right – on the minimum wage, on the Social Chapter, on a Scottish assembly! On the radio John Biffen and George Walden, a couple of smug self-indulgent old farts (who aren't standing, of course) tell us taxes are going to have to go up whatever the Chancellor says – 'everyone knows that'. With friends like these…

TUESDAY 25 FEBRUARY 1997

Anticipating another tight vote last night we hauled in our troops from far and wide – from sickbed and safari – and then ended up with a majority of thirty!

Ted came lumbering up to me, shoulders heaving, wreathed in mischievous smiles: 'See – I'm still with you!' Silly old goat. The PM shrugged, 'People don't take him seriously any more, do they?'

Winston was back from Paris. I had paged him on Thursday night – at the behest of the police who wanted to warn him of a death threat – and he said, 'I got your message. I was at the Paris Opera. You spoilt the second act. I thought I must have missed a vote or something.' I'm impressed his pager works internationally. I suppose with Winston it needs to.

One evening last summer we were coming through the division lobby together and I remarked on his unusually casual appearance.

'Yes,' he said, 'it's maddening. I've been running late since lunch. I didn't have time to change. The service at the Cipriani was dreadfully slow today.'

The DPM had returned from the London Fashion Week dinner. 'I'd only eaten the first course.'

'Why on earth do you go to London Fashion Week?'

'Because I invented it!'

WEDNESDAY 26 FEBRUARY 1997

EDCP with Hezza in the chair. We rattle through the forthcoming attractions. Virginia has an announcement on violence on TV. And she's going to ban another satellite porn channel.

'Can't we have any fun?' murmurs Tony Newton, lighting up. There is momentary consternation. He quickly adds, 'I haven't even got a satellite dish, of course.'

Brian Mawhinney bleats: 'This isn't supposed to be just a diary of events. We're supposed to decide what we're going to *say*. What are we going to say this week?'

'Well,' says Tony, risking a second sortie, 'we could start by saying to the Chancellor and the Foreign Secretary, "Why don't you talk to one another?"'

Nobody laughs.

It's difficult to know when to laugh in this business. Charles Lewington tells me that Page Three lovely Melinda Messenger is about to endorse the PM. 'That's worth twelve points in the polls, isn't it? I'm seeing *The Sun* on Monday. Shall I give it to them? What do you think?'

Desperate times call for desperate measures.

THURSDAY 27 FEBRUARY 1997

I arrived at No. 11 at 9.30 a.m. to find the Chancellor in mellow mood, bleary-eyed but well-scrubbed. It took ten minutes to sort out the coffee. 'Why won't it boil?' He hadn't switched on the kettle. 'We're out of milk – hold on.'

He kept dashing out to the kitchen, into the hallway, but eventually we sat down and I outlined the strategy:

GB: 'The PM doesn't want to go into the election on the back of a lost confidence vote.'
KC: 'Agreed.'

GB: 'The Irish would welcome a concession on airport duty,[642] so why don't we make the concession *now* to show we're willing rather than wait till it's forced out of us?'

KC: 'It's probably illegal. It's certainly illogical. That's why.'

GB: 'Make the concession today and it'll be lost in the papers tomorrow – but it might just encourage a couple of the Irish to stay away if we lose Wirral South and Labour call a No Confidence vote next week.'

KC: 'I don't believe they will.'

GB; 'They might – and isn't there a case to be made that the extra airport duty for Northern Ireland and the highlands and islands is unfair?'

KC: 'Not much of a case! Let's face it. It's simply a bribe for votes. Okay, £7 million for the Reverend Martin Smyth is cheap at the price, and, if it comes to it, I suppose we'll have to do it, but let's not rush into it. It's just a bribe.'

GB: 'But if on the night it'd make a difference you'd agree to it?'

KC: 'Probably.'

I reported that EDCP hoped that he and the Foreign Secretary would be coordinating their two big speeches scheduled for next week.

'I'm going to be talking about the world,' said Ken, twinkling. 'What's he talking about?'

'The world,' I said.

'And they want our two worlds to be the same?' mused the Chancellor. 'Fair enough.'

Lunch at the Treasury was pleasantly chaotic. Michael Jack attempted to persuade Ken to make a speech offering his vision for Britain's economic future. 'That won't get any coverage,' chortled Ken. 'That isn't what politics is about these days. If you want coverage you either have to have a row or do what I did yesterday – go to Bristol and make an idiot of yourself in a balloon factory. And if you want a *front-page* picture there's only one thing to do: wear a silly hat.'

At Cabinet the PM gave strict instructions that the response to the anticipated Wirral South debacle will be as follows: thirty seconds (at most) of regret, then straight on to what will count is the general election when it comes and what Labour has to do is answer the question, 'Where's the money coming from?'

At lunch there was much laughter at the news that Michael Howard is to be the minister on the spot in Wirral South in the morning. 'Couldn't happen to a nicer chap.'

'Poor Michael. It's bound to go wrong,' said Ken. 'If they've got any sense the Labour Party will have people with placards out to greet him: "You're too late, mate! It was yesterday!"'

---

642 The Ulster Unionists were unhappy with the Budget's proposed increase in airport duty. The Chancellor was reluctant to exempt Northern Ireland not only because of the loss of revenue but also because doing so might contravene EU fair competition rules.

FRIDAY 28 FEBRUARY 1997

The Wirral South result is entirely predictable: a 17 per cent swing to Labour. We're doomed.

MONDAY 3 MARCH 1997

Stephen's blown it. 'John Major's government was back on the ropes again last night after Stephen Dorrell, the Secretary of State for Health, smashed the fragile Cabinet agreement on the European single currency.'

Interviewed by Jonathan Dimbleby, Stephen declared 'We shan't be joining a single currency on 1 January 1999' – which may well be true, but isn't the line to take when the poor PM has striven so desperately to get everyone to accept that the government's agreed view is that our joining in 1999 is 'very unlikely, but not impossible.' The headlines tell the story: 'Dear, oh dear, Mr Dorrell. TV blunder over pound spells crisis for Tories' (*Express*). 'Dorrell Does the Splits' (*Daily Mail*). 'Euro Gaffe Wrecks Tory Unity' (*Independent*).

At our end of the Tea Room colleagues are shaking their heads in disbelief. Among Stephen's supporters there's dismay. What was he up to? If it was a deliberate attempt to shift the policy, it was naive. If it was simply a case of going off-message, it was naive. Either way, it's a major blow to his prospects. The 'safe pair of hands' turn out to be covered with goose grease. Now he *is* gaffe-man – his admirers are downcast, his enemies delighted, the generality of the party in despair. This, on top of Wirral, combined with Ted and Tebbit, supplemented by the memoirs of Lord McAlpine[643] and the autobiography of Ian Greer, and there's a sense today that we're in free-fall.

At the A&Q meeting as well as plenty of justified Dorrell-sniping, there was a determined bout of Central Office bashing. The boys are confused about our current line of attack (we're saying that Labour's committed to £30 billion in spending and there's a £12 billion black hole in Gordon Brown's plans and we're putting out both messages simultaneously) and they don't like the weeping lion. 'That poster's not going to win us the election, you know.' I sit next to John Ward who scribbles away furiously. 'I'll pass it all on to the boss – unvarnished.'

I lunched with Sonia Land[644] who told me her Feng Shui guru says that the government's

---

643 1942–2014; Alistair, Lord McAlpine of West Green since 1984; Conservative Party Treasurer 1975–90, deputy chairman 1979–83; a devotee of Margaret Thatcher, he was now advocating support for Sir James Goldsmith.

644 GB's literary agent.

problems stem from the gates at the entrance to Downing Street. They've prevented the good air from getting in and the 'bad vibes' from getting out. Pull down the gates and all will be well. I must pass it on.

TUESDAY 4 MARCH 1997

At breakfast Stephen was contrite – and charming, full of apologies and regrets and shy boyish smiles. 'I don't know how it happened. I found myself saying in public what I've said in private a thousand times – and when I should have heard the alarm bells ringing, I didn't.' We agreed that as far as colleagues are concerned all he should do now is be about and be himself. He shouldn't overdo the self-flagellation or attempt self-justification, just modest regret at any embarrassment caused. As far as the media is concerned, Danny was adamant: 'Do what Hezza does – be enigmatic. Don't give anything away. Let them draw their own conclusions.'

David Faber was nicely consoling: 'Three months from now the gaffe element will be forgotten, but the Eurosceptical spin will linger on.' I wonder… I see that William Hague has announced his engagement.

I walked over to the House with Danny and reported on the A&Q gathering last night and our boys' problem with the poster. He waved his yoghurt carton in the air and roared: 'I'll tell you what the problem is! The problem is eighteen years in power, the Prime Minister's leadership, the fall-out from Wirral South – and two dozen back-benchers want to blame it on the fucking poster! Jeezus!'

This week's message is 'Where's the money coming from, Mr Blair?' Not a bad message, but will we stick with it?

'I don't know,' said Danny, still laughing. 'One of Major's failings is that he won't lock on to a theme. We keep moving from one idea to another, from one target to another.'

'I hope you're enjoying it,' I said.

'Oh, it's wonderful. When I ran computer magazines we had fiascos, but these are much more fun. These are fiascos on a proper scale!'

LATER

I am writing this in the Quiet Room at the end of the Library, where the non-political books are kept and conversation is taboo. Not so snoring. There are eight low green leather chairs set around the fireplace and on nights like tonight when there are several votes they are filled with gentlemen members (I have never seen a woman in here) snoozing fitfully. Within a few inches of me is Peter Mandelson, in his shirtsleeves, gently dozing. He sat down to study the *New Statesman* but, understandably, didn't warm to his task and his eyes quickly closed and now a gentle New Labour *ronflement* is emerging from him. I am resisting the temptation to rifle through his papers and Filofax, now literally within my grasp, but in the fullness of time I look forward to learning how the command structure of New Labour has worked in the run-up to this election. It is self-evidently so much more effective than ours. We have too many power centres and messages insufficiently coordinated and focused – and, perhaps, even no longer a will to win.

Raymond Robertson was with the PM in Scotland on Friday and felt that, for the first time, the boss has accepted we might lose. There's been a sense of free-fall these last twenty-four hours that might just tip him into going for 10 April after all – not just to get it over and done with, but to prevent further fall-out.

An incidental benefit of the Dorrell brouhaha is that it's swamped the speculation over which ministers are planning to break ranks and reject EMU outright in their election addresses. One of the Sundays fingered Angela Browning, our comfortable Minister for Food, and on Saturday night/Sunday morning the lines were hot. The DPM spent an hour on the phone to her – at 1.00 a.m.! – and the PM called her at 7.00. She was dissuaded from resigning and agreed to stick to the line, but if it hadn't been for the Dorrell gaffe the story might have gathered legs.

Hezza's been in fine form today, bullish and playful. We had a meeting to run through his speech for Thursday's debate on public expenditure. William [Waldegrave] seemed unduly exercised about it, but Hezza was gloriously off-hand. In under a minute he ran through the headings – 'it's all pretty obvious – we'll have some fun' – and then chucked the notes to an official, slapped the desk and dismissed us. Clearly, he's not to be discounted.

For well over a year now, in dark corners, colleagues have been muttering about the succession. Now they talk of it openly. In the Tea Room a motley crew is running through the form: Redwood – 'no go, still the man from Mars'; Portillo – 'bruised and unreliable'; Howard – 'brilliant but bloodless'; Clarke – 'sensational, but his views on Europe make it impossible'; Rifkind – 'reality and dandruff are against him'; Dorrell – 'seemed a nice boy for a while, but it's all over'; Hague – '*please*, you can't be serious!'; Gillian – a round of mocking laughter. The consensus: it's got to be Hezza – with, wait for it, as a dark horse, a last-minute surprise runner: Jonathan Aitken.

Ted Heath was at his most twinkly earlier: 'You whips are so busy now controlling the vermin you have no time for controlling the government. We have far too much legislation, poorly drafted, given inadequate time.' Sometimes the old dinosaur gets it spot on.

WEDNESDAY 5 MARCH 1997

Much fluttering in the dovecotes. David Evans, the fat ass with the common touch, has been telling-it-like-it-is at a school in his constituency. On John Major: 'I find him vindictive and not forgiving.' On women in politics: 'Women get promoted, like Virginia Bottomley, who's dead from the neck upwards, right?' On the Birmingham Six: 'You think they hadn't killed hundreds of people before they caught them?'

Evans is holed up at home now, with four camera crews at the door, and he's issued an apology, but the damage is done and, of course, today's the day of the PM's fourth 'presidential' press conference.

EDC (Ministerial Committee on Competitiveness) meets at 10.00 a.m. with a substantial agenda and an early warning from officials that the meeting will be a long one. In the event, the DPM arrives three minutes late and tells us he is due to take a phone call at quarter past. 'Let us proceed ... Consumer affairs – deregulation.' Leafing through the paperwork: 'Do we need this before the election? Do we want to have all the consumers' organisations climbing all over us at this stage in the game? Let's postpone it.'

Greg Knight (Minister for Industry): 'This is just what I—'

DPM: 'Agreed. Next.'

Greg's set piece was due next: competitiveness plans for the English regions. Greg had plenty to say – and began to say it, with giggling on all sides (especially from Gummer). Happily, within a couple of minutes, the penny dropped and he ground to an abrupt halt.

By quarter past we were shuffling out, Douglas Hogg in tweeds, hobbling on crutches.

Waldegrave: What happened to you?

Hogg: I broke my ankle.

Waldegrave: Kicking someone, I trust?

Gummer: Does the countryman's code require one to wear a hacking jacket with a broken leg?

Hogg: I can't hold the crutches with my usual jackets.

Gummer: It's the hat we really miss, Hoggie.

The joshing and the banter and the ragging continued as we rolled out into Whitehall. It's end of term at a minor public school.

THURSDAY 6 MARCH 1997

The Finance Bill faces a couple of hazardous hurdles on Tuesday and the Chancellor of the Exchequer has toddled off to Hong Kong on his way to China. At the Treasury we gather to work out compromises to ensure we avoid defeat. 'Oo, you can't do that!' cluck the officials. (The younger ones all have a slightly camp manner and north country accents). 'Oo, we can't possibly change that at this stage.'

In the 'War Room' at Central Office we meet – at last – to agree the lines of attack on Labour's spending pledges. There are eight young men in shirtsleeves and a leggy girl to take notes. For an hour confusion reigns and we end up exactly where we started. Charles Lewington has to go to No. 10: 'The PM wants to rule out VAT on food.'

'He can't. No one can.'

'If he can't, he'll shoot himself.'

Suppressed giggles all round.

In the Commons Hoggie hops about in the face of accusations of confusion, buck-passing and incompetence in his handling of the BSE crisis in general and the Meat Hygiene Service Report in particular. The PM defends him manfully, but behind the scenes ministers shake their heads and Michael Forsyth [Scottish Secretary] puts the boot in.

Hezza does his 'turn' on the economy and the handful who turn out for it enjoy the show.

....

MONDAY 10 MARCH 1997
....

I was rather dreading last night's 'showfolk party' for the PM at the Ivy. In the event, it was rather fun. There were about 150 in all – Barbara Windsor, Frank Bruno, Joan Collins, Anneka Rice, Ruth Madoc, Anita Harris, Mike Yarwood – more pantoland than *South Bank Show* – but the wine flowed and the PM circulated and a good time was had by all – including the boss, I think, who brought Norma and the children and arrived at eight and was still at it at eleven. Cliff [Richard] looked the business – 'it's all off-the-peg and the shoes cost £55 – I mean, where can you buy a pair of shoes for £55 these days?' – and offered the PM crumbs of comfort: '*Heathcliff* got a terrible press and they said no one would come. Well, we got the biggest advance in history! Forget the critics, John – trust the punters.'

I thought Tim [Rice] and the PM should say a few words. Howell agreed: 'a little bringing of the room together, a little punctuation mark.' The PM wouldn't have it. He was having a night off. He was funny though.

Donald Sinden was telling a fruity story.

'And then,' said Don, 'Lord Alfred Douglas turned to me and remarked…'

The PM chipped in, 'At least you didn't say "And then Lord Alfred Douglas turned over to me and remarked…"'

TUESDAY 11 MARCH 1997

I am writing this sitting on the front bench as we embark on the final stages of the Finance Bill ready, if the minority parties but knew it, to concede absolutely anything rather than lose a vote. The PM has just struggled valiantly through a lacklustre question time and Madam Speaker has just completed one of her music hall turns, playing to the gallery after a good lunch. The Exchequer Secretary [Phillip Oppenheim] has arrived in buoyant mood: 'See that girl in the box. She's Hungarian. Snogs like a hoover.' He's clearly got his mind on the job.

And look who's here: the Chancellor of the Exchequer has wandered in, bleary-eyed and unshaven, just off the plane from Beijing. 'You lot seem to have been panicking somewhat in my absence. Do you know it was 3.30 a.m. when you roused the ambassador's wife to get me onto the radio to deny that silly story about 17 per cent VAT on fuel.'

'How was Beijing?'

'I'm not sure. Seems a long time ago.'

THURSDAY 13 MARCH 1997

Last night I made the mistake of going to a dinner hosted by the BBC. They were eager, intelligent, friendly, hospitable, but the exercise was pointless. They'd invited MPs from all parties which was naive because, as a consequence, we all watched what we said with special care. All we learnt was that the Major–Blair TV debate won't happen.

'We'll see you in court first,' chirruped Archie Kirkwood who looks exactly like an ageing jockey.

The legal advice is that a head-to-head without the Lib Dems isn't on. And what do you do in Scotland? On our side we were resolutely loyal and wouldn't contemplate the possibility of defeat. Menzies Campbell[645] offered Charles Kennedy[646] as his preferred successor to the generally despised (by his colleagues) Paddy Ashdown.

I've just had coffee with Sir Trevor Skeet, an old tortoise, who was dined by the PM last night along with thirty-six other retirees. 'He was very good, but he's got a lot on his mind. He just came and went, you know. He didn't go round the table and say an individual word to each of us. That's what we wanted.' Jesus wept! You simply can't win, can you?

---

645 Liberal then Liberal Democrat MP for Fife North East since 1987; Leader of the Liberal Democrats 2006–7.

646 Liberal then Liberal Democrat MP for Ross Cromarty & Skye 1983–97, Ross Skye & Inverness West 1997–2005, Ross Skye & Lochaber since 2005; Leader of the Liberal Democrats 1999–2006.

At lunch I entertained the Chancellor with an account of Central Office's latest research. Europe and the constitution mean nothing to the bulk of the electorate. 30 per cent of those polled (the same 30 per cent) want us to leave the EU but join EMU!! John Prescott isn't the bogeyman our activists like to think he is. Only 30 per cent of those polled could identify the party he belongs to. Blair is the man they know and rather like. The message for us is ominous: 'People want freshness. They don't like fundamental change.'

FRIDAY 14 MARCH 1997

Albania is disintegrating before our very eyes. How about the Conservative Party? The hapless PM is on his way to Bath to rally the faithful while Edwina is on the radio telling the world that his would-be successors are already readying themselves for the fray and, when the time comes, 'John mustn't hang around. He's got to get on with it – and go.'

She shouldn't be saying it, even if it's true. And it is true, of course. To my knowledge there are least four campaign teams in an advanced state of readiness. Last night, one zealot ran me through the computer program for his man. Anyone likely to be in the new House of Commons is in there (complete with nicknames, numbers, special interests and peculiarities) and rated from one to five – one for a certain supporter, five for 'never-in-a-million-years'.

MONDAY 17 MARCH 1997

It's coming through on the fax right now: 'The Prime Minister has today asked Her Majesty the Queen to proclaim the Dissolution of Parliament. Her Majesty has been graciously pleased to signify that She will comply with this request.'

Last night, at the whips' dinner at No. 12, the PM was surprisingly relaxed, exasperated but not exhausted. 'Bath went well, though you wouldn't have known it from the television pictures. Have you read George Walden's piece in the *Express*? What on earth does he think he's doing? Earning £500 I suppose. God!'

We sneered at Edwina. 'How many doors has she been knocking on?'

'Quite a few publishers' doors, I imagine.' The PM shook his head with a weary smile. 'And who on earth benefits from John Biffen's words of wisdom?' Pause. Glint in eye.

> At the end of the day, when we come to the peerages, let no one assume it comes
> automatically just because you've been in the Cabinet. 'Lady' Biffen needs to

remind her husband of that. There are the likes of Fergus [Montgomery] and Jill Knight to whom I owe a lot more.[647]

He wants the TV debate. 'What have I got to lose? I've forgotten more policy than Blair's ever dreamt of.' The only bleak moment came with the news that our turncoat Alan Howarth has secured a safe Labour seat. 'God, that is depressing.' I wish Alan joy of it. There's a picture of him in the paper today, his elegant toff's head addressing a football at the Newport Working Men's Sports Field.

During the afternoon we went through the charade of the 'party review', each whip giving his (or her) report on the ministers and PPSs in his department in anticipation of the post-election reshuffle. I turned mine into a bestiary – Heseltine the elderly giraffe stalking through the jungle, head aloft, picking off the juiciest leaves; Ken Clarke, the mangy lion; Waldegrave, the anxious llama; little Michael Jack, the eager Chihuahua hopping up at the table etc. It went down quite well during the afternoon, but alarmingly, at the end of dinner, when the post-prandial silence fell, I suddenly heard the Chief saying, 'Gyles, tell the Prime Minister about your little menagerie …' I looked across the table at the PM and suddenly regretted that third Martini, that fourth glass of claret, that top-up of port. I burbled. I was neither impressive (which didn't matter) nor amusing (which did).

This evening Michèle and I had dinner with Stephen in the Strangers' Dining Room. 'What happens if John stays on?' Stephen asked.

'He won't,' I said.

'He might, mightn't he? Perhaps he should – do the decent thing for a year or two, hold us together, maintain the centre ground, allow the National Union time to develop their ideas for an electoral college in which the activists have 20 per cent of the vote.'

Behind us John Gummer was sitting, like a happy pixie, his tie flicked over his shoulder, having a fit of the giggles.

'What does *he* do?' whispered Michèle.

'Supports Ken. Ken's active. Peter Butler [Clarke's PPS] keeps pestering me for phone numbers.'

On the far side of the room, Gillian [Shephard] and Robert Cranborne [Lord Privy Seal], *à deux*, were locked in a conspiratorial huddle. The Chief Whip came in and surveyed the scene.

A little later, scurrying between the Chamber and Tony Newton's room – where the lovely unsung hero of the administration is on his third pack of cigarettes since this morning's announcement – I bump into a wild-eyed Neil Hamilton.

647 In the event, John Biffen and Jill Knight both received peerages and Fergus Montgomery did not. The 'Dissolution Honours' were a disappointment to many and, in certain quarters, fuelled resentment of both John Major and his Chief Whip.

'Look, what am I going to do? Downey[648] isn't going to be able to report now before the election. I've got my AGM on Friday and I needed Downey to exonerate me. Now he can't in time. I'll need a letter from the PM saying "innocent till proved guilty".'

Neil catches John Ward and repeats his plea, but John tells me he doesn't believe the PM can risk overt assistance. 'What if the report leaks during the campaign and it isn't good – and the boss has backed Neil?' I go back to Neil and suggest he gets a letter from Downey, explaining the process, and perhaps something from Mawhinney on how Central Office is going to be pulling out all the stops to win in Tatton. Neil's fear, of course, is that despite one of the healthiest majorities in the land, he could still lose. And then what has he got?

TUESDAY 18 MARCH 1997

By playing it long we thought it could only get better. Perhaps it can only get worse? 'Labour surges to 28-point lead' is the *Telegraph* headline above a shot of JM on his soapbox in Luton. He knows what's coming: that's why he's so relaxed. At yesterday's Cabinet, Hogg was absent (in Brussels) and the Chancellor was late. The PM cast a withering glance at the empty chair and lifted his eyebrows before embarking on his announcement: he would go to the Queen at 11.30, the House would be prorogued on Friday, be dissolved on 8 April and the election would be on 1 May.

This morning it was all very playful in the Tea Room. Our boys were doing their ready-reckoning, who'll be in, who'll be out. 'Edwina's done for. Thank God!' 'Even her friends don't like her.' 'What friends?' 'I met one once!' 'She exudes sexuality,' said Winterton, mouth full of crumpet, 'oozes it, but she doesn't have any sex appeal at all.' 'Yes,' mused Fabricant, 'you can't really see yourself doing it with Edwina. Now I did once picture myself sleeping with Teresa Gorman.' Several of us made our excuses and left.

The Chancellor arrived at his penultimate prayers in high spirits: bright blue shirt, bright yellow tie, cigar in hand, ready for the fray. William was more subdued, but buoyed by his debate in the City with Alistair Darling (shadow Chief Secretary). 'We won the argument. When I said to Alistair, "Mr Blair said yesterday 'there's a black hole in the government's finances', how do you propose to fill it?" Darling didn't have an answer.'

Phillip Oppenheim was fresh from ECOFIN where coinage had been high on the agenda. Apparently the Nordics won't have nickel in their coins. They say it damages your health. And Kohl doesn't like our 20p piece.

There's confusion about who can do what between now and the election. The Chancellor

---

648 Sir Gordon Downey, since 1995 the Parliamentary Commissioner for Standards.

is clear: 'You are ministers until 1 May. You can sign letters, you can make announcements, you can go on visits.' Peter Butler protested that in the outer office the civil servants were saying you couldn't sign letters. Ken leant back contentedly in his chair and waved his cigar smoke about: 'Terry[649] knows bugger all about the way it works. They're pretty unworldly here at times.'

Before the Chancellor arrived I stood alone in the room admiring the Pissaro, the seventeenth-century Dutch still lifes, the portrait of Austen Chamberlain. Forty-four days from now and it'll all be over. Talking to Norma later – she was looking more starlike than ever: she glows – I suggested a chart on the fridge to mark off the days. 'We're taking Easter off. I insisted.' She's mastered the art of being wonderfully intimate without being in the least indiscreet.

WEDNESDAY 19 MARCH 1997

The press are getting away with the implication that the fact the Standards and Privileges Report won't appear before the election is somehow the government's doing. It isn't. It may well be in the government's interest, but that's a rare little bit of good fortune.

The campaign's only just begun, but the bookies are looking over the hill. Today's odds from William Hill on the leadership race: Hague and Portillo, 7–2; Howard and Heseltine 5–1; Clarke, Dorrell and Shephard 10–1. Redwood's stock is dwindling. The problem with John is that when he tries to be nice 'n' normal it comes out all wobbly. As they say in the Tea Room, 'Never do business with a country that has orange in its flag and never trust a man with green blood.'

When I told the PM a few weeks back that I was sure Blair wore make-up at PMQs, he seemed genuinely surprised. 'We need to give that greater currency, don't you think?' So we're going to have a go tomorrow, either with a planted question, 'Can my Right Honourable Friend take this opportunity to salute the cosmetics industry in the United Kingdom etc. …' or by having someone shout out as Blair rises: 'He's wearing make-up!' Yes, it's come to this.

THURSDAY 20 MARCH 1997

What a shambles! Confronted by some hardball from the opposition, Tony Newton has promised an 'interim report' from the Committee on Standards and Privileges at noon today.

---

649 Sir Terence Burns, Permanent Secretary to the Treasury 1991–8; later Barons Burns of Pitshanger.

We now have the worst of both worlds: we're highlighting the problem without resolving it. And, of course, Tony's so decent he won't even tell the Cabinet what the report has in store.

At five to twelve the Members' Lobby is packed with hacks lining up to collect their copies of the report – which then turns out to be a non-event! Downey unreservedly clears a dozen colleagues that we didn't even realise were being investigated while the cloud over Hamilton and co. remains.

At the Treasury we have a last sandwich lunch and the Chancellor makes a gracious little speech. 'Over the past few years we've built an economic recovery round these sandwiches. The trouble is: the buggers out there aren't very grateful. This has been the best ministerial team I've had. And the best private office. Yes, Gyles, I know it seems a bit shambolic, but I don't like to take things too seriously for more than ten minutes at a time. I'm in the business of cheering ourselves up.'

We raised our glasses. William said 'Cheers!' Someone else said 'Britain is booming!' 'God, I hate that expression,' said Ken.

'It's on all our posters, Ken.'

'I know it is. Central Office wanted it. I didn't.'

John Mackay[650] (Social Services Minister in the Lords) had come along and couldn't quite believe it. 'All this drinking and laughing, it's amazing. With Peter Lilley, we just sit there with our heads bowed counting our worry beads.'

There was a full turnout for John Major's last PMQs. The cheering and the jeering were extraordinary – and he was at his best. We had tears in our eyes. It was an amazing spectacle, moving and ridiculous. There was a lovely tribute to Michael Jopling (recovering from his road accident but looking pretty frail) and a last hurrah from Winston. Our absurd cries of 'He's wearing make-up' bounced off Blair unheeded.

MONDAY 24 MARCH 1997

Day 8 of the campaign doesn't begin too badly. Overnight we manage to shift the focus from sleaze to The Great TV Debate – which is amazing since, as yet, it's a non-event (and may prove to be such even if it does materialise) – and today there's a leak from the Labour manifesto suggesting firms could be forced to recognise and negotiate with unions where they are supported by a majority of the workforce. We're dubbing it 'Blair's big pay-off to his union backers.' Is this our first whiff of spring?

Two clerks from the Treasury caught up with me at 7 Millbank. They needed a Lord Commissioner to sign three Treasury Warrants. The first was for £215,096,760 and 90p.

---

650 1938–2001; Lord Mackay of Ardbrecknish since 1991; MP for Argyll 1979–83, Argyll & Bute 1983–7.

The next was for £1,554,472,000 – my first billion-pound cheque. The best was yet to come … in the foyer of 7 Millbank, witnessed by the security man and the lad on the switchboard, amid much giggling, I signed a warrant for £96,861,662,000! I was relieved to see that HM The Queen was my co-signatory and interested to note that her signature is as large and loopy as mine.

TUESDAY 25 MARCH 1997

The English Patient has won nine Oscars. The *Telegraph* tells us that personal incomes have risen by 56 per cent since 1979. John Redwood has been persuaded to cancel the press launch for his anti-EMU tract, *Our Currency, Our Country*. Convicted terrorists have been foiled in their attempt to dig their way out of the Maze Prison. And Allan Stewart, mutton-chopped axe-swinging former Minister, has decided not to contest our safest seat in Scotland for 'health and family reasons' – the tabloids got wind of a dalliance with a lady he encountered at a drying-out clinic! All in all, this has probably been our best day yet. The worst that befalls us is that the PM is photographed visiting a shop called Slees. (Slees Home Hardware of Braunton, Devon.)

WEDNESDAY 26 MARCH 1997

I rather doubt whether anyone is listening, but if they are they'll have noticed that this week we're winning. The unions are back. We've raised the spectre of beer and sandwiches at No. 10. At last, Blair is on the defensive.

At 7.45 a.m. I called Sheila Gunn at Central Office. As she picked up the phone she was shouting across the room, 'You've no idea how *isolated* we feel.' Sheila's i/c the PM on tour and 'We're having teething problems, that's all. We haven't got the bus and the plane yet and communication's terrible, so there we are in the middle of nowhere doing our press conference on education, as agreed, and up here they've decided to switch to the unions and nobody's bothered to tell us. Never mind.'

'Keep smiling.'

'God, I am. I've given strict instructions. At all times we've got to reflect the mood of the boss, take our look from his look.'

'I've seen the pictures – you're beaming beautifully in every one – and you're holding out the recorder to catch every word.'

'Only the machine doesn't pick up half of it – and we're supposed to get it transcribed, but that doesn't seem to be happening either. Happy days.'

Talked to Christine Hamilton who was sounding amazingly chirpy. 'The Association's being just wonderful. It's been terrible and I've had the lot – screaming habdabs, hysterics, crying buckets – but our people locally are being just fantastic. I don't know what we're going to do about the press. Do you know what the Editor of *The Times* said on Friday? At an editorial conference, Michael Gove suggested a piece outlining everything we know about Al-Fayed and Peter Stothard said, "No, that would blunt our attack on the MPs."'

THURSDAY 27 MARCH 1997

Oops! There goes another one … Tim Smith is stepping down in Beaconsfield. 'Ex-minister quits over sleaze – Tory who accepted £25,000 goes, but Hamilton fights on'. I've always rather liked Tim. I didn't know him well at Oxford, but re-encountering him at Westminster, twenty years on, he seemed a decent cove: genial, civilised, intelligent, upright, the sort of person you'd expect to find as a party treasurer and junior minister, *not* the sort you'd expect to see slinking out of the side-door of Harrods clutching brown envelopes stuffed with used banknotes. He was certainly very effective on the Finance Bill and, last night on the box, brave Jenny at his side, he made a dignified fist of his resignation – and looked as upright as ever: ramrod back surmounted by ovoid head, a blanched version of the Green Mekon. Poor man.

Hang on! There's more! News is coming in that Piers Merchant, 46-year-old husband, father and MP for Beckenham, is having an affair with a seventeen-year-old Soho nightclub hostess and was photographed kissing her in the park on Tuesday night. You couldn't make it up! Clean-living, conscientious Piers, vegetarian, teetotal, Peter Lilley's exemplary PPS, so frequently 'in the frame' for promotion but never quite making it on account of his apparent lack of charisma. Little did we know … What an idiot! He's denying it, and wife, family and constituency are right behind him, of course – but it's still morning and I imagine by nightfall he'll be gone.

Hezza was on the radio just now and magnificent – but it's an impossible wicket and the whole thing's a ghastly nightmare. Yesterday Mawhinney wheeled out Margaret Thatcher to bash Blair for toadying to the unions – she's clearly barking, but she's undeniably a superstar, and it was a coup, and it should have, and would have, led the news, and dominated the front pages, but for Tim Smith. Today Gumdrops and the Chancellor are launching our Green manifesto, but thanks to Piers and his teenage sweetheart we can forget it.

It's beyond belief really. The poor PM will be in despair, but at least we have the Easter weekend coming up: then on Tuesday we can pretend the past fortnight hasn't happened and have a go at starting all over again. (Actually, if Neil's going to go eventually – and when the pack want blood they usually get it – he ought to go *now* or we'll have 'sleaze' dogging us all the way …)

....

GOOD FRIDAY, 28 MARCH 1997

....

The nearest the *Today* programme gets to acknowledging Good Friday seems to be an item about a Finn who has rerecorded the hits of Elvis Presley *in Latin* and sent a copy to the Vatican. At the bus stop outside the church I see a respectable-looking, elderly lady engrossed in her morning newspaper. The Good Friday headline: 'I'M SO VERY VERY HORNY'. This is the passion in which the nation is enthralled this Holy Week.

Piers is hanging on. Neil is hanging on. Michael Brown is now under threat. I like Michael: he's a jolly, bouncy Tigger, who fell from grace when the tabloids discovered he'd taken a young man on holiday to the Caribbean… He also accepted £6,000 from Ian Greer Associates for introducing US Tobacco to IGA and campaigning against a ban on Skoal Bandits, a chewing tobacco linked with mouth cancer, and didn't declare the payment in the Register of Members' Interests because he didn't think it necessary. Downey is still to bring in his verdict: meanwhile a friendly Cleethorpes councillor is accusing poor Michael of behaving in an 'unethical and dishonourable' way.

So what do we reckon: three down and three to go? Of course, we haven't had the Sundays yet.

....

SATURDAY 29 MARCH 1997

....

'THIRTY-NINE DIE IN MASS SUICIDE.' Surprisingly, this turns out not to be the campaign team at Central Office, but a bunch of UFO nuts in San Diego. Here on Planet Election '97, it is the Prime Minister's fifty-fourth birthday, and it would be difficult to imagine a worse one. In many ways, the farce is turning to tragedy. Allan Stewart has been admitted to a psychiatric hospital in Paisley and I've just been talking to an alarmingly volatile Christine Hamilton:

> The reptiles are back in force. We've been holed up here for three days. I've just been out and screamed at them 'Get off my property. This is private property. Get off!' I know it doesn't help, but we're at the end of our tethers. The party's got to back us all the way. It's going to, isn't it? If the party lets us down now, I'm warning you … our book'll be out before polling day … and we've got a thing or two to say about leadership … Heseltine should swing for what he said about Piers …

> If Neil goes down the pan … you haven't heard anything yet… If Central Office
> start putting on any pressure, Neil can always stand as an Independent Conserva-
> tive … It's all such a nightmare.

They're in a bad way. Understandably.

Annette Dorrell has had her baby: a 10 lb 1 oz boy ten days overdue. Michèle said: 'Poor Annette!'

....

EASTER DAY, 30 MARCH 1997

....

I am feeling distinctly woozy. The Barlows [Stephen Barlow and Joanna Lumley] took us to Bibendum where Jo spoonfed me my very first oyster – '49-year-old has taste sensation: "A mouthful of the blue lagoon" he says' – and Stevie lavished extravagant wines upon us: champagne sec, pre-pre-prandial; champagne demi-sec, pre-prandial ('we're building now'); Martini ('straight up with a twist'), to brace us while we order; something Alsatian and sensational, for the starters; a red Burgundy and brilliant, with the lamb; a desert wine with a difference ('not too sweet: we need to complement the chocolate truffles') … a happy-happy evening that had us teetering into the street a lit-tle after one. Twelve hours later and I'm teetering still.

Meanwhile, the Tory Party is tottering. Are we on the brink of meltdown? The over-night sensation has been the resignation of Micky Hirst[651] as chairman of the party in Scotland. He has gone with commendable speed in anticipation of the Glasgow *Sunday Mail*'s claim that he has admitted to 'a series of homosexual encounters'. Apparently Paul Martin, a former personal assistant to Hirst, was 'said to have boasted openly' that they were lovers. Is this the same Paul Martin whose 'friend' was also said to be the 'friend' of Michael Brown when he resigned? It's going to get to worse.

It *has* to get worse because Central Office have briefed that Major and Mawhinney want Merchant and Hamilton *out* – and they won't go! The Beckenham crowd have backed Piers 43 to 3, so as far as Piers is concerned that's that. If the Duke of Wellington and Lloyd George and Steve Norris can get away with wholescale philandering, why should a hapless young man entrapped by *The Sun* have to fall on his sword? There was no affair: just a moment of folly in the park.

And Neil, we know, is digging in. He won't like the line in the Sundays: 'Major has also withdrawn his support for Neil Hamilton…. He wants both Hamilton and

---

651 MP for Strathkelvin & Bearsden 1983–87; chairman of the Scottish Conservative and Unionist Party 1993–97; knighted 1992.

Merchant to go before he launches the Tory manifesto on Wednesday.' Teddy Taylor, John Townend, Jim Spicer have all been on the radio just now urging Neil to put party before self, 'however unjust, however unfair'. Judging from my conversation with Christine, they're likely to be disappointed.

When I spoke to Alastair [Goodlad, the Chief Whip] yesterday I told him I was planning to go down to the river to watch the boat race. 'You couldn't contrive to rescue a couple of drowning oarsman, could you? Create a bit of a diversion?'

'What if I have to give them the kiss of life?'

'Oh God! ... Happy Easter.'

EASTER MONDAY, 31 MARCH 1997

The signals are confused. This morning's *Telegraph* is unequivocal: 'Mr Major is determined that Mr Hamilton, the MP for Tatton, has to go before the Conservative manifesto launch on Wednesday. One senior minister said: "It is time to do the decent thing – accept a revolver and a bottle of whisky and get it over with."'

But the radio news takes a very different line: 'Conservative Party sources confirm that it is up to local associations to decide who their candidates will be…' It seems that in the dark watches of the night we've changed tack!

Neil calls. He's amazingly collected. And cool. And funny. Michèle tells him he and Christine looked very pulled together on their way to church.

'Yes,' says Neil, chortling,

> On the way in I had to resist the temptation to deliver my Paschal sermon: 'The message of Easter is that crucifixion is quickly followed by resurrection!' On the way out I did mention to a couple of the reptiles that we'd been praying for the souls of the damned.

He was as resolute as ever:

> I've parked my tanks on the PM's lawn. I spoke to Mawhinney and Lewington yesterday and explained that there's no way I'm going to be moved. I like Lewington, but he's really not up to it. He's certainly no match for Mandelson when it comes to the black arts. Mandelson is very clever, and very nasty. But he may have overplayed his hand. The media don't like him. We should be taking the high moral ground now. We need someone from our side on the *Today* programme saying 'So Labour don't believe in the principle of innocent-till-proved-guilty

any more?' I tried to speak to the Prime Minister last night, but I was told he'd gone to bed. Well, it was 10.15 p.m. I imagine he's one of the Ovaltinies, don't you?

MONDAY 7 APRIL 1997

All the front pages boast a double whammy of absurdity: Elton John, pomaded and peruqued, a perfect fright in silver and white, arriving for his fiftieth birthday fancy dress party, and the BBC's war correspondent, another fright in white, offering himself up as the anti-corruption candidate in Tatton![652] I'm sure both gentlemen will have thought it a fun idea at the time – but I imagine, as the night wore on, Elton wearied of those high heels and that two-foot confection of curls (topped with a bespangled ship in full sail!) and I'm certain that Bell will rue his ill-judged foray into the political arena before the week is out. He says he expects his career as a candidate to be the shortest on record because he hopes and expects Mr Hamilton to stand down. He has underestimated Mr Hamilton...

And Mrs Hamilton! I have just been listening to her on the radio – a galleon in full sail: magnificent. She's revving up to manic overdrive, but she wasn't over the top – yet. (With Bell I imagine it's not so much mania as a delayed mid-life crisis worsened by vanity, a misplaced sense of self-importance, and a sad touch of the poor-me's: 'the BBC don't value/use/understand me any longer').

I called Christine and left a congratulatory message on the machine. I called Joanna to tell her how funny (and seductive) she was on Clive James. When Stephen [Dorrell] called he sounded a bit bleak.

'How's it going?'

'It isn't. I'm treading water. Health isn't an issue, which is good, but Central Office isn't using me, which is frustrating. It's Hezza all the way. And William.'

Yes, and Master Hague is proving very effective.

TUESDAY 8 APRIL 1997

At 6.00 a.m. we left London.

At 11.00 a.m. we were on parade outside the Chester office. At quarter past, on the dot, the Foreign Secretary's limo rolled up. Malcolm was excellent – lots of crinkly charm

---

652 Martin Bell joined the BBC in 1962; the wars he covered, wearing his trademark white suit, ranged from Vietnam and the Gulf to Croatia and Bosnia; Royal Television Society Reporter of the Year 1976 and 1992; MP for Tatton 1997–2001.

and beady-eyed interest. Happily we'd planned a proper programme for him and we had a good turn-out, so there were no *longueurs* and a relative sense that something worthwhile was accomplished. These ministerial visits can be hell: you're advised that a VIP is on his way, it's an honour and a treat and all that, but what on earth are you going to do with him for three hours? We'll have this problem with Tony Newton, one of the loveliest human beings on the planet and one of the most effective members of HMG, but unknown, absolutely utterly unknown to the man or woman in the street.

We had a fair press showing – all the local photographers plus a couple of radio stations. The cow from the BBC began by saying, 'You'll understand that legally we're not allowed to mention Mr Brandreth by name' and then spent most of the interview talking about Messrs Hamilton and Bell. I said, 'Why can you mention the candidates in Tatton by name, but not the candidates in Chester?' She didn't have an answer.

If I'd been desperate to win I'd have found it galling how much of Malcolm's time in my patch was being taken up with the sleaze saga from the other end of the county. As it was, I was simply content that the Foreign Secretary should have an audience and not feel his journey had been wasted. A couple of weeks ago the Chancellor told me he spent seven hours travelling to and from the West Country to talk to one radio station and forty ageing activists in a dismal village hall … It happens all the time. We avoided it by whisking Malcolm round North West Securities and dragooning a hundred (and more) of our faithful to the Club for a sandwich lunch and questions. Having stifled yawns with the hacks and in the car and on the NWS tour, he summoned up the required energy like a trouper and gave a full-blown stump speech, all stops out. Good jokes, good points, good man. He's been an MP for twenty-four years, a minister since '79, but clearly he's still ready for more.

At 7.00 p.m. we went over to the hall for the adoption meeting. There was a full house, generous, supportive, willing us to win. The faces were all familiar. Of course they were. They are exactly the same faces as gazed up at me five years ago at my last adoption. That's our problem in a nutshell: the stalwarts are still there, they're just five years older. Many of my best people are now in their eighties and these are the good folk we call 'activists'!

We got home by ten and turned on the box for news of Cheshire's *other* adoption meeting. Neil secured the necessary endorsement: 182 in favour, thirty-five against, four official abstentions and sixty-one sitting on their hands. The media scrum outside the Dixon Arms was wholly predictable. Christine, dismissing a hack wanting Neil to speak into his tape recorder: 'We do not take orders from *The Observer*.' Neil: 'I feel like Liam Gallagher.' (He cannot resist being funny: it was his joke about the wretched biscuit that really got up the PM's nose and precipitated his forced resignation.)

The most extraordinary feature of the Hamiltons' amazing day was the Duel of Knutsford Heath. Neil and Christine, hand in hand, turned up at Martin Bell's open-air press conference and photo call. With a steely *sang-froid* that would have done Joan of Arc proud, they marched resolutely towards Bell and the surrounding media posse. They pushed their way through and Neil extended his hand. Bell took it. Neil introduced Christine.

'Do you accept that my husband is innocent?'

Bell: 'I don't know. I am standing because a lot of local people have asked me…'

Christine (lip curling *à la* Dame Edna): 'I thought it was at a dinner party – in London…'

Bell: 'There is a question of trust. I cannot judge on questions of innocence until all the facts are made known.'

Portillo, when he's nervous/stressed/on the ropes, has a problem controlling his voice: the pitch alters, an odd seal-like bray brakes in. Neil, with perfect breath control, in his usual light tone, calmly enquired: 'Are you prepared to give me the benefit of the doubt?'

Bell (immediately, without thinking): 'Absolutely.'

Neil had got him! Christine bleated again about innocence, but Neil knew it was enough. He was off – and he'd scored. He knew it. We knew it. Bell knew it too: 'My first mistake was not bringing my flak jacket.'

WEDNESDAY 9 APRIL 1997

The first day of the Brandreth campaign. There's a set pattern to the next twenty-one days: a press conference every morning at nine, two hours walking the streets in one part of the constituency, another two hours in a different part (including a pub lunch), a break for an hour at home (to deal with correspondence, conceive and write tomorrow's press release, call those who've called and have to be called back), two more hours in a third area, another break, then the evening round – tonight it's the Business Club drinks, the YCs and then a gentle grilling at the hands of the Chester Branch of the Society for the Protection of the Unborn Child (three turn up and two of them turn out not to be constituents). At least by planning my own diary I've been able to avoid the things I hate – the railway station at dawn, bearding half-awake commuters; primary school gates as the mums deposit their charges and try to race their pushchairs around and past you without catching your eye; the postal sorting office at 5.00 a.m. when they've been warned you're coming and have hoisted the hostile posters in readiness.

The straightforward street-walking and door-knocking I rather like – especially on a day like today when the sun shines brilliantly and you feel that a few weeks of this and you might even lose a couple of pounds. Sir Fergus and Lady Montgomery join us on the campaign trail. He's a sweetie, a cherubic seventy-one, standing down, as much in love with a certain brand of show business (I first met him at Frankie Howerd's memorial service) as with politics. Joyce [Lady Montgomery] had the solution to Tatton: Neil should have stepped aside and let Fergus stand on 1 May on the understanding that Fergus would resign as soon as Neil is cleared by Downey.

We lunched at the Ring-of-Bells in Christleton. The association chairman's wife is in charge of provisions and she's toured all the pubs we'll be visiting collecting the menus so that we can pre-order. I tell her she belongs to the Nick Soames school of canvassing: 'If you have taken a morale bash in the morning, it is important to have a good lunch. It makes you feel a lot better.' (I don't share with her my favourite Soames story. A former girlfriend is asked what it's like being made love to by Soames ... 'Like having a large wardrobe fall on top of you with the key still in the lock.')

THURSDAY 10 APRIL 1997

'Labour poll lead slashed by the Tories.' That's the headline. According to MORI, we're up six points since last week. I must say it doesn't feel too bad out there ...

The real front page treat in *The Times*, however, is the picture adjacent to the story: a delightful study of Melissa Bell, 24-year-old blonde bombshell daughter of the old fool. She's gloriously photogenic and looks intelligent too. We'll be seeing more of Melissa for sure. We're seeing plenty of Tiger Christine too. Lynda Lee-Potter: 'If there'd been more women like Christine Hamilton we wouldn't have lost the Empire...'

It's Ma's eighty-third birthday and I remember to call. I'm pleased. She's pleased – and sounds in cracking form. I remember too to turn up at the Town Hall to register as a candidate and hand over my £500 deposit. I discover we're getting a Monster Raving Loony Party candidate. I seem to recall that last time the Loonies endorsed me and didn't put up a candidate of their own – so perhaps this is progress... How many votes do they take and from whom?

FRIDAY 11 APRIL 1997

Morning with a Duchess, afternoon at the sewage works, evening ploughing through six courses at the Lord Mayor's Banquet. Such is the candidate's lot.

The Duchess of Westminster is immensely tall and rather stylish and has skin like bubble-wrap that no one remarks upon because she's palpably nice, gloriously wealthy and we do love a duchess, don't we? It was one of the things that struck us most forcibly when we first arrived here: how the Westminsters are treated like local royalty. When Gerald fell out with us (over leasehold reform) and stepped down as Association President, an audible cry of pain emanated from virtually every branch. There was nothing I could do about it. Peter [Morrison] had warned him off me.

Anyway, this morning Her Grace was delightful, opening a home for the homeless. During the ceremony I sat next to David Hanson,[653] Labour candidate for Delyn, and mentioned my ploy for the Tony Newton visit. He said:

> When Gordon Oakes[654] was an MP he went to one of these twilight homes and bent over one of the residents who was sitting in an armchair gazing blankly at the TV screen. 'Do you know who I am?' said Gordon. 'No,' said the patient, 'but ask matron. She'll tell you.'

I've a feeling the story's as old as Dan Leno, but it still makes me smile.

The overnight excitement has been Angela Browning's election newsletter apparently flouting the line on EMU. She doesn't want our gold reserves being carted off to Frankfurt! Quite right too – but do we need to hear this just as the campaign is beginning to go our way? This is exactly what the PM's been dreading.

SATURDAY 12 APRIL 1997

'Cabinet let Eurosceptics off the leash'. Since we have no choice, we might as well make the most of it – and we are. The silence in the Labour ranks reveals the Stalinist nature of New Labour's high command – we, on the other hand, believe in democratic debate and, by the way (nudge-nudge), our candidates are a whole lot more sceptical than theirs …

One who isn't is our star turn for today. John Gummer comes to Chester and is a joy – jolly, impish, giving us just what we need for our photo call in the Handbridge butchers. 'I will gladly inspect the beef, but I will not, repeat not, hold a hamburger.'

Our theme is the importance of local and city centre shops, but John's happiest moment comes when we encounter a lone Labour activist on the parade. The man mutters something derogatory as JG strides past. John spins round: 'What does your candidate have to say on abortion then?'

The man is momentarily stunned, and then declares with some conviction: 'She believes in a woman's right to choose.'

'Oh yes, oh yes,' trills John, voice rising, breath quickening, 'she believes in murdering babies, does she? Just so we know!' The Secretary of State for the Environment is

653 Labour MP for Delyn since 1992.

654 Labour MP for Bolton West 1964–70, Widnes 1971–83, Halton 1983–97.

smacking his lips now: 'You want us to vote for someone who believes in murdering babies. Thank you! Thank you very much!'

At the Cheshire Hunt Point-to-Point the sun shines, 8,000 happy folk cheer the horses (*and* the hounds) and the talk is of the triumph of Aintree rather than the election. Lots of misty-eyed guff about how we defied the IRA last Saturday and proper praise for the police. Lord Leverhulme, still twinkly but struggling on his sticks, tells me he couldn't make it on Monday for the postponed Grand National because cars weren't allowed near the course. Bobbie McAlpine looked after the PM who helicoptered in for the race and found the boss in fighting form: 'Quite extraordinary, considering...' Alastair [Goodlad] was kitted out in what seemed an Ealing comedy version of the countryman's Point-to-Point attire – green cords, brown shoes, hacking jacket and cap. He only had three words to offer on the political front: 'Bloody Angela Browning.'

SUNDAY 13 APRIL 1997

Michèle called. She's back from Bologna, and on her way up. Aphra called from Perth in happy-happy form. ('Dad, did you know some of the kangaroos are six feet tall? We went to the beach today and we saw the dolphins.') Robert Atkins called, 'collecting a bit of a picture from the front' for the boss. I made encouraging noises, both because they were justified and because JM does need to be boosted – his mood does swing. The myth is the even-tempered fellow for ever on an even keel. In fact, he's up and down, hot and cold – and all too sensitive to signals from the front. Today he'll be up. The *Sunday Telegraph* headline guarantees that: 'Labour nosedives in new poll'. How is he? 'Tired,' said Robert, 'but much happier this weekend than last. I told him to remember Gordon Greenidge: it was when he started limping that he went on to score 100.'

Talked to Neil, much happier this week than last. We chuckled at Bell's protests that *he's* now the victim of a smear campaign – 'They have not gone for my politics or for my honesty, which are beyond question. Instead they have gone for my private life. There was an affair, but that was seventeen years ago...' Much chortling from Nether Alderley: 'Can we trust a man who breaks his marriage vows?' cooed Neil. Christine is chirruping in the background. I tell Neil to tell her how magnificent she has been – Boadicea meets Patsy Kensit – and I hear her chorusing, 'I'm a megastar! I'm a megastar!' They sound a lot more relaxed. 'I've gone to ground though. I'm not knocking on any doors, but I'm committed to some public meetings and I don't see that I can get out of them. And there'll be a bit of a media circus on Tuesday when I've got to take in my candidate's form and deposit. I thought I might wear a white suit...'

'And why not take a biscuit—'

'You mean, to give to Bell, say it's an old custom in these parts?'

'No, tell him that his coming up to Tatton from his fastness in London really does take the biscuit – so here it is.' Much guffawing. 'Obviously I want to keep out of the way, lower my profile and his. I've still got a handful of the Association who are making waves, but there weren't a hundred abstentions – there were four. The mix-up was because the old ladies couldn't hold their arms up long enough to be counted.'

My conscience is pricked. Mo Mowlam has been battling with a brain tumour. It's the steroids that have made her bulge and radiotherapy that forced her into a wig. Michèle has long said that I shouldn't make personal remarks.

MONDAY 14 APRIL 1997

What election? It's a non-event. Nothing's happening out there. I've spent the day in the sunshine, on the door-knocker, running up and down pathways in Boughton and Mollington and Christleton and Littleton and everyone's perfectly friendly, there's no hostility, but there's no real interest either. Listening to the radio, watching TV, scanning the papers, it's as though they're covering a movie of an election, a soap opera, that you can tune in to if you're so inclined, but it's not obligatory, it's certainly not real and it isn't really that important either.

Talk to Danny who sounds tired but content. 'The hours are horrendous. I start at six in the morning working on the PM's brief for the day and keep going through meeting after meeting till the last which is with the party chairman at nine. And because there isn't another meeting after it to go on to it can drag on – and on.'

I report on how it's going in the boondocks – no anger, no evidence Labour landslide, the areas you'd expect to be supportive being supportive and really rather positive.

'Yup,' says Danny, 'That's the message we're getting from all over. Honestly, I don't know what's happening any more.'

'I suppose one in ten have a reservation – they're either fed up or it's Europe.'

Danny chuckles. 'If we lose one in ten of our supporters, we're simply washed away!'

'Anyway,' I say, 'You're doing well. We're winning the campaign.'

'Yes, yes, we've softened up Labour, compared with a month ago we've really softened up Blair – but now we need something dramatic to happen.'

TUESDAY 15 APRIL 1997

It has. Suddenly the wait-and-see EMU line is falling apart. After Angela Browning was corralled, we had Angela Rumbold, vice-chairman of the party, coming out firmly against – but we could live with that because she's a backbencher. Danny and co. have rightly taken the view that since we can't stop them let's make a virtue of the fact that we don't stifle debate and let's allow the electorate to know our instincts. Tonight though there's real trouble: John Horam tries to have it both ways – the government's right to negotiate and decide, but when the time comes he'll be against it. *Newsnight* break this – and the first the hapless PM hears of it is as he comes off stage from the *Sunday Times* Q&A forum. I'm slumped in front of the box (Chicken Korma and three-quarters of a bottle of *rosé* down) when the phone goes. It's eleven. I assume it's Michèle. It's *Newsnight*. Through the *rosé* haze I manage to stumble through the agreed line. 'But should he be sacked or can he stay?' There's no line yet issued on this, but knowing what Danny feels and knowing we can't start jettisoning junior ministers left and right at this stage of the game I burble on to the effect that Horam clearly supports the government – but he has a personal view that will only be relevant if and when we need to make a decision. I fall asleep with the radio on and seven hours of World Service later find myself waking up to hear Malcolm Rifkind taking exactly my line, but with greater sobriety and authority.

WEDNESDAY 16 APRIL 1997

The shambles continues. A couple of our tosspot junior ministers have come out against the single currency, but at this stage in the game – and with members of the Cabinet continuing to send out mixed signals – what can the hapless PM do? At the beginning of the week he was in the West Country and realised that the people he was meeting had no idea we were already committed to a referendum on EMU – hence the decision to scrap the planned election broadcast and replace it with his face-to-camera impromptu address to the nation: 'We will never take Britain into EMU. Only the British people can do that.'

THURSDAY 17 APRIL 1997

The PM comes to Chester – or least I think he thinks he's come to Chester. In fact, he's in the adjoining constituency (which we haven't a chance of winning) and the Central Office organisation is so cack-handed that a) he's in a controversial out-of-town shopping precinct where there as many votes to be lost as won, and b) I only get to hear that he's here half an hour after he's gone!

Ah well…

FRIDAY 18 APRIL 1997

Oh dear. The PM, off-the-cuff, has offered a free Commons vote on EMU – but hasn't mentioned the idea in advance to Ken or Hezza so they're both wrong-footed. The PM is unapologetic: 'If I'd said "I'm frightfully sorry, that's a very interesting question but I'd better go and ask Ken Clarke or Joe Bloggs or someone else before I give you an answer" – it's not the way I operate.'

Ken knows he's not being consulted and there's nowt he can do about it. We're making this campaign up on the hoof. Hezza doodled his idea for the ad featuring Blair perched on Kohl's knee while waiting for a plane at Manchester airport. Central Office urged him to check it out with Ken, but he didn't and, deplore it as the high-minded Europhiles do, perhaps it's served its purpose.

MONDAY 21 APRIL 1997

Yesterday morning I did a ring-round of colleagues and the verdict was the same: it doesn't feel too bad, there's no open hostility, you don't sense a rush to Labour. This is naive optimism, isn't it? Look at the detail and one in ten of our supporters have gone wobbly. We're going to be washed away.

David Hunt reckons his majority will be halved and Wirral South could go either way. He hadn't seen the lead story in the Sundays: Redwood readying himself for an immediate putsch and Hunt galvanising 110 middle-of-the-roadsters to urge Major to stay on as long as he can to prevent a precipitate lurch to the right. As we stumble towards the finishing line, the press interest is switching entirely to the leadership struggle. This morning's post has brought a charming handwritten note from one of the potential contenders (Michael Portillo). Nobody writes more notes than Michael. He's almost too good at it: he remembers Michèle's name (and how to spell it), the note doesn't look rushed, and I feel ashamed for thinking he must have sent several hundred in recent weeks. Another contender has generously given time to stomp the streets of Chester: Peter Lilley, who may have the intellectual grasp of a leader-in-waiting, but is alarmingly lacking in the charisma stakes. He did two hours knocking on doors – he was tireless, he was magnificent – but I don't think a soul knew who he was.

On my sortie to London yesterday I caught up with Danny who didn't look nearly as weary as I feared given his dawn-to-dusk routine. How does Central Office rate the campaign so far? Week 1: a wash-out – all sleaze. Week 2: a bit of all right – Labour wobbled. Weeks 3 and 4: Not so bad – we're scoring with Europe. 'We told everybody the party couldn't, wouldn't hold together on EMU. We knew that the election address declarations were coming. We were pretty sure there would be junior ministers who couldn't contain themselves, so all along we knew that when the crisis came all we could do was ride over them. That's what we've done and it's worked.' According to Danny our internal polling suggests we're 12/14 points down – not 19/20 – and it's coming our way. They're contemplating leaking our polling data to give our troops a boost, stifle the mood of meltdown and pre-empt the post-defeat scenario becoming the story.

We gossiped about who had had a good campaign. Hezza – excellent. Howard – invisible. Clarke – 'too all over the place – and Europe kills him'. Hague – an early flourish, but nothing now. Portillo – excellent.

THURSDAY 24 APRIL 1997

Michael Howard came today and I was fearful of a disaster. We'd decided to take him to Christleton, to celebrate the local Neighbourhood Watch and to spare the police the nightmare of closing down half of Chester if we'd taken him on walkabout in the town. My fear was not that the photo call would flop, but simply that once the snappers had snapped we'd have fifty minutes with the Home Secretary and no one for him to see and nothing for him to do. On Tuesday I turned up in the village with a writer and photographer from *The Times* and what greeted us for our mass canvas? Three stalwarts, with an average age of eighty – it was a gift for the hacks: the cast of *Last of the Summer Wine* turn out for Brandreth! I pictured a repeat performance today. In the event, it was a triumph. All the local photographers were on parade: we were pictured by the pump house (yes, really parish pump politics!), and our fifty minutes was packed with action – the nursing home was having a charity day and gave us tea and cheers. A bearded lady kept saying to Michael, 'You're the best Home Secretary we've ever had. You should be PM.' Michael beamed and beamed – and revealed brown teeth which I'd not noticed before. The dentist, the village post office, the pub ('This is superb bitter,' cooed Michael. 'What is it? Bass? Yes, of course'), the mobile library, the parents collecting their offspring from school: we did 'em all. And Rachel Whetstone [Howard's Special Adviser], bless her, brought a bunch of carnations for Michèle.

I spoke at Christleton High School at lunchtime. A large crowd, mostly hostile, including a chippy teacher in a black shirt and seed-packet tie who stood with his hands in his jeans and asked about sleaze. I was loud and theatrical, and almost certainly rather ridiculous. Tonight I spoke to a friendly handful at the Chester College – I was weary but spoke so much better.

Labour press officer quote of the day (quote of the campaign perhaps): 'Later today Tony Blair will be spontaneous. Tomorrow he will be passionate.'

SUNDAY 27 APRIL 1997

To BBC Manchester for a TV debate with an alarmed-looking Tony Lloyd (who'll be a minister by Friday, God help us!) and husky-voiced Liz Lynne.[655] I like them both. Tony was a regular at the French conversation classes: dogged but dim was my assessment.[656] Our discussion on the box was rather fun – we were boisterous but evidently good-humoured, unlike the rather more watchable (and certainly more watched) debate on the other side which had Hezza and Prescott slagging each other off in no uncertain terms.

I reached Alistair and Cecilia's [home near Tarpoley] by about 2.40 p.m. Michèle was already there. The champagne flowed – and the Macon – and the Burgundy – and the salmon was wonderful and the pheasant well-roasted and the apple pie and cream just right. They are good people. Alastair is gathering with the PM and Cranborne and co. at No. 10 on Wednesday night to plan for Friday. Dignity will be the order of the day.

Talked to Seb who didn't know what the Falmouth verdict would be. The PM had been and done well.

'Did you do the warm-up?'

'No, we had Jeffrey. He did his ten-minute bark. It's wearing a bit thin.'

MONDAY 28 APRIL 1997

This election's all over. The focus now is entirely on the next election: who will be leader. Today's papers reckon it'll be between Hezza and Portillo. The confusion at the command centre continues. Indeed, the real confusion is: where is the command centre? In theory, it's Mawhinney, Maurice Saatchi and co. at Central Office. In practice, it's the PM, Robert Cranborne and co. at No. 10 and on the battle bus. Our messages have been all over the place: we abandoned the demon eyes because the PM lost his nerve/didn't like them; we put the weeping lion to rest because he didn't convince anyone; we've highlighted Europe, where we're most divided, when all the research told us Europe isn't an issue for the bulk of the electorate ('it's the economy, stupid'); and we've ended up with posters the length and breadth of the land saying 'Britain is booming' which the Chancellor of the Exchequer loathes and which even the experts agree are risky: see the word boom and you think of bust.

And here in Chester I can only report a dismal day on the Brandreth campaign trail.

655 Liberal Democrat MP for Rochdale 1992–7.

656 Labour MP for Stretford 1983–97, Manchester Central 1997–2012; Minister of State at the Foreign Office 1997–9. Lloyd, GB and a handful of other MPs attended occasional French conversation classes provided at the House of Commons on Wednesday afternoons.

Alternately it drizzles and sleets. The oomph has gone out of the activists and nerves are getting frayed. My support manager (early fifties) and my road manager (early seventies) almost came to blows outside the mobile library in Guilden Sutton. One felt the other was usurping his role: blood pressure and voices were raised. I disappeared inside the library and emerged to find them still at it. Fortunately rain stopped affray! We'd hired a bus for six o'clock to whisk sixty activists round town to show strength in numbers. About fifteen turned up, willing and cheerful, but the rain was driving and we'd have cut a sorry sight trundling round the bleak, deserted streets. Sensibly we aborted the mission.

Virginia [Bottomley] is coming on Wednesday. Her advance guard has just called: 'The Secretary of State would like to arrange a person-to-person phone conversation for tomorrow evening. How late can she call?' I suggested midnight – and could hear the intake of breath. What sort of feeble campaigner turns in at midnight? Two or three at the earliest – and then up again at six.

WEDNESDAY 30 APRIL 1997

Virginia's been and gone and it was another huge success! The walkabout was fine because the sun shone and, hooray, as well visitors from Texas, Germany, Japan, Stoke, Portsmouth, Woking, Plymouth, Flint and Connah's Quay, we did meet Chester folk and they were jolly supportive. You'd still think we could win. As we ambled towards the cathedral Virginia juggled *sotto voces* to me with exuberant forays into the crowd.

'*If I want to get onto a Select Committee, who do I have to speak to?* Hello, I'm Virginia Bottomley, do you come from Chester? *It's the Foreign Affairs Select Committee I want, not to be chairman or anything, just to be on it.* Will you be supporting Gyles Brandreth? Oh, good! He is good, isn't he? *They quite like seeing a woman, whatever Brian says. It's been a funny old campaign, hasn't it? We keep changing tack.* How lovely to see you. You know Gyles, of course. *Should I call Alastair? What about having Hezza as acting leader for a while, like Margaret Beckett?* The Cathedral's had half a million from the Lottery. I haven't forgotten whose millennium it is! *Should I phone Alistair now or wait till Friday?*'

Not one of the Cabinet who has been to Chester during the campaign has any expectation that we'll come within a mile of winning.

The crisis of the hour is that I've discovered a hole in the seat of my trousers – and I don't have another pair. I've been wearing one of my MP's suits day in day out through the campaign and finally it's given out – worn away. Is this a portent?

Five years ago I had no idea what the election outcome would be. I hoped against hope, prayed the opinions polls would be wrong. They were. This time they can't be. What do I reckon the Chester result will be? Con: 20,000? Labour 29,000? Lib Dem: 5,000? Others: 1,000?

THURSDAY 1 MAY 1997

I wasn't far out: Con: 19,253. Lab: 29,806. Lib Dem: 5,353. Referendum: 1,487. Loony and A. N. Other: 358. End of era. Chester RIP.

We voted first thing and then spent the day touring the committee rooms, attempting to boost the flagging morale of our gallant troops. A policewoman noticed the hole in my trousers and mentioned it discreetly to Michèle. When I saw the Superintendent of Police at the count I commended his officer's vigilance.

We had supper with *Blackadder* in front of the box – and when ten o'clock came readied ourselves for the exit poll. It's going to be a Labour landslide. At 10.05 the telephone rang. It was David Davis, our Minister for Europe: 'How's it looking?'

'Haven't you seen the exit poll?'

'Oh never mind that,' said David blithely. 'You'll be all right. We're about 4 per cent down here. Good luck.'

In the event, the swing against him was 9.5 per cent.

A little after midnight we donned our gladrags, adjusted our brave faces, and made our way up the hill to the Town Hall. My opponent was standing on the stairs. I said to her at once, 'Congratulations.' She looked bemused. Our result wasn't due for a couple of hours at least. I spent the time wandering between the press room, the count, and the TV room where a large screen had been erected to display the results. It was so relentlessly bad for us the other parties' supporters had stopped cheering. They just looked on amazed. Of course, there were hurrahs for certain scalps – Neil Hamilton provoked a roar, Norman Lamont a jeer, and poor Portillo's defeat prompted a standing ovation.

FRIDAY 2 MAY 1997

Major has gone, and with some dignity. Mr Blair has arrived and already the messianic fervour is a little too rich for my taste. And as for Cherie...

Talk to Stephen. He sounds dreadful. His voice has gone. He croaks at me in a state of high nervous excitement. I tell him to go to bed and keep quiet. He says he can't. There are calls to make and broadcasts to give. I tell him that wanting to win isn't enough. Others must want him to win too. And to have any chance of winning he needs to look – and sound – like a winner. Michèle tells me, 'You're wasting your time – he doesn't listen to a word you say.' She's right. He's off to do *Newsnight*. We're off for a farewell dinner with our team. They have done all that you could ask of them. The debacle is not their fault.

Nick Winterton calls. He goes through the routine of commiseration (via a good bit of bombast about his and Ann's own splendid results) on his way to asking for Alastair's number. He wants to pitch in early with his thoughts on the leadership. 'Redwood is intellectually the most interesting, but Lilley has strengths – I have had useful meetings with him, at his department, in his room at the House and always been impressed – and, of course, there's William – but that must be for some time down the road. Stephen is supremely competent, but he lacks warmth. I told him months ago that he's got water in his veins instead of blood.' I don't dislike Nick, but he is such a windbag, and so self-opinionated and self-satisfied, that I doubt our paths will be crossing again.

Call Jeremy Hanley. 'This is the Job Centre. How may I help you?' Jeremy is funny, as ever – but devastated. 'The last three elections I was sure I was going to lose – and I won. And this time I thought I'd win and … well, here we are.' I suggest Jeremy puts in to be Director-General of the British Council. He'd be brilliant. He agrees. We also agree that the moment we get back from Sicily we'll all have dinner in the heart of his constituency – 'and we can be as loud as we like and undertip the waiters.'

'I must tell you,' he chuckles, 'my three mad women – the three truly deranged constituents who come to every surgery – I've given each of them my successor's home telephone number…'

Talk to Danny – who gets it spot on:

> Because I haven't always been a Conservative, I know how a lot of people see us. *People loathe the Tories*. That's why we lost. The campaign didn't help. We were Charlton Athletic playing Manchester United. We didn't deliver what we planned. Of course, the PM was our great strength. But he was our liability too. He was running his own campaign alongside ours. You can't win an election if you just come in at eight in the morning and say 'Ooh, it's Wednesday – let's do Europe!' But the campaign wasn't the problem. We were the problem. The election was never about them. It was about us.

And they didn't want us anymore. It was as simple as that.

SATURDAY 3 MAY 1997

We shop. (New Labour, new trousers.) We pack. We hoover through. By noon we're on our way. Lunch at Broxton Hall: poached salmon, salad, new potatoes, and a glass of Sancerre. The sun is shining. I'm forty-nine. I weigh 12 st 9 lbs. I'm out of a job, but for the first time in years I'm beholden to no one. Cry freedom!

POSTSCRIPT

MAY 1997–JUNE 2007

1997

The overnight news is that Hezza is in hospital and has withdrawn from the race [for the Tory leadership]: this has to be good for Stephen; Lilley has thrown his hat into the ring, which must be bad for Howard; the Blair Cabinet is complete and there are no real surprises, except for Dobson at Health.[657] (At least it'll make the officials realise what a class act Stephen has been.)

Ruth Deech (Principal, St Anne's College, Oxford) calls, full of kind concern and heartfelt commiseration. I think she's a little shocked by how jolly I'm sounding – but I do feel free, and easy, and I can't hide it. 'The system's so cruel ... the way you're just thrown out overnight... Poor Peter...' Peter Butler is an old friend of the family, it seems. He had a majority of 14,000. He just assumed he was there for life. A dangerous assumption. 'Poor Peter. He'd moved to Milton Keynes and the children are at school there ... And, of course, there's the loss of status. And the car – he was loaned these wonderful cars – with wonderful soft leather seats...' Dear God, it clearly was time for a change in Milton Keynes!

Stephen calls. He's home at last. The throat's a lot better. He says GMTV went well. I say: 'Now Hezza's out, you're in the frame – but still by default. The press are predicting a final play-off between you and William. As we stand, you'll be the loser. The problem is you're a lot of people's second or third choice, but nobody's first.'

Should he call Ken? No harm in talking to Ken, but Ken will want to stand come what

---

657 Frank Dobson, Labour MP for Holborn & St Pancras since 1979; Secretary of State for Health 1997–9.

may – and to form too early an alliance with the Clarke corner will alienate the Eurosceptics and, like it or not, they are the masters now. We need a clear platform and some key supporters. David Faber, Simon Burns, Peter Luff are lovely, but lightweight. We need Michael Ancram, John Maples, David Curry … My advice is rest, relax, decide on your pitch, and try to secure the support of a few grown-ups.

Richard Ottaway calls. I say that I'm sorry to hear about Michael (odd – I'd have called him Hezza if he hadn't been in hospital with angina): 'Is it serious?'

'He's just being sensible, but it's been a warning for him – better to have had it now than to have let it kill him in a year's time.'

'What do you do now?'

'I don't know. Until 4.00 p.m. yesterday I was Michael's campaign manager. I could end up with Stephen, but…' There's always this 'but': unless we overcome it, we lose. Richard doesn't want Lilley or Hague ('an empty vessel'), but Stephen doesn't deliver for him. 'He comes over as rather soulless. He looked so terrible during the campaign, those bags under the eyes … Some of us have been wondering if we shouldn't look outside the Cabinet.'

'Oh yes?'

'I know three or four who are drawn to Michael Ancram…' Dream on… 'And a couple have mentioned Tom King…'

'Richard. Please. Be serious! We considered that option ten years ago. Don't give up on Stephen … Think: Ancram would be outstanding at the Foreign Office, Lilley at the Treasury, Hague at Central Office. We've got to make sure the centre holds. Don't give up on Stephen…'

MONDAY 5 MAY 1997

Blair has formed his government. It looks tired already. A handful of stars, a bunch of has-beens and a crowd of never-going-to-bes. And out there in voter-land all that naive optimism … On TV at the weekend John Fortune was quite ludicrous. In place of his customary (and enchanting) cynicism there was the most terrible sentimentality – eyes bulging, throat taut, brow glistening, he hailed New Labour as though it were the gateway to the New Jerusalem. 'Yes – and the hawthorn is in bloom!' Pass the sick-bag, Mabel…

TUESDAY 6 MAY 1997

It is Mr Blair's forty-fourth birthday and the century's youngest Prime Minister has completed his government with a little flourish: Tony Banks as Minister for Sport. Better to have the likely lad contained on the front bench than barracking like a barrow boy from the back. Containment is clearly part of the Blair plan. Alastair Campbell has written to the heads of information in every department telling that requests for interviews with ministers should henceforth be cleared with No. 10 – a bureaucratic nightmare! – and that ministers lunching with journalists will be 'frowned upon'. The new ministers will all be 'working too hard building a better Britain for us all' to have time for lunch. Ah well, the road to hell etc.

Last night William Hague did a deal with Michael Howard. Michael as leader, William as deputy and party chairman. Overnight, William thought better of it and reneged. Michael leaked William's change of heart. Stephen's verdict: 'It damages both of them.'

WEDNESDAY 7 MAY 1997

A change of government offers high excitement for the civil service. This morning's post contains the following, dated 2 May: 'I am required to write to you to ask you to return any items of government property which are in your possession. I understand you have a pager and some departmental passes. I should be grateful if you could make arrangements for these items to be returned to me as soon as possible. You are, of course, allowed to keep your black ministerial box as a memento.' Given Mrs Blair's reported aversion to cats I'm also inclined to hang on to my Treasury file on HM government's cats.

SUNDAY 18 MAY 1997

This is perfect. We are in Sicily, in Taormina, and the sun is shining. I am lying on a deckchair by the swimming pool. The season is only just beginning: there is hardly anyone else here. There is a gentle breeze and the smell of spring. It is eleven o'clock and my first cappuccino of the day has just been served.

Michèle booked this for us during the campaign. She knew we'd lose. (She proposed putting our flat in Chester up for sale during the campaign, too. Seriously.) She is very happy with the outcome of the election. Everybody is. Britain is awash with hope. 'A new day has dawned, has it not?' The golden age of Blair is upon us. It'll all go wrong, of course. It always does. But that's not something that you can say out loud at the moment. Everyone (including my wife) believes that Saint Tony will lead us to the Promised Land and that the Conservative Party is not just down, but out – and probably out for good.

I am saying nothing. As an MP, you only meet two types of people: people with problems and people who are right. I marvel that everyone seems to have the answer to everything. What I discovered in Whitehall and Westminster is that, in truth, nobody really knows anything. (Even at the Treasury where they really do think they know it all.)

It is so good to be here, away from all that. I can see Mount Etna in the distance. We are planning an expedition to Syracuse, where the boys come from. But first, lunch: vitello tonnato and a glass of Frascati, I think, don't you?

FRIDAY 30 MAY 1997

I am on the train, going to Leeds, to record *Countdown* – six episodes. (And, yes, madam, since you ask, they do feed you the words through an earpiece. But, no, I won't be wearing any wacky jumpers. 'Time for a change' and all that.) I am so lucky. I am picking up where I left off. *Countdown* called immediately after the election. CBS News called. LBC called. I have a contract for a new novel. I have work – and plenty of it. Many of my colleagues have nothing – nothing and no prospects. People like Derek Conway (who called just now) had huge majorities and still they lost – and now his children will have to be taken out of boarding school. People think there are 'directorships' and all sorts of goodies awaiting ex-MPs. Not so. What use is an ex-Tory MP to anyone? This is Blair's Britain. This is the age of New Labour. Old Tories have nothing to offer. Their contacts are outdated: their skills (such as they are!) irrelevant. It's fine for the few who are famous – e.g. Michael Portillo – but most of my former colleagues are shop-soiled, unknown, unfashionable and the wrong side of fifty. The best they can hope for is something in the charity sector.[658]

MONDAY 2 JUNE 1997

Just before the election, in the Tea Room of the House of Commons, queuing up for a toasted teacake, I found myself standing next to Jack Straw. He was grinning from ear to ear. 'Why are you looking so cheerful?' I asked. 'Because I have been sitting here doing nothing for eighteen years – eighteen years! – and this time next month it looks as if I'll be Home Secretary.' And so he is. And well done him. (He beat me to it, after all.)

After lunch (sole off the bone, at Le Vendome in Dover Street, with Laurie Mansfield,

---

658 Derek Conway (b.1953), Conservative MP for Shrewsbury & Atcham, 1983–97, and a colleague of GB's in the Whips' Office, eventually found work as chief executive of the Cats' Protection League. He later returned to Parliament as Edward Heath's successor as MP for Old Bexley & Sidcup, 2001, falling from grace in 2008 over the misuse of parliamentary expenses.

agent to the stars, organiser of the Royal Variety Performance) I walked to Pimlico, to Stephen Dorrell's campaign headquarters. He hopes to be Leader of the Conservative Party – what's left of it. He is a good man, but it won't happen. He has no following – and I have no interest any more. Either you are in there or you're not. And I'm not.

WEDNESDAY 4 JUNE 1997

Stephen has thrown in the towel. He's backing Ken [Clarke]. We went together to Ken's office this morning. John Gummer, David Curry, Michael Mates were there. They think their man's in with a chance. There was high excitement in the air. I felt the complete outsider. I shouldn't have gone.

THURSDAY 19 JUNE 1997

William Hague has defeated Ken Clarke by twenty-two votes and, at thirty-six, has become the youngest leader of the Conservative Party since Pitt the Younger. 'Much good will it do him,' says Michèle. 'No one is interested in your lot any more. The people have spoken, Gyles. Listen to the people.'

I do. I have. This week I am writing a children's book: *The Adventures of Mouse Village*. Next week I start my novel: *Venice Midnight*. (Jo Lumley gave me the title. I was calling it Venice at Midnight. She said, 'Venice Midnight is much more intriguing.') I am getting on with life in the real world. My friend Seb Coe, by contrast, has thrown in his lot with William. He is already his right-hand man. 'What's the point?' asks M.

'If he sticks with it,' I reply, 'he'll be offered the first safe seat that comes up or a place in the House of Lords.'

'Do you think so?'

'I know so. I know how the system works.'

'Is that what you want?' she asks – and I don't reply. The truth is: I'm not sure. (Actually, the truth is I can't afford to play at politics. I have a living to earn.)

SATURDAY 28 JUNE 1997

We went to Cambridge to watch Benet take his degree. We went on afterwards to the Master's drinks at Magdalene. The sun shone. The young people looked so happy. We parents looked so proud. This is what life is about.

SUNDAY 31 AUGUST 1997

I came down into the kitchen to make the early morning tea and turned on the television and heard the news. Princess Diana is dead.

I called Michèle and we just stood there watching. We just stood there. It was quite difficult to take in. I went out to buy the papers and, amazingly, the *News of the World* had produced a 6.00 a.m. 'shock issue':

> DIANA DEAD. Princess Diana died just after 3.00 a.m. London time today after a horrific car crash in Paris. Her boyfriend Dodi Al-Fayed and the driver of their Mercedes were killed instantly when the car slammed into a wall in a tunnel along the Seine river near the Champs-Elysées.

LATER

It's wall-to-wall Diana. Charles has gone to Paris to collect the body. William and Harry are at Balmoral with the Queen and Prince Philip. Blair has been on the box and brilliant – if you like that sort of thing. William [Hague] botched it utterly.

MONDAY 1 SEPTEMBER 1997

Last night Saethryd went over to Kensington Palace and joined the crowds. They came in all shapes and sizes – a lot of black people, a lot of gays – and they all brought flowers to lay at the palace gates. The outpouring of emotion is extraordinary. There are pictures in the paper of William and Harry being driven to church with Charles yesterday: no tears there, just stiff upper lips. But the rest of the world is awash. And they have all got something to say: Mother Teresa, Lady Thatcher, Bill Clinton, Nelson Mandela. Even James Hewitt's mother Shirley has thrown in her two cents' worth: 'He's in a state of shock.'[659]

I am sorry for Diana, of course. And for her sons. This is a tragedy – but it is their tragedy, not mine. I cannot say that I am feeling this personally, as the rest of the world seems to be doing. I am out of step with the rest of mankind. Mr Blair has his finger on the national pulse: 'She was the people's princess and that is how she will remain in our hearts and our memories forever.'

---

659 James Hewitt, former British household cavalry officer and lover of the Princess of Wales.

FRIDAY 5 SEPTEMBER 1997

It's completely out of hand. The world has lost the plot. The issue of the hour appears to be the Buckingham Palace flagpole. As anyone who knows anything knows, the flagpole is traditionally bare except when the sovereign is in residence when the royal standard is flown. And the royal standard is never flown at half mast, even on the death of a sovereign. But the tabloids are having none of that – they are baying for blood. Actually, they are baying for tears. 'Show us you care, Ma'am!' Well, the Queen doesn't cry – and certainly not in public – but she has bowed to public opinion and the union flag is now flying over Buckingham Palace at half mast.

LATER

I have just watched the Queen's live broadcast. It was perfectly judged. It will have diffused the anger. She did not say anything she did not mean. She did not go over the top. But she did enough.

SATURDAY 6 SEPTEMBER 1997

We sat in the kitchen and watched Diana's funeral. Tony Blair's over-emotional reading of the lesson was an embarrassment, but other than that it all worked. Charles Spencer's tribute to his sister was very touching – even if it didn't quite make sense. (Prince Charles and the royals are William and Harry's 'blood family' too, surely?) When he'd finished, the crowd outside applauded – and the applause was taken up by the congregation inside the abbey. 'The people's princess' indeed. I imagine the Queen is utterly bewildered by it all.

LATER

Interesting call just now. I was surprised to see Prince Philip in the formal funeral procession, walking behind the gun carriage bearing Diana's coffin along the route to Westminster Abbey, but I have now learnt why he was there. Prince Charles and Charles Spencer were expected to walk, with the boys, but it seems that Prince Harry and, in particular, Prince William were initially reluctant. The Duke of Edinburgh, who had not planned to walk (he is merely the ex-father-in-law, after all), said to William, 'If you don't walk, you may regret it later. I think you should do it. If I walk, will you walk with me?'

THURSDAY 9 OCTOBER 1997

Yesterday, I wasted half a day reworking the peroration for William Hague's end-of-conference speech. I have just faxed it over. It won't be used – and William doesn't need help from outsiders anyway. This kind of thing comes naturally to him. Far (far) too much time is spent on the leader's speech at conference. (My favourite conference speech story is John Whittingdale's[660] about Mrs T. and the Monty Python parrot sketch. They had drafted a paragraph for her in which the Liberal Party was likened to the dead parrot – 'This is an ex-party' etc. Mrs T. didn't get it. They explained to her: 'It's a joke, Prime Minister, from Monty Python. It's very funny. It will work. Trust us.' Reluctantly, she went along with it, but she had her reservations to the last. Even as she was approaching the podium to deliver the speech, she said to John Whittingdale: 'This Monty Python – is he one of us?')

1998

TUESDAY 28 APRIL 1998

In advance of next week's referendum, I took part in the Evening Standard/Newsnight 'debate on London'. We don't need a Mayor for London. We certainly don't need a new 'Assembly'.[661] I thought we Conservatives were supposed to believe in less bureaucracy, not more; in containing public expenditure, not extending it; in encouraging grass-roots democracy, not imposing additional tiers of know-it-all, top-down government. We have elected members in thirty-two London boroughs already. Enough's enough. And as for Jeffrey [Archer] promising to work 'nineteen hours a day, 364 days a year' running the capital, heaven forfend! I said some of this tonight, not very well and to little effect. What I didn't say is that I have already been approached about the possibility of becoming the Conservative mayoral candidate – not because they want me, but because they want anyone but Jeffrey. I know they've tried to persuade Seb [Coe], too. The approach was not

---

660 John Whittingdale OBE, Conservative MP for South Colchester & Maldon 1992–7, Maldon since 1997; political secretary to Margaret Thatcher, 1988–92.

661 The referendum, held on 7 May 1998, asked the question: 'Are you in favour of the government's proposals for a Greater London Authority, made up of an elected mayor and a separately elected assembly?' Just 34.1 per cent of the electorate voted, with 72.01 per cent voting Yes and 27.99 per cent voting No. Jeffrey Archer was hoping to be the Conservative Party's first London mayoral candidate.

altogether flattering: 'Don't worry, you won't win. London votes Labour. We expect to lose, but let's lose quietly and with dignity – that means without Jeffrey.'

SUNDAY 10 MAY 1998

Late night, lots of laughs: Joanna and Stevie, Biggins and Neil [Sinclair, his partner] Nikko Grace[662] and Ian, Lynda Bellingham.[663] Non-stop laughter, in fact. (Can't remember what about, but it was good for the soul.) Early start: *Breakfast with Frost* at 11 Downing Street. I told David that Joanna would like to be asked to his summer party: she will be. I told the Chancellor [Gordon Brown] it was good to be back in Downing Street: he said he'd been amused to read my articles about my time at the Treasury. 'You lot seemed to do a lot of eating and drinking and telling jokes. We don't tell jokes.' I can believe it. He is grouchily amiable, but so earnest – and still biting his fingernails to the quick. After the show, he took us upstairs to his flat. He lives above No. 10, while Blair and family are in the No. 11 duplex, which is bigger and more like a proper house. I was intrigued that when he took us into his bedroom, the Chancellor rather ostentatiously opened the built-in wardrobes as if he wanted us to see the women's frocks that were hanging in there. They looked quite large, but I don't think they belong to Gordon. I assume they belong to his girlfriend.[664] I presume he was keen for us to know that he has one – and that she's not a 'beard'. I don't think he does anything without calculation.

TUESDAY 12 MAY 1998

This morning I was on the radio being touted as a possible mayoral candidate. I pointed out to the listeners that last week's referendum showed that three-quarters of Londoners either don't want a Mayor or don't care. I said that if I stand and if I'm elected, I'll do nothing: no press conferences, no initiatives, no grandiose strategies, nothing. Best of all, I'll even give the money back. (The Mayor and Assembly are going to cost £20 million p.a. minimum. It's truly appalling.)

This afternoon, tea at the House of Commons with Virginia Bottomley. We talked about the mysteries of the honours system and her plans for the future. She's going to be a headhunter. Afterwards, as I was walking through Central Lobby, I bumped into Benazir

---

662 Nickolas Grace, English actor, still remembered as Anthony Blanche in *Brideshead Revisited*.

663 Lynda Bellingham, English actress, still remembered as the mum in the Oxo commercials.

664 Sarah Macaulay married Gordon Brown at his home in Fife on 3 August 2000.

Bhutto.[665] I greeted her like a long-lost buddy – which she is – but clearly my cheery informality was not what was expected. I remember her being rather fun at Oxford in the '70s. She took herself very seriously today. I tried to disarm her. 'It's only me,' I said.

'So I see,' she replied.

'It's just us, Benazir,' I persisted.

'We are in the Palace of Westminster,' she answered crisply. 'A certain decorum is called for.'

MONDAY 27 JULY 1998

By coincidence, lunch with Norman Lamont and tea with Julian Clary.[666] I didn't mention one to the other. I don't think they have met since the notorious night when Julian announced on live TV[667] that he had 'just been fisting Norman Lamont ... talk about a red box...' The audience roared and I doubt that Norman minded, but it played badly in the press and, for a while, derailed Julian's career.

Five years on, they are both doing fine, even if the glory days are gone. Norman is stouter, but still fun – obsessed with the dangers of the euro, still brooding on the injustice done to him by John Major, and he appears to have mislaid his nice wife along the way. Julian is tall and slim and beautiful – the beauty of his face is extraordinary. But he is about to turn forty and needs to do something new, hence our meeting. I told him about the bizarre life of Henry Paget, 5th Marquess of Anglesey – 'the dancing marquess'. He died young in 1905, celebrated for his beauty, notorious for his extravagance, his eccentricity (he would lie naked in a coffin covered only in jewels), his non-consummated marriage (he was gay), his love of theatre. He put on his own shows and starred in them, with the estate staff as extras. There's a film in this – it has everything: love, heartache, skulduggery, buggery, Monte Carlo and bust – and, if beautifully written, could be a break-out vehicle for Julian. Except, I don't think he was very interested. And I'm not sure he can act.

THURSDAY 17 DECEMBER 1998

I have decided to like Cherie Blair, partly because others seem to despise her (she doesn't take a good photograph: mouth like a letter box), but mainly because she has

---

665 Benazir Bhutto (1953–2007), Pakistani politician, President of the Oxford Union, 1976. The first woman elected to lead a Muslim state, she was twice Prime Minister of Pakistan (1988–90, 1993–6); assassinated at an election rally in Rawalpindi.

666 Julian Clary, English camp comedian and writer.

667 At the British Comedy Awards in December 1993; both Lamont and Clary were presenting awards that night.

been very helpful and friendly, lending me 'Tony Blair's Teddy Bear' to put on display at our Teddy Bear Museum. The bear is called Lynton (as in Anthony Charles Lynton Blair) and today, after his long holiday with us in Stratford, I took the little fellow back to Downing Street. As Iraq was being bombed,[668] I stood in the hallway of No. 10, holding the bear in my arms, waiting for Cherie, when who should come marching into the building but John Prescott. I said, 'Hello, John.' He simply glowered. His face turned purple with suppressed rage. Anger, rudeness, resentment are his stock-in-trade. (And yet, apparently, he stills gets the girls. It's almost incredible, but they say it's so. There were hacks haunting Chester when I was there, digging for dirt about JP.)

1999

MONDAY 1 FEBRUARY 1999

An evening among the fallen – rather jolly, as it happens. Supper with Neil and Christine Hamilton at their flat on Albert Bridge Road. They fight on – they fight to win.[669] They are like things possessed: Neil drinking too much, Christine on manic overdrive. But they are still fun, still friends, and Christine is a fine cook and a generous hostess. Also of the party: a remarkably sanguine Jonathan Aitken. He thinks prison is a possibility. He seems quite ready for it.[670]

FRIDAY 23 JULY 1999

Breakfast with Jeffrey in the Archer embankment penthouse. I went to interview him for the *Sunday Telegraph*. He wants to be Mayor of London – the first. He is campaigning hard. 'It's going well, Gyles. I don't want anything to go wrong. I've got to be careful. I know I can trust you.'

---

668 From 16 to 19 December 1998, in response to Iraq's failure to comply with certain United Nations Security Council resolutions, US and UK forces bombed Iraqi targets in an operation codenamed Desert Fox.

669 In the event, Neil Hamilton, having already dropped his libel action against *The Guardian* over the 'cash for questions' affair, lost his libel action against Mohammed Al-Fayed in December 1999 and lost the appeal in December 2000. Unable to pay his legal fees, he was declared bankrupt in May 2001 and discharged from bankruptcy three years later.

670 Following his unsuccessful libel action against *The Guardian*, in 1999 Jonathan Aitken was charged with perjury and perverting the cause of justice and sentenced to eighteen months' imprisonment, of which he served seven.

We are not alone. It is 8.20 a.m. and already, up in the gallery, Jeffrey's PA is fielding phone calls. Joseph, the butler (of Middle European extraction and riper years, straight from Central Casting), pads discreetly in and out. While Jeffrey and I tuck in (for the master, a boiled egg, timed to the second; for me, crunchy brown toast and the crispest bacon), two of the mayoral campaign team sit quietly in attendance. They do not eat. Or speak. Jeffrey runs his life as though he's a character in one of his own novels.

I know almost no one who doesn't mock him, but I know few so successful – at least in monetary terms. What is his secret?

> Boundless energy. Determination. And when I see something, I go for it. Long-fellow said, 'The heights that great men reached and kept were not attained by sudden flight, but they, while their companions slept, toiled ever upward through the night.' Later he offered me another gem: 'Energy plus talent, you'll be a king; energy and no talent, you'll be a prince; talent and no energy, you'll be a pauper.'

What fuelled his ambition?

> I didn't do well at school. I failed. I was a disaster. I remember canvassing in Edinburgh with Malcolm Rifkind. We passed his old school and I said, 'I bet you were a prefect.' He said, 'No, I wasn't actually,' and then he told me how, for fun, he had done a test on the Cabinet and three-quarters of the Cabinet had failed to become prefects too. I've often thought failure to succeed at school drives you to want to succeed afterwards. It's ironic how few school captains appear to go on to do anything else. It's almost as if they've achieved what they want to achieve. I still want to achieve.

I mentioned a line of Aristotle Onassis: 'I must keep aiming higher and higher – even though I know how silly it is.'

Jeffrey chuckled, 'That's good. The line I love of Aristotle Onassis is: "If you can count it, you haven't got any."'

MONDAY 6 SEPTEMBER 1999

I am making two films for ITN: one about the nature of leadership, the other about the future of the Conservative Party – is there life after death? I went down to Alfriston in Sussex to see Denis Healey and get some historical perspective. The joy with Denis is that, though he is now eighty-two and beginning to shrink, he remains so certain about everything. Sitting in his handsome mock-Lutyens sun lounge, weighing Clement Attlee and Margaret Thatcher in the scales, the name of the Leader of the Opposition cropped up. 'William Hague?' snorted Denis. 'He's a twerp. A twerp. There's nothing more to be said. Forget him, forget it. Move on.'

Denis is not troubled by self-doubt. And he is blessed in Edna. I like her approach to life. As she brought in the coffee and ginger cake, I said, 'How are you?'

She replied, pleasantly: 'You don't need to know. If you've got worries, keep them to yourself. A trouble shared is a trouble doubled.'

FRIDAY 10 SEPTEMBER 1999

I have been granted the pre-conference interview with the Leader of the Opposition. (Perhaps no one else wanted it?) I went to see him at Central Office in Smith Square. The foyer is now New Conservative: colour scheme by Gap, Sky News on the TV, *The Independent* the one newspaper on the coffee table. The only vestige of William's predecessors is a small bust of Winston Churchill, the last bald leader of the party. Beneath a huge portrait of a purposive Master Hague, finger pointing to the future, is a yellow flyer inviting the faithful to sign up for a seminar at which 'leading professional consultants' will provide 'an excellent opportunity to perfect your skills in three key areas: presentation, personal development, interview technique'. (A four-hour session: £10 including lunch.)

I had a good hour with William, but I came away with nothing. Because of yesterday's excitement,[671] I felt obliged to ask him all sorts of impertinent questions. Was he gay? Had he ever had any homosexual experiences? Would he mind if his children were gay? He played it all with a straight bat. I moved on to confront him, rather rudely, with his failure to make an impact. He answered, genially, 'Time will tell.'

I confronted him with his critics: 'The unkind ones picture you as a foetus in a baseball cap,' I said. 'The others see you as an old man in a young man's body, an odd-looking political nerd reading Hansard at the age of seven. What do you say to that?' He said something anodyne.

Interviewing a safe pair of hands like William will never be easy. He won't drop catches. I asked him if he had a favourite maxim. 'I think Willie Whitelaw said, I think he actually said to me, "Nothing is ever so good or so bad as it first seems in politics."'

671· On 9 September 1999, in an interview with *The Times*, Michael Portillo, who was hoping to become the Conservative candidate in the forthcoming Kensington & Chelsea by-election, admitted to 'some homosexual experiences as a young person'.

Seb (who sat in attendance at the interview, with the glossy-lipped Amanda Platell)[672] claims his boss is 'the most qualified man who ever wanted to be Prime Minister'. Denis Healey says he's a twerp. I reckon the Whitelaw maxim may be nearer the mark. William is thirty-eight, a considerable achiever, likeable, clear-headed, quick-witted, rational, reasonable, intelligent, articulate, thoughtful, shrewd. But something's missing. I was impressed, I wasn't moved. I was charmed, but not inspired. In theatrical terms, he is a first-class leading man: he knows the lines, he won't bump into the furniture, he'll never miss a performance. But he isn't a star in the way Blair is. He won't be Prime Minister. (Foreign Secretary perhaps, twenty years from now, in our next administration.)

WEDNESDAY 6 OCTOBER 1999

I am in Blackpool for the Conservative Party conference. I stood at the back of the hall to listen to Jeffrey's speech. Our mayoral candidate scored a conference triumph. As he and Mary emerged afterwards I hugged them and they beamed. The activists adore him. They love him for what he is: a gung-ho, no-nonsense, tub-thumping rallier to the cause. They love his loyalty. They love his certainty. They love his energy. They feel he is a winner. Of course, what they don't know is that the hierarchy of the Conservative Party would rather have had anyone – anyone – other than Jeffrey as candidate for Mayor. But the activists have the final say, so they've been lumbered with Jeffrey and now they've got to back him to the hilt.

I am having dinner with Adam Boulton.[673] He is very jolly and gets fatter every time I meet him. (I have just seen Tim Rice. Ditto.)

WEDNESDAY 13 OCTOBER 1999

Went to Birmingham to be the MC and warm-up act for John Major. He is on tour with his memoirs. He put a nice inscription in my copy, but whenever I see him nowadays, I feel he is looking at me warily, as though he thinks I know something I shouldn't, as though he can't entirely trust me.[674] (Norma was lovely. Fastidious, intelligent, normal. As ever.)

---

672 Amanda Platell, Australian journalist, press secretary to William Hague, 1997–2001.

673 Adam Boulton, English journalist, political editor of Sky News since 1989.

674 Though a friend of Edwina Currie since their university days, GB had no inkling of her affair with John Major. In March 1997, GB had reported in his diary John Major remarking that he imagined Edwina was then knocking on 'quite a few publishers' doors', but he did not realise the significance of the observation until the publication of her *Diaries: 1987–92* in 2002.

MONDAY 1 NOVEMBER 1999

I am on the train coming back from Salisbury. I have been interviewing Ted Heath. His Queen Anne house in the Cathedral Close is quite perfect. 'When Roy Jenkins came to lunch he looked out of the drawing-room window and said, "Ted, this must be one of the ten finest views in Britain." I said, "Oh really, which do you think are the other nine?"' As he told me the story, Ted's shoulders heaved with happiness. The old monster was in mellow mood. He showed me some of his treasures: his orchids (a present from Fidel Castro), the dish that once belonged to Disraeli, the Richard Strauss manuscript, the Churchill paintings. 'This is the one I prefer. It's got two signatures. Winston signed it when he painted it and then signed it again when he gave it to me. What will you have? Tea, gin, whisky, champagne?' It was not yet four o'clock, so I settled for tea. My proposed theme was the qualities required for successful political leadership. He seemed happy with that. 'You suggest some and I'll respond.'

'Energy,' I began.

'Yes.'

'Stamina.'

'Yes.'

'An ability to perceive reality efficiently and tolerate uncertainty.'

'Hmm. Yes.'

'An ability to inspire loyalty and maintain discipline.'

'Yes, but it depends how it's done. Political leadership is different from military leadership. In politics you can't just lay down the law and expect people to follow it. We see an attempt being made to operate in that way in the Conservative Party now. Hague says, "I'll do it my way!" That's not political leadership. It's an attempt to impose a particular point of view. True political leadership is about persuasion, and about listening to and taking account of others.'

'But also about having a clear personal vision, knowing where you want to go?'

'Yes.'

'And to that end you have to be determined, single-minded, to have what Napoleon admired, the mental power *de fixer les objets longtemps sans être fatigué*?'

'Yes, yes, absolutely. [I knew I'd score with that one.] The great leaders will always concentrate on the big picture, not get too bogged down in the day-to-day. I remember, in the middle of one crisis [in 1958] – three ministers, including the Chancellor of the Exchequer, had just resigned – I went to see Macmillan in his room at No. 10 to talk to him about the timing of the announcement of their replacements. I found him sitting in his armchair with his feet up on a stool, reading in front of the fire. He agreed to what I proposed and then said, "But please don't worry me any more. Can't you see that I'm trying to finish *Dombey and Son* before I go off on this foreign tour tomorrow morning?"'

'Would that approach be possible today?'

'Yes, perfectly. It was that approach that allowed me my music, my concerts; it allowed me my sailing in the spring and the summer. It's a question of how you handle the job. I didn't interfere with departmental ministers just for the sake of it. I only became involved if something appeared to be going wrong.'

'When did that style of government begin to change?'

'With Harold Wilson. He was a workaholic. He had a small group around him and they met constantly, working into the early hours. They say Wilson was a great operator, but to what effect? There's nothing left of Wilson now.'

'And, of course, Mrs Thatcher only needed five hours' sleep and never stopped.'

'Hmm, yes, well. One saw the consequences.'

He gave me plenty of good stuff – scorning Thatcher and Reagan; dismissing Mandela; praising Castro and Chairman Mao. He doesn't care. And mock him as we may, he has his place in history. On 24 January 1972, Ted signed the Treaty of Accession in Brussels. There's no turning back. 'It was the proudest moment of my life.'

SUNDAY 21 NOVEMBER 1999

It's all over. 'Jeffrey Archer destroyed' is the *Sunday Telegraph* headline. The *News of the World* has nailed him as a liar who was prepared to commit perjury in his libel action in 1986. The feeling is he'll end up in gaol. Three to five years, they reckon.[675]

MONDAY 22 NOVEMBER 1999

The press are going to town: 'Lying Archer may face jail: scandal returns to haunt Conservatives' – *The Guardian*; 'Archer faces criminal charges: Hague's judgement questioned as sleaze returns to Tory Party' – *The Times*. On the front page of the *Telegraph* there's a huge picture of Andy Colquhoun [Archer's former mistress and personal assistant], in floods of tears, running the gauntlet of newsmen outside her home. It's a cruel world.

And a ridiculous one. This afternoon I made my way to Kensington Fire Station to film Michael Portillo and William Hague on the hustings. William didn't turn up. Michael

---

675 On 19 July 2001 Archer was found guilty of perjury and perverting the course of justice. He was sentenced to four years' imprisonment. On 21 July 2003 he was released on licence, after serving half of his sentence.

did – and, as he arrived, he was ambushed by Peter Tatchell and friends.[676] In the scrum that followed, I was knocked over. I carried on reporting. Flat on my back from the pavement's edge I declared: 'I'm in the gutter, but I am still looking at the stars!' Maddeningly, the cameraman had stopped rolling. My gem was lost. ('Twas ever thus.)

Also today: Cherie Blair is pregnant, aged forty-five. I did a piece about it for CBS News. The hapless Leader of the Opposition is childless, friendless, sleaze-ridden, but our sainted Prime Minister just goes from strength to strength. Where does he get the time? And the energy? (He is the father: we can be certain of that.)

TUESDAY 7 DECEMBER 1999

Coffee with Christopher Lee,[677] at 6 ft 5 in. the tallest leading actor in the history of cinema. Also, I discovered, the most long-winded. I met up with him at a discreet hotel behind Sloane Square (11 Cadogan Gardens). I got out my recording equipment and, at a little after eleven, I asked him my first question. At a little after twelve, he was still answering it. Fifty minutes later, when he was just getting into his stride with his answer to my second question, I interrupted (which I know was rude), made my excuses and left.

Lunch at the Gay Hussar with Geoffrey Atkinson. He produces the Rory Bremner show[678] and his commitment is humbling. He really cares about politics. (He is more serious about politics than almost any politician I know.) He sees his programme doing what the opposition ought to be doing but isn't: with in-depth research, analysis and understanding, calling the government of the day to account.

Tea with Paul Burrell.[679] His devotion to Diana is not in question, but I do wonder if he was quite as intimate as he implies.

MONDAY 13 DECEMBER 1999

I might tonight have been at Jeffrey's champagne and shepherd's pie party in his penthouse by the Thames. Invitations were sent out a while back, but last week a letter came from our host (in his own hand) saying, with regret, he had decided to cancel. So, instead, tonight I made my way to 14 Cottesmore Gardens, W8, to the gala bash given by Mr and

676 Peter Tatchell, Australian-born political campaigner and gay rights activist.

677 Sir Christopher Lee, leading English film actor, particularly associated with horror films.

678 Geoffrey Atkinson produced *Rory Bremner, Who Else?* from 1993 and, from 1999 to 2010, *Bremner, Bird and Fortune*.

679 Paul Burrell RVM (b.1958), former footman to the Queen and butler to Diana, Princess of Wales.

Mrs Conrad Black.[680] It was generously done, but the crush was incredible: the establishment was out in force, braying smugly at one another and gushing over our shiny and complacent host and his glamorous wife. (I mock, but I gushed and gurgled with the worst of them.) I was pleased to be there: it made an amusing scene: but though, I suppose I am part of it, I don't feel part of it at all. I don't like these events: I don't like these people (certainly not en masse): why do I go? I suppose I feel I can't not be there.

2000

WEDNESDAY 8 MARCH 2000

It is Ash Wednesday and my fifty-second birthday. I am in Dubai taking tea with His Highness General Sheikh Mohammed Bin Raschid Al Maktoum, the Crown Prince and de facto ruler of the kingdom.

Actually, we have coffee not tea – served to me as I sit on a sofa at the end of a drawing room the size of a tennis court. I begin to tell His Highness how wonderful Dubai appears to be. He says nothing. I tell him how wonderful he appears to be. Still he says nothing. I am thinking this is going to be an impossible interview, when a servant steps forward and collects our coffee cups. The Sheikh smiles: 'We Arabs do not talk until we have finished our coffee.'

Throughout our meeting, which lasts two hours, courtiers come and go, messengers approach and retreat: sometimes he receives them, hears what they have to say, takes a document from them, sometimes he raises a hand and silently they back away. I feel I am in a scene from one of Shakespeare's history plays: 'My liege, I bring news from France!'

He charms me and disarms me. 'I am running my country myself, with my people. I do not have advisers. I think they are a waste of time.'

'Will you ever give your people the vote?'

'What is democracy for? To make people happy and safe. My people are happy and they are safe.'

As I leave he gives me a birthday present – beautifully wrapped. 'I think your wife will enjoy these,' he purrs. At once I picture diamonds – or perhaps pearls. It turns out that

---

680 Conrad Black, Baron Black of Crossharbour, Canadian-born newspaper publisher and author, later imprisoned on charges of fraud and obstruction of justice; married, as her fourth husband, to Barbara Amiel, British-Canadian journalist.

His Highness is giving me a collection of his own love poems – translated into so-so English. Does he have a message for me to take away from my visit?

'For you?' He ponders for a moment and then looks me directly in the eye. 'Every morning in Africa a gazelle wakes up. It knows it must outrun the fastest lion or it will be killed. Every morning in Africa a lion wakes up. It knows it must run faster than the slowest gazelle or it will starve. It doesn't matter whether you're a gazelle or a lion, Mr Brandreth. When the sun comes up, you'd better be running.'

THURSDAY 1 JUNE 2000

In October 1997, when Piers Merchant eventually stepped down as MP for Beckenham (it was just a moment's folly in the park!), I got the call from Central Office suggesting I might be just the man for the seat ... I asked for twelve hours to think it over, but I knew at once it was not for me. I don't think Michèle could have borne it and I am not sure I want it any more. Government is exciting, but we won't be in government again for a decade – or more. The backbencher's lot is thankless – mostly futile, relentlessly frustrating and financially quite challenging ... Jacqui Lait (who came second to me when I put up for Chester) became our candidate in Beckenham and I think they are lucky to have her.[681]

And I am lucky to be here in New York. I flew in on Concorde on Monday. I sat in the cockpit with the pilot as we landed. Last night we had dinner with Walter Cronkite, the great CBS news anchor, still voted 'the most trusted man in America'. He took us to the Windows on the World restaurant at the top of the World Trade Center. I am off now to lunch at Sardi's with Barry Humphries. Tomorrow we are seeing his show at the Booth Theater. I reckon Dame Edna is the funniest performer on earth. I am sure Beckenham has its good points, but I like New York in June. How about you?

MONDAY 5 JUNE 2000

4.45 p.m.: Meeting with Alastair Campbell at 10 Downing Street. He's an odd mixture of bluff, gruff and rough-diamond charming. He's clearly in command of the ship.

I went to set up an interview with Tony Blair. 'You're seeing Tony on Wednesday,' he said.

'Am I?'

---

681 She stood down in 2010, having been caught up in the MPs' expenses scandal. She over-claimed for the mortgage interest on her second home, and was told to pay back some £7,000. She was succeeded as MP for Beckenham by Colonel Bob Stewart, commander of the 1st battalion, Cheshire Regiment, when GB first arrived in Chester.

'At Wembley. You're both speaking to the massed ranks of the WI. Ten thousand women.'

'They'll love Tony,' I said. 'He'll have them eating out of his hand.'

'Really? What are they looking for?'

There and then I scribbled a few opening lines for Tony to use. Alastair took them, amused.

As I was leaving, I saw a photo of the Blairs' baby Leo pinned onto a noticeboard on the office wall. I stopped and cooed at the picture.

'Take it,' barked Alastair. 'Take it.' He yanked the picture from the board and thrust it into my hands. 'I don't want it. I can't stand it. Don't know what it was doing there. Take it. I'll be glad to see the back of it.'

WEDNESDAY 7 JUNE 2000

Disaster for Blair at the WI. I arrived as he was finishing – but he was finished, poor man, almost as he began. Wembley is a barn, the acoustic was terrible. I don't know if he used my opening lines or not, but almost at once the audience felt patronised and decided he was giving them a party political broadcast on the wonderful things New Labour is achieving for the NHS and that's not what they were after. He didn't talk to them: he talked at them. And when the barracking and the slow hand-clapping started, he did not know what to do. He should have torn up his script, of course, and just taken questions – been himself, been human. Instead, wide-eyed and sweating, he struggled on with his script as written: because it had already been issued to the press he felt he had to deliver it all.

It was a nightmare for him – a miserable hour that will be followed by days of unforgiving headlines. Whoever had come on next couldn't have failed.

That said, I am happy to report that the good ladies of the WI gave me a standing ovation.

TUESDAY 3 OCTOBER 2000

10.45 a.m.: I set off from London SW13 at the crack of dawn to get to Bournemouth [for the Conservative Party conference, the last before the 2001 general election] in good time for William Hague's unscripted question-and-answer session and here I am, four hours later, stuck on the M3 listening to *Woman's Hour*. There's been a bomb scare. On the motorway the traffic is moving at a snail's pace. On the radio a feisty young lesbian is telling Martha Kearney that the Conservative Party needs to be more inclusive or it is doomed. Hear, hear.

1.30 p.m, Highcliff Hotel, Bournemouth: I may be late, but I have not gone unrewarded. Incredibly, as I arrived, the very first person to greet me was the feisty young lesbian. She's called Karen Gillard.[682] She wants me to come to the Tory Campaign for Homosexual Equality bash, hosted by Steve Norris (natch). 'It's up the other end of town, near the gay guest houses, you'll like it.' I certainly like her. And she says she likes me. (Michèle often says I'm a lesbian's idea of a real man.) Next chance encounter, in the corridor, outside my room, Michael Portillo.[683]

'Gyles, my friend,' he says.

'Michael, my hero,' I respond. He is looking sensational: full tan, full lips, full head of hair. How he makes it stand up and wave like that we'll never know. He's out to wow 'em, without notes, 'from the heart'. He's on a roll. It can't go wrong.

7.30 p.m.: Amazing afternoon. Michael triumphed. In the press room the hacks shook their heads in wonder. 'It's incredible how he's changed' is their line. I don't think he's changed at all. He's abandoned his hectoring style of speaking, he seems happier with himself since sharing his secret past with the wider world, but fundamentally he's the same man. People don't change. But they do grow older. Ted Heath gave me the sweetest smile and shook his shoulders in greeting, but he's not looking good. Wisely, they had him on the platform for the Health debate: Liam Fox, our Health spokesman, is a former GP.

At 4.00 p.m. I made my way to the VIP room behind the stage to join the gathering gaggle of 'Celebrities for a Conservative Victory'. It was exactly like being in the green room before recording a daytime game show for the BBC at Pebble Mill. 'Darling, you look wonderful. Isn't Anthony Andrews looking fantastic? How old is he now? Where's Dana?'

'She couldn't make it. We've got Ed Stewart instead.'

'Stewpot? Stupendous. Crackerjack!' We were happy to see one another, but listening to a couple of party workers whispering over the tea urn was not encouraging.

'Who's that?'

'I don't know.'

'And that?'

'I'm not sure. I think it's Ruth Madoc.'

'Ruth who?'

---

682 She later became a Liberal Democrat councilor in Plymouth and a Lib Dem parliamentary candidate in the 2005 and 2010 general elections.

683 Portillo returned to Parliament as MP for Kensington & Chelsea (1999–2005) following the death of Alan Clark. He was now shadow Chancellor of the Exchequer from 1 February 2000 to 18 September 2001.

'You know, from *Hi-de-Hi!*'

'Actually, I'm Nicky Stevens from Brotherhood of Man.'

'Of course, thank you for being here.'

At 4.40 we were lined up to make our way on to the stage for the Culture, Media and Sport debate. I was supposed to be between Tim Rice and Antony Worrall Thompson ('What about you and Delia Smith, then?' 'Not a barrel-load of laughs, is she?' 'She's the Mary Archer of home cooking.'), but at the last moment a distinguished-looking old boy joined the line next to me. I assumed he was our culture spokesman in the House of Lords and made appropriate small talk. The poor man looked quite bemused. 'He's David Shepherd,' Tim hissed at me.

'The bishop? I thought he was dead.'

'No, world-famous artist. Paints elephants. Makes a fortune.'

'Ah.'

I know the press will mock our line-up, but the hall was full, the mood was good and those they recognised the crowd seemed pleased to see. Mike Yarwood and Bob Champion got the loudest cheers. Patti Boulaye opened the proceedings. We are lucky to have her. She's black and beautiful – not attributes with which the Conservative Party is over-endowed.

1.00 a.m.: The celebs dinner was very jolly, with Jim Davidson in cracking form. He's going to be the warm-up act before the leader's big speech on Thursday. 'I'm going to come on wearing a blue shirt and open my jacket and it'll be drenched – just like Blair's. What d'ya think, Gyles? Fucking great idea, ain't it?'

'Fucking great, Jim.'

'The Tory's Party's changing, Gyles.' It certainly is. I have agreed to be patron of the 'Lesbians for William' campaign. (They really wanted Virginia Bottomley, but I think she demurred.)

At 10.00 p.m. we were herded onto a bus and driven across town to the Bournemouth Pavilion for the Conference Ball. Traditionally, this is a grim affair, peopled by elderly activists jitterbugging sedately to over-amplified music they neither recognise nor enjoy. Tonight it was different. Jim took command of the proceedings. 'Did you hear about the Brad Pitt Lookalike Contest? [Pause] Robin Cook came second. [LONGER pause] Lenny Henry won.' Tim Rice and Michael Ancram did Buddy Holly duets. Jim introduced Tim as the man who has written a musical about the Prime Minister called *The Lying King*. 'Acually,' said Tim, 'It's called *Superstar – Jesus Christ!*'

When William and Ffion appeared on stage the room went berserk. We stamped our feet. We hollered. The girl standing next to me said, 'I love him, I love that man.' William is a sensational performer. On that stage he was as strong, as sharp, as funny as Jim Davidson. 'And look,' he said, 'no sweat.'

When the Hagues departed Faith Brown took to the stage and gave us an impression of Mrs Thatcher crossed with Vera Duckworth (which we loved) followed by a joke about Jeffrey Archer that we didn't want to hear. (Jeffrey is now a non-person. This time last year we were all over him. Tonight we don't even want to hear his name.) Faith (old trouper) fought back with a selection of Abba hits and then went into the title song from *The Full Monty*. For an alarming moment, it looked as if Jim was going to strip for us. He didn't, of course. He gets pretty close to the wire (there was a story about a suppository and the weight of the doctor's hands on his shoulders that left my neighbour a little confused), but he knows his audience and played us to perfection.

I walked back across the park. It is a beautiful night. It has been a good day. The Conservative Party seems more at ease with itself than I have known it in ten years. As I climbed the hill to the hotel I noticed a couple with their arms around each other in the car park. They were kissing. It was Penny and John Gummer.

THURSDAY 5 OCTOBER 2000

4.00 p.m.: Jim's warm-up was a triumph, so hilarious that the laughter and applause drowned out the BBC interview with Hezza in the commentary booth. William's speech raised the roof. He is our best orator in a generation. In the press room, the verdict was that this has been our best conference in years. I rounded on one of the hacks: 'I hope you'll say so.'

'I will – except no one will notice.'

'Why not?'

He pointed at the television screen. 'It seems there's a revolution in Yugoslavia. I'm afraid your friend William is going to be wiped off the front pages. He'll be lucky to make page six.'

The man from *The Guardian* chuckled. 'That's politics.'

WEDNESDAY 18 OCTOBER 2000

Lunch at Grosvenor House, celebrating seventy years of the literary lunches founded by Christina Foyle. Margaret Thatcher was the guest of honour and in fine form. Less so Denis, who drank heavily, sneezed repeatedly and kept dropping off. At one point, he suddenly woke up, looked at Michèle across the table and said, 'Nice titties.' He was smiling. It was meant as a compliment.

It was one of those days. Lord Longford dropped his trousers – right to his ankles. Larry Adler felt off the dais while playing his harmonica and Denis Healey arrived saying, 'Good evening, good evening.' At the end of lunch I gave the vote of thanks and while I was speaking Denis Thatcher slumped forward onto the table. This time I really thought he was dead. I wasn't alone. Norma Major had come with Ian McColl,[684] who crept around the table and managed to get hold of Denis's wrist and take his pulse. He gave a thumbs-up and, as I sat down, Denis sat up and winked at Michèle. Mrs T. looked the other way throughout.

2001

MONDAY 5 MARCH 2001

Brief encounter with one of the great figures of our time: Michael Jackson, in town for Uri Geller's book launch. He looked so strange – and sad. His face has been destroyed. He hobbled in on a crutch, smiled a very weird smile but wouldn't say a word. 'It's a Monday,' one of his minders explained to me, 'Mr Jackson never speaks on a Monday.'

Later, at Sarah Butterfield's art show in Cork Street, John Major was a lot chattier – though in despair at the state of the party and William's apparent lurch to the right. 'I care about the party – not all the people, but the party.' He promised to give me his first post-election interview.

'Thank you,' I said.

'Goodnight,' he said, 'God bless.'

FRIDAY 11 MAY 2001

It doesn't look good for William.[685] Last night, at the Yorkshire Property Awards

---

684 Baron McColl of Dulwich from 1989, physician, surgeon and politician; PPS to John Major in the House of Lords, 1994–7.

685 William Hague led the Conservatives to defeat in the general election on 7 June 2001 and resigned as leader on 13 September 2001. The election result gave Labour 40.7 per cent of the vote; the Conservatives 31.7 per cent; and the Liberal Democrats, under Charles Kennedy, 18.3 per cent.

dinner in Harrogate, I worked the room and at not one table did I find enthusiasm for wee Willie. 'He's a stage Yorkshireman,' sneered a Barnsley millionaire, his companions grunting in agreement.

'He's a real Yorkshireman,' I protested.

They laughed: 'It don't wash with us.'

Coffee with Anthea Turner at her Surrey ranch, Southfork-by-Guildford. If she isn't going to vote Conservative, who is? She claims she's got a soft spot for John Prescott. Actually fancies him.

What hope is there?

Sandwich lunch with Charles Kennedy at his flat in Victoria. He's pottering round in his socks, looking well but smaller and much thinner than I remember. He grins: 'I'm 5 ft 9 in., I won't over-claim.' He's lost at least a stone in weight.

'How?' I ask, 'Exercise?'

He splutters: 'I don't even recognise the word. No, it's being a bit more sensible about food and alcohol consumption.' Does he think he drinks too much? He smiles wanly: 'Because you're seen to be reasonably convivial and because you're a Highlander, and people have a certain perception of Highlanders, what with the distilleries and all that ... these things get said. I smoke too much, I'll admit that.'

How does he rate Blair?

'In terms of general application to the job of being Prime Minister, I think he's a very good Prime Minister.' And Hague? 'A lot of things are not going right for William. The Conservative Party is in an almost psychotic state, incapable of being led.'

By the end of the campaign Charles reckons he will have escaped the Ashdown shadow. His aim is to make the Lib Dems the credible party of opposition and, from there, he reckons government is eventually possible, with or without proportional representation. 'I regard this as marathon, not a sprint.'

'So you could be Prime Minister one day?' I asked, incredulously.

'It is possible, yes.' He said it with an entirely straight face.

When he went to the loo, I poked about the kitchen, looking into the fridge and the cupboards for hidden stashes of booze.

I found a half-bottle of wine, nothing more.

THURSDAY 17 MAY 2001

Anthea's pin-up [John Prescott] has punched a protesting voter in the head and brought the election to life. For this relief much thanks.

Elevenses in Battersea with Neil and Christine Hamilton. Neil is looking pretty punch-drunk himself. He becomes bankrupt next week and is to have the same trus-tee-in-bankruptcy as Jonathan Aitken.

Lunch in a pub in Brentwood with Martin Bell.[686] He is wearing his ludicrous crum-pled white suit and when I tell him it's a gimmick he gets all uppity. Apparently, it's a 'good luck suit' – kept the bullets off him in Sarajevo and should keep the eggs at bay in Ongar. He's put on a stone, maybe two, he's gross, but his daughter Melissa is as beautiful as ever. (His other daughter is not on hand: 'She doesn't want to be known as my daughter. You understand.' I do.) Clearly, he's regretting not standing against Keith Vaz in Leicester, 'but the people here asked me first'.

Tea with Glenda Jackson at the ASLEF headquarters in Hampstead. What does she make of Prescott the street-fighter? 'Poor John. He won't have slept last night. He's a passionate man. We need him.' I tell Glenda that I feel I share the credit for her new, improved, jollier appearance. When she was standing for London Mayor, I urged her to smile more. When she does she looks quite sexy. When I say to her, 'You could be a world-class actress, instead you're a nothing backbencher, why?' she doesn't have an answer. She's sixty-five and doesn't expect to be a minister again. It's raining, so she has called off the afternoon's canvassing. 'I'm not daft.'

MONDAY 21 MAY 2001

The journalists agree: the Kennedy campaign bus is the most friendly; the Blair bus, way, way, the least. En route to Orpington, the Kennedy sandwiches (white bread, dry ham) don't get my vote, but Sarah (Gurling, Kennedy's girlfriend) definitely does. She's thirty, a big girl, not a fashion plate, but 100 per cent normal. 'We've been an item for three years,' Charles tells me.

'Not married?' I say. 'Do you have a commitment problem, Charles?'

'For God's sake, Gyles. We'll get the election out of the way and turn to other issues after that.'[687]

TUESDAY 22 MAY 2001

I am standing in a field on the outskirts of Shrewsbury, gazing at the open sky, awaiting

---

686 The former BBC correspondent, Martin Bell had said he would only serve one term as MP for Tatton (1997–2001) and was now standing as an independent candidate in Brentwood and Ongar, the seat held by Eric Pickles. He came sec-ond in the poll, securing 32 per cent of the vote.

687 They were married in July 2002 and divorced in December 2010.

a vision from heaven. At 2.15 p.m. on the dot the Widdecombe helicopter lands and Ann comes beetling through the long grass towards me.

She is in her element, careering round the country like this, eighteen hours a day.

'How are you surviving?' I ask.

'On Lucozade and catnaps,' she chortles. What is the single most important personal quality a leader needs? 'Moral courage. And William has it to an extraordinary degree. He couldn't have done this without it.'

We crisscross the county, meeting two candidates, six police officers, eight local press, eleven members of the general public ('Good morning! Good morning!' trills Ann, although it is now late afternoon) and twenty-six party activists, average age sixty-plus. 'Is it worth it, Ann?'

'Yes.'

'Are you sure?'

'Yes.' She trembles with zeal.

Ann's off to Cumbria. I want to track down Prescott, but, 'for security reasons', the Labour Party won't release details of his whereabouts. At 6.00 p.m. they concede, 'Tomorrow he is in the north-west. That's all we're saying.' I reckon it will be Chester, my old constituency, where his mother lives.

WEDNESDAY 23 MAY 2001

I am right. At 10.15 a.m. the 'Prescott Express' rolls into town and the bruiser, surrounded by heavies, clambers off the bus and wades through the heaving crowd (mostly media and local Labour stalwarts) to the stone steps where he gives us his stump speech. It is superb: fast, furious, funny. The jokes are current ('Last night Margaret Thatcher said William Hague was cool and gritty – yes, like sand in your ice cream') and the way he wraps up New Labour thinking in Old Labour rhetoric is awe-inspiring. A man who can trumpet the virtues of Tony Blair and Keir Hardie in the same sentence is worth hanging onto.

When it's over and we've had a bit of banter and he's manhandled me joshingly for the cameras, I say, 'Well done. You're a star, though I thought Tony was more into Kir Royale than Keir Hardie.'

JP screws up his face, 'What are you blathering on about, Gyles?' I know his contempt for me and my kind is profound, but today he's all smiles. 'When are you coming over to our side? We'll take you. We're not fussy. Mum sends her best, by the way.'

As we wave the bus farewell, a huge woman standing next to me gives a deep sigh. 'Isn't he fantastic? He's a real man – with a bit of meat on him. That's what this country needs.'

Her friend recognises me and tut-tuts, 'It's you, is it? You only come round when the election's on. You're not getting my vote. We never see you.'

FRIDAY 25 MAY 2001

At 7.40 a.m., outside Conservative Central Office, in a deserted Smith Square, I meet up with the Tory Holy Trinity: William, Ffion and Seb Coe. They seem symbiotically linked. To me, there is something rather touching about their interdependent, mutually nourishing relationship. Others (including several in the shadow Cabinet) find it uncomfortable and excluding. Seb's devotion to William is absolute: 'I would die in the ditch for that man,' he says to me, and he means it literally. As I kiss Ffion I feel immediately guilty: her make-up is mask-like and thick because it has to last the whole day and here I am smudging it before she's even got started. I tell William that I've heard that the Labour focus groups show that, since the punch, Prescott's 'negatives' have turned into 'positives'. William laughs: 'Even so, Gyles, we're still not going to resort to beating up the electorate.' He is looking so cool, so pink and polished, so perky. As one of Blair's aides says to me later, 'If you can keep your head when all about are losing theirs, perhaps you're not reading the situation right.'

Michael Ancram (party chairman) bounces past, 'I'm having so much fun.' His days are numbered. Four years ago I remember getting calls from all and sundry (including Seb, I think) saying, 'What about Ancram for leader?'

TUESDAY 29 MAY 2001

At the Labour press conference, the journalist sitting next to me [Peter Hitchens] has his hand in the air for half an hour without being called. 'Are you ever called?' I ask.

'I'm not waiting to ask a question,' he explains. 'This is a position in tantric yoga designed to suppress nausea.'

Tony Blair clocks me from the platform and flashes me a brilliant smile. William can't do this. Ffion can. She does it to me at lunchtime in Kingston. I melt immediately. Blair can be suddenly cold and distant, but when he focuses on you the sun shines. Hague doesn't blow so hot and cold: he is always the same, even-tempered, serene. His stump speech is completely professional, but somehow he doesn't connect. An elderly Conservative activist in the crowd whispers to me, 'Life hasn't touched him yet. He's still a boy, isn't he? Now we've lost Kenneth Clarke and Douglas Hurd, we haven't got any grown-ups. Labour has all the serious players these days.'

At 8.00 p.m. at Millbank I meet up with Tony. We are alone. (Alastair Campbell, looking thin, pasty, none too well, has disappeared.) The Prime Minister, clutching his mug of tea, is weary but buoyant. 'How are the nights?' I ask.

'Okay, thanks. Leo is sleeping right through. That's made a big difference.' What does Tony think is the single quality most essential to a modern leader? 'Knowing what you believe in, what you want to achieve.' What about energy, stamina, moral courage? 'Yes, they all kick in, but the first essential is to be clear about your aims.'

'Is the Third Way still part of it?'

'Absolutely, Gyles. That's what it's all about. Nothing's changed.'

He looks directly at me. His eyes are wide open and glistening. He squeezes my arm and pushes his eerie, orange, over-made-up face towards mine. 'Gyles, the Third Way – it's real. And it's for you.'

WEDNESDAY 30 MAY 2001

I am expecting to meet William at Central Office at 8.30 a.m. When I arrive, he's gone. The mood has altered: last night, on *Newsnight*, he looked pie-eyed and vulnerable. Today's ICM poll shows the Conservatives losing ground. I gossip with the troops, who know the truth. We're doomed. Four years ago, William's plan was clear: begin by convincing the MPs at Westminster that he can deliver (done); next, shore up the core vote by giving them what they want to hear on Europe (done); finally – having secured our base – broaden the appeal, move back to the centre ground and give a distinctive message in the areas the electorate cares about: the economy, crime, education, health. Alas, not done at all. Perhaps it doesn't matter. We were never going to win anyway. From the electorate's perspective, it isn't yet time for a change.

Fly to Manchester and outside the gates at Old Trafford meet up with Jordan, twenty-three, the surgically enhanced Page Three girl who is standing as an independent in Stetchford. She looks quite rough and completely unreal. The media are out in force. I say to the female reporter from *The Guardian*, 'I don't think this is quite what Emmeline Pankhurst had in mind. Why are you here?'

'Well,' she says gamely, 'We've got to cover this because there's a real shortage of women in the campaign. I mean, Ffion won't say a thing.'

That's right, blame Ffion. The Tories just can't win.[688]

---

688 They didn't and following Hague's post-election resignation the candidates to succeed him included Michael Ancram, David Davis, Michael Portillo, Kenneth Clarke and Iain Duncan Smith. Under new rules, Conservative MPs only voted in the initial rounds of the contest, and the lowest candidate in each round was eliminated; in the final round, involving the membership of the Conservative Party, Iain Duncan Smith secured 60.7 per cent of the popular vote and Kenneth Clarke secured 39.3 per cent.

THURSDAY 28 JUNE 2001

A fun few days on the celebrity merry-go-round. I've just interviewed Ken Clarke, who should become leader of the Conservative Party but won't. Europe does for him every time. I asked him for his motto. 'It's a good life if you don't weaken.' A happy interview with John Major, too. Plenty of white wine and choice Majorisms. When he said Blair is something of a chameleon, I told him he could be something of a chameleon himself, giving everyone he met the impression he was on their side. He responded with a phrase unlikely to fall from the lips of any other Prime Minister: 'I was never in the business of telling porkies.'

I like my life. I like the range of my acquaintance – from Paul Daniels (last night) to Bill Nighy today. (They are both so good at what they do.) I went to a private view of the Vermeer exhibition at the National Gallery organised by Ivan Massow. Peter Mandelson turned up with a handsome black security guy in tow. 'Oh,' squealed Ivan, 'is he my present?' Peter was at the Conrad Black party, too. 'The usual crowd': Trevor McDonald, Melvyn Bragg, Simon Jenkins (all jolly); Portillo ('Hello, darling!' he cried, slapping his palm against mine); Sarah Ferguson (loopier than ever); Angus Ogilvy (sweet); Jack Profumo (eighty-six and still charming); David Frost … 'A joy, Gyles.' 'You're looking well, David.' He was looking terrible. 'I'm on the steady white wine and high protein diet.' I don't know how he is still alive. Andrew Lloyd Webber was looking well. 'I'm 23 pounds lighter after five weeks off alcohol. Shall we write a musical together? A funny one.'

SATURDAY 15 SEPTEMBER 2001

I telephoned Walter Cronkite in New York. 'We can smell the burning still. It's 2 miles away, but we can smell it. And see it. The smoke's still rising.'[689]

'How are you?' I asked, 'How is America?'

'Numb,' he replied. He remembered that he had taken us to the World Trade Center for dinner. 'What can I say? They are burning down our world.' This does not feel like a week when you want Iain Duncan Smith as your leader – nice guy though he is. Everyone is very jittery. I was pre-recording my show at LBC today – in the ITN building in Gray's Inn Road – and the fire alarm went off. My stomach churned. I wasn't alone.

---

689 On 11 September 2001 a series of four coordinated attacks were launched by the terrorist group al-Qaeda on the World Trade Center in New York and on the Pentagon in Washington DC. The attacks killed almost 3,000 people and, as a mark of respect, the announcement of Iain Duncan Smith's victory in the Conservative leadership contest was delayed until 13 September.

2002

....

FRIDAY 1 FEBRUARY 2002

....

Our ten-day try-out of *Zip-a-dee-doo-dah!* is almost done.[690] Given that next week marks the Golden Jubilee, it's appropriate that I am playing at the Palace and staying at the Balmoral – both, of course, in Westcliff-on-Sea. I am getting a fair flavour of the travelling actor's life. My bath at the Balmoral is shallow and narrow and the water is alternately freezing and boiling. There is nothing in between. For lunch I have walked through the windswept town and found a smoke-filled café on the sea front where I am sitting now and where I have been joined at my table by a sweet-faced young man who has explained to me that he is schizophrenic but not dangerous. He says hello to everyone who comes into the café and everyone just wants him to go away.

I have just had a call from Radio 5 Live. They want an interview on who empties the House of Commons. Cue my Paddy Ashdown stories.

....

MONDAY 8 APRIL 2002

....

I walked along the embankment from Millbank to the Savoy, passing the long queues waiting to go in to Westminster Hall to file past the Queen Mother's coffin. The funeral is tomorrow, so I thought it politic to wear a dark suit and black tie tonight even though the Savoy dinner was wholly celebratory and, as it turned out, totally uproarious. Iain Dale was marking the fifth birthday of Politico's, his bookshop and publishing empire, and Margaret Thatcher was his guest of honour. Quite a coup – except that only days ago word reached the world that Lady T. has had a couple of small strokes and consequently, on strict doctor's orders, is never to speak in public again. We thought that might put a bit of a dampener on the proceedings, but, as it turned out, not so. It was a very jolly party. Iain had packed the room with his family (it was his fortieth birthday, too, I think) and her family (Denis and Carol and entourage) and a cast conjured up from all her yesterdays – John Nott, John Redwood, Sir Rex and Mavis Hunt (the salty smell of the Falkands still in their hair), even John Sergeant from outside the embassy in

---

690 The show was conceived by GB and its title changed to *Zipp! 100 Musicals in 100 Minutes or Your Money Back*. With a cast of five, it won the Most Popular Show award at the Edinburgh Festival Fringe in August 2002, toured the UK and played in the West End at the Duchess Theatre.

Paris… Good speeches: Bernard Ingham quite the best. I was the MC and my only task (impressed upon me time and again) was to make absolutely sure that Lady T. heeded her doctor's advice and resisted all temptation to say a word. I failed. As I announced that the great lady was about to leave and reminded the crowd that, while we could salute her she could not address us, suddenly she was at my side – grinning from ear to ear. Without any warning, she lunged towards the podium and grabbed the microphone with both hands. She thanked us for our welcome and told us to keep the faith. She was unstoppable – and glorious. We roared our approval and delight.

The Iron Lady may have fallen silent now, but, tonight, we were there for her last hurrah. Weren't we the lucky ones?

FRIDAY 28 JUNE 2002

Last night: the National Portrait Gallery – where Michèle and I are the curators of an exhibition celebrating a century of children's writers. We were there for the talk on J. M. Barrie, an odd, unhappy man, whose plays are largely forgotten, but whose name will live forever because of his one great creation: Peter Pan.

Tonight: Highgrove for the British Forces' Foundation dinner. Noel Edmonds, Anita Harris, Frederick Forsyth, Will Young, two hugely famous Argentinian polo players whose names I don't catch… Ben Elton provides the cabaret. It doesn't quite work: it's too near the knuckle for this audience and I can sense the poor man, trapped in the spotlight, furiously editing the routine as he goes along. He feels he's dying. He isn't, and afterwards, in a corner of the room, I embrace him with fellow feeling. What do we learn from Ben's performance tonight? Our compère, Jim Davidson, tells me, 'If the audience believe you like them – really like them – they will like you. Put the punters at their ease: make them feel comfortable.' With Ben, some of them were on edge.

Not Charles and Camilla. They laughed obligingly. Their delight in each other's company is palpable. Someone who knew Highgrove in Diana's day whispers to me, 'It's so much happier here now.' The garden is perfect. Charles is so proud of it. 'Do you like it?' he asks, 'I'm so glad. I want you to like it.' He squints at me, brows furrowed. 'Are you still on television?' he enquires. 'Now and then,' I say. 'I don't watch,' he says. 'Not at all?' I ask. 'Not at all,' he says, peering at me closely. 'Are you funny?' he asks. 'I try,' I say wanly. He sighs: 'I know the feeling.'

Camilla is looking lovely (I tell her so, far too fruitily) and seems utterly at home. She is easy with William and Harry, who sit at a table of young ones, conspicuously the only two at the table who do not smoke. When Charles gets up to leave, Camilla creeps around the edge of the room and follows him out at a discreet distance. Ben and I descend on

Harry and William with a flurry of ingratiating banter. Poor lads: they are going to have to endure a lifetime of this.

FRIDAY 13 SEPTEMBER 2002

Theatre Royal, Newcastle. I spent the day in the House Manager's office writing up my interview with John Prescott, Deputy Prime Minister and First Secretary of State. He didn't give much away – beyond a huge dressing gown which had been presented to him as a present in South Africa and which he decided to offload onto me. 'It'll make a change from your bloody ridiculous jumpers.'

He has a colourful way with words. When I arrived at his office – Dover House, White-hall – I was told he was running late. But I knew he was there because I could hear him stomping about and swearing like a trooper. The air was blue with his effing and blind-ing, but when, finally, I was admitted to his presence he was all smiles. It's a nice office – spacious, gracious, overlooking Horse Guards Parade, with its own small garden – and I imagine the trappings of power have helped him go native.

Does he share my misgivings about the impending war against Iraq?

'No. Tony [Blair] has got good judgement and the courage to be a little ahead of one – and that's what you want from your leaders – and, hopefully, it'll work out.'

'Thousands could be killed, John. Innocent people, children. Do you lose sleep about that?'

'I do. I do think about that, and so does Tony, I'm sure. Blimey, you can't help thinking it.'

I filed the interview at 6.00 p.m. and at 7.30 p.m. I was on stage for the show. This is a lovely theatre (Frank Matcham, 1901) and the audience was perfect. Twenty minutes in I had found all the energy I needed. Tonight there really was magic in the air. Halfway through the performance Andrew C. Wadsworth said to me in the wings, 'This is one of my happiest ever nights in the theatre.'

THURSDAY 3 OCTOBER 2002

I am on the train back to Victoria, writing up my interview with Edwina [Currie]. She has been giving me a masterclass in the art of adultery. 'Only meet your lover every two weeks,' she counsels. 'If you leave it much longer between encounters, it's harder to recover the feeling. If you meet too frequently, you get completely overwhelmed. You can get addicted to this sort of thing, you know, so it's unwise to be doing it every week or every night. Once a fortnight is about right.'

My friend knows of what she speaks. In 1984, when she was thirty-seven and a recently elected backbench MP, she embarked on a four-year affair with John Major, then forty-one and a government whip. Her revelation of the affair [in her parliamentary diaries, published this week] has brought the world's press to a handsome, converted malthouse in Nutfield, Surrey, where, with cameras, microphones and notebooks at the ready, they are encamped around the self-confessed adulteress's front door. Because I am a chum and have been invited to lunch, I slip in through the back door unnoticed.

It is a tasty lunch, prepared and served by Edwina's new husband, John Jones, sixty-one, a good-humoured chain-smoking former Metropolitan Police detective, who seems to have the measure of his wife. When Edwina shows him a picture of her and me together at Oxford and giggles, 'Doesn't Gyles look like a young John Major?', Mr Jones chuckles obligingly, pours out the coffee and says, 'I'll leave you two to get on with it.'

Given the media scrum she has been in all week, and the obloquy that, generally, has been heaped upon her, Edwina is looking remarkably pulled together. 'I'm shattered,' she says, 'but I'm okay.'

'Are you really?' I ask.

She doesn't answer. She claps her hands and laughs. 'This Sunday I could have talked to the *News of the World* for £50,000. I'd far rather talk to you for love. Where shall we begin?'

'At the beginning,' I suggest. 'When exactly did the affair start?'

'I can't tell you because I can't remember. It was in the autumn of 1984. I didn't write anything down deliberately because it seemed to me the best camouflage was to leave no traces, but in my little appointments diary there's a big star against a certain date early in December 1984 so I think we'd got there by then.'

I want to discover things the published diaries don't reveal. 'How did you and John Major organise your trysts?'

There were two elements to it. One was fixing up the assignment. Using the House of Commons messenger service, we'd send each other notes: 'May we talk later?' or 'After the seven o'clock vote?' We would then leave the Commons separately. I would go to my flat at the back of Victoria station and, a little later, he would come along, ring the doorbell and say, 'Hello, I've got an envelope for you.' The whip would be bringing me some papers. He'd come upstairs, past Nick Ridley's flat, and arrive at my door. I'd say, 'Come in.' The fact that he was a whip made it all relatively straightforward. He knew the business of the House. He knew when we'd be needed for divisions. I don't think we ever missed a vote because we were making love.

'Sex is important to you,' I say, a little awkwardly.

'I like it,' she says, grinning at me. She opens her eyes wide: 'I like it, Gyles, I like it … I wish John could have been as good a Prime Minister as he was a lover.'

I think he was a good Prime Minister. Edwina disagrees. And that's why she has decided to tell all. 'There has been this huge mystery as to how the party began to collapse so spectacularly. What happened? Whose fault was it? Was it an accident? I don't think it was an accident. I think it could have been avoided. I felt I had a duty to report and put in my piece of the jigsaw – and a hell of a big piece it was.'

'Oh come on, Edwina, let's keep this in perspective. How big a piece was it really? Wasn't it just a four-year bonk?'

'No, no, not at all.' She narrows her eyes. Clearly I am missing the point. Patiently she tries to explain:

'There are two puzzles about John Major. The first puzzle was how this interesting, warm, intelligent man, who, on a personal basis, was a great guy, could come across to the public as so wooden and boring. He did. We can't argue with that. But the greater puzzle was how come someone who was a serious risk-taker, a chancer, an imaginative leaper in the dark, someone who was not by nature cautious, suddenly became a man who found it almost impossible to take a decision and whose entire administration was bedevilled by procrastination, incompetence and lack of intelligence?'

She pauses, smiles coquettishly and raises an eyebrow: 'Could it be that during the '80s, when he was a junior minister, he was getting a lot of help and encouragement from certain quarters that wasn't available later?'

So it wasn't the fiasco of the ERM, the rows over the Maastricht Treaty and a rapidly dwindling majority that brought about the demise of John Major's government. It was the fact that Edwina was no longer on hand to help steel her man and steer the ship of state.

You couldn't make it up – but, amazingly, I think she believes it.

She has not done this for the money – certainly. She has done it because she feels she is being written out of history and wants us to know that she was there. She has done it, too, because John Major (understandably) made no mention of her in his memoirs and that's rankled.

The real horror of what she's done is the hurt she will have caused Norma – the embarrassment that will never go away. I wish she had kept her secret and I tell her so. And to make sure that I don't give her a false impression as to whose side I am on, at the end of our conversation I produce a piece of paper I have brought with me:

'Edwina, you say that you have published your diary as a piece of history. I accept that. But can I read to you what I fear may be the verdict of history on you? I wrote this on the train coming to see you. "As a broadcaster, as a novelist, as a parliamentarian, she was of little consequence. Her only claim to fame was as an aspiring politician's easy lay."'

Edwina interrupts: 'I wasn't easy—'

'Let me finish. "And what is worse, she was guilty of hurting and humiliating someone who did her no harm."'

Edwina's eyes are full of tears.

'Gyles, I have lived my life in a truthful way. It is better to live with the truth, however unpalatable, than to live with a rosy fiction that is actually very cruel to all the people involved. I do not feel guilty. I am not ashamed. When I was a little girl, my mother used to say, "Always remember: God is watching." Well, I do.'

THURSDAY 7 NOVEMBER 2002

I went to the memorial service for Gerald Campion at St Paul's, Covent Garden. His performance as Billy Bunter on TV throughout the '50s was one of the delights of my childhood. It was a privilege to know him.

The memorial service for Iain Duncan Smith will be upon us shortly, I'm sure of that. His support at Westminster has evaporated completely. The week has been a total fiasco. It began with him stamping his foot about gay adoption – demanding support he could not command. By close of play on Monday, when a third of the Conservative Party in Parliament had failed to follow him into the required division lobby, even his friends were shaking their heads wearily. They knew it was a mess, and wholly unnecessary.

What they had not reckoned on – nobody had – was their leader's ability to turn a crisis into a calamity. Monday night's high drama became Tuesday morning's high farce. First, IDS failed to turn up at a scheduled press conference on housing (leaving two hapless front-bench colleagues, unbriefed, facing the cameras and blowing in the wind); next, amid mounting hysteria, he summoned the media to Central Office, managed to be filmed at the window gauchely rehearsing what the hacks took to be his resignation speech, and then appeared, not to fall on his sword, but to brandish it in the face of his colleagues and demand that the party 'unite or die'. It wasn't heroic: it was just embarrassing.

On Monday night, he shot himself in the foot. On Tuesday he shot himself in the face. He is now fatally wounded. The party will survive, but he will die: it is not a question of if, but when.[691]

---

691 In the event, Duncan Smith struggled on until 29 October 2003, when he lost a No Confidence vote among Conservative MPs, 75–90. The parliamentary party then coalesced around the shadow Chancellor of the Exchequer, Michael Howard, who was elected leader, unopposed.

2003

SATURDAY 15 FEBRUARY 2003

We had a wonderful show last night [of *Zipp!* at the Duchess Theatre] and two strong shows today. And in between I joined the peace march along the Strand – my first peace march since I took part in the great anti-Vietnam War march on Washington DC in 1966, when I was eighteen. This war against Iraq is wrong – and if Ken Clarke had become leader of the Conservative Party we might have been spared British involvement. Ken has been against it from the start. Given the number of Labour MPs against it, without whole-hearted Conservative support Blair might not be able to get the vote he needs in the House of Commons.[692]

SUNDAY 23 MARCH 2013

This was the week that war broke out – and I was the subject of *This Is Your Life*. According to President Bush and his sidekick, Tony Blair, the mission is straightforward: 'to disarm Iraq of weapons of mass destruction, to end Saddam Hussein's support for terrorism, and to free the Iraqi people'. It may prove easier said than done, but what do I know? The invasion began on Wednesday. On Thursday the [Duchess] theatre was empty (almost) – though the show went well. And tonight, at 9.45 p.m., on stage, as the curtain fell and we were taking our calls, Michael Aspel suddenly appeared, holding his red book... 'Gyles Brandreth, this is your life...'

It was completely, wholly, utterly unexpected. The cast had dropped not a hint. The 'catch' achieved, I assumed the filming of the show would happen at a later date, but no: it happens right away, before the 'subject' gets a chance to run away or change their mind. By the time we got to the studio it was gone 11.00 p.m. By the time the recording was done, it was one in the morning! I walked through as though in a trance. Only two things that I remember now clearly: 1) feeling sorry for the studio audience who had waited all evening to discover who the subject was and it turned out to be me; 2) feeling

---

692 In the event, Tony Blair secured parliamentary approval to send UK forces into battle against Saddam Hussein on 18 March 2003 and most Conservatives supported him. 217 MPs – Kenneth Clarke, John Gummer, and thirteen other Conservatives, all the Liberal Democrats and 139 Labour backbenchers – backed an amendment opposing the government's stance on Iraq, with 396 opposing the motion. A motion backing the government's position was then passed by 412 votes to 149.

overwhelmed with pride – and joy – and gratitude – when the doors on the set opened and my lovely wife and three gorgeous children walked on. They looked so *beautiful*.

THURSDAY 17 APRIL 2003

Baghdad has fallen; Tikrit has fallen; essentially the Iraq War is won, even if the fighting hasn't stopped. I am having coffee at the Salvador Dali Museum by the St Petersburg Quayside, Sarasota, Florida, USA. The sun is shining brightly. (Perhaps God approves of our victory?) I flew in to Tampa last night to appear on the Home Shopping Network at five o'clock this morning to sell the Teddy Bear Museum range of bears to HSN viewers across the nation. Mission accomplished, I am flying back home tonight. As they say: you couldn't make it up.

THURSDAY 12 JUNE 2003

Rosa Monckton's KIDS Gala at the Grosvenor House Antiques Fair. Rosa's daughter, Domenica, has Down's syndrome and, famously, Diana, Princess of Wales was her godmother. But for her death Diana would have been doing the honours tonight, but in her place we have the next best thing – the actress Elizabeth Hurley – and a very good thing she turns out to be. She even comes equipped with her own equerry: her discreetly charming boyfriend, Ram. As master of ceremonies, before dinner it is my duty to escort Elizabeth around the assorted Antiques Fair stands. I do just that and I have to report that La Hurley plays her part to perfection: she is a princess in all but title. At several of the stands, the people she meets curtsey to her. I promise this is true.

When we have walked the circuit (and Ram has collected the assorted posies and gifts presented to Elizabeth and is clutching them manfully to his chest) it is time to draw the raffle. This we do halfway up the grand staircase in the Great Room: me in the middle, Elizabeth on one side and the Prime Minister's wife, Cherie Blair, on the other. 'Here they are,' I announce, 'Elizabeth Hurley, cutie, and Cherie Booth QC.' The crowd cheers indulgently as we draw ticket after ticket after ticket… There are too many prizes in every raffle in my experience, but what can you do? We do our best and just as we are nearing the end of the ordeal I suddenly feel a hand tugging at my trousers and I hear a voice – an American voice – hissing at me: 'Gyles. Gyles! We've got royalty here. American royalty.' I look down and there is Ruby Wax, on her knees by my knees. 'Come on, kid. Get done with the raffle. Liza Minnelli is waiting.'

And so it proves. Raffle done, Ruby drags me *and* Cherie (plus two-man police escort) *and* Elizabeth (plus Ram) up the stairs and into the midst of the milling throng. 'Where is she? Where is she?' shrieks Ruby. 'She's here's somewhere. And she's royalty. American royalty. Where the fuck's she gone?'

Not far, it turns out. In the middle of the mêlée we find her, slumped in a wheelchair, wrapped in a rug, wearing dark glasses and clearly in a state of desperation. 'How do you do, Miss Minnelli?' I gurgle. 'I need the john,' she gasps. 'I need it now.'

'It's only pee-pee,' says a high-pitched voice above her. It's David Gest, her smooth-checked, orange-faced husband whom I think I've met before. 'David,' I cry. 'It's only pee-pee,' he repeats. 'Don't worry about it.'

'I need the john now,' squawks Liza. 'Now, I tell you.' 'Fear not,' I cry. 'Cherie is here, accompanied by two of Downing Street's finest police officers. We'll sort you out.'

And we did. Cherie's security guys created a path to the lift, we found our way to the floor we needed, we pushed Liza and David through the door to the ladies and waited in the corridor outside. Minutes later, David wheeled Liza out to join us. As she reappeared, she took off her dark glasses in triumph. 'It wasn't just pee-pee.' She looked up at David and snarled, 'He knows *nothing*.'

It was all a bit tame after that. Dinner was served, the speeches came and went, Bob Geldof was good, the auction was a struggle and then, somehow, we managed to lift Liza from her chair and hoist her onto the stage. She teetered to and fro, explaining that she couldn't stand because she had hurt her knee falling off the stage last week while singing with Pavarotti in Rome – or was it Domingo in Madrid? She didn't seem sure. Looking up at a huge photograph of Rosa's daughter Domenica on the screen above the stage, with a catch in her throat, she told us, 'I'm here for her – I'm here for lovely little Jennifer!' 'Domenica!' I hissed from the wings. 'Japonica,' cried Liza. 'Domenica!' I hissed again. 'Veronica,' cried Liza triumphantly, blowing the photograph a kiss. 'We all love Veronica.'

Other highlights of the evening: John Simpson's young wife, Dee; Liz Hurley showing me how a little bit of rolled-up cotton wool can lift a pair of breasts just so; and Cherie. I sat next to Cherie for dinner. I really like her. She is intelligent, funny and nice. We are meeting again next week – at the Tyburn Convent at Marble Arch. Cherie is giving the Tyburn Lecture. I am giving the vote of thanks.

TUESDAY 4 NOVEMBER 2003

I sat with Robin Cook at the *Oldie* literary lunch. Talking about Iraq, he was wholly persuasive. I reminded him how rare it is for ministers to resign on principle. 'Usually it's a scandal that forces them from office,' I said. 'It was Blair's obduracy that drove me out,' he said.[693] 'He wanted the invasion. He would not be moved.' When John Smith died, Robin Cook was the potential Labour leader we most feared. He was a formidable debater – the best of their lot by far. But he looks like a cross between a ginger-nut biscuit and a garden gnome. He hadn't a prayer.

In my time, our only rival to Cook as a forensic debater was Michael Howard – and this week Michael becomes the Conservative leader and the party breathes a collective sigh of relief. After the aberration of IDS, we will have a safe pair of hands – a proper, grown-up leader. Will he become Prime Minister? That, alas, is another matter – though what an adornment Sandra would be to No. 10!

That's where I am just in from – No. 10. An hour or so ago I was sitting in the green drawing room on a sofa, alone with Cherie. (I was early for the Longford Trust reception.) She's sprained her ankle so I sat with her feet by my lap and told her wonderful she is. And she is. Wonderful but needy. She clings to Tony when she sees him because she doesn't see him enough – and (according to Alastair Campbell) Tony resists her because he finds the clinging oppressive.

2004

TUESDAY 6 JANUARY 2004

We were at the pizza parlour in Franschhoek [a small town in the Western Cape Province, South Africa, on holiday] when a call came from Sally [Bulloch] to say that Lady Thatcher would be coming for tea and could we come too. Sally was manager of the Athenaeum Hotel in Piccadilly when the Thatchers were living there 'between houses'. Lady T. likes Sally, trusts her, and here on holiday with Mark (who has a house in Cape Town) is looking for things to do, people to see, ways to pass the time. She was in much brighter form than I had expected – looking wonderfully groomed, elegant and summery, and really pleased to see me – not because she really knows who I am but because she knows that I was an MP and we could talk politics. That's all she wants to do: that's all that interests her. We had a good political gossip – she very much approves of Michael Howard as leader, but she was happiest talking about the old days. She was very funny about the self-indulgence of Peter Morrison, Reggie Maudling and Roy Jenkins – and

---

693 Cook resigned from the Cabinet on 17 March 2003.

absolutely spot-on. I was interested to find that she had the measure of Peter Morrison – that was a surprise.

It was clear that she misses Denis [who died in June 2003] quite dreadfully. She dotes on Mark, but never talks about Carol. There was not much sign of her mental 'frailty', except that she was occasionally fretful – looking around anxiously and saying she wanted to go home. 'I need to be at the House of Lords. There's business to attend to. I should be there – voting. When are we flying back?'

Crawfie [Lady Thatcher's assistant, Cynthia Crawford] was in attendance with her husband – who was dressed in khaki safari shorts like a character from Carry On Up the Zambesi – and clearly in no rush to return to London. 'We're going back in a week or so,' she said.

'I want to go back now,' insisted Lady T.

'You can't go yet,' said Crawfie firmly. 'You must come to tea when we're back in London,' she said to us. We must. Lady T.'s achievement is extraordinary – and she is very sweet. It is a privilege to know her.

FRIDAY 16 JULY 2004

Train to Manningtree. John and Penny Gummer pick me up to take me to Wissett for the 'Annual Lunch'. Penny anxious that I might say the wrong things, John tells the story of being asked on the way to a similar event (by Mrs Michael Grylls, in a neck brace, turning her whole body while driving) 'not to give the talk Teresa Gorman gave last month .. on HRT … We've heard all we need to hear about dry vaginas…'

I spoke in a barn with two tents attached. The rains came. The downpour was torrential. They sat there, in a sauna, with the rain gushing in – under umbrellas. I am pleased to report that my speech went well, but I am so glad (so glad!) I do not have to do this every weekend. Who would be an MP?

MONDAY 19 JULY 2004

Drink with Michael Howard in the leader's office, overlooking the Thames. Half bottle of Chablis on green sofas. He's buttoned up. I make him laugh about our daughters larking about in New York. He relaxes a little – not much. And then we get down to business. It's just the two of us.

Michael has been leader for nine months now. He's known ups and downs, but this has been a bad week – the worst. It's perceived in media-land as being all over. They are not talking about the general election – the result of that is a foregone conclusion. They're talking about the leadership election after the general election.

Michael knows all this. He's no fool. And he's clearly deeply frustrated that his message isn't coming across.

'You have a message?' I say, smiling.

'Oh, yes,' he says, 'I know what I want to do and why…' and as he sits forward and says it, he becomes more real, infinitely more attractive…

I'm there to talk about jokes – but I tell him he doesn't need jokes. People don't need him to be funny: they need him to be human – and convincing. We talk about Bill Clinton and his extraordinary ability to command an emotional response, to inspire and connect.

As Michael gets up and goes to the door to call in the others, I sit there thinking, 'Do I want to become involved? Is there any point? He is a good man, but is this going to get us anywhere?'

The team: Ed[694] is very likeable, Rachel Whetstone has become a bit of a spinny – more than a touch of the bossy-boots schoolmarm. Michael brings them in; cancels the seven o'clock meeting; senses that we're on to something. It can't wait until the party conference. Let's do something now … 'Gyles, 19 July 2004 marks the nadir, the nadir – is that how you pronounce it? Now we have seen the way ahead…'

....

THURSDAY 29 JULY 2004

....

'We're fucked, Gyles, utterly fucked.' Ed Vaizey, speech-writer to the Leader of the Opposition, sums up the prospects for his party and his leader nine months or a year ahead of the next election.

I like Ed. He's droll and savvy and fully aware that the situation is dire and the leader's set-up a shambles. 'All you need to be Leader of the Opposition is to be able to do two things: head up the fund-raising, head-up the strategy.'

'What's the strategy?'

'Exactly.'

I said how much I like Michael, how effective he'd seemed at the Home Office, but how I wasn't yet sure what more there was…

'There isn't.'

'The magic?'

'There won't be.'

---

694 Ed Vaizey, Michael Howard's speech-writer, MP for Wantage since 2005 and Minister for Culture, Communications and Creative Industries since 2010.

Ed was hoping to get to know Michael better this coming week on holiday in Italy. He and Rachel have gone the past few years to stay with Anne Robinson (& Penrose) on holiday in Italy. This year the Howards are coming too. Except that while Ed and are having tea the call comes that it's too hot in Italy and Anne is coming home – but the rest are welcome to go as planned. Michael and Sandra have already bought their tickets.

Ed is anxious about Wantage. He's put in two years and thinks the Lib Dems could win. He's been outed as one of the 'Notting Hill Tories'. The Lib Dems will call him the Member for Notting Hill in Wantage. 'I'm fucked. Michael's fucked. The holiday's fucked. We're all fucked.'

I went on from tea on the terrace at the House of Commons to a drink at the Charlotte Street Hotel with Charlotte Bush – publisher's publicist and the only woman I've met who hasn't fallen for Bill Clinton. 'He's so flabby.' She was looking after the great man's book tour, but barely got beyond the entourage (three cars and a minibus for security) – especially disliking the overweight young woman who was 'the President's scheduler'.

Supper with Joanna Lumley up the road at Tanur, where Jo ordered the mezze and it came: ten starters on a tray. We shan't be going again. Fortunately if you held the Pinot Grigio right up to your nose you could mask the stench from the toilets…

THURSDAY 23 SEPTEMBER 2004

Michael Howard meeting on how to handle PMQs. The outsiders at the meeting (from the world of marketing) don't get it – that Michael has to make it work in the House for the sake of his troops' morale … It has to work in the chamber and on TV … The usual talk: get women into the doughnut, make the sound bite real etc. Nothing has changed in ten years. Even the cast seems much the same: David Cameron (impressive), George Osborne (earnest), Rachel Whetstone (at the far end of the table and very much in command of the show: we worked to her agenda). I sat next to Michael and we smiled at one another knowingly as the young ones rabbited on. The meeting served no purpose whatsoever.

TUESDAY 21 DECEMBER 2004

With Eileen Atkins & Bill Shepherd to Sonny's. Eileen is very funny. She told us about her Women's Reading Group. She joined at the suggestion of John Standing, whose wife

Sarah is a founder ... and it turns out that Kimberley Quinn[695] is a member – and the personification of charm and intelligence: Eileen was almost ready to bed her herself ... The revelations of Kimberley's complex relations with David Blunkett and Simon Hoggart and heaven knows who else have warmed our cockles on these cold winter nights. Anyway, the point is that Eileen wrote to Kimberley to commiserate and, to show fellow-feeling, told a story of one of her own past embarrassments ... and Kimberley sent a lovely eleven-page response full of heart and hurt and humiliation ... Eileen said that all eleven members of the group had written to Kimberley with a confession of their own past wickedness, including Sarah Standing – who is perfect and could only confess to having 'been cross with John once' and feeling so bad about it! ('Sarah is perfect, of course,' said Eileen. 'Michèle, you are probably perfect too – but your saving grace is you have edge.')

On the night of the last Reading Group meeting – when Eileen was making the supper for it – at about three minutes to eight, Harold Pinter telephoned. 'Eileen, will you do my birthday party?' For a moment, Eileen thought he meant cater for it – then she remembered going to some dreadful evening at the Pinters where people read poetry and assumed she was wanted as a kind of cabaret for the party and said, 'Oh, Harold, I hate those sort of things.' Harold responded bleakly, 'But you've done one of my plays before. I thought you liked them.' Then the penny dropped. Eileen is going to do a short tour then a season at the Arts in *The Birthday Party*. She'd like Jude Law as the young man, but the producers won't even ask him.

2005

FRIDAY 6 MAY 2005

The general election result was entirely predictable. Blair is back, but with a majority down to 66 from 160. Labour lost forty-seven seats; we gained thirty-three; the Lib Dems gained eleven. The Lib Dems did well, with a 3.7 per cent swing their way. Labour had a swing against them of 5.5 per cent. The swing our way was just 0.7 per cent. Michael did valiantly – he's a good guy – but we were never going to win. When will we win again? And with whom? And does it matter? (Yes, I think it does. I am not really part of it anymore, but I do still care.)

---

695 American journalist and publisher of *The Spectator* magazine whose three-year affair with Home Secretary David Blunkett was revealed by the *News of the World* in August 2004. Blunkett resigned on 15 December and the *News of the World* revealed that Ms Quinn had also had an affair with the journalist Simon Hoggart.

The Cabinet line-up is entirely predictable. Blair, Prescott, Gordon Brown still chewing his nails and champing at the bit … How long can Blair keep him at bay? Jack Straw is still at the Foreign Office. Blunkett is back – at Work and Pensions. Will that work?[696]

THURSDAY 7 JULY 2005

Yesterday London won the bid to become host city for the 2012 summer Olympics. Well done Seb. (And, indeed, well done Tony Blair. According to Seb, Blair was key and completely hands-on.) Today, London was rocked by bombs.[697] I am calm about it now, but it happened this morning, during the rush hour, and I just held my breath, stomach-churning, until we heard from the children. Aphra [an environmental economist] was at DEFRA in Victoria. Benet [a barrister] was at a solicitor's in Holborn. He went in by bike. They were fine, but fifty-plus have been killed. We were due to go to the British Forces Foundation polo match at Sandhurst. We went, not knowing whether or not it would be cancelled but feeling, somehow, 'the show must go on'. It did. The Prince of Wales didn't appear, but Prince Harry was there and, I must say, is very impressive on horseback.

THURSDAY 6 OCTOBER 2005

A happy outing to Blackpool for the Conservative Party conference at the Winter Gardens. Seb warmed up for me; I warmed up for Michael; Michael warmed the hearts of the crowd with a witty, well-judged, well-delivered farewell. We were all rewarded with standing ovations. Yes, they can still stand – which, given their age, is impressive.

All the leadership candidates were on parade and I wished each of them well because they are all friends and each one has his strengths. But I am sorry to say Ken Clarke is now definitely too fat and too old. Is David Cameron too glossy and too young? He will be thirty-nine on Sunday. He's canny, he's real, he's my kind of Conservative: pragmatic, middle-of-the-road, not obsessive about anything but generally right about most things. And he's very charming. He hugged me as I was about to on stage to do my bit. 'We'll meet soon,' he said. 'We must. We really must.'

---

596 It didn't. David Blunkett resigned from the Cabinet on 2 November 2005 in the wake of press coverage of his extra-parliamentary interests during his time out of government.

597 Four terrorists detonated four bombs: three in quick succession on London Underground trains across the city and, later, a fourth on a double-decker bus in Tavistock Square. As well as the four bombers, fifty-two civilians were killed and over 700 more were injured in the attacks.

David Davis blew it with his speech yesterday. It was lacklustre and wooden. It didn't work. It didn't seduce; it didn't move. I saw him last night, in the hotel foyer, looking so bleak. I like him, but I think I know his ways too well. He was outstanding as DD of the SS, but colleagues won't see him as Prime Minister: they don't trust him enough. I travelled back on the train with Liam Fox. I found him sitting alone in First Class. I told him how well he's done this week – and he has. But there is something about him that's unsettling, too. He's sharp, shrewd, hugely ambitious and achieving, but I think he's a risk too far … Ken's moment has past: DD and Liam will come a cropper. If we want to win – and win next time – it has to be Cameron. He's new. He has the wow factor. And the energy. And steady hands. In fact, I don't think there is a choice: he is the future now.[698]

2006

TUESDAY 7 FEBRUARY 2006

Making my TV series about the Queen[699] I went to interview Mary Soames – Lady of the Garter and Winston Churchill's daughter. She keeps a bronze of her father's hand on her desk. It was taken from life and, as she said, is extraordinary because the hand is so small and so delicate.

'Did you ever meet him?' she asked.

'No,' I said.

'Well, you can shake his hand now' – and she held it out for me … So there you go – another ambition fulfilled. I've shaken hands with Winston Churchill.

Our next stop was Sir Edward Ford, long-serving courtier and the man who conjured up the phrase 'annus horribilis'. He is ninety-five now and completely charming. He said that when the Queen was young her attractiveness lay in her 'complete lack of flirtatiousness'. Other princesses would flirt – Princess Margaret, Princess Marina,

---

698 The first ballot of MPs was held on 18 October 2005. David Davis came top of the poll with 62 votes, followed by David Cameron, 56, Liam Fox, 42, and Kenneth Clarke, 38. Clarke was eliminated and in the second round most of his support went to David Cameron who now secured 90 votes, followed by David Davis with 57 and Liam Fox with 51. Fox was eliminated and the Conservative Party membership was offered a choice between Cameron and Davis. Of the 198,844 members who voted, 32.4 per cent voted for Davis and 67.6 per cent for Cameron.

699 GB's 2004 book, *Philip & Elizabeth: Portrait of a Marriage*, formed the basis of a television series made by ITN for Channel 5.

Princess Diana ... 'The Queen is not flirtatious at all and never has been. That's her secret.' Most people just gush about Her Majesty. Ford was precise and very interesting. 'She lacks imagination,' he said, 'which may have helped keep her steady. Her key strength is that she is blessed with an abundance of common sense.'

SUNDAY 9 APRIL 2006

Went to review the papers on the Andrew Marr programme. (Feeling a tad guilty because I did it so often with David and David was so hurt when they dropped him.[700] A year on, he's still obsessing about it – and 'the awfulness' of his replacement, 'that dreadful little man with the big ears' as Carina [Frost] terms him. In fact, AM is very nice and rather good.) I was on with Katie Melua (singer – pretty but rather serious) and Alan Milburn[701] (MP – not so pretty, nor so serious). In make-up, he said he was still considering standing against Gordon Brown when Tony Blair goes. 'Will anyone stand against him?' I asked.

'Someone should.'

And if Gordon forms a government, I asked, will you be part of it?

'It's highly unlikely he'd want me, though it would be a good idea if he did. I'd certainly consider it.'

It's quite comical how seriously politicians can take themselves. Milburn reckons he's a force to be reckoned with – and perhaps he is? What do I know? (Let's remember: not so long ago Michael Ancram, Alan Duncan, Tim Yeo all thought they might have a chance of becoming Tory leader. 'Vanity, vanity...' as Mrs T. used to say.)

Also on the programme: Foreign Secretary Jack Straw, good with the sound bites, eyes blinking with the contact lenses – and charmingly in the thrall of Condoleezza Rice, US Secretary of State. If Blair is Bush's poodle, Jack is Condi's chihuahua. The other day, when they flew together to the Gulf in the Secretary of State's Boeing 757, Condi offered Jack her on-board bed. Shattered (as all British politicians are) he gratefully accepted and went to snuggle down beneath the Secretary of State's duvet in the front cabin. Mid-flight he got up to go to the loo and found himself stepping over her body in the galley: she was fast asleep, stretched out on the floor. 'I just assumed she had another berth at the back of the plane ... I never thought she was going to have to doss down on the floor.'

---

700 Having worked alongside David Frost at TV-am in the '80s, GB was a regular newspaper reviewer on *Frost on Sunday*, appearing in the 500th and final edition on 29 May 2005. *Sunday AM* with Andrew Marr replaced the Frost programme from 11 September 2005.

701 Labour MP for Darlington 1992–2010; in Tony Blair's Cabinet 1998–2003, 2004–5.

MONDAY 2 OCTOBER 2006

With Kate Hoey and Alison Moore-Gwyn [from the National Playing Fields Association] I went to see Seb [Coe] at Olympic Towers – actually a splendid suite of offices high up in the Barclays HQ at Canary Wharf. The place was awash with beautiful young PAs – 'all chosen personally', said Seb … And then in came the Communications Director. She was huge – I mean truly, preposterously large. We'd gone to give our presentation on what we wanted to see as the 'Olympics Legacy' and our opening slide was all about the need to fight obesity … It was a good meeting, but where it leads I'm not sure. Seb is very at ease with it all. Being a double Olympic gold medallist helps. I think his legacy is not in doubt. MBE, done. OBE, done. Peerage, done. KBE at the New Year. I think CH once the Olympics are done. OM around 2020? Or maybe the Garter. Watch this space.

FRIDAY 13 OCTOBER 2006

We all need a legacy. ('Legacy' is the buzzword of the age.) What's mine to be? (No sniggering at the back, please.) Seriously, what's mine to be? Some people rate my biography of the Queen and Prince Philip – that might last. And I still have hopes for the movie of Nick Saint.[702] And I did introduce the 1994 Marriage Act enabling civil weddings to take place in venues other than register offices: in its small way that has contributed to a happy day in a lot of people's lives. And every time I walk through Trafalgar Square and see something interesting on that plinth I know I'm the one who made that happen … And today I had lunch at The Ivy with Steve Thompson who has written a play about the Whips' Office inspired by my diaries.[703]

FRIDAY 10 NOVEMBER 2006

To No. 1 Knightsbridge; to Al-Jazeera. I have seen the future: it's Muslim. I'm going to be part of it. In a tiny basement studio sits David Frost, facing one camera. There are two other cameras in the room: they appear dormant. Behind David is the logo: *Frost Over the World*. We are piloting a segment of his new show – airing for the first time next week. 'A Conversation with the Four Corners of the World': Al-Jazeera have created

702 The film of GB's 1996 novel *Who Is Nick Saint?* is yet to materialise.

703 *Whipping It Up*, starring Richard Wilson, opened at the Bush Theatre, London, in November 2006 and later transferred to the West End. Stephen Thompson went on to write episodes of *Doctor Who* and *Sherlock*.

'hubs' in Washington DC, Kuala Lumpur, Doha and London and four of us are to have a global chat about the issues of the hour wherever we are … The notion is fine: the reality is dire: the guy in Washington seems to be on a three-second time-delay; the lady in Kuala Lumpur wants to read from a prepared script.

FRIDAY 17 NOVEMBER 2006

Premiere of *Frost Over the World* – David (yellow tie, yellow socks, hands shaking so badly – not nerves: drink and life taking its toll) – I did stuff about Britain's global brands (Frost, James Bond, the royal family – Woolworths are bringing out their William & Kate wedding souvenirs already) – three parts to the show: a 'debate' on religion; the global 'conversation'; and Tony Blair. David scored 'cos Blair conceded that Iraq had been 'pretty much a disaster'. Headlines everywhere. David delivers for Al-Jazeera!

Iraq, 'pretty much a disaster' – is that Blair's legacy? What else has there been? At the start we got the minimum wage and independence for the Bank of England. Has there been anything else – in terms of a lasting legacy? Civil partnerships. That's good, but that's it. And now he's being hounded out of office by his impatient Chancellor and ungrateful backbenchers. The much-maligned John Major managed to keep the show on the road for seven years with virtually no majority and a party split at the heart over Europe. And, *pace* the ERM debacle, we ended up with sound finances and peace in Northern Ireland. And, incredibly, even the privatisation of the railways seems to have worked. What's more, John Major is normal – charmingly so. But there's something about Blair that is really quite strange … Ten years ago Major was written off completely and Blair was the man who walked on water. Now Blair is disappearing fast beneath the waves and, as time goes by, I reckon we are going to find that my friend Mr Major's reputation grows and grows. Wouldn't that be nice? And as it should be.

2007

FRIDAY 2 FEBRUARY 2007

From Derby to St Pancras (being rebuilt) to Millbank to record *How to be Chancellor* for Radio 4 – Lamont very mellow, Clarke on song … Is Blair in free-fall? Adored in the US, derided at home, he is being buffeted on all sides. I bumped into Peter Hain, who is breezily advocating an elected House of Lords – regardless of the PM's policy (if he has one). On to Al-Jazeera, where I bumped into a trim but bug-eyed Andrew Lloyd Webber ('Why are you here?' 'I don't know. David asked me.') The 'global conversation' quite hopeless – the girl from Kuala Lumpur unbroadcastable, I'd have thought… David: 'So good to have you here – a joy.' On to Bertorelli's and Geoff Atkinson – the world now 'beyond parody', according to Geoff. He is obsessed with the government's corrupt core and had some complicated story about a property scam that appeared to involve Meacher, Mandelson, Prescott, Blair and an estate agent with an outlet in Putney … I didn't understand a word of it, but Geoff's heart is good and he bought the lunch.

WEDNESDAY 14 MARCH 2007

On 14 March 1991, I was chosen to succeed Peter Morrison as the prospective parliamentary candidate for the City of Chester. It was a night to remember – seated between Sir Peter and the Duke of Westminster, the acrid smoke rising relentlessly from their forever-burning cigarettes. What's Peter's legacy? The PPS who slept while Margaret Thatcher was turned out of office. That's it, I fear. But why was Peter permanently sozzled? When he was first elected he was twenty-nine, tall and slim, good-looking in a pink-cheeked, curly-headed, English sort of way. When he died, aged fifty-one, he'd become gross, grotesque. He looked seventy. What drove him to drink? And how did he die? Was it a heart attack or did he throw himself down the stairs? And why did he leave instructions that there should be no memorial service – no memorial? Was he a paedophile? Is that the dark secret? I believe he was cautioned once for 'cottaging' in a public lavatory with young men – but they weren't children. Rod Richards and others are convinced he was implicated in the abuse at the children's home in Wrexham, but beyond rumour and conjecture what do we know?

Anyway, today, sixteen years on, we celebrated my darling wife's birthday in quite a different way – but, by bizarre coincidence, the Duke of Westminster was once again on parade. It was a really good day. Lunch at Le Manoir aux Quat' Saisons; a drive to Cholsey to visit Agatha Christie's grave; a race back to town to catch *Boeing-Boeing* at the Comedy Theatre – all-star cast (Mark Rylance sublime), all-star audience (Jamie Oliver and friends). And then, at 10.15 p.m., supper at Le Caprice – where we were followed in by the Duke and Duchess of Westminster. Gerald – in the wake of the revelations about his penchant for prostitutes, courtesy of last month's *News of the World* – did not look well: grim-visaged, brick-red complexion, overweight, dog-tired, and still smoking. Michèle thought he noticed us. I imagine he didn't – or, if he did, couldn't quite place us. It was odd seeing him there, tonight of all nights. We felt luckier and happier than the richest man in the land.

SUNDAY 29 APRIL 2007

Arrive in Stratford-upon-Avon for the Shakespeare birthday celebrations at 3.55 p.m., get out of the car and step up to the Radio Coventry & Warwicks microphone for three minutes. Turn around and there is Susie Sainsbury – a good woman. She could be lolling in a bath of Sainsbury champagne; instead she's giving her all to the Royal Shakespeare Company. She's deputy chairman, Chair of Development, Chair of the American Committee. She's raised £101 million for the capital funds. But all the *Stratford Herald* reports is that they are £14 million short of their target.

Somewhat surprisingly, Gordon Brown is here. Susie is rather cynical about Gordon. She thinks he's 'come to be seen' and brought the children with him. 'He's burnishing his English credentials.' I suppose David [Sainsbury] is a Blairite and they are all anxious about what will happen when Gordon at long last becomes PM. (I can tell them. It will be a shambles. No one who still bites his fingernails aged fifty-six should be allowed to lead the country. Gordon is an obsessive micro-manager with a short fuse and a vile temper. He can be charming and civilised, but after a six-month honeymoon, it will all unravel – there will be blood on the carpet, if not in the streets. My friend David Cameron will be PM within three years, without a doubt.) Susie offers us the remainder of Gordon Brown's little lemon tarts. They are delicious.

I am here to host the Shakespeare quiz.

Two star-studded teams, both alike in dignity: I appoint Ian McKellen and Juliet Stevenson as captains. In the audience, Harriet Walter, coughing. Ian in very happy form. He's come dressed as a mad scientist – beady eyes, King Lear's beard, lab assistant's coat and the Macbeth tartan tie … He's full of Lear: 'Did it last night. It drains you. But then one night we just flew. It simply happened. The question is, once we're there, will I be able to act what I now feel?' … He delivered for us in full measure. When Donald Sinden got the question right about how much older Anne Hathaway was than Shakespeare (eight years), Ian said, 'Of course, Donald had the advantage of knowing them both personally.'

Donald told the Frank Benson cricketing story: how Benson advertised for a fast bowler to play Laertes. A fellow applied. Someone said, 'He's a wonderful fast bowler – not sure if he can play Laertes.' Said Benson: 'Any good fast bowler can play Laertes.'

Judi Dench told a sweet story about being in *The Promise* with Ian – and so nervous on first night she said to Ian, 'I'm just going to concentrate on the front row – focus on the three seats in the centre of the row and think that the Father, the Son and the Holy Ghost are sitting there.'

Said Ian, 'They'd be sitting in the one seat, surely?'

Happy event. Des Barrit fun, Tony Sher fun. Michael Wood fun. Also of the party, and sweet, David Warner – my first Hamlet, 1965.

Post-show, no one seemed to know where to go for the fireworks. The riverside – the Swan garden – the Dell? We saw them through the trees with Susie Sainsbury. Then we had a bite of Indian and joined the party in the tent. We didn't stay because it does get repetitive. Alex Jennings – 'loved you in *The Alchemist*', said Michèle; Mark Rylance – 'loved you in *Boeing-Boeing*'; Simon Russell Beale – 'loved you in … Goodnight!'

And so to bed, weary but mellow. Good to have shared a stage with Ian McKellen and Judi Dench. Long overdue, of course.

THURSDAY 10 MAY 2007

By tube to Ladroke Grove. Sit facing Harriet Walter on the train. She comes over. She's on her way to Brick Lane to rehearse a play about Fallujah. I tell her I'm going to Michael Berkeley's house to record *Private Passions* for Radio 3. She says he's nice and I needn't feel intimidated by his musical knowledge: I just have to concentrate on his hair, not so much a comb-over as a pubic ridge across an otherwise totally bald brow … We talked about the National Portrait Gallery and I said she needed to get in to ensure her immortality. She said that didn't bother her any more. It had once. They'd rejected a drawing of her done by Tony Sher. Pity. A cartoon by Irving of Ellen Terry would be of interest, wouldn't it?

Arrived at Michael Berkeley's way too early: a tall, narrow Victorian house where they've been since 1982 – that's when it was decorated. In the kitchen, a huge table covered with old newspapers, books, bills, old cups of coffee … on the stove last night's bread pudding in one pan, the cold greens in another … a stray cat (literally) on the floor … Michael was amiable. We talked of past guests – Harriet, Barry Humphries (as himself & Dame Edna – but not in costume), John Amis and the programme that was pulled because he told the story of Frank Muir saying, when he heard that Donizetti had died through an excess of masturbation, 'So he literally died by his own hand.'

Just now: William Archer called. He said, 'Is that Mr Brandreth? This is Mr Archer – William Archer, son of Jeffrey' – he could have been Jeffrey! Extraordinary. He's researching a project on Conan Doyle. I'll help him if I can.

And news just in – it's on the radio as I write … A decade and a week after the election that swept him in (and swept me out), Tony Blair is resigning. 'I've been Prime Minister of this country for just over ten years. I think that's long enough, not only for me, but also for the country, and sometimes the only way you conquer the pull of power is to set it down.' He steps down officially on 27 June.

TUESDAY 12 JUNE 2007

The Association of Interior Specialists at the Dorchester. This is my life now. The Drywall has changed the world. The days of wet plaster are long gone! Nice crowd. Afterwards, a cappuccino at Grosvenor House and then I walked all the way to Central Office for the 'Final Farewell to Smith Square'.[704]

The sun shone. I walked via Curzon Street (Benjamin Disraeli lived here – and 'the last courtesan', whoever she may have been) and across the park. Around the Home Office a police cordon was being set up – it was chaos, but it wasn't a bomb: a building that had collapsed.

At 32 Smith Square it was all our yesterdays ... Past chairmen, past leaders ... Chris Patten (he didn't linger), Jeremy Hanley, Michael Ancram, Maurice Saatchi, Norman Lamont, John Gummer, Ken Baker – even Iain Duncan Smith. I was there as MC and to conduct the auction. We raised £155,000. David [Cameron] arrived halfway through ... Jean Searle OBE came over and whispered, 'The leader is here'... I introduced him – explained that an erotic charge had suddenly shot through the room and that we had to get on with it before his hair began to collapse ... He was looking very bouffanted – incredibly crisp: the suit, the shirt, the haircut utterly immaculate – quite perfect, almost unreal.

I introduced 'the next Conservative Prime Minister', who took to the stage and began (unfortunately) with my Anglo-Welsh joke not knowing I'd done it half an hour before[705] ... It didn't matter. He spoke well – but, curiously, there was no magic in the air. When Mrs T. or John Major spoke I always felt oddly moved ... Michèle said later: 'He isn't Prime Minister yet. The office gives the aura.'

When we were both done, David said to me, 'You're brilliant.'

I said to him, 'You're brilliant.'

'You see,' he said, 'we agree on everything. We always have.' He said he was going to the Ritz to have dinner with the Barclay brothers – 'but I'm going to call you. I need you writing speeches for me. I need new jokes. I can count on you?'

---

704 32 Smith Square served as Conservative Central Office between 1958 and 2003. The building stood empty until 2007 when it was sold for £30.5 million to Harcourt Developments who hoped to redevelop it as flats until the 2008 credit crunch derailed the plan. It is now (perhaps ironically, given its heritage) Europe House, the London base of the European Parliament and the European Commission.

705 'I am Anglo-Welsh. My grandparents were Anglo-Welsh. My parents were Anglo-Welsh. Indeed, my parents burnt down their own cottage.'

'Of course,' I said. And he can. I will do his bidding – even though I know the jokes I give him won't be used and my best advice ('you don't need to be funny: you don't even need to be liked; you need to be heroic, you need to inspire') will be routinely ignored.

John Cope (now our Chief Whip in the Lords) stopped me as I was leaving. 'I haven't always approved of everything you've done, but tonight I approved completely...' That was a nice thing to say – and made my day.

....

THURSDAY 28 JUNE 2007

....

This morning I woke up in the City of Chester. Last night I addressed the Chester Business Club. In ten years nothing here seems to have changed – at all.

On the phone from the hotel room just after eight I did a bit on the *Today* programme – about the Queen and her Prime Ministers. Gordon Brown has 'kissed hands' on his appointment and completed his Cabinet. David Miliband is Foreign Secretary. Why not? Jacqui Smith is Home Secretary. Why? Alistair Darling is Chancellor – good. And down the list: Des Browne, John Denham, Ruth Kelly, Andy Burnham ... some of them will be excellent, I'm sure. Many of the best of the ministers in my time – Tony Newton, John MacGregor, David Hunt, David Curry, Roger Freeman etc. – were outstanding but barely noticed beyond the villages of Westminster and Whitehall. I wish them well. We need them to do well.

The merry-go-round keeps turning. I enjoyed my ride, but I'm happy not to be on it any more.

AFTERWORD

JULY 2014

I still keep a diary. I am writing this on Sunday 13 July 2014. It has been a happy week. I went to a party, I went to the theatre, I recorded an episode of *Just a Minute*, I did a day's filming for *The One Show*, I worked on my new book. Yesterday, Michèle and I took one of our six grandchildren for a day-trip to the Isle of Wight. In 1990 I was forty-two and *burning* to be a Member of Parliament. Now I am sixty-six and quite happy just to be 'Grandpa B'.

Today is the final of the 2014 World Cup. I don't know who will win because I am not entirely sure who is taking part. Tomorrow David Cameron starts his government reshuffle. That's a game I shall be following. (I still take an interest in politics. I still contribute the occasional line to a prime ministerial speech.) As a rule, of course, reshuffles make no difference, but this one might.[706]

Tomorrow, too, I am due to deliver all the material for the new edition of this book. It's a pity it wasn't published this week. I have been overwhelmed with 'media interest'. A dozen calls a day, at least. Everyone – *Newsnight*, ITN, Channel 4, all manner of newspaper and radio outlets, stations I'd never heard of – wanting a line on the Whips' Office – the 'black book' – the 'dirt list' – Peter Morrison – paedophilia… Was there a paedophile ring at Westminster? Did the Whips' Office know about it? Did they hush it up?

I let the phone ring and ignored the texts and emails. I said 'no' to the *Today* programme three days' running (not like me) and then – I'm not quite sure why – I said 'yes' to *The Week in Westminster*. I suppose I thought it would be 'safe' – and there was a fee. I played a straight bat – or so I thought. I said there was no 'black book' (well, there wasn't); I said we kept notes (because we did); I said… Never mind what I said. I did myself no favours. Afterwards I made the mistake of checking out the Twittersphere and (this is the price of narcissism) read the usual rants that we 'Tory bastards' seem to inspire.

---

706 It did. Kenneth Clarke and David Willetts were among the 'male, pale and stale' members of the government who were dropped in favour of fresher, female faces, and Michael Gove stepped down as Education Secretary to become Chief Whip.

The tweets had a common thrust: 'Brandreth should stop digging', 'Why is he defending the whips?', 'What's he got to hide?', 'He should think about the victims for a change.'

As it happens, I do think about the victims – quite a lot. I know about the reality of paedophilia. When I was a child I was 'groomed'. Yes, I was 'a victim' once upon a time. The experience lasted two years. It was a long while ago, but I remember it as if it were yesterday.

In the summer of 1959, when I was eleven, my parents sent me away to boarding school. It wasn't that they didn't like me: it was simply what middle-class parents of their generation did. I was sent to a preparatory school in East Kent to prepare me for my Common Entrance examination. I think my mother hoped I would go on to Eton. I think my father had Winchester in mind. I liked my boarding school at once.

It was a happy school. (Bowden, in my dormitory used to cry himself to sleep most nights, but he was only seven, poor mite.) It was a small school – a hundred boys or so – set in a handsome and historic country house in the middle of nowhere. Wet runs, cold showers, lots of Latin. It was a typical English boys' prep school of its time – except there were no beatings. That's how my parents found the school: they were looking for one that did not believe in corporal punishment.

The school had joint headmasters, two thoroughly decent men whose bearing and manner epitomised 'the best of British'. Mr Stocks turned eighty-one in the year I arrived at the school: he was a classicist, scholarly, short-sighted, a little slow on his feet, mild-mannered and infinitely courteous. He believed in hard work above all else: 'a busy boy is a happy boy', he used to say. ('Keep that Latin accurate' was his other mantra.) Mr Burton was a generation younger: a good-hearted, robust and enthusiastic character, keen on games and much liked by me because he produced the school plays and gave me the best parts (Feste in *Twelfth Night* one year, Rosalind in *As You Like It* the next). Mr Burton had silver hair, pink cheeks, leather patches on his elbows and a gammy leg – the result of some heroic action during the war.

The war still echoed around the school. We boys made models of German fighter planes from balsa wood and plastic Airfix kits and, under the bedclothes by torchlight, read Pan paperbacks with lurid covers featuring chilling accounts of the horror of Japanese prisoner-of-war camps. *The Wooden Horse* and *The Cruel Sea* were the films we saw as end-of-term treats. I don't believe any of the masters had professional teaching qualifications, but most of them had impressive war records and were known by their military rank. Colonel Thomas, tall, austere and shy, taught mathematics. Major Douch was smaller, jollier and sported a little moustache that made him look like an odd amalgam of Hitler and Oliver Hardy. He was a kind man, one of my favourites: he taught Latin and, in the army (I discovered this years later), had been best friends with the actor Roger Moore.

Most of the masters were married men and their wives were very much part of school life, supervising at meals, cheering from the touch-line, helping make the costumes for the school plays. The other women I recall were the matrons – one older and a bit of a dragon; two in their twenties and very pretty – and Miss Loewen, who was tiny, ancient, mittel-European, and taught art.

And then there was Mr Harkness. He was a bachelor, in his early thirties, I suppose – perhaps a bit older: his hair was thinning. It was dark brown hair which he wore swept back. He was of medium height and slim build; he dressed well (he owned a pair of blue suede shoes) and his fingers, though stained with nicotine, had nails that were noticeably well manicured. He taught English and music. He was in charge of the school choir. In my first term I joined the choir and, quite quickly, became his pet.

Each evening, by tradition long established, just after 'lights out', there was a close of day musical ritual. It was known as 'Nightingales'. On the landing, outside the boys' dormitories, three or four choristers would gather, in pyjamas and dressing gowns, and stand in a semi-circle around Mr Harkness. He would then strike a tuning fork to give us the note we needed and conduct us as we sang, a capella, a verse or two of 'The day thou gavest, Lord, is ended' or another, similar, evening hymn.

One evening, when we choristers had finished our singing, and were trooping off to our dormitories, Mr Harkness called me back to have a word. Once the others had disappeared and I stood facing him, alone on the darkened landing, he put his hands on my shoulders and bent down to kiss me. He kissed me on the mouth, quite gently. He smelled of tobacco and Old Spice. That is my most vivid recollection of him.

When Mr Harkness kissed me, I did not respond. I just stood there, accepting what was happening. Over the next two years I accepted his attention without questioning it and without complaint. And his attention was considerable. Every day he found a moment when we could be alone – on the landing, in his classroom, in the school chapel, in the vestry of the beautiful church where the choir sang on Sundays, in his bedroom. When he kissed me (which he did daily), when he put his hand on my knee as I sat next to him on the organ bench, when he let his hand stray inside my shorts as I sat on his bed learning my lines for my part in the school play, I knew it was wrong, but I did nothing to stop him. Instinctively I understood that what he was doing was transgressive (without knowing the word), but I acquiesced. I did not complain. I did not protest. I did not like what he did to me, but I did not mind it that much. I felt neutral about it and I felt no pressure – and certainly no desire – to respond. I never touched him. I would not hold his hand. When he said, 'I love you', I did not reply.

I suppose I liked him. At least, I was flattered by his attention. I think I felt it was my due. I was eleven, twelve and thirteen when this was happening and quite full of myself. Mr Harkness took lots of photographs of me. We both admired the results. And

I enjoyed the treats. He allowed me to use his bedroom whenever I wanted and provided little 'feasts' for me: fresh crab in soft white rolls was my favourite. He lent me books (I still have the copy of *Little Boy Lost* by Marghanita Laski that he gave me), he read out loud to me (he was a good reader), he helped 'improve' the poems that I wrote for the school magazine.

I remember that he had an adult friend called Rex who drove down to the school one day and took us on an expedition to Deal or Folkestone. Another boy in my year came with us for the outing. I realised that day that he was another of the choirmaster's pets. 'I don't love him like I love you,' Mr Harkness assured me later. I was not bothered. I was not jealous. I was not emotionally involved.

During term-time, I spent time with Mr Harkness every day. During the holidays I did not see him, but he wrote to me. I have kept the letters. (That is not especially significant. I keep everything.) The letters are affectionate and chatty, but circumspect. They do not give much away. My parents noticed their arrival, of course, not only because twelve-year-olds don't get much correspondence, but also because Mr Harkness wrote in an elegant, rather flowery script and used turquoise ink.

Was it my parents who brought it to a head? Did they speak to the school about it? I don't know. I never discussed it with them. All I know is that during my final term at school, I learnt that Mr Harkness was moving on. He was returning to his own part of the country to teach at a girls' school. And, one day, I was invited to have a chat with Mr Burton, the co-headmaster. Unusually, the conversation did not take place in his study. We went for a walk around the school forecourt, accompanied by another of the masters (the new games master, I think it was). Tentatively, they asked about Mr Harkness and his behaviour towards me. Was it as it should be? They mentioned the police – and wondered if there was something they should be told? I said I didn't think so. It was an awkward walk. As I remember it now, thinking back, I can picture the gravel beneath my feet. I must have been looking down. I am afraid I was not very helpful to them with their enquiries.

Has this experience of being a victim of child abuse had a lasting effect on me? I do not know. I certainly don't feel traumatised by it – nor even resentful. I did not complain then and I am not complaining now. I don't feel that I was robbed of my childhood. I haven't turned to drink or drugs or been haunted by the memory of what happened – though, now I have stopped to think about it, I am startled by how much I do remember and how vivid are the details. Yes, my innocence was violated and it was wrong. It should never have happened. The man should have been stopped – and I hope he was. He was clearly discovered and he moved on. Maybe he mended his ways. We will never know: he is dead now.

Apart from being a reasonably robust and self-confident little lad, and coming from a secure home with a loving family, I suspect that one of the reasons I did not feel traumatised by the experience is that I took it as part and parcel of boarding-school life, something you had to take in your stride, something that happened to lots of people. Perhaps for my generation it was.

And perhaps for the next generation, too. My wife and I decided to send our son to a day school, St Paul's in west London, an outstanding school, I'd say, where, mercifully, he went unmolested. Now I read in the *Daily Mail* that St Paul's and its prep school, Colet Court, have been hotbeds of paedophilia for years. Indeed, my son's old history master has just received a two-year suspended sentence at Southwark Crown Court for possessing hundreds of extreme images of naked boys. And in today's paper I have just seen the headline 'Boris Johnson's former prep school headmaster arrested on suspicion of child sex offences'. I haven't bothered to read on. I can imagine the rest.

From his prep school, Boris went on to Eton. My parents decided that I should go on to Bedales, a co-educational boarding school in Hampshire. I imagine they thought the co-ed element advisable after my prep school experience. And certainly at Bedales I came across no predatory teachers – though a girl in my class did have an affair (and a baby) with one of the French masters. She was a teenager and he was in his twenties, I think. Both left the school and, in time, they were married and had more children, though the marriage did not last.

Adults in positions of trust should not abuse that trust. Older animals should not take advantage of younger ones – emotionally, physically, or in any way at all. We know that. We are all agreed on that – absolutely – and yet, as a society, we appear conflicted, too. In fashion and advertising, we tolerate the sexualisation of pre-adolescent children; the country's bestselling newspaper continues to publish naked pictures of very young women on a daily basis; Sky TV offers pornographic channels where the youth and 'innocence' of the girls on display (seemingly dressed in school uniform) is very much part of the sales pitch: 'barely legal' is the voice-over's killer turn of phrase.

There is nothing new in this confusion. I remember how at TV-am in the 1980s we welcomed Bill Wyman to cosy up with us on the breakfast TV sofa. In 1983 the 47-year-old Rolling Stones bass guitarist had begun a relationship with a thirteen-year-old girl called Mandy Smith. He said, by way of justification, 'She was a woman at thirteen.' When I met Mandy, she told me that she was fourteen when her sexual relationship with Wyman began. He was forty-eight. But we went along for the ride: he was a Rolling Stone, after all, and she was his Lolita. They were married eventually. (In 1989. They divorced in 1991.)

And speaking of *Lolita*, in 1962, in my first year at Bedales, when I was fourteen, I attempted to read Vladimir Nabokov's celebrated novel. I don't remember much beyond the opening paragraph: 'Lolita, light of my life, fire of my loins. My sin, my soul. Lo-lee-ta:

the tip of the tongue taking a trip of three steps down the palate to tap, at three, on the teeth. Lo. Lee. Ta.'

You get the idea. At the start of the story Lolita is twelve and the narrator, Humbert Humbert, is in his late thirties and obsessed with the child, with whom he begins a sexual relationship after he becomes her stepfather. Stanley Kubrick's film version was released in 1962, which is what prompted my interest. James Mason, aged fifty-two, played Humbert Humbert. Sue Lyon, aged fourteen, played Lolita. The film was X-rated so I could not see it at the time; nor, I suppose, could Sue Lyon. You needed to be over eighteen.

We do not approve of child abuse, but depictions of child abuse we seem to tolerate – if they are well enough done. Not long ago *Time* magazine included *Lolita* in its list of the best 100 novels written in English between 1923 and 2005. Nabokov, in an afterword to the book, said, 'There is no moral to the story', echoing Oscar Wilde's line when he was cross-examined about *The Picture of Dorian Gray*: 'There is no such thing as a moral or an immoral book. Books are well written, or badly written. That is all.'

We are certainly 'conflicted' when it comes to Oscar Wilde – whose eldest son, incidentally, was a pupil at Bedales in the 1890s. I am writing this on Sunday morning, having just driven my friend Merlin Holland to St Pancras station to catch the Eurostar. Merlin, Oscar Wilde's only grandson, lives in France, but he was over for a couple of days giving a remarkable talk at the St James's Theatre about the notorious trials of 1895 and his grandfather's tragic downfall. I chaired the Q&A afterwards and I asked Merlin – considering the current press interest in paedophilia in high places and given the age of some of the witnesses produced by the prosecution at the Old Bailey in 1895 – if Oscar Wilde was being tried today might he not end up in prison now, just as he did then? 'Yes,' said Merlin, 'quite possibly, though the boys were sixteen – over the age of consent.'

Could they have been fifteen at the time the offences took place? Did Oscar ask them how old they were? I don't think the detail of their dates of birth was troubling him. By his own admission it was their youth that drew him to them. He was a gentleman, twenty to twenty-five years their senior, hugely famous and successful. They were working-class lads who could barely read nor write. Was Wilde using his position, authority and comparative wealth to exploit their youth, beauty and comparative poverty? Yes. They gave him companionship, an audience and occasional sexual favours. He gave them champagne, cash and an occasional engraved cigarette case. Do we approve? Not really, but that does not stop us from finding his flawed and complex character utterly fascinating and for admiring the charm of his personality and the genius of his works. Next week I am going to yet another production of *The Importance of Being Earnest*. Next month I start writing the seventh in my series of murder mysteries featuring Oscar as my detective. When he was imprisoned, Wilde's very name became taboo and his plays were taken off the stage. Now he is an icon and his plays are box office gold. I wonder: will the day ever come when Rolf Harris singing 'Two Little Boys' is heard again on Radio 2 and his portrait of the Queen is brought up from the basement and put on show once more? (I doubt it, but I suppose Rolf's recordings and paintings don't really rival Oscar's poetry and plays.)

Extraordinary. I have just been down to the kitchen to get a coffee, I was flicking through the *Mail on Sunday* and I have come across a two-page spread by Chris Bryant (Labour MP for Rhondda) featuring Oscar and his boyfriend, Lord Alfred Douglas, and Douglas's brother, Viscount Drumlanrig and *his* rumoured relationship with the Earl of Rosebery, Foreign Secretary and Prime Minister. 'The Cabinet minister who made passes at Etonians, the MP who paid fourteen-year-olds for floggings – the astonishing story of how paedophiles and MPs with bizarre peccadilloes are hardly anything new in the corridors of power...' It's a timely reheating of what the paper likes to call 'the Scandals of Sexminster'. But in the case of young Drumlanrig, sometime secretary to Lord Rosebery, what do we actually know? Rumour was rife, but there is no hard evidence of an unnatural relationship between the two. Drumlanrig was discovered slumped in a ditch at the edge of a turnip field in Somerset on a cold, crisp Thursday in October 1894, his twelve-bore shotgun at his side. Was it murder or suicide or, as the inquest concluded five days later, simply a tragic accident? We will never know.

And will we ever know the truth about Sir Peter Morrison, my predecessor as Member of Parliament for the City of Chester?

When I first met Peter Morrison in 1991 I sensed that he was gay and I could see that he was a heavy drinker. He was stepping down as an MP, aged forty-seven, after eighteen years in Parliament. He was a Privy Counsellor, he was a knight, he had been a minister of state and Parliamentary Private Secretary to the Prime Minister. He told me he knew he wouldn't make it to the Cabinet, so he was giving up politics for business. 'I'm going now while I've got time to start another career,' he told me. 'I want to make some money.' I believed him. But Michèle, whose instinct is always good, said she thought he was jumping before he was pushed.

Was he?

When we arrived in Chester in 1991, the word on the street was that Peter was 'a disgusting pervert'. Out canvassing, knocking on doors in one or other of the large council estates, we were told, in no uncertain terms, that Morrison was a monster who interfered with children. At the time, I don't think I believed it. People do say terrible things without justification. Beyond the fact that his drinking made Morrison appear unprepossessing – Central Casting's idea of what a toff paedophile might look like – no one was offering anything to substantiate their slurs. At the time I never heard anything untoward about Peter from the police or from the local journalists – and I gossiped a good deal with them.

In 2012, Graham Nicholls, a trade union official and former member of the Chester Trades Council, sent an intriguing letter to *The Guardian*. 'After the 1987 general election,' he wrote, 'around 1990, I attended a meeting of Chester Labour Party where we were informed by the agent, Christine Russell, that Peter Morrison would not be standing in 1992. He had been caught in the toilets at Crewe station with a fifteen-year-old boy. A deal was struck between Labour, the local Tories, the local press and the police that if he stood down at the next election the matter would go no further.' I have no reason to disbelieve Mr Nicholls, but I am surprised I heard nothing at all of this at the time.

The first, and only, official acknowledgement of my predecessor's possible involvement in child abuse came my way in 1996 when William Hague, then Secretary of State for Wales, came up to me in the House of Commons to let me know that he had ordered an inquiry into allegations of child abuse in care homes in North Wales between 1974 and 1990 – and that Peter's name might feature in connection with the Bryn Estyn home in Wrexham, twelve miles from Chester. Sir Ronald Waterhouse QC, a retired High Court judge, was appointed to head the inquiry. It took three years, cost £12 million and was reckoned 'the biggest investigation ever held in Britain into allegations of physical, sexual and emotional abuse of children who passed through the care system'.

When the Waterhouse Report appeared, it made grim reading. It named and criticised almost 200 people, for either abusing children or failing to offer them sufficient protection. It found credible evidence of 'widespread sexual abuse, including buggery' and recognised the existence of a paedophile ring in the Wrexham/Chester area, but found no evidence 'to establish that there was a wide-ranging conspiracy involving prominent persons and others with the objective of sexual activity with children in care'. Sir Peter Morrison's name did not feature.

The Waterhouse Report came in for a lot of stick. Some felt its remit had been too narrow and it had let too many people off the hook. Others felt quite differently. In 2005, Richard Webster, a writer of some standing, published *The Secret of Bryn Estyn: The Making of a Modern Witch Hunt*. Webster was highly critical of the Waterhouse Inquiry, arguing that abuse scandals can be 'phenomena created by public hysteria' and detailing cases of apparently innocent care workers imprisoned as a consequence of false or unreliable accusations elicited by police trawling operations.

The accusations against Peter Morrison surfaced again in 2012. Rod Richards (junior minister at the Welsh Office when the Waterhouse Inquiry was being set up) said publicly that Morrison had been named as a regular and unexplained visitor to Bryn Estyn. Channel 4 reported that Morrison had been 'seen' driving away from Bryn Estyn 'with a boy in his car'. And the BBC's *Newsnight* – along with others – wrongly suggested that Lord McAlpine was somehow involved in child abuse, because someone somewhere along the line had confused McAlpine with Morrison.

To calm the furore (or to prolong the hysteria, if you take the Richard Webster view), the Prime Minister and the Home Secretary announced further inquiries into both the original inquiry and any further allegations. Meanwhile, the police were still trawling. In November 2013, they announced that in the past year 235 people had contacted them with information about alleged abuse in care homes in north Wales and they were 'pursuing a large number of active lines of enquiry'. This month the BBC reported that 275 people had made allegations and forty-nine possible suspects were being investigated.

Maybe, eventually, Peter Morrison will be nailed beyond reasonable doubt. But, for now, what do we actually know? Not much.

We do know that in the late 1980s, a *Sunday Mirror* reporter, Chris House, received a tip-off from police officers who said that Peter Morrison had twice been caught 'cottaging' in public lavatories with underaged boys and had been released with a caution. When House confronted Morrison, Morrison threatened legal action. Ten years later, another investigative journalist, Nick Davies, followed up the story and confirmed with the police that Morrison had indeed 'been picked up twice', but added that 'there appeared to be no trace of either incident in any of the official records'.

Was there a cover-up? The story would certainly have been embarrassing. At the beginning of Margaret Thatcher's premiership, Peter Morrison was in the Whips' Office, as a Lord Commissioner of the Treasury and pairing whip. He went on to become a junior minister and then a minister of state. In 1990 he became Mrs Thatcher's PPS. For three years, from 1986 to 1989, he was deputy chairman of the Conservative Party. He was a force to be reckoned with: he was at the heart of the establishment, he was close to the Prime Minister – and, throughout this period, his sister was a friend and lady-in-waiting to the Queen. (Happily, she still is. Indeed, in 2013 Her Majesty made Mary Morrison a Dame Grand Cross of the Royal Victorian Order, the highest rank of the highest order of chivalry in the Queen's personal gift.) This association with the palace adds an undeniable extra frisson to the story. That said, I doubt that Dame Mary knew anything about her younger brother's private life. It's not the sort of thing a chap discusses with his sister.

At Buckingham Palace it would certainly not have worried anybody that Peter Morrison was homosexual – so many who work there are – but child abuse is quite a different matter. Lord Charteris, a devoted courtier and the Queen's former private secretary, came to Chester at Peter's invitation to talk to members of the Conservative Association. I doubt that he would have come if he believed Peter to be a paedophile.

What did Mrs Thatcher know of Peter Morrison's alleged dark side? When I talked to her about him, I felt she had the measure of the man. She knew he was homosexual. She knew he was a drinker. She was fond of him, clearly, but told me that he had ruined himself through 'self-indulgence' – much as Reginald Maudling had done a generation earlier. When it came to the love lives of colleagues, Mrs T. was not judgemental (she was quite ready to forgive Cecil Parkinson for his affair with Sara Keays), but I am sure she would not have countenanced a child abuser as her Parliamentary Private Secretary – let alone have authorised a 'cover-up' on his behalf.

So, if there was a cover-up, who managed it? Peter was a whip and whips do look after their own, so was it the Whips' Office? That has been the suggestion of the week – prompted by a clip from an old TV interview.

In 1995, in a BBC documentary, *Westminster's Secret Service*, a former whip, Tim Fortescue,[707] said this:

> Anyone with any sense, who was in trouble, would come to the whips and tell them the truth, and say, 'Now, I'm in a jam, can you help?' It might be debt, it might be … a scandal involving small boys, or any kind of scandal in which a member seemed likely to be mixed up. They'd come and ask if we could help, and if we could, we did. And we would do everything we can because we would store up brownie points … and if I mean, that sounds a pretty, pretty nasty reason, but it's one of the reasons because if we could get a chap out of trouble then, he will do as we ask forevermore…

'A scandal involving small boys' – what did he mean? He can't have been thinking about Peter Morrison because Tim Fortescue was a whip more than forty years ago, at the beginning of the 1970s, before Peter was even an MP. Did Fortescue have another case in mind? Is child abuse endemic at Westminster? According to a former victim of abuse, now aged sixty, quoted in yesterday's *Daily Mail*, back in the day, young men 'were picked up at King's Cross penniless and handed out like pieces of meat to MPs, celebrities, judges and others in the wealthy elite of London. Many of these guys were under sixteen and had run away from children's homes. They were promised a roof and work, but soon discovered they were being groomed for sex with paedophiles.'

Is it all true? Was there really a paedophile ring at Westminster involving ministers and MPs? And was there a cover-up? Norman Tebbit, among others, now thinks perhaps there was. As I write, the government has promised yet another inquiry, so in the fullness of time we may find out. Who knows?

All I can say is that in my time in the Whips' Office we helped people with mental problems, marital problems, drink problems, financial problems, and more besides, but I don't know of any case where we covered up for anyone who we believed to be guilty of a serious criminal offence.

Reflecting on all this makes me glad that I published this book, even though, in doing

707 Trevor 'Tim' Fortescue, 1916–2008, MP for Liverpool Garston 1966–74.

so, I know that I upset colleagues who felt I had betrayed them. I broke the whips' code of silence – something no whip had ever done before. Whips *never* talk about what they do or how they set about it. That's the rule. As the Chief Whip pointed out to me at the time, 'Our mystery is part of our potency.'

But mystery makes for mischief. Do we want government run like an episode of *House of Cards*? The trouble with operating in secret is that it encourages those not-in-the-know to believe that dark deeds are being done in the murky corridors of power. Occasionally perhaps they are, but mostly they are not. On Monday of this week I went to the party for Sandra Howard's new novel. It was Michael Howard's birthday and a lot of the old gang were there – Ken Clarke, Norman Lamont, John Gummer, Peter Lilley, Norman Fowler, several of them, of course, whips in their day and all of them, in my estimation, good people. In my experience, most politicians are.

INDEX

INDEX